MW00993849

DISPUTE FOR THE SAKE OF HEAVEN

Program in Judaic Studies
Brown University
Box 1826
Providence, RI 02912

BROWN JUDAIC STUDIES

Number 353

DISPUTE FOR THE SAKE OF HEAVEN

Legal Pluralism in the Talmud

by

Richard Hidary

DISPUTE FOR THE SAKE OF HEAVEN

LEGAL PLURALISM IN THE TALMUD

Richard Hidary

Brown Judaic Studies
Providence, Rhode Island

Library of Congress Cataloging-in-Publication Data

Hidary, Richard.
Dispute for the sake of heaven : legal pluralism in the Talmud / by Richard Hidary.
p. cm. — (Brown Judaic studies ; no. 353)
Includes bibliographical references and indexes.
ISBN 978-1-930675-77-3 (cloth binding : alk. paper)
1. Talmud—Hermeneutics. 2. Talmud—Criticism, interpretation, etc. 3. Jewish law—Interpretation and construction. 4. Tannaim. 5. Amoraim. I. Title.

BM503.7.H53 2010
296.1'274—dc22

2010030056

Printed in the United States of America
on acid-free paper

For Esther

שלי שלה

Contents

List of Charts

Acknowledgments

בשם ה' אל עולם

This book is a revised version of my New York University dissertation. I would like to thank my dissertation committee: Professors Lawrence Schiffman, Jeffrey Rubenstein, Dan Fleming, Robert Chazan, and Stuart Miller; my brother, Jack; and Dr. Isaac Sassoon and Uzi Weingarten for their helpful comments and meticulous corrections. Professor Schiffman has mentored me through every stage of research and writing, and I am deeply indebted to his continued personal and professional guidance.

I am grateful to the following for the insights and references they have provided in my conversations with them: Professors Moshe Bernstein, Yaakov Elman, Moshe Halbertal, Goeffrey Hermann, Menachem Lorberbaum, Leib Moscovitz, Ishay Rosen-Zvi, Seth Schwartz, and Rabbis Raymond Harari, Ronnie Hasson, and Moshe Shamah. My gratitude extends also to Professor Suzanne Stone and the Center for Jewish Law and Contemporary Civilization; my time there as a fellow has been invaluable to my research and has greatly enhanced this book.

Special thanks to those who have helped bring this book to publication for their painstaking efforts: Adina Gerver, Paul Kobelski, Professor Michael Satlow, Shaul Seidler-Feller, Isaac Setton, and Shlomo Zuckier.

I thank my parents and in-laws for their support and love. My parents have filled their home with books and instilled in us a love for learning, creating, and giving. I am truly blessed to be able to spend my days studying, writing, and teaching; I owe it all to them. They are my role models, and I pray that their grandchildren and namesakes, David, Ronnie, and Aimee, will continue to learn from them.

My children are my consolation for the loss of my beloved sister, Mariel Hidary, A"H. Mariel inspired self-confidence in her students so that they could look beyond themselves and appreciate the pluralism of humanity. She is dearly missed.

I dedicate this book to my wife, Esther, whose quick insight and wit have helped me think through many perplexing issues. She has a way of intuiting truths that I arrive at only after many hours of research. For over ten years, Esther has been my study partner, my toughest critic, my guide, and my best friend. In so many ways, the credit for writing this book belongs to her.

May our disputes always be for the sake of heaven.

Richard Hidary
Deal, NJ
Tu Be'av, 5770
July 26, 2010

Introduction

> With the sealing of the prophetic voice in rabbinic Judaism, the Jewish canonized text acquires one of its striking features: the codification of controversy.[1]

Rabbinic literature distinguishes itself from most other legal works by including multiple conflicting opinions within one text, often without indicating which is normative and never dismissing any as inauthentic parts of the tradition.[2] This multivocality seems to reflect a relatively nondogmatic worldview that is able to tolerate, if not celebrate, a wide spectrum of opinions about legal and philosophical issues. What is less clear, however, is how the debates on legal questions played out in the practice of normative halakha. How often did each side to any given controversy actually practice its opinion, and how often did controversies remain theoretical while the rabbis came to a consensus of uniform practical law?[3] In fact, rabbinic literature records hundreds of stories and comments indicating that there were significant differences of practice among the rabbis.[4] This does not mean that we can automatically assume that every theoretical debate engendered multiplicity of practice; but these examples

1. Moshe Halbertal, *People of the Book: Canon, Meaning, and Authority* (Cambridge: Harvard University Press, 1997), 49–50.

2. See Yaakov Elman, "Order, Sequence, and Selection: The Mishnah's Anthological Choices," in *The Anthology in Jewish Literature*, ed. D. Stern (New York: Oxford University Press, 2004), 69–70. To be sure, Elman points to examples of Roman and Sasanian law collections that do occasionally "register conflicting opinions." Philip Kreyenbroek, "Ritual and Rituals in the Nerangestan," in *Zoroastrian Rituals in Context*, ed. Michael Stausberg (Leiden: Brill, 2004), 319, similarly notes that in the *Nerangestan*, a Zoroastrian legal text, "mutually exclusive judgements by different priestly commentators are mentioned side by side." Elman concludes, however, that "none of these contains the wealth of disputational material that the Mishnah does" (Elman, ibid., 69).

3. This inquiry is less relevant in nonpractical areas of halakha, such as areas that no longer applied during rabbinic times (most of *Qodashim* and *Ṭeharot* and some of *Zeraᶜim*), or cases that were very rare and only argued about for their conceptual underpinnings (which includes many parts even of *Moᶜed*, *Nashim*, and *Neziqin*). We are concerned rather with diversity in areas of law and liturgy that actually came up in practice.

4. Nearly every story cited in the body of this study recounts a case of diversity in practice between rabbis. See also Catherine Hezser, *The Social Structure of the Rabbinic Movement in Roman Palestine* (Tübingen: Mohr Siebeck, 1997), 243–44.

do reveal that diverse practices were common and manifest throughout rabbinic society.

Perhaps more important than the extent of diversity are the social, political, and philosophical questions of how the rabbis dealt with and thought about diversity of halakhic practice. Did rabbis demand, with whatever power they could muster, that all Jews follow a unified code of law? Did each rabbi merely tolerate the practices of others? Or did the rabbis look positively on pluralism of practice? Furthermore, what are the mechanisms and justifications used by the rabbis to explain their attitudes?

This book will not focus on historical issues, such as describing the actual practices of the rabbis and laypeople, or examining whether or not the rabbis had the political means to enforce their will or how effective any attempts to do so were. Rather, this will be an intellectual history about whether and to what extent the ideal world of the rabbis included multiple groups each practicing one or another variation of halakha, or whether they wished for only one unified set of laws for all Jews. Were the rabbis tolerant of diversity of halakhic practice? Some sources lament factionalism while others accept as a given that each rabbi should follow his own understanding. By tracing the predominance of each of these views through the various works of rabbinic literature, we will create a map of the evolution of the attitudes of the rabbis towards legal diversity.

Throughout this study, I will use the term "monism" to designate the view that there is only one correct way to practice halakha, and "pluralism" to designate the view that there is multiplicity built into the law, and so there may be many valid halakhic practices.[5] Within the former view,

---

5. This is what I call practical monism and pluralism in Richard Hidary, "Right Answers Revisited: Monism and Pluralism in the Talmud," *Dine Israel* 26 (2009). I there distinguish the practical level from theoretical and philosophical monism and pluralism. Theoretical monism/pluralism discusses how many correct solutions exist within a legal system on the level of interpretation and legislation. This is the primary sense of these terms as found in Hanina Ben-Menahem, "Is There Always One Uniquely Correct Answer to a Legal Question in the Talmud?," *Jewish Law Annual* 6 (1987): 165; and Christine Hayes, "Legal Truth, Right Answers and Best Answers: Dworkin and the Rabbis," *Dine Israel* 25 (2008): 73–121. Philosophical monism/pluralism takes a position on whether there exists only one or many legal possibilities on the ontological and metaphysical level. This is the sense of the terms as used by Norman Lamm and Aaron Kirschenbaum, "Freedom and Constraint in the Jewish Judicial Process," *Cardozo Law Review* 1 (1979): 99–133. The unmodifed terms "monism" and "pluralism" in this book will refer to the practical level. I will specify "theoretical" or "philosophical/ontological" monism or pluralism when referring to those concepts or use the general term "pluralism of opinion" to refer to both the theoretical and philosophical levels in contradistinction to pluralism of practice. I do not distinguish between pluralism and tolerance as does Suzanne Last Stone, "Tolerance Versus Pluralism in Judaism," *Journal of Human Rights* 2, no. 1 (2003): 114. Stone's "tolerance" is roughly equivalent to my particular monism; see the following note.

one can further distinguish between "universal monism," in which one invalidates other practices and even protests against them (physically or verbally), thus attempting to make his practice the one universal practice, and "particular monism," in which one invalidates other practices but chooses to ignore them rather than protest them. Particular monists may be content for their practice to remain particular to their own group, even though it is the only correct practice, for at least three reasons (or a combination thereof): (1) they do not care about the welfare of other groups; (2) they do not think protests or persuasion will be effective;[6] and/or (3) they may tolerate another practice even though it is legally invalid because the effort and intention of the practitioner is still valuable. The theoretical basis of monism, whether universal or particular, is either that there exists only one valid opinion even in theory or that there is only one ontological truth. Alternatively, it can admit the possibility of multiple truths but still require that the halakhic system decide one universal practice, be it by majority rule or some other mechanism. According to either theoretical assumption, monism sees diversity as a negative that should not exist in an ideal world.

Within pluralism, one can similarly distinguish between "particular pluralism," according to which the other practice is considered valid for those who follow that view but completely unacceptable for one's own group, and "universal pluralism," in which one accepts practices of other rabbis as equally viable options or at least accepts the results of their decisions even though one might not agree with the bases of those decisions.[7] The theoretical basis of either type of pluralism can also rest on the assumption that there exists only one theoretical or ontological truth but still deem such truth, at least at times, inaccessible or indeterminate, and this legislative doubt leads to multiple normative options.[8] Alternatively,

---

6. This position bears similarity to the political tolerance of liberal philosophers, such as John Locke, *A Letter Concerning Toleration* (Indianapolis: Hackett, 1983). This position may also be represented by Thomas Aquinas; see the discussion of John Rawls, *A Theory of Justice* (Cambridge: Harvard University Press, 2005), 215–16; and Maria Fontana Magee, "A Thomistic Case for Tolerance," at http://www.aquinasonline.com/Topics/tolernce.html. Historically, this form of monism was the policy of governments such as the Roman Empire, which was tolerant of religious minorities simply for political purposes, not necessarily because it thought there was any value in the practices of these minority religions; see Peter Garnsey, "Religious Toleration in Classical Antiquity," in *Persecution and Toleration*, ed. W. J. Sheils, Studies in Church History 21 (Oxford: Ecclesiastical History Society, 1984), 1–27.

7. The use of the terms "particular" and "universal pluralism" here is roughly equivalent to what Richard Claman, "A Philosophic Basis for Halakhic Pluralism," *Conservative Judaism* 54, no. 1 (2002): 68, calls "sectarian pluralism" and "sharing pluralism," respectively. This distinction is somewhat different from what John Griffiths, "What Is Legal Pluralism?" *Journal of Legal Pluralism* 24 (1986): 1–55, labels legal pluralism in the "weak sense" and "strong sense." See further below, p. 9 n. 28.

8. See the discussion on "Indeterminacy and Pluralism," below, pp. 62–77.

pluralism can be based on the belief that there do exist multiple theoretical truths, and so legislating rabbis need not choose only one normative option but can tolerate multiple practices.

Even a pluralistic attitude may view diversity as a negative but still tolerate it. That is, one can wish for an ideal world of uniformity and lament the existence of diversity, but still maintain that now that diversity exists, one should accept those practices as valid halakhic positions. Alternatively, a pluralistic attitude can be based on the view that diversity is positive or perhaps even ideal. The more positively one views diversity, the more universal one's pluralism is likely to be.

Chart 0.1 Range of attitudes toward diverse practices

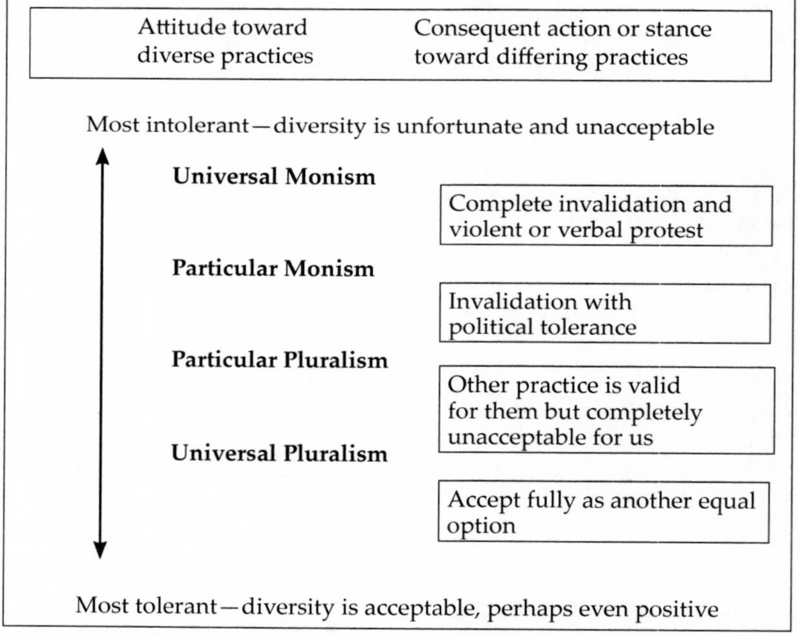

We will use this model in the upcoming chapters in order to help analyze whether those texts that take a negative view toward diversity also take a stance of monism (universal or particular) or pluralism (particular or universal) and whether those texts that take a neutral or positive view toward diversity are based on a stance of particular or universal pluralism.

Of course, one need not accept only one position on all matters. One could be a monist or a particular pluralist when it comes to matters about which a court has made a decision but remain a universal pluralist regarding issues that have not been so decided. One could be a monist when it comes to essential matters of community life, such as the calendar or marriage laws, but be a pluralist in more private matters, such as the laws of vows or the definition of work on Shabbat.[9] Nevertheless, because one's attitude is to a large extent based on certain assumptions about halakhic truth and the nature of the halakhic system, intolerance shown in one area will often indicate an overall monistic view, while a tolerant view regarding one subject will often be part of a pluralistic pattern of thought.

As we will see in detail in the upcoming chapters, one finds a range of views within rabbinic literature with some statements reflecting universal monism or pluralism at the extremes and others advocating the more moderate positions of particular monism and pluralism. A definite pattern, however, emerges when plotting these traditions geographically. Laws and stories from the Yerushalmi generally assume a more monistic view than their parallels in the Bavli. Examples of this split will be shown in each chapter of this book, and the possible reasons for this split will be summarized in the conclusion.

Legal Pluralism in Secular Legal Theory

The topic of this book, halakhic pluralism, intersects two fields of study: Talmudic intellectual history and legal theory. By locating Talmudic pluralism within the larger discussion of pluralism in other systems of law, we can broaden our conceptual framework, build a more precise vocabulary for assessing the nature of halakhic pluralism, and be in a better position to map out the viewpoints of the rabbis. In turn, the example of the Talmud may also contribute some insight into general legal theory itself.[10]

---

9. Thomas Hobbes, *Leviathan* (Cambridge: Cambridge University Press, 1904), part 2, chap. 31, pp. 266–67, makes a similar distinction between public worship of the state religion, which must be uniform, and private worship in which diversity can be tolerated. See Gary Remer, "Hobbes, the Rhetorical Tradition, and Toleration," *Review of Politics* 54, no. 1 (1992): 5–33.

10. This discussion assumes that Talmudic law does constitute a legal system and not simply a collection of religious rites and customs. Talmudic halakha does, after all, maintain an elaborate system of divine punishments and temporal punishments (even if the latter could rarely be fully implemented during the Talmudic period, except for social sanction), and also contains H. L. A. Hart's requirements of primary and secondary rules (*m. ʿEd.* 1:5), and a rule of recognition (rabbinic traditions accepted by the majority as normative). See also Alan Uter, "Is Halakhah Really Law?" *Jewish Law Annual* 8 (1989): 35–52; Aaron Kirschenbaum, "The Role of Punishment in Jewish Criminal Law: A Chapter in Rabbinic Penological Thought," *Jewish Law Annual* 9 (1991): 123–43; idem, "Jewish Penology: Unanswered Questions," *Jewish Law Annual* 18 (2008): 123–30; Jose Faur, "Law and Hermeneutics in Rabbinic Jurisprudence: A Maimonidean Perspective," *Cardozo Law Review* 14 (1992-93): 1657–79; and Hanina Ben-Menahem, "Talmudic Law: A Jurisprudential Perspective," in *The Cambridge History of Judaism IV: The Late Roman-Rabbinic Period,* ed. Steven Katz (Cambridge: Cambridge University Press, 2006), 877–98.

This project in many ways builds on that of Suzanne Last Stone, "In Pursuit of the

Various types of pluralism can be found in most legal systems, a fact that has been appreciated in legal theory only in the past few decades. Traditionally, legal theorists have assumed that legal systems must be centralized in and unified by a hierarchical system of legislation and adjudication that is part of a political state. Hans Kelsen, for example, argues that a legal system cannot contain conflicting norms.[11] If conflicting norms should arise, for some reason, then they "can and must be solved by interpretation,"[12] or else at least one of the norms becomes invalid. As Bernard Jackson puts it, Kelsen sees unity "as the defining characteristic of our notion of legal validity.... The legal system—the one and only legal system—is inter-definable with the state. A state can have only one legal system."[13]

Along the same lines, Owen Fiss defends the authority of the law against the threat of diverse subjective interpretations by appealing to "disciplining rules, which constrain the interpreter and constitute the standards by which the correctness of the interpretation is to be judged."[14] These hermeneutical rules are in turn upheld by an interpretive community, which comprises the legal establishment. Fiss recognizes that there may be disagreement in how to apply rules and deal with challenges to the very authority or existence of a rule. But these disputes can be resolved through "a hierarchy of authority."[15] Fiss states: "Any interpretation of a court, certainly that of the highest court, is prima facie authoritative."[16] For Fiss, law is unitary and hierarchical.[17] Both Kelsen and Fiss agree that law must reside in a single centralized body whose unified interpretation is valid to the exclusion of all others.

The centralized view of law, however, falls short as a description of Talmudic law and even proves inadequate as a theory of modern legal systems, as we shall see below. Halakha during the Tannaitic (70–200 C.E.) and Amoraic (200–500 C.E.) periods was not defined by or dependent on any centralized legislative or judicial body and certainly lacked a framework of independent sovereignty. As Jackson puts it, "With the possible

---

Counter-text: The Turn to the Jewish Legal Model in Contemporary American Legal Theory," *Harvard Law Review* 106, no. 4 (1993): 813–94. I thank Prof. Stone for her personal guidance on this subject.

11. Hans Kelsen, *Pure Theory of Law*, trans. Max Knight (Berkeley: University of California Press, 1967), 205–8.

12. Ibid., 206.

13. Bernard Jackson, "Jewish Law or Jewish Laws," *Jewish Law Annual* 8 (1989): 20.

14. Owen Fiss, "Objectivity and Interpretation," *Stanford Law Review* 34 (1982): 744.

15. Ibid., 747. This need for hierarchichal resolution largely vacates any objectivity gained by the disciplining rules. See Stone, "Pursuit," 860 n. 251; and Paul W. Kahn, "Community in Contemporary Constitutional Theory," *Yale Law Journal* 99 (1989–1990): 47–55.

16. Fiss, "Objectivity and Interpretation," 757.

17. See Mark Tushnet, "Anti-formalism in Recent Constitutional Theory," *Michigan Law Review* 83 (1984–85): 1528.

exception of the Second Commonwealth period, Jewish law has never been centralized in a single state."[18] To be sure, there did exist at various times and places centers of power and rabbinic legislative bodies, but these were of limited jurisdiction. The patriarchs and the exilarchs represent important centers of power, and they often did use that power for religious and judicial matters. However, that power was geographically limited, varied with time, and was often contested by other rabbis.[19] Rabbi Yehudah the Patriarch succeeded in compiling probably the most important codification of halakha in the rabbinic period; but even that work regularly encodes controversy and reports instances of multiple practices.[20] Rabbis often joined together in various courts and academies to vote and legislate on many matters of halakha. However, scholars doubt that there ever existed a single centralized Sanhedrin after 70 C.E. recognized by all rabbis; rather, the rabbis met in smaller courts that either met regularly or on an ad hoc basis.[21] Although smaller academies functioned as centralizing forces for rabbis within their geographic spheres, most scholars question the existence of large highly structured academies during pre-Geonic times.[22] There is clearly evidence for legislation in terms such as נמנו ("they voted"), הורו ("they legislated"), תקנו\התקינו ("they instituted"), גזרו ("they decreed"), but such terms are relatively rare—most laws are not presented on the basis of such legislation—and even laws ratified by vote

18. Jackson, "Jewish Law or Jewish Laws," 24.

19. See further discussion below p. 242 n. 5, and pp. 375–76.

20. See further below pp. 43–45.

21. See *m. Soṭah* 9:11; *t. Soṭah* 15:7; *b. Ketub.* 30a; Lee Levine, *The Rabbinic Class of Roman Palestine in Late Antiquity* (Jerusalem: Yad Izhak Ben-Zvi, 1989), 76–83; David Goodblatt, *The Monarchic Principle: Studies in Jewish Self-Government in Antiquity* (Tübingen: Mohr Siebeck, 1994), 232–76; Martin Jacobs, *Die Institution des jüdischen Patriarchen: Eine quellen- und traditionskritische Studie zur Geschichte der Juden in der Spätantike* (Tübingen: Mohr Siebeck, 1995), 93–99; and Hezser, *Social Structure,* 186–95. For a maximalist view, however, Hayyim Shapira, "Bet ha-din be-Yavneh: maʿamad, samkhuyot ve-tafqidim," in *'Iyyunim be-mishpaṭ 'Ivri uva-halakha: dayyan ve-diyyun,* ed. Yaʿaqov Ḥabah and ʿAmiḥai Radziner (Ramat-Gan: Bar Ilan University, 2007), 305–34, who agrees that there was no Sanhedrin after 70 that enjoyed Roman recognition but still argues for the existence of a central court at Yavneh that legislated on calendrical and other ritual matters. Even assuming the existence of an important central court at Yavneh, a presumption rejected by most scholars, that court functioned for only a small slice of the Talmudic period and also did not succeed in creating a unified code of law for many significant areas of halakha.

22. See Jeffrey Rubenstein, "Social and Institutional Settings of Rabbinic Literature," in *The Cambridge Companion to the Talmud and Rabbinic Literature,* ed. Charlotte Fonrobert and Martin Jaffee (Cambridge: Cambridge University Press, 2007), 58–74; Hezser, *Social Structure,* 195–214; and David Goodblatt, *Rabbinic Instruction in Sasanian Babylonia* (Leiden: Brill, 1975). For a maximalist view see Hayyim Shapira, "Beit ha-Midrash (the House of Study) during the Late Second Temple Period and the Age of the Mishnah: Institutional and Ideological Aspects," (Ph.D. diss., Hebrew University, 2001 [Hebrew]).

were sometimes disregarded by those not present at the voting session.[23] Nevertheless, we can agree with Catherine Hezser that "although particular locations such as Yavneh, Lydda and Sepphoris in the tannaitic period and Lydda, Sepphoris, Tiberias and Caesarea in the amoraic period may have had a larger rabbinic population than other places," overall, "in both the tannaitic and amoraic periods the rabbinic movement seems to have been decentralized."[24] Therefore, legal centralism cannot account for Talmudic law, which operates in a field marked by decentralization.

Legal centralism has also been attacked by secular legal theorists on several fronts. In a seminal essay, John Griffiths has shown that legal centralism fails as an empirical description of legal systems, both ancient and modern. He begins by describing legal pluralism in the weak sense in which a colonial power recognizes all or part of the indigenous practices and commands "different bodies of law for different groups in the population."[25] This form of pluralism, however, still assumes a centralized foundation. Griffiths goes on to define legal pluralism in the strong sense as being present "when in a social field more than one source of 'law,' more than one 'legal order,' is observable."[26] That is, multiple legal systems overlap within a society without recognizing each other's validity or even existence. He argues that this form of legal pluralism is present in virtually all societies.

For all his efforts, however, Griffiths still retains an important tenet of legal centralism, namely, that each individual legal system must be uniform.[27] In the case of Talmudic law, however, dispute and diversity of prac-

23. See E. E. Urbach, *The Halakhah: Its Sources and Development* (Givʿatayim: Yad La-Talmud, 1984), 93–99 (Hebrew); and Catherine Hezser, "Social Fragmentation, Plurality of Opinion, and Nonobservance of Halakha: Rabbis and Community in Late Roman Palestine," *Jewish Studies Quarterly* 1 (1993–94): 178, who writes: "There is no reason to assume that any of the decisions arrived at by vote was representative of or authoritative for the rabbinate as a whole."

24. Hezser, *Social Structure*, 180.

25. Griffiths, "What Is Legal Pluralism?" 5.

26. Ibid., 38.

27. Other writers on legal pluralism have given more attention to pluralism within one legal system. However, the general focus of this field remains the pluralism created by the overlapping of state- and nonstate law within one social field. See Gordon Woodman, "Ideological Combat and Social Observation: Recent Debate about Legal Pluralism," *Journal of Legal Pluralism and Unofficial Law* 21 (1998): 21–59. Overlapping of state- and nonstate law is more relevant to the discussion of halakha and minhag in chapter 1 and would be essential to a study of the interaction between halakha and Roman or Sasanian law. This book, however, focuses on pluralism within one legal system, that of halakha. Halakha is an example of nonstate law but still maintains other (non-Kelsenian) requirements of a legal system; see above p. 5 n. 10. Robert Cover's model, as discussed in the next few pages, best fits the project of this book because he focuses on pluralism within a legal system and also deprives the state of its monopoly on the law and its interpretation. Cover's theory shares this deconstruction of state law with Critical Legal Pluralism, on which see Martha-Marie Kleinhans and

tice occur within a single legal system. Diverse opinions and practices are codified within the same texts and are discussed and practiced by colleagues who identify themselves as members of the same legal order. Halakha is thus distinguished both from centralized systems that allow for little diversity on the one hand, and sectarianism on the other, which is completely decentralized and possesses little unity. Talmudic law is a single legal system, even as it includes multiple conflicting norms.[28]

A better model for Talmudic halakha in modern secular law may be federalism, in which sovereignty is divided between political units that are themselves parts of a single centralized national government. In the United States, for example, state courts have the right and power to interpret the Constitution and issue rulings differently from courts in other states. As Paul Kahn puts it: "Conflicts of interpretation may reflect variations in state experience with respect to a particular value, just as differences in personal experience lead to different moral insights. Different state understandings of constitutional norms should similarly be seen as different insights into a common object of interpretation."[29] However, even federalism, which recognizes multiple practices within one legal order, still assumes that law resides within a political order and that a centralized court and legislature bind the constituent states. Neither of these presumptions is true of Talmudic halakha.

A more expansive description of legal pluralism that extends beyond the confines of the state is offered by the self-described anarchist Robert Cover. In his landmark essay "Nomos and Narrative," Cover contrasts "the more familiar notion of law as social contract" with the concept of *nomos* as "a legal world conceived purely as legal meaning."[30] *Nomos* consists of not only rules and institutions but also the narratives that form the basis and provide meaning to the law. Whereas legal precepts are codified by centralized institutions, *nomos* "requires no state."[31] These narratives "are subject to no formal hierarchical ordering, no central-

---

Roderick MacDonald, "What is Critical Legal Pluralism?" *Canadian Journal of Law and Society* 12 (1997): 25–46. Cover is not sufficiently discussed within the discourse on legal pluralism, a fact noted and somewhat rectified by Emmanuel Melissaris, *Ubiquitous Law: Legal Theory and the Space for Legal Pluralism* (Burlington: Ashgate, 2009), 40f.

28. For this reason, I use the terms "particular" and "universal" legal pluralism to refer to the relative tolerance one side of a dispute shows toward the other within a legal system rather than Griffiths's terms "weak" and "strong" pluralism, which describe the relationship between one legal order and another.

29. Paul W. Kahn, "Interpretation and Authority in State Constitutionalism," *Harvard Law Review* 106, no. 5 (1993): 1161–62.

30. Robert Cover, "Nomos and Narrative," in *Narrative, Violence, and the Law: The Essays of Robert Cover*, ed. Martha Minow et al. (Ann Arbor: University of Michigan Press, 1995), 102–3.

31. Ibid., 103.

ized, authoritative provenance, no necessary pattern of acquiescence."[32] Since one's interpretation of legal precepts depends on one's narrative framework and the state has no power to assert a single authoritative narrative, the state's interpretation of law holds no privileged status over that of any other group. Interpretive communities "identify their own paradigms for lawful behavior and reduce the state to just one element, albeit an important one, in the normative environment."[33]

Cover elaborates on the implications of his approach for the dialectic of unity versus pluralism. Cover distinguishes in this regard between two ideal–typical patterns of normative worlds: the "paideic," which approximates the social world created by narratives, and the "imperial," which approximates the strictly legal order of precepts.[34] In the former, members are personally educated into a common set of narratives and particularistic principles that embody the group's vision for an ideal society and its goals for the future. This normative world obliges its members to create a strong community where members actively engage one another. This group is isolationist, particular, and "culture-specific."[35] The paideic *nomos* is capable of creating a system of meaning *ex nihilo*.

The imperial model, on the other hand, cannot create meaning but can only maintain systems already in place. It ensures that many paideic worlds can coexist by imposing universal and liberal principles on its members. It demands no interpersonal obligations on its members other than to "refrain from the coercion and violence that would make impossible the objective mode of discourse and the impartial and neutral application of norms."[36] It maintains order but does not inspire or create community. Cover summarizes:

> The paideic is an etude on the theme of unity. Its primary psychological motif is attachment. The unity of every paideia is being shattered—shattered, in fact, with its very creation. The imperial is an etude on the theme of diversity. Its primary psychological motif is separation.[37]

Prominent examples of paideic and imperial orders in the modern world are, respectively, religious communities and the liberal nation-state. The nation-state creates an objective environment in which many religious communities can coexist without imposition and violence.[38] Nevertheless,

---

32. Ibid., 111.
33. Ibid., 131.
34. Ibid., 103–13. On the use of these terms see ibid., especially p. 106 nn. 34 and 36.
35. Ibid., 105.
36. Ibid., 106.
37. Ibid., 109–10.
38. In a similar vein, Suzanne Last Stone, "Sinaitic and Noahide Law: Legal Pluralism in Jewish Law," *Cardozo Law Review* 12 (1991): 1212–13, compares the Noahide code, whose

as Cover points out, every normative world actually contains elements of both models. For the moment a paideic order is created, it is already subject to interpretation, criticism, and disagreement. At the very instant that "the divinely ordained normative corpus, common ritual, and strong interpersonal obligations that together from the basis of such a paideic legal order"[38] are combined with a common narrative of its location within the cosmos, the structure already gives birth to variation. Once two members disagree about the content of the *nomos,* an imperial element must enter the system in order to allow both variations to coexist.

Cover writes concerning the paideic *nomos,* "The unification of meaning that stands at its center exists only for an instant, and that instant is itself imaginary."[39] That is, historically speaking, variation and disagreement are already present at the very founding of a new community; often they are remnants from a rift in the group's previous incarnation. Nevertheless, communities often create a narrative about an original unity in order to bind together the current state of diversity. As an example of such a narrative, Cover quotes *b. Sanh.* 88b: "Originally there were not many disputes in Israel.... But when the disciples of Shammai and Hillel who had not studied well enough increased [in number], disputes multiplied in Israel and the Torah became as two Toroth."[40] Cohesion of the community is maintained by emphasizing common roots. Cover further describes the mechanisms of the imperial model: "The sober imperial mode of world maintenance holds the mirror of critical objectivity to meaning, imposes the discipline of institutional justice upon norms, and places the constraint of peace on the void at which strong bonds cease."[41] When these mechanisms fail, those elements that are deemed out of line or antithetical to the *nomos* of the community are expelled, unity of the larger group is destroyed, and the smaller groups must then deal with diversity within themselves.[42]

The relevance of Cover's thesis to Talmudic law is made explicit by

---

purpose is to maintain social peace in the world, to the imperial mode and the Sinaitic code, whose goal is to create a strong covenantal community, to the paideic mode. In this study, I have instead sought out the paideic and imperial elements within "Sinaitic" halakha itself, that is, those principles that create a meaningful and particularistic covenantal community as well as those which maintain peace within the diversity of the larger rabbinic community.

39. Cover, "Nomos and Narrative," 108.

40. Cover's translation, ibid., 109 n. 40. See analysis of this source below, pp. 166f. and 303f.

41. Cover, "Nomos and Narrative," 109.

42. On the expelling of non-rabbinites during the post-destruction period, see below, pp. 31–36. On the increasingly negative view of Samaritans by Tannaim and Amoraim, see James Alan Montgomery, *The Samaritans: The Earliest Jewish Sect, Their History, Theology and Literature* (New York: Ktav, 1968), 165–95. See also Itzhak Hamitovsky, "Rabbi Meir and the Samaritans: The Differences between the Accounts in the Yerushalmi and the Bavli," *Jewish Studies, an Internet Journal* (2009): 1–26 (Hebrew).

Cover himself in the need for halakha to mediate the tension between the diversity created by its paideic aspects with the unity imposed by the imperial aspects. Part of the project of this book will be to identify those laws, institutions, and narratives within the Talmud that encode these various aspects. Of course, this part of Cover's argument is also relevant to all legal systems; Cover applies it most directly to minority religious communities within the secular state. However, Cover also advances a prescriptive and utopian vision that has special relevance to Talmudic law:

> In an imaginary world in which violence played no part in life, law would indeed grow exclusively from the hermeneutic impulse—the human need to create and interpret texts. Law would develop within small communities of mutually committed individuals who cared about the text, about what each made of the text, and about one another and the common life they shared. Such communities might split over major issues of interpretation, but the bonds of social life and mutual concern would permit some interpretive divergence."[43]

As a historical precedent for this imaginary world, Cover points to Talmudic law: "The Jewish legal system has evolved for the past 1900 years without a state and largely without much in the way of coercive powers to be exercised upon the adherents of the faith.... [T]here has been no well defined hierarchy of law articulating voices in Judaism."[44] Suzanne Stone elaborates: "Jewish law provides a test case of a legal system lacking institutional hierarchy, in which law is primarily a system of legal meaning.... [The rabbis] were able to do exactly what modern theory finds problematic—continue in the face of radically inconsistent and plural understandings of the law."[45]

While there may be some differences between Cover's model and Talmudic law,[46] the affinities are significant enough to make Cover's concep-

---

43. Cover, "Nomos and Narrative," 139.

44. Robert Cover, "Obligation: A Jewish Jurisprudence of the Social Order," in *Narrative, Violence, and the Law: The Essays of Robert Cover*, ed. Martha Minow et al. (Ann Arbor: University of Michigan Press, 1995), 242–43.

45. Stone, "Pursuit," 828.

46. One important difference is that while in Cover's vision interpretations by all communities, regardless of their social status, are equally valid, Talmudic law only recognizes interpretations by rabbis. Stone, ibid., 852–55, points to four other aspects of Talmudic law that serve to limit legal pluralism: hermeneutical rules that are agreed upon by the interpretive community, the authority of earlier generations who cannot be challenged, the need to maintain communal uniformity, and anxiety about issuing a mistaken ruling. Even though these aspects do constrain pluralism to some extent, however, they by no means eliminate it. There is plenty of disagreement within the rabbinic class and the rabbis themselves are sometimes found in conversation with women and laymen whose halakhic opinions then enter the rabbinic discourse; see, for example, *t. Kelim Baba Meṣiʿa* 1:6, Alexander Guttmann, "Participation of the Common People in Pharisaic and Rabbinic Legislative Processes," *Jewish Law Association Studies* 1 (1985): 41–51; and Shmuel Safrai, "Ha-ṣibbur ke-gorem bi-qviʿut

tual framework useful for the study of halakhic pluralism. To be sure, the Talmudic reality was not largely the choice of the rabbis but the imposition of historical and political forces laid on them. Legislating halakha without a sovereign state and without coercive powers was not part of a rabbinic utopian vision, at least not at first, but rather the demand of the Roman Empire. Nevertheless, one must still investigate how the rabbis reacted to the new reality: did they give up or go on? Did they continually long for a new order, or did they accept their situation and make the best of it, perhaps even consider it ideal? Cover already notes two major tendencies within the Talmud:

> There have been times when great figures have lamented the cacophony of laws and have understood it to be a condition imposed upon us for our sins. But another strain has almost rejoiced in the plethora of laws and has drawn strength from the traditional solution given by the Talmud to the question of whether the School of Hillel or the School of Shammai was truly correct. "Both are the words of the Living God."[47]

The goal of this study is to identify and analyze the various reactions of the rabbis to the reality of behavioral pluralism and how their attitudes informed their understanding of the past, their hopes for the future, and the policies they should implement in the present. We will seek out both the paideic and imperial forces within the halakha and explain how these forces play off of each other and how they affect and are affected by geographic and political realities. This assessment will provide insight into how the rabbis themselves understood the nature, mechanisms, and motivations of halakhic pluralism.

Previous Research

The most extensive treatment of practical pluralism in the Talmud is by Hanina Ben-Menahem. In one article that addresses this topic directly, Ben-Menahem discusses an important set of texts in which legal doubt

---

ha-halakha," in *Ben samkhut le-'oṭonomiah be-masoret Yisra'el*, ed. Z. Safrai and A. Sagi (Tel-Aviv: Hakibbutz Hameuchad, 1997), 493–500. Hermeneutical rules are themselves subjects of debate (see below, ch. 1, on the rules of R. Yoḥanan, and Michael Chernick, *Midat "gezerah shavah": ṣuroteha ba-Midrashim uva-Talmudim* [Lod: Habermann Institute, 1994]). Statements of earlier generations are routinely interpreted away, and neither will the importance of uniformity nor the anxiety of getting it wrong regularly prevent a scholar who is convinced of his opinion from issuing a divergent practical ruling. Still, Stone is correct that "[s]ometimes, the image of peaceful resolution of conflict through discourse or amicable coexistence with conflicting traditions masks a far more complicated reality" of tension and intolerance (Stone, "Pursuit," 855–56).

47. Cover, "Obligation," 243.

leads to pluralism.[48] He finds that "talmudic Law does contain norms which support the pluralistic position," but that these norms only apply in "exceptional cases"[49] and do not represent the general Talmudic view. Ben-Menahem returns to this subject as a tangent in his book on judicial deviation in Talmudic law.[50] Regarding his main topic, Ben-Menahem summarizes:

> The two Talmudim fundamentally differ in their approach to the concept of judicial power. The Jerusalem Talmud holds that the power of judges is limited strictly to applying the halakhah proper. It does not consider extra-legal considerations as acceptable justifications for judicial decisions. On the other hand, the Babylonian Talmud is more flexible on this issue. It sometimes acquiesces in the power of judges to exceed the limits of the law.[51]

In the context of the chapter proving this thesis, Ben-Menahem tries to find an explanation for the difference between the Talmuds by connecting it with the broader topic of diversity of practice.[52] He finds that the Yerushalmi's insistence on strict conformity with the letter of the law derives from its more general push to unify halakhic practice. Conversely, the Bavli's acceptance of extrajudicial considerations relates to its general tolerance for legal pluralism. He concludes, "While the Yerushalmi rejects any form of legal pluralism and strives to harmonize contradictory accounts, the Bavli accepts legal pluralism as a commonplace to which frequent positive references are made."[53] Ben-Menahem eruditely reviews in broad outlines many of the topics analyzed in this book.[54] Since this is not the main topic of his book, however, he cites only a small sampling of

---

48. Ben-Menahem, "Is There," 164–75. Only the first part of the article is relevant. (The second part deals with the "*kim li* argument," which is a medieval invention not found in the Talmud.) Ben-Menahem cites a few sample texts but does not perform any critical analysis of them and does not compare Yerushalmi and Bavli usages. See further analysis of these texts below, pp. 62–77.

49. Ibid., 166.

50. See Hanina Ben-Menahem, *Judicial Deviation in Talmudic Law* (New York: Harwood Academic Publishers, 1991).

51. Ibid., 181–82. See, interestingly, a possible overlap between Ben-Menahem's characterization of the two Talmuds and that of Rabbi Abraham Isaac Kook at Avinoam Rosenak, *The Prophetic Halakhah: Rabbi A. I. H. Kook's Philosophy of Halakhah* (Jerusalem: Magnes, 2007), 161 (Hebrew).

52. Ben-Menahem, *Judicial Deviation*, 86–98.

53. Ibid., 95. Ben-Menahem's summary of the Yerushalmi's position here is too extreme; the Yerushalmi recognizes many forms of legal pluralism, as we will see below, albeit in more limited form than the Bavli. Otherwise, this statement is fully supported by the current study.

54. I have cited those valuable points that he does make at relevant places throughout the chapters below.

relevant passages and does not analyze any of them with sufficient depth.[55] The present study confirms Ben-Menahem's findings regarding the difference between the Talmuds generally while disputing his explanation for this difference.

The topic of halakhic pluralism has been partially dealt with more recently by Paul Heger.[56] Heger argues that sages before 70 C.E. decided issues on an ad hoc basis with no centralized institution. This created an environment of tolerance for diverse views and practices of halakha in which contradictory decisions were perceived "as legitimate variations in the obligation to fulfill the divine commands expressed in the Torah."[57] After 70, however, the rabbis at Yavneh, in particular Rabban Gamaliel II, attempted to unify halakha and formulate a fixed code, but they were only partially successful. Heger's study, however, is fraught with methodological problems. Having little evidence for the internal workings of the Pharisees before 70, he retrojects what must have been the historical reality from later rabbinic sources—a highly speculative venture.[58] Furthermore, he uses Bavli sources, such as *b. Ber.* 27b, to reflect on the Yavnean period, a methodology now widely discredited.[59] In any case, his conclusions for post-70 are rather indefinite. Heger admits that the attempt at standardization at Yavneh was not successful and, finding evidence for both pluralistic and unifying trends, concludes that "the legal environment post-70 was still quite open and tolerant."[60] Heger is not careful to distinguish Tannaitic versus Amoraic sources, or Yerushalmi versus Bavli texts, thus leaving us with a rather blurred picture.

Besides Ben-Menahem and Heger, this topic has received only superficial treatment by other scholars.[61] For the most part, these authors do not

---

55. He ignores the redactional layers of the texts and misses the more subtle ways in which the two Talmuds express their differences.

56. Paul Heger, *The Pluralistic Halakhah: Legal Innovations in the Late Second Commonwealth and Rabbinic Periods* (Berlin: Walter de Gruyter, 2003).

57. Ibid., 2. See below, p. 31f. for further discussion on the Second Temple and Yavneh periods.

58. See the criticism of Charlotte Fonrobert, "Review of *The Pluralistic Halakhah*," *Review of Biblical Literature* 6 (2004): 352–53.

59. See Jacob Neusner, *Reading and Believing: Ancient Judaism and Contemporary Gullibility* (Atlanta: Scholars Press, 1986); and Daniel Boyarin, "Anecdotal Evidence: The Yavneh Conundrum, *Birkat Hamminim*, and the Problem of Talmudic Historiography," in *The Mishnah in Contemporary Perspective*, ed. Alan Avery-Peck and Jacob Neusner (Leiden: Brill, 2006), 1–35; and discussion below, pp. 269–72.

60. Heger, *Pluralistic Halakhah*, 257.

61. No other book-length treatment of this subject has been written. The most relevant articles and book chapters are Louis Finkelstein, *The Pharisees: The Sociological Background of their Faith*, 3rd ed. (Philadelphia: Jewish Publication Society, 1962), 43–72; Gedaliah Alon, *The Jews in Their Land in the Talmudic Age (70–640 C.E.)*, trans. Gershon Levi (Jerusalem: Magnes, 1984), 308–22, 465–69; David Dishon, *Tarbut ha-maḥloqet be-Yisra'el: ʿiyyun be-mibḥar meqorot* (Jerusalem: Schocken, 1984), 83–106; Levine, *Rabbinic Class*, 76–97; Reuven Kimelman,

treat the subject comprehensively, do not distinguish between time periods and geographies, do not compare parallel versions of each text, do not perform critical or literary readings of these sources, and treat each issue in only a cursory manner. Other articles make only superficial mention of a few obvious Talmudic sources and focus instead on writings of medieval and modern Jewish thinkers.[62] Moreover, most of these works have an agenda of promoting tolerance within the modern Jewish community, which may be praiseworthy but does not necessarily facilitate an objective analysis of all views represented within the rabbinic corpus.[63] To be

---

"Judaism and Pluralism," *Modern Judaism* 7, no. 2 (1987): 131–50; Dov Zlotnick, *The Iron Pillar—Mishnah: Redaction, Form, Intent* (Jerusalem: Bialik Institute, 1988), 194–217; Menachem Elon, *Jewish Law: History, Sources, Principles* (Philadelphia: Jewish Publication Society, 1994), 3:1061–70; and Jackson, "Jewish Law or Jewish Laws," 23–34. The following essays are also relevant but contain only a few paragraphs directly related to rabbinic literature: Jakob Petuchowski, "Plural Models within the Halakhah," *Judaism* 19 (1970): 77–89; W. S. Wurzburger, "Plural Modes and the Authority of the Halakhah," *Judaism* 20, no. 4 (1971): 393; Emanuel Rackman, "Secular Jurisprudence and Halakhah," *Jewish Law Annual* 6 (1987): 49–53; Moshe Ish-Horowicz, "Religious Tolerance and Diversity in Judaism," in *Jerusalem—City of Law and Justice*, ed. Nahum Rakover (Jerusalem: Library of Jewish Law, 1998), 249–62; Bernard Jackson, "Is Diversity Possible within the Halakhah?" *L'Eylah* 29 (1990): 35–38; and Claman, "A Philosophic Basis for Halakhic Pluralism," 60–80.

62. See, for example, Michael Rosensweig, "Elu Va-Elu Divre Elokim Hayyim: Halakhic Pluralism and Theories of Controversy," *Tradition* 26, no. 3 (1992): 4–23; Moshe Sokol, "What Does a Jewish Text Mean? Theories of 'elu ve-elu divrei Elohim hayim' in Rabbinic Literature," *Daat* 32–33 (1994): xxiii–xxxv; Avi Sagi, "'Both are the Words of the Living God': A Typological Analysis of Halakhic Pluralism," *Hebrew Union College Annual* 65 (1995): 105–36; idem, *'Elu va-Elu': A Study on the Meaning of Halakhic Discourse* (Tel-Aviv: Hakibbutz Hameuchad, 1996) (Hebrew); Aviezer Ravitzky, "She'elat ha-sovlanut be-masoret ha-datit-ha-yehudit," in *Ben samkhut le-oṭonomiah be-masoret Yisra'el*, ed. Z. Safrai and A. Sagi (Tel-Aviv: Hakibbutz Hameuchad, 1997), 396–420; and Gilbert S. Rosenthal, "'Both These and Those': Pluralism within Judaism," *Conservative Judaism* 56, no. 3 (2004): 3–20.

See also primary sources from the Talmud and later commentators gathered and analyzed in Hanina Ben-Menahem et al., *Controversy and Dialogue in Halakhic Sources*, 3 vols. (Boston: Boston University School of Law, 1991–2002); and Hanina Ben-Menahem et al., *Controversy and Dialogue in the Jewish Tradition: A Reader* (New York: Routledge, 2005).

63. Although I have sought in this study to document and analyze with equal temperament the spectrum of attitudes toward diversity reflected in rabbinic literature, I also cannot claim to be free of personal bias. I do think that contemporary Jewish communities, and most other groups for that matter, would benefit from more tolerance and respect for opposing viewpoints. I am inspired by the strong pluralistic spirit of Rabbi Shlomo Zalman Auerbach, *Minḥat Shelomo* 1:45, who writes that even though he prohibits *heter mekhira* (fruits grown during the Sabbatical year on land sold to non-Jews), he recognizes the legitimacy of those who permit it to the extent that he himself would have to permit it to a questioner on the basis of the rule, "regarding rabbinic law follow the lenient opinion" (*b. ʿAbod. Zar.* 7a). However, I also recognize the need for groups to define themselves, draw boundaries, and take stands on their beliefs. Neither extreme of the dialectic between inclusivity and exclusivity is healthy. More tolerance and respect can make the world more peaceful, but too much tolerance can lead to moral relativism and the weakening of one's own values and identity.

These issues take on greater significance and complexity in modern times when com-

sure, most of the individual issues covered in the upcoming chapters have received significant scholarly attention, which will be cited and discussed in their appropriate places. However, these studies do not discuss how such issues apply to attitudes toward diversity in general.

Tolerance for Diversity of Opinions

Previous scholarship has given much attention to the closely related topic of the attitude of the rabbis toward argumentation and multiplicity of interpretations and opinions. Did the rabbis believe that there is only one truth, one correct interpretation of Scripture, and one law revealed at Sinai; or did they believe there to be many truths, indeterminacy of meaning, and multivocality of revelation?[64]

Many scholars have pointed to midrash in particular as an area that reflects the rabbis' approval and even celebration of multiple interpretation.[65] In terms of textual praxis, midrash typically lists a series of alterna-

---

munication dissolves borders and when most Jewish communities have been uprooted and joined together in America and Israel. I am moved by the efforts of Rabbi Sabato Morais and Rabbi Ben-Zion Meir Hai Uziel to unify Ashkenazic and Sephardic liturgy and certain halakhic practices. Both rabbis were willing to compromise their own Sephardic traditions and practices for the sake of uniformity, thus recognizing the validity of divergent practices. See Arthur Kiron, "Golden Ages, Promised Lands: The Victorian Rabbinic Humanism of Sabato Morais" (Ph.D. diss., Columbia University, 1999), 164–70; and *Pisqe ᶜUziel bi-she'elot ha-zeman* 1 and 2, and *Mishpeṭe ᶜUziel, 'even ha-ᶜezer* 83. Ironically, the strong pluralistic attitude of these rabbis led them to advocate for greater uniformity. Conversely, Rabbi Abraham Isaac Kook and Rabbi Ovadia Yosef argued that Ashkenazim and Sepharadim should each continue their prior practices because each considers the other's laws to be in some way deficient. Their traditionalism thus ends up advocating for diversity of practice, itself a form of particular pluralism. See *Oraḥ mishpat, oraḥ ḥayyim, simanim* 17 and 18, and *Yabiaᶜ 'omer*, vol. 6, *oraḥ ḥayyim, siman* 43 and *'even ha-ᶜezer, siman* 14. (I thank Rabbi Shmuel Klitsner, David Shasha, and Prof. Arye Edrei for the above references.) Even more complex and pressing are issues involving the implementation of halakha in the sovereign state of Israel and relationships between Jewish denominations. I do not intend in this book to solve or even address any of these modern issues but rather to focus on a historical and textual analysis of Talmudic sources. If the reader finds this analysis to be helpful in assessing such modern issues then that shall be a welcome bonus.

64. On the spectrum of views within rabbinic literature concerning Sinaitic revelation, see Stone, "In Pursuit of the Counter-text," 849–50.

65. See Joseph Heinemann, "Profile of a Midrash: The Art of Composition in Leviticus Rabba," *Journal of the American Academy of Religion* 31 (1971): 146, 149–50; idem, "The Nature of the Aggadah," in *Midrash and Literature*, ed. Geoffrey Hartman and Sanford Budick (New Haven: Yale University Press, 1986), 48–54; James Kugel, "Two Introductions to Midrash," *Prooftexts* 3 (1983): 146; Steven Fraade, *From Tradition to Commentary: Torah and Its Interpretation in the Midrash Sifre to Deuteronomy* (Albany: State University of New York, 1991), 15–17, 123–62; Gerald Bruns, "The Hermeneutics of Midrash," in *Hermeneutics Ancient and Modern* (New Haven: Yale University Press, 1992), 104–23; Richard Sarason, "Interpreting Rabbinic

tive interpretations separated by "דבר אחר—another interpretation," usually without any attempt to reconcile them. To be sure, this is more common in midrash *aggada* than in midrash halakha, but it does occur even in the latter.[66]

In terms of thematization, rabbinic literature offers a number of

---

Biblical Interpretation: The Problem of Midrash, Again," in *Hesed ve-Emet: Studies in Honor of Ernest S. Frerichs*, ed. Jodi Magness and Seymour Gitin (Atlanta: Scholars Press, 1998), 133–54; and David Stern, "Anthology and Polysemy in Classical Midrash," in *The Anthology in Jewish Literature*, ed. idem (New York: Oxford University Press, 2004), 108–39.

Literary critics and Talmudists have debated the extent to which this multiplicity is a forerunner of postmodern theories of indeterminacy present in all texts. See Susan Handelman, *The Slayers of Moses: The Emergence of Rabbinic Interpretation in Modern Literary Theory* (Albany: SUNY, 1982), 66–76; David Stern, "Moses-cide: Midrash and Contemporary Literary Criticism," *Prooftexts* 4 (1985): 193–213; Susan Handelman, "Fragments of the Rock: Contemporary Literary Theory and the Study of Rabbinic Texts—A Response to David Stern," *Prooftexts* 5 (1985): 75–95; idem, "'Everything Is in It': Rabbinic Interpretation and Modern Literary Theory," *Judaism* 35, no. 4 (1986): 429–40; Jose Faur, *Golden Doves with Silver Dots: Semiotics and Textuality in Rabbinic Tradition* (Bloomington: Indiana University Press, 1986); William Scott Green, "Romancing the Tome: Rabbinic Hermeneutics and the Theory of Literature," *Semia* 40 (1987): 147–68; Daniel Boyarin, *Intertextuality and the Reading of Midrash* (Bloomington: Indiana University Press, 1990), 41f.; David Stern, "Midrash and Hermeneutics: Polysemy vs. Indeterminacy," in *Midrash and Theory: Ancient Jewish Exegesis and Contemporary Literary Studies* (Evanston, IL: Northwestern University Press, 1996), 15–38; and Moshe Halbertal, *Interpretive Revolutions in the Making: Values as Interpretive Considerations in Midrashei Halakhah* (Jerusalem: Magnes, 1999), 179–203 (Hebrew). But, even Stern, who does not think midrash reflects indeterminacy as Handelman does, still agrees that the rabbis offered multiple interpretations to the texts they interpreted, which they viewed as polysemous. Green limits even the extent of polysemy in midrash, noting that each interpretation within a series of "דבר אחר" statements is usually no more than an exegetical variation of a single message. In fact, "By providing multiple warrant for that message, the form effectively restricts the interpretive options" ("Romancing," 163). He further posits, "As heirs and practitioners of a levitical piety, rabbis could afford little tolerance of ambiguity, uncertainty, or unclarity" (ibid., 164). Green, however, does not take into account the self-reflective statements within the midrash, on which see further on. Withal, Green agrees that "rabbinic use of scripture was kaleidoscopic" (ibid.).

66. Fraade, *From Tradition to Commentary*, 259 n. 1, calculates that the phrase "דבר אחר" "occurs 2.54 times more frequently in aggadic sections of Sifre Deuteronomy than in halakhic sections of equal length." Even when midrash halakha offers multiple interpretations, it usually includes arguments for and against each side in an attempt to come to a conclusion; Natalie Dorhman, "Reading as Rhetoric in Halakhic Texts," in *Of Scribes and Sages: Early Jewish Interpretation and Transmission of Scripture*, ed. Craig Evans (London: T&T Clark International, 2004), 90–114, argues that *Mekhilta de-R. Ishmael* uses the debate form as rhetoric in order to convince readers (or listeners) of its conclusions. In a similar vein, David Halivni, *Peshat and Derash* (Oxford: Oxford University Press, 1990), 161–62, writes:

> The concession to the reader [that the rabbis read into the text what is not literally there] occasionally encountered in halakha was not an invitation to multiplicity of interpretation. Behavior had to be uniform. The concession was made once and the resulting content stands for all future generations.... The standard was set once and for all for all posterity. Aggada, on the other hand, was never standardized. It required no behavior, so there was less need to be uniform. It was from its very

instances of self-reflection about midrashic hermeneutics. Perhaps the most often quoted is *b. Sanh.* 34a:[67]

> אמר אביי: דאמר קרא: אחת דבר אלהים שתים זו שמעתי כי עז לאלהים—מקרא אחד יוצא לכמה טעמים, ואין טעם אחד יוצא מכמה מקראות.
> דבי רבי ישמעאל תנא: וכפטיש יפצץ סלע, מה פטיש זה מתחלק לכמה ניצוצות—אף מקרא אחד יוצא לכמה טעמים.

> Abaye said: The verse says, *"One thing God has spoken, but two things have I heard, for might belongs to God"* (Ps 62:12). A single verse expresses several meanings, but no two verses ever express the same meaning.
> It was taught in the School of R. Ishmael: *"[Behold, My word is like fire, declares God,] and like a hammer that shatters rock"* (Jer 23:29). Just as this hammer divides into many shivers, so a single verse expresses several meanings.[68]

However, this celebration of polysemy may not be representative of all rabbinic thinking. Azzan Yadin argues that "the Rabbi Ishmael Midrashim do not interpret Scripture as a polysemic text."[69] Regarding *b. Sanh.* 34a, Yadin convincingly shows that its insistence on a polysemic interpretation of the Bible is specific to the Bavli version of this statement. Parallels in Tannaitic sources speak only of God's ability to express two statements in a single utterance, "שני דברים בדיבור אחד," but not that a single statement can have two different meanings.[70] Steven Fraade cites some examples of early

---

> inception more individualistic, less threatened by diversity. It was always more flexible, less defined, and more hospitable to readers' input.

Halivni's description of the distinction between halakha and *aggada* is mostly accurate even if somewhat exaggerated.

67. This and all Hebrew and Aramaic texts in this book are copied from the editions used in the Bar-Ilan University Responsa Project CD-ROM, unless otherwise indicated. Where relevant, I have noted important manuscript variants. All translations of rabbinic texts in this book are my own unless otherwise indicated. Translations of biblical verses are from *JPS Hebrew-English Tanakh* (Philadelphia: Jewish Publication Society, 1999).

68. See parallel at *b. Šabb.* 88b and analysis at Stern, "Midrash and Hermeneutics," 17–18. See also more texts quoted at Steven Fraade, "Rabbinic Polysemy and Pluralism Revisited: Between Praxis and Thematization," *AJS Review* 31, no. 1 (2007): 7 n. 17, 24–31.

69. Azzan Yadin, *Scripture as Logos: Rabbi Ishmael and the Origins of Midrash* (Philadelphia: University of Pennsylvania, 2004), 69–70.

70. Ibid., 71–79. See also Daniel Boyarin, *Border Lines: The Partition of Judaeo-Christianity* (Philadelphia: University of Pennsylvania Press, 2004), 189–92; and Stern, "Anthology," 123–24, esp. n. 43. *Y. Maʿas.* 3:4 (51a) may reflect an attitude of wariness in the Yerushalmi toward multiple interpretations, at least according to R. Zeira:

> דלמא רבי זעירא ורבי אבא בר כהנא ורבי לוי הוון יתבין והוה רבי זעירא מקנתר לאילין דאגדתא וצווח להון סיפרי קיסמי
> אמר ליה רבי בא בר כהנא למה את מקנתר לון שאל ואינון מגיבין לך

thematization of multivocality in Tannaitic texts but admits that they are not as fully developed as in the Bavli's "poster children."[71]

In addition to midrash, scholars have also found openness toward diversity of halakhic opinions in the Mishnah and Talmuds.[72] They cite a common repertoire of Talmudic statements that reflect this attitude explic-

---

אמר ליה מהו הדין דכתיב כי חמת אדם תודך שארית חמות תחגור
אמר ליה כי חמת אדם תודך בעולם הזה שאירית חימות תחגור לעולם הבא
אמר ליה או נימר כי חמת אדם תודך בעולם הבא שאירית חימות תחגור בעולם הזה
אמר רבי לוי כשתעורר המתך על הרשעים צדיקים רואין מה את עושה להן והן מודין לשמך
אמר רבי זעירה היא הפכה והיא מהפכה לא שמעינן מינה כלום

A story: R. Zeira and R. Abba b. Kahana and R. Levi were sitting and R. Zeira was rebuking those [teachers] of *aggada* and called them scribes of magic.

R. Abba b. Kahana asked him, "Why do you rebuke them? Ask them [the meaning of a verse] and they will answer you."

He [R. Zeira] said to him [an *aggada* teacher], "What is that which is written, '*The fury [brought upon] man will [cause him to] acknowledge You; the rest of [God's] fury will catch [him]*' (Ps 76:11)?"

He responded, "*The fury brought upon man will cause him to acknowledge You*—in this world; *the rest of God's fury will catch him*—in the next world."

He told him, "Or we can say, '*The fury brought upon man will cause him to acknowledge You*—in the next world; *the rest of God's fury will catch him*—in this world'?"

R. Levi said, "When Your fury awakens over the evil-doers, the righteous see what You do to them and they acknowledge Your name."

R. Zeira said, "[The interpretation] turns it [the verse] around and it turns it around again and we do not learn anything from it."

R. Zeira seems to have chosen this ambiguous verse because its various interpretations are so loosely tied to the text that one can almost arbitrarily fill in the missing elements, thus rendering the verse itself meaningless. On this basis, R. Zeira criticizes aggadic exegetes because their "magical" techniques produce many arbitrary and opposing interpretations. This *sugya* thus denigrates polysemous interpretations that are found so often in non-halakhic bibilical exegesis.

71. Fraade, "Rabbinic Polysemy," 24f. See chart 0.2 below, p. 27. See also Hananel Mack, "Torah Has Seventy Aspects—The Development of a Saying," in *Rabbi Mordechai Breuer Festschrift: Collected Papers in Jewish Studies*, ed. Moshe Bar-Asher (Jerusalem: Aqademon, 1992), 2:449–62. Even the few examples Fraade brings do not clearly evince polysemy. For example, *Mekhilta de-R. Ishmael, Baḥodesh, par.* 9 (text 9 in Fraade) says that each Israelite at Sinai heard the voices "according to his strength," to which Fraade adds, "hence, as seemingly multiple voices" (p. 25). However, this midrash does not necessarily reflect multiple conflicting interpretations but rather deeper or more superficial understandings of the single message of the voice. Fraade's other examples show evidence of revelation in multiple languages, which, as he notes, "is not identical to polysemy," but he nevertheless argues that polyglosia and polysemy "are two aspects of the all-encompassing multivocality of revelation" (p. 31). Fraade spells out his many arguments with Boyarin and Yadin in nn. 91, 93, 102, 125, and 134.

72. The following discussion focuses more on diverse opinions regarding halakhic matters but applies equally to matters of belief and philosophy. For a presentation of the range of diverse opinions in the latter category, see E. E. Urbach, *The Sages: Their Concepts and Beliefs* (Jerusalem: Magnes, 1971) (Hebrew). See also Menachem Kellner, *Must a Jew Believe Anything?* (London: Littman Library of Jewish Civilization, 1999), 26–43.

itly. This includes oft-quoted statements such as "These and these are the words of the living God,"[73] and *b. Ḥag.* 3b:

> All of them [the words of the sages] *"were given from one shepherd"* (Eccl 12:11). One God gave them, one leader (i.e. Moses) proclaimed them from the mouth of God of all creation, blessed be He, as it is written, *"And God spoke all these words"* (Exod 20:1). Therefore make your ear like the hopper and acquire a perceptive heart to understand the words of those who pronounce impure and the words of those who pronounce pure, the words of those who prohibit and the words of those who permit, the words of those who declare unfit and the words of those who declare fit.[74]

Some scholars make broad generalizations about all of rabbinic literature on the basis of these sources. For example, Shaye Cohen writes, "Rabbinic Judaism is dominated by pluralism, the ideology which allows the existence of conflicting truths."[75] More recently, however, scholarship has been careful to distinguish between different periods and geographies by separating and comparing sources found in Palestinian and Babylonian texts. Shlomo Naeh criticizes David Hartman for not distinguishing between the version of the above-quoted midrash as found in the Bavli *Ḥag.* 3b and that found in the Tosefta *Soṭah* 7:12.[76] He argues that the Tannaitic version is primarily concerned not with the existence or validity of multiple opinions but rather with the practical difficulties facing the student who must memorize this mass of material.[77] Therefore, according to Naeh, only the Bavli version of the midrash can be said to exhibit a positive pluralistic attitude.[78]

---

73. *Y. Yebam.* 1:6 (3b); *b. ʿErub.* 13b; and *b. Giṭ.* 6b. See further below, pp. 30–31 n. 109, 35f., 39 n. 147, and 201 n. 136.

74. Translation slightly modified from Stern, "Midrash and Hermeneutics," 19.

75. Shaye Cohen, "The Significance of Yavneh: Pharisees, Rabbis, and the End of Jewish Sectarianism," *Hebrew Union College Annual* 55 (1984): 47.

76. Shlomo Naeh, "'Make Yourself Many Rooms': Another Look at the Utterances of the Sages about Controversy," in *Renewing Jewish Commitment: The Work and Thought of David Hartman*, ed. Avi Sagi and Zvi Zohar (Jerusalem: Shalom Hartman Institute and Hakibbutz Hameuchad, 2001), 851 (Hebrew), regarding David Hartman, *A Heart of Many Rooms: Celebrating the Many Voices within Judaism* (Woodstock, VT: Jewish Lights Publishing, 1999), 21.

77. Naeh, "Rooms," 851–75; and idem, "On Structures of Memory and the Forms of Text in Rabbinic Literature," *Meḥqere Talmud* 3, no. 2 (2005): 570f. (Hebrew).

78. See, however, Fraade, "Rabbinic Polysemy," 33 n. 115, who criticizes Naeh's attempt to reconstruct the prehistory of the Tosefta rather than to read it as it is. Naeh sees a break between the line "those who come and sit in many assemblies and declare impure what is impure and declare pure what is pure" and the next line, "Since Beth Shammai declares impure and Beth Hillel declares pure ... why (למה) should I learn Torah?" The first line reflects monism and the second presents controversy. Naeh therefore deconstructs the Tosefta into two original sources. However, one can easily explain that the first line describes the consensus within each school while the second line zooms out and notes the contro-

Along these same lines, David Kraemer points to the very form of the Bavli as an indication of the philosophy of its authors that "truth is indeterminable and that alternative views can encompass different aspects of the whole truth."[79] Kraemer's analysis is inspired by David Halivni's characterization of the Bavli as maintaining a "love for the dialectical" and a willingness to defend even rejected opinions "not out of historical necessity but out of love for logical discourse."[80] Halivni argues that the late anonymous editors of the Bavli, whom he labels the "Stammaim,"[81] were responsible for preserving and creating these Amoraic dialogues while the Amoraim themselves did not think their internal arguments were worthy of being transmitted. Kraemer disagrees and thinks that the third- and fourth-generation Bavli Amoraim already valued and preserved argumentation for its own sake. Whatever its provenance, this predilection for argumentation does distinguish the Bavli from earlier works of rabbinic literature. As Kraemer writes, "What is outstanding about the deliberations that the Bavli records is that they so often avoid any conclusion; more often than not they prefer to support competing views rather than

---

versies between one school and another. While members of each school can be satisfied with the monolithic view within their circle, the student who wishes to learn the totality of Torah becomes frustrated: why bother studying the opinions of either school if there is so much confusion as to which views are valid?

While Naeh accuses others of reading the Bavli into the Tosefta ("On Structures," 572 n. 135), it is he who suggests replacing "why (למה)" in the Tosefta with "היאך (how)," as is found in the Bavli (ibid., 574 n. 144). Boyarin, *Border Lines*, 159, similarly mistranslates למה in the Tosefta as "how." Even if Naeh correctly reconstructs the original sources of the Tosefta, its final form does address the theological problem presented by controversy and is mostly similar to the Bavli. However, we can agree that while the Tosefta assumes consensus within each school and addresses only interschool controversy, the Bavli adds that even opposing sides of an intraschool controversy are original and divine. Thus, the Bavli further expands the scope of pluralism of opinions, all of which should be tolerated and even celebrated.

79. David Kraemer, *The Mind of the Talmud* (Oxford: Oxford University Press, 1990), 139. Kraemer elaborates:

> The argumentational form of the Bavli represents a moderation of truth claims and an admission that divine truth is available only in the multifarious play of reasoning and interpretation, and even then, finally only imperfectly.... Because any single interpretation (by definition) grasps only part of the truth, alternative interpretations are always called for. Because any interpretation may embody a kernel of the truth, even views that are for practical reasons rejected should be preserved and studied for their own wisdom. (p. 126)

For another form-critical analysis of the Bavli, see Jack N. Lightstone, *The Rhetoric of the Babylonian Talmud, Its Social Meaning and Context* (Waterloo, ON: Wilfrid Laurier University Press, 1994), who comes to some of the same conclusions: "These exploratory and hypothetical argument-statements especially help create in Bavli the air of valuing ongoing critique and analysis" (p. 174).

80. David Halivni, *Midrash, Mishnah, and Gemara: The Jewish Predilection for Justified Law* (Cambridge: Harvard University Press, 1986), 89–90.

81. This is the plural of "Stam," meaning "anonymous."

deciding in favor of one view or the other."[82] This is not true of the Yerushalmi, which "generally admits only one alternative."[83] Kraemer cites an observation of Jacob Neusner in this regard:

> The sages of the Talmud of the Land of Israel seek certain knowledge about some few, practical things. They therefore reject—from end to beginning—the chaos of speculation, the plurality of possibilities even as to word choice; above all, the daring and confidence to address the world in the name, merely, of sagacity. True, the [Palestinian] Talmud preserves the open-ended discourse of sages, not reduced to cut-and-dried positions. But the [Palestinian] Talmud makes decisions.[84]

Kraemer adds, "This contrast in overall compositional preferences may be the most important difference between the Bavli and the Yerushalmi."[85] Stone summarizes the findings of Kraemer and Ben-Menahem as follows: "According to these studies, the Babylonian Talmud, unlike the Palestinian, is more open to legal pluralism, anti-foundationalist notions of 'truth,' anti-authoritarian modes of decision making, and overt judicial deviation from black letter law."[86]

Yaakov Elman is critical of Kraemer's methodology. Kraemer bases his conclusion on the increasing ratio of argumentation to apodictic material in third- and fourth-generation Amoraim. Elman suggests that this ratio may reflect "not an *increasing* value placed on argumentation but *decreasing* possibility for halakhic innovation.... The result is an entirely different historical reconstruction. The society reflected in B[abylonian] T[almud] is authoritarian rather than pluralistic, a conclusion which is historically highly probable."[87] He writes that the later layers of the Bavli have more argumentation simply because (1) the earlier layers were not transmitted, being further away from the editors; and (2) only after the Tannaitic sources became canonical in the fourth generation was it necessary to extend discussion through interpretation of sources rather than

82. Kraemer, *Mind*, 6.

83. Ibid., 95.

84. Jacob Neusner, *Judaism in Society: The Evidence of the Yerushalmi: Toward the Natural History of Religion* (Atlanta: Scholars Press, 1991), 110–11. This is also quoted and discussed by Boyarin, *Border Lines*, 152. This statement is certainly an overgeneralization, and one can list many Yerushalmi *sugyot* that leave matters open-ended and do not make decisions. Still, it does roughly capture an essential difference between the methodologies of the two Talmuds. See further in Zechariah Frankel, *Mevo ha-Yerushalmi* (Breslau: Schletter, 1870), 28b-36a.

85. Kraemer, *Mind*, 95.

86. Stone, "In Pursuit of the Counter-text," 848.

87. Yaakov Elman, "Argument for the Sake of Heaven: The Mind of the Talmud: A Review Essay," *Jewish Quarterly Review* 84, nos. 2–3 (1994): 269. Elman similarly writes further on: "Rabbinic culture was not pluralistic in the modern sense. While some freedom of opinion was permitted, it was strictly limited" (275).

through new apodictic statements. Elman, however, has since come closer to agreeing with Kraemer's conclusions based on his more recent research.[88]

Catherine Hezser disagrees even more fundamentally with Kraemer. She complains that "Kraemer disregards the harmonizing efforts of the Bavli editors. Even more than the editors of the Yerushalmi, the editors of the Bavli try to reconcile differing opinions."[89] Instead, Hezser argues that the Bavli redactors attempt to minimize the extent of the diversity that existed during Amoraic times. This may be so in some cases, but Hezser does not back this up with any examples.[90] This requires further research.

Jeffrey Rubenstein has confirmed Halivni's findings concerning the value of debate for the Stammaim by analyzing many aggadic traditions of the Bavli. While Halivni based his research on halakhic portions of the Bavli, Rubenstein expands the discussion to include Bavli narratives that "thematize dialectical argumentation and portray it as the highest form of Torah. That this theme is absent from the parallel Palestinian versions of the traditions and from Palestinian sources in general suggests that we are dealing with a late Babylonian concern."[91] Some of these traditions portray the Palestinian sages setting a high value to memorizing traditions, an activity that the Babylonian sages denigrate as trivial.[92] What the

88. Personal communication on September 20, 2007. One of Kraemer's explanations for why the Bavli records argumentation is that the Bavli Amoraim wanted to gain the support of the partially assimilated Jews of Babylonia and had to develop persuasive arguments rather than simply pronounce apodictic declarations. See Kraemer, *Mind*, 119–20. Yaakov Elman, "Acculturation to Elite Persian Norms and Modes of Thought in the Babylonian Jewish Community of Late Antiquity," in *Netiᶜot le-David: Jubilee Volume for David Weiss Halivni*, ed. Yaakov Elman et al. (Jerusalem: Orhot, 2004), 31–56, shows that Rava in particular had to defend the rabbinic positions regarding various issues such as theodicy, rabbinic authority, and oral transmission in the face of challenges by more acculturated Jews.

89. Hezser, *Social Structure*, 243.

90. The tendency in the Bavli to limit controversy is documented by Abraham Goldberg, "Ṣimṣum maḥloqet eṣel Amora'e Bavel," *Meḥqere Talmud* 1 (1990): 135–53. Goldberg shows that late Bavli Amoraim and Stammaim often reinterpret a Tannaitic controversy in such a way as to limit the extent or scope of their argument and make their environment seem more harmonious. However, as Goldberg himself points out, the motivation of the Bavli in most of these cases is not that they were troubled by the existence of controversy itself; rather, the reinterpretation is a byproduct of a different concern, such as, reconciling later controversies with earlier ones, resolving contradictions within the Mishnah, or conceptualizing and correlating one controversy with another. See Leib Moscovitz, *Talmudic Reasoning: From Casuistics to Conceptualization* (Tübingen: Mohr Siebeck, 2002), esp. 339; and Jeffrey Rubenstein, "Perushe meqorot Tanaiim ᶜal yede ᶜeqronot kelaliim u-mufshatim," in *Netiᶜot le-David: Jubilee Volume for David Weiss Halivni*, ed. Yaakov Elman et al. (Jerusalem: Orhot, 2004), 275–304.

91. Jeffrey Rubenstein, "The Thematization of Dialectics in Bavli Aggada," *Journal of Jewish Studies* 54, no. 1 (2003): 72. See also idem, *The Culture of the Babylonian Talmud* (Baltimore, MD: Johns Hopkins University Press, 2003), 39–53.

92. That the Yerushalmi emphasizes the role of tradition more than the Bavli may relate

Stammaim value is dialectical skill, the ability to convincingly argue various sides of an issue, which implies that each of those sides contains some validity. This evaluation of the difference between the sages of each country is expressed explicitly at *b. Sanh.* 24a:

> R. Oshaia said: What is [the meaning] of the verse, *I got two staffs, one of which I named* No'am *(Grace) and the other I named* Hovlin *(Damages)* (Zech 11:7)?
> "Grace"—these are the scholars in the Land of Israel who are gracious (*manᶜimin*) to each other in legal [debate].
> "Damages"—these are the scholars in Babylonia who damage (*meḥablin*) each other in legal [debate].[93]

Menachem Fisch discusses a somewhat different, though closely related, topic of traditionalism in rabbinic texts, which he defines as the tendency to follow preceding sources indiscriminately, versus antitraditionalism, which puts traditions of previous sages to the test of rational inquiry and revises them if necessary.[94] Fisch associates the traditionalist attitude with a philosophy of strong realism, which maintains that there exists one truth (halakhic, aggadic, or exegetical) that humans can attain;

---

to a more general difference between the Talmuds regarding who is greater: "Sinai" or "one who uproots mountains." See Devora Steinmetz, "Distancing and Bringing Near: A New Look at Mishnah Tractates ᶜEduyyot and ᵓAbot," *Hebrew Union College Annual* 73 (2002): 50 n. 3; and David Rosental, "Mesorot Ereṣ-Yisre'eliyot ve-darkan le-Bavel," *Cathedra* 92 (1999): 30–36. Rosental discusses the example of *y. Pesaḥ.* 6:1 (33a) where Hillel offers proofs from logic and from biblical interpretation, which are rejected, and then offers a source from tradition, which is accepted. In the version at *t. Pesaḥ.* 4:13, the biblical derivations are accepted but *t. Pesaḥ.* 4:14 cites another version where Hillel continues to quote from a tradition. The version in *b. Pesaḥ.* 66a has Hillel accepted with just the biblical derivations, although, even in the Bavli, the context makes clear that those derivations were themselves based on a received tradition. See Saul Lieberman, *Tosefta ki-fshuṭah* (New York: Jewish Theological Seminary of America Press, 1955–1988), 4:566–67. The Yerushalmi, however, does include a counterexample where dialectical skill is praised at *y. Sanh.* 4:1 (22a): "R. Yoḥanan said: Whoever is not qualified to offer a hundred arguments for declaring a reptile ritually clean or unclean will not know how to argue for acquittal [in a capital case]." See further on this statement at Richard Hidary, "Classical Rhetorical Arrangement and Reasoning in the Talmud: The Case of Yerushalmi Berakhot 1:1," *AJS Review* 34, no. 1 (2010): 33–64.

93. Translation from Jeffrey Rubenstein, *Talmudic Stories: Narrative Art, Composition, and Culture* (Baltimore: Johns Hopkins University Press, 1999), 277, and see further references at ibid., 403 n. 134. The continuation of this *sugya* calls the Babylonian rabbis "bitter," "arrogant," "poor in Torah," and "dwelling in dark places." Considering the disparaging tone of these remarks, which are all expressed by Palestinian Amoraim, I would consider this *sugya* to be a genuine Palestinian tradition even though it has no parallel in Palestinian texts. This *sugya* reflects the Palestinian sages' evaluation of the Babylonian dialectical style. Presumably, most Babylonians would not agree with this evaluation. Rather, they highly valued diverse opinions and the intense argumentation that they engender.

94. Menachem Fisch, *Rational Rabbis: Science and Talmudic Culture* (Bloomington: Indiana University Press, 1997), 43.

since truth rests in Scripture and other canonical texts (such as Mishnah for the Amoraim), one need only accept tradition to arrive at truth. In this framework, only one opinion can be correct, leaving little room for diversity. The antitraditionalist, on the other hand, can ascribe to either a weak realism, according to which one truth exists in principle but cannot be verifiably attained; or, he can be a conventionalist who does not think there exists only one true interpretation. Fisch correlates antitraditionalism with a pluralistic attitude. By analyzing various textual examples, Fisch finds that the Mishnah contains more antitraditionalist statements than does the Tosefta.[95] The Yerushalmi not only agrees with the traditionalism found in the Tosefta, but it even polemicizes against the antitraditionalist view.[96] He then shows that at least one dominant strand in the Bavli emphasizes the antitraditionalist voice.

Daniel Boyarin brings together the findings of Yadin, Naeh, Kraemer, and Fisch and traces a historical development from earlier exclusivism in Palestinian sources to inclusivism in the editorial layer of the Bavli.[97] While previous scholars considered polysemy to be an intrinsic part of rabbinic thinking, Boyarin argues that it is mainly found at the last stage of a long development. Boyarin writes, "The Palestinian Talmud seems to consider determination of the correctness of one of the views of paramount importance, as did apparently the early strata of Babylonian rabbinism (Amoraic, 200–450 A.C.), whereas for the anonymous redactorial voice of the Babylonian Talmud it is most often the case that such an apparent proof of one view is considered a difficulty (*qushia*) requiring a resolution which, in fact, shows that there is no resolution."[98]

There thus emerges some scholarly consensus that the Bavli, to a greater or lesser extent, supported a polysemic reading of Scripture, favored argumentation, and tolerated differing opinions more than previous texts of rabbinic literature. This knowledge will serve as a good background for analysis of pluralism of practice, which is related to pluralism of opinion, although still not quite the same.

Because the above writers limit their studies to multiplicity in biblical interpretation and theoretical opinion, the texts they use to support their opinions are also limited. Most of the writers focus on the same few texts, which Fraade calls the "poster children" of Talmudic pluralism. In the

95. Ibid., 66–78. See, however, Boyarin, *Border Lines*, 309 n. 31; and below, p. 306 n. 30.

96. Fisch, *Rational Rabbis*, 96f.

97. Boyarin, *Border Lines*, 151f. The same criticism of Boyarin by Fraade regarding polysemy of Scripture, cited above, end of n. 71, applies to the topic of multiplicity of opinion as well, since some of Fraade's examples of early Palestinian texts relate to multiplicity of opinion outside the context of biblical exegesis. See Fraade, "Rabbinic Polysemy," 12–23.

98. Boyarin, *Border Lines*, 152.

following chart, I provide the page numbers on which various authors discuss the six most commonly cited sources:

	t. Sotah 7:12, *b. Ḥag.* 3b "hopper"	*y. Yeb.* 1:6 (3b), *b. ʿErub.* 13b "these and these"	*b. Sanh.* 34a "hammer"	*y. Moʿed Qaṭ.* 3:1 (81c-d), *b. B. Meṣiʿa* 59b "oven of Akhnai"	*y. Ber.* 4:1 (7c-d), *b. Ber.* 27b "Gamaliel's deposition"	*b. Men.* 29b "crowns on letters"
Handelman, *Slayers*, 1982		56	67	40		38
Cohen, "Yavneh," 1984	49 n. 58	48		49	49	
Stern, "Polysemy," 1988	19	21	17	30	34	
Kraemer, *Mind*, 1990		141f.		122f.		
Bruns, "Hermeneutics," 1992	107				121	
Fisch, *Rational*, 1997	91	209		79	65	192
Naeh, "Rooms," 2001	851	856				
Heger, *Pluralistic*, 2003	327	60	43	64	296	236
Boyarin, *Border*, 2004	157	162f.	189	168	185f.	165

Chart 0.2 The "poster children" for pluralism of opinions

As noted above, some of these writers use these texts without proper methodological care to compare parallel versions of each source and distinguish between time periods. Naeh, Rubenstein, Boyarin, Yadin, and Fraade, on the other hand, do use proper methodological caution and thus are able to trace the development of pluralism of opinions from one period to the next. Nevertheless, with a few notable exceptions, these scholars all base their arguments on the same few sources. Kraemer has expanded the discussion to include the form of the Bavli; Rubenstein has called attention to numerous narratives in the Bavli that celebrate dialectics; and Fraade has extended the list to include more Tannaitic thematizations and two instances of textual praxis. These efforts have gone some way toward incorporating more of rabbinic literature into the discussion.

This book proposes to further expand this discussion by assessing the attitudes of the rabbis toward behavioral pluralism. This has the benefit of making available an entire new set of halakhic texts for analysis that are not only interesting in themselves but that can also shed light on rabbinic attitudes toward diversity of opinions. Because the two topics are closely related, one's tolerance for diverse opinion is likely to impact one's tolerance for diverse practice.[99]

Obviously, however, the two issues are not identical and so do not bear a one-to-one correspondence. For example, there is a strong trend found in some sources to tolerate diverse opinions while still requiring uniformity of practice. *m. Sanh.* 11:2, regarding the rebellious elder who hears a ruling from the supreme court, is representative of this view:

> חזר לעיר ושנה ולימד כדרך שהיה למד פטור ואם הורה לעשות חייב שנאמר והאיש אשר יעשה בזדון אינו חייב עד שיורה לעשות
>
> If he returns to his city and repeats and teaches just as he had taught before, he is innocent. However, if he issues a practical ruling, he is liable, as the verse says, "*Should a man act presumptuously*" (Deut 17:12). He is not liable until he issues a practical ruling.[100]

That is, the elder may teach his dissenting view as a theoretical possibility even after the supreme court rules against it; but he may not practice in accordance with it. A similar distinction between theory and practice is found in *y. Sanh.* 4:2 (22a):

> [A] אמר רבי ינאי אילו ניתנה התורה חתוכה לא היתה לרגל עמידה
> [B] מה טעם וידבר ײ׳ אל משה
> [C] אמר לפניו רבונו של עולם הודיעיני היאך היא ההלכה
> [D] אמר לו אחרי רבים להטות רבו המזכין זכו רבו המחייבין חייבו
> [E] כדי שתהא התורה נדרשת מ״ט פנים טמא ומ״ט פנים טהור
> [F] מיניין ודגל״ו
> [G] וכן הוא אומר אמרות ײ׳ אמרות טהורות כסף צרוף בעליל לארץ מזוקק שבעתים
> [H] ואומר מישרים אהבוך
>
> [A] Rabbi Yannai said: Had the Torah been given as clear-cut decisions, it would not have a leg to stand on.[101]

99. As Stern, "Midrash and Hermeneutics," 33–34, writes, "Midrashic polysemy suggests more than just textual stability; it points to a fantasy of social stability, of human community in complete harmony, where disagreement is either resolved agreeably or maintained peacefully." Stern is correct to say that one "suggests" the other but does not necessitate it.

100. See further analysis below, p. 301f.

101. *Qorban ha-ʿedah* explains that had the Torah been given as decisive conclusions then it would not be flexible enough to address the particulars of each situation and would become obsolete. Another explanation is that the Torah could never be fulfilled correctly if it were monistic since the rabbis have no way to assure that they can reliably access the Torah's single correct view. The Torah needs to be multivocal and flexible if the many opinions of

[B] What is the source? "*God spoke to Moses...*" (Num 2:1).[102]
[C] He [Moses] said before Him, "Master of the Universe, inform me what is the halakha."
[D] He responded, "*Incline after the majority* (Exod 23:2). If those who declare innocent are more numerous, then declare innocent. If those who declare guilty are more numerous, then declare guilty."
[E] So that the Torah can be interpreted in forty-nine ways to declare impure and forty-nine ways to declare pure.
[F] From where do we know this? "*His flag (ve-diglo)*" (Ct 2:4).
[G] And so the verse says, "*The words of the Lord are pure words, silver purged in an earthen crucible, refined sevenfold*" (Ps 12:7).[103]
[H] And it says, "*Straightly do they love you*" (Ct 1:4).[104]

Thus, multiplicity of interpretation and opinion is not only tolerated but is an inherent part of Torah as given by God. Nevertheless, when it comes to practice, the judges must use majority rule to decide on only one set of practices. What they decide is not as important as that they come to a uniform decision.

Many scholars, on basis of these and similar sources, assume a monistic position across the board. For example, E. E. Urbach writes:

> Within the academies of the sages a large measure of freedom was allowed for differences of opinion, not only in the area of doctrine and belief but also in that of halakha. Nevertheless, a dissenting member was

rabbis are to be valid. The latter explanation seems preferable based on the version of this statement found at *Soferim* 16:5 and *Pesiqta Rabbati* 21. See further in Ben-Menahem et al., *Controversy and Dialogue in Halakhic Sources*, 3:161.

102. The relevance of the verses cited in this midrash is not self-evident and requires us to fill in some of the gaps with parallel midrashim. See *Num. Rab., pisqa* 2:3, to Num 2:2, which connects דגלו "his flag" (Num 2:2) with ודגלו (Ct 2:4, cited at line F). Thus, here, too, one should read lines E-F as the direct continuation of line B and lines C-D as a parenthetical interruption. Lines E-F interpret Ct 2:4 to mean that God shows His love to Israel by giving them the Torah that can be interpreted in forty-nine ways since the numerical equivalent (*gematria*) of ודגלו is forty-nine. Line B then connects that interpretation to the same word (but lacking the initial ו) in Num 2:2 (although the Talmud only quotes the beginning of 2:1, the continuation to the next verse is implied) to teach that all these interpretations originate at Sinai, which is the setting of Numbers 2. See other parallels to this text cited in Fraade, "Rabbinic Polysemy," 16 n. 44.

103. The midrash interprets the dual form of שבעתים as seven multiplied by itself, which comes to forty-nine. See parallel at *Midrash Tehillim* 12:4; and cf. *Pesiqta de-Rav Kahana, Parah 'adumah, pisqa* 4:2, to Num 19:2 (ed. Mandelbaum, 1:56), which connects a similar idea with Ps 12:8.

104. In contrast to the multivocality of God's word, God's people show their love by practicing one straight path. This verse is used in *Sifra, Shemini*, 1:38, and *Gen. Rab.* 49:17 to describe Abraham's unquestioning devotion in Genesis 22.

obliged to bow to the decision of the majority after it had been taken and could not act in accordance with the rejected opinion.[105]

Along the same lines, Halivni writes:

> In the sphere of belief ... one is not bound by the standard decision-making apparatus of halakha, including majority rule. One may choose the opinion of the minority if that opinion is more appealing. Majority decision does not make its rule inherently true. It is merely a practical necessity, so that whenever feasible, plurality *is* preferable. This applies to almost everything other than practice. Variety of practice was anathema to the rabbis. It was simply inconceivable to them to allow diversity in behavior. Behavior had to be uniform—and majority rule is the most effective way to enforce uniformity.[106]

Regarding *b. Ḥag.* 3b, David Stern summarizes: "Although the sages' opinions may contradict each other, they all are part of Torah, part of a single revelation. They all were spoken by the mouth of one shepherd, Moses, who in turn received them all from God."[107] Stern continues, however: "It should be noted that the student's question is *not* 'How can I practice the law?' The answer to that question would be clear to any disciple of the rabbis: where there is a difference of opinion over the correct law, the halakhah is decided by following the opinion of the majority of sages."[108]

Similarly, after reviewing the Talmudic appreciation for pluralism of ideas and multiple truths, Stone distinguishes this from tolerance for multiple practices:

> Such intellectual tolerance is limited to the realm of ideas and opinions; it does not extend to action or legal practice. Behavioral pluralism, in theory, is either a sin, the disregard of a binding norm or, in the absence of a binding norm, the sad consequence of the failure to reach consensus through rational discourse—the goal of the Halakic community.[109]

---

105. E. E. Urbach, "Self-Isolation or Self-Affirmation in Judaism in the First Three Centuries: Theory and Practice," in *Jewish and Christian Self-Definition: Volume Two, Aspects of Judaism in the Graeco-Roman Period*, ed. E. P. Sanders (Philadelphia: Fortress, 1981), 289–90. In his later book, however, Urbach does recognize various exceptions and limitations to majority rule; see Urbach, *The Halakhah*, 93–99.

106. Halivni, *Peshat and Derash*, 121.

107. Stern, "Midrash and Hermeneutics," 20.

108. Ibid., 21.

109. Stone, "Tolerance Versus Pluralism in Judaism," 112. This assessment is based on sources cited in idem, "In Pursuit of the Counter-text," 838 n. 40. Stone, ibid., 838–39, elaborates:

> On the one hand, the affirmation of multiple halakhic truths paves the way for genuine legal pluralism as each authority pursues his version of the truth by following accepted halakhic methodology. On the other hand, the "these and these"

As we will see, these opinions are based on only a partial sampling of rabbinic texts. In reality, Talmudic jurisprudence contains considerably more complexity. Pluralism of rabbinic opinion does not always translate into pluralism of practice; but neither does the principle of majority rule altogether negate it.

From Sectarianism to Rabbinism

Before we can analyze diversity in the Talmudic period, it is fitting to review what the situation was beforehand and how rabbinic Judaism emerged from those conditions. Second Temple sectarianism lasted from the middle of the Second Temple period until early Tannaitic times, and its shadow must have remained strong for a long time afterward. As we will see, several stories and halakhic discussions in the Talmud reflect a concern that differing halakhic practices might lead to a breakdown in the unity of the Jewish people and a return to sectarianism.[110]

Scholars debate whether to view the sects as variations of Judaism that all share core values and norms or whether they were distinct entities or "Judaisms."[111] In part, this judgment may depend on the identity of the group and the period. Occasionally, sectarian disagreements led to violence or even civil war.[112] However, even when there was no physical violence, each sect still denied the validity of the other sects' halakhic practices.[113] Albert Baumgarten rightly distinguished between various

---

> tradition, which ultimately establishes the Hillel view as the binding law, and other Talmudic traditions suggest that a major goal of the halakhic process is to prevent fragmentation of the law through the eventual identification of a single rule of conduct. In this view, diverse opinions leading to behavioral pluralism are due to the fact that the *halakhah* has not yet been finally determined. Indeed, only on rare occasions does one find cases of true legal pluralism in which the Talmud explicitly regards two contradictory behavior-regulating norms as equally valid, final resolutions of a legal problem.

Stone does, however, provide a more nuanced evaluation of Talmudic pluralism later in the same article; see the quotation above, p. 23.

110. See references below, p. 169 n. 20.

111. This discussion is neatly summarized by Gabriele Boccaccini, *Roots of Rabbinic Judaism: An Intellectual History, from Ezekiel to Daniel* (Grand Rapids, MI: Eerdmans, 2002), 8–14.

112. See Lawrence Schiffman, "Jewish Sectarianism in Second Temple Times," in *Great Schisms in Jewish History*, ed. Raphael Jospe and Stanley Wagner (New York: Ktav and University of Denver, 1981), 27; Anthony J. Saldarini, *Pharisees, Scribes and Sadducees in Palestinian Society: A Sociological Approach* (Wilmington, DE: Michael Glazier, 1988), 79–106; and Richard Hidary, "Tolerance for Diversity of Halakhic Practice in the Talmuds" (Ph.D. diss., New York University, 2008), 26–27.

113. See texts quoted by Emil Schürer, *A History of the Jewish People in the Time of Jesus Christ* (New York: Charles Scribner's Sons, 1896), 2:5–8.

shades of sectarianism: "All would see the Qumran division of the world into sons of light vs. sons of darkness as indicative of an extreme position, which brooks no compromise and has culminated in separatism."[114] Baumgarten classifies the Qumran sect as "introversionist," in distinction from the Sadducees and Pharisees, who were "reformist" sects:[115] "The Pharisees remained loyal to the Temple, in spite of the shifts in control that institution underwent over time, which must have affected Temple practice. They participated in the life of the Hasmonean and Herodian court."[116] The Sadducees and Pharisees made enough of a political compromise to live together and even sit together on the Sanhedrin. Still, this ability to compromise does not reflect an acceptance of the other side. Baumgarten elaborates, "Movements of both sorts insist on the rightness of their way" and the illegitimacy of their opponents' way. They only agreed to live and work together in "hopes of reforming the larger society."[117]

The vast majority of the Jewish population in Palestine during the Second Temple were simple farmers, "people of the land," who most likely knew very little about the different sects.[118] Many Jews were Hellenized to such an extent that the details of Jewish law would not have been important to them.[119] But, for those Jews who were involved in the political arena or religious leadership, especially those who lived near Jerusalem,[120] this was an era of strident divisiveness on political, religious, and social levels without a great amount of tolerance. Baumgarten summarizes, "*Sectarian Jews treated other Jews as outsiders of a new sort.*"[121]

---

114. Albert Baumgarten, *The Flourishing of Jewish Sects in the Maccabean Era: An Interpretation* (Leiden: Brill, 1997), 12.

115. E. P. Sanders, *Paul and Palestinian Judaism* (Philadelphia: Fortress, 1977), 150–57, prefers to reserve the word "sect" for the Essenes but to call the Sadducees a "party" because "although they [the Pharisees] may have thought that the Sadducees were *wrong*, they did not regard them as outside the covenant" (p. 151, italics in original). See also Cohen, "Yavneh," 30 n. 6.

116. Baumgarten, *Flourishing*, 13.

117. Ibid. This is an example of particular monism.

118. See ibid., 42f.; and Shaye Cohen, *From the Maccabees to the Mishnah* (Philadelphia: Westminster, 1987), 172–73.

119. See Erwin R. Goodenough, *Jewish Symbols in the Greco-Roman Period* (New York: Pantheon, 1953), vol. 1; further references in William D. Davies, *The Setting of the Sermon on the Mount* (Cambridge: Cambridge University Press, 1966), 293 n. 1.

120. See Seth Schwartz, *Imperialism and Jewish Society, 200 B.C.E. to 640 C.E.* (Princeton: Princeton University Press, 2001), 91–98.

121. Baumgarten, *Flourishing*, 9; italics in original. For a different assessment of the times, see Boyarin, "Anecdotal Evidence," 2–5, who writes, "The 'sectarianism' of the pre-Yavneh period did not preclude inclusiveness or a sense of a 'pluralistic' Israel" (p. 5). This is based on Josephus's praise of the harmony and unity of the Jewish people in *Contra Apion* 2.179–81. Even if this quotation represents Josephus's true feelings, which is itself doubtful, the perspective of this Hellenized Jew certainly cannot speak for the view of the sectarians themselves. Lawrence Schiffman, "Inter- or Intra-Jewish Conflict?" in *Qumran and Jerusalem:*

What was the primary cause for sectarian mutual rejection? Cohen concludes "that sectarian dispute focused primarily on legal questions."[122] The sects were divided primarily over such halakhic matters as "marriage; Sabbath and festivals; Temple and purity."[123] Once one group differs on details of marriage laws and accuses other groups of breeding *mamzerim*,[124] that group will forbid marriage with nonmembers, thus cutting themselves off socially from the rest of the nation.[125] A major dispute separating the Sadducees from the Pharisees was over the proper date for the first offering of the *ʿomer*.[126] Moshe Halbertal elaborates on the effects of calendrical disputes:

> The various sects definitely rejected one another, for some of the differences between them made coexistence within a single tradition almost impossible. For example, the Dead Sea community rejected the rabbinic lunar calendar. As the two sects had no common calendar, cooperation in a unified community was clearly impossible.[127]

Explaining why the Temple should cause such division, Cohen writes:

> The temple represents monism. "One temple for the one God." Only one holy site, one altar, one cult, and one priesthood can find favor in God's

---

Studies in the Dead Sea Scrolls and the History of Judaism (Grand Rapids, MI: Eerdmans, forthcoming), analyzes the self-perception of the Dead Sea sect based on their own writings. He concludes that the sectarians "seem to have believed that there was only one Judaism, that some followed and most violated."

122. Cohen, *From the Maccabees*, 129. Cohen explains that references in Josephus to the different philosophical schools are written "for the benefit of their intended non-Jewish audience" who could understand philosophical differences better than nitty-gritty points of ritual law. See also idem, "Yavneh," 43f.; Baumgarten, *Flourishing*, 75–80, especially n. 126; and Heger, *Pluralistic Halakhah*, 40 n. 133.

123. Cohen, *From the Maccabees*, 129. See also Yaakov Sussman, "The History of Halakha and the Dead Sea Scrolls: Preliminary Observations on *Miqsat Maʿase ha-Torah* (4QMMT)," *Tarbiz* 59 (1990): 36 (Hebrew), who argues that there were political and philosophical differences between the Dead Sea sect and the Jerusalem groups, but that halakhic differences were the major reason for their breaking away. On the importance of Jewish law in the disputes between the Jesus sect and the Pharisees, see E. P. Sanders, *The Historical Figure of Jesus* (New York: Penguin Books, 1993), 205f. See also idem, *Jewish Law from Jesus to the Mishnah: Five Studies* (London: SCM, 1990); and idem, *Judaism: Practice and Belief, 63 BCE-66 CE* (London: SCM, 1992).

124. Singular, *mamzer*: a child born of incest or adultery.

125. This was a major reason cited by the rabbis for alienating the Samaritans; see *b. Qidd.* 75b. Note that a similar debate existed between the Houses of Shammai and Hillel where the rabbis made special efforts to ensure that the debate would not lead to sectarianism; see below, p. 189 n. 110.

126. Lawrence Schiffman, *Reclaiming the Dead Sea Scrolls* (New York: Doubleday, 1994), 75.

127. Halbertal, *People of the Book*, 50.

> eyes. Sects defined themselves in reference to the temple and therefore arrogated the temple's exclusivistic claims. Only the sect is the true Israel and only the sect correctly fulfills God's wishes. Some of the sects admitted that the temple was still legitimate to one degree or another, but all the sects argued that every variety of Judaism other than its own is illegitimate. This is the monism of the temple transferred to the sect. With the destruction of the temple in 70, the institutional basis of monism is removed.[128]

Cohen sees the limitation of worship at only one Temple as causing an intolerant worldview. He therefore considers the destruction of the Temple to be an important factor contributing to the cessation of sectarianism. The war itself with the Romans also helped to end sectarianism because of the especially high casualties among the revolutionary groups, the Qumran sect, and the Sadducees.[129] As a third factor contributing to the demise of sectarianism, scholars point to the actions of the rabbis at Yavneh. In his effort to show that the Yavnean rabbis were intolerant of diversity, William D. Davies proposes that the Pharisees[130] took advantage of their upper hand after the war to initiate a program of exclusion against the Sadducees and any other remaining sects and succeeded in eradicating them. They declared the Sadducees to be heretics on account of their rejection of certain dogmas, such as that of the resurrection of the dead (*m. Sanh.* 10:1).[131] Davies further argues that the granting of the title "rabbi" to select students helped to "regularize the interpretation of the Law in the interests of unity by delivering it from 'charismatics.'"[132] Rabban Gamaliel of Yavneh seems to have been a strong figure who quashed dissent and excluded many for the sake of the unity of the Jewish people.[133] Along the same lines, Martin Goodman contends that these early rabbis created a

---

128. Cohen, "Yavneh," 47–48; and see also p. 43.

129. Idem, *From the Maccabees*, 277; and George Foot Moore, *Judaism in the First Centuries of the Christian Era, the Age of the Tannaim* (1927; reprint, New York: Schocken Books, 1971), 1:85.

130. The history of scholarship on the relationship between the Pharisees and the rabbis is summarized by Heger, *Pluralistic Halakhah*, 249–52.

131. Moore, *Judaism in the First Centuries*, 1:85–86. See also Davies, *Setting*, 259–60; and Lawrence Schiffman, *Who Was a Jew? Rabbinic and Halakhic Perspectives on the Jewish-Christian Schism* (Hoboken, NJ: Ktav, 1985), 41–46, who similarly identify the beliefs mentioned in *m. Sanh.* 10:1 with Sadducean creeds.

132. Davies, *Setting*, 271. The move to orality also granted the masters great control over what the next generation of rabbis would be taught, thus further helping to regularize the law. See Baumgarten, *Flourishing*, 135.

133. Davies, *Setting*, 277. See also below, p. 242 n. 5.

new term, "*minim*,"[134] in order to designate an entire category of people as heretics.[135]

Shaye Cohen, on the other hand, argues that sectarianism dissolved not because of Yavnean intolerance but rather because the Yavnean rabbis tolerated dissenters and absorbed them into a "grand coalition."[136] He points to a number of sources that portray the rabbis at Yavneh as being pluralistic by declaring, for example, "These and these are the words of the living God." Boyarin, however, emphasizes that the sources for this inclusive portrayal of Yavneh are late, some not even found in Tannaitic texts. Boyarin thus concludes that considering the scanty evidence regarding the historical Yavneh, it is fruitless to make any claims about the relative inclusiveness or exclusiveness of that early group of sages.

A more productive project, Boyarin suggests, is to analyze rabbinic literature in order to reconstruct the outlook of the rabbinic authors and editors about tolerance. By tracing the development of these Talmudic traditions and assuming that each generation retrojected its own positions back to the Yavnean rabbis, we may be able to produce an intellectual history of the rabbis regarding tolerance of diversity. Boyarin is thus able to solve all tensions between these sources diachronically such that the early sources are exclusive and the later ones are pluralistic. He writes, "The two descriptions, one of an exclusivistic and one of a pluralistic Yavneh, are best emplotted diachronically as two stages in the development of Rabbinic ecclesiology itself."[137] As we discussed above, Boyarin sees change from less tolerance for differences in earlier Palestinian texts to greater tolerance in the Bavli.

While I adopt Boyarin's methodology and many of his conclusions in this study, I would also add that these varying accounts of Yavneh can partially be solved synchronically. In the act of defining themselves, the rabbis both excluded certain groups and included others. Most of the exclusivistic statements of the rabbis quoted by Davies and Goodman

134. See Martin Goodman, "The Function of 'Minim' in Early Rabbinic Judaism," in *Geschichte—Tradition—Reflexion I*, ed. Peter Schäfer (Tübingen: Mohr Siebeck, 1996), 504.

135. *Min* in Tannaitic literature does not refer to any one specific group but rather works as a catch-all for anyone whom the rabbis considered heretical or a dangerous influence to their worldview. Tracing the usage of the word *min* throughout Talmudic literature, Reuven Kimelman, "*Birkat Ha-Minim* and the Lack of Evidence for an Anti-Christian Jewish Prayer in Late Antiquity," in *Jewish and Christian Self-Definition: Volume Two, Aspects of Judaism in the Graeco-Roman Period*, ed. E. P. Sanders (Philadelphia: Fortress, 1981), 230, notices that "[i]n Palestinian literature, be it tannaitic or amoraic ... *minim* had a Jewish sectarian denotation and was not used to refer to Gentiles." Only in Babylonia, where the presence of Jewish sectarianism was not as strong, does the term begin to refer to Gentiles as well.

136. Cohen, "Yavneh," 42. For further analysis of this position, see Hidary, "Tolerance for Diversity," 32–35.

137. Boyarin, "Anecdotal Evidence," 11.

apply to those groups who already placed themselves or whom the rabbis already considered outside of the rabbinic circle. The inclusivistic statements, on the other hand, refer to the internal diversity that was tolerated among the rabbis themselves. Even within one time period, the rabbis could have expressed statements rejecting Sadducees and Christians while at the same time describing the tolerance shown by Beth Shammai to Beth Hillel. Boyarin is still correct, however, to show a progression from less to more tolerance within those statements that refer to intrarabbinic controversy.

Thus, statements reflecting pluralism of practice in Talmudic literature apply only within an already circumscribed group. Even the most tolerant rabbi would forcefully exclude a heretic from having any share of legitimacy. Those texts that exclude various groups from the halakhic community have received much scholarly attention, as summarized above, and will not be further analyzed in this study. This study will similarly not deal with the question of tolerance of the rabbis toward sinners, sectarians, *ʿame ha-'areṣ* and Gentiles. Rather, this study will focus on texts dealing with intrarabbinic diversity of practice, a subject that has not previously received adequate attention.

Methodology

This study derives its evidence mostly from rabbinic literature but also makes use of relevant material from extra-Talmudic sources. Each Talmudic text studied will be analyzed using text-critical, source-critical, and literary methods. Available manuscripts will be consulted for important variations. We will pay careful attention to separating the attitudes of the earlier Amoraim from those of the later ones. Of course, attributions are not always reliable, and the redactors sometimes transferred Amoraic statements from other contexts. But with appropriate caution, one can generally use attributions as a tool for reconstructing the evolution of an idea through the generations of the Talmud.[138] We will furthermore attempt to reconstruct the activity of the anonymous redactors of the Talmud (the Stammaim) as they formed each *sugya* (Talmudic pericope, pl. *sugyot*). This is done by seeking parallel texts in other parts of rabbinic literature that may have been used as source material for constructing the *sugya* and also by separating the anonymous statements from the named Amoraic statements within the *sugya*.[139]

---

138. On reliability of attributions see Christine Hayes, *Between the Babylonian and Palestinian Talmuds: Accounting for Halakhic Difference in Selected Sugyot from Tractate Avodah Zarah* (New York: Oxford University Press, 1997), 14–15; and Schwartz, *Imperialism*, 8.

139. For the basis of this methodology, see Shamma Friedman, *Pereq ha-'isha rabbah*

Especially relevant in this study will be comparing parallels between the Palestinian and Babylonian Talmuds. There is scholarly consensus that the Bavli redactors did not have the completed Yerushalmi as recorded in medieval manuscripts. Nevertheless, it is also obvious that much of the Bavli is based on Palestinian traditions that eventually formed the Yerushalmi.[140] The Bavli quotes not only individual statements but even entire structural units of material that are present in the Yerushalmi.[141] Even if the Bavli redactors did not have the Yerushalmi exactly as it exists today, they surely had something close to it. Again, with appropriate caution, we can use the Yerushalmi as a rough estimation for the source materials used by the Bavli.

Rubenstein compares a number of stories found in the Yerushalmi with parallels in the Bavli. He described the method used by the Talmudic redactors to compose the narratives of the Bavli:

> They [the Stammaim] composed these stories by extensively reworking earlier narrative sources, mainly Palestinian traditions that now appear in the P[alestinian] T[almud] in versions similar to those transmitted to Babylonia. The Stammaim revised these sources through processes of embellishment, expansion, and supplementation. They transferred material from other B[abylonian] T[almud] passages, adapted it to their needs, and added stock phrases and common motifs.... However, the redactors

---

ba-Bavli (Jerusalem: Jewish Theological Seminary, 1978); David Halivni, *Meqorot u-mesorot*, 6 vols. (Tel Aviv: Dvir; Jerusalem: Jewish Theological Seminary of America and Magnes, 1968–2003), introductions to volumes 2 and on; Aryeh Cohen, *Rereading Talmud: Gender, Law and the Poetics of Sugyot* (Atlanta: Scholars Press, 1998), 7–42; Rubenstein, *Talmudic Stories*, 15–22; and David Halivni, "Aspects of the Formation of the Talmud," in *Creation and Composition: The Contribution of the Bavli Redactors (Stammaim) to the Aggada*, ed. Jeffrey Rubenstein (Tübingen: Mohr Siebeck, 2005).

140. The literature on this subject is summarized by H. L. Strack and G. Stemberger, *Introduction to the Talmud and Midrash*, trans. Marcus Bockmuehl (Minneapolis: Fortress, 1992), 201: "The Palestinian influence ranges from the mere adoption of halakhic decisions and customs to the transfer of entire *sugyot*, which of course were subject to appropriate revision in Babylonia."

141. Martin Jaffee, "The Babylonian Appropriation of the Talmud Yerushalmi," in *The Literature of Early Rabbinic Judaism*, ed. Alan Avery-Peck (Lanham, MD: University Press of America, 1989), 7, writes: "There is suggestive evidence that the Yerushalmi, in more or less its extant form, shapes the Babylonians' conception of their own task and, moreover, supplies the dominant exegetical themes appropriated by them for amplification or revision." Moreover, "The post-Amoraic editors of the Babylonian Talmud had something like the extant version of the Palestinian Talmud before them and reflected upon the logic of its construction as they composed their own commentary" (ibid., p. 24). See also Hayes, *Between*, 15, and references to Shamma Friedman there; and, more recently, Alyssa Gray, *A Talmud in Exile: The Influence of Yerushalmi Avodah Zarah on the Formation of Bavli Avodah Zarah* (Providence: Brown Judaic Studies, 2005). For an opposing viewpoint see Kraemer, *Mind*, 22 n. 36.

> apparently were unable or unwilling to revise their sources totally, and consequently some interpretive difficulties remain.[142]

Much of this method is used by the Stammaim not only in the composition of stories but in the creation of halakhic *sugyot* as well. Comparing parallels aids in reconstructing the activity of the Stammaim, which in turn affords us an opportunity to see how the Babylonian redactors chose to emphasize, ignore, or polemicize against the Palestinian sources they inherited.

In reconstructing this intellectual history, we will make use of both halakhic statements said by Tannaim and Amoraim as well as narratives told about Tannaim and Amoraim. Statements and stories will be categorized by time period and geography since the realities of the Tannaim were different from those of the Palestinian Amoraim, which again differed from those of the Babylonian Amoraim. Caution must be used, however, when categorizing Talmudic *sugyot* because they often reflect the realities and viewpoints not of the named characters or tradents but rather of their redactors or storytellers. Thus, statements by or stories about Palestinian rabbis found in the Babylonian Talmud may be based on some original Palestinian story or statement, but the Babylonian redactors often add and change aspects of the tradition to reflect their own point of view. When more than one version of the story exists, these changes are easily traceable. In such cases, one often finds important and seemingly intentional differences between Yerushalmi and Bavli versions of a narrative.[143] At the same time, one also finds that the Bavli does sometimes reliably cite the Yerushalmi version even if it later disagrees with it.[144] Therefore, when there is only one version, one cannot be sure how to categorize it. For example, when the Bavli quotes a statement of R. Yoḥanan and no parallel statement exists in the Yerushalmi, are we to presume the statement is authentic and represents a Palestinian viewpoint, or has it been modified to express the Babylonian viewpoint? Conversely, when the Yerushalmi relates a story about Rav that has no parallel in the Bavli, does that story represent a Palestinian or Babylonian perspective? In such cases, we must look for more subtle textual clues to figure out whose point of view is represented in a given story or statement. In some instances, we can hesitantly decide one way or the other based on patterns of thought already established by other, less ambiguous statements.[145]

---

142. Rubenstein, *Talmudic Stories*, 244.

143. Ibid.

144. See below, ch. 1, regarding *b. ʿErub.* 46b–47b, which reliably quotes R. Yoḥanan's rules as they appear in the Yerushalmi even though the Bavli *sugya* then rejects them.

145. See similar methodological considerations at Jeffrey Rubenstein, *The Culture of the Babylonian Talmud* (Baltimore, MD: Johns Hopkins University Press, 2003), 7–11; and Richard Kalmin, *The Sage in Jewish Society of Late Antiquity* (New York: Routledge, 1999), 28. Kalmin

A similar dilemma comes up when the Yerushalmi or Bavli quotes a Tannaitic statement that is not found in any extant Tannaitic work. In some cases, the source is authentic, but in other cases, the Stammaim pseudepigraphically attribute Amoraic statements to the Tannaim.[146] It is usually impossible to determine definitively whether the quoted *baraita* is authentic. However, when the *baraita* expresses views that differ dramatically from all other Tannaitic sources but that do coincide with the Amoraic context or language, then one may tentatively postulate that the *baraita* is likely to be pseudepigraphic.[147] In this study, we avoid basing any major conclusions on such determinations. However, once we are able to show that the Bavli had a distinct viewpoint on a certain issue based on relatively straightforward sources, we will then include such ambiguous sources as further possible examples.

Besides this diachronic analysis, which breaks the *sugya* down into its components, we will also try to put the *sugya* back together and read it synchronically to see how the *sugya* functions as a unit to relate its message.[148] In order to recover the viewpoint of the Talmudic redactor, one must not focus only on a single specific statement found in a *sugya* but rather must find the rhetorical drive of the entire *sugya*. One can be on safest ground when findings based on source criticism coincide with the literary/rhetorical structure of the *sugya*.[149]

---

writes that, with few exceptions, statements attributed to Palestinian rabbis reflect a Palestinian point of view even when recorded in the Bavli. Rubenstein, however, finds that the Bavli Stammaim do very often rework Palestinian traditions to accord with Babylonian values. This study will generally show Rubenstein's view to be more accurate.

146. See Rubenstein, *Culture*, 125, summarizing the findings of Stephen Wald, *BT Pesahim III: Critical Edition with Comprehensive Commentary* (New York: Jewish Theological Seminary, 2000).

147. One such example that is relevant to the topic of this study is presented by Boyarin, *Border Lines*, 163. Naeh presumes that the statement "אלו ואלו דברי אלהים חיים—These and these are the words of the living God," which is cited as a *baraita* in the Talmuds but which is not found in Tannaitic sources, is authentically Tannaitic and is therefore a product of first-century reality. In contrast, Boyarin argues that because this statement contradicts other Tannaitic sources, it must be an Amoraic creation and thus reflects a specifically Amoraic point of view. Boyarin admits, however, that neither view can be proven or disproven.

148. For some examples of literary readings of Bavli *sugyot*, see David Kraemer, *Reading the Rabbis: The Talmud as Literature* (Oxford: Oxford University Press, 1995); Cohen, *Rereading Talmud*, 71f.; Michael Chernick, "An Analysis of BT Berakhot 7a: The Intersection of Talmud Criticism and Literary Appreciation," in *Through Those Near to Me: Essays in Honor of Jerome R. Malino*, ed. Glen Lebetkin (Danbury, CT: United Jewish Center, 1998), 257–65; and David Gordis, "Two Literary Talmudic Readings," in *History and Literature: New Readings of Jewish Texts in Honor of Arnold J. Band*, ed. William Cutter (Providence: Program in Judaic Studies, Brown University, 2002), 3–15.

149. Rubenstein, *Talmudic Stories*, provides many examples of the value of combining diachronic and synchronic analyses of narratives. He concludes:

> That the BT versions of these stories generally diverge from the PT in the parts that relate directly to their BT contexts suggests that the stories were revised and

Outline

Chapter 1 will analyze the attempts of various Amoraim to issue halakhic rulings—sometimes on an individual case and sometimes stating a rule that could apply to many cases (halakha is always like R. X). These are all attempts to impose halakhic unity. Which rabbis make these rules and which rabbis most often follow them or ignore them? This could provide a good sense as to these rabbis' willingness to impose unity or allow flexibility in halakhic practice.

Perhaps the most important and relevant *sugya* on the topic of diversity of practice is found in *b. Yebam.* 13b-16a. This pericope is made up of two parts. The first part discusses diverse customs and practices in light of the prohibition not to make factions, which is based on a midrashic reading of Deut 14:1, "*lo titgodedu.*" This verse is interpreted by the rabbis as a prohibition against acting in a way that resembles sectarianism so that Jewish unity does not disintegrate into factionalism. This could potentially ban any diversity of practice. But, as we will show, this ban is substantially limited in the Bavli, which permits diverse practices in different cities. This will be the subject of chapter 2.

Chapter 3 will then test the findings of chapter 2 regarding halakhic pluralism in different cities by collecting numerous narratives involving visitors from one city to another. We will confirm that the difference between the Yerushalmi and the Bavli found in the halakhic *sugya* of chapter 2 is consistent with these various narratives.

Chapter 4 continues to analyze the second part of the *b. Yebam.* 13b–16a *sugya,* which deals with the historical question of whether or not Beth Shammai and Beth Hillel practiced their own opinions. This analysis is included within a comprehensive study of all significant Talmudic sources that address the relationship between the Houses. We will evaluate how each source portrays the relative tolerance or intolerance displayed by the Houses toward each other.

While the previous chapters focus primarily on large divisions between factions or cities, the next three deal with individual dissenters. Chapter 5 analyzes narratives about individual Tannaim who veer from the mainstream rabbinic practice of halakha. Whereas the Houses are seen

---

> recontextualized simultaneously. This consistent finding supports the claim that the changes should be attributed to the redactors, since the textual location of a story obviously results from the redactional process. Undoubtedly, Babylonian Amoraim transmitted and transformed Palestinian stories. Yet the final form of the story—the extant, redacted story—reveals the hands of redactors who integrated it with a specific Talmudic context. (ibid., 267)

This study applies the same methodology to halakhic *sugyot*. See analyses of *b. ʿErub.* 46b–47b in ch. 1, *b. Yebam.* 13b-16a in chs. 2 and 4, and of *b. Sanh.* 87a-88a in ch. 6.

as two large vying groups, the narratives analyzed in this chapter deal with individuals going against the majority. We will compare how the Yerushalmi and Bavli portray these figures and how they are treated by their colleagues. Included in this chapter is a discussion of the role of the patriarch, particularly Rabban Gamaliel of Yavneh, as a unifying force among the rabbis.

Besides the patriarchate, one of the most important institutions in the effort to establish halakhic unity was the high court or central rabbinical council. Deuteronomy 17:8–13 details the procedures concerning the national judicial system, among them the rule that one must follow the high court in all cases. Chapter 6 will trace the evolution of this law from biblical to Talmudic times when it is dubbed the law of "the rebellious elder." We will highlight differences in the interpretation of this law between time periods and geographical regions.

Closely related and in some tension with the law of the rebellious elder is the law of *Horayot*. Tractate *Horayot* teaches that one who knows that a court issued a mistaken ruling must disobey it. This seems to open the door to recognizing multiple practices, particularly if the court does not admit that it is mistaken. Chapter 7 will delve into the various Tannaitic and Amoraic sources concerning this law. We will explore various ways of reconciling this law with that of the rebellious elder and whether this pair of laws allows room for legal diversity.

The conclusion will summarize the findings of the various chapters and attempt to correlate them with one another. We will gather the various proofs for the thesis of this study that the Yerushalmi usually insists on uniformity of practice while the Bavli more often tolerates legal pluralism. Various possible historical reasons for the differences in attitude present across and within each period and place will be suggested. We will end by discussing whether the tolerance offered by the Talmuds should be classified as particular monism, or particular or universal pluralism, and we will enumerate the halakhic mechanisms that make such tolerance possible.

1

The Rules of Law: The Talmudic Endeavor to Decide Dispute

Every legal system goes through stages of growth followed by efforts at assembling and systematizing this growth through codification. Roman law went through centuries of growth before Hadrian began to unify the unwieldly mass of laws present throughout his empire. This codificatory project continued until Justinian's monumental code was completed four centuries later.[1]

The rabbinic halakhic tradition begins with controversy. *M. ᶜEduyyot* 2:2 introduces the earliest sages of the Second Temple period as pairs of disputants. This trend continues with Shammai and Hillel and their Houses as controversy continues to grow until the full gamut of opinions finds expression in the mouths of the Tannaim at Yavneh and in the Galilee. The task falls to R. Akiba and Rabbi to collect this mass of traditions and arrange it into a code, the Mishnah. The process of codification, however, did not stop there as the Amoraim grappled to decide between the many opinions expressed within the Mishnah. This secondary codification will be the subject of this chapter. By analyzing how the Amoraim went about resolving these disputes, we will gain insight into their views about halakhic uniformity and pluralism in general.

As we will see below, the Yerushalmi formulates and implements a set of rules for deciding disputes while the Bavli rejects these rules explicitly. This suggests that the Yerushalmi has a greater penchant for halakhic uniformity than does the Bavli. The Bavli does, however, assume that most Tannaitic disputes are decided by the Amoraim on an ad hoc basis. Both Talmuds single out a handful of cases in which the normal legislative process breaks down. In some of these cases, the Talmuds allow one to choose any one of the options and practice accordingly. The theoretical implications of this explicit pluralism will be further analyzed. The end of this chapter will offer a reason for the split between the Yerushalmi's and the

1. See further below, pp. 77–80.

Bavli's use of rules based on the historical context of codificatory efforts in the Roman and Sasanian Empires.

Rules for Deciding Halakha in Tannaitic Controversies

Scholars debate whether the Mishnah was meant as a normative law code or an anthology of Tannaitic traditions for study. On the one hand, the Mishnah often presents one opinion anonymously or in the name of the sages,[2] even when that opinion is named in the parallel Tosefta.[3] This would indicate that the redactor intended to choose that opinion as the halakha.[4] On the other hand, the Mishnah often does not indicate which opinion to follow, or contradicts itself in different places.[5] Yaakov Elman, however, denies the basis of this dichotomy: "The division between a code or an anthology was not as great as nineteenth- and twentieth-century scholars imagined. Nor was the division between a formal legal work—code or anthology—and a study text."[6] Rather, Elman suggests, based on parallels to Roman legal writings, that "Rabbi wished to provide a collection that could be used for both study *and* decision making."[7] Stephen Wald similarly bridges the gap between the two extreme possibilities:

---

2. See Hezser, *Social Structure*, 241 and 245.

3. See, for example, *m. Ḥul.* 8:4 compared with *t. Ḥul.* 8:6.

4. The reason the Mishnah records minority opinions at all is addressed at *m. ʿEd.* 1:5–6 and *t. ʿEd.* 1:4; see below, p. 274.

5. See a summary of these arguments in Strack and Stemberger, *Introduction*, 135–38; and further in Louis Ginzberg, *On Jewish Law and Lore* (Philadelphia: Jewish Publication Society of America, 1955), 159f.; Alexander Guttmann, *Rabbinic Judaism in the Making* (Detroit: Wayne State University, 1970), 240–45; Baruch Bokser, "Jacob N. Epstein on the Formation of the Mishnah," and Gary Porton, "Hanokh Albeck on the Mishnah," both published in Alan Avery-Peck and Jacob Neusner, eds., *The Mishnah in Contemporary Perspective* (Leiden: Brill, 2006), 37–55, 209–24; David Halivni, "The Reception Accorded to Rabbi Judah's Mishnah," in *Jewish and Christian Self-Definition: Volume Two, Aspects of Judaism in the Graeco-Roman Period*, ed. E. P. Sanders (Philadelphia: Fortress, 1981), 204–12; Faur, *Golden Doves*, 99; Abraham Goldberg, "The Mishna—A Study Book of Halakha," in *The Literature of the Sages: Part One*, ed. Shmuel Safrai (Philadelphia: Fortress, 1987), 213–14; Zlotnick, *The Iron Pillar*, 181–227; Elon, *Jewish Law: History, Sources, Principles*, 3:1057f.; Fisch, *Rational Rabbis*, 171f.; Heger, *Pluralistic Halakhah*, 175f.; and David Kraemer, "The Mishnah," in *The Cambridge History of Judaism IV: The Late Roman-Rabbinic Period*, ed. S. Katz (Cambridge: Cambridge University Press, 2006), 304–6 and 311–13.

6. Elman, "Order, Sequence, and Selection," 75.

7. Ibid., 70. Cf., however, Jacob Neusner, "The Mishnah in Roman and Christian Contexts," in *The Mishnah in Contemporary Perspective*, ed. Alan Avery-Peck and Jacob Neusner (Leiden: Brill, 2006), 1:121–34, who contends that the Mishnah is not comparable to Roman codes but is rather *sui generis*.

> The question of the form and purpose of the final redaction of the Mishnah has long been a topic of scholarly debate. In the twentieth century this debate focused on the question whether the Mishnah should be seen as a code of relatively self-consistent and authoritative religious practice (Epstein), or as an anthology of frequently contradictory sources (Albeck). As so formulated, this dispute seems somewhat artificial. On the one hand, there is no reason to assume that the final redaction of the Mishnah was governed by one single overriding principle. On the other hand, the redaction of the Mishnah could reflect a preliminary, but as yet incomplete, effort to bring order and consistency to the body of tannaitic halakhah.[8]

Whether or not Rabbi meant the Mishnah to be a code, however, many Amoraim nevertheless looked to it as a source for halakha.[9] These Amoraim formulated meta-halakhic rules that specify how to decide between two sides of a controversy where there is no clear majority and where the Mishnah or relevant *baraitot* provide no indication as to which opinion is preferred. These rules are listed in both Talmuds. First, the Yerushalmi version at *y. Ter.* 3:1 (42a):

[A] רבי יעקב בר אחא בשם רבי יוחנן הלכה כדברי רבי
[B] ...רבי בא בר כהן בעא קומי רבי יוסי לֹא כן אמר רבי חייה בשם רבי יוחנן רבי וחביריו הלֹכה כרבי ואמר רבי יונה ואפילו רבי אצל רבי לֹעזר בי רבי שמעון
[C] אמר ליה בגין דתני לה רבי ישמעאל בי רבי יוסי בשם אביו ואמר רבי יוסי בשם רבי יוחנן רבי יוסי וחביריו הלֹכה כרבי יוסי מחביריו דלֹא תיסבור לֹמימר אוף הכא כן לֹכן צריכה מימר הלכה כרבי
[D] רבי זעירא רבי יעקב בר אידי בשם רבי יוחנן ר׳ מאיר ורבי שמעון הלֹכה כרבי שמעון רבי שמעון ורבי יהודה הלֹכה כרבי יודה ואין צריך לומר רבי מאיר ורבי יהודה שהלֹכה כרבי יהודה

[A] R. Yaʿaqov bar Aḥa [said] in the name of R. Yoḥanan, "The halakha (regarding *t. Ter.* 4:7) follows the view of Rabbi."
[B] ... R. Ba bar Kohen asked in the presence of R. Yose, "Has R. Ḥiyya not said in the name of R. Yoḥanan, '[In a dispute between] Rabbi and his colleagues, the halakha follows Rabbi,' and R. Yonah said, 'Even between Rabbi and R. Eleazar b. R. Shimon'?"
[C] He [R. Yose] said to him [R. Ba bar Kohen], "Because of what

8. Stephen Wald, "Mishnah," *Encyclopedia Judaica* (2007): 14:326. Elizabeth Shanks Alexander, *Transmitting Mishnah: The Shaping Influence of Oral Tradition* (New York: Cambridge University Press, 2006), 173, similarly finds that "the pedagogical and normative functions of the Mishnah are compatible, rather than mutually exclusive."

9. The same interpretive shift happened to the Talmud itself, which was first composed as a work of theoretical law but was then taken by the Geonim to be a code of applied law; see Hanina Ben-Menahem, "The Second Canonization of the Talmud," *California Law Review* 28, no. 1 (2006): 37–51.

is taught by R. Ishmael b. R. Yose in the name of his father [at *t. Ter.* 4:6 and *y. Ter.* 2:3 (41c)]. For R. Yose said in the name of R. Yoḥanan, 'In a dispute between R. Yose and his colleagues, the halakha accords with R. Yose.' So that you not think that here, too, [the halakha follows R. Yose], therefore, [R. Yoḥanan] needed to state that the halakha follows Rabbi."

[D] R. Zeira and R. Yaᶜaqov bar Idi [said] in the name of R. Yoḥanan, "In a dispute between R. Meir and R. Shimon, the halakha follows R. Shimon. [In a dispute between] R. Shimon and R. Yehudah, the halakha follows R. Yehudah. It thus goes without saying [that in a dispute between] R. Meir and R. Yehudah, the halakha follows R. Yehudah."

This *sugya* is the *locus classicus* of the Yerushalmi for the rules of deciding halakha. Significantly, all of the rules are quoted in the name of R. Yoḥanan.[10] We can enumerate at least four basic rules within this *sugya*: (1) Rabbi and his colleagues, the halakha follows Rabbi; (2) R. Yose and his colleagues, the halakha follows R. Yose; (3) R. Meir and R. Shimon, the halakha follows R. Shimon; (4) R. Shimon and R. Yehudah, the halakha follows R. Yehudah. Each of these rules is used throughout the Yerushalmi, as we will see below.

Compare the Yerushalmi above with the *locus classicus* of the Bavli about the rules of decision making at *b. ᶜErub.* 46b-47b:

10. R. Yonah's statement in line B is only a clarification of R. Yoḥanan's broader rule. "R. Yonatan" is named in the continuation of this *sugya* as the author of a rule that is almost exactly the same as line D. However, "Yonatan" there is likely a scribal error and should be corrected to "Yoḥanan"; see Yehuda Brandes, "The Beginnings of the Rules of Halachic Adjudication: Significance, Formation and Development of the Rules Concerning the Tanaic Halacha and Literature" (Ph.D. diss., Hebrew University, 2002), 232 n. 4 (Hebrew). The central role of R. Yoḥanan in formulating these rules of decision making is noted by Yitzhak D. Gilat, "Lo titgodedu," *Bar Ilan* 18–19 (1981): 84 n. 26; Hanokh Albeck, *Introduction to the Talmud Bavli and Yerushalmi* (Tel-Aviv: Dvir, 1987), 184–85 (Hebrew); and Heger, *Pluralistic Halakhah,* 266. See also Ginzberg, *Law and Lore,* 163. R. Yoḥanan, unlike his colleague Resh Laqish, is portrayed in many sources as a staunch supporter of the Patriarch and takes a positive attitude toward kingship and authority in general; see Reuven Kimelman, "Rabbi Yohanan of Tiberias: Aspects of the Social and Religious History of Third Century Palestine" (Ph.D. diss., Yale University, 1977), 107–18. R. Yoḥanan's efforts to impose uniformity on all of the rabbis through these rules is in step with this characterization. Kimelman, ibid., 69–75, also argues that R. Yoḥanan pushed for the "professionalization of the Rabbinate," which included encouraging rabbis to serve as judges on courts. He points to many parallels between instructions of R. Yoḥanan and judicial principles taught by Roman jurists. As we will argue below, pp. 77–80, R. Yoḥanan's formulation of rules is similarly parallel to Roman codificatory efforts and rules.

[A][1] רבי יעקב ורבי זריקא אמרו: הלכה כרבי עקיבא מחבירו, וכרבי יוסי מחבריו, וכרבי מחבירו.[11]

[2] למאי הלכתא? רבי אסי אמר: הלכה, ורבי חייא בר אבא אמר: מטין, ורבי יוסי ברבי חנינא אמר: נראין.

[3] כלשון הזה אמר רבי יעקב בר אידי אמר רבי יוחנן: רבי מאיר ורבי יהודה—הלכה כרבי יהודה. רבי יהודה ורבי יוסי—הלכה כרבי יוסי, ואין צריך לומר רבי מאיר ורבי יוסי—הלכה כרבי יוסי. השתא במקום רבי יהודה—ליתא, במקום רבי יוסי מיבעיא?

[4] אמר רב אסי: אף אני לומד רבי יוסי ורבי שמעון—הלכה כרבי יוסי. דאמר רבי אבא אמר רבי יוחנן: רבי יהודה ורבי שמעון הלכה כרבי יהודה. השתא במקום רבי יהודה ליתא, במקום רבי יוסי מיבעיא?

[5] איבעיא להו: רבי מאיר ורבי שמעון מאי? תיקו.

[B][1] אמר רב משרשיא: ליתנהו להני כללי.
מנא ליה לרב משרשיא הא?
אילימא מהא דתנן, **רבי שמעון אומר...**
ואמר רב חמא בר גוריא אמר רב: הלכה כרבי שמעון. ומאן פליג עליה—רבי יהודה.
והא אמרת: רבי יהודה ורבי שמעון הלכה כרבי יהודה? אלא לאו שמע מינה: ליתנהו.
ומאי קושיא? דילמא: היכא דאיתמר—איתמר, היכא דלא איתמר—לא איתמר?
[2] אלא מהא, דתנן...**דברי רבי יהודה. רבי שמעון אומר...**
ואמר רב חמא בר גוריא אמר רב: הלכה כרבי שמעון. ומאן פליג עליה—רבי יהודה.
והא אמרת: רבי יהודה ורבי שמעון הלכה כרבי יהודה?
ומאי קושיא? דילמא הכא נמי, היכא דאיתמר—איתמר, היכא דלא איתמר—לא איתמר?
[3] אלא מהא, דתנן...**דברי רבי מאיר. רבי יהודה אומר... רבי יוסי אומר... רבי שמעון אומר...**
ואמר רב חמא בר גוריא אמר רב: הלכה כרבי שמעון. ומאן פליג עליה—רבי יהודה?
והא אמרת: רבי יהודה ורבי שמעון הלכה כרבי יהודה?
ומאי קושיא? דלמא הכא נמי, היכא דאיתמר—איתמר, היכא דלא איתמר—לא איתמר?
[4] אלא מהא, דתנן...רבי מאיר אומר... **רבי יהודה אומר: אחד עני ואחד עשיר...**
ומתני ליה רב חייא בר אשי לחייא בר רב קמיה דרב: אחד עני ואחד עשיר, ואמר ליה רב: סיים בה נמי: הלכה כרבי יהודה.
תרתי למה לי? והא אמרת רבי מאיר ורבי יהודה הלכה כרבי יהודה?
ומאי קושיא? דילמא רב לית ליה להני כללי?
[5] אלא מהא, דתנן...**רבי יהודה אומר...רבי יוסי אומר...**
הכי אמר רבי יוחנן: הלכה כרבי יוסי. מכלל דיחידאה פליג עליה? אין, והתניא ... **דברי רבי מאיר. רבי יוסי מתיר...**
למה לי? והא אמרת רבי מאיר ורבי יוסי הלכה כרבי יוסי?
ומאי קושיא? דלמא לאפוקי מדרב נחמן אמר שמואל, דאמר: הלכה כרבי מאיר בגזירותיו?[12]

11. The exact text of this line cannot be determined as it is subject to many textual variants in manuscripts. Ms. Munich reads, "הלכה כר׳ עקיבא מחבירו ולא מחביריו והלכה כר׳ יוסי אפי׳ מחביריו והלכה כר׳ מחביריו." Ms. Vatican 109 reads, "<הלכה> כר׳ עקיבה מחבריו כר׳ יוסי מחברו כר׳ מחברו." See Brandes, "Beginnings of the Rules," 236–37.

12. *B. Ketub.* 57a and 60b.

[6] אלא מהא, דתניא...**אמר רבי יהודה...רבי יוסי אומר...**
ואמר רבי יוחנן: הלכה כרבי יוסי.
ולמה לי? והא אמרת: רבי יהודה ורבי יוסי הלכה כרבי יוסי?

אמר אביי: איצטריך, סלקא דעתך אמינא: הני מילי—במתניתין, אבל בברייתא—אימא לא, קא משמע לן.
אלא הכי קאמר: הני כללי לאו דברי הכל נינהו, דהא רב לית ליה הני כללי.

[A][1] R. Yaʿaqov and R. Zeriqa said: The halakha is always in agreement with R. Akiba when he differs with his colleague, with R. Yose when he differs with his colleagues, and with Rabbi when he differs with his colleague.
[2] How [are these rules] to be applied? R. Assi said, "[They determine] normative practice." R. Ḥiyya bar Abba said, "[They determine which way] we incline." R. Yose son of R. Ḥanina said, "[They determine which view is] apparently preferable."
[3] In the same sense did R. Yaʿaqov b. Idi rule in the name of R. Yoḥanan: [In a dispute between] R. Meir and R. Yehudah, the halakha accords with R. Yehudah; between R. Yehudah and R. Yose, the halakha accords with R. Yose; and there is no need to state that between R. Meir and R. Yose the halakha accords with R. Yose, for, since [it has been established that the opinion of the former is] not normative where it is opposed by that of R. Yehudah, can there be any question where it is opposed by that of R. Yose?
[4] R. Assi said: I also learn that in a dispute between R. Yose and R. Shimon the halakha is in agreement with R. Yose; for R. Abba has said in the name of R. Yoḥanan that in a dispute between R. Yehudah and R. Shimon the halakha is in agreement with R. Yehudah. Now, [since the latter's opinion is] of no consequence where it is opposed by R. Yehudah, can there be any question [as to its inconsequence] where it is opposed by that of R. Yose?
[5] The question was raised: What [is the halakha where a ruling is a matter of dispute between] R. Meir and R. Shimon? This [question] is left standing.

[B][1] Rav Mesharsheya stated: These rules are to be disregarded. From where does Rav Mesharsheya derive this view?
If it be suggested: From the following where we learned, **R. Shimon says ...**
Rav Ḥama bar Goria stated in the name of Rav, "The halakha is in agreement with R. Shimon." And who is it that differs with him? R. Yehudah.

But [this cannot be reconciled with what] you have stated: "[In a dispute between] R. Yehudah and R. Shimon, the halakha is in agreement with R. Yehudah"? Rather, to the contrary, [the rules] are to be disregarded.
But what is the difficulty? Perhaps where a decision to the contrary has been stated the rules are to be disregarded, but where no such decision has been stated the rules remain in force?

[2] [Rav Mesharsheya's view] is rather derived from the following where we learned, **... so R. Yehudah. R. Shimon says ...**
Rav Ḥama bar Goria stated in the name of Rav, "The halakha is in agreement with R. Shimon." And who is it that differed from him? R. Yehudah.
But [this cannot be reconciled with what] you have stated: "[In a dispute between] R. Yehudah and R. Shimon, the halakha is in agreement with R. Yehudah"?
But what is the difficulty? Perhaps here, too, where a decision to the contrary has been stated, the rules are to be disregarded, but where no such decision has been stated the rules remain in force?

[3] [Rav Mesharsheya's view] is rather derived from the following where we learned, **... so R. Meir. R. Yehudah says ... R. Yose says ... R. Shimon says ...**
Rav Ḥama bar Goria stated in the name of Rav, "The halakha is in agreement with R. Shimon." And who is it that differed from him? R. Yehudah.
But [this cannot be reconciled with what] you have stated: "[In a dispute between] R. Yehudah and R. Shimon, the halakha is in agreement with R. Yehudah"?
But what is the difficulty? Perhaps here too where a decision to the contrary has been stated the rules are to be disregarded, but where no such decision has been stated the rules remain in force?

[4] [Rav Mesharsheya's view] is rather derived from the following where we learned, **... R. Meir says ... R. Yehudah says: [It applies to] both rich and poor ...**
And when R. Ḥiyya b. Ashi taught Ḥiyya b. Rav in the presence of Rav [that the halakha applies to] both rich and poor, Rav said to him: "Conclude this also with the statement, 'The halakha is in agreement with R. Yehudah.'"
What need was there for a second statement seeing that you have already stated, "In a dispute between R. Meir and R. Yehudah, the halakha is in agreement with R. Yehudah"?

But what is the difficulty? Perhaps Rav does not accept these rules?
[5] [Rav Mesharsheya's view] is rather derived from the following where we learned **... R. Yehudah says ... R. Yose says ...**
Thus said R. Yoḥanan: "The halakha is in agreement with R. Yose." Does this then imply that only an individual opinion is against him? Yes, and so it was taught **... so R. Meir, but R. Yose permits ...**
What need was there [to state this] seeing that you have already stated, "In a dispute between R. Meir and R. Yose, the halakha is in agreement with R. Yose"?
But what is the difficulty? Perhaps [R. Yoḥanan intended] to indicate that the halakha was not in agreement with Rav Naḥman who said in the name of Shmuel: "The halakha is in agreement with R. Meir in his restrictive decrees"?[12]

[6] [Rav Mesharsheya's view] is rather derived from the following where it was taught **... R. Yehudah said ... R. Yose said ...**
R. Yoḥanan said: "The halakha is in agreement with R. Yose."
But what need was there [for this specific statement] seeing that it has already been laid down, "In a dispute between R. Yehudah and R. Yose, the halakha is in agreement with R. Yose"?
Abaye replied: This was necessary since it might have been presumed that [the rules] applied only to a Mishnah but not to a *baraita*; hence we were informed [here of R. Yoḥanan's decision].
Rather, [Rav Mesharsheya] meant this: Those rules were not unanimously accepted, since Rav in fact did not accept them.

This *sugya* is made up of two parts: [A] a list of the rules and how they should be applied, and [B] a discussion of whether and by whom these rules have been accepted as normative. Thus, the two parts of the *sugya* actually stand in tension with each other, one stating the rules and the other questioning them. The first part is parallel to the Yerushalmi presentation,[13] while the second part is unique to the Bavli. The Yerushalmi never doubts the authority of the rules, not in *y. Ter.* 3:1 (42a) nor anywhere else. Yehuda

13. See Brandes, "Beginnings of the Rules," 235, for a chart comparing the two lists of rules. Significantly, the Bavli confirms that all of the rules originate from R. Yoḥanan and his students. Another rule quoted in the name of R. Yoḥanan, which does not appear in this list (and, in part, contradicts it), is, "אמר רבה בר בר חנה אמר רבי יוחנן: הלכה כרבי יהודה לענין שבת, והלכה כרבי יוסי לענין תרומה—Rabbah bar bar Ḥannah said in the name of R. Yoḥanan: The halakha follows R. Yehudah concerning Shabbat and the halakha follows R. Yose concerning *terumah*" (*b. Šabb.* 35a).

Brandes writes that he cannot find one *sugya* in the entire Yerushalmi that expresses opposition to the rules.[14]

Even within part A, the Bavli quotes a dispute among Palestinian Amoraim about whether these rules always define the halakha absolutely or whether they are mere guidelines or suggestions that can be disregarded based on other considerations. If this dispute is authentic, it probably reflects an early stage in the propagation of the rules in Palestine when they were still being questioned. Even so, it is significant that the Yerushalmi makes no mention of it[15]—perhaps because the editors of the Yerushalmi already accepted the rules as absolute. The Bavli, however, does quote the controversy and leaves it open-ended, suggesting that the Bavli redactors themselves saw reason to doubt the categorical application of these rules.[16]

Brandes attempts to separate between the Amoraic and Stammaitic layers and motivations within part B. He explains that Rav Mesharsheya himself rejected all of the rules listed in part A. The Stam, however, having accepted the rules, did its best to tone down Rav Mesharsheya's statement. The Stam therefore introduced a list of cases in order to prove that the rules were accepted by some and in fact were rejected only by Rav.[17] This reconstruction fits in with Brandes's overall conclusion that these rules were not accepted by Babylonian Amoraim of the early generations but were gradually accepted until, by the time of the Stam, they were fully implemented.[18]

I would like to offer a different reading of this *sugya*. Brandes does not provide sufficient evidence that the rules were accepted by the Stam. In fact, as I will discuss below, he himself cites many texts in which the Stam ignores the rules. Rather, I believe that the motivation of the Stam in this *sugya* is precisely to question the authority of these rules, not to minimize Rav Mesharsheya's rejection.

---

14. Ibid., 334.

15. A decision using מטין does appear in the Yerushalmi in the name of R. Yoḥanan at *y. Ber.* 5:2 (9b). Decisions using נראין appear in the name of R. Yehoshua ben Levi at *y. Šabb.* 2:3 (5a) and R. Yehudah ben Pazzi at *y. Pesaḥ.* 1:5 (27d), et al. However, those decisions are about specific issues, not general rules. Indeed, the Bavli may have borrowed the language of these local decisions that employ מטין and נראין and generalized them to apply to the rules. If this reconstruction is accurate, then the dispute in the Bavli is in large part an invention of the Bavli, probably meant to weaken the authority of the rules right from the start.

16. Brandes, "Beginnings of the Rules," 238–39. Brandes suggests that line 2 applies only to the more general rules in line 1 but not to those in lines 3–4. He further hypothesizes that line 2 originally applied to all the rules but that the editor of this *sugya* moved it in order to limit its impact. Rashi, however, explains that the words כלשון הזה (which appear nowhere else in the Bavli) instruct the reader that the discussion of line 2 applies to the next line as well.

17. Ibid., 188 and 239.

18. Ibid., 283.

Rav Mesharsheya's statement is suspect since it occurs again in a completely different context at *b. ʿErub.* 56a. That *sugya* quotes a *baraita* that lists a number of astronomical laws by which to orient oneself. On that *baraita*, Rav Mesharsheya says, "ליתנהו להני כללי—Those rules are to be disregarded," and proceeds to cite another *baraita* that contradicts those rules. The formula "ליתנהו להני כללי" is also stated by two other Amoraim in two unrelated contexts.[19] Assuming that Rav Mesharsheya did not say the same words twice about different issues, the possibility exists that the editors of this *sugya* transferred the words from *b. ʿErub.* 56a.

In fact, the quotation in *b. ʿErub.* 56a seems to read more smoothly than it does here where the continuation of the *sugya* questions the quotation and ends up reinterpreting it. Rav Mesharsheya at *b. ʿErub.* 56a means to say that everyone should disregard the rules since another *baraita* contradicts them. The issue at hand is astronomical laws in which only one source can be correct. This is also the sense of these words in the other two contexts in which they appear.[20] In *b. ʿErub.* 47a, however, he means only that he himself or some group of rabbis do not recognize the rules. The wording of the statement fits the sense at *b. ʿErub.* 56a better. If it is the Stam who applied Rav Mesharsheya's statement to this context, then it is precisely the Stam who wishes to cast doubt on the rules of R. Yoḥanan.

What might have been the goal of the Stam in constructing part B of this *sugya*? It seems that they first transferred Rav Mesharsheya here to dismiss the rules entirely by challenging whether they were ever accepted. The Gemara then cites six test cases. The first four are all decisions made by Rav. This hardly seems coincidental. The first three attempts all have the same caveat, that is, perhaps the rules apply only in the absence of a decision regarding that specific case. This set of three cases is obviously a literary creation since only the first case is necessary to make the point.[21] Cases

---

19. *B. Yebam.* 64b and *b. Ḥul.* 136a.

20. In *b. Ḥul.* 136a, the suggested rules are rejected based on a *baraita*, and in *b. Yebam.* 64b, they are rejected based on the Mishnah itself. The literal translation of the phrase ליתנהו להני כללי is "these rules do not exist" (see Michael Sokoloff, *A Dictionary of Jewish Babylonian Aramaic of the Talmudic and Geonic Period* (Ramat-Gan: Bar Ilan University Press, 2002), 629). This suggests that the rules are false deductions without logical basis. Such is the usage in all contexts except *b. ʿErub.* 47a where Rav Mesharsheya can only mean that he and his group do not accept the rules of R. Yoḥanan. Rav Mesharsheya cannot say that the rules do not exist since R. Yoḥanan does declare and use them. R. Yoḥanan's rules are not based on any logical deduction but rather on his own authority. The end of the *sugya* must reword the phrase precisely because the original wording does not fit this case. Therefore, we can assume that Rav Mesharsheya did not use this phrase with regard to R. Yoḥanan's rules but rather that it was transferred to *b. ʿErub.* 47a by the Stam.

21. See Halivni, *Meqorot u-mesorot*, *ʿErubin*, 138 n. 1*. On the predominance of lists of three in the Bavli, see Shamma Friedman, "Some Structural Patterns of Talmudic Sugyot," *Proceedings of the Sixth World Congress of Jewish Studies* 3 (Jerusalem: World Union of Jewish Studies, 1977): 389–402 (Hebrew).

2 and 3 do not technically pose any problem since they are also exceptions to the rule in which there was an explicit ruling. Nevertheless, the repetition of such cases does have a rhetorical effect of making the audience realize how futile the rules are if there can be so many exceptions. In the fourth case, Rav adds a decision that happens to accord with R. Yoḥanan's rules, a statement that would be superfluous had Rav accepted the rules in general. This case finally establishes that Rav not only lists exceptions when necessary but that he completely ignores R. Yoḥanan's rules (if, in fact, he had ever heard of them).

The next two cases test whether anyone did accept the rules. After all, even R. Yoḥanan who formulated them seems to ignore them at times. These questions are resolved, and the formula is updated to say that the rules are accepted by some but not by all since Rav does not use them. That the conclusion of the entire *sugya* is the same as the conclusion after the fourth question [B][4] proves that this *sugya* is a literary creation rather than a genuine logical debate. That is, the *sugya* uses proofs and disproofs as a rhetorical device to convey a certain point of view. The addition of two more exceptional cases after establishing that Rav does not use the rules gives the impression that others may also not have used the rules, even though that cannot be proven. The goal of part B of the *sugya* is to deconstruct part A. It casts doubt on the ubiquity and usefulness of the rules set forth so authoritatively by R. Yoḥanan's school by showing that Rav (perhaps representing the Babylonian tradition) never accepted them and by further demonstrating that even R. Yoḥanan (perhaps representing the Palestinian school) needs to constantly defend them against possible exceptions.

Having analyzed where these rules originated, we can also look at where and when these rules were accepted. Ephraim Halivni finds that the rules are never fully accepted but rather are treated like any other Amoraic statement that later Amoraim could disregard. He finds examples of decisions that flout these rules as well as decisions in accordance with the rules in which the rule is not cited; both types of decisions, however, show an indifference to the rules. He finds no distinction between Palestinian and Babylonian or early and late Amoraim; in his view, all Amoraim took the rules with a grain of salt.[22]

Brandes also analyzes each rule set forth in the *sugyot* above. Brandes, however, finds that Palestinian Amoraim generally accept the rules while Babylonian Amoraim use them only sporadically and often ignore them.[23] Brandes further claims in his summary that the rules gain acceptance by

22. Ephraim Halivni, *The Rules for Deciding Halakha in the Talmud* (Lod: Mechon Haberman le-Meḥqere Sifrut, 1999), 142–47.

23. This trend has also been pointed out by Eliyahu Zeni, *Rabanan Sabora'e u-kelale ha-halakha* (Haifa: Ofaqim Rehabim, 1992), 298–99.

the late Babylonian Amoraim and especially by the Stam. This conclusion, however, is not backed up by his own analysis. As we shall see, Brandes himself cites a number of counterexamples.

A general assumption already found in both Talmuds is that when someone decides a case in agreement with a rule but without citing it, then he must not have felt compelled by the rule. If he did, then he would not need to proclaim an explicit decision since the rule makes such a decision superfluous.[24] This assumption is based on the notion that there is a strict economy of words used by the Amoraim, who would never utter a statement that could be logically derived. We should leave open the possibility, however, that an Amora may state such a decision simply in order to confirm the application of the rule in a given case.

Usage of Rules in the Yerushalmi

We will test the theories of Halivni and Brandes with examples from the rules regarding R. Yose and his colleagues. A number of Yerushalmi *sugyot* quote these rules and use them to challenge anyone who decides a halakha against them or even in accordance with them since there is no need to make an explicit ruling once the rules are in effect. For example, *y. Ter.* 11:5 (48b) reads:

> דבי רבי ינאי הלכה כרבי שמעון רבי יעקב בר אחא בשם רבי יאשיה הלכה כרבי שמעון
> ר׳ יוסי צירניא בעא קומי רבי ירמיה דלא כן מה נן אמרין רבי מאיר ורבי שמעון אין הלכה כרבי שמעון
> אמר ליה של בית קודמין היא והא רבי יודה אומר מעין שניהן ור׳ יוסי אומר מעין שניהן ורבי יודה ורבי יוסי הלכה כרבי יוסי
>
> The school of R. Yannai [says], "The halakha accords with R. Shimon." R. Ya'aqov bar Aḥa [says] in the name of R. Yoshiah, "The halakha accords with R. Shimon."
> R. Yose of Sidon asked in the presence of R. Yirmiah, "[Why must they state that the halakha follows R. Shimon?] For if that is not the case, what is it that we say, '[In a dispute between] R. Meir and R. Shimon, does the halakha not accord with R. Shimon?'"
> He said to him, "[The issue was argued] by a previous group. Behold, R. Yehudah's view incorporates aspects of both [R. Meir and R. Shimon] and R. Yose's view incorporates aspects of both. [In a dispute between] R. Yehudah and R. Yose, the halakha accords with R. Yose."

24. This assumption is accepted by Brandes but not by Halivni, *Rules*, 142–43.

The *sugya* addresses how to decide between the four Tannaim listed in *m. Ter.* 11:10. Two traditions of Palestinian Amoraim decide according to R. Shimon. R. Yose of Sidon questions the need for such a ruling since it can be derived from a rule. R. Yirmiah responds that the explicit decision is necessary because it actually opposes the rule. R. Yose and R. Yehudah are also part of this debate; without an explicit ruling according to R. Shimon, one would have applied the rule that the halakha follows R. Yose when in dispute with his colleagues. Paradoxically, the rules are more easily justified against a decision that opposes them, which can be viewed as an exception, than by a decision that agrees with them.

The rules are here cited by R. Yose of Sidon and R. Yirmiah. In most other *sugyot*, the rules are cited by the anonymous voice of the Yerushalmi.[25] In the next two examples, the Stam of the Yerushalmi challenges decisions that agree with the rules. In *y. Yebam.* 4:11 (6a),[26] R. Ḥaninah son of R. Abbahu quotes a decision made by three Palestinian rabbis in accordance with R. Yose. The anonymous voice of the Yerushalmi then wonders why this was necessary when such a decision could be derived from the rules. This question reveals the viewpoint of the Yerushalmi that the rules were accepted by the Amoraim and therefore that any ruling in accordance with them is superfluous.

Even more striking is a similar Yerushalmi *sugya* that has a parallel in the Bavli. *Y. Ber.* 2:4 (4d) relates:

> רב אומר הלכה כדברי שניהן להקל
> דלכן מה כן אמרין סתמה ורבי יוסי הלכה כסתמא רבי יוסי ורבי יודה הלכה כרבי יוסי ומה צריכה למימר רב הלכה כדברי שניהן להקל
> אלא בגין שמע דתני לה ר' חייא בשם ר' מאיר לפום כן צריך למימרא הלכה כדברי שניהן להקל
>
> Rav says the halakha follows the opinion of both of them in their leniencies.
> If that is not the case, what is it that we say, "An anonymous opinion and R. Yose, the halakha follows the anonymous opinion. R. Yose and R. Yehudah, the halakha follows R. Yose"? Why was it necessary to say that Rav rules like both of them in their leniencies?
> Rather, because he heard that we have learned [a *baraita* of] R. Ḥiyya in the name of R. Meir,[27] therefore he needed to say that the halakha follows both of them in their leniencies.

Rav issues a decision concerning *m. Ber.* 2:3 in accordance with the rules. As in the previous text, the Yerushalmi wonders why such an obvious

25. See *y. Maʿas.* 1:5 (49b) and examples below.
26. See parallel at *y. Nid.* 1:34 (49b).
27. Referring to *t. Ber.* 2:13.

ruling needed to be stated. Interestingly, the Yerushalmi here assumes that Rav knew and accepted the rules that were formulated by R. Yoḥanan, his younger contemporary, and which the Bavli explicitly says Rav rejected.[28] This assumption probably reflects the attitude of the Yerushalmi's Stam[29] who did accept the rules as absolutely binding. Compare this with the Bavli at *Ber.* 15b:

> אמר רבי טבי אמר רבי יאשיה: הלכה כדברי שניהם להקל.
>
> R. Ṭabi said in the name of R. Yoshiah: The halakha follows both of them in their leniencies.

The Bavli here quotes the same ruling as the Yerushalmi[30] but does not continue with the question of the Yerushalmi that such a ruling is obvious. This would be especially striking if the Bavli redactors were aware of this question in the Yerushalmi and purposely omitted it. But even if not, it is significant that the Bavli did not ask such a question on its own.

There are also examples of the Yerushalmi ignoring the rules. In *y. Qidd.* 4:6 (66a), for example, R. Yoḥanan says, "The halakha is in accordance with R. Yose," without making reference to his own rule.[31] However, even though the Yerushalmi in some places asks about such "obvious" decisions, this does not mean that the Yerushalmi needs to do so in every case. R. Yoḥanan may just be stating the obvious or preventing his audience from taking some overriding factor into consideration. Additionally, some decisions may date back to a time before the rules were disseminated. We cannot automatically deduce from here that R. Yoḥanan ignored his own rules. Only a case of the Yerushalmi disagreeing with the rules without justification would prove that the Yerushalmi sometimes ignored the rulings. Such cases, however, are rare if they exist at all.[32] We will see in the next chapter that the Yerushalmi considers these rules to be so comprehensive and authoritative that it has difficulty coming up with any cases in which both sides of a controversy could actually be practiced since the halakha is already decided by these rules.[33]

---

28. This is pointed out by Brandes, "Beginnings of the Rules," 338.

29. On the Stam of the Yerushalmi, see Halivni, "Aspects of the Formation of the Talmud," 355–56.

30. Ironically, the Bavli quotes this ruling in the name of the Palestinian Amora R. Yoshiah, a student of R. Yoḥanan, while the Yerushalmi quotes it in the name of Rav the Babylonian.

31. See also *y. Taʿan.* 2:14 (66b) and discussion at Halivni, *Rules*, 41, and Hidary, "Tolerance for Diversity," 411–12.

32. Brandes, "Beginnings of the Rules," 249 n. 51, finds only one case in the Yerushalmi where Amoraim decide against R. Yose, at *y. Šabb.* 6:5 (8c). However, that case involves the colleagues of R. Yanai, the first-generation Palestinian Amora who preceded R. Yoḥanan and therefore would not have known the rules.

33. *Y. Pesaḥ.* 4:1 (30d). See text below, p. 99. This Yerushalmi *sugya* applies the rules

Usage of Rules in the Bavli

Unlike the Yerushalmi, where the rules are generally accepted as binding, the picture in the Bavli is much less consistent. As in the Yerushalmi analysis, we focus on the Bavli's use of rules regarding R. Yose when in dispute with one of his colleagues. The Bavli often records decisions in favor of R. Yose, sometimes attributed to named Amoraim and other times stated by the Stam.[34] Except for *b. ʿErub.* 46b–47b, where the very validity of the rules is in question, the Bavli very rarely asks why such "redundant" decisions are necessary.[35] Of course, the Yerushalmi also does not always ask this question, but it does ask it more often. Even more significantly, there are many decisions in the Bavli that contravene the rules without any attempt at justification.[36] In some cases, a decision only partially agrees with but also partially opposes R. Yose, again without justification.[37] This rarely occurs in the Yerushalmi.[38]

Brandes cites a number of *sugyot* from which he tries to prove that the later Amoraim and the Stam did finally accept the rules. One example is *b. B. Bat.* 168a:

> אמר רב נחמן אמר רבה בר אבוה אמר רב:[39] הלכה כרבי יוסי. כי אתו לקמיה דרבי אמי, אמר להו: וכי מאחר שרבי יוחנן מלמדנו פעם ראשונה ושניה הלכה כרבי יוסי, אני מה אעשה? ואין הלכה כרבי יוסי.
>
> Rav Naḥman [said] in the name of Rabbah bar Abuha in the name of Rav: The halakha accords with R. Yose. When they came before R. Ammi, he said to them: "Since R. Yoḥanan has taught us time

even retroactively and assumes that the Tannaim themselves abided by them and practiced accordingly.

34. Decisions according to R. Yose when in dispute with R. Yehuda are stated in the name of the following: Rav, *b. B. Bat.* 136a, 168a; R. Yoḥanan, *b. ʿAbod. Zar.* 13a; Ula, *b. ʿErub.* 41a; Rav Yosef, *b. Naz.* 39a, *b. Moʿed Qaṭ.* 12a; R. Yirmiah, *b. Beṣah* 4b; Ravina, *b. Moʿed Qaṭ.* 11a; R. Zeira and Stam, *b. Qidd.* 73a.

Decisions according to R. Yose when in dispute with R. Meir are stated in the name of the following: Rav Yehudah in the name of Shmuel, *b. Qidd.* 72b; R. Yoḥanan, *b. Yoma* 12b; and R. Aba, *b. Nid.* 9a.

35. The Bavli never asks such a question regarding the rules relating to R. Yose. *B. B. Meṣiʿa* 38b does ask such a question regarding a different rule.

36. Decisions against the rules are stated by the following Amoraim: Rav Naḥman, *b. Ketub.* 69b; Rava, *b. Nid.* 63b; and Rav Ashi, *b. B. Bat.* 173b. See Brandes, "The Beginnings," 249 n. 51, for more examples.

37. See R. Yoḥanan or R. Yose bar R. Ḥanina, *b. Pesaḥ.* 100a; ʿUla, *b. Moʿed Qaṭ.* 17b; and Stam, *b. Roš Haš.* 19b.

38. See above, n. 32.

39. Ms. Escorial adds אין, and ms. Paris adds אין in the margin. All other mss. follow the text above. The addition of אין brings this *sugya* in closer conformity with the parallel *sugya* at *b. Ned.* 27b; see Tosafot ad loc. According to that version, Rav decided against R. Yose and the Stam decide in agreement with him, but neither opinion cites the rules.

and again that the halakha accords with R. Yose, what can I do?" The halakha, however, does not follow R. Yose.

Brandes sees in this *sugya* the beginnings of the usage of this rule in the Bavli. There are, however, many problems with such a reading. First, as Brandes himself points out, it is not clear if R. Ammi heard R. Yoḥanan many times concerning the rules in general or concerning the law in this specific case only.[40] Second, R. Ammi is a Palestinian Amora. Third, and most importantly, the Stam ends the *sugya* with a ruling against R. Yose. In fact, Minyomi, Rav Naḥman,[41] and Rav Ashi[42] also decide against R. Yose in this matter.[43] This *sugya* actually challenges Brandes' hypothesis that the rules were accepted in Babylonia by the time of the late Amoraim and the Stam.[44]

Brandes further cites three *sugyot* where Rav Naḥman and the Stam decide according to R. Yose because, "רבי יוסי נימוקו עמו—R. Yose's reasons support him."[45] In one such *sugya*, the Stam says that Rabbah falsely quoted a law in R. Yose's name in order to convince Rav Yosef to follow it.[46] These examples do show that there was a preference for R. Yose in Babylonia as well. However, that they do not cite R. Yoḥanan's rules in these cases where it would have been very appropriate to do so shows that these rules were widespread neither among the Babylonian Amoraim nor among the Stam.[47] The phrase, "רבי יוסי נימוקו עמו," derives from a *baraita*[48] and implies a general preference for R. Yose but not an absolute rule that one must follow him. The Bavli, at least in these instances, continues the methodology of decision making used by the late Tannaim and early Amoraim before R. Yoḥanan in which each case was decided on its own merit.[49] There were some general preferences, but no rules.

40. See Brandes, "Beginnings of the Rules," 247 n. 42.

41. *B. B. Meṣiʿa* 66a.

42. *B. B. Bat.* 173b.

43. They do not mention R. Yose explicitly, but they do say, "אסמכתא לא קניא," which is the position attributed by the Gemara (*b. B. Bat.* 68a) to R. Yehudah in opposition to R. Yose who says, "אסמכתא קניא."

44. Notice that the decision of Rav is ignored by subsequent Babylonian Amoraim. The Babylonian Amoraim feel free to challenge not only the rules of R. Yoḥanan, but also decisions by earlier Amoraim about specific issues; more on this below.

45. *B. B. Qam.* 24a, *b. ʿErub.* 14b, and *b. ʿErub.* 51a. See Brandes, "Beginnings of the Rules," 247–49. This statement does not appear in the Yerushalmi.

46. *B. ʿErub.* 51a.

47. Brandes himself points out that the citation of this reason instead of the rule shows that rules were still being ignored by the Amoraim. However, in two of these cases it is the Stam who cites the rule to explain the actions of an Amora. Since the Stam quotes, "R. Yose has his reasons," rather than R. Yoḥanan's formulation, we can deduce that even the Stam never accepted the rules. See also Halivni, *Rules*, 79–80.

48. *B. Giṭ.* 67a.

49. See Brandes, "Beginnings of the Rules," 94–229.

Outside of *b. ʿErub.* 46b, the rules "רבי יהודה ורבי יוסי—הלכה כרבי יוסי" and "רבי יוסי ורבי שמעון—הלכה כרבי יוסי" never appear again in the Bavli. The rule "רבי מאיר ורבי יוסי—הלכה כרבי יוסי," which is a derived rule, is quoted only twice more in the Bavli, both times within one *sugya*. In *b. Sanh.* 27b, Rav Aḥa b. Yaʿaqov uses it against a criminal who tries to go free by following a decision against R. Yose. In *b. Sanh.* 27a, the rule is quoted by the Stam to justify a ruling according to Abaye whose ruling agrees with R. Yose. This shows that some rules were known by some Babylonian Amoraim and Stammaim but the rules rarely appear and are mostly disregarded.

We have analyzed in depth only the three rules involving R. Yose. A full analysis of all of the rules is beyond the scope of this chapter. Based on the conclusions of Halivni and Brandes for rules involving other Tannaim, however, the same seems to hold true for those rules as well. These rules were created by R. Yoḥanan and his students and were widely embraced throughout the Yerushalmi but not in the Bavli where the Amoraim and the Stam seldom refer to them.

Besides the rules that govern the statements of individual Tannaim, the circle of R. Yoḥanan also formulated more general rules such as "הלכה כסתם משנה—the halakha follows the anonymous opinion in the Mishnah."[50] This rule, too, is widely accepted in the Yerushalmi, which seems to think that the halakha follows the anonymous opinion because the anonymous opinion represents the majority opinion.[51] The Bavli, on the other hand, asks over 150 times, "מאן תנא—who is the [anonymous] Tanna?" An individual Tanna is named, in most cases by an early Amora, and the halakha is then decided sometimes according to and sometimes against the anonymous opinion. In these and other cases, the early Babylonian Amoraim treat the anonymous opinion in the Mishnah just like any other named opinion.[52]

Later Amoraim, from the fourth generation on, do think the anonymous opinion represents the halakha. Rather than quote R. Yoḥanan's rule, however, they say, "הלכה כר׳... דסתם לן תנא כוותיה—The halakha follows R. ... because the Tanna [who composed the Mishnah] taught anonymously according to him."[53] That is, even though the anonymous opinion is an identifiable individual, the editor of the Mishnah taught it anonymously

---

50. *B. Yebam.* 16b and see over twenty other citations in the Bavli in Abraham Liss, *The Babylonian Talmud with Variant Readings* (Jerusalem: Yad Harav Herzog, 1983), 1:168 (Hebrew). The Yerushalmi does not quote this rule in R. Yoḥanan's name, but R. Eliezer does quote it to R. Yoḥanan in *y. Taʿan.* 2:13 (66a) = *y. Meg.* 1:4 (70d). See Brandes, "Beginnings of the Rules," 285f.

51. Brandes, "Beginnings of the Rules," 286–97.

52. See ibid., 180f.

53. *B. Pesaḥ.* 13a, *b. Yebam.* 101b, *b. Qidd.* 54b, et al. See Brandes, "Beginnings of the Rules," 183f. and 313f.

because he wanted that to be the halakha.[54] Furthermore, even in the later period, the Bavli does not apply this rule consistently.[55]

Brandes shows that the Bavli only quotes R. Yoḥanan's formula, "הלכה כסתם משנה," in order to challenge a contradictory decision of R. Yoḥanan himself. Every one of the over twenty citations of the rule in the Bavli fits into this pattern. Brandes concludes, "It seems that the Bavli does not ask from the rule of R. Yoḥanan about other Amoraim because it did not accept the rule as a general rule that is binding upon all Amoraim, but rather only upon R. Yoḥanan himself, the author of the rule."[56] That the Stam asks these questions regarding only R. Yoḥanan implies that the rule was not fully accepted in Babylonia even as late as the Stam.

Brandes shows the same pattern to be true regarding other general rules of decision making such as, "הלכה כדברי המכריע—the halakha follows the one who tips the scale," and even, "יחיד ורבים הלכה כרבים—[In a dispute between] an individual and many, the halakha follows the many."[57] All of these rules are formulated within the circle of R. Yoḥanan. Even if some of them are based on prior preferences, the late Tannaim and early Amoraim never treat them as rules. Once the rules are formulated, Palestinian Amoraim accept them as binding, and sometimes the Yerushalmi even retrojects them to early Amoraim. The first three generations of Babylonian Amoraim, on the other hand, do not mention the rules, while later Babylonian Amoraim and the Stam use the rules sometimes but not as systematically as in the Yerushalmi.

Brandes offers explanations for why these rules were formulated. He argues that the rabbis who lived near the time of the Mishnah's publication viewed the Mishnah as just another collection of Tannaitic sayings. A couple of generations later, when the Mishnah came to be viewed as an authoritative halakhic work, the necessity arose for rules that would enable one to know which opinion in Mishnaic controversies was to be followed.

Brandes further argues that the impetus to make rules did not arise out of the blue. The Tannaim themselves yearned for an ideal state of a unified halakha agreed upon by all. The late Tannaim and early Amoraim already began formulating procedures for courts, for travelers, and for one who receives contradictory decisions from two rabbis. They also began to make generalizations from practices that tend to follow certain rabbis. Brandes also explains that R. Yoḥanan was capable of establishing this set of rules because of his towering stature in the Palestinian rabbinic community.

---

54. See Benjamin Lewin, *Iggeret Rav Sherira Gaon* (Jerusalem: Makor, 1972), 55.
55. Brandes, "Beginnings of the Rules," 314–15.
56. Ibid., 292.
57. Ibid., 176–80, 316–22, and 325–31.

While this is all plausible enough, Brandes does not offer any reason why the Babylonians did not formulate rules themselves or, more importantly, why they did not accept R. Yoḥanan's rules. I suggest that the difference between the Talmuds on this issue is one manifestation of a more general difference between the Talmuds regarding tolerance for diversity of halakhic practice. The Yerushalmi seeks uniformity of practice by constructing and upholding these rules. R. Yoḥanan's set of rules ensures that all rabbis, even those in future generations, will come to the same halakhic conclusions when deciding between opinions of the Tannaim. The Bavli, on the other hand, shows tolerance for diversity by deconstructing the rules. According to the Bavli, each rabbi, as a transmitter and interpreter of tradition, must decide each issue on its own merits and cannot be bound by categorical rules. We will see more manifestations of this difference in attitude between the Talmuds in the coming chapters.

In addition to the rules adjudicating Tannaitic controversy, the Bavli also mentions rules regarding controversies between Amoraim such as, "הלכה כרב באיסורי וכשמואל בדיני—The halakha follows Rav in [ritual] prohibitions and Shmuel in civil law," and, "רב ור' יוחנן הלכה כר' יוחנן—Rav and R. Yoḥanan, the halakha follows R. Yoḥanan."[58] These rules are analyzed by Ephraim Halivni who finds that many of the rules cited in the Bavli about how to decide between various Amoraim were not formulated until after the redaction of the Bavli was complete, that is, after the Amoraim and even later than the Stam.[59] Other rules that may have been formulated and used by certain Amoraim were, like the rules regarding Tannaitic dispute, never widely accepted by other Amoraim nor even by the Stam.[60] Therefore, these rules do not serve as evidence of a program of unified codification in the Bavli. To the contrary, the lack of agreement by the Amoraim and the Stam about how to decide such cases reflects a view that the Bavli does not require uniform standards of decision making.

Besides the rules discussed until now, both Talmuds contain hundreds of decisions regarding individual cases. These are introduced by the term "הלכה" when stated by the Amoraim, and "והלכתא" when added by the Stam or the Saboraim. It is difficult to know whether the Amoraim meant such statements to be binding on all of their colleagues. But even if they did, their colleagues evidently thought otherwise. Certainly in the Bavli, and apparently even in the Yerushalmi, decisions about individual

58. *B. Bek.* 49b and *b. Beṣah* 4a, respectively.

59. See further in Robert Brody, *The Geonim of Babylonia and the Shaping of Medieval Jewish Culture* (New Haven and London: Yale University Press, 1998), 165, 181, and citations in footnotes there; Jackob Spiegel, "Later (Saboraic) Additions in the Babylonian Talmud" (Ph.D. diss., Tel Aviv University, 1975), 153–62 (Hebrew); and Zeni, *Rabanan*, 301–66.

60. See Halivni, *Rules*, 84–128; and Hidary, "Tolerance for Diversity," 418–22.

cases by one Amora were often disregarded by their colleagues. They were treated like any other statements by Amoraim, which could be opposed.[61]

Indeterminacy and Pluralism

Despite all the rules and decisions throughout the Talmud, there are still many issues concerning which the halakha is not clearly defined, either because no decision has been given or because contradictory decisions are recorded. Legal theorists discuss the indeterminacy inherent in all legal systems. No matter how much is legislated, there will always be ambiguity due to the open texture of language and the impossibility for humans to predict and legislate for every contingency that may crop up in the future.[62]

The more indeterminate a legal system, the less one can expect the system to produce a single solution to a given question and the more diversity of practice will arise. Halakha, like every legal system, contains indeterminacy,[63] and even the rules discussed above about how to decide between disputes are themselves sometimes indeterminate. How does one act when no rule applies to a particular dispute and no clear halakhic decision has been given regarding it?[64]

In this regard, Ben-Menahem distinguishes between pluralism, which is necessarily built into the law because of general indeterminacy, and "explicit pluralism," which is overtly legislated by the law in a specific

---

61. See examples at *b. Ber.* 27b, *b. Šabb.* 22a and 45b, *y. Šabb.* 3:7 (6c, see parallel cited below, p. 74) and 6:2 (8a), and more general statements at *b. Nid.* 7a, *b. B. Bat.* 130b, and *y. Ḥag.* 1:8 (76d). See further discussion at Hidary, "Tolerance for Diversity," 422–33.

62. See H. L. A. Hart, *The Concept of Law* (Oxford: Oxford University Press, 1994), 124f. See also Nahmanides to Deut 6:18 and Rabbi Vidal Yom Tom of Tolosa in his Magid Mishneh to *Hilkhot Shekhenim* 14:5.

63. See Aryeh Botwinick, "Underdetermination of Meaning by the Talmudic Text," in *Commandment and Community: New Essays in Jewish Legal and Political Philosophy*, ed. D. Frank (New York: State University of New York Press, 1995), 113–40.

64. One solution is provided by *t. ʿEd.* 1:5 (= *b. ʿErub.* 7a):

> היו שנים אחד אוסר ואחד מתיר אחד מטמא ואחד מטהר אם יש חכם אחר נשאלין לו ואם לאו הולכין אחר המחמיר ר׳ יהושע בן קרחה אומר דבר מדברי תורה הולכין אחר המחמיר מדברי סופרים הולכין אחר המיקל.
>
> If there were two [sages], one prohibiting and one permitting, one declaring impure and one declaring pure, if there is another sage, one asks him. If not, one goes according to the stringent view. R. Yehoshua ben Qorḥa says, if it is a matter of Torah law, one follows the stringent view; if it is a matter of rabbinic law, one follows the lenient view.

However, this seems to address an individual who asks different rabbis rather than how rabbis themselves decide between opinions of their predecessors. See Gerald Blidstein, "ʿAl hakhraʿat ha-halakha bi-zman ha-zeh: ʿiyyun ba-Rambam hilkhot mamrim 1, 5," *Dine Israel* 20–21 (2001): 7–9.

case.[65] He searches for legislation that grants its addressee "full autonomy to follow either of the two conflicting modes of behaviour"[66] with no hierarchical preference. He finds such examples in one formulation that the Talmud uses to deal with legal doubt in which the legislator is unable to decide between two competing opinions.

I would like to further explore the contexts and variations of this formula in order to gain a more precise evaluation of the extent and nature of the pluralism they encode. The complete Aramaic formula appears three times in the Bavli:

1. *b. Šabb.* 61a
אמר רב יוסף: השתא דתניא הכי, ואמר רבי יוחנן הכי, דעבד הכי—עבד, ודעבד הכי—עבד.
Rav Yosef said, "Now that we have learned this and R. Yoḥanan has said that, one who acts this way has acted [legitimately] and one who acts that way has acted [legitimately]."

2. *b. Šebu.* 48b
אמר רב חמא: השתא דלא איתמר הלכתא לא כרב ושמואל ולא כרבי אלעזר, האי דיינא דעבד כרב ושמואל—עבד, דעבד כרבי אלעזר—עבד.
Rav Ḥama said, "Since the halakha has not been stated either like Rav and Shmuel or like R. Eleazar, a judge who rules according to Rav and Shmuel has acted [legitimately] and one who rules according to R. Eleazar has acted [legitimately]."

3. *b. Ber.* 27a
השתא דלא אתמר הלכתא לא כמר ולא כמר, דעבד כמר—עבד, ודעבד כמר—עבד.
Since the halakha has not been stated either like this master or like that master, one who acts according to this master has acted [legitimately] and one who acts according to that master has acted [legitimately].

The first text involves a ritual matter concerning the proper order to put on one's shoes. Regarding an unresolved contradiction on this issue between R. Yoḥanan and a *baraita*, Rav Yosef, a third-generation Babylonian, declares both views to be valid.[67] In the second text, Rav Ḥama, a

65. Ben-Menahem, "Is There," 165–66.

66. Ibid., 168.

67. The issue of which shoe to put on first does not seem to be a major halakhic issue or even a custom; nevertheless, the language of this *sugya*, "has acted [legitimately]" (which assumes that one can don shoes in an illegitimate way), implies that this is not considered a trivial matter.

In the continuation of the *sugya* not cited here, Abaye seems to disagree, saying that either R. Yoḥanan did not know the *baraita*—in which case the halakha should follow the

fifth-generation Babylonian Amora, uses the formula concerning a monetary matter of collecting debts from an inheritance.[68] The choice here is given to the judge. The third text concerns a ritual issue of prayer times.[69] The Stam concludes that since the halakha cannot be established either way, both opinions are valid and one may choose which to follow. In all three instances, there is some disagreement about this solution within the *sugya,* but the pluralistic solution is upheld by the final statement.

Ben-Menahem concludes from these examples that the Talmud does not always assume there is one uniquely correct answer to any given question. Christine Hayes, however, has recently questioned Ben-Menahem's use of these examples as evidence of a pluralistic attitude. In her reading, these statements do not endorse two equally correct answers but rather only state that "there are two candidates for the title of 'right answer' between whom we lack the means to choose."[70] That is, these statements endorse two opposing opinions not because they are both correct but rather because we have no means to determine which is correct and so we throw up our hands and accept the legitimacy of both even though one of them is wrong. Hayes posits that these formulae "declare that actions taken in accordance with either view are—*ex post facto*—allowed to stand without challenge."[71] She points to the tense of the verb "עבד" as indicating a past action: "A perfect verb indicates only that rulings already rendered will be respected with no

---

baraita—or he did know it and nevertheless rejected it—in which case the halakha should follow R. Yoḥanan. Either way, both opinions cannot be correct. Rav Naḥman bar Isaac encourages one to be stringent and fulfill both opinions. Rav Ashi ends the *sugya* the way it began, seemingly agreeing with Rav Yosef that either practice is valid.

68. The general law of *m. Šebu.* 7:7 is that if one lends money to someone and both parties die, the lender's children may collect only after swearing that the loan, to their knowledge, was still not collected. In *b. Šebu.* 48b, Rav and Shmuel qualify that this only applies when the lender dies before the borrower, but if the borrower dies first then the lender would already have been obligated to swear to the borrower's children that he was not repaid and that oath cannot be taken by the children because that information cannot be known to them. Since the lender's children cannot fulfill this obligation to swear, they do not get paid. R. Eleazar disagrees and says the lender's children can swear to the best of their knowledge and that is sufficient for them to collect, even if the borrower dies first.

Because no explicit decision by subsequent Amoraim is transmitted regarding which opinion to follow, Rav Ḥama grants a judge of such a case full autonomy to choose between these two equally viable, though contradictory, viewpoints. In the continuation of the *sugya,* Rav Papa, Rav Ḥama's colleague, agrees. An anonymous scholar attempts to challenge a judge who decides according to one view, but Rav Ḥama has the last word.

69. The Talmud endeavors to establish the halakha regarding the latest time one may recite the *minḥa* prayer. In the previous lines of this *sugya,* Rav Isaac remains silent when asked about this issue, indicating that he could not decide and had received no tradition about it. Rav Ḥisda then attempts to bring a proof one way, but it is rejected by the Stam, which has the last word.

70. Hayes, "Legal Truth," 83–84.

71. Ibid., 84.

reference to their correctness or desirability."[72] That these statements only recognize the validity of a ruling after it has been given but do not endorse both views *ante factum*, argues Hayes, suggests that the rabbis adopt a monistic view. She therefore concludes that "the *'de-avad keX/haki avad'* cases are not evidence for a pluralistic view of law in the Talmud."[73]

---

72. Ibid., 82.

73. Ibid., 84. In the context of this chapter, it is sufficient for me to point to the fact of practical pluralism encoded in this formula in order to argue that the more often this formula is offered as a solution and even presented as the conclusion of a *sugya*, the more tolerance this reflects for practical pluralism. I also believe further, though this point is not essential to my argument here, that the formula reflects an attitude of theoretical pluralism, that is, the authenticity of more than one view at the legislative and ontological levels within the legal system (see above, pp. 3-4). This argument is further developed in Richard Hidary, "Right Answers Revisited: Monism and Pluralism in the Talmud," *Dine Israel* 26–27 (2009–2010): 229-55 in response to Hayes's first article.

Hayes subsequently responded to my article in "Theoretical Pluralism in the Talmud: A Response to Richard Hidary," *Dine Israel* 26–27 (2009–2010): 257-307. In her response, Hayes clarifies that she agrees that these and many other statements in the Talmud project practical pluralism and denies that she ever meant to say that these statements endorse practical monism. However, I do not believe that I have misinterpreted Hayes's first article; I suspect that she said what she meant and that her second article reinterprets her first according to her now more clarified views. Just to cite one example, Hayes writes: "Amoraic authorities declare that actions taken in accordance with either view are—*ex post facto*—allowed to stand without challenge. This should not be construed as a declaration that both views are correct and carry an equal endorsement as the course of action to be taken" (Hayes, "Legal Truth," 84). Even her myriad pages of "midrashic pyrotechnics" cannot remove her original statement from its *peshat*.

Be that as it may, we now agree that this formula does encode practical pluralism, but we still disagree on whether it also assumes a stance of theoretical pluralism. Hayes states that "it is certainly *possible* to read these texts as asserting the authenticity or truth value of both positions." However, she continues, "a *better* explanation is that incompatible views are recognized in order to avoid paralysis in the face of a procedural breakdown. This explanation is better because it finds *explicit textual support in three of the five cases*. . . . I did not say that it is *wrong* to claim that the views are authentic, but only that we simply *do not know* and cannot ascertain the authenticity of the two views in question due to a lack of information in these texts—they are *inconclusive* on that point one way or the other" ("Theoretical," 284–85; all italics in the original). My position, however, is that the conjunction of this formula when read in light of programmatic statements lends to a strong argument for theoretical pluralism. Hayes herself says that programmatic statements should be tested to see if legal pronouncements also reflect their sentiments. This formula is precisely the confirmation for which we were looking. In fact, the fifth example of this formula below from *b. Ber.* 11a involved the Houses of Shammai and Hillel, which is also the subject of the most famous programmatic statement, "These and those are the words of the living God."

One important root of our disagreement lies in whether the legitimacy of a law presumes its authenticity. Hayes writes, "A norm can fail to meet authenticity criteria but because it meets validity criteria, it becomes the legitimate halakha. We see this in programmatic texts like the famous oven of Akhnai story in which the halakhic view endorsed by God (and indicator of *authenticity*) is rejected by the procedural principle of majority rule" ("Theoretical," 262). Hayes correctly anticipates the weakness in this argument, which rests on the assumption that "the fundamental *authenticity* criterion is conformity to the will of

I will now revisit Ben-Menahem's analysis of this formula in order to show that it does indeed project a view of pluralism at both the practical and theoretical levels. Hayes's grammatical argument for this phrase being *ex post facto* is problematic. One manuscript actually does read "עביד," indicating a participle.[74] But even for the rest of the versions that read "עבד,"[75] it is not accurate to treat this as a past tense verb. The perfect tense indicates an action that is completed, whether its completion occurs in the past, present, or future.[76] This sense may be more accurately rendered into English by the present tense, as Sokoloff translates: "the one who acts in this manner does so (properly) and the one who acts in that manner does so (properly)."[77] According to this understanding, the phrase can refer to an *ante factum* situation as well.

Furthermore, it is manifest that these formulae do apply *ante factum* based on their contexts. The first case cited above discussed which shoe one should put on first. Rav Yosef declares that one acts properly whether he has put on the right or the left shoe first. How can one understand this statement as being only *post factum*? What is one supposed to do *ante factum*? Does this statement require that one go barefoot because we cannot decide which shoe to put on first? Surely, the permission to allow either foot to go first must apply *ante factum*.

Similarly in the second case, a judge must either rule according to Rav and Shmuel who allow the orphans to swear and collect, or like the sages who do not. The judge cannot simply refuse the case because he cannot decide. This view is affirmed by the statement of Rav Papa, which immediately follows that of Rav Ḥama: "Rav Papa said, 'We do not tear up a document of orphans, nor do we collect with it. We do not collect with it

---

God" (ibid., 261 and see n. 7 there). The point of this story is precisely that the Author's interpretation is irrelevant because authenticity depends solely on the Text that He has given. As the law of *Horayot* teaches, if a court, through normal procedures, issues a ruling in error because it contradicts a learned tradition, then this ruling may not be followed by those who know better and atonement is required for those who follow it (see below, chaper 7). Such a ruling is valid but it is still not legitimate because it is inauthentic in that it does not conform to the sources of written and oral Law. I would thus argue that legitimacy is an indicator of authenticity and therefore rulings that tolerate practical pluralism, especially when alternative solutions are available, are good indicators of theoretical pluralism as well.

In the end, we agree on much more than we disagree about and I thank Prof. Hayes for her collegiality and for helping me to clarify many matters, both in this debate and through her many other writings that have been essential to my development and research.

74. Ms. Oxford of *b. Ber.* 27a.

75. עבד also appears in a quotation of *b. Šebu.* 48b in ms. Sassoon of *Halakhot pesuqot* (ed. S. D. Sassoon, *Sefer halakhot pesuqot* [Jerusalem: Ḥebrat Meqiṣe Nirdamim, 1951], 125). I thank Moshe Morgenstern for this reference.

76. See E. Kautzsch and A. E. Cowley, *Gesenius' Hebrew Grammar* (Oxford: Clarendon, 1910), 309–13. The usage of the tenses in ancient Hebrew and Aramaic are similar.

77. Sokoloff, *A Dictionary of Jewish Babylonian Aramaic*, 836. I thank Moshe Bernstein and Elitzur Avraham Bar-Asher for helping to clarify these grammatical points.

for perhaps we agree with Rav and Shmuel; we do not tear it up because a judge who rules according to R. Eleazar has acted [legitimately].'" Rav Papa addresses the case *ante factum* and states that the loan contract should remain unpaid in the hands of the lender's inheritors and await judgment. If one option were preferable over the other, then Rav Papa should have required that the contract either be destroyed or presented for payment immediately. Thus, we can conclude that Rav Ḥama and Rav Papa deem both options legitimate even *ante factum*.[78]

In the third case, the choice is not between two mutually exclusive options as it is in the previous two. Rather, everyone agrees one can recite *minḥa* before *pelag*; the question is only whether one can still recite it afterward. Therefore, one can be stringent not to pray either *minḥa* or *arbit* between *pelag* and sunset and thus act in agreement with all opinions. In this case, one could assume an *ante factum* preference not to pray at all during this time and then state that *post factum* one has fulfilled his obligation if he did recite either prayer. Such an *ante factum* preference is never stated, however, and so this statement too is likely to be meant *ante factum*.

Once we confirm that this formula applies *ante factum*, we must conclude that the judge has discretion to choose either possibility. We can therefore uphold Ben-Menahem's reasoning that in these cases, the judge is granted "full autonomy to make a choice between conflicting and incompatible norms and that consequently in those instances no one uniquely correct answer exists."[79] These cases describe situations of procedural breakdown where neither law has been established as the halakha. The formula therefore comes to say that although neither has been validated, we will consider both options as valid. In a typical case where there is no procedural breakdown, the rabbis, as legislators, confront a range of authentic and theoretically correct possibilities. From among these possibilities, they choose one as the only legitimate law for practice. However, when, as in the cases discussed here, there is no clear choice, then the range of theoretical possibilities, all of which have truth value, remain available.[80] I will now confirm this reading on the basis of a number of variations on this formula wherein a practical choice is made available even when there is no procedural breakdown or where procedural breakdown is resolved differently.

---

78. Rambam, *Mishneh Torah, Hilkhot malveh ve-loveh* 17:3, however, does think that Rav and Shmuel are to be preferred and that R. Eleazar is only valid *ex post facto*. He derives this from Rav Naḥman's statement earlier in the *sugya* that he would not repeal Rav and Shmuel but would also not add to it, implying that he accepts its present application. Rav Ḥama, however, does not express any preference. Rav Papa's language does seem to prefer Rav and Shmuel ("for perhaps we agree with Rav and Shmuel") over R. Eleazar ("a judge who rules according to R. Eleazar has acted [legitimately]"), but this is not decisive.

79. Ben-Menahem, "Is There," 165.

80. For more on theoretical pluralism in the Talmud, see Hidary, "Right Answers Revisited."

In addition to the three Aramaic statements cited above, there are also two Hebrew parallels to the second half of this formula:

4. *b. B. Bat.* 124a-b
אמר רבה בר חנא אמר ר' חייא: עשה כדברי רבי—עשה, כדברי חכמים—עשה; מספקא ליה: אי הלכה כרבי מחבירו ולא מחביריו, או הלכה כרבי מחבירו ואפילו מחביריו.
Rabbah bar Ḥannah said in the name of R. Ḥiyya, "If one acted according to Rabbi, he has acted [legitimately]; [if one acted] according to the sages, he has acted [legitimately]." He was in doubt whether halakha follows Rabbi [when in dispute] with his colleague but not his colleagues or whether halakha follows Rabbi [when in dispute] with his colleague and even with his colleagues.

5. *b. Ber.* 11a
תני רב יחזקאל: עשה כדברי בית שמאי—עשה, כדברי בית הלל—עשה.
Rav Yeḥezkel learnt: If one acts in accordance with the opinion of Beth Shammai, he has acted [legitimately]; [if he acts] in accordance with the opinion of Beth Hillel, he has acted [legitimately].[81]

These Hebrew Tannaitic formulations are probably earlier than the Amoraic Aramaic variations. The context of statement 4 is a *baraita* discussing a case where the value of an inheritance increases from the time of the father's death to the time when the inheritance is divided. The anonymous opinion rules that the firstborn son is not entitled to a double share of the increased value but only of the original value, while Rabbi rules that the firstborn son does receive a double portion even of the increase. For whatever reason,[82] R. Ḥiyya does not decide between them but rather endorses both options. Since this is a monetary case, a judge must decide between the two opinions and neither is given preference. We can therefore assume that the statement refers to an *ante factum* situation. This is confirmed by contrasting it with a subsequent statement in the same *sugya*:

אמר רבא: אסור לעשות כדברי רבי, ואם עשה עשוי, קא סבר: מטין איתמר.
Rava said, "One may not act according to Rabbi; but if he already did, then it was [legitimately] done." He thought it [the rule about Rabbi and his colleague] was said to incline [towards the sages].

81. See the extended citation and discussion of this statement below, pp. 222–24.

82. The explanation given in the Aramaic part of statement 4, "מספקא ליה ...," is surely a Stammaitic gloss. The rules for deciding between Tannaitic opinions were first formulated by R. Yoḥanan and his students so this explanation is somewhat anachronistic; see above, pp. 44–54.

Rava says one must follow the sages *ante factum*, but Rabbi's opinion is also allowed to stand *post factum*. Note that Rava's statement uses the passive participle (עשוי) in contrast with the perfect (עשה) used in R. Ḥiyya's statement. Even more significantly, Rava's statement clearly distinguishes between *ante* and *post factum* situations; R. Ḥiyya does not. The differences in verb tenses and sentence structures between Rava's statement and the other five statements quoted, Hebrew and Aramaic, confirm that the latter address even *ante factum* situations.

In one sense, Rava's pluralism, although only *post factum*, may actually represent a deeper form of pluralism than the others. The Stammaitic gloss explains that Rava thinks the rule concerning how to decide between Rabbi and his colleagues is not definitive but merely a suggestion to incline toward the opinion of the sages.[83] In contrast, R. Ḥiyya thinks the rule is definitive and only tolerates both options here because he is unsure what the rule is. R. Ḥiyya's pluralism results from a breakdown in the legislative process due to doubt about a legislative principle. Rava's pluralism, although only *post factum*, is built into the legislative process.[84] That Rava still validates Rabbi's view *post factum*, even though he has decided that the halakha follows Rabbi's opponent, suggests that Rava is not a theoretical monist but rather accepts more than one opinion as true. If he thought that Rabbi's opinion had no theoretical truth value, then he should not have allowed a ruling according to Rabbi to stand.

In contrast to the previous four statements, statement 5 does not include a justification for pluralism based on legislative doubt. In the previous statements, pluralism is presented as an unfortunate result of a breakdown in the legislative process. In statement 5, on the other hand, the lack of any justification or apology suggests that this pluralism is perfectly acceptable.[85] No hint is given that one should ultimately triumph over the other; these are simply two valid options. In this sense, statement 5 is similar to that of Rava in statement 4 except that Rava allows only *post factum* pluralism while statement 5 permits it even *ante factum*.

Furthermore, statement 5 appears within the discussion of *m. Ber.* 1:3 regarding whether one must stand during the recitation of *shema* in the morning and lie down during its recitation at night—the opinion of Beth Shammai—or whether the position of recitation does not matter—the opin-

83. This understanding of the rules harks back to the three-way controversy about the nature of these rules recorded in *b. ʿErub.* 46b, above, p. 47.

84. In addition, R. Ḥiyya's pluralism can apply only to a limited number of cases that involve Rabbi versus the sages. On the other hand, if Rava fully adopts the position of R. Assi cited in the previous note, then his *post factum* acceptance of rejected views could apply to all decisions based on these rules.

85. Reading it in light of the other parallel formulae, one could, perhaps, assume a breakdown in the legislative process to decide between the Houses as the basis for this statement as well. However, this statement is a *baraita* and predates its parallels.

ion of Beth Hillel. In this case, unlike the previous ones, it is possible to be stringent like Beth Shammai and fulfill all opinions. If only one view were correct but we were not sure which it was, then the ruling should have been to lie down.[86] Since one is not forced to choose between the two positions, this permission to choose reflects genuine legal pluralism at both the theoretical and practical levels. That is, both views are theoretically authentic possibilities and therefore both views may be legitimately practiced.

Moreover, this statement addresses not only the issue of reciting *shema* but rather all disputes between the Houses.[87] Rav Yeḥezkel's formulation also has a parallel in the Tosefta and the Yerushalmi where it clearly applies to all disputes between the Houses.[88] The Tosefta reads: "Choose either according to Beth Shammai with their leniencies and stringencies or according to Beth Hillel with their leniencies and stringencies." This statement explicitly permits *ante factum* choice between the two Houses and covers all cases, including those where a compromise or stringent position may be possible. This is therefore a significant expression of pluralism. *B. ʿErubin* 7a further extends this choice to controversy between any Tannaim and Amoraim.[89]

One can get added perspective on this formula by comparing it to four others that begin with the same formula as the first three texts cited above but that have different endings. *B. Niddah* 6a (=*b. ʿErub.* 46a) reads:

> תא שמע, מעשה ועשה רבי כרבי אליעזר. לאחר שנזכר אמר: כדי הוא רבי אליעזר לסמוך עליו בשעת הדחק.
> והוינן בה: מאי לאחר שנזכר? אילימא לאחר שנזכר דאין הלכה כרבי אליעזר אלא כרבנן, בשעת הדחק היכי עביד כותיה?
> אלא דלא איתמר הלכתא לא כמר ולא כמר, וכיון שנזכר דלאו יחיד פליג עליה אלא רבים פליגי עליה, אמר כדי הוא רבי אליעזר לסמוך עליו בשעת הדחק.

> Come hear: It happened that Rabbi acted according to R. Eliezer. After he remembered he said, "R. Eliezer is worthy to be relied upon under extenuating circumstances."
>
> We analyzed this: What does "after he remembered" mean? If it means after he remembered that halakha does not follow R. Eliezer but rather the sages, how does he act according to him [R. Eliezer] even under extenuating circumstances?

86. See, however, below, p. 172 n. 33.

87. See the continuation of this *sugya* and Moshe Benovitz, *Talmud ha-Igud: BT Berakhot Chapter I* (Jerusalem: Society for the Interpretation of the Talmud, 2006) (Hebrew), 509 and 513–14.

88. *T. Sukkah* 2:3, *t. Yebam.* 1:13, *t. ʿEd.* 2:3, and *y. Ber.* 1:4 (3b). See further, ibid., 512, and see below, p. 191.

89. See below, p. 232. This point is also made by Ben-Menahem, "Is There," 171.

> Rather, the halakha had been stated neither according to this master nor according to that master. Once he remembered that it is not an individual who disputes him [R. Eliezer] but rather that many dispute him, he said, "R. Eliezer is worthy to be relied upon under extenuating circumstances."

R. Eliezer rules leniently regarding a woman who does not have a period for three months but then sees blood that we do not retroactively declare impure whatever she touched before but assume that this blood is the first occurrence; the rabbis disagree. Rabbi at first follows R. Eliezer but then changes to rule like his detractors while still permitting one to follow R. Eliezer when there is a pressing need. The anonymous redactor explains that at first Rabbi thought the halakha was not established either way between the two views and so he could choose either opinion, as per the formula seen in the previous cases.[90] Once he remembered that it was the majority against R. Eliezer, he had to prefer the majority,[91] but he still upheld some level of legitimacy for R. Eliezer. It is noteworthy that on the original assumption that the disagreement was between individuals, Rabbi did not simply act stringently to prohibit whatever she touched out of doubt. This again suggests that there is more than one correct answer to a question. Otherwise, why not just be stringent?

Here are three more variations on this formula:

> אמר רב הונא בר תחליפא: השתא דלא איתמר הלכתא לא כמר ולא כמר, כל דאלים גבר.
> Rav Huna bar Taḥlifa said, "Since the halakha has not been stated either according to this master or according to that master, whoever is stronger prevails."[92]

> השתא דלא אתמר לא הכי ולא הכי, תפסה—לא מפקינן מינה, לא תפסה—לא יהבינן לה.
> Since [the halakha] has not been stated either this way or that way, if she is in possession of it [her ketubah], then we do not take it from her, but if she is not in possession of it, then we do not give it to her.[93]

> השתא דלא איתמר הלכתא לא כהלל ולא כרבנן—מברך על אכילת מצה ואכיל, והדר מברך על אכילת מרור ואכיל, והדר אכיל מצה וחסא בהדי הדדי בלא ברכה זכר למקדש כהלל.

90. See further analysis in Louis Ginzberg, *A Commentary on the Palestinian Talmud*, 4 vols. (New York: Jewish Theological Seminary of America, 1941), 1:83–84.

91. This criterion is not consistent since two of the cases above also involve an individual opinion against the sages. Apparently, R. Yehudah (*b. Ber.* 27a) and R. Yoḥanan (*b. Šabb.* 61a) were considered of high enough stature to be able to balance the majority.

92. *B. Giṭ.* 60b.

93. *B. Ketub.* 64a.

> Since the halakha has not been stated either according to Hillel or according to the sages, one recites a blessing "on eating *maṣah*" and eats and then recites a blessing "on eating *maror*" and eats, and then eats *maṣah* and *ḥasah* together without reciting a blessing in memory of what Hillel did [during the time of] the Temple.[94]

The first text states that since there is no set halakha, there is no rule of law and the court dismisses the case, thus allowing the parties to settle matters outside of the law.[95] The second text similarly rules that since we cannot decide the halakha, there is no legally rightful claimant to the property, which by default remains with whoever has it; we simply retain the status quo. These two solutions can work for monetary laws but not for ritual law. The third text says that when there is no clear decision, one should try to fulfill both views. This is also the strategy of Rav Naḥman bar Isaac in *b. Šabb.* 61a who advocates fulfilling both opinions, a solution that is not always practicable. None of these three texts simply chooses one view or endorses both views. This suggests that all three assume a monistic view that there is only one right answer, which, in these cases, cannot be accessed.[96]

These are all alternatives to the either-or solution provided by the texts quoted above. *B. Šebuᶜot* 48b is a monetary case in which the Talmud

---

94. *B. Pesaḥ.* 115a.

95. The phrase כל דאלים גבר also occurs twice at *b. B. Bat.* 34b, one of them in the name of Rav Naḥman. See the analysis of Samuel Atlas, *Pathways in Hebrew Law* (New York: American Academy for Jewish Research, 1978), 76–82 (Hebrew). This law is similar to Rav Naḥman's ruling, "עביד אינש דינא לנפשיה—one may take the law into his own hands" (*b. B. Qam.* 27b), on which see Emanuel Quint and Niel Hecht, *Jewish Jurisprudence: Its Sources and Modern Applications* (New York: Harwood Academic Publishers, 1986), 2:91f.

96. These cases of legal doubt are comparable to cases of circumstantial doubt. *Y. Šabb.* 7:1 (9a) and *b. Šabb.* 69b discuss what happens if someone is lost or taken captive and does not know what day is Shabbat. Rav Naḥman bar Yaᶜaqov in the Yerushalmi says that he must rotate which day he observes as Shabbat in order to observe Shabbat at least once every few weeks. Rava in the Bavli says he should do only the minimum amount of work to stay alive every day of the week. Both sages believe that there is only one objective day of Shabbat and therefore prescribe being stringent to try and cover all bases. We thus see that when there is only one correct law that is not known then the rabbis tend to impose stringencies that maximize chances of fulfillment. It then stands to reason that when the rabbis permit one to choose between possibilities, even where they could be stringent, then they do not think there is only one correct answer. In the case of Shabbat, Rav and Shmuel seem to think that there is a subjective element in the day of Shabbat and therefore allow one to begin counting the week from the day he remembers. They do not permit one to randomly choose one day of the week, in which case we could have interpreted their opinion as another way of dealing with doubt about an objective truth. Rather, they require that one recreate the subjective experience of counting the days of creation. For further analysis of this *sugya* see Stephen Wald, *BT Shabbat Chapter VII*, Tamud Ha-Igud (Jerusalem: Society for the Interpretation of the Talmud, 2007) (Hebrew), 59–64.

could have said, "Whoever is stronger prevails," or, "If he is in possession of it, then we do not remove it, but if he is not in possession of it, then we do not give it to him." In *b. Šabb.* 61a, one opinion actually does suggest that one should fulfill both opinions; but the other solutions in that *sugya* do not agree. One could similarly legislate that one should not recite *minḥa* in the late afternoon, just to be stringent, a road not taken by *b. Ber.* 27a. That the Talmud in those three cases decides to leave it up to the judge or the individual to decide which opinion to follow, even where alternative solutions are possible, does not fit well with a monistic view but rather suggests a genuinely pluralistic attitude. If a rabbi chooses to endorse two opposing positions rather than rule stringently, attempt to fulfill both, or excuse himself completely by leaving the status quo or putting the case back into the hands of the litigants, then such a rabbi ascribes some level of authenticity to both positions.

Based on this analysis, I conclude that the above-quoted either-or formulae (statements 1–5) surely permit *ante factum* pluralism of practice. Statements that offer the either-or option only when no legislative solution is possible could be understood as reflecting a negative attitude toward such pluralism. If other less pluralistic options are available, however, and yet the either-or option is still endorsed, then we can detect a somewhat positive outlook even in these statements. Statements that offer the either-or option even when not presented with a legislative breakdown reflect an even higher degree of comfort with halakhic pluralism. Significantly, all of the Bavli *sugyot* that include the either-or formula conclude the *sugya* with a pluralistic ruling, even when more monistic strategies are proposed beforehand.[97]

Yerushalmi Parallels

The Bavli's either-or formula also has a parallel in the Yerushalmi. *Y. ᶜErubin* 1:4 (19a) states:

97. *B. Šebu.* 48b and *b. Ber.* 27a end with the complete pluralistic formula, *b. Šabb.* 61a ends with Rav Kahana, who followed the pluralistic formula, and *b. B. Bat.* 124a and *b. Nid.* 6a end with a limited pluralism (only valid after the fact or in extenuating circumstances). If we assume that the last cited opinion in a *sugya* represents its conclusion, then we may assert that all the Bavli *sugyot* prefer a pluralistic option. However, at least two of these *sugyot* (*b. B. Bat.* 124a and *b. Šabb.* 61a) seem to simply list the opinions in chronological order without necessarily preferring the last cited opinion; these two *sugyot* include about the same number of monistic opinions as pluralistic ones. All opinions cited in *b. Šebu.* 48b are pluralistic, except for that of an anonymous sage, which is rejected. Most significant are *b. Ber.* 27a and *b. Nid.* 6a in which the Stam voice leads the discussion to a pluralistic conclusion (though limited in *b. Nid.* 6a).

רב הונא בשם רב הלכה כרבי מאיר
שמואל אמר הלכה כרבי יודה
רבי יהושע בן לוי אמר הלכה כרבי שמעון
אמר רבי שמעון בר כרסנא מכיון דתימר הלכה כהדין והלכה כהדין מאן דעבד הכין לא חשש ומאן דעבד הכין לא חשש
א"ר מנא מכיון דאיתמר הלכה כרבנן שבקין ליחיד ועבדין כרבנן

> Rav Huna in the name of Rav [says]: The halakha follows R. Meir.
> Shmuel says: The halakha follows R. Yehudah.
> R. Yehoshua ben Levi says: The halakha follows R. Shimon.
> R. Shimon bar Carsena says: Since you say the halakha follows them and the halakha follows them, one who acts this way need not worry and one who acts that way need not worry.
> R. Manna says: Since it is said, "the halakha follows the sages" [i.e., R. Meir, whose view is stated anonymously in *m. ʿErub.* 1:4], we leave the opinion of the individual and we practice according to the sages.[98]

There are three Tannaitic views regarding the size of the crossbeam used for an *eruv.* Each of three early Amoraim establishes the halakha according to a different Tanna. R. Shimon bar Carsena, a fourth-fifth-generation Palestinian Amora, concludes that all options are therefore valid and so one may practice whichever opinion he prefers. In this case, one could be stringent to satisfy all opinions, so the pluralistic option is especially significant. However, R. Manna, also a fifth-generation Palestinian, does decide between the three Tannaim by assuming that R. Meir represents the majority opinion. This is an argument among Amoraim themselves about the rules of decision making (how to interpret the anonymous Mishnah) and the possibility of there being more than one normative option. The continuation of the *sugya* presents a narrative about Rav going to a certain place and invalidating their *eruv,* which was valid only according to R. Yehudah but not R. Meir. Rav himself did not think that people were at liberty to choose other opinions. Thus, although the Yerushalmi entertains the possibility of pluralism, the continuation of the *sugya* seems to reject that possibility in favor of a more monistic view.

The second half of the R. Shimon bar Carsena's formulation is used in *y. Yoma* 5:5 (42d):

שני כהנים ברחו בפולמוסיות אחד אומר עומד הייתי ומחטא ואחד אומר מהלך הייתי ומחטא
אמר רבי יודן הדא אמרה מאן דעבד הכין לא חשש ומאן דעבד הכין לא חשש.

98. A parallel to the beginning of this *sugya* is found at *y. Šabb.* 3:7 (6c).

> Two priests ran away during the wars. One of them said, "I used to stand and sprinkle." The other said, "I used to walk and sprinkle."
> Rav Yudan said, "About this it is said: One who acts this way need not worry and one who acts that way need not worry."

M. Yoma 5:5 records a dispute between the anonymous opinion and R. Eliezer about whether the high priest walks around the altar while sprinkling each corner or whether he stands in one place while sprinkling. Two priests report that they each practiced differently. Rav Yudan concludes that both methods are valid.

Y. Giṭ. 3:1 (44d) expresses a similar point of view to that of R. Shimon bar Carsena, though not using his formulation:

> אתא עובדא קומי רבי ירמיה ועבד כריש לקיש אמר ליה רבי יוסי שבקין רבי יוחנן ועבדין כריש לקיש אמר ליה הוריותיה דרבי יוחנן הורייה והורייתא דריש לקיש לאו הורייה אמר רבי יעקב בר אחא לא ריש לקיש פליג על רבי יוחנן אלא מתניתא שמע ועמד עליה אמר רבי יוסי בי רבי בון לא דריש לקיש מתריס לקבל ר׳ יוחנן בגין דאתפלגי עלה אלא בגין מפקין עובד מיניה כד שמע מתני׳ הוא סמך עליה כד דלא שמע מתני׳ הוא מבטל דעתיה מקומי דעתיה דרבי יוחנן
>
> A case came before R. Yirmiah who acted according to Resh Laqish. R. Yose said, "Do you ignore R. Yoḥanan and act according to Resh Laqish?" He responded, "Is the teaching of R. Yoḥanan a [legitimate] teaching and the teaching of Resh Laqish not a [legitimate] teaching?"
> R. Yaʿaqov bar Aḥa said: "Resh Laqish does not disagree with R. Yoḥanan [fundamentally]. Rather, he [Resh Laqish] learned a [different] *baraita* and relied upon it."
> R. Yose b. R. Bon [said]: "It is not that Resh Laqish objects to accepting the opinion of R. Yoḥanan because he [fundamentally] disagrees with him. Rather, it is because a practical case came before him. When he heard a [different] *baraita,* he relied upon it. If he had not heard the *baraita,* he would have nullified his own view before the view of R. Yoḥanan.

This example is included within a conversation between two Amoraim. R. Yirmiah decides a case according to Resh Laqish and is castigated by R. Yose who assumes that the halakha must follow R. Yoḥanan. R. Yirmiah responds with a powerful retort that both opinions are valid and so one can decide either way.[99] Evidently, there was more than one view in

99. Another Yerushalmi *sugya* quotes a similar conversation:
והוה רבי זעורה מסתכל ביה א״ל מה את מסתכל בי מה ידעת ולא נדע תבין ולא עמנו הוא
R. Zeʿorah was staring at him. He said, "What are you looking at? What do you

Palestine concerning how to deal with halakhic controversy. We see from R. Yose that there were certain expectations already in place about whom to follow in particular situations; but R. Yirmiah shows that not everyone felt bound by these expectations. Still, even R. Yirmiah is only using a pluralistic argument to defend his own position; he does not necessarily advocate individual choice.

The end of the *sugya* discusses what was behind the disagreement between R. Yoḥanan and Resh Laqish. R. Yaʿaqov bar Aḥa explains that their dispute was not over any fundamental principle, but rather that each just happened to learn a different version of a *baraita*. Pene Moshe comments that this comes to justify R. Yirmiah's position, namely, that both sides represent valid rulings since both are well grounded. One could interpret R. Yaʿaqov to have the opposite force, however: R. Yose is correct that only one opinion can be authentic since they are not based on subjective reasoning but rather on two versions of a *baraita*, only one of which can be original. In fact, the last statement of R. Yose b. R. Bon suggests as much by concluding that Resh Laqish would have easily agreed with R. Yoḥanan had he not heard the *baraita*. This implies that his own opinion is not worthy of competing with R. Yoḥanan's decision but that the alternate *baraita* does counter R. Yoḥanan's source. The last two comments are too ambiguous to conclusively determine the outlook of the *sugya* as a whole.

All in all, we find opposing viewpoints within both Talmuds regarding how to deal with indeterminacy. Certain Amoraic statements—both in the Yerushalmi and in the Bavli—tend toward monism while others tend toward pluralism. The structure and flow of most of the Bavli *sugyot* analyzed in this section, however, tend toward pluralism. The editorial hand of the Bavli concludes each *sugya* on a pluralistic note. The Yerushalmi evidence, on the other hand, is inconclusive. The first Yerushalmi *sugya* quoted above ends on a monistic note; the second example is all pluralistic; and the third is unclear. Even if we cannot gain an adequate sense of the preference of the Yerushalmi's editors, however, it is still significant that a number of Palestinian Amoraim do sometimes express pluralistic sentiments.

Paradoxically, the existence of such cases of indeterminacy presumes that the vast majority of cases are determinate. These cases in which "the halakha was not decided either way" are presented as exceptional and reveal a general assumption that most disputes have been conclusively

---

know that we do not know? [What do you] understand that is not [understood] by us?" (*y. Meg.* 4:1 [75a]; the end of the sentence quotes from Job 15:9)

R. Ba in the name of Rav Yehudah offers a radical interpretation of a law. R. Zeʿorah responds with a critical stare. R. Ba retorts that there is more than one way to think about the issue. This comment implies a pluralistic attitude not just on the practical level but perhaps even at the epistemological level.

decided. Indeed, even though the Bavli rejects the absolute authority of the rules of R. Yoḥanan, it does still use them occasionally. Similarly, even though the Bavli sometimes reports that later Amoraim reject the decisions of earlier Amoraim, in most cases a decision of an early Amora does set a precedent for later generations. The Bavli does not advocate a legislative free-for-all in which any rabbi may choose whatever opinion he likes.

Thus, the difference between Yerushalmi and Bavli attitudes toward pluralism should not be exaggerated. Both Talmuds assume a general consensus in most cases about which opinions should be rejected, and both put limits on the freedom of individual rabbis to decide earlier disputes. Conversely, both Talmuds contain genuine expressions of pluralism. Nevertheless, an important distinction between the Talmuds remains. R. Yoḥanan creates rules of law, a comprehensive scheme to decide all cases, and they are by and large accepted by the Palestinian community, at least as represented in the Yerushalmi. The Bavli, however, resists these rules explicitly. The Bavli is far less willing to allow a system of rules to force uniformity of practice and instead allows individual rabbis to deliberate and decide each case independently.

Historical Context

The penchant for codification in the Yerushalmi may be related to similar trends in Roman law during the late Principate and the Dominate. Roman law incorporated an increasingly large number of sources beginning with the publication of the Twelve Tables in 450 B.C.E. and continuing with subsequent legislation by various assemblies, magistrates, and, later on, imperial edicts and senatorial resolutions.[100] This mass of laws that interpreted and sometimes even overturned preceding laws had grown unwieldy over time and place, prompting a sustained effort at codification beginning with Hadrian and culminating with Justinian's *Digest*.[101] This period from the second to the sixth century also saw the production of the Mishnah and the Palestinian Talmud. Previous scholars have noted parallels between Roman codes and the codificatory activity leading up to the publication of the Mishnah. Lee Levine doubts that it is mere coincidence that "R. ʿAqiva and his colleagues began collecting and organizing rab-

100. See O. F. Robinson, *The Sources of Roman Law: Problems and Methods for Ancient Historians* (London: Routledge, 1997); and George Mousourakis, *A Legal History of Rome* (London: Routledge, 2007).

101. Robinson, *Sources of Roman Law*, 16–21; Mousourakis, *A Legal History*, 179–91; and Christine Hayes, "The Abrogation of Torah Law: Rabbinic *Taqqanah* and Praetorian Edict," in *The Talmud Yerushalmi and Graeco-Roman Culture I*, ed. Peter Schäfer (Tübingen: Mohr Siebeck, 1998), 665–67.

binic traditions under Hadrian, when Julianus, Celsus Pomponius, and others were actively involved in making similar compilations in Rome" and "Rabbi Judah the Prince compiled and edited his Mishnah, and tannaitic midrashim were collected under the Severans, at a time when Gaius, Papinianus, Paulus, and Ulpianus were likewise compiling codices and responsa of Roman law and commenting on earlier legal material."[102]

The findings of this chapter suggest that the link between Roman and halakhic codificatory activities extends even past the Mishnah.[103] In 426 C.E., Theodosius II and Valentinian III issued the "Law of Citations," which "aspired to establish a veritable hierarchy for the opinions of celebrated jurists."[104] This law restated an earlier edict issued by Constantine in 321 C.E. that named five jurists (Gaius, Papinianus, Paulus, Ulpianus, and Modestinus) as authorities whose codes should carry the most weight in court. However, the multiplicity of these divergent law codes themselves required further guidelines as to which code to follow. The Law of Citations thus stipulates:

> When conflicting opinions are cited, the greater number of the authors shall prevail, or if the numbers should be equal, the authority of that group shall take precedence in which the man of superior genius, Papinian, shall tower above the rest, and as he defeats a single opponent, so he yields to two.... Furthermore, when their opinions as cited are equally divided and their authority is rated as equal, the regulation of the judge shall choose whose opinion he shall follow.[105]

One must follow the majority of jurists. When they are equally split, then Papinian is to be followed over his four colleagues. This is similar to R. Yoḥanan's rules that also present a hierarchy of sages. If the Law of Citations were written in Hebrew, it might read: "הלכה כפפיניאן מחבירו אבל לא מחביריו." When this rule too cannot solve the dispute, for example, if Papinian did not comment on that matter, then the judge may choose which opinion to follow. In other words, "מאן דעבד הכין לא חשש ומאן דעבד הכין לא חשש." Although

102. Lee Levine, *Judaism and Hellenism in Antiquity: Conflict or Confluence?* (Peabody, MA: Hendrickson, 1999), 135. See also Elman, "Order, Sequence, and Selection," 65–70. E. S. Rosental, "Masoret halakha ve-ḥidushe halakhot be-mishnat ḥakhamim," *Tarbiz* 63 (1994): 321–74, points to a further parallel between Justinian's *Digest* (I, 2, 47–48) and the Houses of Shammai and Hillel regarding tradition and innovation in law.

103. See Catherine Hezser, "The Codification of Legal Knowledge in Late Antiquity: The Talmud Yerushalmi and Roman Law Codes," in *The Talmud Yerushalmi and Graeco-Roman Culture I*, 581–641.

104. George Mousourakis, *The Historical and Institutional Context of Roman Law* (Burlington, VT: Ashgate, 2003), 180.

105. *Codex Theodosianus*, 1.4.3.2–4. Translation from *The Theodosian Code and Novels and the Sirmondian Constitution*, trans. Clyde Pharr (Princeton: Princeton University Press, 1952), 15. For an application of this law, see ibid., 9.43.1.

the Law of Citations is codified later than the Talmudic parallels, it likely has roots in earlier Roman practice.[106] The second part of the Law of Citations is actually already stated ca. 160 C.E. by Gaius in his *Institutes*, 1.7:

> The answers of jurists are the decisions and opinions of persons authorized to lay down the law. If they are unanimous their decision has the force of law; if they disagree, the judge may follow whichever opinion he chooses, as is ruled by a rescript of the late emperor Hadrian.[107]

Tony Honoré argues that Gaius's law, which allowed judges freedom to choose between legal authors as long as they were not unanimous, represents an earlier approach to dealing with indeterminacy. Later on, the Law of Citations significantly curtailed this freedom in order "to promote uniform administration of the law."[108] From now on, "a complex system of head-counting is introduced under which the judge will seldom be free to choose the solution he personally prefers."[109] Even with Theodosian's legislation, however, the either-or option remains viable in cases not covered by the majority rule or not discussed by Papinian.

It is possible that a similar development occurred in rabbinic jurisprudence. At an earlier stage, Tannaitic texts offer the either-or option for certain areas of indeterminacy.[110] R. Yoḥanan then added a hierarchy of authorities, although the either-or option still remained in use in cases not covered by R. Yoḥanan's rules. Whatever is their exact development, the Law of Citations and other similar laws may very well have influenced not only R. Yoḥanan's penchant for uniform rules, but perhaps they even served as a model for the forms of these rules. This historical background may further explain why the rules gained widespread acceptance among the Palestinian Amoraim.

To be sure, there were also legal compilations made in Sasanian Babylonia during this period. Most significant is the *Madayan i hazar dadestan* (*The Book of a Thousand Judgements*), compiled ca. 620 C.E.[111] However, while

106. Just as *Codex Theodosianus* 1.4.3, quoted above, includes laws already declared by Constantine in 321–328 C.E., so too Constantine himself may have been relying on earlier laws or common practices when he formulated his law. R. Yoḥanan died ca. 279 C.E., not long before Constantine's edicts. Also, although the rules are attributed to R. Yoḥanan, they may have been formulated as such only by his students.

107. Edward Poste, *Institutes of Roman Law by Gaius* (Oxford: Clarendon, 1904), 2.

108. Tony Honoré, *Law in the Crisis of Empire, 379–455 AD: The Theodosian Dynasty and Its Quaestors* (Oxford: Clarendon, 1998), 250.

109. Ibid. See also John Methews, *Laying Down the Law: A Study of the Theodosian Code* (New Haven: Yale University Press, 2000), 24–25.

110. See *b. Ber.* 11a, above, p. 68, and references above p. 70 n. 88.

111. For the English translation, see A. G. Perikhanian, *The Book of a Thousand Judgements (A Sasanian Law-Book)*, trans. Nina Garsoian (Costa Mesa, CA: Mazda, 1997). For the German translation, see Maria Macuch, *Das sasanidische Rechtsbuch "Matakdan i hazar datistan" (Teil II)*

this book does quote from a number of previous sources and includes opinions of many jurists, there is no sustained effort at choosing between them nor any general rules about how to decide between these authorities. The *Madayan* can therefore not be classified as a code. In fact, no legal code from Sasanian Babylonia has been preserved.[112] It would seem that diversity of legal sources and opinions was not a major problem for the Sasanians, and they therefore did not have to make concerted efforts at codifying law and developing unifying rules.[113] Ironically, then, it is precisely the great diversity of Roman law that made their legists sensitive to the problems engendered by such diversity and prompted them to codify and systematize their law. Sasanian law, apparently, did not face this challenge. The Babylonian rabbis would therefore also not feel pressure from their surrounding legal culture to codify their laws.[114]

(Wiesbaden: Deutsche Morgenländische Gesellschaft, Kommissionsverlag, F. Steiner, 1981); and idem, *Rechtskasuistik und Gerichtspraxis zu Beginn des siebenten Jahrhunderts in Iran: Die Rechtssammlung des Farrohmard i Wahraman* (Wiesbaden: Otto Harrossowitz, 1993).

112. See A. G. Perikhanian, "Iranian Society and Law," in *The Cambridge History of Iran, Volume 3(2): The Seleucid, Parthian and Sasanian Periods*, ed. Ehsan Yarshater (Cambridge: Cambridge University Press, 1968), 627–80: "Law was not codified on an all-Iran scale in Sasanian times, and this document [the *Madayan*] is not actually a code but a collection of law-cases embracing all branches of private law" (ibid., 628). See also J. P. de Menasce, "Zoroastrian Pahlavi Writings," in *The Cambridge History of Iran, Volume 3(2)*, 1189; Elman, "Order, Sequence, and Selection," 69; and idem, "Scripture Versus Contemporary Needs: A Sasanian/Zoroastrian Example," *Cardozo Law Review* 28, no. 1 (2006): 153–69.

113. See further below, pp. 374–75.

114. I only claim here that Roman law contained more diversity than Sasanian law, not that Palestinian halakhic traditions or halakhic practices were more diverse than those of the Jews in Babylonia. Although the latter claim may be true, I do not have evidence for it. This book focuses on the attitude of the rabbis toward diversity rather than on the reality of how much diversity existed, partly because Talmudic evidence can more readily address the former than the latter. See above, p. 2.

2

Diversity of Customs and the Law of "Do Not Make Factions"

Introduction

The previous chapter dealt with the official legislation and codification of law. We saw there that diversity of practice arises when there is disagreement over which view in a legal debate should be declared normative. However, it is in the realm of custom—*minhag*—that one finds the greatest concentration of diversity of practice.[1] *Minhag* is also the most easily tolerated form of pluralism since even those who might insist on the legitimacy of only one practice of halakha will have an easier time accepting diverse customs. We therefore turn our attention to the place of custom within Jewish law and the level of tolerance held by the Talmud for diverse customs.

This discussion will lead into an analysis of the law of "Do not make factions" based on Deut 14:1, where the Talmuds distinguish between the applicability of this law to *minhag* and halakha. As we will see below, the Yerushalmi permits diversity in matters of custom but rules that law must be uniform; the Bavli, however, permits variant practices among different populations even in legal matters.

The word *halakha* means a regulation or statement of law formulated by a legislator.[2] The word *minhag,* in both its nominal and verbal forms,

1. For a comprehensive treatment of the concept and various connotations of *minhag,* see Moshe Herr and Menachem Elon, "Minhag," *Encyclopedia Judaica* (2007): 14:265f.; and Israel Ta-Shma, *Early Franco-German Ritual and Custom* (Jerusalem: Magnes, 1999), 13–105 (Hebrew).

2. Saul Lieberman, *Hellenism in Jewish Palestine* (New York: Jewish Theological Seminary, 1962), 83 n. 3. Halakha is created when the legislator either decrees a new law or when he codifies existing practice. As Elon writes, "A study of the formative stages of any legal system will reveal that to some extent its directions originated from customs evolved in the practical life of the society concerned, and that only at a later stage was legal recognition con-

is used in rabbinic literature primarily to connote a habitual practice of laypeople that is related to but not directly legislated by halakha.[3] This might be translated as "mere custom." Generally, the rabbis recognize such customs as valid and encourage or require that their practice be continued, even though they are not officially legislated. In some cases, however, the practices of laypeople are considered mistaken by the rabbis because they have no basis in or even contradict the halakha.[4] Rabbinic sources also use the term *minhag* to describe the actual practice of laypeople regarding issues that have already been[5] or are about to be legislated into halakha.[6] In this sense, *minhag* could be translated as the widespread and commonly accepted form of the applied law. It is not always easy to distinguish which sense of the word *minhag* is used in any given text; that Hebrew uses the same word to mean "mere custom" as well as "widespread legal practice" shows that these categories are somewhat fluid.

Secular legal theorists have debated the relationship between custom and legislated law. John Austin draws a strict distinction between custom, which has no legally binding authority since it is not explicitly commanded by the sovereign, and law, which incorporates custom only when officially legislated.[7] Opposing this position is Friedrich Karl von Savigny, who expresses the view that custom arising from the spirit of the folk

---

ferred on such customs—by way of legislation or decision on the part of legislator of judge" (Herr and Elon, "Minhag," 267). See also Burton Leiser, "Custom and Law in Talmudic Jurisprudence," *Judaism* 20 (1971): 396–403; Ronald Brauner, "Some Aspects of Local Custom in Tannaitic Literature," *Jewish Civilization* 2 (1981): 43–54; and Urbach, *The Halakhah,* 27–33. Urbach further proposes that some halakhic arguments between the rabbis have their origins in diverse customs. Each rabbi chooses one among the various customs to legislate into law such that diversity of custom develops directly into diversity of halakha.

3. This is the usage in *m. Pesaḥ.* 4:1–5. Even though these customs are mentioned in the Mishnah, none of them is cited as the opinion of a given rabbi; rather, they describe the practices of laypeople. The Mishnah simply notes the existence and validity of these customs in its attempt to legislate when one is allowed to deviate from a custom. See further discussion below.

4. See, for example, *m. ʿErub.* 10:10. See also the first section of *y. Pesaḥ.* 4:1 (30d) discussed in Hidary, "Tolerance for Diversity," 52–54. Medieval rabbinic literature calls such mistaken customs *minhag ṭaʿut* or *minhag sheṭut*. See further in Daniel Sperber, *Minhage Yisrael: meqorot ve-toladot* (Jerusalem: Mosad Harav Kook, 1990), 31–37.

5. See, for example, *t. Roš Haš.* 2:11, which refers to the controversy in *m. Roš Haš.* 4:5. See also *y. Qidd.* 4:6 (66a), which reports that the priests ignored the halakhic ruling of the rabbis. Nevertheless, R. Abbahu expects the priests to follow their custom and almost whips a priest who violates it! This may reflect the general priority given to custom in the Yerushalmi; see below, pp. 83–84.

6. Under this category would fall cases in which the rabbis decide the law by checking how the public generally practices, such as *y. Peʾah* 7:5 (20c). Also in this category are practices of certain groups that are treated as law, such as "the custom of the sailors" (*t. B. Meṣiʿa* 7:13). See more such examples in Herr and Elon, "Minhag," 266.

7. See John Austin, *Lectures on Jurisprudence; or, The Philosophy of Positive Law* (London:

is valid law.[8] James Coolidge Carter, arguing against the procodification position of Jeremy Bentham, states in even more extreme terms: "Law, Custom, Conduct, Life—different names for almost the same thing—true names for different aspects of the same thing—are so inseparably blended together that one cannot even be thought of without the other."[9]

Rabbinic literature does not maintain a consistent position on the relationship between *minhag* and halakha. Many Talmudic passages clearly distinguish between these categories and play down the importance of custom.[10] Other passages legislate rules about how to deal with customs even at the stage when they are merely habitual practices, such as a stringency practiced by a small group with no precedent in halakha. These laws dictate which customs are acceptable, which customs are binding, who must keep them, when they can be changed, and how visitors to a place that keeps the custom should act. These passages maintain *minhag* as a distinct realm of law but attribute to it a level of legal validity. Yet other passages—especially in the Yerushalmi—blend these categories together by using both *minhag* and halakha to describe the same law,[11] pronouncing penalties for violating customs,[12] and making explicit statements such as, "custom nullifies law."[13]

Prior scholarship has noted the tendency throughout the Yerushalmi to define halakha by the common practice of the people.[14] This is con-

---

John Murray, 1885), 36–37, 101–3. See the criticism of Austin's view of custom in Hart, *The Concept of Law*, 44–48.

8. See Dale Furnish, "Custom as a Source of Law," *American Journal of Comparative Law* 30 (1982): 32–33; and Alan Watson, "An Approach to Customary Law," *University of Illinois Law Review* 561–576 (1984): 564–66.

9. James Coolidge Carter, *Law: Its Origin, Growth and Function* (New York: G. P. Putnam's Sons, 1907), 13. See the discussion in Kunal Parker, "Context in History and Law: A Study of the Late Nineteenth-Century American Jurisprudence of Custom," *Law and History Review* 24, no. 3 (2006): 505–8.

10. See Israel Shepansky, "Torat ha-minhagot," *Or ha-Mizraḥ* 40, no. 1 (1991): 42 n. 32, and the discussion of *b. Pesaḥ.* 50b-51b below.

11. See ibid., 39 n. 9; and Herr and Elon, "Minhag," 268.

12. *Y. Pesaḥ.* 4:3 (30d) = *y. ʿAbod. Zar.* 1:6 (39d). See Shepansky, "Torat ha-minhagot," 42.

13. The Yerushalmi uses the phrase מנהג מבטל הלכה in two contexts: *y. Yebam.* 12:1 (12c) and *y. B. Meṣiʿa* 7:1 (11b). The latter citation is not so significant since it involves contractual agreements in which the general custom simply defines the assumed obligations. The former citation is more significant. See, however, David Henshke, "Minhag mevatel halakha? (Le-ishushah shel hashʿarah)," *Dine Israel* 17 (1994): 135–48, who argues that the phrase in *y. Yebam.* 12:1 (12c) is post-Talmudic. Although there are only these two instances, this phrase does seem to represent the general attitude of the Yerushalmi as seen in other sources. See further analysis in Herr and Elon, "Minhag," 270–71; Stuart Miller, *Sages and Commoners in Late Antique Eretz Israel* (Tübingen: Mohr Siebeck, 2006), 383–85; and the literature cited in Sperber, *Minhage Yisrael*, 1:24; and Mordechai Akiva Friedman, "Teshuva be-ʿinyane tefilah mi-zemano shel Rav Sa'adia Gaon," *Sinai* 109 (1992): 136 n. 77.

14. See Ta-Shma, *Early Franco-German Ritual*, 61–85; and Miller, *Sages and Commoners*, 375–87. One example of the Yerushalmi's use of custom is found in Aviad Stollman, "Hal-

sistent with the general "ancient Palestinian approach," which "placed a greater emphasis on the living, day-to-day tradition and a lesser emphasis on learned argumentation than did the Babylonian."[15] As we will see, the Yerushalmi ascribes great importance to custom, which can sometimes trump official law. The Yerushalmi discourages any change in customs and seeks uniformity of custom within a locale. The Bavli, on the other hand, is more flexible in allowing people to change customs and also more often permits varieties of custom within a locale. Thus, the Yerushalmi's view is closer to that of Savigny and Carter while the Bavli is closer to Austin and Bentham, although the positions of the Talmuds are much less extreme and systematic than those of the legal theorists.

The *locus classicus* for any discussion of custom in rabbinic literature is *m. Pesaḥ.* 4:1–5, which lists a series of issues about which there are varying practices across different locales.[16] Similar cases are found scattered in Tannaitic literature,[17] but this chapter will focus on *m. Pesaḥ.* 4 and Talmudic commentaries on it. The opening Mishnah of the chapter contains the basic formula regarding travelers:

> מקום שנהגו לעשות מלאכה בערבי פסחים עד חצות עושין מקום שנהגו שלא לעשות אין עושין
> ההולך ממקום שעושין למקום שאין עושין או ממקום שאין עושין למקום שעושין נותנין עליו חומרי מקום שיצא משם וחומרי מקום שהלך לשם ואל ישנה אדם מפני המחלוקת.
>
> In a place where they are accustomed to do work on the day before Passover until midday, they may do work. In a place where they are accustomed to refrain from work, they may not do work. One who goes from a place where they do work to a place where they refrain from work or from a place where they refrain from work to a place where they do work, we place upon him the stringencies of his place of origin and the stringencies of his place of destination. One may not differ [from the local custom] because of strife.

This Mishnah mentions a custom not to do any work on the day before Passover from the morning until noon. According to halakha, work is prohibited after noon on that day so that one may focus on preparing the Passover sacrifice. However, some communities extend the prohibited

akhic Development as a Fusion of Hermeneutical Horizons: The Case of the Waiting Period Between Meat and Dairy," *AJS Review* 28, no. 2 (2004): 9–10 (Hebrew).

15. Brody, *Geonim,* 116.

16. See also *t. Pesaḥ.* 2:14–18.

17. Regarding matters of liturgy, see *m. Sukkah* 3:11; *m. Meg.* 4:1; and *t. Ber.* 3:23–24; for monetary law, see *m. B. Meṣiʿa* 4:11; 5:5; 7:1; 9:1; *m. B. Bat.* 1:1–2; 5:11; and *t. Beṣah* 4:10; for laws of mourning, see *t. Moʿed Qaṭ.* 2:17 and *t. Ketub.* 4:2; for agricultural laws, see *t. Šeb.* 1:7–8; 3:14 and 19; for kosher laws, see *t. Ḥul.* 9:7; and for purity laws, see *t. Ṭehar.* 10:12.

time to the morning while other communities allow work to be done until noon. The Mishnah allows each location to follow its custom and adds that one who travels from one place to the other should not work—either because of the custom in his place of origin or out of respect for the custom at his destination. The Mishnah ends with a general principle, "One may not differ [from the local custom] because of strife." Significantly, the Mishnah does not decide in favor of one custom for all. Rather, it recognizes the validity of multiple options and even requires residents of each locale to follow their usual custom.

The Yerushalmi, commenting on *m. Pesaḥ.* 4:1, contains a lengthy discussion about customs, which I have divided into three sections: (A) which customs are valid and when they can be changed, and (B-C) when to tolerate multiple practices. Section B brings examples of both law and custom and tests the pluralism of each against the prohibition of "Do not make factions" based on Deut 14:1. That section and its Bavli parallel constitute the material most directly relevant to our topic. We nevertheless analyze the entire extended *sugya* in order to put section B into proper context as well as to glean important information regarding customs offered in the first section.

Section A—Changing Customs

The first part of the *sugya* in *y. Pesaḥ.* 4:1 (30d), not quoted here, begins with a list of customs that are similar to that in *m. Pesaḥ.* 4:1 in that they all involve women who have a custom not to work on certain days. The *sugya* distinguishes between invalid customs, which the women are encouraged to abandon, and valid customs, which they must continue. The general rule, "all matters depend on custom," opens this section and also closes it.[18] This rule emphasizes that valid customs practiced by laypeople are halakhically binding. This position is consistent with the Palestinian approach, as noted above, and will be further evident in the rest of this Yerushalmi *sugya*.

The continuation of the *sugya* discusses how and when one can change a custom, especially in cases where one travels from a place that keeps one custom to a place that practices differently:[19]

[A] [1] אעין דשיטין הוו במגדל צבעייה. אתון ושאלון לרבי חנניה חברהון דרבנין מהו
מיעבד בהן עבודה
אמר להן מכיון שנהגו בהן אבותיכם באיסור אל תשנו מנהג אבותיכם נוחי נפש.

18. See analysis of this section in Hidary, "Tolerance for Diversity," 52–54.

19. *Y. Pesaḥ.* 4:1 (30d). Tannaitic sources are in bold. The repeating refrain is underlined.

[2] רבי אלעזר בשם רבי אבין כל דבר שאינו יודע שהוא מותר וטועה בו באיסור נשאל והן מתירין לו וכל דבר שהוא יודע בו שהוא מותר והוא נוהג בו באיסור נשאל אין מתירין לו.[20]

[3][a] **יושבין על ספסלו של גוי בשבת. מעשה ברבן גמליאל[21] שישב לו על ספסילו של גוי בשבת בעכו. אמרו לו לא היו נוהגין כן[22] להיות יושבין על ספסילו של גוי בשבת ולא רצה לומר להן מותר לעשות כן אלא עמד והלך לו.**

[b] **מעשה ביהודה ובהלל בניו של רבן גמליאל שנכנסו לרחוץ במרחץ בכבול אמרו להן לא נהגו כן להיות רוחצין שני אחים כאחת ולא רצו לומר מותר כן אלא נכנסו זה אחר זה.**

[c] **ועוד שיצאו לטייל בקורדקיות של זהב בלילי שבת בבירו אמרו להן לא נהגו כאן[23] להיות מטיילין בקורדקיות של זהב בשבת ולא רצו לומר להן מותר כן אלא שילחו ביד עבדיהן.[24]**

[4] ולא סוף דבר פסח אלא אפילו מנהג קיבלו עליהן חרמי טיבריה וגרוסי צפורי דשושי עכו שלא לעשות מלאכה בחולו של מועד.

ניחא גרוסי צפורין דשושי עכו. חרמי טיבריה ואינן ממעטין בשמחת הרגל?

צד הוא בחכה צד הוא במכמורת.

אפילו כן אינן ממעטין בשמחת הרגל?

ר' אימי מיקל לון שהן ממעטין בשמחת הרגל.

גלו ממקום למקום וביקשו לחזור בהן.

[5] ייבא כהדא דאמר רבי בא בני מישא קיבלו עליהן שלא לפרש בים הגדול. אתון שאלון לרבי. אמרין ליה אבותינו נהגו שלא לפרש בים הגדול אנו מה אנו

<u>אמר להן מכיון שנהגו בהן אבותיכם באיסור אל תשנו מנהג אבותיכם נוחי נפש.</u>

ואין אדם נשאל על נדרו?

תמן משנדר נשאל ברם הכא אבותיכם נדרו.

כל שכן יהו מותרים?

אמר רבי חנניה לא מן הדא אלא מן הדא רבי תלמידיה דרבי יודה הוה דרבי יודה אמר אסור לפרש בים הגדול.

[A] [1] There were acacia trees in Magdala of the Dyers. They came and asked R. Ḥananiah the friend of the rabbis, "Can we use them for work?" He told them, "Since your ancestors had a custom to prohibit them, <u>do not change the custom of your ancestors, rest their souls.</u>"

[2] R. Eleazar said in the name of R. Abin: Any matter about which one is not aware that it is permitted, and he mistakenly prohibits it, he can make a request to overturn it and they will permit him. And any matter that one knows to be permitted and yet he prohibits it in practice, if he requests to overturn it they do not permit him.[20]

[3][a] **One may sit on a bench of a Gentile on Shabbat. It once happened that Rabban Gamaliel[21] sat himself upon the bench**

---

20. Section A up until this point is paralleled at *y. Taʿan.* 1:6 (64c).

21. See Aharon Amit, *Talmud ha-Igud: BT Pesaḥim Chapter IV* (Jerusalem: Society for the Interpretation of the Talmud, 2009), 81, concerning which Rabban Gamaliel this is. Amit himself sides with scholars who say that this is Rabban Gamaliel II of Yavneh.

of a Gentile on Shabbat in Acco. They told him, "we are not accustomed here[22] to sit on the bench of a Gentile on Shabbat." He did not want to tell them that it is permitted to do so; rather, he got up and left.

[b] **It once happened that Yehudah and Hillel, the children of Rabban Gamaliel, entered to wash in the bathhouse in Kabul. They told them, "we are not accustomed here for two brothers to wash at the same time." They did not want to tell them that it is permitted to do so; rather, they entered one after the other.**

[c] **Furthermore, they went out for a walk in gilt slippers on Shabbat night in Biro. They told them, "we are not accustomed here[23] to walk in gilt slippers on Shabbat." They did not want to tell them that it is permitted to do so; rather, they sent [the slippers] with their servants.[24]**

[4] Not only regarding Passover [is one required to keep the custom of his origin], but even the custom that the fishermen of Tiberias and the grist-makers of Sepphoris and the threshers of Acco took upon themselves not to perform work on *ḥol hamoᶜed*. It is alright with the grist-makers of Sepphoris and the threshers of Acco; but aren't the fishermen of Tiberias diminishing from the enjoyment of the holiday? He can fish with a hook, he can fish in a small net. Even so, isn't he diminishing the enjoyment of the holiday? R. Ammi would curse them because they diminish the enjoyment of the holiday.

If they were exiled from one place to another and they wanted to change their minds, [would they be allowed]?

[5] Bring that which R. Ba said: The sons of Mesha took upon themselves not to sail in the Mediterranean Sea. They came and asked Rabbi [to overturn it]. They told him, "Our ancestors had the custom not to sail in the Mediterranean Sea but what about us?" He told them, "Since your ancestors practiced prohibitively, do not change from the custom of your ancestors, rest their souls."

---

22. Ms. Leiden reads כן; see Yaakov Sussman, *Talmud Yerushalmi According to Ms. Or. 4720 (Scal. 3) of the Leiden University Library with Restorations and Corrections* (Jerusalem: Academy of the Hebrew Language, 2001), 517. A Geniza fragment, however, reads כאן; see Louis Ginzberg, *Yerushalmi Fragments from the Genizah: Vol. I, Text with Various Readings from the Editio Princeps* (Jerusalem: Jewish Theological Seminary of America, 1909), 111. Ms. Vienna of the Tosefta reads כן in the first and last cases, but many variants appear in other mss. See Saul Lieberman, *The Tosefta According to Codex Vienna ...* (Jerusalem: Jewish Theological Seminary of America, 1955), *Moᶜed*, 372. Lieberman, *Tosefta ki-fshuṭah*, 5:1262, argues that כן in these instances is just short for כאן. I have translated accordingly. However, I translate כן in the second half of each statement as "so," as is evident from the context.

23. Following ms. Leiden, which here reads כאן. Geniza, in this instance, reads כן.

24. *T. Moᶜed Qaṭ.* 2:15–16.

> But can't anyone retract his vow? There, the one who vows retracts; here, your ancestors vowed. All the more so should they be permitted? R. Ḥananiah said, "[Rabbi did] not [prohibit] based on that [i.e. the principle that one cannot change a traditional custom], but based on this: Rabbi was the student of R. Yehudah. R. Yehudah would say it is prohibited to sail in the Mediterranean Sea."

Section A of the Yerushalmi expresses a large measure of conservatism regarding change of customs. Line 1 gives an example of a local custom that the villagers sought to change, seeing it was not based on any law, but were denied permission. Line 2 states as a general rule that only a custom taken on in error can be nullified, but not a stringency to which one consciously committed oneself knowing that it went beyond the letter of the law.

Line 3 quotes three examples from *t. Moʿed Qaṭ.* 2:15–16 of customs that the rabbis did not want to change even though the customs were more stringent than the halakha.[25] We have three stories [a, b, and c] about visiting rabbis who are more lenient than the local residents. For the first case [a], the Tosefta adds a key piece of information not quoted in the Talmuds: "At first they would say that one is not allowed to sit on the bench of a Gentile on Shabbat until R. Akiba came and taught that one may sit on the bench of a Gentile on Shabbat."[26] The custom of Acco thus represents the ancient form of the law, which the rabbinic elite had already changed. Rabban Gamaliel himself keeps the official law of the rabbinic elite even while he tolerates the custom of the commoners. It is likely that the customs of the commoners in the next two stories similarly reflect ancient practice.[27] This series of stories reflects a tension between the official law as legislated by the rabbis and the common practice of the commoners. In each case, the rabbis decide that the locals should continue their traditional custom rather than conform to the official halakha.

Lines 4 and 5 bring two more examples of local or family customs that later members sought to nullify. The Talmud presumes that the response for the case in line 4 should be the same as that for line 5 in which Rabbi did not allow them to change.[28] Rabbi is quoted as responding with the

25. These three stories illustrate R. Abin's principle in line 2. See Amit, *Pesaḥim*, 74.

26. *T. Moʿed Qaṭ.* 2:14. This is missing in some manuscripts of the Tosefta, but it is authentic and was skipped in those Tosefta manuscripts due to homoioteleuton (Lieberman, *The Tosefta, Moʿed*, 372).

27. See Amit, *Pesaḥim*, 74–75. If these stories are about Rabban Gamaliel III, then it is very significant that even though the ancient laws were abolished before 135 C.E., commoners still held onto them at the time of Rabban Gamaliel III, three generations later, ca. 200–220 C.E. However, even if the stories are about Rabban Gamaliel II (see above, n. 21) it still shows that these cities are somewhat disconnected from the central rabbinic authority.

28. This conclusion is all the more surprising considering that R. Ammi condemned the

very same words as R. Ḥananiah in line 1, "Do not change the custom of your ancestors, rest their souls."[29] These words thus serve as a refrain highlighting the primary message of the Yerushalmi that changing customs is highly discouraged and sticking to tradition is of greater value than conforming to official laws.

This entire section of the Yerushalmi has a parallel in *b. Pesaḥ.* 50b-51b:[30]

[1] בני ביישן נהוג דלא הוו אזלין מצור לצידון במעלי שבתא. אתו בנייהו קמיה דרבי יוחנן, אמרו לו: אבהתין אפשר להו, אנן לא אפשר לן. אמר להו: כבר קיבלו אבותיכם עליהם, שנאמר שמע בני מוסר אביך ואל תטש תורת אמך.[31]

[2] בני חוזאי נהגי דמפרשי חלה מארוזא. אתו ואמרו ליה לרב יוסף. אמר להו: ניכלה זר באפייהו. איתיביה אביי: **דברים המותרים ואחרים נהגו בהן איסור אי אתה רשאי להתירן בפניהם.** אמר לו: ולאו מי איתמר עלה, אמר רב חסדא: בכותאי.

כותאי מאי טעמא—משום דמסרכי מילתא, הנך אינשי נמי סרכי מילתא?

אלא אמר רב אשי: חזינן, אי רובן אורז אכלי לא ניכלה זר באפייהו, דילמא משתכחא תורת חלה מינייהו. ואי רובן דגן אכלי ניכלה זר באפייהו, דילמא אתי לאפרושי מן החיוב על הפטור ומן הפטור על החיוב.

[3] גופא, **דברים המותרין ואחרים נהגו בהן איסור אי אתה רשאי להתירן בפניהן.** אמר רב חסדא: בכותאי עסקינן. וכולי עלמא לא? והתניא: **רוחצין שני אחין כאחד, ואין רוחצין שני אחין בכבול. ומעשה ביהודה והלל בניו של רבן גמליאל, שרחצו שניהם כאחד בכבול, ולעזה עליהן כל המדינה, אמרו: מימינו לא ראינו כך. ונשמט הלל ויצא לבית החיצון, ולא רצה לומר להן מותרין אתם.**

יוצאים בקורדקיסון בשבת, ואין יוצאין בקורדקיסון בשבת בבירי. ומעשה ביהודה

custom of the fishermen. This indicates how strongly the Yerushalmi espouses the view that customs are unchangeable.

29. The end of line 5 adds a gloss asking about this from general laws of nullifying vows, which are more permissive. This gloss is very problematic for it contradicts the entire flow of the Talmud until this point. It says that only in this case did Rabbi not undo the vow because he thought the vow concurred with a prohibitive law. This law is quoted in the name of R. Yehudah (Rabbi) in *y. Moʿed Qaṭ.* 3:1 (81c). This implies that in other cases one could simply retract a custom. However, the *sugya* before this one was devoted to differentiating between invalid customs and valid ones, which are unchangeable. R. Abin (line 2) explicitly prohibits undoing valid customs. The opening question in this gloss is also problematic because it should have been asked above when the very same rule, "Do not change from the custom of your ancestors, rest their souls," was first stated. Also, this gloss changes the outcome of the final question of line 4, which line 5 is supposed to answer. If Rabbi only prohibited the retraction because of his opinion about sailing in general, this implies that he would allow change of custom otherwise, including in the case of line 4. This gloss is, therefore, inconsistent with the rest of the *sugya* and may have resulted from incomplete editing or it may be a secondary addition to the core *sugya,* which ended with the repeating refrain. It should be noted that the inclusion of a gloss about *nedarim* may be related to line 2, a version of which is found in *t. Ned.* 4:6; *y. Ned.* 2:1 (37b); *b. Ned.* 15a and 81b. See Amit, *Pesaḥim,* 65–68. The discussion of *nedarim* in this gloss may derive from some proto-*sugya* in the context of *nedarim* that also included a version of line 2.

30. See comparison chart between Tosefta, Yerushalmi, and Bavli at chart 2.1, below, p. 121. Line 4 is paralleled in *b. Ḥul.* 18b, on which see p. 130, below.

והלל בניו של רבן גמליאל שיצאו בקורדקיסון בשבת בבירי, ולעזה עליהן המדינה. ואמרו: מימינו לא ראינו כך, ושמטום ונתנום לעבדיהן, ולא רצו לומר להן מותרין אתם.

ויושבין על ספסלי נכרים בשבת, ואינן יושבין על ספסלי נכרים בשבת בעכו. ומעשה ברבן שמעון בן גמליאל שישב על ספסלי נכרים בשבת בעכו, ולעזה עליו כל המדינה, אמרו: מימינו לא ראינו כך. נשמט על גבי קרקע, ולא רצה לומר להן מותרין אתם.[32]

בני מדינת הים נמי, כיון דלא שכיחי רבנן גבייהו ככותים דמו...[33]

[4] כי אתא רבה בר בר חנה אכל דאייתרא. עול לגביה רב עוירא סבא ורבה בריה דרב הונא, כיון דחזינהו כסייה מינייהו. אתו ואמרו ליה לאביי. אמר להו: שווינכו ככותאי. ורבה בר בר חנה לית ליה הא דתנן **נותנין עליו חומרי המקום שיצא משם וחומרי המקום שהלך לשם.**[34] אמר אביי הני מילי מבבל לבבל, ומארץ ישראל לארץ ישראל. אי נמי מבבל לארץ ישראל. אבל מארץ ישראל לבבל לא, כיון דאנן כייפינן להו עבדינן כוותייהו. רב אשי אמר אפילו תימא מארץ ישראל לבבל. הני מילי היכא דאין דעתו לחזור, ורבה בר בר חנה דעתו לחזור הוה...

[5] בשלמא **ההולך ממקום שעושין למקום שאין עושין נותנין עליו חומרי מקום שהלך לשם, ואל ישנה אדם מפני המחלוקת**[34] ולא ליעביד.

אלא: **ממקום שאין עושין למקום שעושין אל ישנה אדם מפני המחלוקת**,[34] ונעביד?

הא אמרת: **נותנין עליו חומרי מקום שהלך לשם וחומרי מקום שיצא משם**?[34]

אמר אביי: ארישא.

רבא אמר: לעולם אסיפא, והכי קאמר: אין בזו מפני שינוי המחלוקת. מאי קא אמרת: הרואה אומר מלאכה אסורה מימר אמרי: כמה בטלני הוי בשוקא.[35]

[1] The citizens of Bayshan were accustomed not to go from Tyre to Sidon on the eve of Shabbat. Their children came before R. Yoḥanan and said to him, "For our fathers this was possible; for us it is impossible." He said to them, "Your fathers have already taken it upon themselves, as it is said, *My son, heed the instruction of your father, and do not forsake the teaching of your mother*."[31]

[2] The citizens of Ḥozai were accustomed to separate *ḥallah* from rice. They went and told it to Rav Yosef. He said to them, "Let a lay Israelite eat it in front of them." Abaye raised an objection against him: "**Things that are permitted, but that others treat as forbidden, you may not permit in their presence**?" He responded, "Did not Rav Ḥisda say on that, 'This refers to Samaritans'?"

What is the reason in the case of Samaritans? Because they will come to [wrongly] acquire the [easier] practice [in other matters as well]. These people too [being ignorant] will come to acquire the [easier] practice [in other matters]?

Rather, Rav Ashi said, "We check: if most of them eat rice [bread], we will not let a lay Israelite eat [*ḥallah* from rice] in front of them, lest the law of *ḥallah* be forgotten by them; but if most of them eat

31. Proverbs 1:8.

grain [bread], then let a lay Israelite eat [*ḥallah* from rice] in front of them, lest they come to separate [*ḥallah*] from what is required [grain] upon what is exempt [rice], and from what is exempt upon what is required.

[3] We stated above: "**Things that are permitted, but others treat as forbidden, you may not permit in their presence.** Rav Ḥisda said: This refers to Samaritans." Does it not apply to all people? Surely it was taught: **Two brothers may bathe together, but [the custom] in Kabul [is that] two brothers do not bathe [together]. It once happened that Yehudah and Hillel, the sons of Rabban Gamaliel, bathed together in Kabul, and the whole district criticized them, saying, "We have never in our lives seen this." Hillel slipped away and went to the outer chamber rather than tell them, "You are permitted [to do this]."**

One may go out in slippers on Shabbat, but [the custom] in Beri [is that] people do not go out in slippers [on Shabbat]. It once happened that Yehudah and Hillel, the sons of Rabban Gamaliel, went out in slippers on Shabbat in Beri and the whole district criticized them, saying, "We have never in our lives seen this." They removed them and gave them to their [non-Jewish] servants rather than tell them, "You are permitted [to wear them]."

One may sit on the stools of Gentiles on Shabbat, but [the custom] in Acco is that people do not sit on the stools of Gentiles on Shabbat. It once happened that Rabban Shimon ben Gamaliel sat down on the stools of Gentiles on Shabbat in Acco, and the whole district criticized him, saying, "We have never in our lives seen this." He slipped down to the ground rather than tell them, "You are permitted [to do this]."[32] The people of the coastal region are also like Samaritans since rabbis are not common among them....[33]

[4] When Rabbah bar bar Ḥannah came [to Babylonia], he ate of the stomach fat. Rav 'Awira the Elder and Rabbah son of Rav Huna visited him; as soon as he [Rabbah bar bar Ḥannah] saw them, he hid it from them. They came and told it to Abaye who said to them, "He has treated you like Samaritans."

But does not Rabbah bar bar Ḥannah agree with what we have learned: **"We place upon him the stringencies of the place of his origin and the stringencies of his place of destination"?**[34]

Abaye said: That is only [when he goes] from [one town in] Babylonia to [another in] Babylonia, or from [one town in] Israel

32. *T. Moʿed Qaṭ.* 2:15–16.
33. I have omitted a section outlining the reasons for the above three stringencies.
34. *M. Pesaḥ.* 4:1.

> to [another in] Israel, or from Babylonia to Israel; but not [when he goes] from Israel to Babylonia, for since we submit to them, we do as they do.
>
> Rav Ashi said: You may even say [that one must be stringent when he goes] from [one town in] Israel to [one in] Babylonia; however, that is where his intention is not to return; but Rabbah bar bar Ḥannah had the intention of returning…
>
> [5] It is well, "**One who goes from a place where they do work to a place where they refrain from work ... we place upon him ... the stringencies of his place of destination. One may not change [from the local custom] because of strife.**"[34] Therefore, he should not do work.
>
> However, "**... from a place where they refrain from work to a place where they do work ... one may not change [from the local custom] because of strife.**"[34] Should he therefore work? But you have taught, "**We place upon him the stringencies of his place of origin and the stringencies of his place of destination**"?[34]
>
> Abaye said, [The last line of the Mishnah, "One may not change ..."] applies only to the first case [of the Mishnah, "One who goes from a place where they do work ..."].
>
> Rava said, It can even apply to the second case and this is what it means to say: This does not constitute changing [from the local custom] because of strife. What do you think, the onlooker will say work is prohibited? [No, rather] they will say, there are many idlers in the market.[35]

Line 1 records that R. Yoḥanan refused a request by the citizens of Bayshan to discontinue their custom of not traveling on Fridays. This story parallels line A5 of the Yerushalmi above.[36] Line 2 reports that Rav Yosef proactively sought to abolish a custom of the citizens of Ḥozai. Abaye questions his action based on a *baraita* that prohibits one to undo any custom that is more stringent than the law. This *baraita* is related to the statement of R. Abin (line 2 in the Yerushalmi), and they may both come from one original Tannaitic statement.[37] The exact sense of the *baraita* quoted

35. Cf. *b. Ber.* 17b.

36. See Amit, *Pesaḥim*, 58–62, for a discussion of the differences between the Yerushalmi and Bavli versions of the story.

37. See ibid., 71–74. See also the end of n. 29, above, on the relationship of this *baraita* with laws of *nedarim*. This principle is also found in *Sifre Deut.*, *pisqa* 104 (ed. Louis Finkelstein, *Sifre on Deuteronomy* (New York: Jewish Theological Seminary of America, 1969), 163 [Hebrew]). However, Finkelstein does not think it is authentic in *Sifre* but rather a copyist's transfer from the Bavli. The *baraita* appears slightly differently in *b. Ned.* 81b: "דברים המותרים ואחרים נהגו בהן איסור אי אתה רשאי לנהוג בהם היתר כדי לבטלן—Things that are permitted, yet others treat them as forbidden, you may not practice leniently in order to abolish them."

in the Bavli is difficult to determine, but, on the whole, it seems to agree with *m. Pesaḥ.* 4:1.[38] One may not perform a practice or issue a ruling that will go against a stringent custom of a locale. While the Mishnah speaks to any traveler, the *baraita* addresses visiting rabbis whose actions and words have authority.

Rav Ḥisda in this *sugya*, however, greatly limits the *baraita* by confining it only to a case where the custom is performed by Samaritans and all similar populations who are generally ignorant of rabbinic teachings.[39] This means that the rabbis may nullify customs in any city whose residents are cognizant and accepting of rabbinic authority. In such cases, the *baraita* as well as *m. Pesaḥ.* 4:1 do not apply. If one may permit the residents to undo their custom, then the visitor may certainly also ignore the local custom himself, contrary to the Mishnah.

This series of three stories from *t. Moʿed Qaṭ.* 2:14–16 is quoted in the Bavli just as it was in the Yerushalmi, but in opposite order[40] and with opposite effect. The Yerushalmi cites these cases as examples of the principle that customs can never change. The Bavli, on the other hand, brings these cases as questions against Rav Ḥisda's limiting of the *baraita*. Why did the rabbis in all three instances refrain from telling the stringent villagers that their customs were permitted if they were not Samaritans? The Stam responds that the principle also applies to these coastal villages whose dearth of rabbis makes them similar to Samaritans.[41] With this

---

38. Some commentators infer that the *baraita* prohibits the visiting rabbi only from overturning the local practice but permits him to practice leniently in private. See, for example, Amit, *Pesaḥim*, 53 n. 5; and Moshe Halbertal, *By Way of Truth: Nahmanides and the Creation of Tradition* (Jerusalem: Hartman Institute, 2006), 95 (Hebrew). However, such an inference has little basis. In line 2, the reason why Rav Yosef and Abaye debate whether one may allow a lay Israelite to eat the rice *ḥallah* in front of Hozai's citizens is not because they already assume that doing so in private is allowed. Rather, Rav Yosef wishes to undo the custom and have an Israelite eat in protest. We can assume that Abaye would prohibit anyone from contradicting the custom whether in public or in private. In fact, in all three cases in *t. Moʿed Qaṭ.*, the rabbis refrain not only from teaching the residents that their customs have no basis but they also refrain from practicing contrary to the local custom.

39. Rav Ḥisda is quoted saying the same phrase in a completely different situation in *b. Sanh.* 21b. See Amit, *Pesaḥim*, 73, who argues that *b. Pesaḥ.* 50b-51a is the original context.

40. See Amit, *Pesaḥim*, 74.

41. The way these cases are presented in the Bavli already presages this response. The Bavli introduces each story with an additional sentence not found in *t. Moʿed Qaṭ.* 2:15–16 or *y. Pesaḥ.* 4:1 (30d): "Two brothers may bathe together, but [the custom] in Kabul [is that] two brothers do not bathe [together]"; "One may go out in slippers on Shabbat, but [the custom] in Beri [is that] people do not go out in slippers"; and "One may sit on the stools of Gentiles on Shabbat, but [the custom] in Acco [is that] people do not sit on the stools of Gentiles on Shabbat." This presentation sets these cities apart from all other places from the start. More significantly, the words of the citizens of each place are changed from "We are not accustomed here" in the Tosefta and Yerushalmi to "We have never in our lives seen this" in the Bavli. The former implies that they may have heard of the other lenient practice but that it is

move, the Bavli pushes aside these examples as exceptions. Because these towns were generally lax and isolated from rabbinic authority, any leniency might lead them to abandon important laws as well. But in all other cases, it is better to correct local customs to conform to the law.[42]

Line 4 cites a case concerning eating of the stomach fat, which was a controversial issue among the Tannaim and Amoraim. The Palestinian Amoraim permit while the Babylonians prohibit this section of fat.[43] Rabbah bar bar Ḥannah, a Palestinian Amora, travels to Babylonia and eats stomach fat. Two Babylonian rabbis report this to Abaye who, instead of rebuking Rabbah bar bar Ḥannah, simply notes that Rabbah bar bar

---

not the local custom. The latter insinuates that the residents are completely ignorant of other practices and cut off from general rabbinic society. See also Miller, *Sages and Commoners*, 382.

42. The Bavli diverges from R. Abin's ruling in the Yerushalmi in yet another, more subtle way. R. Abin addresses only cases in which the local residents come to the rabbi and request that the custom be undone. In fact, lines 1, 4, and 5 in section A of the Yerushalmi are cases when the residents make such a request. The Bavli, by contrast, interprets the *baraita* to cover cases when the rabbi proactively goes out and undoes a local custom without being asked. If, as Rav Ḥisda explains, the *baraita* only prohibits changing the customs of Samaritans, then when it comes to non-Samaritans one may proactively protest the custom. In line 2, Rav Yosef and, perhaps, Rav Ashi as well promote a protest of the custom even though they are not asked by the local residents for a change. In line 3, the Bavli questions the *baraita* from the cases in the Tosefta when the rabbis visit a city and choose to conform to the local custom rather than educate them. The question assumes that since the residents of these cities are not Samaritans, the rabbis should proactively reject their customs even without being requested to do so.

43. See *t. Ḥul.* 9:11 and *b. Ḥul.* 49a-50b for a discussion about the prohibition of the fat of the stomach. See a detailed analysis of that *sugya* in Amit, *Pesaḥim*, 81–85. One set of stories shows the Palestinian Amoraim eating this fat in practice:

כי הא דאמר רב אויא אמר רבי אמי: מקמצין, וכן אמר רבי ינאי משום זקן אחד: מקמצין.

אמר רב אויא: הוה קאימנא קמיה דרבי אמי, קמצו והבו ליה—ואכל.

שמעיה דרבי חנינא הוה קאי קמיה דרבי חנינא, א"ל: קמוץ, הב לי דאיכול, חזייה דהוי קמחסם, אמר ליה: בבלאה את, גום שדי [יש גורסים, אתגום שרי].

> This accords with the statement of Rav 'Awia in the name of R. Ammi: One must scrape away a little from the surface [and the rest is permitted]. Likewise, R. Yannai said in the name of a certain elder: One must scrape away a little from the surface.
>
> Rav 'Awia said: I was once present before R. Ammi and they scraped it and gave it to him and he ate it.
>
> The attendant of R. Ḥanina was standing before him. R. Ḥanina said to him, "Scrape away a little from the surface and give me to eat." He saw his attendant hesitating. He said to him, "You are evidently a Babylonian, so you had better cut it off and throw it away (other mss. read, cut it off and permit it)" (*b. Ḥul.* 50a).

R. Ammi, a Palestinian Amora, ate this section of fat. R. Ḥanina, also a Palestinian Amora, wishes to eat this fat. When he recognizes that his Babylonian attendant is uncomfortable, he commands him to cut off and discard the prohibited part and permit the rest. R. Ḥanina here shows tolerance for the Babylonian practice (unless one understands the ms. version to mean that R. Ḥanina ordered the attendant to cut and serve the piece and thereby acknowledge that it is permitted). We thus have a case of recognized local customs. See the next chapter for more examples of local practices.

Ḥannah treated the two rabbis like Samaritans.[44] The Gemara wonders how Rabbah bar bar Ḥannah's actions are justified in light of the Mishnah. Abaye offers another restriction on the rule of the Mishnah. One may keep the leniencies of Palestine even in Babylonia because of Palestine's supremacy. Rav Ashi qualifies that this exception is only applicable if one plans to return to Palestine.[45] Line 4 thus directly limits the rule of the Mishnah and further relaxes the need for conformity with local tradition. This falls in line with and adds to the limitations already placed in lines 2 and 3 upon the *baraita* (and indirectly upon the Mishnah as well).

Yet another limit on the Mishnah's rule of keeping the stringencies of one's place of origin and destination is found on the next page of the Bavli *sugya*:

> אמר ליה רב ספרא לר' אבא כגון אנא דידענא בקביעא דירחאביישוב לא עבידנא במדבר מאי
> אמר ליה הכי אמר ר' אמי ביישוב אסור במדבר מותר.
>
> Rav Safra said to R. Abba: "For instance I, who know how to fix the new moon, in inhabited places I do not work; but what about in the desert?"
> Said he to him: Thus did R. Ammi say, "In inhabited regions it is forbidden; in the desert it is permitted."[46]

44. That Abaye is quoted making reference to Cutheans shows that he must have accepted the restriction of Rav Ḥisda that the Mishnah only requires conformity to local stringencies when with Cutheans. This would explain why Abaye did not rebuke Rabbah bar bar Ḥannah for eating the fat in Babylonia at all, even in private. This town must have been generally learned, otherwise Abaye would have agreed with the two students and rebuked Rabbah bar bar Ḥannah. Rabbah bar bar Ḥannah evidently did not trust that the two students would understand his actions, and rightly so, for they immediately go and tell on him.

If Abaye did indeed agree with Rav Ḥisda's principle, then the continuation of the *sugya*, which cites another explanation in the name of Abaye, would be problematic. Similarly, if Rabbah bar bar Ḥannah also accepted this principle, then there is again no need for the question in the next line of the *sugya*. Indeed, most scholars think that the continuation of the *sugya* is not original but was copied from *b. Ḥul.* 18b (see text below, p. 130), though this is based on other considerations. See Amit, *Pesaḥim*, 85–93, who opines that the *sugya* in *b. Pesaḥ.* 51a is original because of significant difficulties fitting the lines into the flow of logic at *b. Ḥul.* 18b. It seems most likely, however, that these lines (the explanations of Abaye and Rav Ashi) existed as an independent unit or were part of some other unknown context and were borrowed by the Bavli redactors of both *b. Pesaḥ.* 51a and *b. Ḥul.* 18b.

45. According to the version in *b. Ḥul.* 18b, Abaye allows one who goes from Babylonia to Palestine to ignore the stringencies of his country of origin. Rav Ashi there qualifies that this is true only if he plans to remain in Palestine.

46. *B. Pesaḥ.* 51b-52a according to ms. Vatican 109. Ms. Oxford and printed editions add, "מפני שינוי המחלוקת," in order to connect this *sugya* with the previous one. See comprehensive analysis at Amit, *Pesaḥim*, 123–27.

This *sugya* discusses the second day added to each holiday in Babylonia, which was too distant to have timely contact with the court in Israel that decided when the new moon appeared. Since the Babylonians were unsure when the month began, they observed each holiday for two days to ensure that at least one of them would be correct.[47] Even if one travels from Israel to Babylonia before the holiday and knows the correct date, if he celebrates the holiday in a Babylonian city where two days are observed, then he must also observe two days according to *m. Pesaḥ.* 4:1. However, if he spends the holiday in the desert of Babylonia where no local custom exists, R. Ammi allows him to observe only one day.[48] Thus, the rule of the Mishnah that one must accept the stringencies of one's destination emerges in the Bavli as simply a political convenience, which can be disregarded when one is alone.[49]

In sum, by comparing section A of the Yerushalmi with the parallel Bavli, we see that the Yerushalmi holds custom as the highest value above official law, while the Bavli pushes to reverse this hierarchy. The Bavli accomplishes its agenda by restricting the *baraita* (and hence the Mishnah as well) to Samaritans and by restricting the Mishnah to exclude leniencies of Palestinian travelers and one who travels to a desert. The disparity between these two *sugyot* reflects the general difference in attitude toward law between the Talmuds, as noted above.[50] The Yerushalmi sees law as a description of the living, day-to-day practice of commoners, whose customs are therefore supreme. Maintaining unity in each locale, even for travelers, ensures that no outside influence will break the continuity of these unchangeable customs. The Bavli, on the other hand, defines law as the result of intellectual argumentation by the rabbis. Therefore, one may protest local custom when that local custom is deemed legally problematic. Local uniformity of custom is made secondary by allowing each rabbi to practice his own custom not only in the desert or when his own custom is superior (because it comes from Palestine), but anywhere there is no danger of ignorant citizens mistaking diversity for impiety.

---

47. See H. J. Zimmels, "The Controversy about the Second Day of the Festival," in *The Abraham Weiss Jubilee Volume* (New York: Abraham Weiss Jubilee Committee, 1964), 139–42; and Ephraim Halivni, "Yom ṭov sheni," *Sinai* 106 (1990): 41–45.

48. See Amit, *Pesaḥim*, 126.

49. Line 5 of the Bavli *sugya* is parallel to section C of the Yerushalmi on which see below, pp. 101–2.

50. Pp. 83–84.

Sections B and C—"Do Not Make Factions"

The last section of the Yerushalmi is the most germane to the question of tolerance for differing halakhic practices. This section brings up the prohibition, based on a midrashic reading of Deut 14:1, not to allow any practice that will create factionalism. Deuteronomy 14:1 prohibits a common ancient Near Eastern mourning practice—"לא תתגודדו—do not cut yourselves." *Sifre Deut., pisqa* 96, taking these words out of context, picks up on an alternative meaning of this same phrase:

> לא תתגודדו, לא תעשו אגודות אלא היו כולכם אגודה אחת וכן הוא אומר הבונה בשמים מעלותיו ואגודתו על ארץ יסדה.
>
> *"Do not cut yourselves"*: Do not make factions, but rather all of you should be one faction, as it is said, *"Who built His chambers in heaven and founded His vault on the earth"* (Amos 9:6).[51]

Finkelstein comments, "The intention of this statement is to oppose the various sects which sprouted during the first generations of Tannaim."[52] This interpretation is also found in Targum Yerushalmi: "לא תעבדון חבורין חבורין לפולחנא נוכריתא—You shall not form companies for idolatry."[53]

Another passage toward the end of the *Sifre* (*pisqa* 346) repeats the same message and adds a parable:

> יחד שבטי ישראל, כשהם עשוים אגודה אחת ולא כשהם עשוים אגודות אגודות, וכן הוא אומר הבונה בשמים מעלותיו ואגודתו על ארץ יסדה. רבי שמעון בן יוחי אומר משל לאחד שהביא שתי ספינות וקשרם בהוגנים ובעשתות והעמידן בלב הים ובנה עליהם פלטרין כל זמן שהספינות קשורות זו בזו פלטרין קיימים פרשו ספינות אין פלטרין קיימים כך ישראל כשעושים רצונו של מקום בונה עליותיו בשמים וכשאין עושים רצונו כביכול אגודתו על

51. Finkelstein, *Sifre*, 158. The word תתגודדו in Deut 14:1, from the root גדד, does not share a root with אגודה, from the root אגד; they only sound similar. The root גדד, however, can mean to gather in groups or divisions of soldiers, as in Jer 5:7 and Mic 4:14. The verse from Amos 9:6 shares a word אגודה with the same word in the midrashic explanation of Deut 14:1. In Amos, it literally refers to the heavens, its parallel in the first half of the verse, which arch overhead like a vaulted ceiling. The midrash, however, assumes that אגודתו refers to the people of Israel, which God placed on earth. Since this word is in the singular, it proves that Israel must be unified. This verse is used to convey a similar message in *b. Ketub.* 6b and *b. Menaḥ.* 27a.

52. Ibid., 158 n. 1. Similarly, Meir Ish Shalom, *Sifre de-ve Rav* (Vienna, 1864), 94 n. 13, comments, "נ"ל דהמדרש הזה בזמנו נדרש בשעה שנעשו אגודות אגודות—It seems to me that this midrash was given in his [R. Shimon bar Yoḥai's] time when [the Jews] separated into many sects." See also Vered Noam, "Beth Shammai veha-halakha ha-kitatit," *Madaʿe ha-Yahadut* 41 (2002): 45.

53. See further at Gilat, "Lo titgodedu," 80 n. 6; and Ben-Menahem et al., *Controversy and Dialogue in Halakhic Sources*, 3:335–36.

ארץ יסדה ... ואף כאן אתה אומר יחד שבטי ישראל כשהם עשוים אגודה אחת ולא כשהם עשוים אגודות אגודות.

"Together the tribes of Israel" (Deut 33:5): [God will become king in Jeshurun] only when they are one faction and not when they split into many factions, as it is said, *"Who built His chambers in heaven and founded His vault on the earth"* (Amos 9:6). R. Shimon ben Yoḥai says, a parable to one who brought two boats and tied them to anchors and iron weights, placed them in the heart of the sea and built upon them a palace. As long as the ships are tied together, the palace stands; once the ships separate, the palace does not stand. So too Israel, when they do the will of God, *"His chamber is built in heaven,"* and when they do not do His will, if one may say so, *"His vault is founded on the earth."*... So too here, you say *"together the tribes of Israel."* When they are one faction and not when they are split into many factions.[54]

The first passage is contained within the halakhic portion of the *Sifre,* while the second comes from the aggadic portion. Scholars believe these two sections of the *Sifre* to be of different provenance—the halakhic section coming from the school of R. Akiba and the aggadic section from the school of R. Ishmael.[55] This could explain the repetition of the same idea within one book. In any case, this message does not have the force of a normative law on any individual or group.[56] The halakhic section itself contains much homiletical content, and the first quotation is too vague to have any direct application. The parable in the aggadic section emphasizes that this is good advice for the community to ensure its continuity. There is no strict prohibition here of any act that differs from the norms of the majority. There is only an opposition to forming sects with all the social and political ramifications that go along with such separations. The Talmuds, however, translate this aggadic teaching into a concrete prohibition, which, at first glance, would prohibit any diversity of practice whatsoever. Yitzhak Gilat argues that the normative concretization of this law coincided with the push for codification at the end of the Tannaitic and beginning of the Amoraic eras. The same fear that the Torah would become split into two that caused R. Yoḥanan to establish rules of deciding dispute also led the early Amoraim to apply "Do not make factions" as a strict legal principle.[57] Each Talmud deals with how this rule can be reconciled with *m. Pesaḥ.* 4:1 and other Tannatitic sources.

---

54. Finkelstein, *Sifre,* 403–4. See parallels in *Midrash Tannaim* on Deut 14:1 and 33:4 and further analysis in Ben-Menahem et al., *Controversy and Dialogue in Halakhic Sources,* 3:337.

55. Strack and Stemberger, *Introduction,* 272–73.

56. See Gilat, "Lo titgodedu," 80.

57. Ibid., 84.

Yerushalmi

Part B of the Yerushalmi *sugya* discusses this topic as a debate between two early Palestinian Amoraim:

[B] [1] רבי שמעון בן לקיש שאל לר׳ יוחנן ואינו אסור משום בל תתגודדו?
אמר ליה בשעה שאילו עושין כבית שמי ואילו עושין כבית הלל
[2] בית שמי ובית הלל אין הלכה כבית הלל?
אמר ליה בשעה שאילו עושין כרבי מאיר ואילו עושין כרבי יוסה
[3] רבי מאיר ור׳ יוסי אין הלכה כרבי יוסי?
אמר ליה תרי תניין אינון על דרבי מאיר ותרין תניין אינון על דרבי יוסי
[4] אמר ליה הרי ראש השנה ויום הכיפורים ביהודה נהגו כר׳ עקיבה ובגליל נהגו כרבי יוחנן בן נורי?[58]
אמר ליה שנייה היא שאם עבר ועשה ביהודה כגליל ובגליל כיהודה יצא
[5] הרי פורים הרי אילו קורין בי״ד ואילו קורין בט״ו?
אמר ליה מי שסידר את המשנה סמכה למקרא משפחה ומשפחה מדינה ומדינה ועיר ועיר
[C] ניחא ממקום שעושין למקום שאין עושין ממקום שאין עושין למקום שעושין ויבטל שהרי כמה בטילין יש לו באותו מקום? רבי סימון בשם רבי יוחנן במתמיה

[B] [1] R. Shimon ben Laqish asked R. Yoḥanan, "Isn't this [having different customs regarding work on the day before Passover] prohibited because of 'Do not make factions'?"
He told him, "[There is only a problem] when some are practicing like the House of Shammai and others are practicing like the House of Hillel."
[2] [But, whenever there is a dispute between] the House of Shammai and the House of Hillel, isn't the halakha like the House of Hillel?
He told him, "[There is only a problem] when some practice like R. Meir and others practice like R. Yose."
[3] [But, whenever there is a dispute between] R. Meir and R. Yose, isn't halakha like R. Yose?
He responded, "When there are two Tannaim concerning R. Meir and two Tannaim concerning R. Yose."
[4] He told him, "But what about Rosh Hashanah and Yom Kippur, in Judea they follow R. Akiba and in the Galilee they follow R. Yoḥanan ben Nuri?"[58]
He responded, "It is different for if one has already acted in Judea as they do in the Galilee or in the Galilee as they do in Judea, he has fulfilled his obligation."

58. This tradition is cited fully in *y. Roš Haš.* 4:6 (59c). Lines 4 and 5 are also cited in *y. Pesaḥ.* 10:5 (37d), on which see Saul Lieberman, *Ha-Yerushalmi ki-fshuṭo* (Jerusalem: Hoṣa'at Darom, 1934), 522–23. The end of line 5 is also cited in *y. Meg.* 1:1 (70b) in a completely different sense.

> [5] But what about Purim? Behold, some read [the book of Esther] on the fourteenth and others read on the fifteenth.
> He told him, "Whoever redacted the Mishnah supported it based on a verse—'Each and every family, each and every province, and each and every city' (Esth 9:28)."
> [C] It is alright with regard to [one who travels] from a place where they do [work on the morning of the day before Passover] to a place where they do not. But from a place where they do not to a place where they do—let him idle since many idlers are in that place? R. Shimon [said] in the name of R. Yoḥanan, "where he will cause others to inquire [since he is usually a busy person]."[59]

This section tests the law of *m. Pesaḥ.* 4:1[60] against the principle set up by the *Sifre,* "Do not make factions." The homiletic message of the Tannaitic Midrashim takes on normative force in the Yerushalmi and challenges all diversity of practice. R. Yoḥanan responds (line 1) that the prohibition does not apply to varying customs regarding work on the day before Passover because this is a matter of mere custom.[61] Each locale can and must follow its own ancestral customs. "Do not make factions" only applies in cases where different groups follow different named laws, such as if some follow Beth Shammai and others follow Beth Hillel.

This answer is not accepted because one must follow the established rules of how to decide between two opinions and so there cannot be any diversity of valid halakhic practice (line 2).[62] It is inconceivable to the Yerushalmi that such a case could arise when one could legitimately follow Beth Shammai, and so the problem of creating factions is irrelevant to this category. The Talmud attempts a different example of controversy that was not yet decided, such as a dispute between R. Yose and R. Meir. It turns out that in this case too, however, the law always favors R. Yose (line 3). The Yerushalmi presumes an elaborate and consistent system of decid-

---

59. *Y. Pesaḥ.* 4:1 (30d).

60. *Qorban ha-ʿedah* and *Pene Moshe* ad loc. explain that the opening question goes back to the law of the Mishnah. However, one can also argue that it asks about the immediately preceding case about fishermen who are accustomed not to work on *ḥol hamoʿed* but move to a place where people do work. It can also refer to the sons of Mesha who did not sail on the sea while others did. These cases both have the potential to create factions. See further in Ben-Menahem et al., *Controversy and Dialogue in Halakhic Sources,* 3:338.

61. See *Qorban ha-ʿedah* and *Pene Moshe* ad loc. The *sugya* does not make this distinction explicitly; in fact, it does not include any word meaning "law" (such as איסורא, דין, or הלכה). Nevertheless, the distinction is implied by the examples used. The distinction is made explicit in the parallel Bavli, see below.

62. See below, p. 201, where the Yerushalmi says that one who follows Beth Shammai is liable to death.

ing halakhot in all cases of dispute, as discussed in chapter 1.[63] Finally, the third attempt is successful: a case where some Tannaim transmit one version of the dispute and other Tannaim transmit a different version. In a case where there is a dispute about the details of a previous dispute, then tolerance must be granted to followers of both opinions and there would thus arise a problem of "Do not make factions." The Talmud does not attempt to suggest how one should act in such a situation. But at least the case of varying customs in *m. Pesaḥ.* 4:1 does not violate this law.

The Talmud cites a counterexample in which two different named opinions are followed in two different places (line 4). In this case, however, both sides would agree that the other practice is still valid. In other words, this law is similar to a custom in that there is no critical difference as to which practice one follows. Another counterexample is brought from the varying days of reading *Megillah* where it is a single authority, namely, the Mishnah, which legislates different laws for different groups (line 5). However, this example is deflected on the grounds that Scripture itself had provided more than one unique date for the reading of the *Megillah* and is thus an exception to the rule.

All in all, the Yerushalmi distinguishes between custom and law. The law of "Do not make factions" does not apply to *minhag.* Variation in customs from one locale to another are not only tolerated (section B), they also must never even be changed (section A). Regarding halakha, on the other hand, everyone must follow the established rules of decision making, otherwise they are outside the boundaries of halakha. Only in an undecided case, where each side may have halakhic validity, does the problem of "Do not make factions" arise and one must find a way to agree.

Section C then returns to the Mishnah. Two principles are established at the end of the Mishnah that can potentially come into conflict with each other. The first principle of *m. Pesaḥ.* 4:1 states: "One who goes from a place where they do work to a place where they refrain from work or from a place where they refrain from work to a place where they do work, we place on him the stringencies of the place of his origin and the stringencies of his place of destination." The second principle demands, "One may not differ [from the local custom] because of strife." These two principles coincide when going to a place that does not do work. But, if one idles in a place where everyone else does work, he will be acting differently from the locals. This is not a problem in most cases since some people in any case are not working. However, R. Yoḥanan suggests that when a person's idling will stand out, this violates the second principle, and such a per-

63. Above, p. 45. Most of these rules are created by R. Yoḥanan himself and his students.

son must work despite the custom of his place of origin. The second rule trumps the first.

This possible contradiction is also addressed in the Bavli cited above (line 5 of *b. Pesaḥ.* 51b) where the question in part C is more fleshed out.[64] Abaye interprets the second rule to apply only to one who travels to a place where they do not work; but if one who does not work in his hometown travels to a place where they do work, he must idle even if it will be conspicuous. Rava says that the second rule can apply even to one who travels to a place where they do work since there are many idlers in the town. He does not take into consideration the case of R. Yoḥanan in which a normally busy person will stand out if he idles. Rava and, even more so, Abaye tolerate some diversity of practice even within one locale while R. Yoḥanan pushes for almost complete unity.[65]

In sum, the Yerushalmi evinces a strong push for uniformity of both halakhic and customary practice. In most cases, the halakha is decided by preset rules. If one were to practice the rejected side of a dispute, it is simply not a halakhically valid act and would therefore not even constitute a problem of "Do not make factions." The prohibition only applies when there are two possible valid options for the halakha. This can occur only in a case where the rules of decision making cannot be applied, such as when there is confusion as to which viewpoint belongs to each Tanna. It is here that the law of not making factions enjoins all sides to agree one way or the other.

In cases of custom, there is much more leeway for local regions to follow their own tradition. In fact, local traditions and customs taken upon oneself cannot be changed. But even when it comes to customs, a traveler should make sure to follow local tradition, certainly in a case of stringency and even in a case of leniency if such leniency will be noticed. Thus, the Yerushalmi tolerates diversity only regarding issues of custom and, even then, it requires conformity by all Jewish denizens of a particular region—whether permanent or transient.

The Yerushalmi does not explicitly define what is custom and what is law. From the examples brought, however, we can deduce some principles. First, law is generally associated with an opinion of a given sage while custom is associated with the practices of citizens of a given place. Second, law consists of issues about which only one practice is legitimate while custom includes issues not addressed by any law[66] or about which

---

64. See text above, p. 90, and last row of chart 2.1 (p. 123). See also Amit, *Pesaḥim,* 107–17, for a theoretical reconstruction of the development of this *sugya.*

65. R. Yoḥanan would only allow one to deviate if he is idle and if his idling will not be noticed.

66. Such as *m. Pesaḥ.* 4:1.

the law allows for two equally viable options.[67] The latter criterion creates something of a tautology: multiple local practices are allowed in cases of customs, and customs are themselves defined as issues where multiple options are viable. Thus, custom in reality may be defined as any issue about which differences of practice exist across multiple regions. Distinguishing between each of these categories is thus subjective and open to dispute, but the Yerushalmi nevertheless assumes that such categories exist and that it is possible to determine whether any given issue is a custom or a law.

Bavli

While much of sections A and C of the Yerushalmi have parallels in Bavli *Pesaḥim,* the parallel for section B is found only in Bavli *Yebamot.* This transfer from one context to another is the first hint that this *sugya* will undergo significant changes in the Bavli. The new context in *Yebamot* is the controversy between Beth Hillel and Beth Shammai regarding the daughter's cowife.[68] *M. Yebamot* 1:4 states, "Though these forbade what the others permitted, nevertheless, Beth Shammai did not refrain from marrying women from Beth Hillel, nor did Beth Hillel [refrain from marrying women] from Beth Shammai." The possibility that the two Houses not only followed their own opinions, but even married each other despite them, flies in the face of the *sugya* at *y. Pesaḥ.* 4:1 (30d), which assumes uniformity of practice in all areas of halakha.[69] The *sugya* at *b. Yebam.* 13b-14a attempts to alleviate the tension between the pluralism described in *m. Yebam.* 1:4 with the unity prescribed by "Do not make factions." Here is the Bavli *sugya* (*Yebam.* 13b-14a):[70]

[1] תנן התם: **מגילה נקראת באחד עשר, ובשנים עשר, ובשלשה עשר, ובארבעה עשר, ובחמשה עשר, לא פחות ולא יותר.**[71] אמר ליה ריש לקיש לר' יוחנן, איקרי כאן: **לא תתגודדו,**[72] **לא תעשו אגודות אגודות.**[73]
האי לא תתגודדו מיבעי ליה לגופיה, דאמר רחמנא: לא תעשו חבורה על מת?[74] אם כן, לימא קרא לא תגודדו, מאי תתגודדו? שמע מינה להכי הוא דאתא. ואימא: כוליה להכי הוא דאתא? אם כן, לימא קרא לא תגודדו, מאי לא תתגודדו? שמע מינה תרתי.

67. Such as the liturgy of the holidays (line 4). There are examples of laws where two options are deemed legitimate; see above, pp. 62–77. However, these are rather exceptional cases.

68. For a detailed analysis of this case see below, pp. 189–222.

69. The Yerushalmi deals with this issue at *y. Yebam.* 1:6 (3a-b), see below, pp. 201–4.

70. Tannaitic texts are in bold. Text follows the printed edition, but see manuscript variants in Liss, *The Babylonian Talmud with Variant Readings,* 1:132–45; and Hidary, "Tolerance for Diversity," 100–102, chart 1.3.

[2] אמר ליה, עד כאן לא שנית: **מקום שנהגו לעשות מלאכה בערבי פסחים עד חצות—עושין, מקום שנהגו שלא לעשות—אין עושין?**[75]

[3] אמר ליה: אמינא לך אנא איסורא, דאמר רב שמן בר אבא אמר ר׳ יוחנן: לקיים את ימי הפורים בזמניהם[76] זמנים הרבה תיקנו להם חכמים[77] ואת אמרת לי מנהגא?
[4] והתם לאו איסורא הויא? והתנן: **בלילה—בית שמאי אוסרין, ובית הלל מתירין?**[78]

[5] אמר ליה התם, הרואה אומר מלאכה הוא דלית ליה.
[6] והא **בית שמאי מתירין הצרות לאחים, ובית הלל אוסרים?**[79]

[7] מי סברת עשו בית שמאי כדבריהם? לא עשו בית שמאי כדבריהם.
[8] ור׳ יוחנן אמר: עשו ועשו.[80]

[9] ובפלוגתא [דרב ושמואל], דרב אומר: לא עשו בית שמאי כדבריהם, ושמואל אמר: עשו ועשו.[81]
אימת? אילימא קודם בת קול,[82] מאי טעמא דמאן דאמר לא עשו? ואלא לאחר בת קול, מאי טעמא דמאן דאמר עשו? אי בעית אימא: קודם בת קול, ואי בעית אימא: לאחר בת קול. אי בעית אימא קודם בת קול, וכגון דבית הלל רובא, למאן דאמר לא עשו, דהא בית הלל רובא. ומאן דאמר עשו, כי אזלינן בתר רובא היכא דכי הדדי נינהו, הכא בית שמאי מחדדי טפי. ואי בעית אימא לאחר בת קול, מאן דאמר לא עשו, דהא נפקא בת קול. ומאן דאמר עשו, רבי יהושע היא, דאמר: אין משגיחין בבת קול. ומאן דאמר עשו, קרינן כאן: **לא תתגודדו, לא תעשו אגודות אגודות?**[73]
[10][a] אמר אביי: כי אמרינן לא תתגודדו כגון שתי בתי דינים בעיר אחת,[83] הללו מורים כדברי בית שמאי והללו מורים כדברי בית הלל, אבל שתי בתי דינים בשתי עיירות—לית לן בה.
[b] אמר ליה רבא: והא בית שמאי ובית הלל כשתי בתי דינים בעיר אחת דמי? אלא אמר רבא: כי אמרינן לא תתגודדו כגון בית דין בעיר אחת, פלג מורין כדברי בית שמאי ופלג מורין כדברי בית הלל. אבל שתי בתי דינין בעיר אחת לית לן בה.

[11] תא שמע: **במקומו של רבי אליעזר היו כורתים עצים לעשות פחמים בשבת לעשות ברזל, במקומו של ר׳ יוסי הגלילי היו אוכלים בשר עוף בחלב.**[84] במקומו של רבי אליעזר אין, במקומו של רבי עקיבא לא. דתניא, **כלל אמר רבי עקיבא: כל מלאכה שאפשר לעשותה מערב שבת אין דוחה את השבת?**[85] והאי מאי תיובתא? מקומות מקומות שאני. ודקארי לה מאי קארי לה? סלקא דעתך אמינא, משום חומרא דשבת כמקום אחד דמי, קא משמע לן.
[12] תא שמע: דרבי אבהו כי איקלע לאתריה דרבי יהושע בן לוי הוה מטלטל שרגא, וכי איקלע לאתריה דר׳ יוחנן לא הוה מטלטל שרגא?[86] והאי מאי קושיא? ולא אמרינן מקומות שאני? אנן הכי קאמרינן: ר׳ אבהו היכי עביד הכא הכי, והיכי עביד הכא הכי? רבי אבהו כר׳ יהושע בן לוי סבירא ליה, וכי מקלע לאתריה דרבי יוחנן, לא הוה מטלטל משום כבודו דרבי יוחנן. והאיכא שמעא? דמודע ליה לשמעא.

[1] We learned there: **The Scroll of Esther is recited on the eleventh, twelfth, thirteenth, fourteenth, and fifteenth, but not ear-**

lier or later.[71] Resh Laqish said to R. Yoḥanan: I can apply here: ***lo titgodedu,***[72] **do not form factions?**[73]
(This mention of *lo titgodedu* is required for its own context, for the Merciful said: Do not inflict a wound over the dead?[74] If so, let Scripture say *lo tegodedu.* What is *titgodedu*? I conclude that it comes for this [to teach about factions]. But say all of it comes for this [to teach making factions]. If so, let Scripture say *lo tagodu.* What is *lo titgodedu*? We learn from it two laws.)
[2] He [R. Yoḥanan] said to him [Resh Laqish]: Have you not yet learned: **In a place where they are accustomed to do work on the day before Passover until midday, they may do work. In a place where they are accustomed to refrain from work, they may not do work?**[75]

[3] He said to him: I tell you a prohibition, as R. Shaman bar Abba said [in the name of] R. Yoḥanan], "*To fulfill these days of Purim at their designated times*[76]—the rabbis instituted many times for them,"[77] and you tell me a custom?
[4] And there [regarding Passover], is it not a prohibition? Have we not learned: **At night, Beth Shammai prohibits and Beth Hillel permits [doing work].**[78]

[5] He said to him: There, an onlooker will assume that he has no work to do.
[6] But, **Beth Shammai permits the cowives to the brothers and Beth Hillel prohibits.**[79]

[7] Do you think that Beth Shammai practiced according to their opinions? Beth Shammai did not practice according to their opinions.
[8] R. Yoḥanan says, they certainly did practice [according to their opinions].[80]

---

71. *M. Meg.* 1:1.
72. Deuteronomy 14:1.
73. *Sifre Deut., pisqa* 96 (ed. Finkelstein, 158).
74. There is no verse with this wording. Rather this is a paraphrase of Deut 14:1, probably based on the language of the Targum Yerushalmi. See above, p. 97.
75. *M. Pesaḥ.* 4:1.
76. Esther 9:31.
77. Cited also in *b. Meg.* 2a; and see Gilat, "Lo titgodedu," 82 n. 15.
78. *M. Pesaḥ.* 4:5.
79. *M. Yebam.* 1:4. See analysis of this topic on pp. 189–222.
80. This contradicts *y. Yebam.* 1:6 (3b) = *y. Qidd.* 1:1 (58d) where R. Yoḥanan states that Beth Shammai followed Beth Hillel; see below, p. 201.

[9] This relates to a controversy between Rav and Shmuel. Rav says, Beth Shammai did not practice according to their opinions. Shmuel says, they certainly did practice.[81]
When [did Beth Shammai practice]? If one says before the divine voice,[82] what is the reasoning of the one who says they did not practice? If it was after the divine voice, what is the reasoning of the one who says they did practice? If you want I can say it is before the divine voice and if you want I can say it is after the divine voice. If you want I can say it is before the divine voice and Beth Hillel was the majority. According to the one who says they did not practice it is because Beth Hillel was the majority. According to the one who says they did practice, we only follow the majority when both sides are equally talented, but here, Beth Shammai is sharper. If you want I can say it is after the divine voice. According to the one who says they did not practice, it is because the divine voice came forth. According to the one who says they did practice, we apply here: ***lo titgodedu*, do not form factions.**[72]
[10][a] Abaye said: We apply *lo titgodedu* in cases such as two courts in one city,[83] these teach according to Beth Shammai and those teach according to Beth Hillel. But, we do not apply it to two courts in two cities.
[b] Rava said to him: But Beth Shammai and Beth Hillel are like two courts in one city? Rather, Rava says: We apply *lo titgodedu* in cases such as one court in one city, half [of whose judges] teach according to Beth Shammai and half according to Beth Hillel. But, we do not apply it to two courts in one city.

[11] Come and hear: **In the place of R. Eliezer, they used to chop wood to make charcoal on Shabbat to make iron [to make a knife for use in a circumcision]. In the place of R. Yose the Galilean, they used to eat fowl with milk.**[84] In the place of R. Eliezer,

81. The controversy between Rav and Shmuel also appears in the Yerushalmi; see the previous note. A similar controversy involving these same three sages appears in *b. Yebam.* 96b in a completely different context. Since these three opinions are cited already in the Yerushalmi in the context of Beth Shammai's practice, *b. Yebam.* 14a must be the original context and the redactor of *b. Yebam.* 96b borrowed these words and applied them to a different case.

82. Literally, the daughter of a voice or echo. This refers to the voice that declared halakha according to Beth Hillel at *b. ʿErub.* 13b.

83. The existence of competing courts within the same city reflects a decentralized structure where neither court needs to answer to a higher authority. This structure may reflect the reality in Babylonia during Rava's time. See the next chapter.

84. This is cited as a *baraita* in *b. Šabb.* 130a and *b. Ḥul.* 116a. See analysis of this text below, pp. 148–53.

yes [they did act so], but in the place of R. Akiba, no [they did not do so], as it was taught: **R. Akiba pronounced a rule, Any work which can be done before Shabbat does not supersede Shabbat?** [85] And what is the question here? Each place is different. When he discussed it what did he discuss [since the answer is obvious]? You might have thought that because of the stringency of Shabbat it is considered like one place. This teaches us [otherwise].

[12] Come and hear: When R. Abbahu would come to the place of R. Yehoshua ben Levi, he would carry a lamp. When he would come to the place of R. Yoḥanan he would not carry a lamp.[86] And what is the question here? Do we not say each place is different? We [meant to] say as follows: How could R. Abbahu practice here like this and there like that? R. Abbahu agrees with R. Yehoshua ben Levi. When he would come to the place of R. Yoḥanan he would not carry a lamp in deference to the honor of R. Yoḥanan. But isn't there an attendant [who will become confused about the law]? He [R. Abbahu] informs the attendant.

This *sugya* defines the parameters of the prohibition "Do not make factions." A number of cases are tested against this principle, and the rule is alternatively defined by several Amoraim. Many interpretive and literary problems become apparent upon close analysis of the *sugya*. Textual criticism and source criticism can help explain some of these issues, but the *sugya* remains problematic if we insist on finding a clear logical flow.

We will first analyze previous commentaries on this *sugya*. Traditional commentaries generally assume that the *sugya*, at least until statement 8, is one long conversation between R. Yoḥanan and Resh Laqish. This is historically problematic right off the bat. The statements in the Bavli, except for statement 1 and, in part, statements 2 and 5, are not found in the parallel conversation as recorded in the Yerushalmi. Even if almost none of this dialogue was pronounced by R. Yoḥanan and Resh Laqish, however, the more significant question is what the redactors of this *sugya* meant for their audience to understand. Is the listener meant to assume that this is one long dialogue between these two Amoraim?

Manuscripts differ widely about how many times "אמר ליה" appears. Ed. Pizaro (1509) has only one; ms. Vatican 114 has two;[87] most manuscripts have three; recent printed editions have four; and one Geniza frag-

85. *M. Pesaḥ.* 6:2.

86. This case also appears in *b. Šabb.* 46a (quoted below, p. 142). See parallel in *y. Ber.* 8:1 (12a), quoted below, p. 145.

87. Ed. Pizaro only reads א"ל in statement [1] and has אלא in statement [3]. All manuscripts read א"ל in statements [1] and [3]. Vat 114 lacks א"ל in statement [2], but it is added between the lines.

ment has five.[88] Halivni notes that the words "אמר ליה" are never reliable in extended dialogue.[89] Laying this problem aside, this *sugya* does still have the form of a single dialogue. We will now attempt to find a continuous logical progression from each statement to the next in order to test whether it is possible to read the *sugya* as a cohesive dialogue.

(1) The *sugya* begins with a quotation from *m. Meg.* 1:1 and the question of Resh Laqish that this Mishnah seems to contradict the verse "Do not make factions." Next, follows a technical analysis of how one verse can be used to teach two different laws and precisely which letters are extra. This is certainly a Stammaitic addition.[90]

(2) It is not immediately clear what is meant by R. Yoḥanan's first response, which simply quotes a Mishnah. Apparently, R. Yoḥanan himself does not have a problem with either *m. Meg.* 1:1 or *m. Pesaḥ.* 4:1—either because he thinks Deut 14:1 does not prohibit factions at all[91] or, more likely, because he has a more limited view of when the law applies.[92] Assuming the latter approach, R. Yoḥanan shows from *m. Pesaḥ.* 4:1 that the prohibition does not apply when different cities have varying practices but only when there is diversity of practice within one location.[93] This

88. Ed. Vilna and Geniza fragment Adler 3652,4–5 read א"ל at the beginning of statement [5]. Eds. Pizaro and Venice (1520) do not have א"ל at this point, but it was added by R. Shelomo Luria and included in subsequent printings. Interestingly, no witness begins statement [4] with אמר ליה. The Geniza fragment also has אמר ליה before האי לא תתגודדו in statement [1], a reading also cited but rejected by Riṭva (R. Yom Tov Ashbili [of Seville], ca. 1250–1330). *Tosafot Rid* seems to read אמר ליה in statements [6] and [7], and perhaps so does Riṭva unless he added these words as commentary.

89. Halivni, *Meqorot u-mesorot*, Nashim, 17 n. 11*.

90. See Gilat, "Lo titgodedu," 81 n. 14. The style of this section and its concern for technical grammatical points is demonstrably Stammaitic. Nevertheless, Rashba, s.v. ואימא, quotes a *responsum* of Hai Gaon or Sherira Gaon according to which this section is part of the dialogue between R. Yoḥanan and Resh Laqish. See above, n. 88. According to this, R. Yoḥanan challenges the entire prohibition not to make factions.

91. According to the Geonim and Rashba mentioned in the previous note, R. Yoḥanan thinks that the entire prohibition not to make factions does not exist. Therefore, in each of his responses to Resh Laqish, R. Yoḥanan is only asking rhetorically why Resh Laqish does not also ask about more cases.

92. Riṭva thinks that R. Yoḥanan does have a prohibition not to make factions but that he interprets it along the lines of the conclusions of Abaye and Rava below. (In fact, they were arguing about what exactly were R. Yoḥanan's intentions.) That is why R. Yoḥanan does not himself have any difficulty with any of the cases presented by Resh Laqish. R. Yoḥanan's responses are meant only to add to Resh Laqish's difficulties: "If you have a problem with that case then you will also have a problem with this one...." Rashba and Riṭva agree, for different reasons, that R. Yoḥanan does not mean to solve Resh Laqish's question but rather to add to it and thereby show that Resh Laqish's assumptions about the applicability of this law must be wrong—a classic *reductio ad absurdum.*

93. Of course, this discussion is relevant only to the Bavli's representation of R. Yoḥanan. The parallel dialogue in the Yerushalmi makes no allowance for diversity in different locations.

limitation of the law of "Do not make factions" would resolve *m. Meg.* 1:1as well.[94]

(3) Resh Laqish now responds by making an important distinction between *m. Meg.* 1:1, which legislates a law, and *m. Pesaḥ.* 4:1, which only regulates a custom. Resh Laqish argues that diversity of practice in two locations is tolerable only in a case of differing customs, but different laws cannot exist even in two locales.[95] Therefore, *m. Meg.* 1:1 remains problematic.

(4) R. Yoḥanan[96] cites a controversy between Beth Shammai and Beth Hillel about working on the night before Passover. The point of this citation seems to be that since performing work at night is treated as an issue of law and not custom, so too we should view the controversy about working in the morning also as one about law and not custom. Therefore, R. Yoḥanan's response in line 2 is upheld.[97]

(5) Resh Laqish puts to rest all arguments from varying customs regarding performing work since one can always be idle without anyone noticing that he is actually following a deviant practice that does not allow work.[98]

---

94. Although, this only resolves the difference between cities reading on the 14th and 15th days of Adar, not the villagers who read on the preceding days. These villagers read when they come to the cities on market days thus causing diverse practices within one place. R. Asher ben Yeḥiel (Rosh, d. 1327) therefore explains that R. Yoḥanan thinks that *m. Meg.* 1:1 is not a problem since the differing practices are simply dependent on location and do not involve any rabbinic controversy. Accordingly, R. Yoḥanan offers *m. Pesaḥ.* 4:1 only as a rhetorical argument that Resh Laqish should have asked a better question.

95. The view of Resh Laqish here concurs with the view of the Yerushalmi, which also does not allow for diversity in different cities.

96. Although statement 4 does not begin with אמר ליה, the flow of the *sugya* suggests that we are to read this as a continuation of the dialogue.

97. An alternate explanation is that R. Yoḥanan shifts to a new line of reasoning and does not continue to convince Resh Laqish that diversity in two locations is allowed. Rather, he steps up his *reductio ad absurdum* argument by citing a case that is not a custom and was even practiced in the same place. This would have to assume either, like the Geonim, that R. Yoḥanan does not agree with the entire law of factions or that he anticipates the response of Rava. I prefer the explanation given above because it preserves a more natural flow of the argument. R. Yoḥanan seems to be continuing with his argument from *m. Pesaḥ.* 4:1 since he begins this sentence with והתם. See, however, Riṭva, s.v. והתם; *b. Pesaḥ.* 55a and discussion in Ben-Menahem et al., *Controversy and Dialogue in Halakhic Sources*, 3:444–45.

98. This response confirms that line 4 continues the line of reasoning based on *m. Pesaḥ.* 4:1 and does not switch to the case of the night before Passover (see previous note). If one explains that R. Yoḥanan did switch to an argument based on *m. Pesaḥ.* 4:5, then Resh Laqish's answer would not make sense since Beth Shammai and Beth Hillel live in the same place and a problem would arise when the Hillelites performed work in front of the Shammaites. Resh Laqish's response that one can be passive only works regarding *m. Pesaḥ.* 4:1 where one who travels from a place that does not work to a place that does work can be passive without raising any eyebrows.

(6) This line continues the Beth Shammai and Beth Hillel theme begun in statement 4 and finds another example that does not involve passively refraining from work but rather requires taking certain actions. Medieval commentaries understand this and the next two lines as a continuation of the dialogue between Resh Laqish and R. Yoḥanan. R. Yoḥanan thus presents this difficult case as a challenge to Resh Laqish's wide application of the law not to make factions.[99] What is not clear, however, is how R. Yoḥanan himself would account for this case unless he does not agree with the prohibition against factions at all or has a very limited view of it such as that of Rava below.[100] David Halivni, on the other hand, argues that this line is not said by R. Yoḥanan but rather by the Stam. This would be a new line of reasoning against both Resh Laqish and R. Yoḥanan.[101] Even R. Yoḥanan, who thinks diverse practices in different locations are allowed, must explain how Beth Shammai could practice against Beth Hillel with whom they resided. The problem with this interpretation is that the dialogue between Resh Laqish and R. Yoḥanan ends abruptly without resolution and creates a *non sequitur*.

(7) Resh Laqish (for the medieval commentators) or the Stam (for Halivni) objects that Beth Shammai never followed their own opinions in practice, and so there is no problem of factions. For Resh Laqish, the only example from all the proposed cases of differing practices that is a law (not a custom), which one performs actively (and does not passively refrain from doing it) and which was actually carried out by different groups, is *m. Meg.* 1:1.

(8) R Yoḥanan, or the Stam speaking for him, argues that Beth Shammai did follow its own practice.[102] The next line will pick up on the problem presented by this case.

---

99. Comparison with the parallel Yerushalmi dialogue where R. Yoḥanan does respond to Resh Laqish by citing Beth Shammai and Beth Hillel may suggest that this line in the Bavli should also be read as a continuation of the dialogue. In both Talmuds, Resh Laqish then responds that Beth Shammai did not practice its own opinion. However, R. Yoḥanan in the Yerushalmi argues that the law of factions should apply only to cases like Beth Shammai and Beth Hillel while in the Bavli R. Yoḥanan seems to say that it does not apply in these cases. Thus, this source is used for very different purposes in each *sugya*, which should warn us against using the Yerushalmi to explain the Bavli.

100. See above, nn. 91–92.

101. Halivni, *Meqorot u-mesorot*, Pesaḥim, 16–17.

102. Halivni, ibid., thinks that the historical R. Yoḥanan believed that Beth Shammai did not follow its opinion, which is his explicit view in *y. Yebam.* 1:6 (3b) (see above, n. 80) and his implied view in *y. Pesaḥ.* 4:1 (30d) [B1] above, p. 99. According to Halivni, statement 8 is written by the Stam based on a mistaken inference from statement 6, which it believed was asked by R. Yoḥanan. However, continues Halivni, statement 6 was actually itself written by an earlier Stam and not R. Yoḥanan. Another possibility is that the Bavli deduced that R. Yoḥanan must have thought that Beth Shammai practiced its own opinion from his response to Resh Laqish in the Yerushalmi [B1], "בשעה שאילו עושין כבית שמי ואילו עושין כבית הלל." Resh

(9) The Stam now notes that this controversy was also played out by the Babylonian first-generation Amoraim. Then a tangent begins concerning whether they disagreed about the practice of Beth Shammai before or after the heavenly voice that announced that halakha is like Beth Hillel. The Stam then resumes its line of questioning against those who believe that Beth Shammai did practice their own opinions, that is, R. Yoḥanan and Shmuel.[103] Even medieval commentators must agree that this question is not part of the previous dialogue.[104] Therefore, whether one interprets that the dialogue between R. Yoḥanan and Resh Laqish ends in line 5 or in line 8, the original question of Resh Laqish is not directly resolved within the dialogue. It is possible that Abaye answers the *m. Meg.* 1:1 question indirectly,[105] but it should have been the main point. There is no resolution to the primary dialogue.

(10) Two limitations of the law of factions are offered as answers to the question in statement 9. They are spoken by two fourth-generation Babylonian Amoraim far removed from the original dialogue of the first-generation Palestinian Amoraim. Strangely, they introduce courts, which were not previously mentioned.[106] Even more surprisingly, Abaye's answer does not solve the problem at all. His solution could resolve the case of *m. Meg.* 1:1 but not the case of Beth Shammai and Beth Hillel, which was the immediately preceding question. Therefore, the statements of Abaye

---

Laqish responds that Beth Shammai followed Beth Hillel but R. Yoḥanan may not have agreed and only carried on the conversation according to the assumptions of Resh Laqish.

103. Rashba, s.v. ולמ"ד, questions why the Gemara would ask this question to R. Yoḥanan since, according to the Geonim, R. Yoḥanan does not prohibit factions at all. Rashba concludes that this question is not asked to R. Yoḥanan but to anyone, perhaps Shmuel or perhaps only a theoretical viewpoint, who might think that Beth Shammai followed their opinion and also thinks there is a prohibition against making factions.

104. See Riṭva, s.v. ולמ"ד, and Rashba in previous note.

105. Ramban notes that Abaye's answer still does not solve the *Megillah* problem since the villagers are reading on the day they come into the city, which can be a different day than the city dwellers themselves read. Rava's answer does solve all the problems, though. Rosh thinks even Rava does not answer the question from *m. Meg.* 1:1 since this is like one court in one city where half read on one day and half on the other. Instead, Rosh explains that *m. Meg.* 1:1 was implicitly answered by R. Yoḥanan above (see n. 94). He also quotes Rabbenu Ḥayyim who says that Abaye could answer the *Megillah* question since, according to the Yerushalmi, the villagers would read in their own villages on those days and so there would not be two different customs within one city.

106. The cases up until now involved either customs of different cities or opinions of individual rabbis. It is not clear how either of these circumstances line up with a system of courts. Perhaps Abaye and Rava's statements were originally said in another context that did involve courts.

In their original statements, Abaye and Rava may not have necessarily disagreed with each other. Abaye lived in Pumbedita, a small town where there was likely only one court. Rava lived in Maḥoza, a suburb of Ctesiphon, which must have contained many courts. The differences in formulation between their statements may simply reflect differences in their local contexts.

and Rava seem to stand somewhat independently from the dialogical and logical flow of the *sugya*.

(11) and (12) These cases are surely not part of the conversation between R. Yoḥanan and Resh Laqish. These are two examples of rabbis following different laws in different places. The first case examines practices of two Tannaim in two locations while the second examines the practices of one Amora in two locations. The cases are brought as a challenge to "Do not make factions." As the Stam here points out, however, they present no problem once we accept the interpretations of Abaye and Rava. These questions might have been appropriate in a pre-Abaye version of the *sugya,* but as it stands now they are simply out of place.[107] The Stam therefore invents reasons why they are nevertheless appropriate.

In sum, all interpretations that try to trace a clear logical exchange of ideas from one statement to the next end up with difficulties. There is a problem with the flow of the dialogue. The *sugya* begins as a conversation between Resh Laqish and R. Yoḥanan but, after a few steps,[108] it morphs into an anonymous give-and-take.[109] The *sugya* begins with a concern about *m. Meg.* 1:1 and then jumps to the controversies of Beth Shammai and Beth Hillel without returning to address *m. Meg.* 1:1. There is a lack of continuity from the beginning of the *sugya* to the end of it both regarding the characters in the conversation and the focus of its discussion. Furthermore, Abaye and Rava introduce courts, which do not relate to any previous case, and Abaye's answer does not solve the preceding question. Lastly, the last two cases in line 11 seem superfluous and add little substantive information.

Is this *sugya* just a jumble of somewhat related statements? It is obviously not an actual report of a conversation and does not even try to mimic such a report. There is no apparent concern to maintain a consistent dialogical voice. Some logical threads are brought to a close while others are left dangling. Is it a game of free association or is there a literary unity in this *sugya*? What is the point of this *sugya* and what is the rhetorical effect of its structure? Perhaps we can get a better idea of what the redactors of this *sugya* had in mind if we compare this *sugya* to its earlier parallel in the Yerushalmi, which does maintain a clear dialogical flow and logical consistency.[110] Both *sugyot* try to reconcile the law of factions with various

107. See Halivni, *Meqorot u-mesorot*, Pesaḥim, 15–16.

108. The interpretation of the medieval commentators is able to sustain the dialogue longer than that of Halivni. But both admit that the Stam takes over the dialogue at some point and leaves the original discussion without closure.

109. R. Yoḥanan's name does appear again in statement 8, but this is only a quotation by the anonymous redactor, not part of the dialogue.

110. See above, pp. 37–39, concerning the theory that the Bavli redactors used something like the Yerushalmi as a base text, which they then modified.

Tannaitic instances of diverse practices. However, each Talmud comes to very different conclusions.

The primary distinction made in the Yerushalmi is that the prohibition of making factions applies only to laws but not to diverse customs or other cases where both disputants agree that the other side is valid if only *ex post facto*. Laws, however, rarely present any problem because of the comprehensive rules of decision making assumed by the Yerushalmi.[111] The Yerushalmi thus successfully reconciles "Do not make factions" with these various Tannaitic sources.

The Bavli agrees with the Yerushalmi that "Do not make factions" does not apply to customs. However, the Bavli, which rejects R. Yoḥanan's rules of decision making and further believes that Beth Shammai did practice differently from Beth Hillel,[112] must also reconcile a whole set of sources about diverse practices of law with the prohibition against factions. This requires the Bavli to place more severe limitations on the application of this law. Abaye and Rava therefore conclude that the law does not apply to diverse legal practices in different cities or even in different courts within the same city. Thus, the Yerushalmi and the Bavli have vastly different interpretations of the law of "Do not make factions" based, in part, on their fundamentally different assumptions about the existence of diversity of halakhic practice.

I propose that the redactors of the Bavli *sugya* rearranged, deleted, expanded and reinterpreted elements of the Yerushalmi *sugya* in order to argue for its fundamentally different point of view. The *non sequiturs* and loose ends found in the Bavli *sugya* can be explained on the basis of this redactional history. The overall structure of the Bavli forms a carefully arranged polemic against the Yerushalmi. It pieces together parts of various dialogues and sources to create a rhetorical argument.

The first major difference between the two *sugyot* is that while *m. Meg.* 1:1 is mentioned last in the Yerushalmi and is dismissed as an exception, it becomes first in the Bavli and the center of its opening dialogue.[113] There is no apparent reason why the Bavli, which comments on *m. Yebam.* 1:4, should begin with *m. Meg.* 1:1. Neither *m. Meg.* 1:1 nor the verse from Deut 14:1 has any immediate connection to any previous statement in *b.*

111. The rules of decision making are so comprehensive, in fact, that the Yerushalmi actually has trouble finding a case where "Do not make factions" could apply. If custom is excluded and law is always determined then nothing is left. The Yerushalmi settles on a case of doubtful attributions. Thus, both the Yerushalmi and the Bavli limit the law of "Do not make factions" to a very small area, but they do so for vastly different reasons. The Bavli does so because it tolerates diversity of practice. The Yerushalmi does so because diversity of practice is already removed by the rules of decision making.

112. See further below, pp. 204–16.

113. See comparison table in chart 2.2 below, p. 124.

Yebam.[114] Why does it begin with the example of *m. Meg.* 1:1 when many other more problematic examples could have been chosen?[115] If this *sugya* appeared in *b. Meg.*, then such a move would link it to the literary context. But the primary placement of *m. Meg.* 1:1 in *b. Yebam.* 13b is striking. It would be difficult to argue that this is simply how the historical argument happened because in the original *sugya* of *y. Pesaḥ.* 4:1 (30d), *m. Meg.* 1:1 is quoted at the end of the dialogue. Why did the Bavli promote it to be first?

The promotion of *m. Meg.* 1:1 in the Bavli may be related to the different explanations given to this source in each Talmud. The Yerushalmi says that *m. Meg.* 1:1 does not violate the prohibition against making factions because it is based on a verse (Esth 9:28) and so is an exception. The Bavli also quotes a similar verse (Esth 9:31) that is near the verse used by the Yerushalmi but to opposite effect. The verse in the Yerushalmi is used to prove that there is no problem of making factions in *m. Meg.* 1:1.[116] The verse in the Bavli proves that *m. Meg.* 1:1 is a problem because the requirement for each city to read on its given day is based on law and not merely custom. The verse in the Bavli further problematizes *m. Meg.* 1:1 rather than solves it.

The Bavli finds the Yerushalmi's resolution of "Do not make factions" with cases of Tannaitic dispute to be insufficient. In order to explain this disagreement, the Bavli proceeds to point out the problems with the Yerushalmi's view. First it focuses attention on *m. Meg.* 1:1. By placing this source up front, the Bavli argues that this cannot just be written off as an exception but rather shows that a broader set of limitations on "Do not make factions" will be necessary. This begins to prepare the way toward the Bavli's new definitions of the law.

The Bavli next has R. Yoḥanan cite *m. Pesaḥ.* 4:1 as a proof that diversity in different cities is permitted, thus prefiguring Abaye's more explicit statement. This source serves a very different function in the Yerushalmi where it is the subject of Resh Laqish's opening question. Instead of functioning as a question, *m. Pesaḥ.* 4:1 functions as an answer in the Bavli. Next, Resh Laqish suggests distinguishing between custom and law, which was precisely the response of R. Yoḥanan in the Yerushalmi. R. Yoḥanan, however, shows that *m. Pesaḥ.* 4 also involves law. Therefore, the entire distinction of the Yerushalmi between law and custom is shown

---

114. In fact, this *sugya* looks like it could have been formed independently from the present context and then copied here on account of its reference to *m. Yebam.* 1. However, there is no parallel to this *sugya* in *b. Meg.* nor anywhere else in the Bavli.

115. Calendrical controversies, such as recorded at *m. Roš Haš.* 2:9, surely have greater potential to create factions. See herein, pp. 33 and 264–69. In the case of *m. Meg.* 1:1, everyone agrees that each locale should read on its given days and therefore does not present much danger of creating opposing factions.

116. Perhaps the Bavli was not satisfied with the Yerushalmi making an arbitrary exception. Also, how can a verse from *Ketubim* reject a verse from the Pentateuch?

to be not only unhelpful, since *m. Pesaḥ.* 4 does involve law,[117] but also unnecessary, since diversity in different cities is allowed.

The Bavli then puts aside any lessons from *m. Pesaḥ.* 4 since one may simply be passive in those cases.[118] However, an even more problematic case of *m. Yebam.* 1:4 is then cited that surely cannot be dismissed as mere custom or acting passively. The Yerushalmi also cited the example of Beth Shammai and Beth Hillel as an answer. Unlike the Yerushalmi, which dismissed such cases as nonexistant, however, the Bavli cannot so easily ignore the possibility that Beth Shammai did practice differently from its rival.

Now that the Yerushalmi's view has been rejected and the full range of problematic sources has been laid out, the way is paved for the Bavli to present its own resolution. It first cites Abaye, who excludes diverse practices in different cities from the prohibition against factions. This view was already implied in the preceding dialogue and does succeed in solving many of the previously cited cases. As Rava notes,[119] however, Abaye's definition of the law does not solve the cases of Beth Shammai and Beth Hillel. He therefore proposes that the prohibition is limited to diversity within a court and does not apply to two courts even within a city.

To review, the case of *m. Meg.* 1:1 refutes the Yerushalmi's simple custom-vs.-law distinction and raises the need for Abaye's solution. This explains the promotion and reinterpretation of this case by the Bavli. The case of *m. Yebam.* 1:4, however, further problematizes all previous solutions and raises the need for Rava's solution. This explains its central role in the Bavli *sugya,* where it derails the previous dialogue and dominates the discussion. The central role of *m. Yebam.* 1:4 may also explain why

117. Also, *m. Pesah.* 4:1 shows that diversity of custom within one city is also problematic. See the next note.

118. This line may be an echo of part C of the Yerushalmi, which also notes that travelers from a place that does not work to a place that does work may simply idle. The Yerushalmi, however, concludes that one should do work in a place where the custom is to work if he will attract attention by not working. This is a case of a custom where diversity is still prohibited because it occurs in the same place and is noticeable. Thus, the Yerushalmi allows diversity only in areas of custom that are practiced in different places but prohibits all cases of laws and even prohibits diverse customs in the same place.

To be sure, *m. Pesaḥ.* 4:1 itself prohibits a traveler from a place that does work to a place that does not do work to continue his usual practice of working since he must conform to the practice of his destination. Thus all agree that even diversity of customs is prohibited if it can be avoided by being passive. However, only the Yerushalmi requires that one actively disobey one's usual custom for the sake of conformity with the local custom. See also above, p. 102 n. 65.

119. The attribution of this line to Rava results in two statements back to back said by Rava making the second אמר רבא superfluous. This may suggest that only the second of Rava's attributions is authentic and the first is pseudepigraphically attributed to him by the Stam in order to explain why Rava needed to present a more radical view.

the Bavli moved the *sugya* from *m. Pesaḥ.* 4:1 in the Yerushalmi to its current placement in the Bavli. While *m. Pesaḥ.* 4:1 was the main concern of the Yerushalmi, the Bavli recasts this source as part of its rejection of the Yerushalmi's view. Thus, the shift in literary contexts from *m. Pesaḥ.* to *m. Yebam.* is another example of the dramatic transformation of the Yerushalmi *sugya* by the Bavli redactors.[120]

This is the extent of the overlap between the two Talmuds. Notice all the material that is in the Yerushalmi that is not present in the Bavli. Line B3 of the Yerushalmi, which denies the possibility of any normative halakhic diversity, is not found in the Bavli. In the Yerushalmi, Resh Laqish argues that nobody could follow Beth Shammai or any other minority view, not only because of Deut 14:1, but because their opinion has no halakhic validity. The Bavli, which rejects the rules of decision making presented by R. Yoḥanan, has no need to address this issue.

B4, about the Rosh Hashanah liturgy, is also missing in the Bavli. First of all, this describes a Palestinian controversy, which would be irrelevant in Babylonia. More importantly, this case would be solved by the Bavli's allowance for diversity in different cities. That the Yerushalmi responds to this case instead by fitting into the custom-vs.-law distinction shows that the Yerushalmi does not tolerate diversity in different cities. This is also evident from the Yerushalmi's need to dismiss *m. Meg.* 1:1 as an exception rather than permit it on account of its diverse practices occurring in different cities.

I have been working under the assumption that the redactors of the Bavli had a version of the Yerushalmi very similar to our Yerushalmi. This assumption is certainly questionable. In fact, many of the omissions, reinterpretations, and rearrangements found in the Bavli may stem from another version of the Palestinian *sugya* that served as the basis for the Bavli *sugya* and was very different from the version preserved in the Yerushalmi. However, the Yerushalmi as we have it is still the best, and only, approximation to the source material used by the Bavli redactors, and so our working assumption is that if something in the Bavli is different from the Yerushalmi, then it is at least plausible that it was intentionally changed. More importantly, when all the changes from the Yerushalmi to the Bavli fit into the explicity stated viewpoint of the Bavli, as they do in this *sugya*, then we may propose a high probability that most of these changes were conscious and purposeful.[121]

---

120. Rubenstein, *Talmudic Stories*, 59, states, regarding the oven of Akhnai story, which appears in Yerushalmi *Ḥagigah* but is transferred to *Baba Meṣiʿa* in the Bavli, "The BT redactors seem to have reworked and recontextualized the story simultaneously. That is, the redactors have tailored the text of the story to fit the context they chose." Cf. ibid., 50.

121. The Bavli *sugya* achieves its rhetorical effect even without comparison with the Yerushalmi. Each step of the dialogue raises another problematic source to challenge the validity of the prohibition against factions until we are forced into the radical interpretations

In sum, the Bavli's position can be seen most clearly in the explicit statements of the Bavli *sugya*. Different practices that are not noticeable by the public are tolerated (*b. Pesaḥ.* 51b). Abaye and Rava effectively reject the law of *lo titgodedu*. By defining the prohibition in terms of acts of a court, they exclude customs and practices of individuals. Furthermore, multiple practices across different cities or, for Rava, even separate groups within one city, are tolerated. It is actually not easy to come up with a case that Rava would include in the prohibition.

Along the same lines, the Stammaitic tangent about what changed from before and after the heavenly voice (statement 9) shows great ambivalence about rejecting Beth Shammai. Compare this with the parallel in *y. Yebam.* 1:6 (3b), which legislates the death penalty for those following Beth Shammai after the heavenly voice.[122] The Bavli recognizes Beth Shammai's superior astuteness, which can possibly justify their practice even against the majority. The Bavli denies the effectiveness of both the heavenly voice and the majority rule in favor of individual intellectual honesty and the need for pluralism that results from it.[123]

The position of the Bavli is reflected not only in these explicit statements but also in the activity of the Bavli redactors. This analysis goes a long way to explain why the Bavli seems so fragmented upon first reading. It does not follow a straight logical flow of ideas because its redactors reworked a preexisting *sugya* instead of writing one from scratch. What at first looks like a confused flow of ideas and fragmented quotations emerges, on comparison with the Yerushalmi material, as a carefully selected and meticulously placed mosaic of citations from older sources combined with new Babylonian Amoraic and Stammaitic material. Like hearing only one side of a telephone conversation, the gaps in the Bavli *sugya* result from its reacting to the earlier Yerushalmi *sugya*. By view-

---

of Rava. This is true especially if we understand, with the Geonim, that R. Yoḥanan rejects the entire prohibition against factions; see above, nn. 90–92. In this reading, Resh Laqish questions the law and R. Yoḥanan, rather than answering the question and defending the prohibition (as he does in the Yerushalmi), undermines Resh Laqish's very assumption that there is a prohibition at all by adducing more problematic sources. The dialogue reads like a competition for who can find the most problematic Mishnah. As Kraemer, *Reading the Rabbis*, 73–74, writes: "R. Yoḥanan, surprisingly, responds to the problem raised by Resh Laqish not by answering it but by saying, in effect, 'And is this the first time you have noticed the problem? There are other prominent examples of such "factionalism" as well!' Resh Laqish tries to explain why the problem he raised was the more difficult one." R. Yoḥanan is transformed from the defender of the prohibition against factions in the Yerushalmi to its greatest detractor in the Bavli.

122. See the last line of the Yerushalmi on p. 201 and analysis at p. 216, below. This Bavli discussion is mostly repeated in *b. Pesaḥ.* 114a; *b. ʿErub.* 6b; and *b. Ḥul.* 44a.

123. See David Kraemer, *Reading the Rabbis: The Talmud as Literature* (Oxford: Oxford University Press, 1996), 79–81; idem, *Mind*, 140–41; and Ben-Menahem, *Judicial Deviation*, 94 n. 134.

ing the Bavli over the backdrop of the Yerushalmi, we come to appreciate its polemical reworking of the Yerushalmi's dialogue and the viewpoints expressed therein.

Louis Jacobs argues that most Bavli *sugyot* are "artificial constructions." Jacobs writes: "The typical Talmudic *sugya* is so arranged that the argument proceeds, in true dramatic fashion, so as to lead by stages to a climax."[124] Using Jacobs's model, we can better appreciate the structure of this *sugya*. The statements of Abaye and Rava are the climax of the *sugya*. The rest of the *sugya*, with its fragmentary dialogues and loose ends, all serve to build up to Abaye and Rava. The Bavli first challenges the Yerushalmi's viewpoint by promoting and reexamining the question presented by *m. Meg.* 1:1. This introduces the allowance for diversity in different cities. The Bavli then discusses allowance for diversity in cases of custom and in cases where one can be passive. All of these limitations are shown to be insufficient, however, because of the cases of Beth Shammai and Beth Hillel in *m. Yebam.* 1:4. The Talmud establishes, tentatively now and conclusively in the continuation of the *sugya* (see below, p. 210), that Beth Shammai did follow their own opinion. Statements 1–5 serve to build up to the tension created by the problematic case of *m. Yebam.* 1:4, which is introduced in statement 6. Statements 7–9 then continue the suspense of the question of statement 6. All of this emphasizes the highly problematical nature of this issue in order to prepare us for the radical reinterpretation of the prohibition against making factions offered by Abaye and Rava. Statement 10 is the climax of the *sugya*. Statements 11 and 12 already take the interpretations of Abaye and Rava for granted and test them out on two other cases. These cases teach that diverse practices in different places are tolerated even regarding important laws like Shabbat and even in the case of a single person traveling between two places.[125] In sum, we see that the Bavli redactors carefully cite, rearrange, and rework

---

124. Louis Jacobs, *Structure and Form in the Babylonian Talmud* (Cambridge: Cambridge University Press, 1991), 100.

125. Kraemer, *Reading the Rabbis*, 82–83, elaborates on the rhetorical effect of these two cases:

> Rhetorically, these flawed objections accomplish two things. First, they illustrate prominent cases in which, even in matters as serious as shabbat and kashrut, a variety of practices was tolerated. Secondly, by pointing out that, in light of the interpretations of Abbaye and Rava, the opinion that demands "don't separate into factions" applies only (possibly) in the same town, the "restrictive" opinion turns out to be very tolerant indeed. By means of the qualifying remarks of Abbaye and Rava, which the Gemara, in these "objections," insists that we notice, the denial of legitimate alternatives in practice is far more restrictive. The objections don't work precisely because the other party *already agrees* that alternatives should be supported.

See also idem, "New Meaning in Ancient Talmudic Texts: A Rhetorical Reading and the Case for Pluralism," *Proceedings of the Rabbinical Assembly* 49 (1988): 212.

fragments of prior sources and join them together to create a cogent and powerful rhetorical presentation.

Conclusion

Y. Pesaḥ. 4:1 (30d) covers two related topics: stability and uniformity of customs (sections A and C) and diversity of legal practice (section B). Regarding the first, the Yerushalmi requires all cities to retain their ancestral customs and even obliges visitors to conform to local stringencies. This conservatism ensures uniformity of practice within each geographical locale. Regarding the second, the Yerushalmi refuses to recognize the possibility of more than one valid practice for all Jews. The prohibition of "Do not make factions" stands as a bulwark against any diversity of halakhic practice. Both of these attitudes stem, in part, from the view of halakha as a practical system of living. Conservatism of custom and unity of law are both important values for effectively putting halakha into practice.

The Yerushalmi's view of custom may also be related to the place of custom in Roman law. Roman law going back to the era of the Republic distinguished between *ius scriptum* and *ius non scriptum* (written law and unwritten law). Customs based on ancient traditions were part of the *ius non scriptum* and were "a source of norms which derived their binding force from the tacit consent of the people and their long-standing practice within the community."[126] Once Rome extended citizenship to all free inhabitants of its empire in 212 C.E. under the enactment of the *constitutio Antoniniana,* law became uniform for all citizens. However, this did not abolish the variety of local practices across various regions and cultures. Rather, as George Mousourakis points out, "During the Dominate the role of custom as a supplementary source of law was further recognized.... The centralization of law-making activity seems to have contributed, in an indirect way, to the enlargement of the role of custom as a source of law during this period."[127] As we noted at the end of chapter 1, Hadrian began a program of unification and codification of Roman law. But this unifying program paradoxically strengthened the importance of custom. The various communities throughout the Roman Empire did not simply abandon their previous laws and practices on becoming citizens and reading a code

---

126. Mousourakis, *The Historical and Institutional Context of Roman Law,* 20. See also H. F. Jolowicz and B. Nicholas, *Historical Introduction to the Study of Roman Law* (Cambridge: Cambridge University Press, 1972), 353–55; Robinson, *Sources of Roman Law,* 25–29. See also David Daube, "Rabbinic Methods of Interpretation and Hellenistic Rhetoric," *Hebrew Union College Annual* 22 (1949): 248 and 58–59, who relates these two concepts in Roman law to the rabbinic belief in the written and oral Torahs.

127. Mousourakis, *The Historical and Institutional Context of Roman Law,* 355.

that contradicted their own laws. Rather, many of these previous traditions continued under the category of custom.

In a similar vein, the Yerushalmi's emphasis on the importance of local custom may actually have resulted from its insistence on unity of law. Once one establishes that only one law may be valid, one still needs a way to justify the existence of variations of practice throughout pious rabbinic communities. Recognizing multiplicity of practice in the area of custom allows one to be more intolerant regarding multiple practices of law.[128]

For the Bavli, on the other hand, halakha is produced by and must stand the test of rabbinic argumentation.[129] Therefore, local customs of commoners cannot compete with reasoned conclusions based on the pool of traditional sources transmitted by the rabbis. The conclusions of the *beth midrash* are more important than the customs and actual practice of the Jewish community.[130]

When it comes to law, the Bavli greatly limits the application of "Do not make factions." Abaye requires uniformity of practice within a city but allows the authorities in different cities to determine the law for their own constituents, even if this results in multiplicity of practice from one locale to the next. Rava, however, goes even further. He recognizes the need for uniformity within a jurisdiction of a court but does not define a jurisdiction based on geography. Even within one city, there may be two courts, with each having its own following, such as Beth Shammai and Beth Hillel. Each court can decide halakha as it sees fit according to its understanding of halakha as long as all members of the court are able to speak with one voice.[131] For both Abaye and Rava, national uniformity—a worthy goal by itself—does not trump the calling of each rabbi to practice the correct law as he understands it. The rabbis of each city or of each court have the right and obligation to legislate halakha for their constituents according to their own reasoned conclusions. For the Bavli, no rabbi can ask his colleague to relinquish his own idea of truth, and so tolerance for both must be accepted.

---

128. Ibid.

129. See further above, pp. 22–26, and below, pp. 378–85.

130. Furthermore, the Bavli's tolerance for pluralism in law dilutes the need for the concept of custom. If a practice is judged primarily based on its status as legitimate law and law can accommodate multiple views, then custom becomes just an unwanted back door for unexamined practices to enter. For the Bavli, no practice can hide under the guise of ancient ancestral tradition if it cannot pass the rabbis' review based on reason. Further investigation is required regarding how the Yerushalmi and Bavli each define the border between law and custom and whether the Bavli places into the category of law any issues that are treated as customs in the Yerushalmi.

131. For further analysis of the views of Abaye and Rava see below, p. 153 n. 74.

Chart 2.1 Comparison chart for sections A and C of *y. Pesaḥ.* 4:1 (30d) and parallels at *t. Moᶜed Qaṭ.* 2:12–14 and *b. Pesaḥ.* 50b–51

***b. Pesaḥ*. 50b-51b**	***y. Pesaḥ*. 4:1 (30d)**	***t. Moᶜed Qaṭ*. 2:14–16**
בני ביישן נהוג דלא הוו אזלין מצור לצידון במעלי שבתא. אתו בנייהו קמיה דרבי יוחנן, אמרו לו: אבהתין אפשר להו, אנן לא אפשר לן.—אמר להו: כבר קיבלו אבותיכם עליהם, שנאמר שמע בני מוסר אביך ואל תטש תורת אמך.	See below, line 5.	
	Section A [1] אעין דשיטין הוו במגדל צבעייה. אתון ושאלון לרבי חנניה חברהון דרבנין מהו מיעבד בהן עבודה אמר להן מכיון שנהגו בהן אבותיכם באיסור אל תשנו מנהג אבותיכם נוחי נפש.	
בני חוזאי נהגי דמפרשי חלה מארוזא. אתו ואמרו ליה לרב יוסף. אמר להו: ניכלה זר באפייהו. איתיביה אביי: **דברים המותרים ואחרים נהגו בהן איסור אי אתה רשאי להתירן בפניהם.** אמר לו: ולאו מי איתמר עלה, אמר רב חסדא: בכותאי. כותאי מאי טעמא משום דמסרכי מילתא, הנך אינשי נמי סרכי מילתא? אלא אמר רב אשי: חזינן, אי רובן אורז אכלי לא ניכלה זר באפייהו, דילמא משתכחא תורת חלה מינייהו. ואי רובן דגן אכלי ניכלה זר באפייהו, דילמא אתי לאפרושי מן החיוב על הפטור ומן הפטור על החיוב.		

הלכה יד **יושבין על ספסל של גוים בשבת שבראשונה היו אומ' אין יושבין על ספסל של גוים בשבת עד שבא ר' עקיבא ולימד שיושבין על ספסל של גוים בשבת** **הלכה טו** **ומעשה ברבן גמליאל שהיה יושב על ספסל של גוים בשבת בעכו אמרו לו לא היו נוהגין כן להיות יושבין על ספסל של גוים בשבת ולא רצה לומר מותרין אתם אלא עמד והלך לו** **מעשה ביהודה והלל בניו של רבן גמליאל שנכנסו לרחוץ בכבול אמרו להם לא היו נוהגין להיות רוחצין שני אחין כאחד לא רצו לומר להם מותרין אתם אלא נכנסו ורחצו זה אחר זה** **הלכה טז** **שוב מעשה ביהודה והלל בניו של רבן גמליאל שהיו יוצאין בקורדקיסין של זהב בשבת בבירי אמ' להם לא היו נוהגין כן להיות יוצאין בקורד־קיסין של זהב בשבת לא רצו לומר להם מותרין אתם אלא שלחום ביד עבדיהם**	[2] רבי אלעזר בשם רבי אבין כל דבר שאינו יודע שהוא מותר וטועה בו באיסור נשאל והן מתירין לו וכל דבר שהוא יודע בו שהוא מותר והוא נוהג בו באיסור נשאל אין מתירין לו. [3][a] **יושבין על ספסלו של גוי בשבת. מעשה ברבן גמליאל שישב לו על ספסילו של גוי בשבת בעכו. אמרו לו לא היו נוהגין כן להיות יושבין על ספסילו של גוי בשבת ולא רצה לומר להן מותר לעשות כן אלא עמד והלך לו.** [b] **מעשה ביהודה ובהלל בניו של רבן גמליאל שנכנסו לרחוץ במרחץ בכבול אמרו להן לא נהגו כן להיות רוחצין שני אחים כאחת ולא רצו לומר מותר כן אלא נכנסו זה אחר זה.** [c] **ועוד שיצאו לטייל בקורדקיות של זהב בלילי שבת בבירו אמרו להן לא נהגו כאן להיות מטיילין בקורדקיות של זהב בשבת ולא רצו לומר להן מותר כן אלא שילחו ביד עבדיהן.**	גופא, **דברים המותרין ואחרים נהגו בהן איסור אי אתה רשאי להתירן בפניהן.** אמר רב חסדא: בכותאי עסקינן. וכולי עלמא לא? והתניא: **רוחצין שני אחין כאחד, ואין רוח־צין שני אחין בכבול.** **ומעשה ביהודה והלל בניו של רבן גמליאל, שרחצו שניהם כאחד בכבול, ולעזה עליהן כל המדינה, אמרו: מימינו לא ראינו כך. ונשמט הלל ויצא לבית החיצון, ולא רצה לומר להן מותרין אתם.** **יוצאים בקורדקיסון בשבת, ואין יוצאין בקורדקיסון בשבת בבירי.** **ומעשה ביהודה והלל בניו של רבן גמליאל שיצאו בקורדקיסון בשבת בבירי, ולעזה עליהן המדינה.** **ואמרו: מימינו לא ראינו כך, ושמ־טום ונתנום לעבדיהן, ולא רצו לומר להן מותרין אתם.** **ויושבין על ספסלי נכרים בשבת, ואינן יושבין על ספסלי נכרים בשבת בעכו.** **ומעשה ברבן שמעון בן גמליאל שישב על ספסלי נכרים בשבת בעכו, ולעזה עליו כל המדינה, אמרו: מימינו לא ראינו כך. נשמט על גבי קרקע, ולא רצה לומר להן מותרין אתם.** בני מדינת הים נמי, כיון דלא שכיחי רבנן גבייהו—ככותים דמו...
	[4] ולא סוף דבר פסח אלא אפילו מנהג קיבלו עליהן חרמי טיבריה וגרוסי צפורי דשושי עכו שלא לעשות מלאכה בחולו של מועד. ניחא גרוסי צפורין דשושי עכו. חרמי טיבריה ואינן ממעטין בשמחת הרגל. צד הוא בחכה צד הוא במכמורת אפילו כן אינן ממעטין בשמחת הרגל? ר' אימי מיקל לון שהן ממעטין בשמחת הרגל גלו ממקום למקום וביקשו לחזור בהן.	

See first row.	[5] ייבא כהדא דאמר רבי בא בני מישא קיבלו עליהן שלא לפרש בים הגדול. אתון שאלון לרבי. אמרין ליה אבותינו נהגו שלא לפרש בים הגדול אנו מה אנו אמר להן מכיון שנהגו בהן אבותיכם באיסור אל תשנו מנהג אבו־תיכם נוחי נפש. ואין אדם נשאל על נדרו תמן משנדר נשאל ברם הכא אבותיכם נדרו כל שכן יהו מותרים אמר רבי חנניה לא מן הדא אלא מן הדא רבי תלמידיה דרבי יודה הוה דרבי יודה אמר אסור לפרש בים הגדול.	
… Rabbah bar bar Ḥannah eats stomach fat in Babylonia … eating leftovers during Shevi^cit …		
	Section B … discussion of *lo titgodedu* …	
בשלמא **ההולך ממקום שעושין למקום שאין עושין נותנין עליו חומרי מקום שהלך לשם, ואל ישנה אדם מפני המחלוקת** ולא ליעביד. אלא: **ממקום שאין עושין למקום שעושין—אל ישנה אדם מפני המחלוקת,** ונעביד? הא אמרת: **נות־נין עליו חומרי מקום שהלך לשם וחומרי מקום שיצא משם**? אמר אביי: ארישא. רבא אמר: לעולם אסיפא, והכי קאמר: אין בזו מפני שינוי המחלוקת. מאי קא אמרת: הרואה אומר מלאכה אסורה—מימר אמרי: כמה בטלני הוי בשוקא.	Section C ניחא ממקום שעושין למקום שאין עושין ממקום שאין עושין למקום שעושין ויבטל שהרי כמה בטילין יש לו באותו מקום רבי סימון בשם רבי יוחנן במתמיה	

Chart 2.2 Comparison chart for section B of *y. Pesaḥ*. 4:1 (30d) and *b. Yebam*. 13b–14a

***b. Yebam*. 13b–14a**	***y. Pesaḥ*. 4:1 (30d)**
[1] תנן התם: מגילה נקראת באחד עשר, ובשנים עשר, ובשלשה עשר, ובארבעה עשר, ובחמשה עשר, לא פחות ולא יותר. (משנה מגילה א, א)	
אמר ליה ריש לקיש לר׳ יוחנן, איקרי כאן: לא תתגודדו, לא תעשו אגודות אגודות.	[B][1]רבי שמעון בן לקיש שאל לר׳ יוחנן ואינו אסור משום בל תתגודדו
האי לא תתגודדו מיבעי ליה לגופיה, דאמר רחמנא: לא תעשו חבורה על מת? אם כן, לימא קרא לא תגודדו, מאי תתגודדו? שמע מינה להכי הוא דאתא. ואימא: כוליה להכי הוא דאתא? אם כן, לימא קרא לא תגודו, מאי לא תתגודדו? שמע מינה תרתי.	
	אמר ליה בשעה שאילו עושין כבית שמאי ואילו עושין כבית הלל
	[2] בית שמאי ובית הלל אין הלכה כבית הלל אמר ליה בשעה שאילו עושין כרבי מאיר ואילו עושין כרבי יוסה
	[3] רבי מאיר ור׳ יוסי אין הלכה כרבי יוסי אמר ליה תרי תניין אינון על דרבי מאיר ותרין תניין אינון על דרבי יוסי
	[4] אמר ליה הרי ראש השנה ויום הכיפורים ביהודה נהגו כר׳ עקיבה ובגליל נהגו כרבי יוחנן בן נורי אמר ליה שנייה היא שאם עבר ועשה ביהודה כגליל ובגליל כיהודה יצא
	[5] הרי פורים הרי אילו קורין בי״ד ואילו קורין בט״ו
[2] אמר ליה, עד כאן לא שנית: מקום שנהגו לעשות מלאכה בערבי פסחים עד חצות עושין, מקום שנהגו שלא לעשות אין עושין? (משנה פסחים ד, א)	
[3] אמר ליה: אמינא לך אנא איסורא, דאמר רב שמן בר אבא אמר ר׳ יוחנן: לקיים את ימי הפורים בזמניהם (אסתר ט, לא) זמנים הרבה תיקנו להם חכמים ואת אמרת לי מנהגא.	אמר ליה מי שסידר את המשנה סמכה למקרא משפחה ומשפחה מדינה ומדינה ועיר ועיר (אסתר ט, כח)
[4] והתם לאו איסורא הויא? והתנן: בלילה בית שמאי אוסרין, ובית הלל מתירין? (משנה פסחים ד, ה)	
[5] (אמר ליה) התם, הרואה אומר מלאכה הוא דלית ליה.	[C] ניחא ממקום שעושין למקום שאין עושין ממקום שאין עושין למקום שעושין ויבטל שהרי כמה בטילין יש לו באותו מקום? רבי סימון בשם רבי יוחנן במתמיה

[6] והא בית שמאי מתירין הצרות לאחים, ובית הלל אוסרים? (משנה יבמות א, ד) [7] מי סברת עשו בית שמאי כדבריהם? לא עשו בית שמאי כדבריהם. [8] ור' יוחנן אמר: עשו ועשו. [9] ובפלוגתא [דרב ושמואל], דרב אומר: לא עשו בית שמאי כדבריהם, ושמואל אמר: עשו ועשו. אימת? אילימא קודם בת קול, מאי טעמא דמאן דאמר לא עשו? ואלא לאחר בת קול, מאי טעמא דמאן דאמר עשו? אי בעית אימא: קודם בת קול, ואי בעית אימא: לאחר בת קול. אי בעית אימא קודם בת קול, וכגון דבית הלל רובא, למאן דאמר לא עשו, דהא בית הלל רובא. ומאן דאמר עשו, כי אזלינן בתר רובא היכא דכי הדדי נינהו, הכא בית שמאי מחדדי טפי. ואי בעית אימא לאחר בת קול, מאן דאמר לא עשו, דהא נפקא בת קול. ומאן דאמר עשו, רבי יהושע היא, דאמר: אין משגיחין בבת קול. ומאן דאמר עשו, קרינן כאן: לא תתגודדו, לא תעשו אגו־דות אגודות? [10][a] אמר אביי: כי אמרינן לא תתגודדו כגון שתי בתי דינים בעיר אחת, הללו מורים כדברי בית שמאי והללו מורים כדברי בית הלל, אבל שתי בתי דינים בשתי עיירות לית לן בה. [b] אמר ליה רבא: והא בית שמאי ובית הלל כשתי בתי דינים בעיר אחת דמי! אלא אמר רבא: כי אמרינן לא תתגודדו כגון בית דין בעיר אחת, פלג מורין כדברי בית שמאי ופלג מורין כדברי בית הלל, אבל שתי בתי דינין בעיר אחת לית לן בה.	

3

"Each River Follows Its Own Course": Rabbis as Local Authorities

Diverse Practices in Different Cities

We saw in the previous chapter that both Talmuds tolerate diverse practices in different cities regarding matters of custom. However, diverse practices in different cities regarding matters of halakha are prohibited according to the Yerushalmi's definition of "Do not make factions," but permitted by Abaye and Rava in the Bavli. Numerous stories recorded in both Talmuds make it clear that this discussion of intercity diversity was not only theoretical but was a real-life concern.[1] This chapter evaluates these stories in light of the findings of chapter 2 in order to test whether the difference found between the Yerushalmi and Bavli in a legal context also bears out in narrative contexts. That is, are the differing attitudes of the Yerushalmi and Bavli toward diversity of practice as evidenced in their interpretations of "Do not make factions" also reflected in the way each Talmud retells rabbinic stories that involve such diversity. As we will see, this analysis not only substantiates the conclusions of chapter 2, but these stories also provide further insight into the reasons for the difference between the Yerushalmi and Bavli attitudes toward diversity.

It should be made clear that we are not interested in stories concerning differences of practice that are due only to different local circumstances. The practice in one city may differ from that in another city when the law is based on such realities as language and terminology,[2] dress,[3] common

1. Regardless of the historicity of these stories, analysis of the attitudes reflected in the way these narratives are told can offer insight into the viewpoints of their editors regarding legal pluralism.

2. See, for example, *b. Pesaḥ.* 3a; *b. Pesaḥ.* 37a = *b. Beṣah* 22b; *b. Yoma* 55a; *b. Beṣah* 15a; *b. Ned.* 49a, 52b; *b. B. Qam.* 119b; *b. Ḥul.* 66a. In all of these cases and the ones in the following notes, it is usually the Stam that locates the source of a dispute in different regional circumstances. In some cases, this explanation may be based on historical information and in others it is just one conjecture among many possibilities. In providing such explanations, the Stam assumes that these disputes are not only theoretical but that both sides were practiced in each locale.

3. See *b. Šabb.* 12a.

practices of the citizens,[4] market regulations,[5] other local regulations,[6] access to resources,[7] or when different practices are legislated by the law itself.[8] In other cases, however, different practices in cities are based on

---

4. See *b. ʿErub.* 28a-b, where Rav changed the blessing on a vegetable because it was eaten in Babylonia but not in Palestine. *Y. Ter.* 8:2 (45c) reports that in the place of R. Ḥiyya people would purposely make holes in fruit and so R. Ḥiyya ignored the law against eating such fruit. See also *b. Giṭ.* 54a=*b. Bek.* 30a. *B. Bek.* 32a cites a difference in law based on common use of bone.

5. See *b. Šabb.* 148b; *b. B. Meṣiʿa* 40a, 117a; and *b. B. Bat.* 12a.

6. See *b. Giṭ.* 81a on court regulations regarding rumors. Another example is in *b. Yebam.* 99b (=*b. Ketub.* 28b; and see parallels in *y. Yebam.* 11:5 [12a]; *y. Ketub.* 2:7 [26d] and 2:10 [26d)), which discusses conventions regarding how to judge priestly lineage:

> דתניא: **אין חולקין תרומה לעבד אלא אם כן רבו עמו, דברי ר׳ יהודה; ר׳ יוסי אומר, יכול שיאמר: אם כהן אני תנו לי בשביל עצמי, ואם עבד כהן אני תנו לי בשביל רבי. במקומו של ר׳ יהודה היו מעלין מתרומה ליוחסין, במקומו של ר׳ יוסי לא היו מעלין מתרומה ליוחסין.**
>
> תניא: **אמר רבי אלעזר בר צדוק: מימי לא העדתי אלא עדות אחד, והעלו עבד לכהונה על פי.** העלו ס״ד? השתא בהמתן של צדיקים אין הקב״ה מביא תקלה על ידן, צדיקים עצמן לא כ״ש! אלא אימא: בקשו להעלות עבד לכהונה על פי, חזא באתריה דר׳ יוסי, ואזל ואסהיד באתריה דרבי יהודה.
>
> For it was taught: **We do not distribute *terumah* to a slave unless his master is with him, these are the words of R. Yehudah. R. Yose says, the slave may claim, "If I am a priest, give me for my own sake; and if I am a priest's slave, give me for the sake of my master."**
>
> **In the place of R. Yehudah, they would judge a person to be of proper priestly status based on [whether he was given] *terumah*. In the place of R. Yose, they would not judge a person's status based on [whether he was given] *terumah*.**
>
> It was taught: **R. Eleazar bar Ṣadoq said, "During the whole of my lifetime I have testified only once, and they [mistakenly] raised a slave to the status of priesthood based on my testimony."** Can it really be that they raised? If the Holy One, blessed be He, does not cause an offense to be committed through the animals of the righteous, how much less through the righteous themselves! Rather, read: "They desired to raise a slave to the status of priesthood through my testimony." He witnessed [the occurrence] in the place of R. Yose but went and testified in the place of R. Yehudah.

The Gemara quotes *t. Yebam.* 12:6 concerning a dispute in the case of a child of a priestess who was confused with the child of the priestess' maid. Both children may eat *terumah*. R. Yehudah, however, requires that both be present together in order to receive *terumah*. The continuation of the Gemara testifies that the towns of each rabbi actually practiced these opinions. The Gemara explains that R. Yehudah's position is based on the convention in R. Yehudah's town that receiving *terumah* by an individual is proof of his proper lineage. Therefore, a slave who receives *terumah* by himself will later be mistakenly taken for a priest even when freed from his priestly master. R. Yose says they may receive *terumah* separately because in his town, no such judgment was made regarding lineage.

R. Eleazar bar Ṣadoq saw a slave receive individually in the place of R. Yose and testified as such in the place of R. Yehudah. R. Yehudah's place thus wrongly assumed he was a priest. In this case, the importance of following local practice is because of a convention about how to judge who is a proper priest. R. Yose would in fact agree that the slave is not a priest.

7. For example a law based on the rarity of oil in *b. Šabb.* 111b and *b. B. Bat.* 91a; of earth for clay in *b. B. Meṣiʿa* 74a; of animals and birds in *b. Menaḥ.* 107b; or wine in *b. Pesaḥ.* 107a.

8. Such as *m. Meg.* 1:1. In this category also falls the extra day of festivals practiced in

substantive halakhic disputes.[9] We will focus attention on the latter category.

One telling formula appears twice in the Bavli and sums up the Bavli's point of view: "Each river follows its own course."[10] Both citations regard food laws and neither has a parallel in the Yerushalmi.[11] One occurrence of the formula appears at *b. Ḥul.* 57a in relation to conflicting traditions from two cities:

> אמר רב הונא אמר רב: שמוטת ירך בעוף כשרה. א"ל רבה בר רב הונא לרב הונא, והא רבנן דאתו מפומבדיתא אמרו: רב יהודה משמיה דרב אמר שמוטת ירך בעוף טרפה! אמר ליה: ברי, נהרא נהרא ופשטיה.
>
> Rav Huna said in the name of Rav: "If the femur of a bird was dislodged, it is permitted." Rabbah the son of Rav Huna said to Rav Huna, "But the rabbis who came from Pumbedita said: 'Rav Yehudah in the name of Rav said, If the femur of a bird was dislodged it is *ṭerefah*!'" He replied: "My son, each river follows its own course."

Rav Huna quotes Rav permitting a bird with a dislodged leg while the rabbis of Pumbedita quote Rav prohibiting it. Rav Huna's son questions his father about this contradiction. Rav Huna responds that each river follows its own course. There are two contradictory traditions concerning what Rav said, only one of which can be authentic.[12] What is significant

Babylonia. Palestine and parts of Babylonia close to Jerusalem practice one day of festival while the rest of Babylonia practices two. This difference is due not to a dispute among rabbis but to geographic reality. There is some controversy regarding certain cities and festivals (on which see *b. Roš Haš.* 21a; *b. Pesaḥ.* 52a, quoted partially above, p. 95), and other details (see *b. Beṣah* 4b); however, nobody diputes the basic law. See articles cited above, p. 96 n. 47.

9. See examples in stories below. Some issues are on the border between local customary practices and halakha, and it is not always easy to distinguish between the two categories. For example, in Nehardea they would read *Ketubim* during Minḥa on Shabbat but not in other places (*b. Šabb.* 116b). In some places, people walked in front of the coffin while, in other places, they walked in back of it (*b. Šabb.* 153a).

10. See below. Cf. *b. Giṭ.* 60b, where the literal sense of this phrase is meant and refers to an actual river, "נהרא כפשטיה ליזיל—Let the river follow its course."

11. The prevalence of this concept of tolerance for local practices in the Yerushalmi will be discussed in a later section of this chapter.

12. Rashi here explains that both traditions are authentic. Rav permitted such a bird in his hometown of Sura. When he went to visit Pumbedita and saw that they were stringent, however, he did not give them permission to be lenient. According to Rashi, Rav apparently accepted the constraint of the *baraita* "Things that are permitted, yet others treat them as forbidden, you may not permit them in their presence" (*b. Pesaḥ.* 50b-51a; see above, p. 89). Rav recognized the validity of opposite laws in a different city and insisted that each locale continue its own prevailing practice. Rashi's explanation, however, seems apologetic; nothing in the Talmud suggests that Rav changed his ruling depending on where he was. Rather,

here is that Rav Huna does not respond by either changing his mind or by rejecting the Pumbeditan tradition. Rather, he recognizes that there are two possibilities and takes a pluralistic stance that each place may follow its own received tradition.

The other context in which this formula appears is *b. Ḥul.* 18b:

כי סליק רבי זירא אכל מוגרמת דרב ושמואל, אמרי ליה: לאו מאתריה דרב ושמואל את? אמר להו: מאן אמרה? יוסף בר חייא, יוסף בר חייא מכולי עלמא גמיר שמע רב יוסף איקפד...

ור׳ זירא לית ליה **נותנין עליו חומרי המקום שיצא משם וחומרי המקום שהלך לשם**?[13]

אמר אביי: הני מילי מבבל לבבל ומארץ ישראל לארץ ישראל, אי נמי מארץ ישראל לבבל, אבל מבבל לארץ ישראל, כיון דאנן כייפינן להו עבדינן כוותייהו.

רב אשי אמר: אפילו תימא מבבל לארץ ישראל, הני מילי היכא דדעתו לחזור, ר׳ זירא אין דעתו לחזור הוה.[14]

אמר ליה אביי לרב יוסף: והא רבנן דאתו ממחוזא אמרי, אמר רבי זירא משמיה דרב נחמן: מוגרמת כשרה! א״ל: נהרא נהרא ופשטיה.

When R. Zeira went up [to Palestine] he ate an animal slaughtered by a slanting cut [and thus prohibited] according to Rav and Shmuel. They [the residents of Palestine] told him, "Are you not from the place of Rav and Shmuel?" He told them, "Who said this [tradition about Rav and Shmuel]? Yosef bar Ḥiyya? Yosef bar Ḥiyya learns from everyone [and is mistaken about this attribution]. Rav Yosef heard and took exception...."

But does R. Zeira not agree that "**We place upon him the stringencies of the place of his origin and the stringencies of his place of destination**"?[13]

Abaye said: That is only [when he goes] from [one town in] Babylonia to [another in] Babylonia, or from [one town in] Israel to [another in] Israel, or from [a town in] Israel to [one in] Babylonia; but not [when he goes] from [a town in] Babylonia to [one in] Israel, for since we submit to them, we do as they do.

Rav Ashi said: You may even say [that one must be stringent when he goes] from [one town in] Babylonia to [one in] Israel; however, that is where his intention is to return; but R. Zeira had no intention of returning.[14]

Abaye said to Rav Yosef, "But the rabbis who came from Maḥoza said: 'R. Zeira said in the name of Rav Naḥman that an animal

---

Rav Huna advises that each city should practice according to its version of Rav's ruling even though only one can be authentic. This tolerance is therefore not based on multivocality of Sinaitic revelation but rather on an acceptance of the confusions that naturally develop in the legislation and transmission of a legal system.

13. *M. Pesaḥ.* 4:1.

14. This *sugya* has a parallel at *b. Pesaḥ.* 51a; see pp. 90 and 94–95, esp. nn. 44–45.

> slaughtered by a slanting cut is kosher'?" He responded, "Each river follows its own course."

The citizens of Palestine, who were lenient regarding an animal slaughtered in a certain way, questioned R. Zeira for eating with them because R. Zeira came from Babylonia where Rav and Shmuel prohibit such an animal. These citizens recognize the existence of different practices but also know the rule of *m. Pesaḥ.* 4:1 that one must keep the stringency of his place of origin. R. Zeira answers that he is not sure whether the tradition in the name of Rav and Shmuel is authentic. The rabbi who was responsible for transmitting this tradition then expresses his personal affront and insists that his traditions are trustworthy. Abaye then offers a second explanation—that when one goes from Babylonia to Israel then one may practice the leniencies of Israel whose laws are superior. A third explanation, given by Rav Ashi, is that R. Zeira was allowed to adopt the local custom because he intended to remain there.

Abaye then points out that even in Babylonia there is one city that is lenient on the matter.[15] To this Rav Yosef responds, "Each river follows its own course." Every city should follow its own practice and that level of diversity is tolerated. Ben-Menahem, based on these sources, writes that the Bavli "often comments, without objection, that in Babylon [*sic*] the people of a given locale followed the ruling of Rabbi A while those of another area observed the contradictory ruling of Rabbi B."[16] Questions only arise when one travels from one place to another.

Having established that diverse practices from one Babylonian city to the next were tolerated, we can investigate how rabbis from different cities treated one another when they met. Most stories about two colleagues meeting involve one rabbi going to visit the city where the other rabbi lives. When the opinions of the visiting and local rabbi differ, a number of questions arise. Does the visiting rabbi have to conform to local practice or at least hide his own deviant practice? Can the local rabbi force the visitor to conform? If the visiting rabbi is asked a question, can he give a halakhic decision differing from that of the local rabbi?

---

15. In the current form of the *sugya*, Abaye's conversation with Rav Yosef does not seem to flow from what comes before it. Abaye's comment may be a fourth explanation for R. Zeira's actions. This explanation says that although R. Zeira was from Babylonia where most cities prohibit, he was from a city that was lenient. However, we only find R. Zeira studying under Rav Huna in Sura and under Rav Yehudah in Pumbedita (*b. Ber.* 39a), which are the cities of Rav and Shmuel, and never in Maḥoza. Abaye's comment may therefore stand alone as an interesting point about the variety of practice between various cities. Indeed, Rav Yosef's response expresses this thought explicitly. Amit, *Pesaḥim*, 86–89, reconstructs the original *sugya* in which this conversation directly continues Rav Yosef's statement at the beginning of the story, partially cited here.

16. Ben-Menahem, *Judicial Deviation*, 87.

The second text quoted above deals with a traveler between Palestine and Babylonia and treats such intercountry cases as exceptional.[17] But what about travelers within each country? Examples used in the following sections have been extracted from a search across both Talmuds for the terms אתריה ד... and במקומו של ("the place of").[18] I have underlined these words when they appear in texts below. I have chosen those texts from within this search that are most relevant to the issue of diversity of practice, and I have included parallel, nearby, and other directly relevant texts where appropriate. Hopefully, the result is a representative sampling of the full contents of the Talmuds.[19]

Visiting Colleagues Issuing Rulings

One set of stories that may shed light on tolerance for diverse practice involves cases in which one rabbi visits the town of another and finds himself in a position to rule on a legal matter about which he disagrees with the local authority. Many of these stories recount times when Rav and Shmuel visited each other's towns. These narratives reveal some degree of tolerance in their portrayal of the respect that each showed for the other's local authority. One such story, found at *b. B. Bat.* 153a, involves second-generation students of Rav and Shmuel:

---

17. Regarding diversity of practice between Palestine and Babylonia, both Talmuds generally seem comfortable that such differences should exist. The Talmuds report many such instances in which no indication is given that this is problematic. See, for example, *y. Ber.* 1:6 (3d) and examples collected in Amos Sofer, "Ha lan ve-ha le-hu," *Sinai* 113 (1994): 84–89. To be sure, there was much tension between sages of the two countries; see Saul Lieberman, "Kakh hayah ve-kakh yihyeh," *Cathedra* 17 (1981) (Hebrew): 3–10; and Joshua Schwartz, "Tension Between Palestinian Scholars and Babylonian Olim in Amoraic Palestine," *Journal for the Study of Judaism* 11 (1980): 78–94. However, the examples cited in those articles indicate that those tensions were caused by personal and cultural differences and resentments more than by legal differences.

In order to facilitate comparison between Yerushalmi and Bavli attitudes toward local authority, we focus in this chapter on diversity of practice across cities within each country. Although beyond the scope of this study, an expanded study on all cases of travelers between the countries remains a desideratum.

18. Other relevant terms that sometimes occur in conjuction with "the place of" are: "איקלע—to happen to come," "אזל—went," "נחית—went (down)," and "על—entered." These terms, however, are too broad to be very useful.

19. The results of my search include and expand on the Talmudic texts selected by Ben-Menahem et al., *Controversy and Dialogue in Halakhic Sources*, 2:753–55. I did not discuss *b. Nid.* 20b because the reason ʿUla did not issue a ruling in the place of R. Yehudah there is necessarily not out of deference to him as the local authority for all matters but rather in deference to his expertise in the area of *niddah* laws.

ההוא דאתא לקמיה דרב נחמן לנהרדעא, שדריה לקמיה דר' ירמיה בר אבא לשום טמיא,
אמר: הכא אתרא דשמואל, היכי נעביד כוותיה דרב.

> A certain person once came before Rav Naḥman in Nehardea [to receive a ruling]. He [Rav Naḥman] sent him to R. Yirmiah b. Abba in Shumtamya, saying, "This is Shmuel's place. How could we rule in accordance with Rav?"[20]

Rav and Shmuel dispute whether a person who gifted his property when sick using the formula "in life or in death" may retract the gift if he recovers. Rav permits while Shmuel prohibits. One such recovered philanthropist came before Rav Naḥman expecting a ruling in accordance with Rav. Rav Naḥman, however, refers him to R. Yirmiah bar Abba, a student of Rav who lived in another town, because Rav Naḥman would not issue a ruling against Shmuel in the latter's town.

In two other stories involving Rav and Shmuel themselves, it is the Stam that infers from the details of the story that each of these Amoraim refused to rule in accordance with his own opinion when in the place of a colleague.[21] In both of these instances, the stories themselves make no indication of where the rabbis were situated or why they refrained from ruling. The explanation of the Stam that these sages respected one another's domain therefore reflects more about the assumptions of the Stam than about the Amoraim themselves.

The consequences for one who does rule against the local rabbi are spelled out at *b. Šabb.* 19b:

ההוא תלמידא דאורי בחרתא דארגיז כרבי שמעון, שמתיה רב המנונא. והא כרבי שמעון
סבירא לן![22] באתריה דרב הוה, לא איבעי ליה למיעבד הכי.

> A certain disciple issued a ruling in Ḥarta of Argiz in accordance with R. Shimon. R. Hamnuna banned him. But we agree with R. Shimon![22] It was in Rav's town, and so he should have acted accordingly.

Regarding certain cases of *muqṣeh* (handling unusable items on Shabbat), Rav rules strictly in accordance with R. Yehudah while Shmuel rules leniently in accordance with R. Shimon. A student who ruled in accordance with Shmuel in the place of Rav[23] was excommunicated even though

---

20. See futher analysis of this story in Aharon Oppenheimer, *Babylonia Judaica in the Talmudic Period* (Wiesbaden: Ludwig Reichert, 1983), 408–10.

21. See *b. Pesaḥ.* 30a, *b. Ḥul.* 53b, and further analysis at Hidary, "Tolerance for Diversity," 110–12.

22. See Halivni, *Meqorot u-mesorot*, Shabbat, 58–59, for alternative readings.

23. This does not mean that Rav lived there or was even necessarily alive at the time. Rather, this city practiced according to Rav in this matter. R. Hamnuna was actually the rabbi of Ḥarta of Argiz (*b. ʿErub.* 63a). See ibid., 60.

Shmuel represented the majority opinion. This heavy punishment may have been appropriate in this case because the traveler was a student and had no right to contradict the local elder rabbi on two accounts. This story, at least according to the Stam's reading, confirms that the local authority of a rabbi is strictly guarded even when it opposes the widespread practice outside that city.[24]

At a countrywide level, the respect shown by visiting rabbis for the local authority reflects an attitude of pluralism. There is no one absolute law for all places that any one rabbi can impose on all Jews. Rather, each rabbi has authority to decide the law for his town and that authority is respected by visiting rabbis.

At a local level, however, the inability of a visitor to contradict the local rabbi shows relative intolerance for any deviation of practice within that locale.[25] This is similar to the pattern seen in the previous chapter regarding customs. Varying customs in different cities are acceptable, and each locale is expected to continue its traditions. However, a person traveling from one place to another is expected to conform to the local custom or at least to hide the custom of his place of origin in order not to display any diversity within a town.

The motivation to keep unity of customs within a town, seen in the previous chapter, seems to be a more genuine expression of intolerance of diversity and a wish for unity than the examples examined in this chapter. In these cases, the goal is not so much unity of practice as much as upholding the respect and authority due to the local rabbi. A dissenting visitor not only disrupts unity among the residents but also challenges the power of the local rabbi. Nevertheless, the net effect of upholding the sole power of the local rabbi to make all decisions is to create an environment that does not tolerate opposing legal decisions.[26] In sum, on a local level

---

24. Two other possible sources that seem to confirm this conclusion are *b. Ber.* 63a and *b. Nid.* 20b. However, see David Halivni, "The Role of the Mara D'atra in Jewish Law," *Proceedings of the Rabbinical Assembly of America* 38 (1976): 124–29, who argues that these sources are not relevant.

25. Rabbinic sources do not provide enough information about how two resident rabbis of a town would settle a dispute and how one rabbi would become the local authority rather than his colleague. Perhaps the cities themselves were split into two sections or perhaps one rabbi was generally recognized—either by his colleagues or by the populus—as more competent than the other, or was appointed—either by the previous authority or by the patriarch. Different mechanisms may have applied in different times and places. Regardless of how one became the local authority, it is clear that the stories analyzed in this chapter do assume that certain Babylonian cities were under the jurisdiction of certain rabbis.

26. Another limitation on legal pluralism besides local authority is the authority of the rabbi who first rules on a given case. *T. ʿEd.* 1:5 prohibits one from asking for a second opinion, thus precluding the possibility of having more than one valid option to choose from:

נישאל לחכם אחד וטימא לו לא ישאל לחכם אחר נשאל לחכם וטיהר לו לא ישאל לחכם אחר

If one asked one sage who declared impure, one may not ask another sage. If one

resident rabbis were usually intolerant of any visitor teaching divergent practices. As a corollary to local intolerance, visiting rabbis respected the authority of the local rabbi thus maintaining a high level of tolerance for multiple practices on a country-wide level.

Practice of Visiting Colleagues

In other cases, the visiting rabbi is faced with the question not of proclaiming decisions for others against the local rabbi but rather deciding whether he should himself practice in opposition to the local halakha. In one such case involving the laws of *eruvin,* Rav keeps the stringency of his place of origin. *B. ʿErubin* 93b-94a relates:

> אתמר, כותל שבין שתי חצירות שנפל, רב אמר: אין מטלטלין בו אלא בארבע אמות, ושמואל אמר: זה מטלטל עד עיקר מחיצה, וזה מטלטל עד עיקר מחיצה.
> והא דרב לאו בפירוש אתמר, אלא מכללא אתמר. דרב ושמואל הוו יתבי בההוא חצר, נפל גודא דביני ביני. אמר להו שמואל: שקולו גלימא נגידו בה. אהדרינהו רב לאפיה. אמר להו שמואל: אי קפיד אבא שקולו הימניה וקטרו בה.
> ולשמואל למה לי הא? הא אמר: זה מטלטל עד עיקר מחיצה, וזה מטלטל עד עיקר מחיצה! שמואל עביד לצניעותא בעלמא. ורב, אי סבירא ליה דאסיר לימא ליה! אתריה דשמואל הוה. אי הכי, מאי טעמא אהדרינהו לאפיה? דלא נימרו כשמואל סבירא ליה, והדר ביה משמעתיה.
>
> It was said: If a wall between two courtyards fell, Rav says, "One may not carry in it except four cubits," but Shmuel said, "Both parties may carry until the foundation of the wall."
> This statement of Rav, however, was not said explicitly but only derived. For Rav and Shmuel were once sitting in a certain courtyard. The wall between them collapsed. Shmuel said to them

---

asked one sage who declared pure one may not ask another sage. (*t. ʿEd.* 1:5 following ms. Erfurt)

This legislation creates an environment similar to that created by local authorities. Each rabbi has authority to preside over any case that comes before him first. All other rabbis must respect the first rabbi's decision and may not rule differently on it even if they disagree. See discussion of this rule at Charlotte Fonrobert, *Menstrual Purity: Rabbinic and Christian Reconstructions of Biblical Gender* (Stanford: Stanford University Press, 2000), 263 nn. 48–49.

Ms. Vienna and the first printing of this Tosefta have only the first half, "נשאל לחכם וטמא לו לא ישאל לחכם," and omit the second half. According to this version, the Tosefta may be in agreement with an alternate version of the *baraita* quoted in the Talmuds: "והתניא, חכם שטימא—אין חבירו רשאי לטהר, אסר—אין חבירו רשאי להתיר" (*b. Ḥul.* 44b=*b. Nid.* 20b=*b. ʿAbod. Zar.* 7a). In this version one may not ask for a second opinion after receiving a stringent ruling. This implies that one may seek a second opinion after receiving a lenient ruling. This is made explicit in *y. Šabb.* 19:1 (16d) and *b. Ber.* 63b. In this version, the law is simply meant to prevent one from shopping around for a leniency.

> [his attendants], "Take a cloak and spread it out." Rav turned away his face. Shmuel said to them, "If Abba is annoyed let him take his belt and tie it."
> Why did Shmuel need this? After all he said, "Both parties may carry until the foundation of the wall." Shmuel made it only for privacy. And Rav, if he thinks it is forbidden why does he not say so to him? It was <u>the place of Shmuel</u>. If so, why did he [Rav] turn away his face? So that nobody should think that he changed his mind and agrees with Shmuel.

Rav and Shmuel were sitting in neighboring courtyards when the wall between them fell down. Shmuel, who permitted carrying in such a case, ordered that a cloak be carried and spread for privacy in place of the wall. Rav expressed his dissatisfaction that Shmuel permitted carrying by turning away his head. Shmuel retorts with a sarcastic remark.[27] This give-and-take reflects some tension between the two rabbis over their differences of practice.

The Stam comment wonders why Rav does not rebuke Shmuel for permitting carrying and explains that it was the place of Shmuel. So, although Rav does not carry himself and even turns away to send the message that he disagrees, Rav still respected Shmuel's authority enough to tolerate others carrying. He would not issue an opposing ruling in the place of Shmuel. Even though Rav and Shmuel have different practices and even express some antagonism toward each other on that account, they still respect each other's authority enough to tolerate their differences. Rav does not rebuke Shmuel in Shmuel's hometown, and neither does Shmuel force Rav to conform despite it being Shmuel's jurisdiction.

We find a similar story also regarding an *eruv* at Yerushalmi ʿ*Erubin* 1:1 (18c):

> רבי יוחנן וריש לקיש הוון שריין בשקקה דרבי יצחק ריש לקיש טילטל כדעתיה ר' יוחנן לא אסר ולא טילטל

27. Halivni, *Meqorot u-mesorot*, ʿ*Erubin*, 239–40, explains that the original dispute in this story seems to be about whether or not one may build a temporary partition on Shabbat. The Bavli redactors later applied the story to the context of carrying in an area that was permitted at the start of Shabbat but that has changed since, as here where the partition wall fell down during Shabbat. In the original story, Rav turns away because he prohibits building a partition. Shmuel sarcastically retorts that if Rav is unhappy with the partition, Rav should come and make it stronger with his belt. Of course, Rav's objection was not with the flimsiness of the partition but with building it at all. The point of the sarcasm is slightly dulled once the story is placed in this new context. Nevertheless, even in the new context one can make sense of the line. Rav opposes carrying the sheet to build the building. Shmuel ridicules Rav's opposition by assuming that Rav opposes only the flimsiness of the partition and so tells him to make is stronger. See Me'iri ad loc. who similarly explains that Shmuel spoke sarcastically, "דרך בדיחותא."

אמ׳ ר׳ יוחנן הניחו לבני מבוי שיהו שוגגין ואל יהו מזידין.
מה טילטל לא טילטל? אין תימר טילטל מחלפה שיטת רבי יוחנן אין תימר לא טילטל יואסר לבני המבוי?
רבי יוחנן ביטל רשותו.
אמר רבי אחא כף ריש לקיש לרבי יוחנן וטלטל.
אמר רבי מתניה ויאות.

R. Yoḥanan and Resh Laqish were staying on the street of R. Isaac. Resh Laqish carried according to his own opinion. R. Yoḥanan did not prohibit carrying but also did not carry himself.
R. Yoḥanan said, "Leave the residents of the alley to be inadvertent sinners and not be deliberate sinners."
Did [R. Yoḥanan] carry or not carry? If you say he carried, this contradicts R. Yoḥanan's opinion. If you say he did not carry, he should prohibit the other members of the alley?
R. Yoḥanan relinquished dominion over his property.
R. Aḥa said, "Resh Laqish forced[28] R. Yoḥanan and he carried.
R. Matnaya said, "It is good [that Resh Laqish forced R. Yoḥanan to carry].

Resh Laqish was more lenient than R. Yoḥanan regarding the status of a street that bends.[29] When on one occasion these two rabbis were staying on such a street, Resh Laqish permitted carrying and acted accordingly. R. Yoḥanan did not permit and did not carry himself. Normally, when one resident opposes the *eruv* the entire *eruv* is void.[30] Here, however, R. Yoḥanan allowed others to carry by relinquishing his own property rights. R. Aḥa adds another scene to the story in which Resh Laqish actually forced R. Yoḥanan to carry. This seems to be an alternate response to the previous question of how they could make an *eruv* without R. Yoḥanan's participation. R. Matnaya commends this forced participation because even relinquishing possession leaves open the possibility that he can regain it later.[31]

The story up to R. Aḥa's addition paints a picture similar to the Bavli story about Rav and Shmuel where one rabbi carries and the other does not and each side tolerates the other. The Bavli does add that Rav turned away in order to show his disagreement. This does not seem to have been necessary for R. Yoḥanan since his position was known; the dispute in the Yerushalmi was ongoing while the case in the Bavli came up only once the wall fell and so Rav had to clarify his position on the spot.

---

28. For this translation of כף, see Michael Sokoloff, *A Dictionary of Jewish Palestinian Aramaic of the Byzantine Period* (Ramat-Gan: Bar Ilan University, 1992), 267.
29. This dispute appears before this story. See also parallel discussion at *b. ʿErub.* 6a–b.
30. *M. ʿErub.* 6:1.
31. See the continuation of the *sugya*.

Another difference between the stories is that in the Yerushalmi story the place is not identified as the hometown of either Amora but rather they both seem to be guests of R. Isaac. The most significant difference between the stories, however, is R. Aḥa's addendum that Resh Laqish forced[32] R. Yoḥanan to conform.[33] This forced conformity does not necessarily reflect intolerance of diversity as much as a need for R. Yoḥanan to participate in order that the entire *eruv* should be legitimate. Still, the very assumption of R. Aḥa that resignation of possession is not enough and that every resident must completely participate in the *eruv* may itself reflect a push toward unity.[34]

One should not deduce from the above two sources that Bavli stories always portray more tolerance than Yerushalmi stories. Here is an example in the opposite direction. Bavli *Šabbat* 50a reports:

> רפרם בר פפא איקלע לבי כנישתא דאבי גיבר, קם קרא בספרא ואמר: ברכו את ה׳, ואשתיק ולא אמר המבורך. אוושו כולי עלמא: ברכו את ה׳ המבורך! אמר רבא: פתיא אוכמא, בהדי פלוגתא למה לך! ועוד: הא נהוג עלמא כרבי ישמעאל.
>
> Rafram bar Papa happened upon the synagogue of Abi Gobar. He rose to read in the Scripture and he said "Bless the Lord,"

32. *Pene Moshe* and *Qorban ha-ʿedah* explain, rather apologetically, that Resh Laqish forced R. Yoḥanan by convincing him with strong arguments and proofs. More likely, however, Resh Laqish applied political pressure to force R. Yoḥanan's action. I could not find any other use in the Talmud of the verb כף in the context of one rabbi forcing another rabbi.

33. If R. Isaac's street represents neutral ground, not the hometown of either R. Yoḥanan or Resh Laqish, then it is noteworthy that Resh Laqish is said to have forced R. Yoḥanan to carry even though it was not his hometown. It does seem, however, that the town favored the position of Resh Laqish since they all agreed to the *eruv*.

34. The continuation of the *sugya* explains that a Sadducee cannot be included in an *eruv* even if he relinquishes his property because he might take it back and cannot be trusted. (*y. ʿErub.* 6:3 [23c] uses this same logic to explain why property of a non-Jew may not also be included within the *eruv* even if he relinquishes his dominion). R. Aḥa thinks that R. Yoḥanan, because he opposes this *eruv*, should also be treated as a Sadducee, and so his resignation of property is not accepted. The only way to validate this *eruv* must therefore be to force R. Yoḥanan to agree to it.

The goal of an *eruv* is, at least in part, to create a community. See Charlotte Fonrobert, "From Separatism to Urbanism: The Dead Sea Scrolls and the Origins of the Rabbinic Eruv," *Dead Sea Discoveries* 11, no. 1 (2004): 43–71; and idem, "The Political Symbolism of the Eruv," *Jewish Social Studies* 11, no. 3 (2005): 9–35. An exclusivist attitude, which allows only like-minded people in the *eruv*, reflects a wish for a homogeneous community where all members follow the same *halakhic* practice. Greater inclusivity, on the other hand, may imply tolerance for a more diverse community. Y. N. Epstein, *Mavo le-nusah ha-Mishnah* (Jerusalem: Magnes, 1948; reprint, 2000), 609, argues that the Bavli did not read the words או עם מי שאינו מודה בערוב in its version of *m. ʿErub.* 6:1. The Bavli thus requires only that the property of a non-Jew be leased while property of a dissenting Jew can simply be relinquished. More research is needed to compare how the Yerushalmi and Bavli deal with dissenters to the *eruv*, whether the dissenters are Sadducees who oppose the entire concept of *eruv* or rabbis who oppose a certain detail of a specific *eruv*.

> but stopped and did not say, "Who is Blessed." The whole congregation cried out, "Bless the Lord who is blessed." Rava said: "You black bucket! Why do you enter into this controversy? And besides, the general custom is to follow R. Ishmael.[35]

Rafram b. Papa, who is from Pumbedita, does not say "Who is Blessed" when he travels to Abi Gobar, thus violating the local custom. He is first corrected by the congregation. Then Rava, who lives in Maḥoza, which is near Abi Gobar, addresses Rafram with a derogatory name[36] and rebukes him for causing controversy. Rava adds that the general custom in most places is to say "Who is Blessed." If, in fact, the general custom in most places was to say "Who is Blessed" then Rafram was not simply continuing his local custom but was rather moving to change the prevailing custom. This would explain Rava's harsh reaction. Whatever were the exact circumstances, we see that Rava did not tolerate the different practice of a traveler near his own hometown. A similar case on the same topic is found in *y. Ber.* 7:3 (11c):[37]

> רבי חייא בר אשי קם מקרי באורייתא ואמר ברכו ולא אמר המבורך בעון מישתקיניה אמר להון רב ארפוניה דנהיג כרבי עקיבה
> רבי זעירא קם מקרי כהן במקום לוי ובירך לפניה ולאחריה ובעון מישתוקניה אמ׳ לון רבי חייא בר אשי ארפוניה דכן אינון נהיגין גבייהו
> Rav Ḥiyya bar Ashi rose up to read in the Torah. He said, "Bless ..." but did not say, "Who is Blessed." They [the congregation] wanted to shut him up. Rav told them, "Leave him alone for he practices according to R. Akiba."
> R. Zeira rose up to read Kohen instead of Levi. He recited a blessing before and after his portion. They [the congregation] wanted to shut him up. Rav Ḥiyya bar Ashi told them, "Leave him alone for so do they practice in their circles."

In this case, R. Ḥiyya bar Ashi, a Babylonian Amora of the second generation and a student of Rav, practices in accordance with R. Akiba. The congregation does not want to tolerate it. Obviously, he diverges from the local custom. Rav, however, steps in and lets him follow his own practice even though it is against the local practice. The story does not say explicitly that Rav Ḥiyya bar Ashi traveled anywhere, though we can assume that he did travel to a new place because the congregation did not expect his behavior.

---

35. R. Ishmael rules that one should recite the complete formula in *m. Ber.* 7:3.

36. Rashi here explains that he called him a "black bucket" because of his dark complexion. See, however, Rashi to *b. ʿAbod. Zar.* 16b.

37. Since this case involves different people and has the opposite outcome, it seems to be unrelated to the Bavli story. Still, a comparison is instructive.

In the next scene, a traveler from Palestine to Babylonia keeps his Palestinian custom.[38] Once again the congregation wishes to shut him up, but Rav Ḥiyya bar Ashi tells them to leave him alone. In both cases, the local rabbi does not insist that the traveler conform to the practice of the local synagogue but rather recognizes the right of the visitor to follow his own tradition.[39] Even though these stories appear in the Yerushalmi, they both involve Babylonian rabbis and are set in Babylonia. It is therefore difficult to determine which society is reflected here. Also, in both cases in this Yerushalmi, as well as in the Bavli parallel, the visitor violates the practice of the local commoners, but in none of these cases is that practice identified as being based on the ruling of the local rabbinic authority.

Most recorded stories are about rabbis who come to visit another town, but at least one story at *b. Meg.* 5b involves a layperson:

ורבי, היכי נטע נטיעה בפורים? והתני רב יוסף: שמחה ומשתה ויום טוב, שמחה—מלמד שאסורים בהספד, משתה—מלמד שאסור בתענית, ויום טוב—מלמד שאסור בעשיית מלאכה!

אלא: רבי בר ארביסר הוה, וכי נטע בחמיסר נטע...

איני? רב חזייה לההוא גברא דהוה קא שדי כיתנא בפוריא, ולטייה ולא צמח כיתניה?

התם בר יומא הוה.

רבה בריה דרבא אמר: אפילו תימא ביומיה, הספד ותענית קבילו עלייהו, מלאכה לא קבילו עלייהו. דמעיקרא כתיב שמחה ומשתה ויום טוב, ולבסוף כתיב לעשות אותם ימי משתה ושמחה, ואילו יום טוב לא כתיב.

ואלא רב, מאי טעמא לטייה לההוא גברא? **דברים המותרין ואחרים נהגו בהן איסור** הוה, ובאתריה דרבי לא נהוג.

How did Rabbi plant on Purim? Didn't Rav Yosef teach: "*Joy, feasting and holiday*" (Esth 9:19). *Joy*: teaches that one may not eulogize; *Feasting*: teaches that one may not fast; *holiday*: teaches that performing work is prohibited?

Rather, Rabbi [lived in a place where Purim was celebrated] on the fourteenth and he planted on the fifteenth.

Is that so? But, Rav saw a man sowing flax on Purim, and cursed him, and the flax did not grow?

There, he [the man] was doing it on the day that he ought to have observed.

Rabbah the son of Rava said. You may even say [that Rabbi planted] on the day [that he ought to have observed]. [The Jews]

38. See *b. ʿAbod. Zar.* 16b, which reports that R. Zeira did visit Rav Ḥiyya bar Ashi in Korkunia.

39. The Yerushalmi may show more tolerance in these cases because they deal with liturgy, which is more like custom than law. However, this only makes the Bavli's intolerance more perplexing. It is possible that Rava in the Bavli story had some personal grudge against Rafram bar Papa, as might be inferred from his insult, "You black bucket."

accepted upon themselves to abstain from eulogizing and fasting, but did not accept refraining from working, for first it is written, *"Joy, feasting and holiday,"* but afterward it is written, *"That they should make them days of feasting and joy"* (Esth 9:22), and *"holiday"* is not mentioned.

Why then did Rav curse that man? It was a case of "**things that are permitted but others are accustomed to prohibit.**" [40] But in Rabbi's place this was not the practice.

Assuming that work on Purim is prohibited, the report that Rabbi did work on Purim is interpreted to mean that he worked on the day not celebrated in his place. Recognizing the difficult in this interpretation, Rabbah the son of Rava explains that Rabbi actually permitted work on Purim. In order to explain why Rav cursed the man even though no less an authority than Rabbi permitted it, the Stam concludes that the occurrence happened in a city where the usual custom was to prohibit work. In Rabbi's city, however, work was permitted.

This conclusion is not based on a tradition received from Palestine, where Rabbi lived, but rather is based on the Bavli's give-and-take. The use of the term "Rabbi's place," which never occurs in the Yerushalmi, must therefore derive from the hands of the Bavli editors. Rav did not show tolerance for the layperson who worked on Purim even though other rabbis permitted such work. The Stam assumes that such intolerance could have occurred only in a place where the general practice was to prohibit.

In some cases the host rabbi is tolerant of an alternate practice by his guest. *B. Pesaḥim* 106b relates:

בעא מיניה רב חנא בר חיננא מרב הונא: טעם מהו שיבדיל? אמר ליה: אני אומר טעם מבדיל, ורב אסי אמר: טעם אינו מבדיל.

רב ירמיה בר אבא איקלע לבי רב אסי, אישתלי וטעים מידי. הבו ליה כסא ואבדיל. אמרה ליה דביתהו: והא מר לא עביד הכי! אמר לה: שבקיה, כרביה סבירא ליה.

R. Ḥana bar Ḥinena asked Rav Huna: "One who has tasted [food], may he [subsequently] recite *havdalah*?" He replied, "I say that one who has tasted recites *havdalah*. But Rav Assi said: One who has tasted may not recite *havdalah*."

R. Yirmiah bar Abba visited the house of Rav Assi. He forgot himself and ate something. They gave him a cup [of wine] and he recited *havdalah*. His [Rav Assi's] wife said to him [Rav Assi]: "But the master [you] does not act thus!" He replied, "Leave him alone, he adopts the opinion of his master."

40. By quoting the *baraita,* the Gemara treats the stringent practice not to work as a mere custom. The Gemara earlier, however, derives the prohibition from a verse, which makes it seem like a law. The line between custom and law here is blurred.

Generally, one must recite *havdalah* after Shabbat before one may eat. If one eats by mistake before *havdalah,* then he may still recite it according to Rav Huna but has lost his opportunity to recite it according to Rav Assi. When, on one occasion, R Yirmiah bar Abba visited R. Assi, R. Yirmiah recited *havdalah* even after eating, which prompted an inquiry by Rav Assi's wife. Rav Assi, however, did not rebuke R. Yirmiah or force him to follow the local custom. Rather, he tolerated R. Yirmiah practicing according to his own tradition. The expression, "Leave him alone, he adopts the opinion of his master," recurs a few times in the Bavli.[41]

Some cases, however, show that a visiting rabbi would make sure to conform to local practice. *B. Šabbat* 46a relates:

> רב מלכיא איקלע לבי רבי שמלאי וטילטל שרגא ואיקפד רבי שמלאי.
> רבי יוסי גלילאה איקלע לאתריה דרבי יוסי ברבי חנינא, טילטל שרגא ואיקפד רבי יוסי ברבי חנינא.
> רבי אבהו, כי איקלע לאתריה דרבי יהושע בן לוי הוה מטלטל שרגא, כי איקלע לאתריה דרבי יוחנן לא הוה מטלטל שרגא. מה נפשך, אי כרבי יהודה סבירא ליה ליעבד כרבי יהודה, אי כרבי שמעון סבירא ליה ליעבד כרבי שמעון? לעולם כרבי שמעון סבירא ליה, ומשום כבודו דרבי יוחנן הוא דלא הוה עביד.
>
> R. Malkia visited R. Simlai's home and moved a lamp, which caused R. Simlai to be angry.
> R. Yose of Galilee visited the town of R. Yose son of R. Ḥaninah and he moved a lamp, which caused R. Yose son of R. Ḥaninah to be angry.
> When R. Abbahu visited the town of R. Yehoshua ben Levi, he would move a lamp. When he visited the town of R. Yoḥanan he would not move a lamp. What is your choice? If he agrees with R. Yehudah, let him act accordingly; if he agrees with R. Shimon, let him act accordingly? Rather, he agreed with R. Shimon, but did not act accordingly out of deference to R. Yoḥanan.[42]

In the first two cases, a visitor keeps the practice of his place of origin in opposition to the local rabbi who becomes upset by this nonconformity. The third case offers a contrasting action of R. Abbahu, who conforms to the local practice wherever he goes. R. Abbahu would change his own practice in order to conform to the local practice at his destination. On

41. See *b. Šabb.* 12b and 53b. The former citation includes a conversation identical with *b. Pesaḥ.* 106b regarding R. Yirmiah and R. Assi except it involves a different issue. The same exact conversation is not likely to have occurred twice. Rather, the narrative must have been transferred from one issue to the other by the Bavli redactors. Regardless of whether either story ever happened, we do see that the Bavli redactors regularly envisioned a host rabbi being tolerant of the deviant practices of his guest.

42. This text has a parallel at *b. Yebam.* 14a (quoted above, p. 104).

the one hand, this shows conformity to the local custom to be the highest value. On the other hand, it also shows that there were different practices in each place and that at least R. Abbahu was respectful of both and did not insist on maintaining only one practice. So we see tolerance of diversity across different cities but not within one city. This story has a parallel in the Yerushalmi, which we will discuss in the next section.[43]

The continuation of that Gemara has a story of intolerance caused by a personal insult:

> רב אויא איקלע לבי רבא, הוה מאיסן בי כרעיה בטינא, אתיבי אפוריא קמיה דרבא. איקפד רבא, בעא לצעוריה. אמר ליה: מאי טעמא רבה ורב יוסף דאמרי תרוייהו שרגא דנפטא נמי שרי לטלטוליה? אמר ליה: הואיל וחזיא לכסויי בה מנא. אלא מעתה כל צרורות שבחצר מטלטלין, הואיל וחזיא לכסויי בהו מנא! אמר ליה: הא איכא תורת כלי עליה, הני ליכא תורת כלי עליה. מי לא תניא **השירים והנזמים והטבעות הרי הן ככל הכלים הנטלים בחצר**, ואמר עולא: מה טעם הואיל ואיכא תורת כלי עליה. הכא נמי הואיל ואיכא תורת כלי עליה. אמר רב נחמן בר יצחק: בריך רחמנא דלא כסיפיה רבא לרב אויא.
>
> Rav 'Awia visited Rava's home. His [Rav 'Awia's] feet were dirty with clay. He sat down on a bed before Rava. Rava became angry and wished to vex him. He [Rava] said to him: "What is the reason that Rabbah and Rav Yosef both maintain that a naphtha lamp too may be handled [on Shabbat]?" He replied, "Because it is fit for covering a utensil." [Rava said,] "If so, all of the pebbles in the couryard may be handled, since they are fit to cover a utensil?" [Rav 'Awia replied], "This [the naphtha lamp] is in the category of a utensil; those are not in the category of utensils. Was it not taught: **Bracelets, earrings and rings are like all utensils that may be handled in a courtyard.** And ʿUla said: 'What is the reason? Since they are in the category of utensils.' Here too, since it is in the category of a utensil." Rav Naḥman b. Isaac observed: Blessed is the Merciful One, that Rava did embarrass Rav 'Awia.[44]

This is not a case of differing practice but rather a theoretical debate about the reason for a certain law of *muqṣeh*. Yet, it does provide a rare admission that one rabbi was motivated by personal insult to subject his colleague to a difficult line of questioning.[45] In most cases, we are not aware of personal tensions between participants in a discussion or characters in a story. It is nevertheless likely that some cases of intolerance by one rabbi toward the practice of his colleague may be motivated not purely by the rabbi's attitude toward pluralism but rather by personal hostilities arising from nonlegal considerations.

---

43. See below, pp. 145–46.
44. *B. Šabb.* 46a-b.
45. See also the treatment by R. Eleazar be-R. Shimon of Rabbi at *b. B. Meṣiʿa* 84b.

Reviewing the Bavli stories, although visiting rabbis consistently refrain from issuing decisions against their host rabbis, they are not as consistent regarding their own practices. Rav does not violate his own practice even in Shmuel's place; Shmuel makes a remark but, overall, does not object. Rafram bar Papa, however, opposes the local practice by refusing to recite "Who is Blessed," and is rebuked. R. Yirmiah b. Abba follows his own practice, which is tolerated by his host. R. Abbahu is careful to conform to the practice of his host while other rabbis violate the local practice and are rebuked by their hosts.

Another series of stories in *b. Ḥul.* 109b–111b confirms these conclusions.[46] This section discusses various controversial foods such as udders and livers and the tensions created when rabbis eat at each other's homes. These stories confirm that rabbis had authority to enforce unity only within the borders of their own cities but tolerated differences outside their cities. This distinction is taken extremely literally by one Rami bar Tamri, who would travel from Pumbedita, where udders were eaten, to Sura, where udders were not eaten, collect all the discarded udders, and eat them beyond the city limits.[47] Abaye, on the other hand, berates Rabin for refusing to eat the udder when visiting Rav Pape's house where they did eat the udder.[48] Rav Ashi does not tolerate a family member following a viewpoint regarding the liver that differs from the accepted halakha.[49] Shmuel shows intolerance toward a dissenting student but respected the dissenting practice of Rav, his colleague, on the same issue.[50] Thus, we can perhaps hypothesize that tolerance for visitors fluctuated according to the relationship of the host to his visitor and other personal variables. There was no overriding ethic of pluralism for visitors that these Amoraim applied to all cases.

In none of these cases, however, does the visitor ever invalidate the practice of the host. This confirms the widespread recognition and respect for local authorities. Beyond that generalization, even this small sample of cases reveals that neither visitors nor hosts followed a consistent pattern. Visitors generally try not to flagrantly oppose the local practice, but they are also not likely to change their usual practice. The reaction of host rabbis depends to some extent on the relationship between the host and the visitor, that is, whether the host is of higher status (a teacher or an elder), whether the visitor is a family member, or whether there is any preexisting tension between them.

---

46. See Hidary, "Tolerance for Diversity," 128–38, for a detailed analysis of this section. Below is a brief summary of this analysis.

47. *B. Ḥul.* 110a.

48. *B. Ḥul.* 109b.

49. *B. Ḥul.* 111a-b.

50. *B. Ḥul.* 111b.

Local Authorities in Palestine

Do we find evidence for the existence of local authorities in various cities in Palestine just as we have seen above in Babylonia? In chapter 2, we saw that the Yerushalmi does recognize local customs and protects those customs adamantly. Residents of a town may not change from their traditional custom, and visitors should conform to the local custom. In none of those cases, however, are the customs based on the decision of a local rabbi. They are rather based on mimetic traditions of laypeople.

We have seen two examples above of stories in the Bavli that have parallels in the Yerushalmi. In the first example, the Bavli says that Rav did not forbid the *eruv* because he was "in the place of Shmuel." A similar Yerushalmi story involving R. Yoḥanan and Resh Laqish occurred on the street of R. Isaac rather than in the town of either rabbi. Rav and Shmuel, the foremost Babylonian Amoraim of the first generation, lived in separate cities and had full jurisdiction in their hometowns. We therefore find many stories about one rabbi visiting and showing respect to the other. In contrast, R. Yoḥanan and Resh Laqish, the two most prominent Palestinian Amoraim of their generation, lived near each other, and so neither had absolute authority over a specific area. In the second example, about adding "Who is Blessed," neither the Bavli nor the Yerushalmi stories occur in a place that is under the jurisdiction of a particular rabbi. In fact, there are very few Yerushalmi passages that identify a rabbi as the local authority of a particular city.[51]

The Yerushalmi story that most closely reflects an environment of local authorities is in *y. Ber.* 8:1 (12a):

יום טוב שחל להיות במוצאי שבת
רבי יוחנן אמר יקנ״ה יין קידוש נר הבדלה...
רבי חנינא אמר ינה״ק
[וכן] שמואל (לא)[52] אמר כהדא דרבי חנינא דאמר רבי אחא בשם רבי יהושע בן לוי מלך יוצא ושלטון נכנס מלוין את המלך ואח״כ מכניסין את השלטון...
רבי אבהו כד הוה אזיל לדרומה הוה עבד כר׳ חנינא וכד הוה נחית לטיבריא הוה עבד כרבי יוחנן דלא מפלג על בר נש באתריה.

A festival that falls at the end of Shabbat:
R. Yoḥanan says, "Wine, *Kiddush*, Lamp, *Havdalah* ..."
R. Ḥaninah says, "Wine, Lamp, *Havdalah*, *Kiddush*."
Shmuel agrees with the statement of R. Ḥaninah for R. Aḥa in the name of R. Yehoshua ben Levi says, "If a king is leaving and a governor is entering, first one escorts the king out and then welcomes the governor."...

51. This is based on searches for terms such as מקום, אתר, אזל, and city names.
52. Following the correction of *Pene Moshe*.

> When R. Abbahu went to the South, he practiced according to R. Ḥaninah; when he went to Tiberias, he practiced according to R. Yoḥanan in order not to conflict with anyone in his own place.[53]

This story is parallel to that quoted above concerning R. Abbahu,[54] which also involves a controversy over a lamp and Shabbat but in a somewhat different case. R. Abbahu changes his practice when in the South or when in Tiberias—perhaps a metonym for the North—in order not to disagree with "anyone in his own place." Not that R. Ḥaninah was in the South.[55] Rather, the sentence means that when R. Abbahu went to the South, he practiced according to R. Ḥaninah, who is in agreement with R. Yehoshua ben Levi, in order not to contradict R. Yehoshua ben Levi in his place, which was Lydda in the South.[56]

Even this source, which comes very close to calling R. Yoḥanan the local authority in Tiberias and R. Yehoshua ben Levi that of the South, does not spell this out as clearly as in the Bavli stories above regarding Rav and Shmuel. We do not find, as we do in the stories above, any local rabbi instructing R. Abbahu to conform. He seems to do so more out of a diplomatic spirit than a sense of obligation. It may be telling that unlike the Bavli parallel, the last line of the Yerushalmi uses R. Ḥaninah's name instead of R. Yehoshua ben Levi's. The focus is not on the personal authority of the local master but rather on the local practice, which happens to be taught by that rabbi. One could even interpret the words "בר נש—anyone" as a reference not to the local rabbis but to the local populace. Compare this to the language of the Bavli, רבי אבהו, כי איקלע לאתריה דרבי יהושע בן לוי הוה מטלטל שרגא, כי איקלע לאתריה דרבי יוחנן לא הוה מטלטל שרגא—"When R. Abbahu visited R. Yehoshua ben Levi's town he would move a lamp; when he visited R. Yoḥanan's town he would not move a lamp."[57] The Bavli does not even provide names for the cities, which are referred to only by association with their rabbis. The Bavli emphasizes that each locale is governed by the decisions of the local rabbi with the consequence that all visitors fall under the rabbi's jurisdiction. The Yerushalmi version does recognize that there were differing practices in the North and South but does not directly name each region as being the jurisdiction of a particular rabbi.[58]

---

53. See parallel discussion at *b. Pesaḥ.* 102b-103a.

54. See *b. Šabb.* 46a (above, p. 142) and *b. Yebam.* 14a (above, p. 104).

55. R. Ḥanina bar Ḥama actually lived in Sepphoris in the North; see texts below and Stuart Miller, "R. Hanina bar Hama at Sepphoris," in *The Galilee in Late Antiquity*, ed. Lee Levine (New York and Jerusalem: Jewish Theological Seminary, 1992), 175–200; and idem, *Sages and Commoners*, 63–99, 289 n. 235 and 419–23.

56. This explanation is confirmed by the Bavli parallels (above, n. 54), which name R. Yehoshua ben Levi explicitly as the authority in the South.

57. *B. Šabb.* 46a (above, p. 142) and *b. Yebam.* 14a (above, p. 104)

58. See also *y. Šabb.* 1:7 (4a) in which a student of R. Simai travels to Antipatris and eats

Perhaps we can get some sense of the authority structure of the rabbis in Palestine from these two Yerushalmi texts:

> רבי חנינה הורי לציפוראיי[59] בספחי חרדל ובביצה כרבי יודה
> עאל רבי יוחנן ודרש להון כרבנן דהכא וכרבנן דתמן
> רבי אבא בר זמינא בשם רבי יוצדק מן קומי אילין תרתין מילייא נחת רבי יוחנן מן ציפורין לטיבריא אמר מה איתיתון לי ההן סבא דאנא שרי והוא אסר ואסר והוא שרי
>
> R. Ḥaninah issued a ruling to the Sepphorites[59] concerning the aftergrowth of mustard [seeds in the Seventh Year] and concerning the egg in accordance with the view of R. Yehudah.
> R. Yoḥanan entered and taught them in accordance with the rabbis in this case and in accord with the rabbis in that case.
> R. Abba bar Zamina in the name of R. Yoṣedeq: Because of these two matters, R. Yoḥanan went down from Sepphoris to Tiberias. He said, "Why do you bring me [together with] that elder [R. Ḥaninah], for what I permit he prohibits, and [what I] prohibit, he permits."[60]

> ר' חנינה הוה שרי בציפורין והוון אתאי קומוי עובדין ומפק מן תרתין זימנין והוון רבי יוחנן ורבי שמעון בן לקיש שריין תמן ולא הוה מצרף לון עימיה אמרין חכים הוא ההוא סבא דפרזלוי חריפין
> חד זמן צרפון עימיה אמרין מה חמא רבי משגח עלינן יומא דין אמר לון ייתי עלי אם לא כל מעשה ומעשה שהייתי מוציא אם לא שמעתי אותו מר' להלכה כשערות ראשי ולמעשה שלשה פעמים והן עובדא לא אתא קומי רבי אלא תרין זימנין מן בגין כן צריפתכון עמי
>
> R. Ḥaninah was living in Sepphoris. Cases came before him and he made decisions twice.[61] Now R. Yoḥanan and R. Shimon ben Laqish were living there, but he never joined them to himself [for consultation]. They said, "That old man knows that his tools are sharp."

Damascene plums, and a student of R. Yehoshua ben Levi also travels there but does not eat of the plums. When the student of the latter reports this to his master, R. Yehoshua ben Levi responds that the other student is simply following the ruling of his teacher. This does reflect tolerance for the rulings of other rabbis and a degree of particular pluralism. However, notice that the two students travel away from their masters so there is no suggestion here that these Palestinian rabbis held geographical authority. Their authority stems from their roles as teachers and not as rabbis of a certain locale. See further at Hidary, "Tolerance for Diversity," 149–53.

59. On this term, see Miller, *Sages and Commoners*, 31–106.

60. *Y. Beṣah* 1:1 (60a). See analysis of this *sugya* in ibid., 81–86 and passim; and Hayim Lapin, "Rabbis and Cities: Some Aspects of the Rabbinic Movement in Its Graeco-Roman Environment," in *The Talmud Yerushalmi and Graeco-Roman Culture II*, ed. Peter Schäfer and Catherine Hezser (Tübingen: Mohr Siebeck, 1998), 57–58.

61. See Sokoloff, *A Dictionary of Jewish Palestinian Aramaic*, 358, for this translation. I suppose that this means that he decided each case carefully and double-checked his conclusions. Cf. Miller, *Sages and Commoners*, 420, who translates, "Cases would be brought before him, and they would often be brought repeatedly."

One time he did join them to himself. They said, "Why did the master see fit to take us into consideration today?" He said to them, "May [afflictions] befall me, if it is not so that each and every case that I sent forth I learned from Rabbi as a valid law as many times as there are hairs on my head [and if I also did not see my teacher apply these laws] in practice at least three times. And on that account I rely on my own teaching. But this particular case came before Rabbi only twice. On that account I have joined you with me."[62]

It is clear from these two sources that R. Ḥanina bar Ḥama was the dominant personality in Sepphoris in the early Amoraic period.[63] When R. Yoḥanan taught two laws there, he was contradicted by R. Ḥanina and felt that his presence there was useless and so decided to move to Tiberias. Most cases of *niddah* law came R. Ḥanina's way, which he decided alone. He invited R. Yoḥanan and Resh Laqish, who were also living there at the time, only on a single occasion when he was less sure of himself. So there definitely were, at least in some cases, dominant rabbis in various cities. Even in these texts, however, we do not find that Sepphoris is called "the place of R. Ḥanina." R. Yoḥanan feels free to teach a ruling differently from R. Ḥanina and is not condemned for having ruled against the local authority. He leaves only because he feels powerless to accomplish anything in the face of R. Ḥanina.

The few cases of local authorities in Palestine, that is, rabbis who preside over the practice of a certain town, are recorded only in the Bavli. *B. Šabbat* 130a quotes a *baraita* about two of the most famous differences of practice between cities:

> תנו רבנן: **במקומו של רבי אליעזר היו כורתין עצים לעשות פחמין לעשות ברזל בשבת.**
> במקומו של רבי יוסי הגלילי היו אוכלין בשר עוף בחלב.
> Our rabbis taught: **In the place of R. Eliezer, they used to chop wood to make charcoal to make iron [to make a knife for circumcision] on Shabbat.**
> In the place of R. Yose the Galilean they used to eat fowl with milk.[64]

62. *Y. Nid.* 2:7 (50b).

63. See reference above, n. 55.

64. See parallels in *b. Ḥul.* 116a and partially at *b. Yebam.* 14a, cited on p. 104 above. Similar language is used in *b. ʿAbod. Zar.* 40b.

The Mishnah already records the opinions of these two Tannaim,[65] but only this *baraita* in the Bavli reports that these two regions actually followed these opinions in practice. If this *baraita* is an authentic and historical Tannaitic tradition, then we might be able to use it to partially reconstruct Palestinian reality.[66] Since it only appears in the Bavli, however, it may actually be better understood as a reflection of the Bavli's attitude toward diversity.[67] *B. Šabbat* 130a cites other stories on this subject, which are also absent from the Yerushalmi:

> אמר רבי יצחק: עיר אחת היתה בארץ ישראל שהיו עושין כרבי אליעזר, והיו מתים בזמנן. ולא עוד אלא שפעם אחת גזרה מלכות הרשעה גזרה על ישראל על המילה, ועל אותה העיר לא גזרה.
>
> R. Isaac said: There was one city in Israel that used to practice according to R. Eliezer and its citizens would die at their proper times. Moreover, one time the evil kingdom decreed a ban on the Jews regarding circumcision but on that city it did not decree.

R. Isaac is a second–third generation Palestinian citing a tradition about a city that at some time in the past followed R. Eliezer and violated Shabbat to prepare for circumcisions. The city was blessed because of this action. Its residents were allowed to continue performing circumcision even when a general decree was issued forbidding circumcision. The reason seems to be that they showed so much respect for the law of circumcision by putting even preparations for circumcision above Shabbat.

This tradition is related by a Palestinian rabbi about a Palestinian city. Yet, it does not appear in the Yerushalmi but only in the Bavli. We cannot prove that the Yerushalmi omitted it deliberately or that the Bavli invented it. It is nevertheless significant that only the Bavli includes a tradition that

---

65. *M. Šabb.* 19:1 and *m. Ḥul.* 8:4. In both cases, R. Akiba disagrees.

66. Such a reconstruction might read as follows: The majority of the people followed R. Akiba in both cases, but the minority opinion was followed in the towns of the dissenting rabbis. These examples are presented as exceptional—perhaps because usually rabbis did not practice their opinion or perhaps because they usually did but these examples are especially surprising because they involve what appear to be flagrant violations of kosher and Shabbat laws. Nevertheless, we see that R. Eliezer's local influence sufficed to have his entire town follow his opinion despite the widespread practice against him. (See Halivni, *Rules*, 75.) We can extrapolate from this source that there were likely other cities as well that followed the minority opinions of their local rabbis.

67. Ben-Menahem, *Judicial Deviation*, 88, suggests that "these reports are late Babylonian traditions, perhaps fabricated in order to justify the great variation of the halakhah in Babylon [*sic*]." He further notes that "the sequence of *b. Šabb.* 130a has a strong polemical flavor." At the same time, he also entertains the possibility that "The Yerushalmi deliberately suppressed old Tannaitic traditions which were not congruent with later Palestinian developments" (ibid., 88 n. 109).

celebrates the divergence of such a city. In another story pertaining to this subject, however, the Yerushalmi and Bavli are very similar. *Y. Šabbat* 19:1 (16d) discusses whether Rabbi followed R. Eliezer:

תני מעשה היה והורה רבי כרבי אליעזר
אמר רבי יוחנן חבורה[68] היתה מקשה מה ראה רבי להניח דברי חכמים ולעשות כרבי אליעזר
אמר רבי הושעיה שאלנו את רבי יהודה הגוזר ואמר לנו במבוי שאינו מפולש

It has been taught: There was a case when Rabbi ruled in accordance with R. Eliezer.
R. Yoḥanan said, "The scholars questioned: Why did Rabbi see fit to ignore the view of the sages and act in accordance with R. Eliezer?"
R. Hoshaiah said, "We asked R. Yehudah the circumciser, and he told us that it took place in an alleyway that was not open on both sides."

The opening *baraita* reports that Rabbi once, probably to save himself in a pinch, permitted the practice of R. Eliezer. The subsequent discussion, however, proceeds to explain that Rabbi actually did not practice according to R. Eliezer but rather relied on a different opinion that allowed carrying in that situation for a different reason. We do not know whether to trust the *baraita* or the tradition of the circumciser, so it is difficult to know what actually happened. However, it is clear that R. Yoḥanan, as well as the editor of this *sugya*, was not comfortable with the possibility that Rabbi acted in accordance with R. Eliezer, and he therefore sought a different explanation for Rabbi's actions. We find a parallel story in *b. Šabb.* 130b:

[A] זימנין אשכחיה דיתיב וקאמר: אמר רבי שמעון בן לקיש משום רבי יהודה הנשיא: פעם אחת שכחו ולא הביאו איזמל מערב שבת, והביאוהו בשבת,
[B] והיה הדבר קשה לחכמים: היאך מניחין דברי חכמים ועושין כרבי אליעזר.
[C] חדא דרבי אליעזר שמותי הוא, ועוד יחיד ורבים הלכה כרבים.
[D] ואמר רבי אושעיא: שאילית את רבי יהודה הגוזר, ואמר לי: מבוי שלא נשתתפו בו הוה, ואייתוהו מהאי רישא להאי רישא.

[A] On one occasion, [R. Zeira] found him [R. Assi] sitting and stating, "R. Shimon ben Laqish said in the name of R. Yehudah the Patriarch: One time, they forgot and did not bring a knife from before Shabbath eve so they brought it on Shabbat.
[B] The matter was very distressing to the sages; how could they abandon the words of the sages and practice according to R. Eliezer?"

68. On the term חברייא in the Yerushalmi see Miller, *Sages and Commoners*, 395–99.

> [C] First, R. Eliezer is a Shammaite and further, [in a controversy between] an individual and the many, the halakha follows the many.
> [D] R. Oshaia said, I asked R. Yehudah the circumciser who told me, "It was a courtyard whose residents had not partnered together and they brought it from one end to the other end."

The Bavli differs slightly but is otherwise very similar to the Yerushalmi. In the Bavli, Rabbi only reports the incident[69] but is not the one who permits it, as he does in the Yerushalmi. Still, both Talmuds reinterpret and thus deny a *baraita* that attests to a single incident where R. Eliezer was followed. It is difficult to judge whether the Bavli's redactors share the Yerushalmi's discomfort with this incident or whether the Bavli is simply faithfully quoting its source. However, this case may differ from the usual case in that R. Eliezer's opinion was not consistently followed by either Rabbi or any of the sages. The actors in these cases were not part of his town of followers but rather used his leniency on one occasion. Also, the opinion of R. Akiba probably had already become so widespread that R. Eliezer could no longer be countenanced.[70] Based on these texts, it seems that rabbis would not tolerate an individual following a minority opinion on an ad hoc basis, but would tolerate an entire city that followed the opinion of its rabbi.

This is confirmed in many stories about travelers to and from cities that follow minority practice. One such story in *b. Ḥull.* 116a has to do with R. Yose the Galilean's opinion that poultry and milk may be eaten together:

> לוי איקלע לבי יוסף רישבא, אייתו לקמיה רישא דטיוסא בחלבא, ולא אמר להו ולא מידי, כי אתא לקמיה דרבי, אמר ליה: אמאי לא תשמתינהו? אמר ליה: אתריה דרבי יהודה בן בתירא הוא, ואמינא, דרש להו כרבי יוסי הגלילי דאמר יצא עוף שאין לו חלב אם.
> Levi visited the house of Yosef the fowler. They brought to him a head of a peacock in milk. He [Levi] did not say anything to them. When he came before Rabbi, [Rabbi] said to him [Levi]: "Why did you not ban him?" He said to him, "It was the place of R. Yehudah b. Betera and I assumed that he explained it [the law of poultry

69. It is not clear whether the statement of Rabbi is meant to include only [A] or also [B]. [B] may be the words of R. Assi. It does seem clear that [C] is Stammaitic since it begins in Aramaic.

70. Even though R. Eliezer was not generally followed, both Talmuds quote many instances of rabbis who find loopholes within the laws of carrying when under pressure. The Yerushalmi quotes stories when various rabbis carried objects using a human chain or in a shoe, but other rabbis insisted that the circumcision be delayed to Sunday. The Bavli quotes a story in which the circumcision knife was carried by way of courtyards.

and milk] like R. Yose the Galilean who said, 'poultry is excluded since it does not have mother's milk.'"[71]

This story shows that the practice according to R. Yose the Galilean probably extended beyond his own town.[72] Rabbi wants to excommunicate Yosef for violating the law. This itself is notable for the way Rabbi would deal with halakhic deviation. Levi's response, however, diffuses the attack. Assuming that Rabbi accepted this response, it seems that even Rabbi would consent to pluralism if the practice was done in a city that accepts a different opinion as law. Once again, we should point out that this story involves Palestinian rabbis yet it appears only in the Bavli.

Summarizing this set of texts about R. Eliezer and R. Yose the Galilean, we find one Bavli story in which the possibility that Rabbi followed the same minority opinion is questioned and reinterpreted. This story reflects a negative attitude toward diverse practices. This Bavli story, however, is a quotation from the parallel version found in the Yerushalmi. Furthermore, neither version of the story says that Rabbi's city practiced according to R. Eliezer but rather that he decided so on one occasion, probably against the common practice of the city. Two other stories about Palestinian rabbis, which appear only in the Bavli, tolerate and even praise those places that follow these minority opinions.

The *baraita* and other texts quoted in the Bavli about R. Eliezer and R. Yose the Galilean may have some historical basis. Nevertheless, it is noteworthy that they are absent from the Yerushalmi. The Yerushalmi knew that R. Eliezer permitted preparations for circumcision, but does not state that his town followed this practice. It is therefore likely that the Bavli sources relate authentic Palestinian traditions, but the terminology used in these texts may reflect Bavli conceptions. In other words, even assuming that R. Yose the Galilean, along with many of his students and townspeople, did eat poultry and milk, the phrase, "במקומו של רבי יוסי הגלילי—in the locality of R. Yose the Galilean," which implies that he was a recognized authority of that area, may be a Bavli formulation. Similarly in the last story quoted above, Levi may actually have told Rabbi that his host was a follower of R. Yose the Galilean, and it is only the Bavli storytellers who inserted "אתריה דרבי יהודה בן בתירא—the place of Yehudah b. Betera." Of course, this is very speculative. It is also possible that these stories represent the few exceptions where there were local authorities in Palestine.[73]

71. See the parallel in *b. Šabb.* 130a, which has slight variations.

72. R. Yehudah b. Betera was active in Nisibis in Babylonia. This source does not tell us if the whole town followed this practice.

73. Another passage cited as exceptional by Ben-Menahem, *Judicial Deviation*, 87 n. 106, is *y. Ber.* 7:1 (11a) regarding whether two people who ate together may invite each other to recite the blessing over the meal or whether three are necessary. R. Yasa (a Palestinian)

Nevertheless, the phenomenon seems to be much rarer in Palestine than it was in Babylonia.

Conclusion

This chapter confirms through many stories that, unlike the Yerushalmi, the Bavli reflects tolerance for diversity of practice from one city to the next. This corroborates that the view of Abaye that "Do not make factions" does not apply from one city to the next is not just a theoretical statement of tolerance, but reflects the reality in Babylonia, at least as recorded by the Talmudic memory.[74] Each city or region in Babylonia was expected to follow its local rabbinic authority even against the widespread practice in other cities. Along with this intercity tolerance came a certain degree of intolerance for diversity within a city. Nevertheless, because the rabbi of each city respected the authority of the rabbi in the next city, this created an atmosphere of tolerance for diversity across the country.

According to the Bavli stories discussed in this chapter, traveling rabbis always respected the halakhic decisions of the local rabbi for his own constituency. The visitor did not usually feel a need to conform to the local custom himself, nor did the host usually force him to do so. Less frequently, however, some visitors did submit to the host, and some hosts did force their visitors to conform. Personal considerations are likely to have come into play in each case. Tolerance is dependent on what the issue is and, more importantly, who is involved. Opposition by commoners is not tolerated;[75] visitors are subject to the jurisdiction of their hosts; students are subject to the authority of their teachers;[76] and personal grievances can influence how a rabbi will react to a dissenting colleague.[77] But overall, the

---

requires three while R. Zeira in the name of Abba (Rabbah) bar Yirmiah (a Suran) allows two. The Gemara concludes, "The rabbis of here according to their opinion and the rabbis of there according to their opinion." Apparently, R. Zeira who came from Babylonia retained the Babylonian view even after moving to Palestine. However, this example does not state that the dissenting parties practiced what they preached, only that they expressed the viewpoint of their places of origin.

74. I have not found stories that address cases of two courts within a city, and so I cannot test Rava's view empirically. It is possible that Rava's statement was a necessary conclusion to resolve the contradiction between Deut 14:1 and *m. Yebam.* 1:4, which Abaye's answer does not sufficiently explain. As noted above, p. 117, it is difficult to come up with any case that Rava would include in the prohibition of "Do not make factions." It therefore seems likely that Abaye's statement is based on an empirical evaluation while Rava's results from theoretical argumentation.

75. See above, p. 140, and below, p. 256.

76. See above, pp. 133, 144 n. 50, 146 n. 58 and further on this point at Hidary, "Tolerance for Diversity," 149–53.

77. See above, pp. 132 n. 17, 140 n. 39, 143, and below, p. 181 n. 67.

Bavli viewpoint can be summed up in the saying: "Each river follows its own course." In the Yerushalmi, on the other hand, tolerance for diversity between cities and the role of the rabbi as a local authority are not found to be dominant themes. What can account for this difference?

In the previous chapter, we pointed to one factor contributing to the different attitudes found in each Talmud toward legal pluralism as rooted in their views of the nature of halakha. The Yerushalmi emphasizes custom and mimetic tradition, which favors conservatism and uniformity, while the Bavli favors legal argumentation, which allows for a certain degree of change and diversity. The findings of the current chapter point to two additional but related factors that may have contributed to the differences laid out above. The first is the difference in the distribution of the Jewish population in Palestine and Babylonia, and the second relates to differences in the role of the rabbi in each country. These two factors may, in turn, help explain the basis for the different views in the Talmuds about the nature of halakha as outlined in chapter 2. To be sure, we have little direct access to the actual history of Amoraic Babylonia since our primary source is the Talmud itself. Thus, I cannot prove that the historical Babylonian rabbis were tolerant of one another, but only that the Bavli redactors portray them as such. Still, this lack of direct access to the past does not preclude the possibility that the Bavli portrayal is inspired by and based on the real facts on the ground during the Amoraic period. In fact, historians of the Talmudic era have already pointed out these relevant factors.

Regarding the difference in population distribution, Kraemer writes:

> The rabbinic movement in Palestine had been a relatively confined, relatively centralized community, reflecting the concentration of the Jewish community at large in the Galilee during the Talmudic period. Not so the rabbinic community in Babylonia, which was geographically far more diverse and which coexisted with a larger Jewish community that continued, as far as we can tell, to be incompletely assimilated into the rabbinic form of Judaism.... [T]he decentralized rabbinic community is an obvious influence in determining the plurality of practices and opinions that the Bavli records. Its variety is formed in the image of the community that was its home.[78]

Kraemer posits that the geographic decentralization of Babylonian Jewry influences the halakhic decentralization of the rabbis. This decentralization brings about increased diversity of practice within the rabbinic community itself.[79] The more physical distance there is between two rab-

---

78. Kraemer, *Mind*, 119. See further discussion of Kraemer below, p. 376.

79. Kraemer also writes that the geographic decentralization results in greater nonconformity among the general community to rabbinic authority. It is not clear whether the "plurality of practices and opinions that the Bavli records" refers to plurality across the gen-

binic authorities, the less likely they are to pressure one another to conform to a single standard; diverse practices that exist remain and even increase as each group decreases its communication with other groups. Greater geographic centralization, on the other hand, increases opportunities for each rabbi to rival his colleagues over whose opinion will become normative; diverse practices that do exist eventually converge into one practice as various groups assimilate. Kraemer cites little proof for his assertions, but the following sources show it to be well founded. In at least one case of a differing practice, the Bavli goes so far as to define the borders of each rabbi's jurisdiction. *Bavli Ketubot* 54a states:

> בבל וכל פרוודהא נהוג כרב, נהרדעא וכל פרוודהא נהוג כשמואל. ההיא בת מחוזא דהות נסיבא לנהרדעא, אתו לקמיה דרב נחמן, שמעה לקלה דבת מחוזא היא, אמר להו: בבל וכל פרוודהא נהוג כרב. אמרו ליה: והא לנהרדעא נסיבא! אמר להו: אי הכי, נהרדעא וכל פרוודהא נהוג כשמואל. ועד היכא נהרדעא? עד היכא דסגי קבא דנהרדעא.
>
> Babylon and all its environs follow the practice of Rav; Nehardea and all its environs follow the practice of Shmuel. A woman of Maḥoza was married to a Nehardean. They came before Rav Naḥman. He recognized from her voice that she was a Maḥozan. He said to them, "Babylon and all its environs follow the practice of Rav [so you must practice according to his opinion]." They said to him, "But she is married to a Nehardean." He said to them, "If so, Nehardea and all its environs follow Shmuel [and you must practice accordingly]." Until where is Nehardea? As far as the Nahardean *qab* is used.[80]

---

eral Jewish community or among the rabbis. I take it to mean the latter since the diversity recorded in the Bavli is mainly intrarabbinic dispute. I argue below that the rabbis in Babylonia actually had a more important role within their communities than they did in Palestine where the community was led by laypeople. This may suggest greater conformity among the general Jewish population in Babylonia to rabbinic authority, although it is also possible that Babylonian rabbis held strong authority only over their devotees while most other Jews were not rabbinized at all. In any case, the practice of the general Jewish community is outside the scope of this study, which focuses on intrarabbinic dispute.

80. Another *sugya* identifies various rabbis with specific cities in Babylonia:

דייני דפומבדיתא—רב פפא בר שמואל, דייני דנהרדעא—רב אדא בר מניומי, סבי דסורא—רב הונא ורב חסדא. סבי דפומבדיתא—רב יהודה ורב עינא, חריפי דפומבדיתא—עיפה ואבימי בני רחבה. אמוראי דפומבדיתא—רבה ורב יוסף. אמוראי דנהרדעי—רב חמא. נהרבלאי מתנו—רמי בר ברבי. אמרי בי רב—רב הונא.

"The judges of Pumbedita,"—Rav Papa bar Shmuel, "the judges of Nehardea"—R. Adda bar Minyomi, "the elders of Sura"—Rav Huna and Rav Ḥisda, "the elders of Pumbedita"—Rav Yehudah and R. 'Aina, "the acute sages of Pumbedita"—'Efa and Abimi the sons of Reḥabah, "the Amoraim of Pumbedita"—Rabbah and Rav Yosef, "the Amoraim of Nehardea"—R. Ḥama. "Those of Neharbelai taught,"—Rammi bar Berabi. Be Rav say—Rav Huna (*b. Sanh.* 17b).

See analysis at David Goodblatt, "Local Traditions in the Babylonian Talmud," *Hebrew Union College Annual* 48 (1977): 196–201 and 207.

Geoffrey Herman describes the administrative structure of Sasanian Babylonia in similar terms based on sigillographic evidence from the fifth and sixth centuries.[81] The country was divided into provinces, which were each ruled by a local governor.[82] The city called Maḥoza in rabbinic sources was called Weh-Ardasir by the Persians and was the capital of the province by the same name. Nehardea was close to the provincial center of Peroz-Sabur, which was itself likely to have been subordinated under Weh-Ardasir. Pumbedita was to the north of Peroz-Sabur. Sura and Meḥaseya were within the province of Weh-Kavad, which had the city of Babylon as its capital.[83] Therefore, "Babylon and its environs" in *b. Ketub.* 54a includes Meḥaseya and Sura, the domain of Rav;[84] "Nehardea and its environs" was the domain of Shmuel, though it is not clear what other cities that included.

Herman concludes, "One can assume that the administrative regions of the Sasanian Empire influenced the regions defined by the Jews and the spheres of influence of the various Torah centers just as it apparently influenced the experience of the Christians."[85] The stories above, especially those concerning Rav and Shmuel, come into much sharper focus when read with this regional map in mind. The Jewish population of Babylonia divided itself along the same regional lines used by the Sasanid government, and recognized the authority of certain rabbinic masters in each province.

Compare this with Roman Palestine, which, from 135 C.E. on, was all one administrative province of Syria-Palestina including Judea, Samaria, and Galilee, with the governor situated in Caesarea.[86] Only in the late fourth century was this province subdivided into Palestina Prima, Secunda, and Tertia.[87] Palestina Secunda included the Galilee and had Scythopolis as its capital. To be sure, even though the land of Israel was officially one

81. Some of these seals can be viewed at http://ecai.org/sasanianweb/ and http://www.grifterrec.com/coins/sasania/sas_seals/sas_seal.html.

82. Geoffrey Herman, "The Exilarchate in the Sasanian Era" (Ph.D. diss., Hebrew University, 2005), 22–23 (Hebrew).

83. Ibid., 24–26.

84. See *b. Ta'an.* 28b, where Rav travels to Babylon and feels he has authority to correct their liturgical practice. He refrains from correcting them only because he realizes that their practice is actually in line with his opinion. He was the authority not only for Sura, where he lived, but for the entire region of Weh-Kavad.

85. Herman, "Exilarchate," 26.

86. See Martin Goodman, *State and Society in Roman Galilee, A.D. 132–212* (Totowa, NJ: Rowman & Allanheld, 1983), 135; Michael Avi-Yonah, *The Holy Land from the Persian to the Arab Conquests (536 B.C. to A.D. 640)* (Grand Rapids: Baker Book House, 1966), 110; and Alon, *The Jews in Their Land*, 596.

87. See Avi-Yonah, *Holy Land*, 121; Abraham Schalit, *Roman Administration in Palestine* (Jerusalem: Mosad Bialik, 1937), 11–16 (Hebrew); and E. Mary Smallwood, *The Jews under Roman Rule from Pompey to Diocletian* (Leiden: Brill, 1981), 534 n. 29.

province for most of the Talmudic period, there were still municipal subdivisions within it,[88] and the areas of Judea and Galilee were generally viewed as distinct regions.[89] However, the Yerushalmi does not designate these territories as the jurisdiction of any particular rabbis, as does the Bavli. Interestingly, Rav and Shmuel in *b. Ketub.* 54a (cited above) disagree about an issue already recorded in *m. Ketub.* 4:12 as a matter practiced differently by "the people of Jerusalem," "the people of Galilee," and "the people of Judea."[90] Notice that the Mishnah identifies the differing parties as "the people of" each region, that is, the commoners.[91] The practice in each region is upheld by a mimetic tradition.[92] It is not based on a decision by the local rabbi, as in the Bavli where each region is said to follow a certain rabbi's ruling.[93]

---

88. Avi-Yonah, *Holy Land*, 127.

89. Reference to these regions is made in *m. Šeb.* 9:2; *m. Ketub.* 13:10; *m. B. Bat.* 3:2.

90. This not a matter of halakhic dispute in the Mishnah but simply a different law dependent on local custom. The people of Jerusalem and the Galilee were accustomed to write in the *ketubah* a different formulation than the people of Judea regarding maintenance of the wife after the death of the husband. Even if that line is not written in the *ketubah*, it is still assumed and required by the court. Thus, when that line is absent in Jerusalem or the Galilee, the court requires what the Jerusalemites and Galileans usually have written there, and the same goes for Judea. This falls into the category of regional differences listed above, pp. 127–29 nn. 2–8. (The same is true for *m. Ketub.* 1:5.) *B. Ketub.* 54a, however, uses the phrase "halakha is like R. X," meaning it is a halakhic dispute. It seems that the Babylonian Amoraim disputed which Palestinian practice is or should be the practice in Babylonia.

91. Aharon Oppenheimer, *Between Rome and Babylon: Studies in Jewish Leadership and Society* (Tübingen: Mohr Siebeck, 2005), 30–46, notes various echoes in Talmudic literature of changes in administrative divisions in Palestine. I have yet to find, however, an indication that a particular Palestinian rabbi was the recognized authority over a region.

92. The same seems to be true regarding other example of diversity within Palestine discussed by Finkelstein, *The Pharisees*, 43–72; and Levine, *Rabbinic Class*, 89.

93. Isaiah Gafni, *The Jews of Babylonia in the Talmudic Era: A Social and Cultural History* (Jerusalem: Zalman Shazar Center for Jewish History, 1990), 124–25 (Hebrew), discusses other differences between the two countries that are potentially relevant here. He finds that Babylonians felt a strong connection to their native cities. This is reflected by insults hurled by residents of one city against residents of other cities within Babylonia. This could help explain why residents of a city follow the authority in that city as a way of distinguishing themselves from competing cities. This can also account for the intolerance felt by visitors from one city to the next who practice according to their place of origin. However, we also find insults hurled within Palestine between the North and the South. See Joshua Schwartz, "Tension Between Scholars of Judea in the South and Scholars of the Galilee During the Era of the Mishna and Talmud (Bar-Kokhba)," *Sinai* 93 (1983): 102–9 (Hebrew).

Gafni, *Jews of Babylonia*, 124, also points to traditions quoted in the name of anonymous rabbis of a certain city such as אמרי נהרדעא—"Nehardeans say," as proof for local patriotism. Goodblatt, "Local Traditions," 187–217, argues that this and similar formulae refer to a specific group of rabbis in each town. Based on this, one could argue that by referring to the local circle of rabbis as speaking for the whole town, the Bavli reveals a society where the rabbis of each city wielded authority over its citizens. However, terms such as ציפוראי and טיבראי are also used in the Yerushalmi when quoting rabbinic statements. It is true that the Yerushalmi

These findings overlap those of Richard Kalmin, who has similarly shown that the rabbis in Babylonia were decentralized and had only occasional contact with one another[94] while rabbis in Palestine were better organized and sometimes cooperated in joint ventures.[95] He argues that "Babylonian rabbis in their own localities, part of a city, or an entire city and its environs, presided over their own 'fiefdoms.'"[96] Kalmin finds a correlation between the decentralization of the Babylonian rabbinic movement and the decentralized nature of the Sasanian Empire which was organized according to a feudal structure with a few noble families holding the power. In contrast, "the rabbinic movement in Palestine," claims Kalmin, "was influenced by centralizing trends in the Roman Empire," which had a strong central government.[97]

The rabbis of Palestine were mainly concentrated in urban areas of the Galilee, "usually in the immediate vicinity of Tiberias or Sepphoris."[98] That "their geographical diffusion was not in fact very great"[99] goes a long way in explaining why rabbis of Palestine were not recognized as local authorities in their respective cities. Most of them lived near each other and were competing to control the very same Jewish population.[100] This competition engendered less tolerance for diverse practices.

This leads us to another closely related factor contributing to the difference between the Talmuds, which is the stronger role of the rabbi in

---

terms sometimes refer to nonrabbinic residents of these towns; see Miller, *Sages and Commoners*, 31f. However, Goodblat also find cases where the Bavli formulae refer to laypeople. He writes: "In the four disputes at Ket. 55a 'the Pumbeditans' seem to be the townspeople in general. This is suggested by the contrast with the unqualified 'people of Mata Mehasya.' In other words, the 'disputes' consist of varying legal practice in the two towns" (Goodblatt, "Local Traditions," 207). These examples are similar to the mimetic traditions of Palestinian communities. More research is needed to compare the usage of these terms in the two Talmuds.

94. Richard Kalmin, *Sages, Stories, Authors, and Editors in Rabbinic Babylonia* (Atlanta: Scholars Press, 1994), especially 175–214.

95. Miller, *Sages and Commoners*, 457–58; and Hezser, *Social Structure*, 171–80, show that rabbinic society in Palestine was also rather decentralized. Nevertheless, interaction between rabbis in Palestine still seems to have been much greater in Palestine than in Babylonia.

96. Kalmin, *The Sage in Jewish Society*, 11.

97. Ibid., 13..

98. Schwartz, *Imperialism*, 124. Goodman, *State and Society*, 29, adds that villages in the Galilee are "often found remarkably close together." See also Hayim Lapin, "Rabbis and Cities in Later Roman Palestine: The Literary Evidence," *Journal of Jewish Studies* 50, no. 2 (1999): 187–207.

99. Schwartz, *Imperialism*, 123.

100. See Hezser, *Social Structure*, 179–84. Hezser shows that "at least two rabbis of the same generation are mentioned in connection with Sepphoris, Tiberias, and Caesarea, while only one rabbi tends to be mentioned for each village" (p. 181). It is possible that rabbis in villages had more independence than those in the cities; however, there were many more rabbis in cities and it is their voice that is primarily heard in the Yerushalmi.

Babylonia compared with the more prominent position of layleaders in Palestinian communities. This is relevant to the findings of Isaiah Gafni regarding the leadership of Palestinian communities compared with that of Babylonian communities. Gafni has found that concerning the issue of collecting charity, for example, the communities in Palestine appointed lay leaders to collect and manage charities while in Babylonia those tasks were undertaken by the rabbis. The same is true regarding market regulation and administration of education.[101] Palestinian communities had their own lay leadership and organizations of which the rabbis were only one component. In Babylonia, on the other hand, the rabbi was the official and recognized administrator for all such matters. Gafni explicitly relates such differences in administrative matters to the status of the rabbi in each country. He points to *b. Mo*ᶜ*ed Qaṭ.* 6a as representative of the Babylonian view:

> אמר אביי: שמע מינה: צורבא מרבנן דאיכא במתא כל מילי דמתא עליה רמיא.
> Abaye said: We can conclude from this that if a scholar is present in a town, all matters of the town are placed upon him.[102]

In Palestine, the community was run by lay leadership and had an identity independent of the rabbi. The Palestinian communities had their own sense of strong mimetic tradition that may have sometimes been in tension with the decisions of the rabbis.[103] Stuart Miller describes a "complex common Judaism" practiced by common Jews in Palestine, based mostly on the Bible.[104] Hence, the strong emphasis on *minhag* in Palestine, as discussed in the previous chapter.[105] The recognition of the rabbi as

---

101. See Gafni, *Jews of Babylonia*, 98–109, esp. citations at 102 n. 57. This finding is confirmed by Ze'ev Safrai, *The Jewish Community in the Talmudic Period* (Jerusalem: Zalman Shazar Center for Jewish History, 1995), 50–62 (Hebrew).

102. See further elaboration in Gafni, *Jews of Babylonia*, 106 n. 78.

103. See Goodman, *State and Society*, 93–111, who argues that at least for the second century, rabbinic authority among the masses of Palestinian Jews was rather weak. He sees a resuscitation of such authority in the third century but cites only *y. Ḥag.* 1:7 (76c) and *y. Yebam.* 12:6 (13a) in this regard (ibid., 110). Schwartz, *Imperialism*, 121–23, rejects the significance of those two Yerushalmi texts. Schwartz summarizes his findings: "Even though the rabbis established a foothold in urban and suburban Palestine in the course of the third century, … the rabbis did not have any officially recognized legal authority until the end of the fourth century. Even then it was severely restricted and in any case not limited to rabbis" (ibid., 103–4). Even Miller, *Sages and Commoners*, 446–66, who argues for a somewhat greater role for the rabbis in society, agrees that the movement remained rather insular.

104. See Stuart Miller, "Roman Imperialism, Jewish Self-Definition, and Rabbinic Society: Belayche's *Iudaea-Palaestina*; Schwartz's *Imperialism and Jewish Society*; and Boyarin's *Border Lines* Reconsidered," *AJS Review* 31, no. 2 (2007): 348–50; and Miller, *Sages and Commoners*, 21–28.

105. See especially the quote from Brody on p. 84, above.

administrator in Babylonian communities goes hand in hand with the recognition of the rabbi as the halakhic authority in all matters.[106]

Babylonian society often looked to the rabbi as their leader and administrator in many areas.[107] This resulted in local Babylonian communities centered around a particular rabbinic figure in each region, although this structure may have varied over time and place.[108] The vast number of stories about Rav and Shmuel certainly depict them as the local authorities of their times in their respective regions. This is unlike Palestinian society where the community had its own sense of identity independent of the rabbi. Regarding the leadership of Palestine, Ze'ev Safrai writes, "There was no rabbi in Jewish cities during the period of the Mishnah and Talmud. The rabbi of the city is not mentioned in the sources even in those tens of places where his mention would be expected had there been a role such as this."[109]

The weaker role of the rabbi in Palestine, caused by the geographic concentration of rabbis in the Galilee and their resulting competition, may in turn have caused Palestinian rabbinic society to remain with a mimetic view of halakha.[110] The stronger role of the rabbi in Babylonia, itself promoted by geographic decentralization and rabbinic "fiefdoms," may have in turn caused Babylonian rabbinic society to move toward a more intellectual and legislative model of halakha.

In sum, the rabbi as local authority was more institutionalized in Babylonia than in Palestine. Pluralism for local practice was built into the Babylonian social and political framework in a way that it was not in Palestine. Since each rabbi in Babylonia was recognized as the authority for his town, and visiting rabbis generally respected that authority, each town

---

106. Kalmin, *The Sage in Jewish Society*, 6–7, similarly writes, "Palestinian rabbis wish to strengthen their precarious status and be counted among the leaders of Jewish society.... Babylonian sources, in contrast, depict a rabbinic movement more secure in its social position, less economically dependent on outsiders, and more powerful than its Palestinian counterpart." This is not to say that the masses always followed the rabbis. Indeed, the Bavli makes note of various people who did not fully accept the authority of the rabbis (*b. Sanh.* 99b-100a). But, to the extent that they did submit to rabbinic authority, they would follow the opinions of the local rabbi.

107. Daniel Friedenberg and Norman Gold, *Sasanian Jewry and Its Culture* (Chicago: University of Illinois Press, 2009), 9, write that the Babylonian Amoraim "often doubled as district magistrates."

108. We should further assume that the local rabbi was considered the authority only by those Jews who closely identified with the rabbinic leadership generally. The rabbis did not have influence over the entire Jewish population of either Palestine or Babylonia. In any case, we are less interested in historical reality than in the way the Talmud portrays the position of the rabbis.

109. Safrai, *The Jewish Community in the Talmudic Period*, 157. My translation.

110. See the previous chapter. Of course, it is also possible that a mimetic view of halakha, perhaps the default view of previous generations, caused the diminished role of the rabbi in Palestine. Geographic centralization and competition would then just be another contributing factor to the rabbis' weaker role in Palestine.

could follow its own set of practices in peace. Ironically, this authority also sometimes bred intolerance for deviation within that town. Some Babylonian hosts, however, were gracious enough to tolerate different practices of their guests, as we saw above.

In Palestine, where communities did not define themselves based on their local rabbis, each rabbi pushed for his opinion to be the universal practice. There was therefore little recognition of any particular rabbi as the sole authority over any particular region. Certain outstanding personalities may have been recognized and respected by others who would think twice before disagreeing with that master. Such people would act as a unifying force throughout Palestine. However, there were no borders to authority and therefore no automatic tolerance built into the structure of society. As Hayim Lapin writes, "Concentration of rabbis in a few places facilitated both the cultivation of long-term relationships ... as well as competition and hostility."[111] Each master vied with his colleagues to gain authority over all Jews instead of carving up regions within which each master's authority was absolute but delimited. This resulted in there being less tolerance for diverse practices.

This conclusion fits well with the different attitudes in each Talmud regarding the prohibition not to make factions, as discussed in the previous chapter. The Yerushalmi prohibited any difference of halakha. Abaye and Rava, however, limit the law to multiple practices within a city or within the jurisdiction of a certain court. They do tolerate diversity across different cities or jurisdictions. This definition of the prohibition of *lo titgodedu* may partly derive from the social reality in Babylonia where each city had its own authority. Babylonians were evidently comfortable with such regional diversity.

The next two chapters will continue to compare rabbinic stories in the Talmuds involving diversity of practice, but now involving Tannaim. Chapter 4 will analyze narratives about Beth Shammai and Beth Hillel while chapter 5 will review those about Rabban Gamaliel and other figures.

111. Lapin, "Rabbis and Cities: Some Aspects," 57.

4

The Houses of Shammai and Hillel: Did They Live under the Same Roof?

What is a dispute for the sake of heaven?
This is the dispute between Hillel and Shammai.

m. ʾAbot 5:17

Introduction

It can be argued that the most prominent and pervasive example of halakhic multiplicity in all of rabbinic literature involves the multigenerational split between the Houses of Shammai and Hillel. The Houses began with the personages of Shammai and Hillel themselves near the beginning of the first century C.E.,[1] increased during the following decades,[2] and seem to have ceased around 70 C.E.[3] As we will see in the examples

1. Some of the controversies between the Houses may have predated even their founders, although the only example we have of this is the *semikha* controversy recorded in *m. Ḥag.* 2:2. See also Moshe Weiss, "Traces of Pre-Bet Shammai–Bet Hillel Explicit Halakhic Decisions," *Sidra* 8 (1992): 39–51 (Hebrew). However, the attribution of the Houses to these two personalities suggests that these disputes multiplied and became increasingly contentious during their lifetimes and those of their students.

2. See *t. Ḥag.* 2:9 quoted below, p. 167.

3. To be sure, followers of both Houses can be found throughout the Tannaitic period and even into the Amoraic period when Beth Hillel gradually became ascendant; see below, pp. 186–89 and 222–28. Nevertheless, it seems appropriate to mark 70 C.E. as an important turning point in the nature of the Houses. Alexander Guttmann, "The End of the 'Houses'," in *The Abraham Weiss Jubilee Volume* (New York: Abraham Weiss Jubilee Committee, 1964), 89–105, argues that the Houses ended shortly after 70 C.E. See also idem, "Hillelites and Shammaites: A Clarification," *Hebrew Union College Annual* 28 (1957): 115–26. Guttman's reliance on the Yerushalmi's testimony that at Yavneh a *bat qol* declared that "the law is according to Beth Hillel" is certainly problematic. The *bat qol* does not appear in any Tannaitic sources; see Boyarin, *Border Lines*, 162–63. See also Brandes, "Beginnings of the Rules," 154–66, who shows that the Tannaim did not yet have any established rule that halakha follows Beth Hillel. However, Guttmann adduces more convincing evidence from Tannaitic texts in which Tannaim active at the end of the first century were themselves debating the

analyzed in this chapter, the Houses did not debate merely at the theoretical level but actually practiced divergent sets of laws in numerous areas of halakha.[4] We will not analyze here the divergent practices themselves but rather the relationship engendered by them. As portrayed in rabbinic sources, did these differences in halakhic practice cause tension and hostility between the groups, or was there room for tolerance and mutual respect despite their divergences?

The earliest sources we have for the Houses are the Mishnah and Tosefta, which, although completed well over a century after the flourishing

---

proper interpretation of the opinions of the Houses, such as *t. Peʿah* 3:2; *t. Ḥag.* 2:10; and *t. Yebam.* 5:1 = *t. ʿEd.* 2:9. Guttmann, "End," 93, notes: "Existing schools, no doubt, would have been able to clarify their own views without admitting a controversy concerning the case in question." Cohen, "Yavneh," 28, agrees with Guttmann that the Houses ended soon after 70 C.E. at Yavneh "in consequence of the destruction of the Temple."

However, even if the Houses officially ended, there were still many individual proponents of each side. As Guttmann, "End," 95, writes: "Termination of the School does not mean the extermination of its members. As individuals they continued live [*sic*] for some time. They even may have continued as a sectarian school. Yet, as the recognized School of Shammai, they did not exist [after 70 C.E.]."

While the sources used by Guttmann do indicate that there was no formal school after 70 C.E., he does not verify that there ever was a formal school even before 70 C.E. There was surely no physical location for the school since its members tended to meet haphazardly in people's homes. See *m. Šabb.* 1:4, and the discussion of the term "houses" in Hezser, *Social Structure*, 308–15. See also Rubenstein, "Social and Institutional Settings," 60. Isaak Halevy, *Dorot ha-rishonim* (Jerusalem: 1966), 2:554, also notes that no leader of either House is ever mentioned. The "schools" may have been no more than two loosely organized groups of sages. The most significant change to happen after 70 C.E. is that the Houses are no longer anonymous, and "from now on, the controversies proceed under the name of individual sages" (Guttmann, "End," 95). The sages of the Houses themselves are almost always quoted anonymously in Tannaitic sources. In fact, we know the names of only a handful of sages belonging to each school; see Shmuel Safrai, "Bet Hillel and Bet Shammai," *Encyclopedia Judaica* (2007): 3:531. Cohen relates this shift not to any change in the Houses themselves but rather to a wider shift affecting all sects who spoke with one voice before 70 C.E. but as individuals afterward. See Cohen, "Yavneh," 46–47, for a possible explanation for this shift. See also Yonah Frenkel, *Sippur ha-agadah, aḥdut shel tokhen ve-ṣurah: koveṣ meḥqarim* (Tel Aviv: Hakibbutz Hameuchad, 2001), 346–48; and Heger, *Pluralistic Halakhah*, 245 n. 16, quoting Hayim Lapin, "Early Rabbinic Civil Law and the Literature of the Second Temple Period," *Jewish Studies Quarterly* 2 (1995): 149–83.

4. It may be worthwhile to cite a few examples here of Tannaitic sources that record cases dating to pre-70 C.E. times in which the Houses did practice their own opinions. *M. Sukkah* 2:8 tells us that Shammai followed his own opinions and had his family do so as well. *M. Yebam.* 1:4 claims that the Houses married each other despite their halakhic differences. This implies that the Houses must have been following different practices for otherwise we would have no reason to think that they would not marry each other. The patriarchal family preceding R. Gamaliel II followed Beth Shammai in three laws (*m. Beṣah* 2:6=*m. ʿEd.* 3:10). We learn in *m. Demai* 6:6 that a group called "the modest of Beth Hillel" would practice like Beth Shammai regarding certain laws. Conversely, R. Yoḥanan ben Haḥorani was a student of Beth Shammai but he always practiced according to Beth Hillel (*t. Sukkah* 2:3; *t. ʿEd.* 2:2). See more examples below, p. 186.

of the Houses, may still reliably preserve ancient traditions in some cases.[5] However, even when later Tannaitic and certainly Amoraic sources retroject contemporary reality into pre-70 C.E. stories or paint an idealized (or villianized) picture of a past that never existed, they are still significant for what they tell us about the attitudes of the authors and editors of these traditions. In fact, it is precisely when the later sources are out of step with history that we can most clearly detect their agenda.[6] We will therefore look to the Tannaitic and Amoraic sources not so much for what they might reveal about the historical Houses but more for what they reveal about the attitudes of their authors in the way they portray the Houses.[7] Our working assumption is that rabbinic sources about the past often describe "what 'ought to have been' according to the belief of the sages" who wish "to substantiate their own ideological preferences by attributing such beliefs to earlier periods."[8] What can we glean from the various rabbinic statements concerning the Houses about the attitudes of the Tannaim and Amoraim toward diversity of halakhic practice? Does the relationship between the Houses as portrayed in the Mishnah and Tosefta differ from the way it is portrayed in the Talmuds? Can we find any pattern in the interpretation of Tannaitic sources by the Yerushalmi and Bavli? What can such patterns teach us about the relative tolerance for diversity of practice in each era and country?

While most scholars consider the Houses to be two schools within the Pharisees,[9] others propose that they were more like two vying

---

5. The most significant nonrabbinic sources on the Houses are two paragraphs from Jerome relating to Shammai and Hillel. See quotes at Strack and Stemberger, *Introduction,* 65–66.

6. For the theoretical basis of this methodology, see Boyarin, "Anecdotal Evidence," 11–24.

7. On the problem of attribution of statements to the Houses, see Jacob Neusner, "Why We Cannot Assume the Historical Reliability of Attributions: The Case of the Houses in Mishnah-Tosefta Makhshirin," in *The Mishnah in Contemporary Perspective,* ed. Alan Avery-Peck and Jacob Neusner (Leiden: Brill, 2006), 190–212; Israel Ben-Shalom, *The School of Shammai and the Zealots' Struggle against Rome* (Jerusalem: Yad Izhak Ben-Zvi and Ben-Gurion University of the Negev Press, 1993), 234–35 (Hebrew); Moshe Weiss, "The Authenticity of the Explicit Discussions in Bet Shammai-Bet Hillel Disputes," *Sidra* 4 (1988) (Hebrew); and Y. N. Epstein, *Mevo'ot le-sifrut ha-Tannaim, Mishnah, Tosefta, u-midreshe halakha,* ed. E. Z. Melamed (Jerusalem: Magnes, 1947), 60–61. Epstein suggests that all disputes and dialogues recorded in the Mishnah between the Houses were actually collected and redacted by R. Yehoshua. See also Heger, *Pluralistic Halakhah,* 358–59, for the suggestion that Yavnean sages attributed strict laws to Beth Shammai and lenient laws to Beth Hillel. Heger also puts forward the possibility that "the Sages of later generations who decided that the halakha was always to be decided according to Beit Hillel may have reversed the attributions of specific declarations." If true, this would make it impossible to reconstruct the reality of the historical Houses from the Tannaitic sources.

8. Heger, *Pluralistic Halakhah,* 247.

9. Cohen, *From the Maccabees,* 157. For proponents of this view see Davies, *Setting,* 264; Jacob Neusner, *Rabbinic Traditions about the Pharisees before 70,* vol. 2 (Leiden: Brill, 1970),

sects.[10] The difficulty that historians have in determining the relationship between the Houses is due to the varying presentations within the rabbinic sources themselves. These sources present a range of attitudes toward diversity from outright violence, coercion, and delegitimization at one extreme, to cordial disagreement and attempts to reconcile in the middle, to good social relations and tolerance at the other extreme. We will review the most relevant Tannaitic statements regarding the Houses, beginning with their founding, and then analyze how the Talmuds re-present and interpret those sources. We will find that the Tannaitic sources include a variegated set of portrayals of the Houses from irenic to acrimonious. The Yerushalmi generally emphasizes the acrimonious traditions while the Bavli gives more weight to the irenic sources.

The Rise of the Houses

Tosefta Ḥagigah 2:9 laments the rise of the Houses as a regrettable and unwelcome event:[11]

192–93; and Yitzhak D. Gilat, "Le-maḥloqet Beth Shamai u-Beth Hillel," in *Yad le-Gilat* (Jerusalem: Bialik Institute, 2002), 166.

10. Proponents of the first view point out that the content of their arguments fits into what we know about the Pharisees from other sources. However, as Cohen, *From the Maccabees*, 158, notes, the issues about which the Houses disagree, such as purity laws and festivals, are topics that also divide the various sects, and there is no evident reason why the Houses should not have similarly separated into sects. Cohen defines "sect" in ibid., 124–27. See also Baumgarten, *Flourishing*, 56, who concludes based on the similarity in terminology used by the sects that "the law as observed by one group was not that different from the way it was fulfilled by others ... all were offering more or less the same merchandise." Nevertheless, Baumgarten, ibid., 78, argues that they remained a single movement despite differences in legal practice because they still agreed "on the source of *legal authority*" (italics in original). This view is based on Morton Smith, "What Is Implied by the Variety of Messianic Figures?" *Journal of Biblical Literature* 78 (1959): 66–72. See, however, Noam, "Beth Shammai veha-halakha ha-kitatit," 49, who argues that Beth Shammai shared the same "*halakhic* mindset" as the Qumran sect.

Cohen, *From the Maccabees*, 158, concludes that he prefers "to admit ignorance." He admits to knowing "neither the social reality that the houses represent nor the relationship of the houses to the Pharisees." Indeed, even if the Houses considered themselves members of the Pharisaic movement, we can still question the extent to which they lived peacefully, tolerating each other's differences, or felt hostile tension toward each other, each vying to define proper Pharisaism. The two Houses may have felt fairly close to each other because they had much more in common with the other than with the non-Pharisaic sects. On the other hand, one argues most often and sometimes most vehemently with those most similar to oneself. Cohen himself assumes sectarian-like acrimony between the Houses. He says that the "wishful thinking" of *m. Yebam.* 1:4 "cannot disguise the truth" (idem, "Yavneh," 48).

11. A similar sentiment regarding diversity of opinion in general is found in *m. B. Bat.* 9:10; see below, p. 390. The following text is further analyzed below, pp. 303–7.

אמר רבי יוסי כתחלה לא היו מחלוקות[12] בישראל אלא בית דין של שבעים ואחד היו בלשכת הגזית....[13] נשאלה הלכה אם שמעו אמרו להן ואם לאו עומדין על המנין רבו המטמאין טמאו רבו המטהרין טהרו ומשם הלכה יוצא ורווחת בישראל. משרבו תלמידי שמאי והלל שלא שמשו כל צרכן רבו המחלוקות בישראל.[14]

R. Yose said: At first, there were no divisions[12] within Israel. Rather, there was a court of seventy members in the chamber of hewn stone....[13] A question would be asked. If they heard [a tradition answering that question] they [the judges] informed them [the inquirers]. If not, they would take it to a vote. If those who declared it impure had the majority, they declared it impure; if those who declared it pure had the majority, they declared it pure. From there did the law emanate and spread throughout Israel. Once the students of Shammai and Hillel, who did not serve sufficiently, became numerous, divisions multiplied in Israel.[14]

---

12. The word מחלוקת (the spelling is different in each manuscript, see chart at Hidary, "Tolerance for Diversity," 355–57) in rabbinic literature can mean both "argument" and "faction." It is not always clear which definition is meant. It always means "division" in biblical usage; see Josh 11:23; 1 Sam 23:28; Neh 12:36; 1 Chron 27:1, and passim. Naeh, "Rooms," 853–56, esp. nn. 23, 25, shows that the word מחלוקת in most Tannaitic contexts refers not to differences of opinion but rather to camps or parties. Thus, early rabbinic usage is similar to biblical usage. He argues that we should also understand מחלוקות in *t. Ḥag.* 2:9 as "factions," as is confirmed by the word כיתות in the Yerushalmi parallel (see below, p. 169). If correct, this means that the Tosefta thinks of the Houses as two factions or even sects. Naeh argues that the phrase "מחלוקת קרח ועדתו" in *m. ʾAbot* 5:17 should also be translated as "the faction of Qoraḥ and his assembly." However, as he notes, ibid., 855 n. 19, the phrase "מחלוקת שמאי והילל" must be translated as "the dispute between Shammai and Hillel." Since it is the latter who argue for the sake of heaven, I have chosen the word "dispute" in the title of this book. See also Ben-Menahem et al., *Controversy and Dialogue in the Jewish Tradition: A Reader,* 4–5; and Ben-Menahem et al., *Controversy and Dialogue in Halakhic Sources*, xx-xxii. For a broader discussion of Hebrew and Aramaic terms connoting "to differ," see David Daube, "Dissent in Bible and Talmud," *California Law Review* 59 (1971): 784–87.

13. For the significance of this chamber see Joshua Efron, *Studies on the Hasmonean Period* (Leiden: Brill, 1987), 297, and p. 301 n. 12.

14. Text is based on ms. London. Ms. Vienna, both here and in *t. Sanh.* 7:1, adds "ונעשו שתי תורות—and there arose two Torahs." Ms. Erfurt, both here and in *t. Sanh.* 7:1, omits these words. See Lieberman, *The Tosefta*, Moed, 384, and idem, *Tosefta ki-fshuṭah*, ad loc. These words are also present in *y. Sanh.* 1:4 (19c) and in slightly subdued form in *b. Sanh.* 88b, "ונע־שית תורה כשתי תורות—the Torah became as two Torahs."

David Hoffmann, *The First Mishna and the Controversies of the Tannaim: The Highest Court in the City of the Sanctuary* (New York: Maurosho Publications of Cong. Kehillath Yaakov, 1977), 79–82 (Hebrew), argues that the entire sentence from משרבו תלמידי until תורות was borrowed from *t. Soṭah* 14:9 by the editors of the Tosefta and is not original to R. Yose's statement in *t. Ḥag.* 2:9 and *t. Sanh.* 7:1 because it interrupts the flow of ideas from משם היתה יוצאת הלכה to ומשם שולחין ובודקין. See also Avi Sagi, *'Elu va-Elu': A Study on the Meaning of Halakhic Discourse* (Tel-Aviv: Hakibbutz Hameuchad, 1996), 176–79 (Hebrew); Naeh, "Rooms," 856 n. 25; and Ben-Menahem et al., *Controversy and Dialogue in Halakhic Sources*, 3:511, who agree with Hoffman. Hoffmann is certainly correct to notice that this Tosefta is made up of parts that do not hold together smoothly. However, taking out this sentence ignores the literary structure of

In this Tosefta, R. Yose provides two reasons for the rise of factionalism: the demise of the high court[15] and the multiplying of students of Shammai and Hillel.[16] *T. Soṭah* 14:9 focuses only on the latter and adds that the split between the Houses gave rise to "two Torahs."[17] The rabbis imagine the "good old days" as a time when one rabbinic high court presided over a hierarchical national judicial and legislative system that regulated and unified all aspects of Jewish law. Because this description has little basis in historical reality, it is all the more important as a reflection of the ideal society imagined by R. Yose and probably a good number of other Tannaim as well.[18] This rewriting of history reflects their discomfort with halakhic dispute and a hankering after an imaginary utopia of halakhic homogeneity.[19] We find little mention of Second Temple sectarianism in

---

the Tosefta. *T. Ḥagigah* and *t. Sanhedrin* begin, "At first there was no controversy in Israel," which is the counterpart to "controversy multiplied in Israel." The sentence that Hoffmann strikes is the semantic completion of the opening sentence contrasting the original situation with the new reality. The sentence must therefore be an integral part of *t. Ḥag.* 2:9 as we have it. Rather, it seems that the original tradition was similar to that stated anonymously at *y. Ḥag.* 2:2 (77d), cited below, which focuses only on the history of the Houses as the reason for the rise of factions, and the discussion of the court system was added to this statement.See Ishay Rosen-Zvi, "Ha-'umnam 'protocol' bet ha-din be-Yavne? ʿIyyun meḥudash be-Tosefta sanhedrin perek 7" (forthcoming). See further textual issues discussed below, pp. 303–4 nn. 16–21.

15. This source assumes that all halakha was originally based on a unified received set of traditions. If a local court received the tradition on a given matter there is no need to go to the higher court, and it is assumed that every local court knows the same set of received traditions. Only if a local court has not received a tradition regarding a certain matter do they consult the higher court. Even this source admits that there could be differences of opinion regarding matters about which even the high court has no tradition, but these differences are put to a final majority vote so there is only one final ruling in all matters. See Brandes, "Beginnings of the Rules," 94–95.

16. Hoffmann, *First Mishnah*, 82–83, convincingly argues that these two reasons are not mutually exclusive. Rather, the lack of diligence by the students caused forgetting of laws based on tradition while the loss of the Sanhedrin caused a problem only in deciding new laws for which there was no tradition (see previous note).

17. See above, n. 14. This source also blames another group for the rise of factionalism, "משרבו זחוחי הלב רבו מחלוקות בישראל והן הן שופכי דמים—When the arrogant of spirit multiplied, division multiplied in Israel, and these very people are murderers." It is not clear if this refers to some specific sect or just arrogant people in general. Lieberman, *Tosefta ki-fshuṭah*, 8:755, opts for the latter. See further in Ben-Menahem et al., *Controversy and Dialogue in Halakhic Sources*, 3:507–8.

18. It is interesting to note that similar descriptions of the origins of controversy are found regarding the Platonic academy; see Shaye Cohen, "A Virgin Defiled: Some Rabbinic and Christian Views on the Origins of Heresy," *Union Seminary Quarterly Review* 36 (1980): 8; Boyarin, *Border Lines*, 162; and Rosen-Zvi, "Ha-'umnam," nn. 144–45. Cf. Rosental, "Masoret halakha," 321–24.

19. See *m. ʿEd.* 8:7. According to R. Shimon, when Eliyahu comes at the end of days he will reconcile all controversy, "רבי שמעון אומר להשוות המחלוקת." See further on this text below, p. 276.

Tannaitic literature, certainly nothing that could prepare us for what we know based on pre-Talmudic sources.[20] Instead, the rabbis retroject themselves as representative of the mainstream throughout the Second Temple period. They trace their traditions directly back to Sinai in an unbroken chain[21] and record only one controversial issue in the days before Shammai and Hillel.[22] This longing for the single authentic truth goes hand in hand with the rabbis' need to establish their own teachings as the only authentic interpretation of the Torah.[23] Sectarianism and controversy only weaken this claim by relegating each rabbi's opinion to just one possibility among many. The Yerushalmi parallel to this Tosefta, *y. Ḥag.* 2:2 (77d) further amplifies the same longing for unity:

> בראשונה לא היתה מחלוקת בישראל אלא על הסמיכה בלבד ועמדו שמי והלל ועשו אותן ארבע משרבו תלמידי בית שמי ותלמידי בית הלל ולא שימשו את רביהן כל צורכן ורבו המחלוקות בישראל ונחלקו לשתי כיתות אילו מטמאין ואילו מטהרין ועוד אינה עתידה לחזור למקומה עד שיבוא בן דוד.
>
> At first, there was no controversy in Israel except concerning the issue of laying the hands. Shammai and Hillel came and made them [the number of controversies] four. Once the students of the House of Shammai and the students of the House of Hillel

---

20. Baumgarten, *Flourishing,* 4, points to one Talmudic text that possibly refers to Second Temple sectarianism, אמר רבי יוחנן לא גלו ישראל עד שנעשו עשרים וארבע כיתות של מינים—"R. Yoḥanan said, Israel was not exiled until it split up into twenty-four sects of heretics" (*y. Sanh.* 10:3, 29c). See Saul Lieberman, *Texts and Studies* (New York: Ktav, 1974), 199 n. 69. The prohibition "Do not make factions" and the laws of the rebellious elder and *Horayot* may each be reactions to sectarianism (see respectively, above, p. 97 n. 52, and below, pp. 320–21 and 361 n. 59). See also below, n. 23 and p. 189 n. 110. Many texts mention Sadducees and Boethusians, but always as part of a fringe group outside the mainstream rabbinic community. Naeh, "Rooms," 855 n. 20, suggests that "Qoraḥ and his assembly" in *m. ʾAbot* 5:17 may be a veiled reference to a sectarian group similar to the way the Dead Sea sect used various pseudonyms for contemporary groups.

21. Brandes, "Beginnings of the Rules," 96 n. 3, justifies the rabbinic history because he claims that *t. Ḥag.* 2:9 focuses only on strife within the Pharisaic movement. This, however, also cannot be historically accurate because *t. Ḥag.* 2:9 assumes the reality of a Pharisaic Sanhedrin, which likely never existed. See Moore, *Judaism in the First Centuries,* 82, for a description of the constitution of the Sanhedrin. In addition, Strack and Stemberger, *Introduction,* 4, point out that even in the chain of tradition of *m. ʾAbot* 1–2, "there is a break after Hillel and Shammai; after them, only Yoḥanan ben Zakkai is described in the same language of tradition (*qibbel-masar*), while the appended list of patriarchs and the enumeration of the other rabbis does not employ this typical terminology."

22. *M. Ḥag.* 2:2, *t. Ḥag.* 2:8. See Brandes, "Beginnings of the Rules," 97 n. 7.

23. One wonders whether this rewriting of history is inspired by a polemic against the Sadducees who, foreshadowing the attacks of the Karaites, rejected the authenticity of the oral law and looked to rabbinic controversy as proof that they had no such tradition. Even if it was not intended by the rabbis as such, the Geonim do cite the idea of a unified tradition from Sinai in their polemics against Karaite attacks regarding the authenticity of the oral Torah. See Halbertal, *People of the Book,* 52–72.

> became numerous and did not serve their masters[24] sufficiently, controversies multiplied in Israel and [Israel] split into two sects. These declared impure and those declared pure. The situation will not return to its first place in the future until the son of David arrives.

The Yerushalmi includes more detail about the history of controversy before the Houses, lacks reference to the high court, and instead places all the blame on the irresponsible students of Shammai and Hillel. The Yerushalmi explicitly calls the Houses sects (כתות), further emphasizing the magnitude of the split between them. It sees controversy as an enduring part of the new state of affairs, irreversible until the end of days as part of a messianic hope.[25] As we will see below, the Yerushalmi consistently reads more tension into Tannaitic recollections of the Houses than is present in the original sources.

R. Yoḥanan ben Haḥorani's *Sukkah*

While the above sources bemoan the rise of the Houses and describe them as two factions, they do not provide much detail about how the two groups treated each other. However, a number of incisive narratives about the Houses do reveal much more. *M. Sukkah* 2:7 relates that Beth Shammai requires one's table to be with him inside his *sukkah* while Beth Hillel permits the table to be outside the *sukkah* as long as his body is mostly inside. On one occasion, members of both Houses went to visit R. Yoḥanan ben Haḥorani, who had his table outside his *sukkah*. Beth Shammai audaciously told R. Yoḥanan ben Haḥorani, "If you have so practiced, then you have not fulfilled the law of *sukkah* in your life."[26] It is possible that they dealt more harshly with R. Yoḥanan ben Haḥorani than they would have with another sage who followed Beth Hillel because R. Yoḥanan was a student of Beth Shammai.[27] Be that as it may, we have here one example

24. On the concept of service in the master-disciple relationship see Martin Jaffee, *Torah in the Mouth: Writing and Oral Tradition in Palestinian Judaism 200 BCE–400 CE* (Oxford: Oxford University Press, 2001), 147–51; Shaye Cohen, "The Rabbis in Second-Century Jewish Society," in *The Cambridge History of Judaism. Vol. 3: The Early Roman Period*, ed. W. Horbury et al. (Cambridge: Cambridge University Press, 1999), 952–54; Hezser, *Social Structure*, 332–46; Levine, *Rabbinic Class*, 59–61; and further citations in Miller, *Sages and Commoners*, 372 n. 96.

25. See also above, n. 19.

26. The text of *m. Sukkah* 2:7 can be found below, p. 222.

27. See *t. Sukkah* 2:3. It is also possible that this particular issue was exceptional because the opinion of Beth Shammai was generally accepted in this case. See *y. Sukkah* 2:8 (53b), cited below p. 224, and *b. Sukkah* 3a where various Amoraim decide halakha in

where, according to the Mishnah, Beth Shammai utterly invalidates the opinion of Beth Hillel.

Reciting the *Shema* Standing or Reclining

In another case, the Houses argue about the proper position in which one should recite *Shema*. Beth Shammai, applying a pedantically literal interpretation to Deut 6:7, says that one should recline when reciting at night and stand during the day. Beth Hillel says any position is fine. *M. Berakot* 1:3 relates:

> אמר ר׳ טרפון אני הייתי בא בדרך והטיתי לקרות כדברי בית שמאי וסכנתי בעצמי מפני הלסטים אמרו לו כדי היית לחוב בעצמך שעברת על דברי בית הלל.
>
> R. Ṭarfon said, "I was traveling on the road and I lay down to recite in accordance with Beth Shammai and I put myself in danger from robbers." They told him, "You deserved to come to harm for you transgressed the words of Beth Hillel."

R. Ṭarfon, a second-generation Tanna, reports that he once lay down to recite the *Shema* while on the road thus putting himself in danger from robbers. Presumably, R. Ṭarfon would always lie down according to the opinion of Beth Shammai;[28] but this occurrence was more remarkable because of the danger. We have here a report of a mainstream and important rabbi actually practicing according to the view of Beth Shammai. The Mishnah portrays R. Ṭarfon's colleagues as being fairly intolerant of any practice that follows Beth Shammai and go so far as to rebuke him severely for his actions.[29] It is not clear if we are meant to understand R. Ṭarfon as expressing regret about his practice in this case because of the unanticipated danger or boasting about how seriously he takes the law that he would even

---

accordance with Beth Shammai in this case. See, however, below, p. 223 n. 189, regarding *b. Sukkah* 3a.

28. R. Ṭarfon's allegiance to Beth Shammai is also seen in *y. Šeb.* 4:2 (35b). On the other hand, R. Ṭarfon expresses desire to reject Beth Shammai in *t. Yebam.* 1:10; see below, p. 193. A plain reading of *t. Ḥag.* 2:13 also reflects R. Ṭarfon following Beth Shammai. R. Ṭarfon will not eulogize on the day after the holiday (*yom teboaḥ)* even though Beth Hillel says, "there is no *teboaḥ*." However, see Lieberman, *Tosefta ki-fshuṭah,* 5:1305–6, quoting *Tosfot Rid,* who explains that Beth Hillel also recognized an optional *yom teboaḥ*. See also Rabbi Hayyim Yosef David Azulai, *Sefer birke Yosef* (Jerusalem: Siaḥ Yisra'el, 2000), *siman* 494:4, p. 467.

29. We cannot be sure if this is a transcript of an actual dialogue and if the curse represents the opinion of the majority of rabbis at the time of R. Ṭarfon. It is possible that the dialogue was created or intensified by a later redactor. Either way, the inclusion of this story in the Mishnah, which does not regularly record narrative, is significant for assessing the views of the Mishnah's redactors.

intentionally risk his life for it.[30] According to the first reading, the rabbis emphatically confirm that R. Ṭarfon used poor judgment and therefore deserved to come to harm.[31] According to the second reading, R. Ṭarfon's colleagues may not have condemned him had he already expressed regret for his actions. Rather, they gave such harsh rebuke precisely because of R. Ṭarfon's boasting.[32] The strong reaction of the rabbis is all the more outstanding in the first reading; the rabbis feel so antagonistic to Beth Shammai that they rebuke R. Ṭarfon even after his unsolicited apology.

The condemnation is even more significant because Beth Hillel allows one to recite lying down as well, so R. Ṭarfon violated no prohibition.[33] Rather, it was simply his intention to follow Beth Shammai that bothered his colleagues. This antagonism seems to reflect widespread tension between the followers of each of the Houses, at least as perceived by the tellers of this narrative.

We read of a similar story involving younger contemporaries of R. Ṭarfon. This story appears in a number of places, but I will cite the Tosefta version at *Ber.* 1:4:[34]

[A] מעשה בר׳ ישמעאל ור׳ אלעזר בן עזריה שהיו שרויין במקום אחד והיה ר׳ ישמעאל מוטה ור׳ אלעזר בן עזריה זקוף
[B] הגיע זמן קרית שמע נזקף ר׳ ישמעאל והטה ר׳ אלעזר בן עזריה
[C] אמ׳ לו ר׳ ישמעאל מה זה אלעזר
[D] אמ׳ לו ישמעאל אחי לאחד אומר לו מפני מה זקנך מגודל והוא אומר להם יהיה כנגד המשחיתים אני שהייתי זקוף הטיתי ואת שהייתה מוטה נזקפתה

30. For the latter reading, see Azulai, ibid., and others quoted there; and Mordechai Sabato, "Qeri'at shemaᶜ shel R. Ishmaᶜel ve-shel R. 'Eleazar ben ᶜAzariah veha-hakhraᶜah ke-Beth Hillel," *Sidra* 22 (2007): 51–52. *B. ᶜErub.* 21b reports that R. Akiba also endangered his life in order to fulfill a relatively minor law.

31. The robbers seem to be a threat not only to his property but also to his life. See *y. Ber.* 1:4 (3b) = *y. Sanh.* 11:4 (30a) = *y. ᶜAbod. Zar.* 2:7 (41c), and *b. Ber.* 11a, which assume that the response of the rabbis here is that he deserved to die in the hands of the robbers.

32. The Talmuds, however, taking the story out of context, do not assume that the condemnation was dependent on the boasting or even on R. Ṭarfon's placing himself in danger. Rather, the Yerushalmi (*y. Ber.* 1:4, 3b) assumes that the rebuke of the rabbis was justified because he violated rabbinic law, which is more beloved to God than biblical law. According to the wording of the Yerushalmi, even had R. Ṭarfon not put himself in danger, he would still have been liable to death for rejecting Beth Hillel. Similarly, Rav Naḥman bar Isaac derives the universal principle from this Mishnah that "If one follows the opinion of Beth Shammai he is liable to death" (*b. Ber.* 11a, see below, p. 222).

33. *M. Ber.* 1:3 quotes Beth Hillel ruling, "One may recite in his usual manner." See also *b. Ber.* 11a. See, however, Amram Tropper, ""Ub-lekhtekha ba-derekh": Beth Hillel kedarkan," (forthcoming), who explains based on Amram Gaon that Beth Hillel would allow one to remain in whatever position he was in before but not move into the position required by Beth Shammai.

34. Ms. Vienna. The story also appears in *Sifre Deut.*, *pisqa* 34 (ed. Finkelstein, 62–63); *y. Ber.* 1:3 (3b); and *b. Ber.* 11a. See the comparison in chart 4.1 below, p. 234.

[E] אמר לו אתה הטיתה לקיים דברי בית שמאי ואני נזקפתי לקיים [דברי] בית הלל
[F] דבר אחר שלא יראו התלמידים ויעשו קבע הלכה כדבריך

[A] It happened that R. Ishmael and R. Eleazar ben Azariah were lodging in the same place. R. Ishmael had been reclining and R. Eleazar ben Azariah had been standing.
[B] The time to recite *Shema* arrived. R. Ishmael stood up [after][35] R. Eleazar ben Azariah reclined.
[C] R. Ishmael asked, "What is this Eleazar?"
[D] He responded, "Ishmael, my brother, [this is similar to] one who is asked, 'Why is your beard overgrown?' And he responds to them, 'So that it should protest against those who shave with a razor.'[36] I, who was standing, reclined, and you, who were reclining, stood up!"
[D] [R. Ishmael] told him, "You reclined in order to fulfill the words of Beth Shammai. I stood up in order to fulfill the words of Beth Hillel."
[E] Another version, [R. Ishmael told him, "I stood up] so that the students should not see me [reclining] and set the law permanently according to your view."

R. Eleazar ben Azariah reclines in accordance with the teaching of Beth Shammai. His colleague, R. Ishmael, stands up just to show his disagreement. This story reflects a slightly more cordial relationship than the previous story. R. Ishmael does not condemn R. Eleazar, but he does ask, "מה זה אלעזר—What is this Eleazar?"[37] The phrase מה זה often has an accusatory or critical connotation.[38] In the Sifre, Tosefta, and Bavli versions of this story, R. Eleazar addresses his colleague with the diplomatic term, "ישמעאל אחי—Ishmael, my brother." This term is used a handful of times in conversations of the Tannaim.[39] It is missing, however, in the Yerushalmi (see chart 4.1, p. 234). This may be a simple scribal error,[40] but it may also reflect a slightly less friendly atmosphere in the Yerushalmi version.

---

35. In the Tosefta version as well as in *Sifre Deut.*, *pisqa* 34, R. Ishmael acts first. *Y. Ber.* 1:3 (3b) and *b. Ber.* 11a, however, have R. Eleazar acting first. See chart 4.1, p. 231. Lieberman, *Tosefta ki-fshuṭah*, 1:4, line 20, explains that the Tosefta version too must be interpreted to mean that R. Eleazar acted first based on the context. See, however, Sabato, "Qeri'at shemaᶜ," 49–51, who rejects Lieberman's reading.

36. See Lieberman, *Tosefta ki-fshuṭah*, 1:5, line 22.

37. This question is quoted only in the Sifre and Tosefta but not in the Yerushalmi or Bavli.

38. See *m. Pesaḥ.* 6:2; *m. Naz.* 7:4; *t. Yoma* 1:4; *t. Sukkah* 2:1; *t. Ḥag.* 2:12; *t. B. Qam.* 7:13; and *t. ʾOhal* 3:7.

39. Ginzberg, *Commentary*, 146 n. 5. See also Lieberman, *Tosefta ki-fshuṭah*, 1:5 n.17.

40. Ginzberg, ibid.

Another difference between the versions may contribute to the hypothesis that the Yerushalmi assumes a more hostile atmosphere. Each version of the story, except the *Sifri,* uses a different word to express that the two rabbis were together in the same place.[41] The Tosefta uses the word שרויין as does the Yerushalmi in ms. Leiden. This is a neutral word that simply means "dwelling." Significantly, a Geniza manuscript of the Yerushalmi reads נתונים,[42] which has a negative connotation, implying that the two rabbis were forced to be together against their wills.[43]

Furthermore, the Yerushalmi places the event during the day such that R. Eleazar stands in accordance with Beth Shammai and R. Ishmael lays down in accordance with Beth Hillel. Ginzberg says that the Palestinian custom, certainly in Geonic times and probably also at the time this *sugya* was redacted, was to always stand during the *Shema,* be it day or night.[44] The Yerushalmi therefore changed the setting from nighttime to daytime. Had R. Ishmael stood at night, this would not have expressed an act of defiance since he would have stood in any case. Changing the setting to the daytime, on the other hand, greatly increases the polemical aspect of R. Ishmael's defiant act. R. Ishmael goes so far as to violate a custom of standing during *Shema* just to lie down in protest of R. Eleazar's standing. This move in the Yerushalmi again reflects a more acrimonious atmosphere.

R. Eleazar compares the reaction of R. Ishmael to those Jews who do not trim their beards as a protest against those who shave with a razor.[45]

---

41. This is noted in the story because the two rabbis did not live nearby. R. Ishmael lived in Kikar Aziz near Edom in Southern Judea (*m. Ketub.* 5:8 and *m. Kil.* 6:4). R. Eleazar ben Azariah was involved in the politics at Yavneh (*m. Zebah.* 1:3; *m. Yad.* 4:2; *y. Ber.* 4:1 (7d); *b. Ber.* 27b–28a) and so must have lived there for at least a significant part of his life. See also Tropper, "Ub-lekhtekha ba-derekh," who argues that the Sifre version is the most original and that the later versions needed to add this background to the story after they omitted ודורש in the original Sifre version.

42. Ginzberg, *Yerushalmi Fragments,* 5.

43. Idem, *Commentary,* 144 n. 3. The Bavli replaces this word with מסובין (lit., surrounding [the table]), which may suggest that they were dining together in a more congenial setting. Ginzberg, ibid., 144, claims that שרויין, from the root שרי in the sense of "dwelling," is common in Palestinian Aramaic but not in Babylonian Aramaic. He thereby explains the change from the Tosefta and Yerushalmi (ms. Leiden) to the Bavli. However, there are many examples of שרא in the sense of dwelling in the Bavli, such as *b. Ber.* 64a; *b. Šabb.* 6b, 88b; *b. ʿErub.* 48b, 70a-b. Binyamin Katzoff, "Ha-yaḥas ben ha-Tosefta veha-Yerushalmi le-masekhet Berakhot" (Ph.D. diss., Bar-Ilan University, 2004), 101 n. 16, explains that the Bavli changes שרויין in the Palestinian version to מסובין in order to update the verb to be more commonplace and clear. While this explanation is plausible, it does not rule out the possibility that the change may also reflect an underlying assumption about the atmosphere surrounding this incident.

44. Ginzberg, *Commentary,* 146–47. See also Benovitz, *Berakhot,* 510.

45. See various possible explanations of this line discussed in Sabato, "Qeri'at shemaʿ," 44–49.

The narrator then offers two alternative responses on behalf of R. Ishmael. In the first, R. Ishmael explains that he acted in accordance with Beth Hillel and was therefore justified while R. Eleazar acted according to Beth Shammai and was therefore not justified. This response reflects a fundamental delegitimization by R. Ishmael of Beth Shammai. In the second response, R. Ishmael does not condemn R. Eleazar but is concerned only that the watching students will get the wrong impression that he agrees with Beth Shammai as well. In this version, R. Ishmael does not necessarily intend to delegitimize Beth Shammai as much as to clarify his own stance on the matter.

Significantly, *b. Ber.* 11a, commenting on the words דבר אחר[46] at end of this *baraita,* offers a telling interpretation:

> מאי דבר אחר וכי תימא במטין נמי שוין הני מילי היכא דמטי ואתי מעיקרא אבל הכא כיון דעד השתא זקוף והשתא מוטה שמע מינה כבית שמאי סבירא להו שמא יראו התלמידים ויקבעו הלכה לדורות.[47]
>
> What is "another statement"? If you should say that [Beth Hillel] also agree [with Beth Shammai] that one may recline, this is only if he had been reclining already. But in this case, since you [R. Eleazar] had been standing and you only now reclined, [onlookers will say,] "therefore he must agree with Beth Shammai." Perhaps students will see this and set the law [according to Beth Shammai] for generations.

The Bavli wonders why the *baraita* offers a second response in the name of R. Ishmael if the first was sufficient. It therefore presents a rejection of the first response: R. Ishmael did not stand in order to follow Beth Hillel since even Beth Hillel agrees that one may lie down. Rather, R. Ishmael stood only so that onlookers would not mistake his lying down along with R. Eleazar who had been standing as a sign that R. Ishmael follows Beth Shammai. In the Palestinian versions, the first response has R. Ishmael offer a highly polemical response; R. Ishmael lay down even though Beth Hillel permitted standing as well just to show his objection to R. Eleazar's action. The Bavli, however, takes all of the punch out of the first response. The Stammaitic discussion explains that the second response is necessary

46. Bavli witnesses do not all agree on these words. Ms. Oxford, a Gaonic responsum, the glossator to ms. Munich, and *Midrash hag-gadol* (ed. Fisch, 5:135) all read דבר אחר. See Sabato, "Qeri'at shemaᶜ," 44 n. 27. Mss. Florence, Paris, the body text of Munich, and printed editions read ולא עוד. Lieberman, *Tosefta ki-fshuṭah,* 1:5 n. 20, calls the latter a corrupt version. It seems that the Bavli's explanation of the words דבר אחר in *b. Ber.* 11a, discussed below, led to the change to ולא עוד. Since the Bavli rejects the first response spoken by R. Ishmael, later copyists deemed it more readable if the second response was not presented as an alternative but as an addition to the first.

47. Ms. Oxford.

because according to the first there indeed would be no reason for R. Ishmael to stand up. In effect, the Bavli erases the first possibility and leaves us with only the second, less polemical explanation for R. Ishmael's action.

In sum, this story is retold a number of times, each with slight variations that affect the tone of the relationship between the two characters. The Tannaitic versions show these two rabbis acting with some amount of congeniality, using the address "my brother," and having a productive conversation about their dispute. This is certainly more amicable than the conversation between R. Ṭarfon and his colleagues on the same subject. Still, the two clearly do not recognize each other's practices as legitimate and chastise each other for their actions. We get the sense of two colleagues who respect each other and consider themselves part of the same group, but who feel a significant amount of tension in their relationship regarding certain issues.

The Tannaitic story is then refracted through two retellings in the Talmuds. The most negative reading is that in the Yerushalmi. The Geniza version has them placed together unwillingly, and the term of endearment "my brother" is absent from R. Eleazar's question. The Yerushalmi also increases the stakes by placing the story during the day when R. Ishmael would have to violate a custom in order to protest R. Eleazar. If Ginzberg's theory is correct, then the change to the daytime combines with the first two more subtle changes in the Yerushalmi (נתונים instead of שרויין, and omission of אחי) to create a story that reflects little congeniality between these two rabbis and even a deep rejection of each other's opinions to the extent that one would violate his own custom just to protest his colleague's practice.

The most amicable version of the story is that of the Bavli. Here they are found dining together, and one calls the other "my brother," even in the midst of his cross-examination. The accusation found in the Tosefta, מה זה אלעזר, is absent in the Bavli (though it is also absent in the Yerushalmi). Most importantly, the Bavli presents only one possible reading of R. Ishmael's motive, which was simply to make his own opinion clear before watching students. The Bavli removes the hostility present in the Yerushalmi version of the story in which R. Ishmael acted in order to demonstrate a personal protest against R. Eleazar.

Each of these changes is quite subtle, and there is no proof that any of them was consciously (or subconsciously) made because of different agendas (or assumptions) on the part of the redactors of each document. The differences in this story do seem significant, however, when placed in the context of other comparisons between Yerushalmi and Bavli *sugyot*. I propose that this is just one example of many where the Yerushalmi assumes that differences in practice tend to yield animosity while the Bavli takes for granted that multiple practices can live side by side in relative peace.

In the Loft of Ḥananiah

One story stands out among all the stories about the Houses as by far the most acrimonious, though here we find even more significant differences between the sources. The Mishnah reports rather neutrally that a series of eighteen decrees were enacted one day in the "loft of Ḥananiah ben Ḥezekiah ben Gurion[48] when [the rabbis] went to visit him. They voted and Beth Shammai outnumbered Beth Hillel."[49] The Tosefta reveals a completely negative view of the event: "והיה אותו היום קשה להם לישראל כיום שנעשה בו העגל—That day was as difficult for Israel as the day the Golden Calf was made."[50] The Tosefta does not explain why that day was considered so tragic. However, this comment does show that there is something more to the story that is not revealed in the Tosefta. The Talmuds, as we will see below, fill in the gap.[51]

The next Tosefta provides only a hint at what could have been so problematic with the events of that day. R. Eliezer and R. Yehoshua compare the enactments to filling up a *se'ah* measurement. R. Yehoshua says that they leveled off the measurement such that any further filling would cause an overflow. R. Eliezer says they overfilled the measurement. The Tosefta version is a bit terse, making it difficult to determine whether either Rabbi is giving a positive or negative assessment of the enactments. The Talmuds also elaborate on this debate.

What is interesting about these sources is their claim that the two Houses did get together for a binding vote.[52] Although we have testimony for a handful of laws on which the Houses voted,[53] this does not seem

48. He was probably himself an important member of Beth Shammai. See Abraham Goldberg, *Commentary to the Mishna: Shabbat* (Jerusalem: Jewish Theological Seminary of America, 1976), 15 (Hebrew), and Ben-Shalom, *Shammai*, 235–37.

49. *M. Šabb.* 1:4. See Goldberg, *Commentary to the Mishna: Shabbat*, 16–22, for various views on the identification of these eighteen enactments.

50. *T. Šabb.* 1:16.

51. This is similar to Oven of Akhnai over which the Tosefta says there was much controversy but does not get into any details, and the Talmuds fill in the missing information. See below, p. 276.

52. In another case, the elders of both Houses get together and agree on a certain matter without recourse to a vote. See *Sifre Num.*, 115 (ed. Hayyim Saul Horovitz, *Sifre d'Be Rab: Sifre on Numbers and Sifre Zutta* [Jerusalem: Shalem Books, 1992], 124), and parallel in *b. Menaḥ.* 41b.

53. See *m. Šabb.* 1:4–8, *t. Šabb.* 1:18–19, and *m. Miqw.* 4:1 (though R. Yose disputes the existence or the acceptance of the vote in the last case). Interestingly, all of these sources use the phrase "נמנו ורבו בית שמיי על בית הלל—they voted and Beth Shammai outnumbered Beth Hillel." The term ורבו is never used for votes involving rabbis other than the Houses. Votes by other rabbis use either נמנו alone (*m. Giṭ.* 5:6; *m. Ohal* 18:9; *t. Šeb.* 4:21) or "נמנו וגמרו—they voted and concluded" (*m. Yad.* 4:1, 3) followed by the law that they decided. This difference in terminology may reflect a different atmosphere in which each vote is taken. With later rabbis, once the court votes it can speak with a unanimous voice since the outcome of the

to be a regular event.[54] These rabbis did not come to have a meeting but rather for a visit, and Beth Shammai took advantage of the opportunity while they were in the majority to vote on some laws. Still, that Beth Hillel would submit themselves to the authority of the majority even if it ruled like Beth Shammai does show that, at least according this Mishnah and Tosefta, Beth Hillel considered the views of Beth Shammai to be legitimate regarding some issues.[55]

Yerushalmi *Šabb.* 1:4, 3c, presents the incident as follows:

[A] אותו היום היה קשה לישראל כיום שנעשה בו העגל
[B] רבי ליעזר אומר בו ביום גדשו את הסאה רבי יהושע אומר בו ביום מחקו אותה
[C] אמר לו ר׳ ליעזר אילו היתה חסירה ומילאוה יאות לחבית שהיא מליאה אגוזין כל מה שאתה נותן לתוכה שומשמין היא מחזקת
[D] אמר לו ר׳ יהושע אילו היתה מליאה וחיסרוה יאות לחבית שהיתה מליאה שמן כל מה שאתה נותן לתוכה מים היא מפזרת את השמן
[E] תנא רבי יהושע אונייא תלמידי ב״ש עמדו להן מלמטה והיו הורגין בתלמידי בית הלל
[F] תני ששה מהן עלו והשאר עמדו עליהן בחרבות וברמחים

[A] That day was as difficult for Israel as the day the [golden] calf was made.

[B] R. Eliezer said, "On that day they overfilled the measure." R. Yehoshua says, "On that day they leveled the measure."

---

vote is the decision of the entire court (see *m. Sanh.* 3:7). *M. Giṭ.* 5:6, for example, can say "בית דין...אמרו—the court ... said." Regarding the Houses, the tradition records that there was a majority who outnumbered and forced out the minority and their opinion, reminding us that the vote included dissent. The language sounds more like a partisan contest in which Beth Shammai beat out Beth Hillel rather than the conclusions of a nonpartisan group of experts. For more on votes in the Talmud see Urbach, *The Halakhah*, 93–99.

54. See Moore, *Judaism in the First Centuries*, 1:81. Based on the dearth of cases showing cooperation and the numerous cases showing diversity of practice, we can probably assume that the two Houses each practiced their own opinions in the vast majority of the hundreds of arguments recorded in their names.

55. From the Mishnah and Tosefta it would seem that the eighteen enactments are the matters on which they voted. The Talmuds, however, explain that eighteen enactments were made besides the other matters on which they voted. The Yerushalmi mentions three different categories of laws, "תני שמונה עשר דבר גזרו ובשמונה עשרה רבו, ובשמונה עשרה נחלקו—It was taught, they made eighteen enactments, in eighteen they outvoted, and in eighteen they were split." The Bavli has a slightly different categorization, "אמר רב יהודה אמר שמואל: שמנה עשר גזרו, ובשמנה עשר נחלקו.—והתניא: הושוו!—בו ביום נחלקו, ולמחר הושוו," or Maimonides' reconstructed version, "שמונה עשר גזרו, ובשמונה עשר נחלקו, ובשמונה עשר הושוו, Eighteen enactments were made, and in eighteen they were split, and in eighteen they agreed." See Lieberman, *Tosefta ki-fshuṭah*, 3:13–15; Goldberg, *Commentary to the Mishna: Shabbat*, 16–22; and Ben-Shalom, *Shammai*, 262–63. That the body "was split" can mean that there were an even number of people and the vote was evenly split. Another possibility is that some of the members refused to put those matters to a vote, that is, they would not concede to the majority. The second understanding opens the possibility that Beth Hillel did delegitimize Beth Shammai in some matters such that they would not submit to them even if Beth Shammai were the majority.

[C] R. Eliezer told him, "If it had been lacking and they filled it, that would be good. This is similar to a barrel that is full of nuts; the more sesame seeds you put in it the better it will hold."
[D] R. Yehoshua told him, "If it had been full and they emptied some from it, that would be good. This is similar to a barrel full of oil; the more one adds water to it, the more it will displace the oil.
[E] It was taught by R. Yehoshua of Onaiah: The students of Beth Shammai stood below and were killing the students of Beth Hillel.
[F] It was taught, "Six of [Beth Hillel] were allowed to enter and the rest were guarded by swords and spears."[56]

Lieberman explains that both rabbis provide a negative assessment of the enactments, thus elaborating on why that day was compared to the day of the making of the golden calf.[57] They argued only on the nature of the problem with the enactments. R. Eliezer thinks that the ideal is for the measure to be full but level. On that day, they added too many enactments, thus overfilling the measure and causing some laws to overflow and be lost. In real terms, this means that the stringencies were overbearing and impossible for the masses to fulfill, thus causing them to violate the law. R. Yehoshua thinks that the ideal is for the measure to be slightly underfilled to ensure that nothing should fall out. Filling to the brim is too precarious. In real terms, he teaches that one should leave room for some leniency in rabbinic enactments so that people can concentrate on the biblical essence of the laws. R. Yehoshua responds that it is still best to fill it to the brim because enactments act like sesame seeds between nuts. Rabbinic enactments themselves ensure that people will not violate the biblical laws. R. Eliezer counters that biblical laws and enactments do not mix. If the masses are given too many rabbinic enactments they will lose focus on some of the biblical laws just as water displaces oil.[58] Both rabbis agree, however, that it was a tragic day because the enactments were too stringent.

The Yerushalmi adds a scene that is not found in the Tannaitic compilations. Beth Shammai was able to win out in the legislation of these laws

56. Translation of line F follows *Pene Moshe*. *Qorban ha-ʿedah*, however, thinks Beth Shammai is the subject. According to this explanation, the sentence translates, "six of [Beth Shammai] went up and the rest guarded them with swords and spears." See Ben-Shalom, *Shammai*, 262 n. 57.

57. Lieberman, *Ha-Yerushalmi ki-fshuṭo*, 37–38, and idem, *Tosefta Ki-Fshuṭah*, 3:15–16.

58. The Bavli version of this dispute is found in *b. Šabb.* 153b connected to one of the eighteen enactments (*b. Šabb.* 17b) but without the first halves of C and D. Rashi explains that R. Eliezer praises the enactments of that day—the more the better. Only R. Yehoshua criticizes their severity because they will lead to loss of the essential laws. One can explain the Bavli in the same fashion as Lieberman explained the Yerushalmi; however, the dialogue does not proceed as smoothly without the first halves of C and D.

with the help of some violence against Beth Hillel. According to a Tannaitic tradition preserved by R. Yehoshua of Onaiah, an early Palestinian Amora, Beth Shammai went so far as to murder some members of Beth Hillel. According to a second Tannaitic tradition, Beth Shammai stood guard with swords and spears, that is, they only threatened students of Beth Hillel but did not actually kill them. These two *baraitot* seem to offer alternative histories, the second much more toned down that the first.[59]

Pene Moshe assumes that even the first *baraita* does not mean that there was actually any blood spilled but rather that Beth Shammai threatened to kill them if they should enter. Lieberman, however, points to a comment later on in the Yerushalmi to confirm that the murder did indeed take place: "בתוך שמונה עשרה אפילו גדול אינה מבטל מפני שעמדה להן בנפשותיהן—Regarding the eighteen [enactments] even a great [court] may not overturn them because they were established with their lives."[60] This passage assumes that the killings are literal. Lieberman thinks that the Tosefta compared this day with that of the golden calf not because of the stringencies themselves, but because of the violence surrounding them.[61] Some historians agree that these murders are based on historical reality. Graetz explains that Beth Shammai included themselves among the Zealots looking for any opportunity to fight Rome. These enactments were meant to separate the Jews from the Gentiles by prohibiting the purchase of "wine, oil, bread, or any other articles of food from their heathen neighbors."[62] The murder of the students of Beth Hillel recorded in the Yerushalmi resulted from a combination of "religious fervor and political zealotry."[63] This theory was supported more recently by Ben-Shalom[64], though it also has its detractors.[65] If indeed this violent story is based on some historical reality, then this tradition certainly predates the Yerushalmi. Even if the Yerushalmi did not invent it, however, it is still significant that the Yerushalmi is the only rabbinic document to record it explicitly.[66] If, on the other hand, the Yeru-

---

59. One could also read the two lines cumulatively; students of Beth Shammai first killed some of Beth Hillel and then held the rest captive.

60. *Y. Šabb.* 1:4 (3d). Lieberman, *Ha-Yerushalmi ki-fshuṭo*, 38.

61. Idem, *Tosefta Ki-Fshuṭah*, 3:15.

62. Heinrich Graetz, *History of the Jews*, 6 vols. (Philadelphia: Jewish Publication Society of America, 1891–98), 2:270.

63. Ibid.

64. Ben-Shalom, *Shammai*, 252f. See also evidence from *Sifre Zuṭa* published in Y. N. Epstein, "Sifri zuṭa, parashat parah," *Tarbiz* 1 (1930): 52 and 70, discussed in Lieberman, *Ha-Yerushalmi ki-fshuṭo*, 38; Urbach, *The Halakhah*, 175; and Ben-Shalom, *Shammai*, 236–37. See also references in Davies, *Setting*, 264 n. 1.

65. See Ben-Shalom, *Shammai*, 253 n. 7; and Vered Noam, *Megillat Taʿanit: Versions, Interpretation, History with a Critical Edition* (Jerusalem: Tad Ben-Zvi Press, 2003), 333–36 (Hebrew).

66. Also, the Yerushalmi makes no record of the political background, giving the impression that the violence was over purely *halakhic* matters.

shalmi did invent or exaggerate the murderous violence, then this testimony is all the more significant for revealing the Yerushalmi's ideology.[67]

The Bavli version of this story is considerably different. *B. Šabbat* 17a reads:

> הבוצר לגת, שמאי אומר: הוכשר, הלל אומר: לא הוכשר. אמר לו הלל לשמאי: מפני מה בוצרין בטהרה, ואין מוסקין בטהרה? אמר לו: אם תקניטני—גוזרני טומאה אף על המסיקה. נעצו חרב בבית המדרש, אמרו: הנכנס יכנס והיוצא אל יצא. ואותו היום היה הלל כפוף ויושב לפני שמאי כאחד מן התלמידים, והיה קשה לישראל כיום שנעשה בו העגל. וגזור שמאי והלל—ולא קבלו מינייהו, ואתו תלמידייהו גזור וקבלו מינייהו.
>
> One who prunes grapes for pressing wine: Shammai says [those grapes] are susceptible [to becoming impure]. Hillel says they are not susceptible [to impurity]. Hillel said to Shammai, "Why do we cut in purity but do not harvest olives in purity?" He responded, "If you incite me, I will decree impurity even on harvesting olives." They planted a sword in the *beth midrash* and said, "Whoever wants to enter may enter but whoever wants to leave may not leave." Hillel sat submissively before Shammai as one of his students. That day was as difficult for Israel as the day on which the [golden] calf was made. Shammai and Hillel decreed [regarding the grapes] but it was not accepted. Then their students came and decreed and it was accepted.

In the Bavli version, the violent argument does not surround the entire meeting but only flares up regarding one of the eighteen enactments in which Shammai is more stringent about the purity status of harvested grapes. The argument is recorded between Shammai and Hillel themselves and begins with Hillel asking Shammai a seemingly fair question about why Shammai distinguishes between grapes and olives. In response, Shammai threatens to be stringent on both grapes and olives if provoked further. This is an interesting example of an action taken only for polemical ends, like the story above regarding posture during *Shema*.[68]

Someone then declares that nobody may leave the house of study[69] under the threat of the sword.[70] Although the Bavli does not state explic-

---

67. Hezser, *Social Structure*, 243, warns that the Yerushalmi's claim of murder should not be taken "too literally" but that it "nevertheless indicates the hostility which went with disagreement."

68. In that case, the polemic caused R. Ishmael to change his action only on that occasion in order to express his disagreement. The polemic here is more significant in that Shammai threatens to change an entire law based on a personal pique.

69. The action is moved from the loft of Ḥananiah to the *beth midrash*, a shift performed by the Bavli's redactors in many other narratives as well. See Rubenstein, *Culture*, 26–27.

70. The image of planting a sword in the middle of the house of study is borrowed from *y. Yebam.* 8:3 (9c) (where the sword is planted in a courtroom; see previous note). The

itly who made this threat, it is clear from the continuation that it was the supporters of Shammai, realizing they had the upper hand that day, who did not want to let the humiliated Hillel escape. The Bavli makes no mention of a vote and even says that the enactment, although unanimously backed by both Shammai and Hillel, failed at first. The enactment only stuck when their students reenacted it.

The Bavli version is far removed from the historical event; it brings in Shammai and Hillel even though this meeting, if based on some historical event, must have happened closer to the time of the revolt.[71] The tradition about not letting anyone out of the meeting reverses the second *baraita* in the Yerushalmi where nobody was allowed into the meeting. In that *baraita,* Beth Hillel was kept out so that Beth Shammai would keep the majority. In the Bavli, the Hillelites are kept in so that they can be forcibly humiliated. The Bavli makes no mention of any bloodshed, although it does include a threat of violence with the sword planted in the center of the room.

Each version of this famous meeting must have passed through a complicated transmission process, which we are no longer able to trace. Many aspects of this event are shrouded in mystery. However, we can at least observe that the Yerushalmi describes a much more horrific scene than the Bavli. The Yerushalmi, oblivious to any of the political overtones that modern historians find in its narrative, nonchalantly depicts a massacre of one group of rabbis by another without further comment. To be sure, the Yerushalmi does offer a second, less violent possibility, but the first is confirmed on the next page. The Yerushalmi seems open to the possibility that an argument over halakha can become extremely nasty. The Bavli, on the other hand, does not mention any killing and does not even focus attention on the sword, which is dug into the middle of the room as more of a symbolic threat rather than being held by guards at the doors. The major tragedy in the Bavli was that Hillel was humiliated and made to feel like a student before Shammai. The Bavli never imagines actual violence resulting from a legal dispute.[72] Rather, the worst case the Bavli can envision is that of a rabbi being disgraced.[73] Once again, comparing the Yerushalmi with the Bavli, we can see that the Yerushalmi depicts a dispute between the Houses as being more acrimonious than the description of the same debate in the Bavli.

---

image of the sword is also found in *Shir haShirim Zuta* 29 in the context of the oven-of-Akhnai story: "On the day that Rabbi Eliezer ben Hyrkanus took his seat in the Academy, each man girded on his sword."

71. Ben-Shalom, *Shammai,* 258.

72. Even though the Bavli often depicts debate using violent imagery, that violence is not real. See Rubenstein, *Culture,* 54–66 and esp. 179 n. 32.

73. On the prime importance of shame in the Bavli, see ibid., 67–69.

The *Semikha* Controversy

The narratives about the loft of Ḥananiah might be the most hostile and violent traditions involving the Houses, or any other group of rabbis for that matter, in all of rabbinic literature. There are some sources, however, such as *t. Ḥag.* 2:11–12 regarding the longstanding *semikha* controversy,[74] that reflect a nonviolent but still forceful attempt by the Shammaites to overcome the Hillelites:[75]

מעשה בהלל הזקן שסמך על העולה בעזרה חברו עליו תלמידי בית שמאי[76] אמר להן בואו וראו שהיא נקבה וצריך אני לעשותה זבחי שלמים הפליגן בדברים והלכו להם
מיד[77] גברה ידם של בית שמאי ובקשו לקבוע הלכה כדבריהם והיה שם בבא בן בוטא מתלמידי בית שמאי שהיה יודע שהלכה כבית הלל הלך והביא כל צאן קדר[78] והעמידן בעזרה ואמר כל מי שצריך עולות ושלמים יבא ויטול ויסמוך באו ונטלו את הבהמה והעלו עולות ושלמים וסמכו עליהן בו ביום[79] נקבעה הלכה כדברי בית הלל ולא ערער אדם על דבר
שוב מעשה בתלמיד אחד מתלמידי בית הלל שסמך על העולה בעזרה מצאו תלמיד אחד מתלמידי בית שמאי אמר לו מה זה סמכיא אמר לו מה זה שתקיה שיתקו בנזיפה.[80]

It happened that Hillel the Elder placed his hands upon a sacrificial animal in the courtyard [of the Temple on the holiday] and the students of Beth Shammai[76] ganged up on him. He told them, "Come and see that it is a female and I must sacrifice it as a *shelamim*." He diverted them with [other] matters and they left. As a result,[77] Beth Shammai gained the upper hand and they sought to establish the law according to their opinion. Baba ben Buṭa was among them who, although a student of Beth Shammai, knew that the law follows Beth Hillel. He brought all the sheep from Qedar,[78] placed them in the courtyard and announced, "whoever needs *olot* or *shelamim* should come take an animal and place his hands upon it. [The people] came, took animals and

74. On the significance of and motivation behind each side of this issue, see E. E. Hallewy, "The First Mishnaic Controversy," *Tarbiz* 28 (1958): 154–57 (Hebrew).

75. *T. Ḥag.* 1:11–12 according to ms. London. See parallel versions at *y. Ḥag.* 2:3 (78a) = *y. Beṣah* 2:4 (61c) and *b. Beṣah* 20a-b. See the comparison in chart 4.2, p. 235.

76. It is interesting that the followers of Shammai are already called Beth Shammai even while Hillel the Elder was alive. This is most probably an anachronism. Ms. Vienna, the Yerushalmi, and some mss. of the Bavli omit בית here, but all versions read בית later on in the story.

77. Literally, "immediately." Yerushalmi reads לאחר ימים and Bavli reads ואותו יום. What must be emphasized in any of these versions is not immediacy in time but a causal link between the events. Even if the second event happened much later than the first, the narrative can still say מיד to imply that the first event caused the second. The rabbinic storytellers regularly link events together by joining them in time; see Isaak Heinemann, *Darkhe ha-'aggada* (Jerusalem: Magnes, 1970), 27.

78. I.e., the best cattle. See Isa 60:7; and Lieberman, *Hellenism in Jewish Palestine*, 153.

> made them *olot* and *shelamim*, and placed their hands upon them. On that very day,[79] the law was established according to Beth Hillel and nobody questioned the matter.
> Another story occurred with a student of Beth Hillel who placed his hands upon his *olah* in the courtyard. One student of Beth Shammai found him and rebuked him, "What is this *semikha*?" He responded, "What is this silence?" He shut him up with a rebuke.[80]

T. Ḥagigah 2:11 reports that when Hillel the Elder laid his hands on an *olah* sacrifice on the holiday, which was in his opinion permitted and required, the students of Shammai ganged up on him and he only got them to leave by lying to them that the animal was female, thus unfit for *olah,* and then diverting their attention.[81] One wonders whether Hillel was forced to humiliate himself before the students of Shammai because they actually threatened violence against him or if he simply buckled under social pressure. In either case, this weak stance by Hillel opened an opportunity for Beth Shammai to strengthen its own position and establish the halakha. The tide changed only when Baba ben Buṭa,[82] a well-respected sage of Beth Shammai, performed such a strong spectacle in favor of Hillel that

---

79. See above, n. 77. However, in this instance, בו ביום may be literal considering the public scene that took place.

80. נזיפה may denote more than just verbal harassment. It can be a minor form of excommunication. See the *baraita* in *b. Moʿed Qaṭ.* 16a = *y. Moʿed Qaṭ.* 31 (81c): "Excommunication (נידוי) is not less than thirty days, rebuke (נזיפה) is not less than seven days." See Michelle Hammer-Kossoy, "Divine Justice in Rabbinic Hands: Talmudic Reconstitution of the Penal System" (Ph.D. diss., New York University, 2005), 475–83. Ms. Erfurt reads, בגערה. Bavli ms. Vatican 109 reads, בטיפה, a simple scribal error.

81. Beth Shammai agreed that one could bring a *shelamim* on *yom ṭov* (see *m. Ḥag.* 2:3), although they still prohibited placing the hands. This raises the question why the students of Shammai were satisfied that it was a *shelamim* offering and did not continue to badger Hillel on his performing *semikha*. Tosafot (at *b. Ḥag.* 7b) assumes that the students did not see Hillel perform *semikha*. See also *Pene Moshe* (at *y. Ḥag.* 78a) and Lieberman, *Tosefta ki-fshuṭah*, 1303.

However, it seems more likely that they did see the *semikha,* which prompted them to confront Hillel in the first place. The story does not specify the content of their criticism (although the Bavli does formulate what their criticism must have been based on Hillel's response). Hillel only diffuses the *olah* issue by claiming the animal to be a female, but he still must divert the conversation to other matters—perhaps because he never addressed the *semikha* problem. (This verbal diversion is replaced in the Bavli with a physical diversion of shaking its tail. Also in the Bavli, Hillel does not invite them to inspect the animal.) See Urbach, *The Halakhah*, 300 n. 18. The students are content to see Hillel subjugate himself before them and deny that he is opposing Shammai. They do not further question about *semikha* just as they do not inspect the animal. They were less interested in having a sincere legal discussion and more interested in picking a fight for the honor of their master. Seeing Hillel humiliated, forced to make excuses and lie about the obvious, satisfied their desires. See Yonah Frenkel, "Hermeneutic Problems in the Study of the Aggadic Narrative," *Tarbiz* 47, no. 3/4 (2001): 147 n. 24 (Hebrew).

82. On his lineage, see below p. 187 n. 90 and Urbach, *Sages*, 528 n. 80.

nobody could argue with him. This story shows the two groups fighting it out not in the halls of study but in the courtyard of the Temple. They did not discuss the matter intellectually nor put the matter to a vote. Rather, each side tries to influence the masses using whatever political and demagogic means at their disposal.

The next story in the Tosefta repeats the main elements of the plot of the first story. Now, a student of Beth Hillel performs *semikha* on his *olah* and is again rebuked by a student of Beth Shammai. This time, however, the student responds with strength, thus allaying the need for any further intervention and establishing Beth Hillel as the norm.

It is noteworthy that both Talmuds learn lessons from these stories about how to respond to criticism (see the comparison in chart 4.2, p. 235). The Yerushalmi formulates the moral as a parable: "In the beginning, a cup [of water] requires [a basket] full of wormwood [to heat it up]. [One can also derive the lesson from the fuel] itself. Any coal that does not burn in its time will not burn."[83] The basic point of this parable is: respond immediately when provoked or you will never be able to stand up for yourself. This is meant both as criticism of Hillel the Elder and as praise for Baba ben Buṭa.[84] The Bavli derives a lesson from the second story: "Therefore a young scholar should not answer back to his friend more than he had spoken to him." Both of these are lessons in politics and maintenance of personal dignity. They are not lessons in compromise and peace. The emphasis of each, however, is different. While the Yerushalmi encourages one to respond to a challenge immediately and with strength, the Bavli encourages one to control his anger, and not to let it exceed the original incitement. The Bavli focuses on the more subdued reaction of the student in the second story while the Yerushalmi holds up Baba ben Buṭa's grand protest as the model reaction.

---

83. See Aramaic below, p. 235. The same proverb also appears at *y. Maʿas Š.* 5:3 (56c) where R. Eleazar is forced to practice like R. Akiba after the former does not respond to the initial rebuke of the latter. The first half of the Yerushalmi's proverb is unclear. See Sokoloff, *A Dictionary of Jewish Palestinian Aramaic*, p. 270, s.v. כשירו and p. 295, s.v. מוליי. This translation follows *Qorban ha-ʿedah* who explains that when one wishes to heat up a cup of water from scratch (שירותא = beginning) one needs a basketful of wood, but once it is heated only a little wood is required to keep it hot. מיניה וביה is understood by *Qorban ha-ʿedah* as an introduction to the next proverb, which derives the lesson from the fuel itself (coal). See also *Pene Moshe* at *y. Beṣah* 2:4 (61c) and *y. Maʿas Š.* 5:3 (56c).

84. Frenkel, "Hermeneutic Problems," 146–49, derives a similar interpretation based on the structure of the Bavli version of this story. The Bavli includes two parallel phrases: "ואותו היום גברה ידם של בית שמאי על בית הלל, ובקשו לקבוע הלכה כמותן" and "ואותו היום גברה ידן של בית הלל וקבעו הלכה כמותן." These two phrases divide the story into two parts: the first about Hillel and the second about Baba ben Buṭa. Frenkel explains: "Hillel is the contrasting character to Baba ben Buṭa. Baba ben Buṭa is successful because he acts against many others with inner-strength according to his conviction. Hillel fails because in his weakness, he bows to those who gang up on him" (ibid., 148).

The Yerushalmi emphasizes Baba ben Buṭa's reaction in yet another way. The Yerushalmi includes a scene that is not found in either the Tosefta or in the Bavli. In this scene, the strengthening of Beth Shammai causes the Temple to become desolate, since Beth Shammai did not allow most types of sacrifices on the holiday. Baba ben Buṭa then proceeds to curse Beth Shammai, "ישמו בתיהן של אילו שהישמו את בית אלהינו—Let the houses of these people [Beth Shammai] become desolate for they have made desolate the house of our God." This introduces a new level of animosity that is not present in the Tosefta. The Tosefta version of the story reflects an atmosphere of political struggle between the two camps over legal practice that could often become confrontational and heated. The Yerushalmi's retelling slightly exaggerates the level of anger by encouraging confrontation and introducing a curse of Beth Shammai.[85]

Cooperation

Despite all the stories of conflict analyzed until now, another set of sources shows friendliness, compromise, and peace between the Houses. There are a number of cases where Beth Hillel changes its mind to rule (להורות) like Beth Shammai,[86] and vice versa.[87] This shows that, at least in some cases, there was discussion between the two groups who tried to convince each other and that they were able to shed their group pride for the sake of intellectual honesty.

Perhaps more telling are numerous examples of members of one group practicing according to the opinions of the other group. We have already seen in *t. Ḥag.* 2:11 that Baba ben Buṭa, a student of Shammai, is presented as the leading champion for a certain law of Beth Hillel. Similarly, R. Yoḥanan ben Haḥorani was a student of Beth Shammai, but he always

---

85. Ironically, it is said by a member of Beth Shammai against his own group. See next section for more examples of such crossing of allegiances between the Houses.

86. *M. ʿEd.* 1:12 (=*m. Yebam.* 15:2–3); 13 (=*m. Giṭ.* 4:5); 14 (=*m. Kelim* 9:2); and *m. ʾOhal.* 5:3.

87. See *m. Ter.* 5:4 and explanation in *y. Ter.* 5:2 (43c-d) where Beth Shammai seems to have agreed with Beth Hillel. See Lieberman, *Tosefta ki-fshuṭah,* 1:382–83. Kimelman, "Judaism and Pluralism," 138, notices that Beth Hillel reverses its position in many cases but Beth Shammai does so only once. This same observation may be the basis of R. Yuda bar Pazzi's statement that halakha follows Beth Hillel because when "they agreed with the opinion of Beth Shammai they changed their minds" (*y. Sukkah* 2:8 (53b); see text below, p. 224).

Kimelman further derives from this and from *b. ʿErub.* 13b that Beth Hillel had a "pluralistic mentality" that could "sustain collegiality in the face of diversity" (ibid.). However, the Yerushalmi and Bavli seem to disagree on how to describe Beth Hillel's character. The Yerushalmi mentions only Beth Hillel's intellectual honesty in their search for truth, not their congeniality or modesty. See below, pp. 224–28.

practiced according to Beth Hillel.[88] Conversely, the "modest of Beth Hillel" would act stringently in matters of tithes following Beth Shammai.[89] This crossing of borders shows that, at least according to the authors of these sources, the lines dividing the groups were not absolute. There was enough social cohesion between the two groups for individuals to break from their own party lines in certain matters and still not be ejected from their original party. All the above cases of cross-practicing are set in the early decades of the first century, certainly before the destruction of the Temple.[90]

Even after 70 C.E., when the scholars of the Houses lost their anonymity and the rabbis began to speak as individuals,[91] there were still individual rabbis following opinions previously attributed to each House. Among the rabbis mentioned in the Mishnah, the opinions of Beth Hillel were already generally ascendant;[92] yet, we still find examples of rabbis who followed Beth Shammai on certain issues.[93] R. Ṭarfon and R. Eleazar ben Azariah practiced according to Beth Shammai in the matter of reciting the *Shema*.[94] R. Ṭarfon followed Beth Shammai in other cases as well.[95] Regarding the case of "the daughter's cowife," Rabban Gamaliel II practiced according to Beth Shammai,[96] and R. Yoḥanan ben Nuri and R. Shimon ben Gamaliel II were afraid to reject Beth Shammai.[97] In one case, the masses followed Beth Shammai while Rabban Gamaliel II and

88. *M. Sukkah* 2:7; *t. Sukkah* 2:3; *t. ʿEd.* 2:2; *b. Yebam.* 15b. Abraham Büchler, "Halakhot le-maʿaseh ke-Beth Shammai bi-zman ha-bayit ve-'aḥar ha-ḥurban," in *Sefer ha-yovel li-khevod R. Mosheh Aryeh Bloch*, ed. Sámuel Krausz and Miksa Weisz (Budapest, 1905), 22, assumes that R. Yoḥanan ben Haḥorani held only by Beth Hillel's stringencies but not his leniencies. However, in *m. Sukkah* 2:7 he follows Beth Hillel's leniency to sit in a small Sukkah.

89. *M. Demai* 6:6. See Urbach, *Sages*, 531 n. 94, and Ben-Shalom, *Shammai*, 238–39.

90. Baba ben Buṭa certainly was active during the Second Temple Period, as seen from this story. He is also mentioned interacting with Herod in *b. B. Bat.* 3b-4a, and he may be related to "the sons of Baba" mentioned by Josephus as opponents of Herod (*Antiquities*, 15.7.10). R. Yoḥanan ben Haḥorani was active during the Second Temple and even had a student, R. Eleazar bar Ṣadoq, who was himself active before the destruction. See Yitzhak D. Gilat, "Eleazar (Eliezer) ben Zadok," *Encyclopedia Judaica* (2007): 6:309. The "modest of Beth Hillel" were fulfilling the laws of tithes, which indicates they were living during the Temple period.

91. See above, p. 163 n. 3. This loss of anonymity goes hand in hand with a shift from two organized parties/institutions to more decentralized groups of rabbis who no longer considered membership in either House a primary source of identity.

92. Avigdor Bitman, "Le-ṭivo shel ha-kelal halakha ke-Beth Hillel," *Sinai* 82 (1988): 185–96 (Hebrew).

93. See Halivni, *Rules*, 132–39; and Shmuel Safrai, "Ha-hakhraʿah ke-Beth Hillel be-Yavneh," *Proceedings of the Seventh World Congress of Jewish Studies: Studies in the Talmud, Halacha, and Midrash* (1977): 21–43, for a comprehensive list of such cases.

94. See above, pp. 171–76.

95. See above, n. 28.

96. *B. Yebam.* 15a; and see Halivni, *Rules*, 133 n. 1.

97. *T. Yebam.* 1:9–10. See more on this issue below.

R. Yehoshua practiced according to Beth Hillel.[98] In other cases, Rabban Gamaliel II himself follows Beth Shammai's stringencies,[99] as was the practice of the patriarchal family before him.[100] R. Akiba practices a stringency of Beth Shammai.[101]

Besides the cases quoted above where Tannaim of all generations actually practice the view of Beth Shammai, there are many more texts in which a later Tanna espouses the view of Beth Shammai without explicitly indicating his own practice. R. Eliezer ben Hyrcanus rules according to Beth Shammai on a number of occasions and is even labeled a "שמותי—Shammaite."[102] R. Yehudah twice rules in accordance with Beth Shammai, in one case even against the practice of the masses.[103] R. Yose[104] and R. Meir[105] rule according to Beth Shammai in various cases. An anonymous *baraita* rules according to Beth Shammai.[106] Sometimes the controversy between the Houses continued as controversy between later Tannaim[107] or even Amoraim.[108]

These sources show that both before and after 70 C.E., the members of

---

98. *M. Sukkah* 3:9. Some versions say the opposite; see Halivni, *Rules*, 133–34.

99. *M. Šabb.* 1:8–9; *b. Ber.* 43b.

100. *M. Beṣah* 2:6=*m. ʿEd.* 3:10. The Mishnah reports that the patriarchal family were only stringent with themselves but lenient with others. In a story on this topic at *t. Beṣah* 2:12, however, R. Gamaliel does try to stop R. Akiba following a leniency of Beth Hillel. It is interesting that the patriarchal family, who are descendents of Hillel, should practice according to Beth Shammai. This may have been a political move to be accepted by all. See David Goodblatt, "The End of Sectarianism and the Patriarchs," in *For Uriel: Studies in the History of Israel in Antiquity Presented to Professor Uriel Rappaport*, ed. M. Mor et al. (Jerusalem: Zalman Shazar Center for Jewish History, 2005), 52–72.

101. *T. Šeb.* 4:21.

102. See Halivni, *Rules*, 73–75, 138; Jacob Neusner, *Eliezer Ben Hyrcanus: The Tradition and the Man*, 2 vols. (Leiden: Brill, 1973), 2:95–97, 115–18, 351–52; Alexander Guttmann, "Hillelites and Shammaites: A Clarification," *Hebrew Union College Annual* 28 (1957): 115f.; and Yitzhak D. Gilat, *The Teachings of R. Eliezer Ben Hyrcanos and Their Position in the History of the Halakha* (Tel Aviv: Dvir, 1968), 309–29 (Hebrew).

103. *T. Miqw.* 5:2 and against the masses in *t. Ter.* 3:12. The latter source may indicate that the tendency toward Beth Hillel was driven by the custom of the masses and not by the rulings of the rabbis. *Y. Ter.* 3:3 (42a), commenting on this Tosefta, adds an interesting line, "R. Shimon says, 'The words of Beth Shammai are better suited for the time of the Temple and the words of Beth Hillel for nowadays.'" The shift to Beth Hillel was a gradual process, and we usually cannot identify precise events or people contributing to the shift. But here we have at least one explicit case of the masses shifting from ruling like Beth Shammai to Beth Hillel. Because this is a case concerning tithes and ritual purity, Beth Hillel's ruling is better suited for post-Temple times, but this reasoning does not apply to most of their controversies.

104. *T. Kelim, B. Batra*, 1:12.

105. *T. Nid.* 9:9.

106. *T. Maʿas. Š.* 3:15.

107. *T. ʿArak.* 4:5.

108. See below, n. 189.

the same social network followed rulings of both Houses. This is a far cry from the sectarian antagonism witnessed in the texts above. Most of these sources are Tannaitic or are about Tannaim. As we will discuss below, Beth Shammai was only gradually excluded from halakha during Amoraic times, so we should not be surprised to find various Tannaim following Beth Shammai in some instances. At certain times and places, practices of both Houses might have been tolerated. The transition from tenuous coexistence to the rejection of Beth Shammai must have been facilitated by a number of defining events in which such cooperation would be condemned. More on this below.

The Daughter's Cowife

By far, the most harmonious picture of the Houses is presented in *m. Yebam.* 1:4:

> בית שמאי מתירין הצרות לאחים ובית הלל אוסרים חלצו בית שמאי פוסלין מן הכהונה ובית הלל מכשירים נתיבמו בית שמאי מכשירים ובית הלל פוסלין
> אף על פי שאלו אוסרין ואלו מתירין אלו פוסלין ואלו מכשירין לא נמנעו בית שמאי מלישא נשים מבית הלל ולא בית הלל מבית שמאי כל הטהרות והטומאות שהיו אלו מטהרין ואלו מטמאין לא נמנעו עושין טהרות אלו על גבי אלו
> Beth Shammai permit the cowives to the [surviving] brothers but Beth Hillel prohibit. If they perform *ḥaliṣa,*[109] Beth Shammai disqualify [the children of the cowives] from [marrying into] the priesthood but Beth Hillel qualify them. If they perform *yibbum,* Beth Shammai qualify them but Beth Hillel disqualify them.
> Even though these prohibit and these permit, Beth Shammai did not refrain from marrying women from Beth Hillel, nor did Beth Hillel [refrain from marrying women] from Beth Shammai. They [also] did not refrain from using any pure and impure items that these declared pure and these declared impure one on top of the other to prepare pure [foods].[110]

Normally, the law of *yibbum* prescribes that a man whose brother dies without children must marry one of his sisters-in-law in order to propagate the name of the deceased brother. This law becomes more complicated, however, when potential incest arises. If, for example, a man mar-

109. A ceremony to cancel the levirate obligation.

110. This statement explicitly, and perhaps even consciously, rejects the behavior of the Dead Sea sect as presented in 4QMMT who refused to marry other groups and who "could not accept as pure foods prepared under other standards" than their own (Baumgarten, *Flourishing,* 103 n. 60). See also Sussman, "History of Halakha," 36–37.

ried his niece and then died without children, it is obvious that the living brother would not be allowed to marry his own daughter. In such a case, the woman would be free from the obligation of *yibbum* and could marry any man. If, however, a man married two women—one of them being his niece and the other not related to him—then Beth Shammai required the living brother to perform *yibbum* (or *ḥaliṣa*) on the woman who is not related while Beth Hillel forbade him to do so.[111]

Even though this controversy is only one of many between Beth Shammai and Beth Hillel, it receives great attention because of the potentially acute problems that it could engender. If the brother does perform *yibbum*, then the child of that relationship will be judged perfectly legitimate according to Beth Shammai but a *mamzer* according to Beth Hillel since relations with one's brother's wife is incest when not required by *yibbum*. If, on the other hand, they perform *ḥaliṣa* and the cowife marries a priest, the child of that relationship will be perfectly legitimate according to Beth Hillel but *pagum* (blemished) according to Beth Shammai.[112]

Considering the consequences, this Mishnah is extraordinary. A controversy that impacts the marriageable status of involved parties and their descendants has the potential to divide the community in two. Yet, the Mishnah says that the two groups married into each other despite their significant differences, thus overcoming the threat of sectarianism. At face value, this Mishnah assumes an attitude of universal pluralism. Even though Beth Hillel fully believed the law to be one way, they were open to the possibility of a contradictory law also being valid for another group. More significantly, each side accepted the other side as valid to the extent that they would marry into their families. Beth Shammai respected Beth Hillel's practice so much that they would act on Beth Hillel's decisions even though they disagreed with the basis of that decision and vice versa. In a straightforward reading of this Mishnah, Beth Hillel would marry off their children even to a definite *mamzer* according to their own standards because they defer to the decision of Beth Shammai for members of Beth

111. On the prevalence of marrying nieces during the Second Temple period and early rabbinic eras, see Adiel Schremer, "Qumran Polemic on Marital Law: CD 4:20–5:11 and Its Social Background," in *The Damascus Document*, ed. Joseph Baumgarten et al. (Leiden: Brill, 2000), 155–56. On the prevalence of polygamy during the rabbinic period, see idem, "How Much Jewish Polygamy in Roman Palestine?" *Proceedings of the American Academy for Jewish Research* 63 (2001): 181–223; Michael Satlow, *Jewish Marriage in Antiquity* (Princeton: Princeton University Press, 2001), 189–92; Rachel Biale, *Women and Jewish Law* (New York: Schoken Books, 1984), 49–50; and S. Lowy, "The Extent of Jewish Polygamy in Talmudic Times," *Journal of Jewish Studies* 9 (1958): 115–38.

112. A woman who was obligated to marry the brother of her deceased husband but performs *ḥaliṣa* instead may not marry a priest just as a divorced woman cannot. The child of an illicit marriage that is not incestuous or adulterous is called *pagum*, blemished. This is a lesser problem than *mamzer*. A *mamzer* may marry only another *mamzer* while a *pagum* may marry any Jew except a priest.

Shammai's circle. Admittedly, this seems too idyllic to be true. The Talmuds have trouble believing it,[113] as do some modern historians.[114] The rabbis at the time and for long afterward struggled with this case, which they termed "צרת הבת—the daughter's cowife."[115]

Tosefta

We will now analyze the substantial Talmudic literature surrounding this case. We begin with *t. Yebam.* 1:9–13:

[A][9] נתיבמו בית שמיי אומר הן כשירות והולד כשר בית הלל אומר הן פסולות והולד ממזר

אמר ר׳ יוחנן בן נורי בא וראה היאך הלכה זו רווחת בישראל לקיים כדברי בית שמיי הולד ממזר כדברי בית הלל אם לקיים כדברי בית הלל הוולד פגום כדברי בית שמאי אלא בוא ונתקין שיהו הצרות חולצות ולא מתיבמות ולא הספיקו לגמור את הדבר עד שנטרפה שעה

[B][10] אמר רבן שמעון בן גמליאל מה נעשה להם לצרות הראשונות

[C] שאלו את ר׳ יהושע בני צרות מהן אמר להם למה אתם מכניסין ראשי לבין שני הרים גדולים לבין בית שמיי ובין בית הלל שיריצו את ראשי אלא מעיד אני על משפחת בית עלובאי מבית צבאים ועל משפחת בית קיפאי מבית מקושש שהן בני צרות ומהם כהנים גדולים והיו מקריבין לגבי מזבח

[D] אמר ר׳ טרפון תאיב אני שתהא לי צרת הבת ואסיאנה לכהונה

[E] אמר ר׳ אלעזר אף על פי שנחלקו בית שמיי כנגד בית הלל בצרות מודים שאין הולד ממזר שאין ממזר אלא מן האשה שאיסורה איסור ערוה וחייבין עליה כרת

[F] אף על פי שנחלקו בית שמיי כנגד בית הלל בצרות ובאחיות ובספק אשת איש ובגט ישן ובמקדש את האשה בשוה פרוטה והמגרש את אשתו ולנה עמו בפונדקי לא נמנעו בית שמיי לישא נשים מבית הלל ולא בית הלל מבית שמיי אלא נהגו האמת והשלום ביניהן שנאמר האמת והשלום אהבו

[G][11] אף על פי שאילו אוסרין ואילו מתירין לא נמנעו עושין טהרות אילו על גב אילו לקיים מה שנאמר כל דרך איש זך בעיניו ותכן לבות ה׳

[H][12] ר׳ שמעון אומר מן הספק לא היו נמנעין אבל נמנעין הן מן הודיי

[I][13] לעולם הלכה כדברי בית הלל הרוצה להחמיר על עצמו לנהוג כדברי בית שמיי וכדברי בית הלל על זה נאמר הכסיל בחשך ילך התופס קולי בית שמיי וקולי בית הלל

113. See below, pp. 201–4 and 207–16.

114. Cohen, "Yavneh," 48, writes, "As part of this irenic trend someone (at Yavneh?) even asserted that the disputes between the Houses did not prevent them from intermarrying or from respecting each other's purities but this wishful thinking cannot disguise the truth." See also Büchler, "Halakha le-maʿaseh," 21–22; and Ben-Menahem et al., *Controversy and Dialogue in Halakhic Sources*, 3:477–78.

115. The daughter is only one of fifteen close relations listed in *m. Yebam.* 1:1 who would be subject to the same law. However, the Talmud refers to this entire set of cases as "צרת הבת—the daughter's cowife," perhaps because that was the most common example. We will use the same shorthand in this book.

רשע אלא אם כדברי בית שמיי כקוליהן וכחומריהון אם כדברי בית הלל כקוליהון וכחומ־
ריהון

[A][9] If they performed *yibbum*, Beth Shammai says they are kosher and the child is kosher; Beth Hillel says they are invalid and the child is a *mamzer*. R. Yoḥanan ben Nuri said, "Come see the ramifications of this law [lit., how this law spreads] in Israel. [If one wants] to fulfill the words of Beth Shammai then the child will be a *mamzer* according to Beth Hillel. [If one wants] to fulfill the words of Beth Hillel then the child is blemished according to Beth Shammai. Rather, come and let us institute that the cowives should perform *ḥaliṣa* and not *yibbum*." They did not get a chance to finalize the matter before the times became troubled [with political persecution].

[B][10] Rabban Shimon ben Gamaliel said, "What should we do about the previous cowives?"

[C] They asked R. Yehoshua, "What about the children of cowives?" He told them, "Why do you place my head in between two great mountains, between Beth Shammai and Beth Hillel, who will crush my head? But, I do testify that the family of Beth Aluvai from Beth S(eva'im and the family of Beth Qipai from Beth Meqoshesh are the descendants of cowives and High Priests came from them who sacrificed upon the altar."

[D] R. Ṭarfon said, "I desire that [a case of] a cowife should come before me so that I can marry her to a priest."

[E] R. Eleazar said, "Even though Beth Shammai argues with Beth Hillel regarding the cowife, they agree that the offspring is not a *mamzer,* for a *mamzer* only results from a woman who is prohibited because of incest and whose punishment is cutting-off."

[F] Even though Beth Shammai and Beth Hillel argue about cowives, sisters, a doubtful adulteress, an outdated divorce paper, one who betroths a woman with the worth of a *peruṭah,* one who divorces his wife and sleeps with her at an inn, still Beth Shammai did not refrain from marrying women of Beth Hillel nor did Beth Hillel from Beth Shammai. Rather they practiced with truth and peace between them as the verse states, "*Truth and peace do they love*" (Zech 8:19).

[G][11] Even though these prohibit and these permit, they did not abstain from handling pure objects one upon the other to fulfill what is stated, "All the ways of a man seem right to him, but the Lord probes motives" (Prov 16:2).

[H][12] R. Shimon says, "They did not refrain from [marrying] the uncertain [women] but they did refrain from the definite ones."

[I][13] Halakha always follows Beth Hillel. One who wants to be stringent upon himself to practice the stringencies of Beth Shammai as well as the stringencies of Beth Hillel, upon him the verse states, "*The fool walks in darkness*" (Eccl 2:14). One who seizes the leniencies of both Beth Shammai and Beth Hillel is wicked. Rather, choose either according to Beth Shammai with their leniencies and stringencies, or according to Beth Hillel with their leniencies and stringencies.[116]

[A] The Tosefta elaborates on the phrase נתיבמו בית שמאי מכשירים ובית הלל פוסלין from *m. Yebam.* 1:4, adding that the status of the mother if they should perform *yibbum* also has ramifications for the child born from that relationship. R. Yoḥanan ben Nuri then offers a practical compromise in order to mitigate the problems that arise when two groups follow different laws. This this attempt fails, however, because "the times became troubled."[117] [B] One of the possible objections is voiced by Rabban Shimon ben Gamaliel (of the fourth generation, a later contemporary of R. Yoḥanan ben Nuri). If they do legislate that all such cases should perform *ḥaliṣa*, then what happens to women in past cases who either performed *yibbum* or did nothing?

The continuation of the Tosefta shows even more clearly that Beth Shammai had an enduring following. [C] R. Yehoshua was reluctant to explicitly divulge his opinion about the status of the children born from cowives who married priests outside the family. Even though he agrees with Beth Hillel, it is still interesting that he did not want to explicitly rule like Beth Hillel because of his fear of the followers of Beth Shammai. [D] R. Ṭarfon also agrees with Beth Hillel and wishes that such a case should come before him so that he can marry her off to a priest without performing *ḥaliṣa*. He wanted to publicly demonstrate his alliance with Beth Hillel. The fear of disagreeing with Beth Shammai, as well as the zeal to protest against them reflected by various Tannaim, reflects a tense climate between the houses.

The next three statements attempt to reduce the gap between Beth Shammai and Beth Hillel. They each begin with אף על פי. [E] R. Eleazar says that Beth Shammai and Beth Hillel agree that a *mamzer* results only from a limited number of cases, and the daughter's cowife is not one of them. Certainly, Beth Shammai agrees that if cowives marry without *ḥaliṣa*, even though not permitted, their children are not *mamzerim*. This agrees with R. Yoḥanan ben Nuri [A].[118] R. Eleazar also claims that Beth Hillel agrees that

116. Translation based on Jacob Neusner, *The Tosefta* (Peabody: Hendrickson, 2002), 1:686–88.

117. Ginzberg, *Commentary*, 159–60, explains that the Bar Kokhba revolt began and the rabbis had no opportunity to meet and finalize discussion of the matter.

118. All manuscripts of the Tosefta as well as all manuscripts of the Bavli say that if one follows Beth Hillel then the child is considered *pagum* (blemished) according to Beth

if cowives perform *yibbum*, even though not permitted, their children are not *mamzerim*.[119] R. Eleazar thus argues with R. Yoḥanan ben Nuri about the severity of the issue and goes one step toward alleviating the problem brought up by R. Yoḥanan ben Nuri above.

[F] The next statement further closes the gap by stating that even though there was great theoretical controversy between the Houses on multiple issues, in practice, they continued to marry each other. The Tosefta adds that they acted in a spirit of truth and peace, thus fulfilling Zech 8:19. This verse may imply that there is sometimes tension between truth and peace, but ultimately peace must prevail. One must forgo what he believes to be the true law in order to maintain peace with those who disagree.[120]

[G] The next statement also adds a comment concerning the willingness to tolerate different purity laws. The quotations from Prov 16:2 and 21:2[121] teach that the differences between the details of the laws of the two Houses seem important to man, but God is concerned with man's intention.[122] The basis for legal pluralism here is not simply pragmatic that man cannot reach absolute certainty regarding the "correct" law. Rather, any set of rules that are thoughtfully formulated and are followed with sincere devotion are equally acceptable to God.[123] The implications of such a philosophy of law

---

Shammai. The Yerushalmi, however, says that Beth Shammai considers him a *mamzer*, which would follow the opinion of R. Akiba (*m. Yebam.* 4:13; see *Pene Moshe*). Lieberman, *Tosefta ki-fshuṭah*, 6:5, suggests that even the Yerushalmi did not mean that he is literally a *mamzer* but was simply exaggerating.

119. This interpretation of R. Eleazar is rejected by the Bavli, which assumes that marrying a daughter's cowife is punishable by *kareth*, and so, according to R. Eleazar, the child is a *mamzer*. However, see Halivni, *Meqorot u-mesorot*, Nashim, 18–19, who reconstructs the original intention of R. Eleazar based on the derivation of Rabbi in *b. Yebam.* 8a that the daughter's cowife is merely a negative prohibition, not punishable by *kareth*, and therefore would not produce a *mamzer*.

120. See further in the conclusion, below, p. 392.

121. These verses are slightly different, and the Tosefta combines elements of each to create a combination verse.

122. NJPS translates, "All the ways of a man seem right to him, but the Lord probes motives [or, the mind]." The plain meaning of this verse is meant to denigrate one who acts in whatever way he wishes thinking it is correct and not giving enough thought to what God wants. Such a person will not succeed for God knows his true motivation. In this context, however, the verse is given a positive spin, i.e., the Houses accepted each other's rulings because even though each side believed its own opinions to be correct, it still recognized that God will accept any action motivated by a sincere heart. The phrase תכן לבות is also found in Prov 24:12. *Exodus Rabbah* 33:5 applies this verse to Phineas who was not sure what to do, but he assured himself in his decision to kill the sinners because God knows his intention is good (see commentary of David Luria in the Vilna edition ad loc.). A similar idea is found in *b. Sanh.* 106b, "הקדוש ברוך הוא ליבא בעי דכתיב וה' יראה ללבב (1 Sam 16:7)." However, see Lieberman, *Tosefta ki-fshuṭah*, 6:8, who interprets the Tosefta differently.

123. The assumption here may be that there is one objectively true law but that God does not require that one achieve that law since intention is of primary import. This is also

are certainly far reaching. The Tosefta thus amplifies and gives a theoretical basis for the universal pluralism reflected in the Mishnah.[124]

The next statement of the Tosefta [H], however, dampens the spirit of the Mishnah. R. Shimon limits the Mishnah's tolerance to cases of doubt. If one side was unsure of the status of a particular case, then it would rely on the other opinion only to grant the benefit of the doubt. However, if one side was sure that marriage to a certain person was prohibited, it did not bend. This denies that the full measure of pluralism described above existed, but still admits to a relatively high degree of respect for the opposing viewpoint.

[I] Finally, the last section declares that halakha is officially like Beth Hillel. It then discredits any attempt to combine the laws of the two Houses, either for stringency or leniency. Section I ends with a requirement that one consistently follow one school exclusively, be it Beth Shammai or Beth Hillel. This last statement contradicts the first one that halakha follows Beth Hillel.[125] It is possible that only the second statement is original while the first line is a later addition appended after Beth Hillel became ascendant and Beth Shammai was no longer practically viable.[126] But, even if we read the Tosefta as is, it does not completely eliminate Beth Shammai. Rather, it seeks to formulate a middle position that recognizes the ascendancy of Beth Hillel (see line D) but at the same time keeps alive the validity of Beth Shammai.[127] Taken as a whole, the Tosefta tries to

---

the argument for tolerance proposed by J. S. Mill, *On Liberty* (Indianapolis: Hackett, 1978), ch. 2. Alternatively, the Tosefta may be suggesting that there is no one "correct" law and that any set of rules that are properly motivated are equally valid. This unreservedly relativistic argument comes close to the view of Nietzsche, who relativizes all notions of truth and falsehood. See Moshe Halbertal, "Jews and Pagans in the Mishnah," in *Tolerance and Intolerance in Early Judaism and Christianity*, ed. G. Stanton and G. Stroumsa (Cambridge: Cambridge University Press, 1998), 160–61.

124. See further in the conclusion, below, p. 392.

125. *B. ʿErub.* 6b notices the contradiction between the first and last lines of statement I and offers three solutions. Scholars have also made various attempts to solve this contradiction using source-critical means.

126. Ginzberg, *Commentary*, 152, 155–56, suggests that the second part of I, which allows one to follow either House as long as one is consistent, was originally separate from the first line. The first line was created later than the rest, after the law was decided according to Beth Hillel, while the earlier statement reflects the reality before such a decision was made. The contradiction in this Tosefta results from a rather sloppy conflation of the two traditions. This is essentially the first answer given in *b. ʿErub.* 6b. See also Halivni, *Rules*, 130.

127. Hanokh Albeck, *Six Orders of Mishnah*, 6 vols. (Jerusalem: Mossad Bialik, 1959) (Hebrew), *Yevamot*, 332, suggests that the original statement, "הלכה כבית הלל," only described the general practice among the masses to follow Beth Hillel but was not a prescriptive requirement to follow them. As the rest of the statement goes on to say, one may choose either set of laws. Only later did the meaning of the first statement become prescriptive. See similarly at Bitman, "Le-tivo," 187. Safrai, "Ha-hakhraʿah," 43, makes a similar suggestion that originally the first line was not meant as a blanket statement that the law follows Beth

reconcile and minimize the controversy regarding the daughter's cowife, even while taking note of some of the hostility surrounding this case. It expands on the ideal of living in peace and tolerance but also limits the full range of possible pluralism.

Yerushalmi

We will now analyze how the Yerushalmi and Bavli deal with this important Tosefta. The Yerushalmi quotes much of the Tosefta but adds interpretive material, that significantly alters the thrust of its statements. *Y. Yebamot* 1:6 (3a-b) begins with a discussion about the scriptural source for Beth Shammai:

רבי סימון בשם ר׳ יוסי בשם נהוריי טעמון דבית שמאי לא תהיה אשת המת החוצה לאיש זר החיצונה לא תהיה לאיש זר

אתייא דבית שמאי כאילין כותייא שהן מייבמין את הארוסות ומוציאין את הנשואות דאינון דרשין חוצה החיצונה

מה מקיימין בית שמאי[128] ובן אין לו אמר רבי יעקב דרומייא קומי רבי יוסי ובן אין לו מן הנשואה החיצונה לא תהיה לאיש זר אמר ליה לא יחסדונך כותאי דאת מקיים דרשיהון

תני רבי שמעון בן אלעזר **נומיתי לסופרי כותים מי גרם לכם לטעות דלית אתון דרשין כר׳ נחמיה** דתני בשם ר׳ נחמיה **כל דבר שהוא צריך למד מתחילתו ולא ניתן לו ניתן לו הא בסופו כגון לחוץ חוצה לשעיר שעירה לסוכות סוכותה.** מתיבין לרבי נחמיה והא כתיב ישובו רשעים לשאולה אמר רבא בר זבדא לדייטי התחתונה של שאול.[129]

R. Simon in the name of R. Yose in the name of Nahorai: "The scriptural basis for the position of the Beth Shammai is this: *'The wife of the deceased shall not be married outside to a stranger'* (Deut 25:5). The woman who is outside [of a consanguinous relationship with the living brother] should not marry a stranger."

[In interpreting "outside" to refer to the woman's status], the view of the House of Shammai accords with the opinion of these Samaritans who enter into levirate marriage with those who have been betrothed but who send away those who have been in a fully

Hillel in every case, only most of the time. Menachem Katz, "The First Chapter of Tractate Qiddushin of the Talmud Yerushalmi: Text, Commentary, and Studies in the Editorial Process" (Ph.D. diss., Bar-Ilan University, 2003), 286–290, explains that Beth Shammai was not completely rejected even after the halakha was established according to Beth Hillel and individuals were permitted to follow Beth Shammai. Sabato, "Qeri'at shemaʿ," 52–53, agrees that Katz's explanation best fits the plain sense of the words.

128. *Pene Moshe* and *Qorban ha-ʿedah* emend to כותאי. I have followed this emendation in the translation.

129. The *baraita* of R. Nehemiah, the question, and the answer of Raba bar Zabda are also found in *Genesis Rabbah* 50, 68, and 86.

> consummated marriage. For they interpret "outside" to mean "an outsider."
>
> How do the Samaritans[128] interpret the statement, "And has no sons" (Deut 25:5)? Said R. Yaᶜaqov from Ruma before R. Yose, "If he has no son from the woman to whom he is married then one who is an outsider [betrothed] should not marry a stranger." He said to him, "The Samaritans should not denigrate you since you uphold their interpretations."
>
> R. Shimon ben Eleazar taught, **"I remarked to Samaritan scribes, 'Who made you err? It was that you do not interpret Scripture as does R. Nehemiah."** For it has been taught in the name of R. Nehemiah, **"Any word that requires a *lamed* at the beginning of the word, and such a letter has not been supplied, gets a *heh* at the end. This would, for example, be in the contrast between, 'to outside' and 'outside-ward,' 'to Seir,' and 'Seir-ward,' 'to Sukkoth' and 'Sukkoth-ward.'"** They objected to R. Nehemiah, "But it is written, 'the wicked will return to Sheol-ward' (Ps 9:17)." Said R. Raba bar Zabda, "It means to the lowest level of Sheol."

It is not clear to whom each of the names in the opening chain of tradition refers, but R. Simon is probably the Palestinian Amora of the second/third generation. He interprets החוצה—"outside" to be an adjective for the wife who is an outsider since she is not related to the living brother and therefore can marry him. The Talmud then points out that it so happens that the Samaritans also interpret this word as an adjective describing the woman. This places Beth Shammai in the uncomfortable position of being allied with the heretical Samaritans.

In the next paragraph, R. Yaᶜaqov from Ruma defends the interpretation of the Samaritans and is ridiculed by his teacher. This leads the reader to apply the same ridicule to Beth Shammai. R. Shimon ben Eleazar, a late Tanna, then proves the interpretation of the Samaritans to be incorrect.[130] The less-than-subtle implication is that Beth Shammai also interpreted the verse wrongly, and so their ruling has no basis. The attempt to find scriptural basis for Beth Shammai thus ends up placing them in the Samaritan camp, who are not only the enemy but who also do not know basic Hebrew grammar. The *sugya* so far not only disfavors Beth Shammai but even finds opportunities to insult them.

The next section of the Yerushalmi quotes the Tosefta almost exactly except that it has a different order for the statements, namely, A, B, E, D,

---

130. R. Eleazar b. R. Shimon has a similar anti-Samaritan statement in *y. Soṭah* 7:3 (21c). The similarity between the names of these two unrelated Tannaim suggests that only one of these Tannaim debated the Samaritans and the name of the other has been confused for the former.

C, F, I.[131] (See chart 4.3, p. 236, for a comparison of the Yerushalmi and the Tosefta.) After quoting statement [C], which is an account of students asking a rabbi about the law of the cowife, the Yerushalmi interrupts its quotation of the Tosefta with the following story, which is also about students asking about this subject:

ר׳ יעקב בר אידי בשם ר׳ יהושע בן לוי מעשה שנכנסו זקינים אצל ר׳ דוסא בן הרכינס לשאול לו על צרת הבת. אמרו לו את הוא שאת מתיר בצרות אמר לון מה שמעתון דוסא בן הרכינס. אמרו לו בן הרכינס. אמר לון יונתן אחי הוה בכור שטן ומתלמידי בית שמאי היזהרו ממנו שלש מאות תשובות יש לו על צרת הבת. אזלון לגביה. שלח וכתב ליה היזהר שחכמי ישראל נכנסין אצלך.

עלון ויתיב להו קומוי הוה מסביר להון ולא סברין מיסבר להון ולא סברין. שריין מתנמנמין. אמר להן מה אתון מתנמנמין שרי מישדי עליהון צרירין. ואית דמרין בחד תרע עלון ובתלתא נפקין. שלח אמר ליה מה שלחת לי בני נש בעו מילף ואמרת לי אינון חכמי ישראל.

אתו לגביה אמרון ליה את מה את אמר. אמר להן על המדוכה הזאת ישב חגי הנביא והעיד שלשה דברים על צרת הבת שתינשא לכהונה ועל עמון ומואב שהן מעשרין מעשר עני בשביעית ועל גירי תדמור שהן כשירין לבוא בקהל. אמר תלון שני עיני דניחמי לחכמי ישראל ראה את רבי יהושע וקרא עליו את מי יורה דיעה זכור אני שהיתה אמו מולכת עריסתו לבית הכנסת בשביל שיתדבקו אזניו בדברי תורה. את רבי עקיבה וקרא עליו כפירים רשו ורעבו מכירו אני שאדם גיבור בתורה הוא. ראה את רבי לעזר בן עזריה וקרא עליו נער הייתי גם זקנתי מכירו אני שהוא דור עשירי לעזרא ועינוי דמיין לדידיה.

אמר רבי חנינה דציפורין אף רבי טרפון הוה עמהן וקרא עליו כהדא דרבי לעזר בן עזריה.

R. Yaʿaqov bar Idi in the name of R. Yehoshua ben Levi [related] a story: when the elders visited R. Dosa ben Harkinas to ask him about the case of the daughter's cowife, they said to him, are you the one who permits cowives? He told them, "Did you hear [that rumor about] Dosa ben Harkinas?" They responded, "Ben Harkinas." He told them, "My brother Yonatan is the firstborn of Satan and is a student of Beth Shammai. Be wary of him for he has three hundred responses concerning the daughter's cowife." They went to him. [R. Dosa] sent a letter to him writing, "Be wary as the sages of Israel are coming to you."

They entered and he sat himself before them. He was explaining it to them but they did not understand. He explained it to them again but they did not understand. They began to doze. He told them, "Why are you dozing?" He began to throw pebbles at them. Some say that they entered through one doorway and exited through three. He sent and told him [R. Dosa], "What did you send me? These people have yet to learn and you tell me they are the sages of Israel?!"

---

131. This basically follows the order of the Tosefta except switching [C] and [E]. This switch does not make any substantive difference in meaning but rather seems to reflect a different version of the Tosefta.

> They came to him [R. Dosa] and asked him, "As for you, what do you say [about the cowife]?" He told them, "Upon this very mortar stood Ḥaggai the prophet and testified concerning three matters: concerning the daughter's cowife that she may marry a priest, concerning the lands Amon and Moab that they require tithing of the poor man's tithe in the Seventh year, and concerning the converts of Palmyra that they may marry into the congregation." He added, "Lift up my two eyes that I may look upon <u>the sages of Israel</u>." He saw R. Yehoshua and applied to him the verse, *"To whom would he give instruction? [To whom expound a message? To those newly weaned from milk, just taken away from the breast]"* (Isa 28:9). I remember that his mother would carry his cradle to the synagogue so that his ears would cleave to words of Torah." [He saw] R. Akiba and applied to him the verse, *"Lions have been reduced to starvation, [but those who turn to the* Lord *shall not lack any good]* (Ps 34:11). I recognize him to be a man who is mighty in Torah." He saw R. Eleazar ben Azariah and applied to him the verse, *"I have been young and am now old, [but I have never seen a righteous man abandoned, or his children seeking bread]* (Ps 37:25). I recognize him to be a tenth-generation descendent of Ezra and his eyes are similar to his [Ezra's]." R. Ḥaninah of Sepphoris said, "R. Ṭarfon was also with them, and he [R. Dosa] applied the same verse as he did for R. Eleazar ben Azariah.[132]

In this story, the tension between the two schools is dramatically represented by two brothers, R. Dosa ben Harkinas and Yonatan ben Harkinas. The students, based on a rumor, believe that R. Dosa ben Harkinas permitted one to perform *yibbum* with a daughter's cowife. The students, troubled that he would rule like Beth Shammai, visit him to clarify the matter. R. Dosa ben Harkinas explains that it is actually his brother who rules like Beth Shammai. R. Dosa ben Harkinas describes his brother as Satan's firstborn who must be approached with caution since he has three hundred responses for his view. R. Dosa also warns his brother that the sages of Israel are coming to him. The first warning turns out to be well warranted, unlike the second, which comes back to haunt R. Dosa. The explanations of Yonatan ben Harkinas are so complex that the students are unable to comprehend them. After falling asleep and getting pelted with pebbles, they leave ashamed. They entered together with poise and self-confidence through one doorway and leave humiliated through three doorways, as if they had to sneak out.[133] Yonatan chastises his brother for describing

---

132. *Y. Yebam.* 1:6 (3a-b). I have underlined what seems to be a key theme throughout this story, i.e., competition over who is to be considered the sage.

133. See the second explanation of *Qorban ha-ʿedah* ad loc. The contrast between enter-

these students, who need to learn the basics, as "the sages of Israel." The students now return to R. Dosa to gain back their confidence and see how he deals with the three hundred responses of Yonatan.[134] R. Dosa invokes a prophetic tradition to prove his position.[135] R. Dosa confirms that he still considers them "sages of Israel" and proceeds to praise each one of them.

The story recognizes that Yonatan ben Harkinas has more intellectual prowess. It still claims that Beth Hillel is correct, however, and that its sages are of high caliber. The story is both about the intellectual competition between Beth Shammai and Beth Hillel and also about the personal dignity of the rabbis. The tension in this story arises from the possibility that Yonatan may have better insight and possess the true halakha. But such a possibility is ultimately rejected, the law of Beth Hillel is established, and the honor of the rabbis is restored.

The story provides a more elaborate example of the position taken by R. Yehoshua in part C of the Tosefta just before the story. Although R. Yehoshua decides in favor of Beth Hillel, he still is afraid to offend Beth Shammai. R. Yehoshua is afraid his head will be smashed between arguments of the two schools. The students in the story of R. Dosa actually get intellectually overpowered and pelted with stones. In both stories, Beth Hillel wins out, not because a better argument is brought for their side, but because of a historical precedent, the high priestly family or the prophecy of Ḥaggai.

The *sugya* continues with a discussion of accepting proselytes from places other than those mentioned in the story. We omit this section since

---

ing through the same door or different doors also comes up in *y. Šabb.* 19:5 (17b) where R. Ḥaggai explains his refusal to have a legal discussion with Yaʿaqov of Kefar Nevoraia with this phrase: "If you and I were going in the same door, perhaps maybe we could discuss this point." Yaʿaqov is a controversial figure, sometimes considered a heretic; see Oded Ir-Shai, "Yaʿaqov 'Ish Kefar Nevoraia—Ḥakham she-nikhshal be-minut," *Meḥqere Yerushalayim be-Maḥshevet Yisrael* 2, no. 2 (1983): 153–68, and see below, pp. 278–80. In that context, going through a door together indicates comradery, and refusal to go through the same door indicates rejection; see Boyarin, *Border Lines*, 177. That meaning, however, is not precisely relevant in our pericope. The students do feel rejected by Yonatan but they do not reject each other. Rather, it serves here as a sign of disgrace.

134. Yonatan's three hundred responses do not guarantee that he is correct but only that his position is well reasoned and not easily disproven. See Rubenstein, "Thematization," 78, who says that the hyperbolic number of responses in the Bavli points "to the inherent worth of the most intricate and complex argumentation for the Stammaim." In this case, however, the number of responses has the same function in the Yerushalmi and so does not indicate an innovation of the Stammaim.

135. The three laws quoted in the name of Ḥagai all have in common that they were controversial. For the tithe in Amon and Moab, see *m. Yad.* 4:3, *t. Yad.* 2:17, and *b. Ḥag.* 3b, where this law is similarly quoted as an ancient prophetic tradition (although it is known only to R. Yose ben Durmaskit). For the converts of Palmyra see *y. Yebam.* 1:6 (3b) and *y. Qidd.* 4:1 (65c); these sources, however, provide no indication of a prophetic tradition nor do they give the impression that the controversy surrounding them was particularly intense.

it is only a tangent and not relevant to our topic. The *sugya* then goes on to quote the remainder of the Tosefta and elaborates on it.[136]

[F] **אף על פי שנחלקו בית שמאי ובית הלל בצרות ובאחיות ובגט ישן ובספק אשת איש ובמקדש בשוה פרוטה והמגרש את אשתו ולנה עמו בפונדקי והאשה מתקדשת בדינר ובשוה דינר לא נמנעו בית שמאי מלישא נשים מבית הלל ולא בית הלל מבית שמאי אלא נוהגין באמת ובשלום שנאמר והאמת והשלום אהבו**

ממזירות בנתיים ואת אמר הכין...

[1] ר׳ יעקב בר אחא בשם רבי יוחנן מודין בית שמאי לבית הלל לחומרין

מעתה בית שמאי ישאו נשים מבית הלל דאינון מודיי להון ובית הלל לא ישאו נשים מבית שמאי דלית אינון מודיי להון[137]

[2] רבי הילא בשם ר׳ יוחנן אילו ואילו כהלכה היו עושין

אם כהלכה היו עושין בדא תנינן **שלחו להן בית שמאי ופחתוה שבית שמאי אומרים עד שיפחות את רובה**[138]

[3] אמר רבי יוסי בי רבי בון עד שלא בא מעשה אצל בית הלל היו בית שמאי נוגעין בו

משבא מעשה אצל בית הלל לא היו בית שמאי נוגעין בו

אמר רבי אבמרי יאות מה תנינן טימאו טהרות למפרע לא מיכן ולהבא

[4] רבי יוסי בי רבי בון אמר רב ושמואל חד אמר אילו ואילו כהלכה היו עושין וחד אמר אילו כהילכתן ואילו כהילכתן

ממזרות בנתיים ואת אמר הכין[139]

המקום משמר ולא אורע מעשה מעולם

[I] כהדא דתני **כל הרוצה להחמיר על עצמו לנהוג כחומרי בית שמאי וכחומרי בית הלל על זה נאמר והכסיל בחושך הולך כקולי אילו ואילו נקרא רשע אלא או כדברי בית שמאי כקוליהם וכחומריהן או כדברי בית הלל וכקוליהם וכחומריהן**

הדא דתימר עד שלא יצאת בת קול אבל משיצאת בת קול **לעולם הלכה כדברי בית הלל** וכל העובר על דברי בית הלל חייב מיתה תני **יצאתה בת קול ואמרה אילו ואילו דברי אלהים חיים הם אבל הלכה כבית הלל לעולם** באיכן יצאת בת קול רבי ביבי בשם רבי יוחנן אמר ביבנה יצאת בת קול.

[F] **Even though Beth Shammai and Beth Hillel argue about cowives, sisters, an outdated divorce paper, a doubtful adulteress, one who betroths with the worth of a *peruṭah*, one who divorces his wife and sleeps with her at an inn, and a women who is betrothed with a *dinar* or the worth of a *dinar*, still Beth Shammai did not refrain from marrying women of Beth Hillel nor did Beth Hillel from Beth Shammai. Rather they practiced with truth and peace as the verse states, "*Truth and peace do they love*"** (Zech 8:19).

How can you say this when they disagree about an issue that includes *mamzerut?*...

[1] R. Yaʿaqov bar Aḥa in the name of R. Yoḥanan [said], "Beth

136. *Y. Yebam.* 1:6 (3b). This entire section has a parallel in *y. Qidd.* 1:1 (58d). The tradition of the heavenly voice (part I) also appears in the Yerushalmi at *y. Ber.* 1:4 (3b) and *y. Soṭah* 3:4 (19a).

Shammai agrees to the stringencies of Beth Hillel." If so, Beth Shammai should marry women of Beth Hillel since they [Beth Shammai] agree with them [Beth Hillel], but Beth Hillel should not marry women of Beth Shammai since they [Beth Hillel] do not agree with them [Beth Shammai]?[137]

[2] R. Hila in the name of R. Yoḥanan [said], "Both these and those followed halakha." If they both followed halakha then what about that which we have learned in the Mishnah, **Beth Shammai sent people to widen [the hole] since Beth Shammai says [it is not valid] until one hollows out most of it**?[138]

[3] R. Yose said in the name of R. Bun, "Before a case reached Beth Hillel, Beth Shammai would get involved in it, but once a case came before Beth Hillel, Beth Shammai would no longer get involved with it." R. Abamari said, "This is correct. What have we learned, that they defiled the pure items retroactively? No, only from now on."

[4] R. Yose said in the name of R. Bun, "Rav and Shmuel, one of them said 'these and those followed one halakha' and the other said 'these followed their halakha and those followed their halakha.'"

<u>How can you say this when they disagree about an issue that includes *mamzerut*?</u>[139]

God watches and no [problematic] case ever occurred.

[I] This is similar to that which we learned: **Anyone who wants to be stringent upon himself to practice the stringencies of Beth Shammai as well as the stringencies of Beth Hillel, upon him the verse states, "*The fool walks in darkness*" (Eccl 2:14). One who follows the leniencies of these and those is called wicked. Rather, choose either according to Beth Shammai with their leniencies and stringencies, or according to Beth Hillel with their leniencies and stringencies.**

You say this before the heavenly voice sounded, but since the heavenly voice went out halakha is always like Beth Hillel and anyone who transgresses the words of Beth Hillel deserves death. We learned, **the heavenly voice came out and said these and those are the words of the living God; however, the halakha**

---

137. *Qorban ha-ʿedah* suggests that the text is corrupt and that the names in this statement should be swapped. If Beth Shammai kept the stringencies of Beth Hillel then Beth Hillel would agree to marry Beth Shammai, but Beth Shammai would still have a problem marrying Beth Hillel because of cases where Beth Hillel was more lenient.

138. *M. Miqw.* 4:5.

139. This question is underlined because it is repeated like a refrain; it highlights the basic problem addressed by the *sugya*.

> **follows Beth Hillel always.** Where did the heavenly voice come out? R. Bevai in the name of R. Yoḥanan said, "The heavenly voice came out at Yavneh."

The Gemara quotes the next portion of the Tosefta [F] stating that members of Beth Shammai and Beth Hillel married each other despite all their differences regarding laws of marriage. (It does not quote [G], however.) Then it asks the obvious question, how could they be so tolerant when they have such far-reaching controversies? Several answers to this question follow. Each of them limits the original sense of the Mishnah and Tosefta [F-G] in some way and in that sense are parallel to part [H] of the Tosefta, which is not quoted in the Yerushalmi. [1] R. Yaʿaqov bar Aḥa in the name of R. Yoḥanan says that Beth Shammai practiced not only their own stringencies but also the stringencies of Beth Hillel so that their children would be acceptable to those of Beth Hillel. However, this does not work since Beth Shammai would still not accept the children of Beth Hillel on account of their leniencies. [2] R. Hila, also in the name of R. Yoḥanan, suggests that Beth Shammai practiced entirely like Beth Hillel. However, *m. Miqw.* 4:5 relates a story in which Beth Shammai did follow their own opinion. [3] R. Yose then proposes that Beth Shammai did follow their own opinion in public cases in which Beth Hillel was not involved and, presumably, in private as well. This does not answer the original question of how they could marry each other since Beth Shammai did still follow their own practices some of the time. Rather, it attempts to reconcile R. Hila's statement in line [2] with *m. Miqw.* 4:5.

[4] Another statement from the same R. Yose refers us to a controversy between Rav and Shmuel on this topic. One of these Babylonian sages agrees with R. Hila in the name of R. Yoḥanan quoted above that Beth Shammai followed one halakha along with Beth Hillel. The other opinion admits that they followed their own halakha. The Gemara now reiterates its original question to the sage that holds this opinion. The Gemara gives its final answer that even though each House follows its own opinion, they still married each other because they relied on God to make sure that no problematic marriage would result. This answer could have been given only after the time when people actually had different practices. It is a way to get out of the problem on a theoretical level but would not help people at the time of the controversy who witnessed such problematic cases in front of their eyes. Furthermore, the invocation of divine providence to thwart any possible halakhic problems denies the possibility that the Houses compromised a halakhic principle for the sake of peace and unity. Although it admits the historical occurrence of diversity, it eviscerates any value of pluralism encoded in such diversity with its guarantee that neither side will lose anything by cooperating and do not need to recognize any legitimacy in the view of the other. The Yerushalmi's version

of diversity could never serve as a model for future cooperation between opposing parties.[140]

The Gemara quotes the rest of the Tosefta but transfers the line that halakha is like Beth Hillel to the next paragraph. The Yerushalmi cannot let the Tosefta stand since the Tosefta tolerates one who decides to wholly follow Beth Shammai. It therefore limits that tolerance to the time period before the heavenly voice decided in favor of Beth Hillel. The Yerushalmi places the ruling in favor of Beth Hillel in the mouth of a heavenly voice and enforces it by threat of death, which is not clearly defensible in terms of general Talmudic law,[141] but which does bring home the point that following Beth Shammai is not acceptable. Finally, the *sugya* further specifies exactly when the heavenly voice came forth in order to make it more concrete and therefore more authoritative.

In sum, the Yerushalmi inherits the text of the Tosefta and quotes it almost verbatim, as is the usual practice of the Yerushalmi. The Yerushalmi, however, does not agree with the tolerance for Beth Shammai that is reflected in the Tosefta. The Yerushalmi therefore adds commentary that limits the impact of the Tosefta and promotes a unified halakha following Beth Hillel. The first two explanations for part F of the Tosefta effectively say that Beth Shammai followed the rulings of Beth Hillel. The third explanation limits the cooperation between the Houses to public cases, but only the last opinion admits to the possibility that they followed their own opinion even in open disputes with Beth Hillel. The Yerushalmi must admit such a possibility in any case because of part [I]. But that historical reality is confined to a prior time period and no longer relevant.

Bavli

Bavli *Yebamot* 13b-16a[142] begins with a *sugya* that parallels the opening *sugya* of the Yerushalmi concerning the derivation for Beth Shammai's ruling. The Bavli, however, takes the *sugya* in a drastically different direction

---

140. See Kraemer, "New Meaning," 205.

141. A person would be liable to death only if it involved a case in which the punishment for violating is death, such as Shabbat, but not for cases like lying down while reciting *Shema.* Even under the law of the rebellious elder, only one who has attained the status of *hora'ah* is liable to death but not a student or layman; see *m. Sanh.* 11:2 and discussion below, pp. 302–7.

142. This *sugya* continues from the discussion of *lo titgodedu,* discussed in chapter 2. That section quoted a controversy between Rav and Shmuel about whether Beth Shammai followed their own opinion (see above, p. 104). This part of the *sugya* picks up on that question and cites eleven different cases, one of which is the daughter's cowife, from which it tries to prove whether or not there was actually diversity of practice between the houses.

by legitimating Beth Shammai rather than denigrating them. The Bavli begins:

[1] אמר רבי שמעון בן פזי מאי טעמא דבית שמאי דכתיב (דברים כה:ה) לא תהיה אשת המת החוצה לאיש זר חוצה מכלל דאיכא פנימית ואמר רחמנא לא תהיה
[2] ובית הלל מיבעי להו לכדרב יהודה אמר רב דאמר רב יהודה אמר רב מנין שאין קידושין תופסין ביבמה שנאמר לא תהיה אשת המת החוצה לאיש זר לא תהיה בה הויה לזר
[3] ובית שמאי מי כתיב לחוץ חוצה כתיב
[4] ובית הלל כיון דכתיב חוצה כמאן דכתיב לחוץ דמי דתניא **ר' נחמיה אומר כל תיבה שצריכה למ"ד בתחלתה הטיל לה הכתוב ה"א בסופה** ותנא דבי ר' ישמעאל **כגון אלים אלימה מחנים מחנימה מצרים מצרימה דבלתימה ירושלימה מדברה**
[5] ובית שמאי דרב יהודה אמר רב מנא להו מלאיש זר נפקא
[6] ובית הלל נמי תיפוק להו מלאיש זר אין הכי נמי
[7] חוצה למה לי לרבות הארוסה
[8] ואידך מחוצה החוצה
[9] ואידך חוצה החוצה לא משמע להו
[10] רבא אמר טעמייהו דבית שמאי דאין איסור חל על איסור תינח היכא דנשא מת ואחר כך נשא חי לא אתי איסור אחות אשה וחייל אאיסור אשת אח אלא נשא חי ואחר כך נשא מת אחות אשה קדים[143] כיון דלא אתי איסור אשת אח וחייל אאיסור אחות אשה הויא לה צרת ערוה שלא במקום מצוה ושריא

[1] R. Shimon ben Pazzi said, what is the reason of Beth Shammai? For it is written, "*The wife of the deceased shall not be married outside to a stranger*" (Deut 25:5). This implies that there is an inside [wife who is related to the brother]; yet, the Merciful One said, [the unrelated wife] "*shall not be married…*"
[2] Beth Hillel requires [the word "*outside*"] as Rav Yehudah said in the name of Rav, for Rav Yehudah said in the name of Rav, "From where do we know that betrothal of a levirate woman is not effective? For it is written, '*The wife of the deceased shall not be married outside to a stranger*'—she cannot be married to a stranger.
[3] Beth Shammai [counters], is it written *la-ḥuṣ*? Rather, it is written *ḥuṣa*.
[4] Beth Hillel [counters], since it is written *ḥuṣa*, it is as if it is written *la-ḥuṣ*. For it has been taught, **R. Nehemiah says, "Any word that requires a *lamed* at the beginning of the word, Scripture attaches to it a *heh* at the end."** The house of R. Ishmael teaches, **"Such as *'elim 'elimah* (Exod 15:27), *maḥanaim maḥanaimah* (2 Sam 17:24), *miṣrayim miṣrayimah* (Gen 12:10), *diblataimah* (Num 33:46), *yerushalaimah* (Ez 8:3), *midbarah* (1 Chron 5:9)."**

143. See the parallel in *b. Ḥul.* 8a.

[5] From where does Beth Shammai derive the ruling of Rav Yehudah in the name of Rav? From *"to a stranger."*
[6] Then let Beth Hillel also derive this ruling from *"to a stranger"*? Indeed, this is so.
[7] [According to Beth Hillel,] why do I need *"outside"*? To include the betrothed woman.
[8] And the other one? [Beth Shammai could derive the betrothed woman] from [the extra *heh* in] *ḥuṣa—haḥuṣa.*
[9] And the other one? [Beth Hillel] does not derive from [the extra *heh* in] *ḥuṣa—haḥuṣa.*
[10] Rava says, the reason of Beth Shammai is that a prohibition cannot apply when there is already another prohibition. This is acceptable in a case where the deceased brother had married and then the living brother married since the prohibition of the wife's sister does not apply to the prohibition of the brother's wife. However, if the living brother had married and then the deceased brother married then the prohibition of the wife's sister precedes?[143] Since the prohibition of the brother's wife does not apply to the prohibition of the wife's sister, she is a cowife of an incestual relation who is not is not included in the commandment [of *yibbum*] and therefore permitted.

The Bavli *sugya* opens with the same derivation for Beth Shammai's ruling as does the Yerushalmi with added explanation. In line [2], the Bavli does not reject the interpretation, as does the Yerushalmi, but rather turns the line of questioning against Beth Hillel—how would they explain the word *"outside"*? Beth Hillel derives from this word that betrothal of a *yebama* by another man is ineffective. In lines [3–4], the two interpretations for "outside" are juxtaposed without giving preference to either one. Lines [5–6] teach that Beth Shammai derives the law of betrothal to a *yebama* from *"to a stranger"* and Beth Hillel agrees. This once again frees the word *"outside."* Beth Hillel and Beth Shammai agree that this word teaches that a betrothed women whose husband dies childless is also required to perform *yibbum*. Beth Shammai, however, also derive the law of the daughter's cowife from the first letter of this word. Unlike the Yerushalmi, the Bavli makes no mention of Samaritans and also does not reject the view or derivation of Beth Shammai.

In line [10], the Bavli adds another source for Beth Shammai's view, not from a verse but from a general legal principle. This legal principle is widely used and accepted throughout the Bavli. In fact, some commentators wonder why Beth Hillel would not agree with this reasoning.[144] In

144. See *Tosafot Yeshanim* and Riṭva.

complete contrast to the Yerushalmi's sharp rejection of Beth Shammai, the Bavli treats Beth Shammai's view as equal to that of Beth Hillel and even seems to prefer it by having Beth Hillel agree to Beth Shammai's derivation in line [6] and especially by citing two sources for his view both from a verse and from a widespread principle.

It is difficult to know if the redactors of the Bavli *sugya* knew of the Yerushalmi *sugya* as we have it. However, it is evident that something resembling the current Yerushalmi served as the basis for the Bavli *sugya* since both *sugyot* share a skeletal outline. Both cite the derivation for Beth Shammai from "*outside*"; both discuss the betrothed woman; and both cite the *baraita* of R. Nehemiah. This similarity only serves to highlight their differences. The Yerushalmi rejects the derivation of Beth Shammai and compares it to that of the Samaritans that *yibbum* does not apply to a betrothed woman. The Bavli accepts the derivation of Beth Shammai as legitimate and makes a point of saying that both Beth Shammai and Beth Hillel agree that *yibbum* applies to a betrothed woman. The Yerushalmi cites the *baraita* of R. Nehemiah in order to reject the interpretation of the Samaritans and Beth Shammai while the Bavli cites it as an equal alternative to the interpretation of Beth Shammai.

If our Yerusahlmi *sugya* was known to the Bavli editors, then the Bavli redactor's omission of any reference to Samaritans and inclusion of material that shows the legitimacy of Beth Shammai would be very significant. However, even if both *sugyot* are based on a proto-*sugya* with only the skeletal structure delineated above, the Yerushalmi can still serve as an Archimedean point in order to assess the intention of the Bavli redactor.[145] The Yerushalmi presents the path not taken by the Bavli redactors and vice versa. The choices made by the redactors of each *sugya* fit the general tendency toward intolerance of halakhic diversity in the Yerushalmi and a stronger sense of pluralism in the Bavli.

The next *sugya* places the Tosefta within an extended deliberation about whether the rabbis of each House actually practiced their opinions:

[1] תא שמע: **אף על פי שאלו אוסרים ואלו מתירים, לא נמנעו בית שמאי מלישא נשים מבית הלל, ולא בית הלל מבית שמאי.**[146] אי אמרת בשלמא לא עשו, משום הכי לא נמנעו, אלא אי אמרת עשו, אמאי לא נמנעו? בשלמא בית שמאי מבית הלל לא נמנעו, דבני חייבי לאוין נינהו, אלא בית הלל מבית שמאי אמאי לא נמנעו? בני חייבי כריתות—ממזרים נינהו! וכי תימא, קסברי בית הלל דאין ממזר מחייבי כריתות, **והאמר רבי אלעזר: אף על פי שנחלקו בית שמאי ובית הלל בצרות, מודים שאין ממזר אלא ממי שאיסורו איסור ערוה וענוש כרת**[147] אלא לאו שמע מינה: לא עשו

145. See Yaakov Zussman, "Ve-shuv le-Yerushalmi neziqin," in *Meḥqere Talmud 1*, ed. Yaakov Zussman and David Rosental (Jerusalem: Magnes, 1990), 114 n. 213.

146. *M. Yebam.* 1:4.

147. *T. Yebam.* 1:10.

לא, לעולם עשו, דמודעי להו ופרשי. והכי נמי מסתברא, דקתני סיפא: **כל הטהרות...**אלא לאו דמודעי להו, שמע מינה.

[2] תא שמע: **אף על פי שנחלקו בית שמאי ובית הלל בצרות ... לא נמנעו בית שמאי מלישא נשים מבית הלל, ולא בית הלל מבית שמאי, ללמדך, שחיבה וריעות נוהגים זה בזה, לקיים מה שנאמר: האמת והשלום אהבו.**[148] **ר"ש אומר: נמנעו הן מן הודאי, ולא נמנעו מן הספק.**[149] אי אמרת בשלמא עשו, משום הכי נמנעו, אלא אי אמרת לא עשו, אמאי נמנעו?

... כדאמר רב נחמן בר יצחק ...

ומאי שנא מן הודאי? דאיסורא הוא? ספק נמי איסורא הוא! לא תימא מן הספק, אלא אימא מן הסתם, דמודעי להו ופרשי. ומאי קא משמע לן? דאהבה וריעות נוהגים זה בזה...

[3] תא שמע, **דאמר רבי יוחנן בן נורי:...בואו ונתקן להן לצרות, שיהו חולצות ולא מתייבמות...אמר לו רבן שמעון בן גמליאל: מה נעשה להם לצרות הראשונות מעתה?**[150] אי אמרת בשלמא עשו, היינו דקאמר מה נעשה, אלא אי אמרת לא עשו, מאי מה נעשה?

אמר רב נחמן בר יצחק: לא נצרכה אלא לצרה עצמה...[151]

[4] ת"ש, **דא"ר טרפון: תאבני, מתי תבא צרת הבת לידי ואשאנה?**[152]

אימא: ואשיאנה. והא תאבני קאמר! לאפוקי מדרבי יוחנן בן נורי.

[5] ת"ש: מעשה בבתו של רבן גמליאל שהיתה נשואה לאבא אחיו, ומת בלא בנים, וייבם רבן גמליאל את צרתה. ותסברא? רבן גמליאל מתלמידי ב"ש הוא?

אלא, שאני בתו של רבן גמליאל, דאילונית הואי...

[6] מתיב רב משרשיא: **מעשה בר' עקיבא שליקט אתרוג באחד בשבט, ונהג בו ב' עשורין, אחד כדברי ב"ש ואחד כדברי ב"ה.**[153] שמע מינה: עשו?

---

148. Ibid. See further below, p. 392.

149. Ibid. 1:12. In the Tosefta, R. Shimon [H] qualifies the statement concerning purity laws [G]. The application in the Bavli of R. Shimon [H] to the previous statement [F] regarding various marriage laws is still valid since even in the original Tosefta it is likely that R. Shimon [H] applies to both prior statements [F and G].

150. *T. Yebam.* 1:9–10. In the version cited in *b. Yebam.* 27a, Rav Naḥman bar Isaac adds that afterward they did in fact make such a decree.

151. Rav Naḥman explains that Beth Shammai did not in fact practice their opinion and so there is no problem for Beth Hillel to marry their children. Beth Shammai, however, will still have a problem with the cowives who remarried according to Beth Hillel without anybody performing *ḥaliṣa*. It is thus possible to exaplain the statement of Rabban Shimon ben Gamaliel even assuming that Beth Shammai practiced according to Beth Hillel.

152. *T. Yebam.* 1:10.

153. See *T. Šeb.* 4:21 and parallel *sugyot* at *y. Bik.* 2:4 (65b), *y. Roš Haš.* 1:2 (57a), *b. Roš Haš.* 14a-b and *b. ʿErub.* 6b-7a. It seems that in the original version of the story, as the questioner in this case correctly perceives, R. Akiba did attempt to follow the stringencies of both Beth Shammai and Beth Hillel. R. Yose in the Tosefta and the Yerushalmi, perhaps because they did not find it acceptable that R. Akiba—living after Yavneh—should be worrying about the

ר' עקיבא גמריה אסתפק ליה, ולא ידע אי בית הלל באחד בשבט אמור, או בט"ו בשבט אמור.

[7] מתיב מר זוטרא: **מעשה וילדה כלתו של שמאי הזקן, ופיחת את המעזיבה וסיכך על גבי מטה בשביל קטן,**[154] ש"מ: עשו?
התם, הרואה אומר לאפושי אויר קעביד.[155]

[8] מתיב מר זוטרא: **מעשה בשוקת יהוא שהיתה בירושלים, והיתה נקובה למקוה, וכל טהרות שהיו בירושלים נעשים על גבה, ושלחו בית שמאי והרחיבוה, שבית שמאי אומרים: עד שתיפחת ברובה.**[156] ...שמע מינה: עשו
התם, הרואה אומר לאפושי מיא הוא דקא עביד.[157]

[9] תא שמע, **דא"ר אלעזר בר צדוק: כשהייתי לומד תורה אצל ר' יוחנן החורני, ראיתי...**[158] **ואף על פי שתלמיד שמאי היה, כל מעשיו לא עשה אלא כדברי בית הלל.**[159]
אי אמרת בשלמא עשו, היינו רבותיה, אלא אי אמרת לא עשו, מאי רבותיה?

[10] תא שמע, **שאלו את ר' יהושע: צרת הבת, מהו?...אמר להם: מפני מה אתם מכניסין ראשי בין שני הרים גדולים, בין שתי מחלוקות גדולות בין בית שמאי ובין בית הלל? מתיירא אני שמא ירוצו גלגלתי...**[160]
אי אמרת בשלמא עשו, היינו דקאמר מתיירא אני, אלא אי אמרת לא עשו, אמאי קאמר מתיירא אני?...

---

view of Beth Shammai, reinterpreted the case. That the fruit happened to be an *etrog* opened for R. Yose the interpretive possibility that R. Akiba wanted to follow the stringencies of both Rabban Gamaliel and R. Eliezer in *m. Bik.* 2:6. The Bavli here, as in *b. ʿErub.* 6b-7a, applies a different reinterpretation—that R. Akiba forgot which opinion belonged to Beth Hillel. *B. Roš Haš.* 14a-b combines the reinterpretations of both the Tosefta/Yerushalmi and the Bavli.

154. *M. Sukkah* 2:8.

155. See below, n. 157.

156. *M. Miqw.* 4:5.

157. This answer is similar to the explanation in line 7 that if there is another reason to explain the action it is not a problem. The Bavli explains that even the opinion that says Beth Shammai did not act according to their opinions could agree that Beth Shammai would try to follow their opinion as long as such action was not noticeable. The Yerushalmi (line 2) also cites *m. Miqw.* 4:5 but instead explains that Beth Shammai would follow their own opinion as long as Beth Hillel was not involved. Both explanations thus admit that Beth Shammai did sometimes follow their own opinion as long as it was not in confrontation with Beth Hillel. The Yerushalmi's explanation for this case allows for greater freedom for Beth Shammai to follow its own opinion, whether for stringency or for leniency, while the Bavli only allows for Beth Shammai to practice certain stringencies if the action can be interpreted otherwise. The Bavli, on the other hand, would allow Beth Shammai to perform such actions in public cases in which Beth Hillel was already involved, which would be prohibited according to the Yerushalmi. In any case, the Bavli's explanation here is only tentative; according to its concusion that Beth Shammai always practiced according to its own opinion, the limitation given at this stage would no longer be necessary.

158. *M. ʿEd.* 4:6.

159. *T. Sukkah* 2:3

160. *T. Yebam.* 1:10.

[11] תא שמע: בימי רבי דוסא בן הרכינס הותרה צרת הבת לאחין,
שמע מינה: עשו, שמע מינה.

[1] **Come and hear: Even though these prohibit and these permit, Beth Shammai did not refrain from marrying women from Beth Hillel, nor did Beth Hillel from Beth Shammai.**[146] If you say they [Beth Shammai] did not act [according to their opinions] it is well; for that reason they did not refrain [from marrying]. But if you say they did act, why did they not refrain? It is well that Beth Shammai did not refrain [from marrying] Beth Hillel since they [those prohibited by Beth Shammai are only] liable to a negative precept. However, why did Beth Hillel not refrain [from marrying] Beth Shammai since they [those prohibited by Beth Hillel] are liable to *karet* and their children are *mamzerim*? If you say that Beth Hillel thinks that [a child from a relationship of people who are] liable to *karet* does not produce *mamzerim*, but behold **R. Eleazar said: "Even though Beth Shammai argues with Beth Hillel regarding the cowife, they agree that the offspring is not a *mamzer* for a *mamzer* only results from a woman who is prohibited because of incest and whose punishment is cutting-off."**[147] Rather, conclude that they did not act.
No, they did act but they informed them [of controversial cases] and kept away. This is also confirmed from the continuation of the Mishnah, **All the pure objects....** Rather, they informed each other. We have concluded from it.

[2] Come and hear: **Even though Beth Shammai argues with Beth Hillel regarding cowives ... still Beth Shammai did not refrain from marrying women of Beth Hillel nor did Beth Hillel [refrain from marrying women] of Beth Shammai. This teaches you that they practiced with truth and peace between them, as the verse states, "*Truth and peace do they love*" (Zech 8:19).**[148] **R. Shimon says, "They did refrain from the definite [women] but not from the doubtful ones."**[149] If you say they [Beth Shammai] did act [according to their opinions] it is well; for that reason they refrained [from marrying]. But if you say they did not act, why did they refrain?
... As Rav Naḥman bar Isaac said ...
How is [a doubtful case] different from a definite case? Because it [the definite case] is prohibited? A doubtful case is also prohibited. Rather, do not say "from the doubtful ones" but "from unknown cases." [In problematic cases,] they [Beth Shammai] would inform them [Beth Hillel] and they [Beth Hillel] would

keep away. What does this teach us? That they treated each other with love and friendship....

[3] Come and hear: **R. Yoḥanan ben Nuri said, "... Come and let us institute that the cowives should perform *ḥaliṣa* and not *yibbum*." ... Rabban Shimon ben Gamaliel said, "What should we do about the previous cowives?"**[150] If you say they [Beth Shammai] did act [according to their opinions] it is well; for that reason he said "What should we do." But if you say they did not act, what does "What should we do" mean?
Rav Naḥman bar Isaac replied: "This was required only in the case of the cowife herself...."[151]

[4] Come and hear: **R. Ṭarfon said, "I desire that [a case of] a cowife should come before me so that I can marry her to a priest."**[152] Say, "that I could make her marry [someone else]." But he said, "I desire." He only wanted to reject the decree of R. Yoḥanan ben Nuri.

[5] Come and hear: It happened that Rabban Gamaliel's daughter was married to Abba, his brother, who died without children, and Rabban Gamaliel performed *yibbum* with her cowife. How can you explain this? Was Rabban Gamaliel a student of Beth Shammai?
Rather, the daughter of Rabban Gamaliel is different because she was infertile....

[6] Rav Mesharsheya asked: **It happened that R. Akiba gathered an *etrog* on the first of Shevat and subjected it to two tithes, one according to the view of Beth Shammai and the other according to the view of Beth Hillel.**[153] Conclude from this that they did act [according to Beth Shammai]?
R. Akiba was uncertain of his learning and he did not know whether Beth Hillel said the first of Shevat or the fifteenth of Shevat.

[7] Mar Zuṭra asked: **It happened that the daughter-in-law of Shammai the Elder gave birth and he broke a hole through the ceiling and covered it above the bed [thus making a *sukkah*] for the sake of the child.**[154] Conclude from this that they did act [according to Beth Shammai]?
In that case, one who sees it can assume that he made it to increase the airspace.[155]

[8] Mar Zuṭra asked: **<u>It happened</u> with the trough of Yehu in Jerusalem, which had a hole in it [and was connected] to a ritual bath, and all the utensils in Jerusalem were made pure in it, that Beth Shammai sent and had the hole widened. For Beth Shammai says [that the connection is not valid] until a majority of [the wall] is broken through.**[156] ... Conclude from this that they did act [according to Beth Shammai]?
In that case, one who sees it can assume that he made it to increase the water flow.[157]

[9] Come and hear: **R. Eleazar bar Ṣadoq said: "When I was learning Torah with R. Yoḥanan Haḥorani I noticed that.... "**[158] **And even though he was a student of Shammai, he always practiced according to the view of Beth Hillel.**[159]
If you say they [Beth Shammai] did act [according to their opinions] it is well; that is why [R. Yoḥanan's conformity with Beth Hillel] needed to be stated. But if you say they did not act, then what does that statement add?

[10] Come and hear: **They asked R. Yehoshua, "What is the law regarding the duaghter's cowife? ... He said to them, "Why do you insert my head between two great mountains, between two great factions, between Beth Shammai and Beth Hillel? I am afraid that they will crush my head...**[160]
If you say they [Beth Shammai] did act [according to their opinions] it is well; that is why he said, "I am afraid." But if you say they did not act, then why did he say, "I am afraid"?

[11] Come and hear: In the days of R. Dosa ben Harkinas the daughter's cowife was permitted to the brothers.
Conclude from this that they did act [according to Beth Shammai]. It is proven.

This section continues the תא שמע statements from the end of the *sugya* analyzed in chapter 2.[161] The source material used in this section comes mostly from the Tosefta quoted above but also from the parallel Yerushalmi as well as other Tannaitic and Amoraic sources. The Bavli combines all of these sources together with Amoraic and Stammaitic material to create a completely new composition. By way of contrast, the Yerushalmi quotes the Tosefta almost completely (missing G and H) and in almost the same order (C, D, and E are reversed) and only periodically inserts an Amoraic discussion (after C, F, and H). The Bavli, on the other hand,

---

161. See p. 104.

completely changes the order of sources as they are presented in either the Tosefta or the Yerushalmi and integrates the Tosefta material into the middle of anonymous discussions. The earlier sources are broken down into component pieces and only then reconnected in a different way to build the Bavli *sugya*. In order to appreciate the thrust of this *sugya*and what this list of eleven proofs builds up to, we will review the arguments presented while keeping in mind a key form-critical question: If the Bavli does not follow the order of Tosefta, then what order is followed in this list of eleven cases?[162]

The Bavli begins with the *m. Yebam.* 1:4, which is the focus of the entire extended pericope. Statement 1 attempts to prove from this Mishnah that Beth Shammai could not have followed their own opinion since they agreed to intermarry with Beth Hillel. Of course, such a conclusion is impossible since there would be no need for the Mishnah to say that they married each other had they all followed the laws of Beth Hillel. A simple explanation of the Mishnah might be that even though they practiced differently regarding certain marriage laws, they overlooked their differences—even when it impinged on *mamzerut*—in order to prevent schism. The Bavli, however, like the Yerushalmi, is not willing to entertain the possibility that they would put tolerance above risking *mamzerut*.

The Bavli quotes R. Eleazar from the Tosefta [E]. In its original context, R. Eleazar says that he does not think that the daughter's cowife created a situation of *mamzerut* at all—thus diminishing the severity of the problem. The Bavli, however, reinterprets R. Eleazar to mean that only Beth Shammai would agree that if one follows Beth Hillel the child is not a *mamzer* but not the other way around.[163] The Bavli therefore uses R. Eleazar not to resolve the problem but to reconfirm that there is a problem for Beth Hillel to marry into Beth Shammai. The Gemara finally concludes that each side did practice its own opinion but that they informed each other of problematic families whom they refrained from marrying.[164] This explanation is supported by the end of the Mishnah regarding purity laws and is conclusive enough for the Bavli to cease trying to prove that Beth Shammai conformed to Beth Hillel.[165] The next ten cases, therefore, all attempt

162. Even if the Bavli is not based on our Tosefta or the Yerusahlmi but on some Babylonian version of the Tosefta, one must still explain the order of statements within it.

163. See above, n. 119. Perhaps the Bavli wanted to maintain a stricter definition of *mamzer* as part of a general tendency to be careful with matters of lineage, which pervaded Persian culture. See Rubenstein, *Culture*, 80–101.

164. This is somewhat similar to the final answer in the Yerushalmi, only with a naturalistic explanation of how problems were avoided instead of faith in supernatural intervention to prevent problematic marriages. Kraemer, "New Meaning," 213, points out that R. Abbahu informing his servant about the reason for his practice above foreshadows the answer here that the Houses informed each other.

165. According to the printed edition and most manuscripts, one could still explain

to prove, with more or less success, that Beth Shammai did follow their opinion, unlike the first case, which began from the opposite premise.

The second proof comes from the Tosefta [F and H], which, just like the Mishnah above, boasts that despite their many differences, the Houses still intermarried. R. Shimon, however, limits this tolerance only to cases of doubt. The Bavli uses R. Shimon to prove that Beth Shammai did follow their opinion for otherwise why would they refrain from marrying each other in some cases? Even though this case is fairly conclusive, the Bavli seeks further proofs in order to present a comprehensive analysis. The next six cases, however, will turn out not to be conclusive at all. The structure of the next few cases is based on association of ideas and words. Each of the next proofs has some literary connection with the one before, creating a chain-link between them.

The third case quotes from the beginning of the Tosefta. Like case 2, it also quotes Rav Naḥman bar Isaac to ward off a possible disproof. The fourth comes next because its discussion again quotes line A of the Tosefta as did the third case—לאפוקי מדרבי יוחנן בן נורי. Having quoted one rabbi who himself evidently wanted to perform *yibbum* on his daughter's cowife, the Bavli next quotes a case of another rabbi who actually did so. Case 5 is the first of four cases introduced by מעשה, but while case 5 was on the subject of the cowife, the next three cases bring in completely different topics. Cases 7 and 8 are both questions asked by Mar Zuṭra, and both conclude that Beth Shammai would at least try to uphold their stringencies as long as they did not obviously contradict Beth Hillel. Case 9 follows case 8 since they both concern purity laws. Even though the interpretations of cases 3 to 8 are rather forced, the possibility that one could conceive of an explanation for which these cases could conform with the thesis of uniform practice urges the redactors to search for more conclusive proofs.

The Bavli saves the three most conclusive cases for last. Case 9 paradoxically proves that most students of Beth Shammai did practice the law of Beth Shammai because the Tosefta singles out R. Yoḥanan Haḥorani as one who practiced like Beth Hillel even though he was a student of Beth Shammai. Cases 10 and 11 return to the original deliberation about the daughter's cowife. Case 10 requires extended deliberation, but its basic thrust is rather conclusive. Case 11 deals the final blow with an explicit reference to a story in which the law was decided in accordance with Beth Shammai. The details of this story will be discussed below.

---

for both sections of the Mishnah that they married each other and mingled utensils because Beth Shammai did not practice their own opinions. However, Geniza fragment Oxford 2675 reverses the order of these names in the second proof, "בלשמא בית הלל לא נמנעו מבית שמאי. . . ," which makes sense since Beth Shammai is generally more stringent in purity laws. According the reading of the Geniza, the added proof from the end of the Mishnah is more conclusive. See Tosafot s.v. אמלשב, Ramban, Rashba, and Riṭva ad loc.

We can now explain the order in which these cases are presented. The *sugya* begins with an attempt to prove that Beth Shammai did not practice their opinions. That attempt fails, showing that such a position is not defensible. The redactors begin as devil's advocates in order to preempt such arguments.[166] The redactors can then devote the rest of the *sugya* to proving that Beth Shammai did practice their opinions. Cases 2 through 9 are all linked to one another by association such that any two adjacent cases share some key word, source, or theme. The editors place a good proof at the beginning in order to start with a bang and then save the best three proofs for the end to create a dramatic conclusion.[167] David Kraemer aptly writes:

> [T]he context established by the Gemara, and the overall deliberation, with its careful turns and manipulations, together serve to create a surprisingly forceful statement on behalf of the legitimacy of different practices in different rabbinic communities. Given the care with which this argument was formulated, there can be little doubt that this was the author's purpose from the very beginning.[168]

In sum, the thrust of the arguments in the Bavli is consistently to prove that Beth Shammai did follow their own opinion. Analysis of the structure of the *sugya* reveals its agenda—to confirm the existence of pluralism of practice at the time of the Houses. Along the way, we see reservations at accepting the full measure of pluralism implied by a plain reading of the Mishnah and Tosefta. The Bavli will not accept the possibility that Beth Hillel overlooked the existence of *mamzerim*. The first two cases limit their tolerance by assuming that they informed each other of problematic families. Still, the Bavli does admit to a basic tolerance between the Houses and agrees that historically Beth Shammai definitely did follow their own opinions. In fact, the Bavli, in its quotation of line F of the Tosefta, includes slightly different wording. Rather than "נהגו האמת והשלום ביניהן—they prac-

166. Kraemer, *Mind,* 111, calls this type of argument a "rhetorical objection," which "should be understood not only as an objection to the opinion being considered, but as a defense. The more objections against which the Gemara successfully defends the opinion of rabbi so-and-so, the more secure his view will appear." In this regard, Kraemer cites Chaim Perelman and L. Olbrechts-Tyteca, *The New Rhetoric: A Treatise on Argumentation* (Notre Dame, IN, and London: University of Notre Dame Press, 1969), 457: "Everything that furnishes an argument against the thesis being defended by the speaker, including objections to his own hypotheses, becomes an indication of sincerity and straightforwardness and increases the hearers' confidence."

167. This follows the typical order of classical rhetorical arrangement to place the best proof last, the second best first, and the least convincing one in the middle. See further at Hidary, "Classical Rhetorical Arrangement," n. 83.

168. David Kraemer, "Composition and Meaning in the Bavli," *Prooftexts* 8, no. 3 (1988): 281; and idem, *Reading the Rabbis,* 84.

ticed truth and peace between them" in the Tosefta, the Bavli reads "שחיבה וריעות נוהגים זה בזה—they treated each other with love and friendship," thus emphasizing that the Houses were not just at peace but they were genuinely friendly and felt comradery toward each other.[169]

This is unlike the Yerushalmi, which refrains as much as possible from admitting even to the historical reality of diversity. Even when the Yerushalmi is confronted with the position of the Amora who says there was diversity of practice, it proposes that God's providence prevented any problems; the Yerushalmi will not accept that the rabbis themselves could have compromised to accept each other's differences. It further limits the legitimacy of Beth Shammai to ancient times by relegating the freedom of choice offered in section I of the Tosefta to the era before the *bat qol*.

The Bavli, on the other hand, even though it omits section I of the Tosefta here, addressed the view that Beth Shammai did follow its opinions in the previous *sugya*[170] where it specifically argues that the heavenly voice is irrelevant—seemingly, a direct polemic against the Yerushalmi. The *bat qol* is discussed in *b. Pesaḥ.* 114a, *b. ʿErub.* 6b, and *b. Ḥul.* 44a, and in all cases it is similarly deemed irrelevant. The Bavli *sugya* thus proves conclusively that Beth Shammai did follow its opinions and lends legitimacy to practicing according to Beth Shammai even after the Yavnean period.

R. Dosa Story

The pericope ends with a story about the dispute over the daughter's cowife. What binds the four parts of the Bavli pericope together (the search for the sources of Beth Shammai's ruling, the discussion of *lo titgodedu* quoted in chapter 2, the eleven proofs just analyzed, and this story) is not only the case of the daughter's cowife, the subject of the Mishnah, but also a fascination with the prospect that multiple views can be halakhically valid. This story reexamines the roles of argumentation as well as rabbinic respect in the creation of halakha.[171]

בימי רבי דוסא בן הרכינס התירו צרת הבת לאחין, והיה הדבר קשה לחכמים, מפני שחכם גדול היה,[172] ועיניו קמו מלבא לבית המדרש.

אמרו מי ילך ויודיעו? אמר להן רבי יהושע: אני אלך. ואחריו מי? רבי אלעזר בן עזריה. ואחריו מי? רבי עקיבא.

169. This change is pointed out in Heger, *Pluralistic Halakhah*, 284. Note that the Yerushalmi quotes the Tosefta in its original form.

170. See text above, p. 201, and analysis on p. 204.

171. For discussion of this story in scholarly literature see Rubenstein, *Culture*, 27, 44–45, 56.

172. Manuscripts add וזקן גדול היה. This was skipped in the printed editions due to homoioteleuton. See Liss, *Babylonian Talmud*, 160.

הלכו ועמדו על פתח ביתו. נכנסה שפחתו, אמרה לו: רבי, חכמי ישראל באין אצלך, אמר לה: יכנסו, ונכנסו. תפסו לרבי יהושע והושיבהו על מטה של זהב.
אמר לו: רבי, אמור לתלמידך אחר וישב, אמר לו: מי הוא? רבי אלעזר בן עזריה. אמר: ויש לו בן לעזריה חבירנו? קרא עליו המקרא הזה: נער הייתי גם זקנתי ולא ראיתי צדיק נעזב וזרעו מבקש לחם,[173] תפסו והושיבו עאמר לו: רבי, אמור לתלמידך אחר וישב, אמר לו: ומי הוא? עקיבא בן יוסף. אמר לו: אתה הוא עקיבא בן יוסף, ששמך הולך מסוף העולם ועד סופו? שב, בני, שב, כמותך ירבו בישראל.
התחילו מסבבים אותו בהלכות, עד שהגיעו לצרת הבת. אמרו ליה: צרת הבת, מהו? אמר להן: מחלוקת בית שמאי ובית הלל. הלכה כדברי מי? אמר להן: הלכה כבית הלל. אמרו ליה, והלא משמך אמרו: הלכה כבית שמאי! אמר להם: דוסא שמעתם, או בן הרכינס שמעתם? אמרו ליה: חיי רבי, סתם שמענו. אמר להם: אח קטן יש לי, בכור שטן הוא, ויונתן שמו, והוא מתלמידי שמאי, והזהרו שלא יקפח אתכם בהלכות, לפי שיש עמו שלש מאות תשובות בצרת הבת שהיא מותרת, אבל מעיד אני עלי שמים וארץ, שעל מדוכה זו ישב חגי הנביא, ואמר שלשה דברים: צרת הבת אסורה...
תנא: **כשנכנסו, נכנסו בפתח אחד, כשיצאו, יצאו בשלשה פתחים.** פגע בו ברבי עקיבא, אקשי ליה ואוקמיה. אמר לו: אתה הוא עקיבא,[174] ששמך הולך מסוף העולם ועד סופו? אשריך שזכית לשם, ועדיין לא הגעת לרועי בקר! אמר לו רבי עקיבא: ואפילו לרועי צאן!

In the days of R. Dosa ben Harkinas they permitted the daughter's cowife to the brothers but this matter was distressing to the sages because he [R. Dosa ben Harkinas] was a great sage. His failing eyes kept him from coming to the House of Study.
They said, "Who will go and inform him?" R. Yehoshua said to them, "I will go." And after him who? R. Eleazar ben Azariah. And after him who? R. Akiba.
They went and stood at the entrance to his house. His maid entered. She said to him [R. Dosa], "Master, the sages of Israel are coming to you." He said to her, "Let them enter," and they entered. He seized R. Yehoshua and sat him down upon a golden bed.
He [R. Yehoshua] said to him [R. Dosa], "Master, tell your other student to sit." He replied, "Who is he?" "R. Eleazar ben Azariah." He said, "Does our friend Azariah have a son!" He applied to him the verse: "*I have been young and am now old, but I have never seen a righteous man abandoned or his children seeking bread.*"[173] He seized him and sat him down upon a golden bed.
He said to him, "Master, tell your other student to sit." He replied, "And who is he?" "Akiba ben Yosef." He said to him, "Are you Akiba ben Yosef whose reputation spreads from one end of the world to the other? Sit, my son, sit. May there be many like you in Israel."
They began to surround him with laws until they arrived at the daughter's cowife. They said to him, "What is the law regarding

173. Ps 37:25.
174. Some mss. add הדרשן. See Liss, ibid., 165.

> the daughter's cowife?" He said to them, "It is the subject of a dispute between Beth Shammai and Beth Hillel." "According to whom is the halakha?" He said to them, "The halakha follows Beth Hillel." They said to him, "But it was said in your name that halakha follows Beth Shammai?" He said to them, "Did you hear 'Dosa' or did you hear 'the son of Harkinas'?" They said to him, "By the life of our master, we heard it without designation [of the name of the son]." He said to them, "I have a little brother who is the firstborn of Satan. His name is Yonatan and he is a student of Beth Shammai. Be careful that he does not overwhelm you with laws,[175] for he posseses three hundred explanations for why the daughter's cowife is permitted. However, I testify by heaven and earth that Ḥaggai the prophet sat upon this mortar and said three things: the daughter's cowife is prohibited...."
> It was taught: **When they entered, they entered through one doorway, but when they left, they left through three doorways.** He [R. Yonatan ben Harkinas] bumped into R. Akiba. He [R. Yonatan] challenged him [R. Akiba] and made him stand silent. He said to him, "Are you Akiba whose reputation spreads from one end of the world to the other? Praised are you that you merited such a reputation even though you have not yet reached the level of ox herders." R. Akiba said to him, "Not even the level of shepherds."[176]

The extended discussion in the *sugya* before this story concluded that Beth Shammai did act according to their opinion. This story now comes to emphasize the tension that existed between the groups who followed Beth Shammai and Beth Hillel, a tension that caused personal strife between rabbis. This story highlights the dual, and sometimes opposing, roles of strict rational argumentation, on the one hand, and personal honor, on the other, in creating halakhic institutions.

The story begins with the vague declaration, "In the days of R. Dosa ben Harkinas, they permitted the daughter's cowife to the brothers." This sentence purposely leaves the name of the person responsible for permitting ambiguous because that information is itself a crux in the plot of the story. This ruling was very distressing to "the sages," which means a certain group of Hillelites,[177] who assume that R. Dosa ben Harkinas himself permitted it. R. Dosa's approval of the opinion of Beth Shammai is

---

175. Literally, "strike"; see the use of this verb in *b. Qidd.* 52b. See also Rubenstein, *Culture*, 56, on the use of violent terminology in the Bavli.

176. *B. Yebam.* 16a.

177. Perhaps they are called simply "the rabbis" anachronistically since the story is being told by later rabbis at a time when everyone followed Beth Hillel.

particularly troublesome because a man of R. Dosa's stature could make a permanent effect on the future of halakha.

While the Yerushalmi reports that these rabbis simply went and asked R. Dosa about the matter, the Bavli creates a minidrama about this point.[178] The rabbis all feel too apprehensive to approach R. Dosa, and even the three brave souls who volunteer have to beat around the bush before bringing up their real concern. The only reason they would be so anxious is if they were not merely asking for a clarification but further seeking to accuse and reprimand R. Dosa for his decision. Compare the language here, "They said, 'Who will go and inform him?' R. Yehoshua said to them, 'I will go.' And after him who? R. Eleazar ben Azariah. And after him who? R. Akiba,"with that in *b. B. Meṣiᶜa* 59b, "They said, 'Who will go and inform him?' R. Akiva said to them, 'I will go,'"or its source in *y. Moᶜed Qaṭ*. 3:1 (81c) "Who will go and inform him? R. Akiba said, I will go."[179] In that context the rabbis were afraid to tell R. Eliezer that they had voted to ban him because they knew that dangerous ramifications could ensue. R. Akiba there, presumably like the three colleagues here, volunteers only because he wants to make sure it is done with careful tact.[180]

Similar language is also used in the Bavli version of the deposition of Rabban Gamaliel. Once R. Yehoshua forgave Rabban Gamaliel, they sought a messenger to go and tell the rabbis in the *beth midrash*, especially R. Akiba and R. Eleazar: "Who will go and tell the rabbis?" R. Yehoshua was apprehensive about telling them this news with good reason, as R. Akiba responded by locking the doors.[181] Here too, this language suggests that the rabbis felt so threatened by R. Dosa's purported defection that they wanted to reprove the elder rabbi and perhaps even threaten him with excommunication. This is a first example of the Bavli adding

178. See comparison in chart 4.4, p. 238. For a short discussion of how the Bavli expands on the Yerushalmi, see Aryeh Karlin, *Divre sefer: masot* (Tel Aviv: Maḥbarot le-sifrut, 1952), 8–10.

179. The redactors of the R. Dosa story may have listed R. Akiba last in volunteering because that is also the order used when they are introduced to R. Dosa. See below for the significance of R. Akiba being last. R. Yehoshua, who volunteers first in this story and stands up to the *bat qol* in *b. B. Mesiᶜa* 59b, also volunteers to go on a potentially hazardous mission in *b. Šabb.* 127b and *Kallah Rabbati* 8:2. In addition to the above sources, the phrase "Who will go" is also found in *b. Meᶜil.* 17a and *Lev. Rab.* 10 [ed. Margaliot, p. 197]; every instance involves a dangerous mission.

180. Another similar phrase common to the two stories is that in *b. Meṣiᶜa* 59b where the rabbis surrounded R. Eliezer with words, "שהקיפו דברים"; here too the rabbis encircle R. Dosa with laws, "מסבבים אותו בהלכות." See Rubenstein, *Talmudic Stories*, 316 n. 14. Devora Steinmetz, "Agada Unbound: Inter-Agadic Characterization of Sages in the Bavli and Implications for Reading Agada," in *Creation and Composition*, ed. Jeffrey Rubenstein (Tübingen: Mohr Siebeck, 2005), 315 n. 48, however, argues that the oven is the object being surrounded in *b. Meṣiᶜa* 59b, not R. Eliezer.

181. See more on this story below, pp. 269–72 and Hebrew text in chart 5.3 below, p. 287.

dramatic effect to the original Yerushalmi story. This brazen attempt to reprove the great R. Dosa shows how self-assured these three rabbis are about the correctness of their opinion. This self-assurance will serve to contrast with R. Akiba's later humiliation before Yonatan ben Harkinas.

R. Yehoshua is made to sit on a golden chair as a sign of great honor. The Bavli changes the order of the rabbis as they are introduced before R. Dosa from that in the Yerushalmi. In the Yerushalmi we find: R. Yehoshua, R. Akiba, and R. Eleazar ben Azariah; in the Bavli we have: R. Yehoshua, R. Eleazar ben Azariah, and R. Akiba. R. Dosa's praises increase from no praise for R. Yehoshua, praise of lineage for R. Eleazar ben Azariah, and highest praise for R. Akiba. This props up R. Akiba and sets him up for the greater humiliation in the final scene.

There are significant differences between the praise given by R. Dosa to R. Akiba in the Yerushalmi compared with that given to him in the Bavli. In the Yerushalmi, R. Dosa quotes a verse that perhaps makes reference to R. Akiba's poor background when he was not yet "a man who is mighty in Torah." In the Bavli, however, he is praised for his great reputation—"אתה הוא עקיבא בן יוסף ששמך הולך מסוף העולם ועד סופו," invited to sit with endearing words, "שב בני שב," and given a blessing that there should be more like him, "כמותך ירבו בישראל." The Bavli significantly inflates R. Dosa's praise of R. Akiba, once again to set him up for his final fall. Yonatan will use the exact same words, "אתה הוא עקיבא, ששמך הולך מסוף העולם ועד סופו?" except that he adds a twist to transform it into a backhanded insult.

After R. Dosa untangles the name mix-up and provides prophetic backing for his position, the rabbis are satisfied, and there is no indication that they are looking to find Yonatan. The rabbis now leave through three exits from before R. Dosa, instead of from before Yonatan as in the Yerushalmi. If leaving through separate doorways was a sign of humiliation in the Yerushalmi, then why is it now applied to their exit from before R. Dosa? Perhaps they leave in shame for wrongly suspecting R. Dosa. Or, perhaps they leave separately simply to show that their mission to put things straight with R. Dosa has been accomplished. Frenkel suggests that the three rabbis leave from separate doorways because they wanted to disperse in order not to be spotted on the road and be forced to confront Yonatan.[182] They felt intimidated by R. Dosa's description of Yonatan as the firstborn of Satan with three hundred proofs at hand and therefore sought to avoid him. Unlike the Yerushalmi where all three rab-

---

182. Frenkel, *Sippur ha-agadah*, 354. Tosafot offers this as one of two contradictory explanations. Either they left from separate entrances so that R. Yonatan would not find them altogether, convince them, and be forced to decide halakha like him, or they split up in order to more easily locate him so they could ask him about the matter. Another possibility is that this is simply a remnant from the Yerushalmi story but has no relevant context in the Bavli where the rabbis do not meet R. Yonatan together.

bis go to meet Yonatan, in the Bavli, Yonatan just happens upon R. Akiba alone. Yonatan silences R. Akiba with his questions and then insults him. Yonatan admits that R. Akiba has a widespread reputation but thinks it is undeserved. R. Akiba, deeply humbled, concedes and lowers himself even further (perhaps, though, with a touch of sarcasm).

The most important difference between the two versions of the story is the order of the plot. In the Yerushalmi, R. Dosa first clears up the mistaken rumor, and the rabbis immediately go to Yonatan. Only after they are all humiliated by Yonatan do they return to R. Dosa seeking guidance and comfort. R. Dosa amply provides both. The story ends on a positive note. Yonatan looks like a bully, using his intellectual muscle to intimidate these three students who are comforted to know that they have the prophecy of Ḥaggai on their side.

In the Bavli, on the other hand, R. Dosa immediately praises the rabbis, clears up the misunderstanding, and explains his own position. The rabbis, who are confident from the beginning, are further reassured knowing that the great R. Dosa holds them in esteem, agrees with their position, and even has a tradition of prophecy to prove it. However, there is something fake about this strength in numbers. The rabbis deep down still feel uneasy knowing that Yonatan has three hundred proofs and they are too intimidated to go and confront him. The last scene shows their fear to have been warranted when even the great R. Akiba is defeated by arguments and stripped of his Torah status to the point that he feels himself revert back to his youth as a sheepherder. The Bavli ends with Yonatan triumphant, and the rabbis of Beth Hillel humiliated.[183]

The structure of the Bavli version of the R. Dosa story parallels the structure of the first part of the Bavli (the eleven cases). The Bavli begins with trying to prove that everyone practiced according Beth Hillel but then concludes that Beth Shammai followed their own opinions. Similarly, the Bavli version of the R. Dosa story begins with the three rabbis of Beth Hillel being praised but ends with Yonatan, who agrees with Beth Shammai, being triumphant. The Yerushalmi, by way of contrast, has the order reversed. The Yerushalmi *sugya* concludes by insisting that the law must always follow Beth Hillel.[184] Similarly, the Yerushalmi version of the R. Dosa story first has the rabbis who wish to follow Beth Hillel insulted but ends with their vindication. The Bavli *sugya*, and this story in particular, recognizes the superior intellect of Beth Shammai.[185] Only prophecy

---

183. Another example of the Bavli redactors changing the order of events as they are in the Yerushalmi for rhetorical function is pointed out by Rubenstein, *Talmudic Stories*, 50. Concerning the oven-of-Akhnai story, Rubenstein writes, "This different sequence of events in the BT completely changes the fundamental tension."

184. See Kraemer, "Composition and Meaning," 278; and idem, *Reading the Rabbis*, 78.

185. See also below, p. 227.

comes to the rescue of Beth Hillel. This recognition fits with the Bavli's general tolerance toward Beth Shammai and its willingness to admit that its laws were once followed.

By performing a literary and source critical analysis of the extended *sugya* in *b. Yebam.* 13b-16a (including the discussion of *lo titgodedu* in chapter 2), we see that the redactors of this *sugya* had an agenda. They wished to establish that Beth Shammai did at one time follow their own opinion and that it was perfectly legitimate for them to do so; first, because they may have been correct, and, second, because the law of *lo titgodedu* allows for different groups to follow multiple practices at the same time. This does not mean that the Bavli redactors would allow their contemporaries to follow Beth Shammai. Its opinions were thoroughly rejected during the Amoraic period.[186] Rather, it seems that the Bavli wishes to hold the Houses up as a model for how multiplicity of halakhic practice generally can coexist legitimately and peacefully.

The Gradual Exclusion of Beth Shammai

Beth Hillel did not gain supremacy overnight but did so through a long process whose traces are left in various Talmudic sources. In the following *sugya*, some of the Tannaitic sources discussed earlier in this chapter are used by various Amoraim to back up their own views about the legitimacy of following Beth Shammai's halakha. We can trace here the evolution of the attitudes of the Babylonian Amoraim toward Beth Shammai from tolerance to exclusion. *B. Ber.* 11a states:

תני רב יחזקאל: **עשה כדברי בית שמאי—עשה, כדברי בית הלל—עשה.**

רב יוסף אמר: עשה כדברי בית שמאי—לא עשה ולא כלום, דתנן: **מי שהיה ראשו ורובו בסוכה ושלחנו בתוך הבית—בית שמאי פוסלין, ובית הלל מכשירין. אמרו להם בית הלל לבית שמאי: מעשה שהלכו זקני בית שמאי וזקני בית הלל לבקר את רבי יוחנן בן החורנית. מצאוהו שהיה ראשו ורובו בסוכה ושלחנו בתוך הבית, ולא אמרו לו כלום. אמרו להם: משם ראיה? אף הם אמרו לו: אם כן היית נוהג, לא קיימת מצות סוכה מימיך.**[187]

רב נחמן בר יצחק אמר: עשה כדברי בית שמאי—חייב מיתה, דתנן **אמר רבי טרפון: אני הייתי בא בדרך והטתי לקרות כדברי בית שמאי, וסכנתי בעצמי מפני הלסטים. אמרו לו: כדאי היית לחוב בעצמך, שעברת על דברי בית הלל.**[188]

Rav Ezekiel learnt: **If one acts in accordance with the opinion of**

186. Halivni, *Rules*, 138, does list a few cases of Amoraim deciding law on the side of Beth Shammai. However, he concludes, p. 141, that Amoraim generally rejected completely any possibility of deciding like Beth Shammai. See further in the next section, "The Gradual Exclusion of Beth Shammai."

187. *M. Sukkah* 2:7. See above, p. 170.

188. *M. Ber.* 1:3. See above, p. 171.

> **Beth Shammai he has acted [legitimately]; if he acts in accordance with the opinion of Beth Hillel he has acted [legitimately].**
> Rav Joseph said: If one acts in accordance with the opinion of Beth Shammai, his action is worthless, as we have learnt: **One whose head and most of his body are in the *sukkah* but his table is in the house: Beth Shammai declares this invalid and Beth Hillel declares this valid. Beth Hillel told Beth Shammai, "Did it not happen that the elders of Beth Shammai and the elders of Beth Hillel went to visit R. Yoḥanan ben Haḥorani and they found him sitting with his head and most of his body in the *sukkah* and his table in the house and they did not tell him a word?" Beth Shammai responded, "Is that a proof! In fact, they did tell him, 'If you have so practiced, then you have never fulfilled the commandment of *sukkah* in your life.'"**[187]
> Rav Naḥman bar Isaac said: If one acts in accordance with the opinion of Beth Shammai, he deserves the death penalty, as we have learnt: **R. Ṭarfon said, "I was traveling on the road and I lay down to recite in accordance with Beth Shammai and I put myself in danger from robbers." They told him, "You deserved to come to harm for you transgressed the words of Beth Hillel."**[188]

Rav Yeḥezkel, the first-generation Babylonian Amora, quotes a *baraita* that offers a choice to follow either House, similar to *t. Yebam.* 1:13. Rav Yosef, a third-generation Pumbeditan, is the student of Rav Yeḥezkel's son, Rav Yehudah. He has a less tolerant view toward Beth Shammai, namely, one who follows its law has not fulfilled the law at all. The proof from *m. Sukkah* 2:7 is interesting because in the Mishnah, it is the students of Beth Shammai who declare the practice of Beth Hillel invalid. Rav Yosef turns the source back on itself, assuming that if one side invalidates the other then the other side would reciprocate in kind.[189]

Rav Naḥman bar Isaac, the fourth-generation Suran, goes to the ultimate extreme by declaring the death penalty for anyone who follows Beth Shammai. We see that the attitudes of these Amoraim become less and less tolerant as time goes on. By the time we get to the Stammaim, we find the following statement repeated a number of times: "בית שמאי במקום בית הלל

189. Ironically, *y. Sukkah* 2:8 (53b) (see text immediately below) reports that Rav decided halakha in favor of Beth Shammai in this Mishnah, the very case that Rav Yosef uses to prove that Beth Shammai is invalid. *B. Sukkah* 3a, according to printed editions, also suggests that R. Shmuel b. Isaac, a third-generation Palestinian Amora, decided according to Beth Shammai. However, Israel Burgansky, "Masekhet Sukkah shel Talmud Bavli: mekoroteha ve-darkhe ʿarikhatah" (PhD diss., Bar-Ilan University, 1979), 62–69, shows, based on manuscript versions, that the Amoraic layer of this *sugya* does not relate to the case in *m. Sukkah* 2:8. Other cases of Amoraim practicing according to Beth Shammai are found in *b. Ber.* 52b, 53b, and *b. Šabb.* 21b. See Halivni, *Rules*, 138–39; and Safrai, "Ha-hakhraʿah," 26.

אינה משנה—Beth Shammai, when in conflict with Beth Hillel, is not a [valid] Mishnah."[190] In many cases, the Stam rejects out of hand any possibility that a Tanna or Amora should agree with Beth Shammai.[191]

Another *sugya* addresses the reason why halakha is established according to Beth Hillel. A comparison between the Yerushalmi and Bavli versions of this *sugya* is instructive.[192] First, *y. Sukkah* 2:8 (53b):

[A] מה זכו בית הלל שתיקבע הלכה כדבריהן
[B] אמר רבי יודה בר פזי שהיו מקדימין דברי בית שמי לדבריהן
[C] ולא עוד אלא שהיו רואין דברי בית שמי וחוזרין בהן
[D] התיב רבי סימון בר זבד קומי רבי אילא או נאמר תנייה חמתון סבין מינון ואקדמון
[E] והא תני **מעשה שהלכו זקני בית שמי וזקני בית הלל לבקר את יוחנן בן החורוני**[193]
[F] נאמר זקינינו וזקניכם[194]
[G] אמר רבי זעורה רב חונה בשם רב הלכה כבית שמי
רבי ירמיה רבי שמואל בר רב יצחק בשם רב ממה שסילקו בית שמי לבית הלל הדא אמרה הלכה כדבריהן

[A] Why did Beth Hillel merit that halakha should be established according to their views?
[B] R. Yuda bar Pazzi says, "Because they quoted the opinion of Beth Shammai before their own opinion.
[C] Moreover, [when] they agreed with the opinion of Beth Shammai they changed their minds."
[D] R. Simon bar Zebed asked before R. Ila, "Or one could say that the Tanna [R. Yehudah the Patriarch] saw that they [Beth Shammai] were older than them [Beth Hillel] and therefore introduced them first?"
[E] But behold it is taught: **It happened that the elders of Beth**

---

190. *B. Ber.* 36a; *b. Beṣah* 11b; and *b. Yebam.* 9a. Halivni, *Rules*, 131, comments on this: "The Stam adds that the opinions of Beth Shammai have a lower status than the words of other sages whose opinions are rejected from Halakha." Cf. the usage of the phrase אינה משנה in *b. Šabb.* 106a (=*b. B. Qam.* 34b) and *b. Beṣah* 12b, where the person reciting the invalid teaching is ordered to leave the study hall. In *b. Ḥul.* 82b and *b. Nid.* 13b the phrase is used to suggest a textual emendation to the Mishnah. If we apply this meaning also to *b. Ber.* 36a, then we confront the surprising stance that Beth Shammai should be removed from the canon even after the Tannaitic period when Beth Shammai was included in the Mishnah and firmly established as theoretically legitimate (*b. ʿErub.* 13b). Some Tannaitic sources, such as the more intolerant stories discussed above, may not take this for granted and therefore may be discussing the status of Beth Shammai as a valid part of the canon; but it is unlikely that the Stam seeks to remove Beth Shammai from the Mishnah. More likely, the Bavli uses such extreme language only rhetorically to emphasize that one should not practice their views. In fact, this is the usage of אינה משנה in *b. Yebam.* 43a where two Amoraim discuss whether halakha follows the view of a certain Mishnah. (The phrase appears again only in *b. Ketub.* 81b, 82a, and *b. Bek.* 56a, where the precise meaning is more difficult to assess.)

191. See Halivni, *Rules*, 141.

192. See comparison in chart 4.5 below, p. 240.

> **Shammai and the elders of Beth Hillel went to visit Yoḥanan ben Haḥorani.**[193]
> [F] It should have said, "Our elders and your elders."[194]
> [G] R. Ze'orah said [in the name of] Rav Huna in the name of Rav: "The law follows Beth Shammai [in the case of *m. Sukkah* 2:7]. R. Yirmiyah [said in the name of] R. Shmuel bar R. Isaac in the name of Rav: "Since Beth Shammai rejected Beth Hillel, this teaches us that the law follows their [Beth Shammai's] opinion [in this case]."

The Yerushalmi asks why the halakha has been decided according to Beth Hillel and offers two reasons. The first, that Beth Hillel mentioned Beth Shammai's opinion before its own, is rejected in the course of the *sugya*. That we find Beth Shammai mentioned first in the Mishnah is due only to the Mishnah's editor and does not necessarily reflect Beth Hillel's own wording. Neither house, according to the Yerushalmi, quoted the other first. We are left with the second, that Beth Hillel had the intellectual honesty to change their minds whenever they recognized the correctness of Beth Shammai's opinion.[195] So ironically, the reason why halakha follows Beth Hillel is because they sometimes accept the opinion of Beth Shammai. Beth Hillel is followed because they are flexible enough to be convinced by Beth Shammai and thus better able to access the truth.

The *sugya* concludes with another ironic twist. R. Ze'orah proclaims that regarding *m. Sukkah* 2:7, the law follows Beth Shammai. After a whole discussion about why the law follows Beth Hillel, a discussion that incorporates *m. Sukkah* 2:7 in its arguments, we end with an exceptional case in which Beth Hillel is not followed! The reason for this exception is that Beth Shammai has rejected Beth Hillel. R. Yirmiyah uses the verb סילק, which in other contexts similarly means to utterly reject as completely wrong.[196] The

193. *M. Sukkah* 2:7. This citation is introduced in the Mishnah as a statement by Beth Hillel. Therefore, these must be the exact words of Beth Hillel and not of the editor.

194. R. Ila retorts that the statement in the Mishnah must have been written by the editor since Beth Hillel would not have referred to themselves in the third person. In fact, Beth Hillel mentioned themselves first, and it was only the later editor who switched the order. Thus, there is no proof from this Mishnah that Beth Hillel put Beth Shammai first, and we should rather assume that it was only the editor of the Mishnah who placed the elder sage first. This explanation follows *Pene Moshe*. See, however, *Qorban ha-'edah*.

195. This may be based not on any specific tradition but rather on a plain reading of the Mishnah. See above, nn. 86 and 87.

196. See *y. Ta'an.* 1:1 (60d) where, after a long discussion between R. Eliezer and R. Yehoshua about a nonhalakhic matter, R. Eliezer is dealt a final blow and his position is rejected, "איסתלק רבי ליעזר." See also *y. Ter.* 5:2 (43c) where Bet Shammai abandons their own position and admits Beth Hillel is correct and the Gemara wonders, "בית שמאי מסלקין לון ואינון מודיי לון," i.e., if Beth Shammai prevailed in their argument over Beth Hillel then why would they admit to Beth Hillel rather than the other way around. See also *y. Kil.* 9:2 (32a) and *y. Hor.* 1:2 (45d) cited below, p. 352.

Yerushalmi assumes that if Beth Shammai offers a strong rejection of Beth Hillel then they must be right. There is no indication in the Mishnah that Beth Hillel accepted Beth Shammai's position in the end. Presumably not, for otherwise R. Zeʿorah would say that Beth Hillel changed their minds rather than say that the law follows Beth Shammai, implying that the dispute remains. R. Yirmiah's statement as well as the context of the Yerushalmi, however, seem to indicate that since Beth Hillel was proven wrong they must have changed their minds. Thus, according to the Yerushalmi the yardstick for deciding the law is to follow whoever has better access to the truth. The law usually follows Beth Hillel only because they were agreeable and honest enough to admit their mistake when proven wrong. But when Beth Shammai offers a strong rejection and no response from Beth Hillel is recorded, then we can assume that Beth Shammai is correct.

Compare this with *b. ʿErub.* 13b:[197]

א״ר אבא אמר שמואל שלש שנים נחלקו בית שמאי ובית הלל הללו אומרים הלכה כמותנו והללו אומרים הלכה כמותנו יצאה בת קול ואמרה אלו ואלו דברי אלהים חיים הן והלכה כבית הלל

[A] וכי מאחר שאלו ואלו דברי אלהים חיים מפני מה זכו בית הלל לקבוע הלכה כמותן?

[C] מפני שנוחין ועלובין היו

[B] ושונין דבריהן ודברי בית שמאי ולא עוד אלא שמקדימין דברי בית שמאי לדבריהן

[E] כאותה ששנינו **מי שהיה ראשו ורובו בסוכה...**[198]

R. Abba said in the name of Shmuel: "For three years Beth Shammai and Beth Hillel disputed, these saying 'the law is like us,' and these saying 'the law is like us.' A heavenly voice emerged and said '[Both] these and these are the words of the living God, and the law is according to Beth Hillel.'"

[A] If both these and those are the words of the living God then by what merit did Beth Hillel have the law fixed according to them?

[C] Because they were pleasing and humble,

[B] and they taught their own words and the words of Beth Shammai, and not only that, but they [even] gave priority to the words of Beth Shammai before their own words.

[E] Like that which we have taught: **One whose head and most of his body are in the *sukkah*....**

The Bavli offers three reasons for the decision in favor of Beth Hillel. The first reason, that they are pleasing and humble, significantly alters the second reason in the Yerushalmi, that they acquiesced when proven wrong.[199]

---

197. The lettered headings in this text correspond to lines in the Yerushalmi. See chart 4.5 below, p. 240.

198. *M. Sukkah* 2:7. The continuation of this Mishnah can be found above, p. 222.

199. Heger, *Pluralistic Halakhah*, 357, also notices this change.

The Bavli broadens and transforms the Yerushalmi's reason into a praise of Beth Hillel's fine character traits of pleasantness and humility. In its next two reasons, the Bavli echoes the Yerushalmi's first reason for the law to follow Beth Hillel—that they quoted Beth Shammai first. The Bavli, however, does not reject this reason as does the Yerushalmi; rather, *m. Sukkah* 2:7 is cited as a good proof.[200] In fact, the Bavli expands on this reason by noting two praiseworthy aspects of it: that they mention Beth Shammai at all, and that they mention them first.

Kraemer points out that these reasons "are striking for what they are not: no claim is made that the Hillelites are more brilliant than the Shammaites.... What matters, at this stage of the answer in any case, is not their relationship to God and God's revelation but their relationship to other human beings."[201] The Bavli *sugya* thus holds pleasantness and civility as the highest value in determining the law, and not accuracy of tradition or brilliance of interpretation. The Bavli reads into the history of Beth Hillel an environment of peace and tolerance for opposing halakhic views[202] even though it rejects Beth Shammai for contemporary practice.[203]

---

200. Kraemer, commenting on the Bavli, echoes the same problems with this proof as already expressed by the Yerushalmi quoted above. Kraemer, *Reading the Rabbis*, 68, notes that "the choice of the present Mishnah is particularly puzzling." However, based on comparison with the Yerushalmi, we see that the Bavli redactors did not make this choice but simply repeated an element already present in the *sugya* they had received. The Bavli ignores the Yerushalmi's disproof, assuming it knew it, in order to establish the importance of civility for Beth Hillel.

201. Ibid., 67.

202. While Kraemer and Boyarin, in the context of their chapters about recognizing multiple truths, focus on multiplicity of opinion in this *sugya*, the current reading focuses on what the *sugya* says about tolerance for multiplicity of practice. After all, the opening of the Bavli *sugya* actually addresses not opinion or truth but halakhic practice. This opening scene describes a three-year competition between the Houses for halakhic dominance. Only after this period does the heavenly voice address multiplicity of opinion. Boyarin, *Border Lines*, 163–64, points to this three-year struggle as one of "vigorous and exclusivistic dispute.... However, in this latter period, the 'now' of the text ... is to be found in the description of the House of Hillel as 'pleasant and modest.'" Boyarin's reading is not precise. The Bavli here recalls a time when both Houses practiced their own opinions, thus causing themselves to be "divided—נחלקו." It does not say that they fought (רבו) or otherwise paint it as a time of strife. On the contrary, at least Beth Hillel was extremely cordial and tolerant toward Beth Shammai. It is Beth Hillel's pleasant attitude *during* the three years that is given as the reason for them winning out. The three characteristics of Beth Hillel listed in the *sugya* describe Hillel's tolerance in the face of halakhic opposition. They are not character traits that Beth Hillel developed after the heavenly voice, as Boyarin suggests.

203. Naeh, "Rooms," 857, shows that the words דברי אלהים חיים reference Jer 23:36 in order to make the point that neither opinion is false. Both contain divine truth and are part of Torah, and so neither group should be rejected as a heretical sect. Before the heavenly voice, therefore, Beth Hillel could—and according to the Bavli did—tolerate Beth Shammai's practice as a valid alternative. Only after the heavenly voice does Beth Shammai's practice become invalid for practice.

The Yerushalmi, on the other hand, praises Beth Hillel not for acting with civility in the face of disagreement but for changing their minds in the face of truth. For the Yerushalmi there can be only one valid practice—that which most closely conforms to the truth. Therefore, either Beth Hillel holds the truth and so Beth Shammai is rejected, or Beth Shammai is correct, in which case Beth Hillel would accede to Bet Shammai's view. There is no middle ground in the Yerushalmi and no suggestion that each House follows an alternate but equally valid viewpoint.

The recollection in this Bavli *sugya* of a past where both Houses practiced their own halakha coincides with other passages in the Bavli discussed above, which similarly recognize that the Houses each followed its own views. As we have shown above, the Bavli (contrary to the Yerushalmi) consistently emphasizes tolerance and peace and deemphasizes violence and tension in Tannaitic sources that mention divergent practices of the Houses. This suggests that such readings reflect a perspective of tolerance for halakhic pluralism by the Bavli redactors, which they read into the idealized past.

Of course, the Bavli too has limits, and ever since the halakha of Beth Hillel has been established no one has the right to follow Beth Shammai.[204] However, even this *sugya,* which ascribes the rejection of Beth Shammai to a divine voice, still leaves room for a broader message. Congeniality and civility trump truth and exclusivity as the ultimate values of Jewish law. Beth Shammai's views may no longer be valid—but the Bavli still holds up Beth Hillel's tolerance toward them as a model for dealing with divergent opinions and practices in later times.

Conclusion

The rabbinic sources concerning the relationship between the Houses describe a full range of possibilities including peaceful coexistence, two groups with fluid borders, productive discussion, voting sessions, delegitimization, curses, threats, and violence. What can these various recollections teach us about the attitudes of the Tannaim and Amoraim toward legal pluralism in general? We must divide our conclusions into two parts: those regarding the Tannaitic texts and those regarding the Amoraic texts.

204. Halivni, *Rules,* 140–41, notes that the rejection of Beth Shammai is uniquely severe among all cases of opinions rejected as halakha. Thus, the Bavli's rejection of Beth Shammai should not necessarily be taken as an indication of intolerance toward diversity of practice in general.

Tannaitic Sources

When we see different attitudes within the Mishnah or Tosefta, we should not assume that this reflects different editors for each tractate but rather that the editors of these documents are quoting from sources originating at different times. The relationship between the Houses was not static over the decades of their existence, and so stories about the Houses should reflect that dynamic.

The various Tannaitic statements reflecting the most tolerance toward Beth Shammai seem to derive from a late period—probably from the editorial layer of the Mishnah and Tosefta. *T. Yebamot* 1:13, granting permission to follow either opinion, is anonymous and therefore probably late. The idyllic history of *m. Yebam.* 1:4 also seems to be a creation of a later redactor. Unlike the other stories about the Houses, this Mishnah lacks any specific details or names. *M. ʾAbot* 5:17, which holds up the Houses as an ideal model of "controversy for the sake of heaven," also seems to have been formulated at the end of the Tannaitic period.[205] Living long after the historical Houses and their rivalries, these editors could more easily portray an atmosphere of congeniality and pluralism.

Based on this, we can say that the editors of the Mishnah and Tosefta were tolerant of diversity. This may explain their tendency to include many different opinions side by side. The trend toward the practice of Beth Hillel begins during this period, even as Beth Shammai is firmly established as part of the canon. The Mishnah does show a pro–Beth Hillel bias in its tendency to record many opinions of the students of Beth Hillel throughout the Tannaitic period but not many students of Beth Shammai after the generation of the Bar Kokhba revolt. Still, for the earlier period, the Mishnah does make sure to include opinions of both Houses side-by-side as a matter of principle.[206]

The editors of these documents, however, not being authors, still included older material that reflects a tense coexistence between the two groups. On the one hand, we find reports of individuals who crossed party lines—following the practice of one party even while retaining the identity of the other. These reports suggest that the Houses were not two absolute fronts but rather loose alliances of sages linked to each of the Houses without absolute consistency or partisanship. This shows a cer-

205. This assumption is based on the fact that this Mishnah, as well as most of the fifth chapter of *ʾAbot*, is anonymous. This chapter furthermore follows the chronological list of generations in the first four chapters, which ends with some of the last Tannaim in the fifth generation. If chapter 5 is meant to continue the chronology, this indicates that the contents of the fifth chapter are of even later provenance. See Amram Tropper, "Avot," *Encyclopedia Judaica* (2007).

206. See *t. ʿEd.* 1:1.

tain amount of fluidity between the groups not normally found in rival sects. On the other hand, some of these very individuals (R. Yoḥanan ben Haḥorani in *m. Sukkah* 2:7 and Baba ben Buṭa in *t. Ḥag.* 2:11–12) were subject to invalidation and had to deal with political rivalry. Others who followed Beth Shammai regarding reciting the *Shema* (*m. Ber.* 1:3 and *t. Ber.* 1:4) were the recipients of harsh rebuke and polemical reactions. Hillel himself also experienced humiliation and perhaps even threats of violence (*t. Ḥag.* 2:11–12). Such stories are not normally told about colleagues.

The Tannaim thus remember the relationship between the Houses as being complex and variegated. They seem to wish that everything was peaceful and friendly; but they also report traditions that reveal tension and rivalry. The Houses are not portrayed as discrete antagonistic sects; there is a sense of unity among the members of both groups. Sometimes they interact quite amicably, but at other times they can verge on becoming outright enemies. This complexity and ambiguity in the Tannaitic sources allows much leeway for the Amoraim to provide a wide range of interpretations.

Amoraic Sources

During Amoraic times, halakha was definitively decided according to Beth Hillel. The Amoraic sources contain little independent knowledge of the history of the Houses. Rather, their importance lies is how they interpret the Tannaitic sources. Comparing the interpretations presented in the Palestinian and Babylonian sources is instructive. Even though Beth Shammai is no longer a normative option for the Babylonian Amoraim, these sages still express tolerance for the Beth Shammai of the past when Beth Shammai's view was a normative possibility. The Yerushalmi, on the other hand, consistently seeks to minimize the historical practice of Beth Shammai and exaggerates the level of tension present whenever such practice did occur.

We have found this pattern within Talmudic interpretations of *t. Ḥag.* 2:9 concerning reclining during *Shema.* In the Bavli, one rabbi calls his disputant "my brother" (quoting the Tannaitic sources), and both rabbis are pictured as eating together (surpassing the amicability in the Tannaitic sources). The Bavli then chooses the less hostile reading from the two versions in the Tannaitic sources. The Yerushalmi omits "my brother," pictures them as being forced to be together, and changes the setting in order to increase the level of defiance with which one rabbi acts toward the other.

While Tannaitic sources are rather vague regarding the events surrounding the "eighteen enactments," the Talmuds provide very detailed narratives. The Yerushalmi describes a most horrific, violent, and even bloody scene at the loft of Ḥananiah in which terrorism, murder, and force are the preferred tools of resolving debate. This is not meant to suggest that the Yerushalmi advocated such measures; to the contrary, it laments the events of that day. Still, it is significant that the Yerushalmi considered it within the realm of possibility for such an event to have occurred. The Bavli, on the other hand, offers a much more toned-down version of an argument in the house of study in which a sword was thrown down in a symbolic gesture and those present were locked in and were humiliated.

In the context of the *semikha* disputes, the Yerushalmi teaches that one should respond to criticism quickly and forcefully while the Bavli urges one to have a self-controlled and measured response. This is an explicit indication that the Talmuds read these stories of earlier controversies as educational models of how to act in their own contemporary disputes. The Yerushalmi not only criticizes Hillel for not standing up for himself, but also inserts an inflammatory curse into the mouth of Baba ben Buṭa. The Yerushalmi celebrates Baba ben Buṭa's ability to unify halakhic practice by taking an uncompromising stance. By contrast, the Bavli commends the ability of one student to fend off criticism, follow his own opinion, and leave the others to follow theirs.

In the most extended *sugya* on the subject of the practice of the Houses, that of the daughter's cowife, we see that the Yerushalmi first links Beth Shammai with the Samaritans—implying that their view is not valid. The Yerushalmi, interpreting the Tosefta against the grain, then minimizes the extent to which Beth Shammai actually practiced its own opinion. The Bavli, on the other hand, legitimates Beth Shammai's derivation and even adds another line of reasoning on their behalf. It then proves comprehensively from a massive barrage of cases that Beth Shammai did in fact follow its own opinion. The Yerushalmi retells the R. Dosa story, which places the Hillelite students in the best light, while the Bavli ends the story on a sour note for the Hillelites, showing that Beth Shammai's opinions must be taken seriously.

Taken together, the Yerushalmi consistently seeks to deny that Beth Shammai followed its own practice at all. When it must admit that Beth Shammai followed its opinions, the Yerushalmi assumes that such actions must have caused great tension between the Houses. Only the Yerushalmi calls the Houses "two sects." The Bavli, in contrast, willingly admits that Beth Shammai practiced what they preached and also tends to paint a rosier picture of the relationship between the Houses.

One can never be sure whether a change from the Yerushalmi to the Bavli is due to a deliberate reworking by a redactor, a subconscious alteration by a transmitter (which can still be a significant indication of the attitude of the transmitter, a kind of Freudian slip), or simply an error by an incompetent student. However, the accumulation, in this case, of so many examples following the same pattern, does shift the balance in favor of regarding such changes as part of a purposeful, even if not planned or organized, rereading of Tannaitic texts based on a certain point of view.[207] While in some cases, the Bavli versions of older stories may be based on traditions independent of the Yerushalmi, it seems unlikely that the Babylonian rabbis would have consistently received more pacifistic traditions than did their Palestinian counterparts.

If, indeed, differences between the two Talmuds are not simply coincidences of transmission history, then what can such changes teach us about the outlooks of the redactors of each Talmud? We propose that these changes reflect a different attitude in each Talmud regarding the existence of more than one practice of halakha within the rabbinic community. The rivalry between the Houses is the most significant and longest sustained example of two vying halakhic schools, each practicing its own set of opinions. Perhaps Beth Shammai and Beth Hillel here should be thought of as the prototype for all later controversy. *B. ᶜErubin* 7a actually applies *t. Yebam.* 1:13 regarding the Houses to all rabbinic controversy:

> כל היכא דמשכחת תרי תנאי ותרי אמוראי דפליגי אהדדי כעין מחלוקת בית שמאי ובית הלל—לא ליעבד כי קוליה דמר וכי קוליה דמר, ולא כחומריה דמר וכי חומריה דמר. אלא, או כי קוליה דמר וכחומריה עביד, או כקוליה דמר וכחומריה עביד.
>
> Anytime one finds two Tannaim or two Amoraim arguing with each other like the dispute between Beth Shammai and Beth Hillel, do not act according to the leniencies of both nor according to the stringencies of both. Rather, either like the leniencies and stringencies of one or the leniencies and stringencies of the other.

In this *sugya,* the Houses represent the quintessential *maḥloqet,* which serves as the model for dealing with all subsequent controversy. The dispute between the Houses stretched the limits of tolerance and almost created a rift within the Jewish people; yet they remained a single community. If Beth Shammai and Beth Hillel were able to tolerate each other, then certainly later disputants should be able to live together peacefully. The redactors of the Talmuds used these various sources regarding the Houses not to say anything about Beth Shammai and Beth Hillel themselves (whose controversy is moot in any case), but rather to present their ideas on controversy and the practice of halakha in general. The Yerushalmi, in interpreting stories about this period in an acrimonious light, divulges its own presupposition that multiplicity of practice usually leads to aggression. The Bavli, in its emphasis on the peaceful environment and congeniality of the Houses, reveals the Bavli's own conviction that it is

207. If this generalization is correct, then we should expect to find similar trends in other passages as well. See the next chapter for an analysis of the Yerushalmi and Bavli versions of stories about Rabban Gamaliel II and R. Eliezer b. Hyrcanus.

possible for pluralism of practice to exist and for the parties to still remain socially unified and living under one roof.

Chapter 2 analyzed the law addressed to the community at large not to break up into factions. Chapter 3 and the current chapter similarly identified narratives in which one segment of the Jewish population practiced differently from another group—whether the groups were defined by geography or by allegiance to a certain school. The Houses are the prime example of two large divisions within the rabbinic community. The next three chapters, however, concentrate on individual rabbis who oppose the mainstream of the community. Chapter 5 analyzes narratives about dissident rabbis, and chapters 6 and 7 analyze laws that regulate diversity of practice but are addressed to individuals—the laws of the rebellious elder and *Horayot.*

Chart 4.1 Comparison chart for *Sifre Deut. pisqa* 34 (ed. Finkelstein, 62–63), *t. Ber.* 1:4 (ms. Vienna), *y. Ber.* 1:3 (3b) (ms. Leiden), and *b. Ber.* 11a (ms. Oxford) on the debate about reclining during *Shema*

***b. Ber.* 11a**	***y. Ber.* 1:3 (3b)**	***t. Ber.* 1:4**	***Sifre Deut.* 34**
A. מעשה ברבי ישמעאל ורבי אלעזר בן עזריה שהיו **מסובין** במקום אחד, והיה רבי ישמעאל מוטה ורבי אלעזר בן עזריה זקוף.	A. תני מעשה בר' אלעזר בן עזריה ור' ישמעאל שהיו **שרויין** **[נתונים]**[208] במקום אחד והיה ר' אלעזר בן עזריה מוטה ור' ישמעאל זקוף	A. מעשה בר' ישמעאל ור' אלעזר בן עזריה שהיו **שרויין** במקום אחד והיה ר' ישמעאל מוטה ור' אלעזר בן עזריה זקוף	A. וכבר היה רבי ישמעאל מוטה ודורש ורבי אלעזר בן עזריה זקוף,
B. כיון שהגיע זמן קריאת שמע, הטה רבי אלעזר בן עזריה וזקף רבי ישמעאל.	B. הגיע זמן עונת קרית שמע זקף ר' אלעזר בן עזריה והיטה רבי ישמעאל	B. הגיע זמן קרית שמע נזקף ר' ישמעאל והטה ר' אלעזר בן עזריה	B. הגיע זמן קריית שמע נזקף רבי ישמעאל והטה רבי אלעזר בן עזריה
		C. אמ' לו ר' ישמעאל מה זה אלעזר	C. אמר לו רבי ישמעאל, מה זה אלעזר
D. אמר לו: ישמעאל **אחי**, אמשול לך משל למה הדבר דומה? לאדם שאומר לו זקנך מגודל. אמר לו: יהיה כנגד המשחיתים. אף אתה, כל זמן שאני זקפתי אתה הטיתה, ועכשו שהטיתי אתה זקפת.	D. א"ר אלעזר לר' ישמעאל אומר לאחד בשוק מה לך זקנך מגודל והוא אומר יהיה כנגד המשחיתים אני שהייתי מוטה נזקפתי ואת' שהיית זקוף הטית	D. אמ' לו ישמעאל אחי לאחד אומר לו מפני מה זקנך מגודל והוא אומר להם יהיה כנגד המשחיתים אני שהייתי זקוף הטיתי ואת שהייתה מוטה נזקפתה	D. אמר לו, ישמעאל אחי, אמרו לאחד, מפני מה זקנך מגודל, אמר להם יהי כנגד המשחיתים
E. אמ' לו אתה עשית כדברי בית שמאי ואני עשיתי כדברי בית הלל.	E. אמר לו אתה נזקפת כדברי בית שמאי ואני היטיתי כדברי בית הלל	E. אמר לו אתה הטיתה לקיים דברי בית שמאי ואני נזקפתי לקיים [דברי] בית הלל	E. אמר לו, אתה הטיתה כדברי בית שמיי ואני נזקפתי כדברי בית הלל.
F. דבר אחר שמא יראו התלמידים ויקבעו הלכה לדורות.	F. דבר אחר שלא יראוני התלמידים ויעשו הלכה קבע כדברי בית שמאי	F. דבר אחר שלא יראו התלמידים ויעשו קבע הלכה כדבריך	F. דבר אחר שלא יקבע הדבר חובה שבית שמיי אומרים בערב כל אדם יטו ויקראו ובבוקר יעמדו

208. This word appears in Geniza fragment TS F17.6 instead of שרויין.

Chart 4.2 Comparison chart for *t. Ḥag.* 1:11–12 (ms. London); *y. Ḥag.* 2:3 (78a) (ms. Leiden), and *b. Beṣah* 20a–b (ms. Oxford). Tannaitic sources are in bold.

***b. Beṣah* 20a–b**	***y. Ḥag.* 2:3 (78a)**	***t. Ḥag.* 1:11–12**
תנו רבנן **מעשה בהלל הזקן שהביא עולתו לעזרה וסמך עליה וחברו עליו תלמידי ב״ש אמרו לו מה טיבה של זו אמ׳ להן נקבה היא ולזבח שלמים הבאתיה כשכש להן בזנבה והלכו להם** **ואותו היום גברה ידן של ב״ש על ב״ה ובקשו לקבוע הלכה כמותן והיה שם זקן אחד מתלמידי ב״ש ובבא בן בוטא שמו שהיה יודע שהלכה כדברי ב״ה**	**מעשה בהלל הזקן שהביא עולתו לעזרה וסמך עליה חברו עליו תלמידי בית שמי התחיל מכשכש בזנבה אמר להן ראו נקיבה היא ושלמים הבאתיה הפליגן בדברים והלכו להן** **לאחר ימים גברה ידן שלבית שמי וביקשו לקבוע הלכה כדבריהם והיה שם בבא בן בוטא מתלמידי בית שמי ויודע שהלכה כבית הלל**	**מעשה בהלל הזקן שסמך על העולה בעזרה חברו עליו תלמידי בית שמאי אמר להן בואו וראו שהיא נקבה וצריך אני לעשותה זבחי שלמים הפליגן בדברים והלכו להם** **מיד גברה ידם של בית שמאי ובקשו לקבוע הלכה כדבריהם והיה שם בבא בן בוטא מתלמידי בית שמאי שהיה יודע שהלכה כבית הלל**
	פעם אחת נכנס לעזרה ומצאה שוממת אמר ישמו בתיהן של אילו שהישמו את בית אלהינו	
שלח והביא כל צאן קדר שבירושלם והעמידן ואמ׳ כל מי שירצה להביא עולה יביא ויסמוך ואתו היום גברה ידן של ב״ה וקבעו הלכה כמותן ולא היה שם אדם אחר שערער בדבר כלום	**מה עשה שלח והביא שלשת אלפים טלים מצאן קדר וביקרן ממומין והעמידן בהר הבית ואמר להן שמעוני אחיי בית ישראל כל מי שהוא רוצה יביא עולות יביא ויסמוך יביא שלמים ויסמוך באותה השעה נקבעה הלכה כבית הלל ולא אמר אדם דבר**	**הלך והביא כל צאן קדר והעמידן בעזרה ואמר כל מי שצריך עולות ושלמים יבא ויטול ויסמוך באו ונטלו את הבהמה והעלו עולות ושלמים וסמכו עליהן בו ביום נקבעה הלכה כדברי בית הלל ולא ערער אדם על דבר**
	אמר רבי יצחק ביר׳ לעזר הדא כסא בשירותה בעייא מוליי ססא דקיסא מיניה וביה כל גומרא דלא כוויא בשעתה לא כווייא	
שוב מעשה בתלמיד אחד שהביא עולתו לעזרה לסמוך עליה ומצאו תלמיד אחד מתלמידי ב״ש אמ׳ ליה מה זו סמיכה אמ׳ ליה מה זו שתיקה שתקו בנזיפה והלך לו	**מעשה באחד מתלמידי בית הלל שהביא עולתו לעזרה וסמך עליה וראהו אחד מתלמידי בית שמי אמר להן מה זו סמיכה אמר לו מה זו שתיקה ושיתקו בנזיפה והלך לו**	**שוב מעשה בתלמיד אחד מתלמידי בית הלל שסמך על העולה בעזרה מצאו תלמיד אחד מתלמידי בית שמאי אמר לו מה סמכיא אמר לו מה זה שתקיה שיתקו בנזיפה.**
אמר אביי הלכך האי צורבא מרבנן לא ליהדר לחבריה מילתא טפי ממאי דאמ׳ ליה איהו אמ׳ ליה מה זו סמיכה איהו מאהדר ליה מה זו שתיקה		

Chart 4.3 Comparison chart of *t. Yebam.* 1:9–13 and *y. Yebam.* 1:6 (3a–b). Tannaitic sources are in bold.

y. Yebam. **1:6 (3a–b)**	*t. Yebam.* **1:9–13**
Links between Beth Shammai and Samaritan interpretation …	
[A] תני אמר רבי יוחנן בן נורי ראה היאך הלכה זו רווחת בישראל אם לקיים דברי בית שמאי הוולד ממזר מדברי בית הלל אם לקיים דברי בית הלל הוולד ממזר מדברי בית שמאי בואו ונתקן שיהו הצרות חולצות ולא מתייבמות תני לא הספיקו להתקין עד שנטרפה השעה	[A] הלכה ט—נתיבמו בית שמיי או׳ הן כשירות והולד כשר בית הלל או׳ הן פסולות והולד ממזר אמר ר׳ יוחנן בן נורי בא וראה היאך הלכה זו רווחת בישראל לקיים כדברי בית שמיי הולד ממזר כדברי בית הלל אם לקיים כדברי בית הלל הוולד פגום כדברי בית שמאי אלא בוא ונתקין שיהו הצרות חולצות ולא מתיבמות ולא הספיקו לגמור את הדבר עד שנטרפה שעה
[B] אמר רבן שמעון בן גמליאל ואם כן מה נעשה לצרות הראשונות שנישאו	[B] הלכה י—אמ׳ רבן שמעון בן גמליאל מה נעשה להם לצרות הראשונות
[E] אמר רבי לעזר אף על פי שנחלקו בית שמאי ובית הלל בצרות מודין היו שאין הוולד ממזר שאין ממזר אלא מאשה שהיא אסורה עליו איסור ערוה וחייבין עליה כרת	[C] שאלו את ר׳ יהושע בני צרות מהן אמ׳ להם למה אתם מכניסין ראשי לבין שני הרים גדולים לבין בית שמיי ובין בית הלל שיריצו את ראשי אלא מעיד אני על משפחת בית עלובאי מבית צבאים ועל משפחת בית קיפאי מבית מקושש שהן בני צרות ומהם כהנים גדולים והיו מקריבין לגבי מזבח
[D] אמר רבי טרפון תאב אני שיהא לי צרת הבת שאשיאה לכהונה	[D] אמ׳ ר׳ טרפון תאיב אני שתהא לי צרת הבת ואסיאנה לכהונה
[C] שאלו את רבי יהושע בני צרת מה הן אמר להן הרי אתה מכניסין את ראשי בין שני ההרים הגבוהים בין דברי בית שמאי ובין דברי בית הלל בשביל שיריצו את מוחי אבל מעיד אני על משפחת בית ענוביי מבית צבועים ועל משפחת בית נקיפי מבית קושש שהיו בני צרות והיו בני בניהם כהנים גדולים עומדין ומקריבין על גבי המזבח	[E] אמ׳ ר׳ אלעזר אף על פי שנחלקו בית שמיי כנגד בית הלל בצרות מודים שאין הולד ממזר שאין ממזר אלא מן האשה שאיסורה איסור ערוה וחייבין עליה כרת
R. Dosa story…	
[F] אף על פי שנחלקו בית שמאי ובית הלל בצרות ובאחיות ובגט ישן ובספק אשת איש ובמקדש בשוה פרוטה והמגרש את אשתו ולנה עמו בפונדקי והאשה מתקדשת בדינר ובשוה דינר לא נמנעו בית שמאי מלישא נשים מבית הלל ולא בית הלל מבית שמאי אלא נוהגין באמת ובשלום שנאמר והאמת והשלום אהבו	[F] אף על פי שנחלקו בית שמיי כנגד בית הלל בצרות ובאחיות ובספק אשת איש ובגט ישן ובמקדש את האשה בשוה פרוטה והמגרש את אשתו ולנה עמו בפונדקי לא נמנעו בית שמיי לישא נשים מבית הלל ולא בית הלל מבית שמיי אלא נהגו האמת והשלום ביניהן שנ׳ האמת והשלום אהבו
	[G] הלכה יא—אף על פי שאילו אוסרין ואילו מתירין לא נמנעו עושין טהרות אילו על גב אילו לקיים מה שנ׳ כל דרך איש זך בעיניו ותכן לבות ה׳

[H] הלכה יב—**ר׳ שמעון או׳ מן הספק לא היו נמנעין אבל נמנעין הן מן הודיי**	ממזירות בנתיים ואת אמר הכין היך עבידא קידש הראשון בשוה פרוטה והשיני בדינר על דעתיה דבית שמאי מקודשת לשיני והוולד ממזר מן הראשון על דעתי׳ דבית הלל מקודשת לראשון והוולד ממזר מן השיני. Four Explanations…
[I] הלכה יג—**לעולם הלכה כדברי בית הלל הרוצה להחמיר על עצמו לנהוג כדברי בית שמיי וכדברי בית הלל על זה נאמ׳ הכסיל בחשך ילך התופס קולי בית שמיי וקולי בית הלל רשע אלא אם כדברי בית שמיי כקוליהן וכחומריהון אם כדברי בית הלל כקוליהון וכחומריהון**	[I] כהדא דתני **כל הרוצה להחמיר על עצמו לנהוג כחומרי בית שמאי וכחומרי בית הלל על זה נאמר והכסיל בחושך הולך כקולי אילו ואילו נקרא רשע אלא או כדברי בית שמאי כקוליהם וכחומריהן או כדברי בית הלל וכקוליהם וכחומריהן** הדא דתימר עד שלא יצאת בת קול אבל משיצאת בת קול **לעולם הלכה כדברי בית הלל** וכל העובר על דברי בית הלל חייב מיתה תני **יצאתה בת קול ואמרה אילו ואילו דברי אלהים חיים הם אבל הלכה כבית הלל לעולם** באיכן יצאת בת קול רבי ביבי בשם רבי יוחנן אמ׳ ביבנה יצאת בת קול.

Chart 4.4 Comparison chart of *y. Yebam.* 1:6 (3a–b) and *b. Yebam.* 16a versions of the R. Dosa story

***b. Yebam.* 16a**	***y. Yebam.* 1:6 (3a–b)**
גופא: בימי רבי דוסא בן הרכינס התירו צרת הבת לאחין, והיה הדבר קשה לחכמים, מפני שחכם גדול היה, ועיניו קמו מלבא לבית המדרש. אמרו מי ילך ויודיעו? אמר להן רבי יהושע: אני אלך. ואחריו מי? רבי אלעזר בן עזריה. ואחריו מי? ר׳ עקיבא.	ר׳ יעקב בר אידי בשם ר׳ יהושע בן לוי מעשה שנכנסו זקינים אצל ר׳ דוסא בן הרכינס לשאול לו על צרת הבת
הלכו ועמדו על פתח ביתו. נכנסה שפחתו, אמרה לו: רבי, חכמי ישראל באין אצלך, אמר לה: יכנסו, ונכנסו. תפסו לרבי יהושע והושיבהו על מטה של זהב. אמר לו: רבי, אמור לתלמידך אחר וישב, אמר לו: מי הוא? רבי אלעזר בן עזריה. אמר: ויש לו בן לעזריה חבירנו? קרא עליו המקרא הזה: נער הייתי גם זקנתי ולא ראיתי צדיק נעזב וזרעו מבקש לחם, תפסו והושיבו על מטה של זהב. אמר לו: רבי, אמור לתלמידך אחר וישב, אמר לו: ומי הוא? עקיבא בן יוסף. אמר לו: אתה הוא עקיבא בן יוסף, ששמך הולך מסוף העולם ועד סופו? שב, בני, שב, כמותך ירבו בישראל.	
התחילו מסבבים אותו בהלכות, עד שהגיעו לצרת הבת. אמרו ליה: צרת הבת, מהו? אמר להן: מחלוקת בית שמאי ובית הלל. הלכה כדברי מי? אמר להן: הלכה כבית הלל. אמרו ליה, והלא משמך אמרו: הלכה כבית שמאי! אמר להם: דוסא שמעתם, או בן הרכינס שמעתם? אמרו ליה: חיי רבי, סתם שמענו. אמר להם: אח קטן יש לי, בכור שטן הוא, ויונתן שמו, והוא מתלמידי שמאי, והזהרו שלא יקפח אתכם בהלכות, לפי שיש עמו שלש מאות תשובות בצרת הבת שהיא מותרת,	אמרו לו את הוא שאת מתיר בצרות אמר לון מה שמעתון דוסא בן הרכינס אמרו לו בן הרכינס אמ׳ לון יונתן אחי הוה בכור שטן ומתלמידי בית שמאי היזהרו ממנו שלש מאות תשובו׳ יש לו על צרת הבת
	אזלון לגביה שלח וכתב ליה היזהר שחכמי ישראל נכנסין אצלך עלון ויתיב להו קומוי הוה מסביר להון ולא סברין מיסבר להון ולא סברין שריין מתנמנמין אמר להן מה אתון מתנמנמין שרי מישדי עליהון צרירין ואית דמרין בחד תרע עלון ובתלתא נפקין שלח אמר ליה מה שלחת לי בני נש בעו מילף ואמרת לי אינון חכמי ישראל אתו לגביה אמרון ליה את מה את אמר
אבל מעיד אני עלי שמים וארץ, שעל מדוכה זו ישב חגי הנביא, ואמר שלשה דברים: צרת הבת אסורה, עמון ומואב מעשרין מעשר עני בשביעית, ומקבלים גרים מן הקרדויין ומן התרמודים.	אמר להן על המדוכה הזאת ישב חגי הנביא והעיד שלשה דברים על צרת הבת שתינשא לכהונה ועל עמון ומואב שהן מעשרין מעשר עני בשביעית ועל גירי תדמור שהן כשירין לבוא בקהל

	אמר תלון שני עיני דניחמי לחכמי ישראל ראה את רבי יהושע וקרא עליו את מי יורה דיעה זכור אני שהיתה אמו מולכת עריסתו לבית הכנסת בשביל שיתדבקו אזניו בדברי תורה את רבי עקיבה וקרא עליו כפירים רשו ורעבו מכירו אני שאדם גיבור בתורה הוא ראה את רבי לעזר בן עזריה וקרא עליו נער הייתי גם זקנתי מכירו אני שהוא דור עשירי לעזרא ועינוי דמיין לדידיה אמר רבי חנינה דציפורין אף רבי טרפון הוה עמהן וקרא עליו כהדא דרבי לעזר בן עזריה
תנא: **כשנכנסו, נכנסו בפתח אחד, כשיצאו, יצאו בשלשה פתחים**. פגע בו רבי עקיבא, אקשי ליה ואוקמיה. אמר לו: אתה הוא עקיבא, ששמך הולך מסוף העולם ועד סופו? אשריך שזכית לשם, ועדיין לא הגעת לרועי בקר! אמר לו רבי עקיבא: ואפילו לרועי צאן!	

Chart 4.5 Comparison chart for *y. Sukkah* 2:8 (53b) and *b. ʿErub.* 13b on why halakha follows Beth Hillel

***b. ʿErub.* 13b**	***y. Sukkah* 2:8 (53b)**
א״ר אבא אמר שמואל שלש שנים נחלקו בית שמאי ובית הלל הללו אומרים הלכה כמותנו והללו אומרים הלכה כמותנו יצאה בת קול ואמרה אלו ואלו דברי אלהים חיים הן והלכה כבית הלל	
A. וכי מאחר שאלו ואלו דברי אלהים חיים מפני מה זכו בית הלל לקבוע הלכה כמותן?	A. מה זכו בית הלל שתיקבע הלכה כדבריהן
C. מפני שנוחין ועלובין היו	B. אמר רבי יודה בר פזי שהיו מקדימין דברי בית שמאי לדבריהן
B. ושונין דבריהן ודברי בית שמאי ולא עוד אלא שמקדימין דברי בית שמאי לדבריהן	C. ולא עוד אלא שהיו רואין דברי בית שמאי וחוזרין בהן
	D. התיב רבי סימון בר זבד קומי רבי אילא או נאמר תנייה חמתון סבין מינון ואקדמון
E. כאותה ששנינו **מי שהיה ראשו ורובו בסוכה ושלחנו בתוך הבית בית שמאי פוסלין ובית הלל מכשירין אמרו בית הלל לבית שמאי לא כך היה מעשה שהלכו זקני בית שמאי וזקני בית הלל לבקר את ר׳ יוחנן בן החורנית ומצאוהו יושב ראשו ורובו בסוכה ושלחנו בתוך הבית אמרו להן בית שמאי משם ראיה אף הן אמרו לו אם כך היית נוהג לא קיימת מצות סוכה מימיך**	E. והא תני **מעשה שהלכו זקני בית שמאי וזקני בית הלל לבקר את יוחנן בן החורוני**
	F. נאמר זקינינו וזקניכם
	G. אמר רבי זעורה רב חונה בשם רב הלכה כבית שמאי רבי ירמיה רבי שמואל בר רב יצחק בשם רב ממה שסילקו בית שמאי לבית הלל הדא אמרה הלכה כדבריהן

5

Rabban Gamaliel of Yavneh and Other Rabbinic Dissidents

The current chapter uses the same methodology as the previous one, that is, comparing Yerushalmi and Bavli narratives about Tannaim and analyzing how these stories reflect on diversity of practice. Rabbinic literature records many stories about rabbinic dissidents who opposed the majority ruling on one or more occasions. The Mishnah and Talmuds evidently tolerate diversity of halakhic opinion since nearly every page of these texts includes multiple views. However, as these narratives show, we should not assume that this tolerance for diverse opinions necessarily transferred to diverse practices. By comparing the way these stories are presented in Tannaitic sources and interpreted by the Yerushalmi and Bavli, we can gain insight into how each rabbinic corpus approaches halakhic pluralism generally. As we will see, the Bavli more readily admits to diversity of practice among the Tannaim even when the Yerushalmi denies such diversity, and the Bavli is also quicker to criticize attempts at unification than is the Yerushalmi.

Rabban Gamaliel of Yavneh

Tannaitic sources include many stories that portray Rabban Gamaliel II of Yavneh as someone who did not feel himself bound by the practice of the majority of sages. The Mishnah includes many reports of Rabban Gamaliel practicing contrary to the sages.[1] *T. Berakot* 4:15 reports that

1. See *m. Demai* 3:1, examples analyzed below, and citations below p. 262 n. 66. These narratives are collected and analyzed in Alexei Siverstev, *Households, Sects, and the Origins of Rabbinic Judaism* (Leiden: Brill, 2005), 218–31; Jacob Neusner, "From Biography to Theology: Gamaliel and the Patriarchate," *Review of Rabbinic Judaism* 7 (2004): 52–97; Hanah Kohat, "Ben 'aristoqratyah le-democratyah—Rabban Gamaliel ve-Rabbi Yehoshua," in *Sefer yeshurun*, ed. Michael Shashar (Jerusalem: Shashar, 1999), 213–28; Shamai Kanter, *Rabban Gamaliel II: The Legal Traditions* (Ann Arbor, MI: Brown University Press, 1980), 238–42, 246–51; and Ben-Zion Wacholder, "Sippure Rabban Gamaliel ba-Mishna uba-Tosefta," *World Congress for*

Rabban Gamaliel disagreed with his colleagues on the appropriate blessing after eating from the seven fruits of Israel: Rabban Gamaliel prescribes three blessings while the sages require one blessing. On one occasion, R. Akiba took preemptive action in accordance with the sages, knowing that otherwise Rabban Gamaliel would follow his own opinion:

> מעשה ברבן גמליאל וזקנים שהיו מסובין ביריחו הביאו לפניהם כותבות ואכלו קפץ ר׳ עקיבא ברך אחריהן אחת אמר לו רבן גמליאל עקיבא למה אתה מכניס ראשך לבין המח־לקות אמר לו למדתנו אחרי רבים להטות[2] אף על פי שאתה אומר כך וחביריך אומרים כך הלכה כדברי המרובין.
>
> It happened that Rabban Gamaliel and the elders were eating together in Jericho. Dates were brought to them, which they ate. R. Akiba preempted [lit., jumped] and blessed one [blessing]. Rabban Gamaliel told him, "Akiba, why do you poke your head into controversies?" He responded, "You taught us to incline after the majority. Even though you say this and your colleagues say that, the halakha follows the words of the majority."[3]

Rabban Gamaliel rebukes R. Akiba for making such a point of opposing him. R. Akiba, however, counters with the principle, which Rabban Gamaliel himself teaches, that the majority rules.[4] Rabban Gamaliel not only practiced according to his own opinion but he even reportedly used his power as patriarch to force others to accede to his view.[5] The picture

---

Jewish Studies 4, no. 1 (1967): 143–44. Rabban Gamaliel is also portrayed as feeling himself above the rules regarding learning Greek studies (*b. Soṭah* 49b); cf. *m. ʿAbod. Zar.* 3:4; and Azzan Yadin, "Rabban Gamliel, Aphrodite's Bath, and the Question of Pagan Monotheism," *Jewish Quarterly Review* 96, no. 2 (2006): 149–79. Rabban Gamaliel I is also portrayed as maintaining special halakhic privilege in the Temple; see *m. Šeqal.* 3:3 and 6:1.

2. Exodus 23:2 as interpreted in *Mekhilta de-R. Ishmael, Mishpatim, Masekhta d'Kaspa*, 20, "לא תהיה"; *m. Sanh.* 1:6; and *b. Ḥul.* 11a.

3. *T. Ber.* 4:15.

4. A similar dialogue between Rabban Gamaliel and R. Akiba appears again in *t. Beṣah* 2:12, and cf. *t. Demai* 5:24, *Sifre Deut.*, *pisqa* 1 (ed. Finkelstein, 3–4), and *b. Sukkah* 23a. The motif of R. Akiba "jumping" appears also in *Sifre Num.*, *pisqa* 118 (ed. Horovitz, 141) = Midrash Tannaim to Deut 15:20, *Sifre Zuta* 9:2 and 19:16 (ed. Horovitz, 257 and 312).

5. See *m. Roš Haš.* 2:8–9 and the story of his deposition analyzed below, pp. 264–72. Many scholars doubt that the official position of patriarch recognized by the Romans even existed before the fourth century. I make no claim here concerning the historical role of Rabban Gamaliel of Yavneh as patriarch. My goal is only to analyze how the Talmud represents and remembers Rabban Gamaliel; in that context, his purported role as patriarch is significant. On the history of the patriarchate in general see below pp. 375–76 nn. 31–33 and 37. See also Shaye Cohen, "Patriarchs and Scholarchs," *Proceedings of the American Academy for Jewish Research* 48 (1981): 57–85; Martin Goodman, "The Roman State and the Jewish Patriarch in the Third Century," in *The Galilee in Late Antiquity*, ed. Lee Levine (New York: Jewish Theological Seminary of America, 1994), 107–19; Jacobs, *Die Institution* ; Lee Levine, "The Status of the Patriarch in the Third and Fourth Centuries: Sources and Methodology," *Journal of*

formed by these rabbinic sources, whether historically accurate or not, is that Rabban Gamaliel's independence was not based on tolerance for diversity but rather intolerance for anyone who did not agree with him.[6]

We will here analyze a few of these sources regarding Rabban Gamaliel as a dissident and as a domineering leader. In each case, we will compare the Yerushalmi and Bavli readings of these Tannaitic sources in order to gain clues as to the general outlook of the Talmuds toward diversity and coercion.

The Time for Shema (m. Ber. *1:1*)

One story about Rabban Gamaliel contradicting the rabbis is found at *m. Ber.* 1:1:[7]

[A] מאמתי קורין את שמע בערבים משעה שהכהנים נכנסים לאכל בתרומתן.
[B] עד סוף האשמורת הראשונה דברי ר׳ אליעזר וחכמים אומרים עד חצות רבן גמליאל אומר עד שיעלה עמוד השחר.
[C] מעשה שבאו בניו מבית המשתה אמרו לו לא קרינו את שמע אמר להם אם לא עלה עמוד השחר מותרין[8] אתם ליקרות.
[D] ולא זו בלבד[9] אלא כל שאמרו חכמים עד חצות מצותן עד שיעלה עמוד השחר הקטר חלבים ואברים ואכילת פסחים[10] מצוותן עד שיעלה עמוד השחר כל הנאכלין ליום אחד מצוותן עד שיעלה עמוד השחר אם כן למה אמרו חכמים עד חצות אלא[11] להרחיק את האדם מן העבירה:

Jewish Studies 47, no. 1 (1996): 1–32; Seth Schwartz, "The Patriarchs and the Diaspora," *Journal of Jewish Studies* 51, no. 2 (2000): 208–318; idem, *Imperialism*, 103–28 (and see references there on p. 111 n. 20); Heger, *Pluralistic Halakhah*, 289–309; Sacha Stern, "Rabbi and the Origins of the Patriarchate," *Journal of Jewish Studies* 54, no. 2 (2003): 193–215; and Goodblatt, "End of Sectarianism," 32.

6. See Ginzberg, *Commentary*, 91; Stern, "Midrash and Hermeneutics," 34; and Heger, *Pluralistic Halakhah*, 309–34. For a different view of Rabban Gamaliel see Goodblatt, "End of Sectarianism," 32–36, who bases his stance on historical assumptions and trends rather than on rabbinic texts.

7. Text follows ms. Kaufman.

8. Mss. Kaufman, Parma, Geniza TS E 2.3 and 2.4, and Bavli ms. Paris read מותרין. Geniza TS E 2.2 reads חייבין, which is changed to מותרין in the margin. The Mishnah in the Bavli printed edition and mss. Munich and Florence read חייבין. See Ginzberg, *Commentary*, 1:92 n. 11.

9. The Mishnah in the Bavli adds אמרו here.

10. Printed editions of Mishnah and Mishnah in Bavli (printed edition and mss. Florence, and Paris) omit אכילת פסחים. Ms. Munich of the Bavli has these words, but they are erased. The Yerushalmi already reports that some include these words and some do not. See *y. Ber.* 1:1 (3a) (the *sugya* after the one analyzed below). Cf. *Mekhilta de-R. Yishmael, Bo, Pisḥa*, 6; *m. Zebaḥ.* 5:8; *b. Zebaḥ.* 57b; and see Ginzberg, *Commentary*, 1:100–101; and Epstein, *Mavo le-nusah ha-Mishnah*, 76–78, 165, and 713.

11. Mss. Kaufman, Parma, Geniza TS E 2.2, 2.3 and 2.4, read אלא. Printed editions have כדי. Ms. Munich of the Bavli reads אלא but adds כדי in the margin.

> [A] From what time may one recite *shema* in the evening? From the time that the priests enter to eat their *terumah*.[12]
> [B] [One may continue to recite *shema*] until the end of the first watch (i.e. the fourth hour of the night). These are the words of R. Eliezer. But the sages say until midnight. Rabban Gamaliel says until dawn arrives.
> [C] It happened that his [Rabban Gamaliel's] sons came from the banquet hall. They told him, "We did not recite *shema*." He responded, "If dawn has not yet arrived you may recite.
> [D] "Moreover, any matter that the sages say one may do 'until midnight,' the obligation applies until dawn arrives. The obligation of burning fats and limbs applies until dawn arrives and everything that must be eaten in one day one may eat until dawn arrives. If so, why did the sages say [only] until midnight? In order to distance one from sin."

Line B records three opinions: R. Eliezer says one may recite *shema* only until the first watch, the sages say only until midnight, and Rabban Gamaliel says even until dawn. Line C recounts a story in which Rabban Gamaliel instructed his sons to follow his opinion. Line D then explains that the sages agree in essence with Rabban Gamaliel that one may recite until dawn but that they instruct people to recite before midnight as a safeguard. Some read line D as an editorial explanation,[13] but others include it within Rabban Gamaliel's quote.[14] Line D does not flow smoothly from lines A-C[15] and reads like a secondary gloss.[16] Without line D, one gets the impression that the sages invalidate recitation after midnight just as R. Eliezer invalidates it after the first watch. If so, Rabban Gamaliel breaks with his colleagues in allowing his sons to recite after midnight.

---

12. I.e., priests who had been impure and who must bathe and wait until dark to become pure in order to eat *terumah*.

13. See Shamma Friedman, *Tosefta ʿatikta: masekhet pesah rishon* (Ramat-Gan: Bar-Ilan University, 2002), 455.

14. See *b. Ber.* 9a, and Benovitz, *Berakhot*, 354 n. 1. The punctuation of the translation above follows this option. Even according to this explanation, line D may be a later editorial gloss; however, the glossator meant for it to be understood as an extension of Rabban Gamaliel's words.

15. *B. Ber.* 9a already notices some disjunction when it asks, ורבן גמליאל מי קאמר עד חצות דקתני ולא זו בלבד אמרו—"Did Rabban Gamaliel say 'until midnight' that he should say 'Moreover [whenever they say until midnight…]?'" If, on the other hand, line D is read as the voice of the editor, then a similar problem arises; the sages had not said earlier that *shema* could be recited until dawn for line D to introduce more examples of actions that can be performed until dawn with the phrase, "Moreover…." Line D is also problematic in that it contradicts other Mishnayot; see *m. Meg.* 2:6 and see explanation of Rashi s.v. כדי להרחיק, and n. 11 above.

16. See Neusner, *Eliezer Ben Hyrcanus*, 1:19–20; and Kanter, *Rabban Gamaliel*, 3–4, who opine that line D is "a later harmonization of the sages' position with Gamaliel's" (ibid., p. 3).

The purpose of this gloss may be to reconcile the dispute between Rabban Gamaliel and the sages, thus removing the possibility that Rabban Gamaliel acted against the opinion of the sages. According to line D, the sages would have agreed that if one did not recite *shema* before midnight then one still must do so afterward. If they disagree at all,[17] Rabban Gamaliel is only slightly more lenient in allowing one to recite until dawn *ab initio* while the sages allow one to recite only if one has already missed the preferred window.[18]

The above summary represents the Bavli's understanding of line D as presented in *b. Ber.* 9a:

> ועד השתא לא שמיע להו הא דרבן גמליאל? הכי קאמרי ליה: רבנן פליגי עילווך ויחיד ורבים הלכה כרבים, או דלמא רבנן כוותך סבירא להו, והאי דקאמרי עד חצות כדי להרחיק אדם מן העבירה? אמר להו: רבנן כוותי סבירא להו, וחייבין אתם. והאי דקאמרי עד חצות כדי להרחיק אדם מן העבירה.
>
> Until now did [his sons] never hear the opinion of Rabban Gamaliel? This is what they [his sons] told him, "Do the sages disagree with you, and [in a dispute between] an individual and the many the halakha follows the many, or perhaps the sages agree with you and that which they have said, 'until midnight,' is only to distance one from sin?" He [Rabban Gamaliel] told them, "The sages agree with me and so you are required [to recite]. That which they said 'until midnight' is only to distance one from sin."

This *sugya* reads a question into the gap between lines C and D; namely, did Rabban Gamaliel issue a decision against the sages? The purpose of line D, then, is to clarify that the sages would agree. It may be impossible to reconstruct who added line D and why, but it is clear that the Bavli understood it as a way to remove the possibility that Rabban Gamaliel opposed the sages and followed his own opinion. Compare this with the Yerushalmi, which either ignores line D or interprets it differently and assumes that Rabban Gamaliel did oppose the sages and therefore makes its own attempt at reconciling Rabban Gamaliel with the sages. This Yerushalmi *sugya* is one of the most significant treatments of the general question of legal pluralism in the Talmud, and we therefore analyze it at length.[19] *Y. Berakot* 1:1 (3a) reads:

---

17. It is possible that even Rabban Gamaliel agrees that one should recite before midnight *ab initio*. However, if they agree completely then the Mishnah would not need to record them separately.

18. See Benovitz, *Berakhot*, 355. This explanation introduces an inconsistency within line B, where R. Eliezer and Rabban Gamaliel address the biblically mandated time period and the sages address the rabbinic law. A similar explanation is suggested for *m. Zebaḥ.* 5:8 by Abaye in *b. Zebaḥ.* 57b but is rejected.

19. See also further analysis in Hidary, "Classical Rhetorical Arrangement and Reason-

[A] **מעשה שבאו בניו מבית המשתה אמרו לו לא קרינו את שמע אמר להן אם לא עלה עמוד השחר חייבין[20] אתם לקרות.**
ורבן גמליאל פליג על רבנין ועבד עובדא כוותיה?
והא רבי מאיר פליג על רבנין ולא עבד עובדא כוותיה.
והא רבי עקיבא פליג על רבנין ולא עבד עובדא כוותיה.
[והא רבי שמעון פליג על רבנין ולא עבד עובדא כוותיה.][21]

[B] והן אשכחנן דרבי מאיר פליג על רבנין ולא עבד עובדא כוותיה? דתני **סכין אלוונתית לחולה בשבת אימתי בזמן שטרפו ביין ושמן מערב שבת אבל אם לא טרפו מערב שבת אסור**
תני **אמר ר׳ שמעון בן אלעזר מתיר היה רבי מאיר לטרוף יין ושמן ולסוך לחולה בשבת וכבר חלה ובקשנו לעשות לו כן ולא הניח לנו ואמרנו לו רבי דבריך מבטל בחייך ואמר לן אף על פי שאני מיקל לאחרים מחמיר אני על עצמי דהא פליגי עלי חברי.**[22]

[C] והן אשכחנן דרבי עקיבה פליג על רבנין ולא עבד עובדא כוותיה כיי דתנינן תמן **השדרה והגולגולת מב׳ מתים רביעית דם מב׳ מתים ורובע עצמות מב׳ מתים אבר מן המת מב׳ מתים אבר מן החי מב׳ אנשים רבי עקיבא מטמא וחכמים מטהרין.**[23]
תני **מעשה שהביאו קופה מליאה עצמות מכפר טבי והניחוה באויר[24] הכנסת בלוד ונכנס תודרוס הרופא ונכנסו כל הרופאים עמו אמר תודרוס הרופא אין כאן שדרה ממת אחד ולא גולגולת ממת אחד אמרו הואיל ויש כאן מטהרין ויש כאן מטמאין נעמוד על המניין התחילו מרבי עקיבה וטיהר אמרו לו הואיל והיית מטמא וטיהרת טהור.**[25]

[D] והן אשכחנן דר׳ שמעון פליג על רבנין ולא עבד עובדא כוותיה כיי דתנינן תמן **רבי שמעון אומר כל הספחין מותרין חוץ מספיחי כרוב שאין כיוצא בהן בירקות שדה[26] וחכמים אומרים כל הספחין אסורין.**[27]
ר׳ שמעון בן יוחי עבר[28] בשמיטתא חמא חד מלקט ספיחי שביעית אמר ליה ולית אסור

---

ing in the Talmud: The Case of Yerushalmi Berakhot 1:1," *AJS Review* 34, no. 1 (2010), which explicates the structure and mode of reasoning used in this *sugya* on the basis of the Greco-Roman rhetorical tradition.

20. Ms. Leiden and printed editions read חייבין. See, however, above, n. 8.

21. This line is missing in printed editions due to homoioteleuton. The base text of ms. Leiden does have this line for R. Akiba and R. Shimon but omits it for R. Meir. An attempt is made to correct this between the lines, which results in the text found in the printed editions.

22. See *t. Šabb.* 12:12, *b. Šabb.* 134a, and discussion below.

23. *M. ʾOhal.* 2:6 and cf. *t. ʿEd.* 1:7.

24. Where there was no roof to create a problem of *ohel*. However, see commentary of R. Eleazar Azikri (Safed, 1533–1600), *Perush mi-baʿal sefer ḥaredim*, s.v. והניחוהו (printed in standard editions of the Yerushalmi) who says it was hung inside the synagogue so that nobody would touch it, which would cause impurity according to all opinions. See also Saul Lieberman, *Tosefeth rishonim* (New York: Jewish Theological Seminary, 1999), 3:102.

25. *T. ʾOhal.* 4:2 and *b. Naz.* 52a.

26. Cabbages do not generally grow ownerless in the wild. Therefore, even R. Shimon bar Yoḥai prohibits picking them during the seventh year.

27. *M. Šeb.* 9:1.

28. Following Geniza and *y. Šeb.* 9:1 (38d). See Ginzberg, *Yerushalmi Fragments*, 2, line 8. Ms. Leiden here reads עבד עובדא instead of עבר.

ולאו ספיחי אינון אמר[29] ליה ולא את הוא שאת מתיר אמר ליה ואין חבירי חולקין עלי וקרי עלוי ופורץ גדר ישכנו נחש[30] וכן הות ליה.

[E] ורבן גמליאל פליג על רבנן ועבד עובדא כוותיה?

שנייא הכא שהיא לשינון. מעתה אף משיעלה עמוד השחר?

ואית דבעי מימר תמן היו יכולין לקיים דברי חכמים ברם הכא כבר עבר חצות ולא היו יכולין לקיים דברי חכמים אמר לון עובדין עובדא כותיה.

[A] **It happened that his [Rabban Gamaliel's] sons came from the banquet hall.**

They told him, "We did not recite *shema*." He told them, "If dawn has not yet arrived, you are obligated to recite."

Does Rabban Gamaliel disagree with the rabbis and did he perform a deed according to his own opinion?

Behold R. Meir disagrees with the rabbis but did not perform a deed according his own opinion.

Behold R. Akiba disagrees with the rabbis but did not perform a deed according to his own opinion.

[Behold R. Shimon disagrees with the rabbis but did not perform a deed according to his own opinion.][21]

[B] Where do we find that R. Meir disagrees with the rabbis but did not perform a deed according to his own opinion? As it was taught: **One may oil a cloth for a sick person on Shabbat only when he has mixed it with wine and oil from before Shabbat. But if he had not mixed it from before Shabbat, it is forbidden.** It was taught, **R. Shimon ben Eleazar said, R. Meir used to permit one to mix wine and oil and to anoint a sick person on Shabbat. It once happened that [R. Meir] became sick and we wanted to do so for him but he did not let us. We told him, "Rabbi, your ruling will become nullified in your lifetime." He responded, "Even though I am lenient for others, I am stringent upon myself for behold my colleagues disagree with me."**[22]

[C] Where do we find that R. Akiba disagrees with the rabbis but did not perform a deed according to his own opinion? As we have learned there: **The spine or the skull from two corpses, a quarter [of a *log*] of blood from two corpses, a quarter [of a *qab*] of bones from two corpses, a severed limb of a corpse from two corpses, or a severed limb of a live person from two people, R. Akiba declares impure and the sages declare pure.**[23]

It was taught: **It happened that a basket full of bones was brought from Kefar Ṭabi and placed it in the open air**[24] **of the synagogue of Lydda. Theodorus the physician entered and all**

29. Following Geniza, which has 'א. Ms. Leiden reads אמרי. See also Ginzberg, *Commentary,* 1:90, regarding the placement of this verb.

30. Ecclesiastes 10:8. This verse is used often in a similar sense of threatening those who disobey the rabbis; see below, p. 316 n. 63.

the doctors entered with him. Theodorus the doctor declared, "There is neither a spine from one corpse nor a skull from one corpse here." They said, "Since there are some who declare pure and some who declare impure here let us put it to a vote." They began with R. Akiba who declared pure. They said, "Since you used to declare impure and now you have declared it pure, it is pure."[25]

[D] Where do we find that R. Shimon disagrees with the rabbis but did not perform a deed according to his own opinion? As we have learned there: **R. Shimon says, All the aftergrowths are permitted [during the seventh year] except for the aftergrowths of cabbage for other vegetables of the field are not similar to them.**[26] **But the sages say all aftergrowths are prohibited.**[27] R. Shimon ben Yoḥai was passing by during the seventh year. He saw someone gathering aftergrowths of the seventh year. He told him, "Isn't this prohibited? Aren't they aftergrowths?" He responded, "Aren't you the one who permits?" He told him, "Don't my colleagues disagree with me?" R. Shimon applied to him the verse, "*One who breaches a fence will be bitten by a snake*."[30] And so it happened to him.

[E] Does Rabban Gamaliel disagree with the rabbis and did he perform a deed according to his own opinion?

Here it is different for it [the recitation of *shema*] is simply repetition [a form of learning]. According to this, [his sons should be allowed to recite *shema*] even after dawn has arrived?

Others explain that there [in all three cases involving other Tannaim], they were able to fulfill the opinion of the sages. Here, however, midnight had already passed, and they were not able to fulfill the opinion of the sages [in any case]. [Therefore, Rabban Gamaliel] told them to perform a deed according to his own opinion.

[A] ***Rabban Gamaliel***

The opening question assumes that the sages completely invalidate (i.e., even from Torah law) recitation of *shema* after midnight, which probably represents their original opinion without line D of the Mishnah. Commentators struggle to understand how the Yerushalmi accounts for line D.[31] For whatever reason, this *sugya* did not know of or did not accept

31. One radical possibility is that the author of this *sugya* had a version of the Mishnah without line D. However, that the next *sugya* of the Yerushalmi quotes and discusses line D makes this option unlikely.

Azikri, *Perush mi-ba`al sefer ḥaredim*, s.v. אמרו לא, explains that line D does not mean to include reciting *shema* before midnight as an example of a rabbinic safeguard; midnight is the biblical deadline for reciting *shema* according to the sages. Rather, Rabban Gamaliel's

the plain sense of line D as understood in the Bavli, which does reconcile the sages with Rabban Gamaliel. It therefore proceeds to make its own inquiry into Rabban Gamaliel's alleged contradiction of the sages.[32] The *sugya* thus reveals at the outset its driving motivation: to make the case that no sage could possibly have practiced in opposition to the majority.

---

point is that even the sages admit that biblical law allows performance until dawn regarding other issues, and so the same should be true here. This explanation is adopted by Chaim Malinowitz et al., eds., *The Schottenstein Edition: Talmud Yerushalmi* (Brooklyn: Mesorah Publications, 2005), 1a1 nn. 6–7 and variant A; 1a2 n. 10; and 8b1 n. 1. However, this does not fit well with the plain sense of the Mishnah; after all, line D begins with the phrase ולא זו בלבד—"Moreover," which denotes that what comes next includes and adds to what came before. It is difficult to believe that the Yerushalmi would assume such a forced interpretation of the Mishnah.

Ginzberg, *Commentary*, 1:96, explains that line D represents only the opinion of Rabban Gamaliel, who disagrees with the sages not only regarding *shema* but regarding all matters that the sages forbid after midnight. The sages use midnight as the biblical time limit in all these matters while Rabban Gamaliel views midnight as only a rabbinic safeguard to the biblical time limit of dawn. (Ginzberg thinks this is also the explanation assumed by *b. Ber.* 4a. However, a better explanation is that *b. Ber.* 4a simply asked the obvious as a rhetorical device in order to clarify the opinions on the basis of a *baraita* that it quotes. See Benovitz, *Berakhot*, 130f.) However, this interpretation is impossible because the last few words of line D read, "If so, why did the sages say…?" It is clear from these words that line D elaborates the view of the sages, not Rabban Gamaliel. Benovitz, ibid., 355–56, agrees with Ginzberg's interpretation but notes that it is problematic (356 n. 4) and ends up hinting at the solution given in the next paragraph.

R. Moshe Margaliot (d. 1781) explains that the Yerushalmi assumes that the rabbinic boundary applies even to an *ex post facto* case. See *Mareh HaPanim*, s.v. הלכה כחכמים and ורבן גמליאל. R. Margaliot's student, R. Elijah of Vilna (1720–1797), also follows this interpretation; see *Biur HaGra* to *Shulḥan Arukh, Oraḥ Ḥaim*, 235:3 s.v. וזמנה. See also Ginzberg, *Commentary*, 1:85 n. 5, 94, and 95 n. 1, who points to other places where a rabbinic safeguard uproots the biblical law. Thus, line D does include *shema* and does describe the position of the sages, which is that the Bible permits these laws until dawn but the rabbis invalidate their fulfillment after midnight. This introduces the same inconsistency noted above, n. 18, a problem that is bothersome but not unprecedented (cf. *b. Ḥul.* 104a). Since the sages invalidate recitation of *shema* after midnight, the Yerushalmi appropriately asks how Rabban Gamaliel could ignore their safeguard.

To review the evolution of the interpretation of this Mishnah, the original Mishnah (lines A-C) presented a three-way dispute as to the biblical time limit for reciting *shema*. A later editor, evidently bothered by the story in which Rabban Gamaliel opposes the sages in practice, added line D in order to reconcile the sages, who offer midnight only as an a priori safeguard, with Rabban Gamaliel. This understanding of line D is represented in the Bavli. The Yerushalmi, however, remains faithful to the original sense of lines A-C according to which the sages invalidate recitation after midnight.

32. Perhaps the Yerushalmi purposely ignored line D precisely in order to make explicit and elaborate on its insistence that diversity of practice by an individual against the sages can never be tolerated. But even if the Yerushalmi simply inherited a different interpretation of line D according to which the sages are not reconciled with Rabban Gamaliel (thus remaining faithful to the original view of the sages), this *sugya*'s opening question still does reveal its basic assumption that no sage could possibly have practiced in opposition to the majority.

[B] *R. Meir*

The agenda of the Yerushalmi in this *sugya* is made further apparent by analyzing each of its proofs, all of which are problematic. The Yerushalmi brings three cases in which various Tannaim who had differing opinions nevertheless followed the majority. The first case, quoted from *t. Šabb.* 12:12, reports that the sages prohibit the preparation of a wine-and-oil ointment for a sick person on Shabbat but R. Meir permits. When, on one occasion, R. Meir was himself sick, his students offered to prepare this ointment, to which R. Meir replied, "Even though I am lenient for others, I am stringent upon myself for behold my colleagues disagree with me." The *sugya* focuses on the second half of R. Meir's statement, "I am stringent upon myself," in order to prove that R. Meir conformed to the majority opinion. However, R. Meir also says, "I am lenient for others." That R. Meir issued practical decisions based on his own opinion is confirmed earlier in this source, which states, "R. Meir used to permit…." This source contains elements of both conformity (R. Meir for himself) and nonconformity (R. Meir for others).

The Yerushalmi version of this *baraita* does not fit well into the overall argument of the Yerushalmi *sugya*. The *sugya* is trying to prove that other rabbis conformed to the majority in order to question how Rabban Gamaliel could have taught his sons to contradict the majority. If R. Meir taught others to follow his own opinion, however, even if he was stringent for himself, then he poses no problem for Rabban Gamaliel, who is also lenient for others. Yet, the Yerushalmi includes this as a proof for R. Meir's conformity and a challenge to Rabban Gamaliel without further comment.[33]

---

33. R. Eleazar Azikri, *Perush mi-ba`al sefer ḥaredim*, s.v. וכבר חלה, appropriately asks:
קשיא טובא וכי לא ידעו דיחיד ורבים הלכה כרבים? ועוד מה שהשיב ר׳ מאיר אע״פ שאני מיקל כו׳ הרי זה מעשה לסתור דפליגי רבנן עליה והוא עביד עובדא כוותיה וכל שכן להורות לרבים?

> This is highly problematic. Did they [R. Meir's students] not know that [in a dispute between] an individual and the majority the law follows the majority? Furthermore, that which R. Meir responds, "Even though I am lenient…," is a story that contradicts [what the Talmud sets out to prove], for the sages oppose him yet he practices in a case according to his own opinion and even teaches it to the public?

Azikri answers that R. Meir did not actually permit others to rely on his leniency but did not protest if they did so because this is a matter of health. This, however, does not fit well with the words of the *baraita*, which suggest that R. Meir did permit it for others outright.

As a possible explanation, Ginzberg, *Commentary*, 1:81–86, posits that since Rabban Gamaliel was deciding for his sons, not his students or laymen, we should assume that he held his household up to the same standard as he would for himself. If R. Meir was stringent on himself then Rabban Gamaliel should have been stringent on himself and his children as well. This explanation is part of his more general thesis that during the Tannaitic period, the rabbis had not yet voted on most matters and so individual rabbis would regularly teach others according to their own opinion, even against the majority. Even during this period, however, Tannaim would usually be stringent on themselves in order not to personally offend their colleagues. Accordingly, this *baraita* of R. Meir makes perfect sense and is a good proof against Rabban Gamaliel, who permitted his own children—extensions of himself—to act against the majority. (*B. Pesaḥ.* 51a-b, discussed below, similarly suggests that the sage's immediate circle of students is also an extension of himself but perhaps only when in the

The Yerushalmi version of this *baraita* is substantially different from that in the Tosefta:

b. Šabb. 134a[34]	*y. Ber.* 1:1 (3a)	*t. Šabb.* 12:12
אמר ליה אביי לרב יוסף...יין ושמן חזי נמי בשבת לחולה!		
	דתני סכין אלוונתית לחולה בשבת אימתי בזמן שטרפו ביין ושמן מערב שבת אבל אם לא טרפו מערב שבת אסור	עושין אלנתית לחולה בשבת אימתי בזמן שטרפה מערב שבת לא טרפה מערב שבת אסורה שאין טורפין בתחלה בשבת
דתניא: אין טורפין יין ושמן לחולה בשבת.		אין טורפין יין ושמן לחולה בשבת
אמר רבי שמעון בן אלעזר משום רבי מאיר: אף טורפין יין ושמן.	תני אמר ר' שמעון בן אלעזר מתיר היה רבי מאיר לטרוף יין ושמן ולסוך לחולה בשבת	רבי שמעון בן אלעזר אומר משום רבי מאיר טורפין יין ושמן לחולה בשבת
אמר רבי שמעון בן אלעזר: פעם אחת חש רבי מאיר במעיו, ובקשנו לטרוף לו יין ושמן, ולא הנחנו.	וכבר חלה ובקשנו לעשות לו כן ולא הניח לנו	אמר ר' שמעון בן לעזר פעם אחת חלה ר' מאיר ובקשנו לעשות לו ולא הניחני
אמרנו לו: דבריך יבטלו בחייך? אמר לנו: אף על פי שאני אומר כך, וחבירי אומרים כך — מימי לא מלאני לבי לעבור על דברי חבירי.	ואמרנו לו רבי דבריך מבטל בחייך ואמר לן אף על פי שאני מיקל לאחרים מחמיר אני על עצמי דהא פליגי עלי חברי	אמר לו רבינו תבטל דבריך בחייך אמר לנו אף על פי שאני אומר כן לא מלאני לבי מימי[35] לעבור על דברי חבירי[36]
הוא ניהו דמחמיר אנפשיה, אבל לכולי עלמא שרי!...		

master's presence. See also Hidary, "Tolerance for Diversity," 152–53.) This general thesis has little foundation, but the particular application to this case is helpful.

Even accepting this explanation, however, R. Meir's case is far from an absolute proof for universal uniformity. R. Meir seems to have acted not out of a halakhic duty to follow the majority but rather took upon himself a supererogatory stringency out of respect for his colleagues. He could be stringent on himself but could not impose this stringency on others when he thought it was actually permitted. This source does not pose a serious difficulty for Rabban Gamaliel who was not deciding for his own person and may not have felt particularly obligated to his colleagues. Furthermore, if Rabban Gamaliel would forbid his sons from reciting *shema*, he would cause them to sin by neglecting a halakhic obligation, whereas R. Meir's stringency did not compromise his own halakhic views. One cannot prove that Rabban Gamaliel should violate his own halakha because of the majority from R. Meir's case in which no violation was caused.

34. See the English translation of this source on the next page.

35. The language of the Tosefta, "I never in my life had the conviction to transgress the words of my colleagues," suggests that R. Meir would always follow the standard view. Ms. London omits מימי so that R. Meir may have felt uncertain only in this case but would contradict them when he was more confident. It is interesting that R. Meir's students assume he will allow it and R. Meir has to make a statement to explain his refusal. This may suggest that such conformist behavior was not the norm.

36. In *t. B. Qam.* 8:13, the phrase לעבור על דברי חבירי is used for an otherwise unanimous law that only one rabbi transgresses.

Only the last line of the Yerushalmi explicitly states that R. Meir allowed others to follow his opinion. The Yerushalmi further reads "מתיר היה רבי מאיר," which also suggests that he permitted it in practice. The Tosefta version, on the other hand, simply quotes R. Meir, saying that one may mix them on Shabbat but is more ambiguous about whether that was only his theoretical opinion or whether he also put it into practice. The end of the Tosefta adds that R. Meir would never contradict his colleagues, implying that R. Meir did not permit it to others either. Ironically, the Tosefta version would fit better into the Yerushalmi's argument than the Yerushalmi's version of the *baraita*.

It is unlikely that the Yerushalmi changed the original wording intentionally, because the Tosefta version would actually have fit better into the Yerushalmi context.[37] Rather, the Yerushalmi must have been working with an alternate Tannaitic tradition. That the Yerushalmi would include this tradition, even though it actually proves the opposite of what the Yerushalmi seeks, shows how forcefully the Yerushalmi's redactors were willing to strain interpretation of their sources in order to reflect an environment of unity.

Compare this with how the Tosefta is used in the Bavli context. Abaye asks Rav Yosef why *m. Šabb.* 19:2 prohibits preparing a wine-and-oil salve for a baby after circumcision on Shabbat considering that R. Meir permitted preparing the same formula for a sick person. *B. Šabbat* 134a reads:

> Abaye asked Rav Yosef ... wine and oil may also be used on Shabbat for a sick person, as we have learned in a baraita: **One may not mix wine and oil for a sick person on Shabbat. R. Shimon ben Eleazar said in the name of R. Meir, "One may even mix wine and oil [on Shabbat]." R. Shimon ben Eleazar said, "One time, R. Meir became sick in his bowels and we wanted to mix wine and oil for him but he did not let us. We told him, 'Rabbi, your words will become nullified in your lifetime.' He responded, 'Even though I say this and my colleagues say that, I never in my life had the conviction to transgress the words of my colleagues.'"** He was stringent upon himself but for everyone else he permitted.[38]

The Bavli here quotes the version of the *baraita* found in the Tosefta, but manages to interpret it such that it reaches the same conclusion as the Yerushalmi version. The Tosefta itself says only that R. Meir conformed and gives no explicit indication about what he taught others. Yet the Bavli,

37. This point is made by R. Yehoshua Benveniste (1590–1668) in his *S'deh Yehoshua* cited in Malinowitz et al., eds., *The Schottenstein Edition: Talmud Yerushalmi,* 1:8b1 n. 7.

38. See the Hebrew in the chart on the previous page.

through a midrashic derivation, uses this source as a proof that R. Meir ruled leniently for others. The Bavli thus ignores R. Meir's own confession of conformity and instead focuses on what he allegedly taught others. Conversely, the Yerushalmi ignores the report that R. Meir permitted it to others and focuses only on R. Meir's conformity. In an ironic case of role reversal, the Yerushalmi version of the *baraita* would fit better into the Bavli *sugya* and the Bavli's version is better suited to the Yerushalmi![39] That each Talmud nevertheless uses the *baraita* to prove opposite conclusions reveals that each *sugya* is motivated not by the *baraita* itself, which contains both conformity and diversity, but rather by the redactors' preconceived notions. The Yerushalmi seeks to prove that all Tannaim conformed to the majority opinion while the Bavli assumes that R. Meir must have allowed others to practice his opinion. Both *sugyot* find what they are looking for in this *baraita*.

[C] *R. Akiba*

In the previous case, R. Meir had a more lenient view than the rabbis, and so he could act stringently without compromising his own principle. In this case, however, R. Akiba had a more stringent view than the majority. A case came up in Lydda when many rabbis were present. They decided to take a vote knowing that R. Akiba disagreed with the majority. R. Akiba was called upon first, he voted pure, and the vote stopped right there.[40] This shows that R. Akiba voted according to the majority opinion even though he himself opined that the basket was impure.

The Tosefta version of this story at *ʾOhal.* 4:2, which is also found in *b. Naz.* 52a-b, surrounds the narrative with a discussion by two of R. Akiba's disciples:

אמ׳ ר׳ יהודה ששה דברים היה ר׳ עקיבא מטמא וחזר בו
מעשה שהביאו קופות של עצמות מכפר טביא והניחום באויר בית הכנסת בלוד ונכנס
תיאודו רוס הרופא וכל הרופאים עמו אמרו אין כאן שדרה ממת אחד ולא גולגולת ממת

39. While one could suggest that the original Yerushalmi *sugya* had a version of the R. Meir story similar to that in the Tosefta and the Bavli and that the words "Even though I am lenient for others" were added by a later copyist on the basis of the Bavli's interpretation, I find this extremely unlikely for three reasons: (1) The language used by the Bavli to say that R. Meir permitted it to others bears no resemblance to that in the Yerushalmi. (2) The Yerushalmi also includes מתיר היה ר׳ מאיר, which has no parallel in the Bavli. (3) If this copyist were sophisticated enough to insert the Bavli's interpretation so smoothly in two places in the Yerushalmi *baraita*, then he would have known better than to change the Yerushalmi's *baraita* in such a way that destroyed the Yerushalmi's entire proof.

40. It is noteworthy that the rabbis did not assume that R. Akiba would concede and therefore thought that they had to outvote him. It is also possible, however, that they were really asking him respectfully to concede, which he does.

אחד[41] אמרו הואיל ויש כאן מטמאין ויש כאן מטהרין נעמוד למניין התחילו מר' עקיבא וטיהר אמרו לו הואיל ואתה שהייתה מטמא טיהרתה יהו טהורין
אמר ר' שמעון ועד יום מיתתו של ר' עקיבא היה מטמא ואם משמת חזר בו איני יודע.[42]

R. Yehudah said: Regarding six issues, R. Akiba used to declare impure but then changed his mind.
It happened that baskets of bones were brought from Kefar Ṭabi and placed in the open air of the synagogue of Lydda. Theodorus the doctor entered together with all the doctors. They declared, "There is neither a spine from one corpse nor a skull from one corpse here." They [the rabbis] said, "Since there are some who declare pure and some who declare impure here let us put it to a vote." They began with R. Akiba who declared pure. They said, "Since you used to declare impure and now you have declared it pure, let them be pure."
R. Shimon said: R. Akiba declared impure until the day of his death. If he changed his mind after he died, I am not aware of it.

According to R. Yehudah, R. Akiba had changed his mind from his original position and actually agreed with the majority. The reason he voted with the majority is not because he wanted to conform despite his differences, but rather because he had reversed his opinion. R. Akiba is not an opposing sage who compromises for the sake of uniformity of practice but rather a previously opposing sage who changed his mind. This fact spoils the entire argument of the Yerushalmi. R. Eleazar Azikri asks this very question:

וקשה דבנזיר פרק כהן גדול מייתי ברייתא בבלי דהדר ביה ר' עקיבא. אם כן, אין מכאן ראיה דלא עבד עובדא כוותיה דאילו לא הדר דלמא הוה מטמא. וי"ל דהירושלמי אדר' שמעון סמך דאמר התם דכל ימיו לא חזר בו ומסתמא לא הכחיש ר' שמעון המעשה הזה המפורסם אלא שהבין דמשום דלא למעבד עובדא נגד הרבים טיהר כדעתם לא משום דחזר בו.

It is difficult because in *b. Nazir* 52a a baraita is cited saying that R. Akiba changed his mind. If so, there is no proof from here that he did not perform a deed according to his own opinion, for if he had not changed his mind perhaps he would not have declared impure. One may answer that the Yerushalmi relied on R. Shimon there who says that [R. Akiba] did not change his mind all of his days. Presumably, R. Shimon did not doubt this famous story but rather understood that he declared pure like the sages in order not to perform a deed against the majority and not because he had changed his mind.[43]

---

41. Ms. Vienna reads אחר. I have emended to אחד based on the first edition.

42. Based on ms. Vienna. The manuscript reads אינו in the second to last word, which I have emended to איני based on the first edition. *B. Naz.* 52b also reads איני in all witnesses.

43. *Perush mi-baʿal sefer ḥaredim*, s.v. הואיל. Ginzberg, *Commentary*, 1:88–89, follows this interpretation.

Azikri explains that the Yerushalmi assumes the view of R. Shimon that R. Akiba did not change his mind. Still, if the Yerushalmi redactors had before them our version of this Tosefta with the comments of both R. Yehudah and R. Shimon, then their argument here would be severely weakened by assuming one interpretation of the story without providing reasons to reject the other.[44]

Rather, we should probably assume that the Yerushalmi redactors had only the story itself without the comments by R. Akiba's two students. That is, the Yerushalmi preserves the earliest version of this Tannaitic tradition, which included only the story, while the Tosefta and the Bavli record a later version with the added comments by R. Yehudah and R. Shimon.[45] Rabbis often extracted apodictic laws from stories and transmitted them as independent traditions.[46] In this case too, it seems most likely that R. Yehudah did not receive a tradition that R. Akiba had changed his mind, especially considering that R. Shimon, a fellow student of R. Akiba, so adamantly denies its veracity. Rather, R. Yehudah reasoned that if R. Akiba voted with the majority then he obviously agreed with them and therefore must have reversed his opinion as stated in *m. ʾOhal.* 2:6.[47] The story is not the proof of R. Yehudah's statement but rather its source.[48]

Even if we accept that the Yerushalmi redactors disagreed with or did not know of R. Yehudah's position, R. Yehudah's interpretation of the story, which is quoted in the Bavli, represents an interpretive possibility not taken by the Yerushalmi. Furthermore, even if the redactors did not think of this interpretation, this source still does not serve as a solid proof.

---

44. R. Yehudah's statement comes before the story and uses the story as proof. R. Shimon's comes after the story, which suggests that he denies the story ever happened. (Azikri's only counter-argument is that R. Shimon must have accepted this "famous" story. See also Lieberman, *Tosefeth rishonim*, 3:102.) According to this reconstruction, perhaps the Yerushalmi purposely and conveniently left out this background information concerning R. Akiba's change of heart in order to force the story to conform to its agenda of proving that individuals would always accede to the majority practice even when they disagree in theory. The Bavli, which has no such agenda, preserves the original background of the story. See, however, the next paragraph.

45. The Tosefta as we have it was not used by the Yerushalmi. On the relationship between Tannaitic statements found in the Tosefta and the Talmuds, see Binyamin Katzoff, "The Relationship Between the Baraitot in the Tosefta and Their Talmudic Parallels: The Evidence of Tractate Berachot," *Hebrew Union College Annual* 75 (2004): 1–24 (Hebrew).

46. Hanokh Albeck, *Introduction to the Mishna* (Jerusalem: Mossad Bialik, 1959), 92 (Hebrew).

47. Otherwise, R. Akiba should have voted according to his own opinion and then let the vote decide the outcome. He should have conformed to the majority only after he lost the vote, as is recommended in *m. Sanh.* 3:7. See Ginzberg, *Commentary*, 1:88, who incorrectly applies *m. Sanh.* 3:7 to the deliberation of the judges when the vote is taken even though the Mishnah explicitly says, "When one of the judges leaves" the deliberation.

R. Yehudah may also have inferred that R. Akiva changed his mind from the use of the perfect, שהייתה מטהר, rather than the a present tense verb in the statement of the rabbis.

48. I thank Michal Bar-Asher Siegal for this insight.

Perhaps R. Akiba conformed to the majority only because it was a public vote and he would have lost the vote anyway. We cannot prove from here that Rabban Gamaliel, who was deciding alone and in private, could not have decided against the majority.[49] Once again, the Yerushalmi's use of this source despite these difficulties reveals its bias.

[D] *R. Shimon bar Yoḥai*

R. Shimon bar Yoḥai is more lenient than his colleagues concerning picking the aftergrowth of vegetables during the Sabbatical year when farming is prohibited. A story is recounted in which R. Shimon tells a farmer to follow the stringent view of the sages despite his own lenient position; presumably, he would act stringently himself as well. The story is repeated in *y. Šeb.* 9:1 (38d) where another story follows in which R. Shimon bar Yoḥai also rebukes and curses someone and which also ends with וכן הוות.[50] In that context, the story is one example of R. Shimon bar Yoḥai's intensity and zeal; he is portrayed in these stories as impatient and impulsive.[51] Furthermore, the tone of the story with its repeated use of sarcasm, introduced by the words ולית ... ולאו ... ולא ... ואין, shows that this story involves a personal tiff rather than an earnest halakhic discussion. R. Shimon bar Yoḥai was offended by this farmer's actions and cursed him. Rabbi Shimon bar Yoḥai might have been more tolerant if he had seen a rabbinic colleague gathering vegetation. He seems to have been particularly upset by the farmer because he was a layman who was simply taking advantage of R. Shimon's leniency regarding this issue. The Yerushalmi uses this story as a proof that no rabbi may follow a minority opinion even though the story only describes an exceptional case of an impatient rabbi dealing with an opportunistic layperson.

Compare this story to the following report in *b. Pesaḥ.* 51a-b:

דאמר רבה בר בר חנה: סח לי רבי יוחנן בן אלעזר: פעם אחת נכנסתי אחר רבי שמעון בן רבי יוסי בן לקוניא לגינה, ונטל ספיחי כרוב,[52] ואכל ונתן לי. ואמר לי: בני, בפני אכול, שלא בפני לא תאכל. אני שראיתי את רבי שמעון בן יוחי שאכל כדי הוא רבי שמעון בן יוחי לסמוך עליו, בפניו ושלא בפניו. אתה, בפני אכול, שלא בפני לא תאכל.

49. Ginzberg, ibid., asks this question and concludes that the Yerushalmi only compares one aspect of the cases even though they are fundamentally different. Ginzberg, ibid., 91, is forced to say that "the cases of R. Akiba and R. Shimon were only cited here as a mere example since they also were particular to honor their colleagues, but the main question on Rabban Gamaliel is from R. Meir."

50. The order of the stories is reversed in *Genesis Rabbah* 79:6.

51. See more on this story in Rubenstein, *Talmudic Stories*, 121f.

52. The Bavli subsequently cites a *baraita* stating that R. Shimon bar Yoḥai prohibits aftergrowth of all vegetation except the cabbage, which is the opposite of *m. Šeb.* 9:1. The Bavli story about R. Shimon bar Yoḥai eating of the cabbage concurs with the Bavli *baraita*. See Tosafot *b. Naz.* 51a, s.v. כל.

> For Rabbah bar bar Ḥannah said: R. Yoḥanan ben Eleazar told me, "One time I followed R. Shimon ben R. Yose ben Laqunia into a garden. He took an aftergrowth of cabbage,[52] ate it, gave it to me and told me, 'My son, you may eat in my presence but you may not eat when outside my presence. I saw R. Shimon bar Yoḥai eating and R. Shimon bar Yoḥai is worthy to rely on in his presence and outside his presence. You [who only saw me eat] may eat in my presence but may not eat when outside my presence.'"

According to the Bavli, R. Shimon does, in fact, follow his own opinion and even advises his student to do so. This is completely opposite from the Yerushalmi story and may reflect the general tendency of the Bavli to be more tolerant of diversity.[53] Tosafot wonders about this contradiction and insightfully explains that in the Yerushalmi case the source of R. Shimon's anger is not the lenient practice itself, but rather the character of the *am ha'areṣ,* who just follows the leniency blindly.[54] Of course, we cannot assume that the Yerushalmi's redactors knew of this Bavli story.[55] As noted above, however, even if they did not know of it, it seems evident from the Yerushalmi story alone that R. Shimon was particularly upset by the farmer because he was a layman who was simply taking advantage of R. Shimon's leniency. One could easily imagine an alternate *sugya* trying to prove the opposite view citing this story and concluding, עם הארץ שאני—"a layman is different," just as Tosafot does.

The Yerushalmi uses this story as a proof that no rabbi may follow a minority opinion even though the story only describes an exceptional case of an impatient rabbi dealing with an opportunistic layperson. Furthermore, as was the case for R. Meir, R. Shimon is stringent in a way that does not cause him to violate any of his own norms. This can only prove that a rabbi should be stringent in consideration of the majority, but it cannot prove that a rabbi may transgress what he thinks is a norm because of the majority. Thus, the R. Shimon story cannot prove that Rabban Gamaliel must forgo what he views as an obligation to recite *shema*.[56]

53. See Ben-Menahem, *Judicial Deviation*, 89.

54. Tosafot *b. Pesaḥ.* 51b, s.v. אני. Ginzberg, *Commentary*, 90, does not accept the resolution of Tosafot because when read back into the Yerushalmi *sugya* it suggests that Rabban Gamaliel should have treated his sons like *amei haʾareṣ*. Instead, he explains that the Yerushalmi simply was not aware of the Bavli story.

55. Duberush Ashkenazi, *Shaʿare Yerushalmi* (Warsaw: Drukerni N. Schriftgisser, 1866), 2b, in fact takes the position that the Yerushalmi did not know of the Bavli story in order to resolve the difficulty that the Bavli story would pose to the Yerushalmi argument. I think, however, that the interpretation of Tosafot is evident from a literary reading of the Yerushalmi story even independent of the need to reconcile it with the Bavli.

56. See Aryeh Leib Gunzberg, *Shaʾagat aryeh* (New York: Israel Wolf, 1958), *siman* 4, p. 11, who writes:

The Yerushalmi's use of this story to prove that no rabbi practiced against the majority is, at best, somewhat of a leap. We can most clearly see the agenda of the Yerushalmi when it reads a source against the grain and forces it to prove something that it does not.

[E] ***Resolution***

The Yerushalmi offers two answers. The first is that Rabban Gamaliel told his sons to read even though he did not think they could fulfill their obligation, that is, he completely agreed with the sages that reciting after midnight is not valid but only permitted them to read it as a form of study. This is not accepted because Rabban Gamaliel says, "If dawn has not yet arrived...," and one could study *shema* even after dawn. The second response is that Rabban Gamaliel did rely on his opinion *ex post facto* and thought that they could fulfill their obligation. This allows for diversity of practice only where it is in any case impossible to fulfill the law according to the majority. Still, Rabban Gamaliel would not oppose his colleagues before the fact.

In sum, both Talmuds reject the possibility that Rabban Gamaliel acted against the sages in *m. Ber.* 1:1. However, the Bavli only clarifies what is already embedded in line D of the Mishnah, while the Yerushalmi, which ignores line D, introduces its line of questioning from scratch. More significantly, all three proofs of the Yerushalmi are problematic in that they do not prove conformity and may even reflect diversity. That the Yerushalmi nevertheless uses these three sources to prove halakhic conformity within the Tannaitic community reveals the Yerushalmi's push to read uniformity into the past. It is uncomfortable with diversity of practice among the Tannaim and interprets examples of it out of existence. The Bavli, by contrast, does not include a parallel to the entire *sugya* but does

---

The main question of the Yerushalmi is only from the case of R. Akiba, for there is no question from R. Meir and R. Shimon who act stringently according to the majority who disagree with them, since there is no stringency that leads to a leniency in their controversies. Therefore, they acted according to the majority and were stringent. However, regarding the recitation of *shema* after midnight, since according to Rabban Gamaliel this is still the time for the recitation of *shema* and they may recite, therefore, they are necessarily obligated to recite. If they would act stringently according to the sages, even if the majority prohibits them from reading as a rabbinic enactment, this would be a stringency that would lead to a leniency.... The cases of R. Meir and R. Shimon were only dragged in incidentally by the Yerushalmi. Since it cited that R. Akiba did not perform an act according to his own opinion it cites the cases of R. Meir and R. Shimon as well who did not perform acts according to their own opinions even though the main question is only from R. Akiba. This is the way of the Yerushalmi in all places to drag in many things that are similar even though they are not very relevant to the topic of the *sugya* and this is clear to whoever is acquainted with the Talmud Yerushalmi.

Cf. n. 49, above. These comments indicate how problematic the proofs in this *sugya* are.

have parallels to each of the proofs; in each case, the Bavli emphasizes the diversity that does exist regarding each issue.

Roasting the *Pesaḥ* (*m. Pesaḥ.* 7:2)

M. Pesaḥim 7:2 records another case in which Rabban Gamaliel practiced against the accepted opinion:

> אין צולין את הפסח לא על השפוד ולא על האסכלא
> אמר רבי צדוק מעשה ברבן גמליאל שאמר לטבי עבדו צא וצלה לנו את הפסח על האסכלא
> One may not roast the *pesaḥ* offering neither on a metal spit nor on a grill.
> R. Ṣadoq says: It happened that Rabban Gamaliel told Ṭabi his servant, "Go roast for us the *pesaḥ* on a grill."

The Yerushalmi is uncomfortable that Rabban Gamaliel practiced in opposition to his colleagues and questions his behavior using language that is very similar to its question in *y. Ber.* 1:1 (3a) above. *Y. Pesaḥim* 7:2 (34b) reads:

> רבן גמליאל חלוק על חכמים ועושה הלכה כיוצא בו?
> Does Rabban Gamaliel disagree with the sages and practice halakha accordingly?

The Yerushalmi provides no answer and simply leaves the question hanging. Bavli *Pesaḥim* 75a, on the other hand, says the following:

> מעשה לסתור? חסורי מיחסרא והכי קתני: ואם אסכלא מנוקבת מותר. ואמר רבי צדוק: מעשה ברבן גמליאל שאמר לטבי עבדו צא וצלה לנו את הפסח על האסכלא מנוקבת.
> [Does the Tanna cite] a story to contradict [the law before it]? [The Mishnah] is lacking and should be taught thus: "But if the grill is perforated it is permissible. R. Ṣadoq says, 'It happened that Rabban Gamaliel told Ṭabi his servant, 'Go roast for us the *pesaḥ* on a perforated grill.'"

The result of the emendation (or explanation)[57] here is that Rabban Gamaliel's practice no longer opposes the sages. The formula מעשה לסתור? חסורי מיחסרא והכי קתני is quoted numerous times in the Bavli. The Bavli solves these cases with two different strategies. In most cases, it updates the

57. On the various ways this term is used in the Bavli, see Epstein, *Mavo le-nusah ha-Mishnah*, 595–673. On the use of the term in this case see ibid., 599.

understanding of the law so that the opposition is removed.[58] In these cases, the story is meant to add nuance to the law by providing an exception. In other cases, it adds an opinion to the Mishnah to make it clear that the story does indeed contradict the law of the Mishnah and instead follows an alternate view. In some of these cases the alternate view is more stringent,[59] but in some it is more lenient.[60] That *b. Pesaḥ.* 75a chooses the former strategy and does not say something like, "It is lacking and one should add, 'Rabban Gamaliel permits on a metal spit...,'" suggests that the Bavli's motivation was to remove the opposition in this story. It did not want to recognize that there could have been such diversity of practice about this issue. Still, the Bavli is not as explicit about it as is the Yerushalmi.

The language used by the Yerushalmi in the above two cases to question Rabban Gamaliel's nonconformity is also found in two other Yerushalmi passages regarding actions of other Tannaim. *M. ᶜAbodah Zarah* 3:7 records a dispute regarding whether a tree with an idol at its feet is considered *asherah*; the sages are stringent and R. Shimon is lenient. The Mishnah continues to recount a story in which R. Shimon actually permitted such a case. *Y. ᶜAbodah Zarah* 3:10 (43b) poses that this is problematic: וקשיא ר' שמעון חלוק על החכמים ועושה מעשה כיוצא בו–"It is difficult; does R. Shimon disagree with the sages and perform an act in accordance [with his own opinion]!" The Yerushalmi offers no response. The Bavli, on the other hand, which makes no comment on this issue, does not seem to be bothered by this problem. Similarly, *y. Demai* 3:3 (23c), commenting on R. Yose's position allowing one to send food that was definitely not tithed to a friend as long as the sender informs the receiver of its status, states: אף על גב דו פליג על רבנין לא עבד עובדא דכוותיה—"Even though [R. Yose] argues with the sages, he did not act according to his own opinion."[61] Therefore, a concern about individuals practicing in opposition to the majority is not an isolated phenomenon in the Yerushalmi but rather runs through many Yerushalmi pericopae, perhaps indicating a concerted effort on the redactional level to address such issues.[62] Getting back to Rabban Gamaliel, the following is another context in which the Yerushalmi discusses his nonconformity, albeit not using the formula analyzed above.

---

58. See *b. Ned.* 48a; *b. Naz.* 11a; and *b. Giṭ.* 66a. Cf. *b. Ber.* 16b; *b. Meṣiᶜa* 86a, 102b; *b. ᶜAbod. Zar.* 65b; and *b. ᶜArak.* 19b.

59. See *b. Sukkah* 26b and 28b. Since the protagonists in these stories are more stringent, they do not pose such a problem of opposing the law of the Mishnah.

60. See *b. Beṣah* 24a (cited below) and *b. Ned.* 66a.

61. See further discussion in Ginzberg, *Commentary*, 1:84–85.

62. See also *y. Seb.* 9:4 (39a) where an Amora rules against his own view in order to conform to the majority, and *y. Šabb.* 5:4 (7c) analyzed by Ben-Menahem, *Judicial Deviation*, 89–90.

Trapping Animals on Yom Ṭov *(m.* Beṣah *3:2)*

One Mishnah that has a similar structure to *m. Pesaḥ.* 7:2 is *m. Beṣah* 3:2:

מצודות חיה ועוף ודגים שעשאן מערב יום טוב לא יטול מהן ביום טוב, אלא אם כן יודע שנצודו מערב יום טוב.
ומעשה בנכרי אחד שהביא דגים לרבן גמליאל, ואמר: מותרין הן, אלא שאין רצוני לקבל הימנו.

One may not remove animals, birds, or fish from a trap that one set up before a festival [*yom ṭov* on which work is prohibited] unless he knows that they were caught before the festival.
It happened that a certain Gentile brought fish to Rabban Gamaliel [on *yom ṭov*]. He [Rabban Gamaliel] said, "They are permitted but I do not wish to accept them from him [for personal reasons]."

Once again, Rabban Gamaliel seems to have opposed the anonymous opinion, which would prohibit the Gentile's fish because it was presumably caught on *yom ṭov*, in favor of his own lenient view.[63] Bothered by this act of nonconformity, the Yerushalmi (*y. Beṣah* 3:2, 62a) cites Rav, who says that even Rabban Gamaliel prohibits the Gentile fish on *yom ṭov* and he only said, "They are permitted" regarding the next day after *yom ṭov*. That the Yerushalmi offers such a forced interpretation of the Mishnah shows just how much it was bothered by the possibility that Rabban Gamaliel could have opposed the sages on this matter. Rav's explanation succeeds in removing opposition from Rabban Gamaliel's story altogether.

The Yerushalmi further cites the possibility that Rabban Gamaliel did permit himself to eat the fish on *yom ṭov* because he held that a case of doubt is permitted or that food from Gentiles does not need to be prepared before *yom ṭov*. Although there are disagreements about both of these issues, they are ancillary to the topic of the Mishnah itself. Accordingly, Rabban Gamaliel follows one side of a controversy but does not oppose the anonymous law of the Mishnah.

Compare this with the Bavli treatment of this Mishnah at *Beṣah* 24a:

מעשה לסתור? חסורי מחסרא והכי קתני: ספק מוכן אסור, ורבן גמליאל מתיר. ומעשה נמי בנכרי אחד שהביא דגים לרבן גמליאל, ואמר: מותרין הן, אלא שאין רצוני לקבל הימנו.

[Does the Tanna cite] a story to contradict [the law before it]? [The Mishnah] is lacking and should be taught thus: "If one is in doubt

63. Historically, Rabban Gamaliel may not have known of any other opinion, and this entire controversy may be the creation of the Mishnah's redactor, who juxtaposed the two views. Nevertheless, the Mishnah as we have it does present a dispute, and it is this dispute that the Talmuds interpret.

> whether something was prepared [before *yom ṭov*] it is prohibited. Rabban Gamaliel permits. In fact, it happened that a certain Gentile brought fish to Rabban Gamaliel [on *yom ṭov*]. He said, 'They are permitted but I do not wish to accept them from him.'"

Rabban Gamaliel still opposes the anonymous ruling, even after the Bavli's textual emendation (unlike in the previous case at *b. Pesaḥ.* 75a[64]). The emendation only serves to insert an anchor into the story so that we know what the issue is and that Rabban Gamaliel is not simply violating the halakha but rather following his own view. This *sugya* assumes, as does one interpretation of the Yerushalmi, that the issue at hand is how to rule in cases of doubt. Unlike the Yerushalmi, however, the Bavli inserts an anonymous ruling into the Mishnah that prohibits cases of doubt so that Rabban Gamaliel now opposes an anonymous Mishnah. That the Bavli does not emend the text to remove the possibility that Rabban Gamaliel opposed the rabbis (as it did in *m. Pesaḥ.* 7:2) but rather inserts opposition into the Mishnah suggests that it tolerates diversity of practice in this case.

The continuation of the Bavli, however, offers an alternate explanation[65] of the Mishnah, which does lessen the extent of diversity it reflects. The Bavli (*b. Beṣah* 24b) quotes Rav as explaining that Rabban Gamaliel allowed himself only to take the fish from the Gentile but not to eat it. This significantly limits the extent of Rabban Gamaliel's opposition from a disagreement about biblical prohibition of work on *yom ṭov* to one about the rabbinic prohibition of *muqṣeh*.

The Yerushalmi and Bavli do not reflect significant difference in their treatment of *m. Beṣah* 3:2. It is, however, noteworthy that in their citations of Rav, the Yerushalmi removes all opposition while the Bavli only limits it to a rabbinic prohibition. Also, the Bavli assumes that Rabban Gamaliel opposed the anonymous opinion in the Mishnah regarding cases of doubt while the Yerushalmi does not connect the issue of doubt with the dispute in the Mishnah.

In the above three cases, Rabban Gamaliel is more lenient than the sages.[66] This provokes questioning by the Talmuds. In all three cases, the Yerusahlmi explicitly questions his dissent (*m. Pesaḥ.* 7:2), and in two of the cases it proceeds to reinterpret the Mishnah in order to eliminate (*m.*

---

64. On the uniqueness of the use of חסורי מחסרא in this case versus other occurrences in the Bavli see Goldberg, "Ṣimṣum maḥloket eṣel Amora'e Bavel," 147.

65. The explanations do not fit together, for if Rabban Gamaliel permits cases of doubt then there would be no reason to refrain from eating the fish.

66. In other cases, Rabban Gamaliel is more stringent; see *m. Ber.* 2:5; *m. Beṣah* 2:6; *m. Sukkah* 2:5; and *t. Šabb.* 1:22. The Talmuds do not address Rabban Gamaliel's deviance in these cases because being more stringent is not usually viewed as a threat to the lenient opinion. An exception, however, is found in *y. ʿAbod. Zar.* 2:8 (41d), on which see below, pp. 327–28.

Beṣah 3:2) or limit (*m. Ber.* 1:1) the extent of his disagreement. The Bavli also eliminates controversy in these three cases; however, it does not seem to do so because of the same agenda that is made so explicit in the Yerushalmi. In the case of *m. Ber.* 1:1, the Bavli simply follows the cue of the last part of the Mishnah. In *m. Pesaḥ.* 7:2 and *m. Beṣah* 3:2 it is bothered by the lack of flow in the Mishnah, which cites a law and then a contradictory narrative. Its solutions seem to be aimed at emending the Mishnah to read more smoothly rather than at the alleged nonconformity itself. In yet another case, the plain meaning of a Mishnah does not indicate any disagreement between Rabban Gamaliel and the sages, yet the Bavli inserts diversity into it.[67]

---

67. See *m. ʿErub.* 6:1–2, where Rabban Gamaliel reports about his father's practice regarding a controversial issue:

[1] הדר עם הנכרי בחצר או עם מי שאינו מודה בערוב הרי זה אוסר עליו...

[2] אמר רבן גמליאל מעשה בצדוקי אחד שהיה דר עמנו במבוי בירושלים ואמר לנו אבא מהרו והוציאו את כל הכלים למבוי עד שלא יוציא ויאסר עליכם

רבי יהודה אומר בלשון אחר מהרו ועשו צרכיכם במבוי עד שלא יוציא ויאסר עליכם:

[1] One who lives with a Gentile in a courtyard or with someone [a Jew] who does not agree to the *eruv*, he [the Gentile or disagreeing Jew] prohibits him [from creating an *eruv*]…

[2] Rabban Gamaliel said: It happened that a certain Sadducee lived with us in a courtyard in Jerusalem. Our father told us, "Hurry and take all of the utensils out to the courtyard before he [the Sadducee] takes out [his utensils] and prohibits you [from using the *eruv*]."

R. Yehudah recounts [the story] differently, "[Rabban Gamaliel's father said,] Hurry and accomplish what you need to in the courtyard before he [the Sadducee] takes out [his utensils] and prohibits you [from using the *eruv*]."

Mishnah 1 simply reports that Gentiles and Jews who oppose the *eruv* render the entire *eruv* invalid. In general, the property of a Gentile must be rented out by the other members of the courtyard in order to make an *eruv*, while the Jew who opposes the *eruv* must agree to relinquish his right to the courtyard. Rabban Gamaliel's story deals with the status of a Sadducee who is ethnically considered Jewish but who does not accept the law of *eruv* and is not part of the rabbinic community. The Mishnah records two versions of the story. According to the first version, Rabban Gamaliel's father equated the Sadducee with a Jew who can relinquish his property rights and therefore they must make a claim to the courtyard before the Sadducee changes his mind and uses it. R. Yehudah, according to his version of the story, agrees that the Sadducee can relinquish his property but does not think that making a claim to the courtyard does any good. (See statement of R. Aḥa in *y. ʿErub.* 6:2 (23b) and Rashi in *b. ʿErub.* 61b, s.v. מהרו. *B. ʿErub.* 69a, however, explains that according to R. Yehudah's version of the story, Rabban Gamaliel does consider the Sadducee as a Gentile. See the various interpretations explicated by Abraham Goldberg, *The Mishna Treatise Eruvin* (Jerusalem: Magnes, 1986), 161–66.)

Neither version of the story opposes the original law, which does not comment on the status of a Sadducee (i.e., whether he is treated like a Gentile or a Jew). This straightforward reading of the Mishnah is assumed by the Yerushalmi whose comment on this Mishnah is simply: רבי אחא רבי חיננא בשם כהנא אין הלכה כרבי יהודה — "R. Aḥa [in the name of] R. Ḥinena in the name of Kahana [said], the halakha does not follow R. Yehudah."

Bavli ʿErub. 68b, however, reads the Mishnah differently:

These examples reveal a consistent pattern throughout many Yerushalmi *sugyot* to assume uniformity of practice among the Tannaim and question examples of dissent. This pattern suggests that it reflects the attitude of the Yerushalmi's redactors. The Yerushalmi's viewpoint is especially evident in the extended discussion at *y. Ber.* 1:1 (3a). While the Bavli also addresses this diversity it does not do so with the same level of consistency or explicitness.

Rabban Gamaliel as Unifier

Controversies over the Calendar

Other stories involving Rabban Gamaliel are also revealing. He is portrayed not only as someone who follows his own view even against the majority but also as a strong leader who imposes his opinion on others. *M. Roš Haššanah* 2:8–9 reports that when, on one occasion, Rabban Gamaliel declared that the new moon had arrived based on controversial testimony, he nevertheless forced R. Yehoshua to accept his calendar.[68] The calendar may be a special example in which Rabban Gamaliel was recognized by his colleagues as the authority.[69] In fact, R. Akiba encourages R. Yehoshua to bow to Rabban Gamaliel's authority precisely because the Torah has left calendrical decisions up to the sages and so whatever date Rabban Gamaliel's court chooses is valid.[70]

צדוקי מאן דכר שמיה? חסורי מיחסרא והכי קתני: צדוקי הרי הוא כנכרי. ורבן גמליאל אומר: צדוקי אינו כנכרי. ואמר רבן גמליאל: מעשה....

> Who mentioned anything about Sadducees [in *m. ʿErub.* 6:1 that it should be discussed in 6:2]? [The Mishnah] is lacking and should be taught thus: "A Sadducee is like a Gentile. Rabban Gamaliel says a Sadducee is not like a Gentile. Rabban Gamaliel said, it once happened....

According to the Bavli, Rabban Gamaliel disagrees with the sages who say a Sadducee is like a Gentile. The Bavli follows this with a proof from a *baraita*. In this reading, the story presents Rabban Gamaliel's father performing a deed according to his own opinion and in opposition to his colleagues. In this example, the Bavli assumes there was diversity of practice while the plain sense of the Mishnah, which is the same as the Yerushalmi's reading of the Mishnah, does not reflect any diversity.

68. See text below, p. 282, chart 5.1.

69. See *M. ʿEd.* 7:7.

70. Although, the second argument offered in *m. Ber.* 2:9 is not calendar specific but rather declares the decisions of a court on any matter as authoritative. It is not clear whether this second argument is expressed by R. Dosa or R. Yehoshua. If the former, then it is ironic that R. Dosa, who tells R. Yehoshua here not to question the court, is the one who questioned Rabban Gamaliel's decision in the first place! Perhaps R. Yehoshua conceded only after R. Dosa's advice (and not after R. Akiba's) precisely because R. Dosa is the one who challenged Rabban Gamaliel first. R. Yehoshua only seconded R. Dosa's challenge, so once R. Dosa con-

The Bavli transmits a shorter version of this story with small but perhaps significant differences:

> It was taught: R. Akiba went and found R. Yehoshua distressed. He said to him, "Master, why are you distressed?" He responded, "R. Akiba, it is better for one to fall to his bed for twelve months than have such a decree decreed upon him."
> He said to him, "Master, allow me to say something before you that you have taught me." He responded, "Speak." He said to him, "Behold [Scripture] states, 'you' (Lev 23:2), 'you' (23:4), 'you' (23:37), three times: 'you'—even inadvertently, 'you'—even deliberately, 'you'—even in error." With this language did he respond, "Akiba, you have comforted me, you have comforted me."

***b. Roš Haš.* 25a**	***m. Roš Haš.* 2:8**
דתניא הלך רבי עקיבא ומצאו לרבי יהושע כשהוא מיצר, אמר לו: רבי, מפני מה אתה מיצר? אמר לו: רבי עקיבא, ראוי לו שיפול למטה שנים עשר חדש ואל יגזור עליו גזירה זו.	הלך ומצאו רבי עקיבא מיצר
אמר לו: רבי, תרשיני לומר לפניך דבר אחד שלמד־תני. אמר לו: אמור. אמר לו: הרי הוא אומר (ויקרא כג:ב) אתם, (ויקרא כג:ד) אתם, (ויקרא כג:לז) אתם, שלש פעמים, אתם—אפילו שוגגין, אתם—אפילו מזידין, אתם—אפילו מוטעין. בלשון הזה אמר לו: עקיבא, נחמתני, נחמתני.	אמר לו יש לי ללמוד שכל מה שעשה רבן גמליאל עשוי שנאמר (ויקרא כג:ד) אלה מועדי ה׳ מקראי קודש אשר תקראו אתם בין בזמנן בין שלא בזמנן אין לי מועדות אלא אלו

cedes so does R. Yehoshua. See, however, Daniel Schwartz, "From Priests at Their Right to Christians at Their Left?: On the Interpretation and Development of a Mishnaic Story (M. Rosh Hashanah 2:8–9)," *Tarbiz* 74, no. 1 (2005): 25–33 (Hebrew), who argues that this line was said by R. Yehoshua. It is R. Yehoshua who tries, unsucessfuly, to convince R. Dosa to concede to Rabban Gamaliel's decision. According to this reading, however, we would expect R. Yehoshua to use R. Akiba's argument, which addresses the specific issue at hand, rather than invent a broad argument. If R. Yehoshua knew this broad argument beforehand then he should not have opposed Rabban Gamaliel in the first place. If he did not know it and did not learn it from R. Akiba, then what inspired him to think of it now? On the other hand, it is R. Yehoshua who approaches R. Dosa, which suggests that R. Yehoshua now had something to contribute. Perhaps R. Yehoshua had internalized and extended R. Akiba's argument to the point that he was ready to challenge his original position that he learned from R. Dosa. In addition, the transition to R. Yehoshua as the subject of the next sentence, "He took his staff," without repeating his name suggests that R. Yehoshua was also the subject of the verb "said" in the previous sentence. See also David Henshke, "R. Joshua's Acceptance of the Authority of Rabban Gamaliel II: A Study of Two Versions of the Same Event," *Tarbiz* 76, nos. 1–2 (2007): 81–98, who argues that the first argument was also said by R. Yehoshua and that R. Akiba's name did not appear in the original Mishnah.

The Bavli *baraita* includes a more detailed conversation between R. Yehoshua and R. Akiba about the suffering of the former on account of Rabban Gamaliel's pronouncement. R. Yehoshua's statement that he would rather be sick for one year than be subject to such an injunction causes the audience to sympathize with R. Yehoshua's plight. The *baraita* also utilizes a different midrash to extrapolate that the court's calendrical rulings are binding even when wrong. The Mishnah derives from the words "*you shall proclaim*" that the holidays are declared holy on whatever day the court proclaims, "whether they are at their [correct] times or whether they are not at their [correct] times." The *baraita,* however, derives from the revocalization of the thrice repeated word אתם that the court's decision is binding whether the court declares the wrong date inadvertently, deliberately, or in error. Only the Bavli *baraita* includes "deliberately," which may be a subtle criticism of Rabban Gamaliel's actions.[71] Based on these and other differences between the Mishnah and Bavli *baraita,* David Henshke concludes:

> The author of the Baraita wanted to paint Rabban Gamaliel—and as a consequence the patriarchate in general—in a manner very different from that painted in the Mishnah. [In the *baraita,*] the opposition of R. Yehoshua was palpable; the patriarch was severe and cruel and was not necessarily correct.[72]

Henshke goes on to attribute the reason for the positive view of Rabban Gamaliel in the Mishnah to R. Yehudah ha-Nasi's role in editing that work and seeking to protect the reputation of his lineage. He further speculates that the *baraita* derives from an anti-establishment group of Akiban students. I suggest, rather, that the Bavli's version reflects a general tendency in the Bavli to denounce halakhic intolerance,[73] especially on the part of Rabban Gamaliel.[74] Significantly, *b. Ber.* 27b includes this event as one of the reasons cited by the crowd to depose Rabban Gamaliel, as we will see below. The Yerushalmi, which cites only a couple of lines of this *baraita,* is indeterminate on this matter.

Controversy over the right to set the calendar plays out again in the following generation between Rabban Gamaliel's grandson, Rabbi (not named in the Bavli), and R. Yehoshua's nephew, Ḥananiah (or Ḥanina

---

71. "Deliberately" is also not found in the parallel Sifra, *'Emor, parasha* 9, *perek* 10:3. See further at Henshke, "R. Joshua's Acceptance," 95. Cf. *m. Hor.* 1:4.

72. Henshke, "R. Joshua's Acceptance," 97.

73. The differences in the Bavli *baraita* may be due to modification of the *baraita* in Babylonia. However, even if the *baraita* is authentically Palestinian, it still seems significant that it was preserved and recorded only in the Bavli.

74. See further below on the deposition of Rabban Gamaliel and on standardizing the liturgy.

in the Bavli).[75] The story appears in both the Yerushalmi and the Bavli.[76] According to both versions, Ḥananiah attempts to intercalate the year in Babylonia, and Rabbi uses a carefully planned and forceful strategy to stop Ḥananiah from doing so. Rabbi sends messengers who feign friendly motives in order to receive public honor from Ḥananiah, which they can later use against him. The messengers tell Ḥananiah that his actions are equivalent to opening a competing Temple to that in Jerusalem and (in the Bavli) separating themselves from Israel. In the Yerushalmi version, the messengers insert errors into their Bible readings in the synagogue in order to mock Ḥananiah. In the Bavli version, the messengers threaten Ḥaninah with excommunication if he does not desist, and they contradict each ruling of Ḥaninah by permitting whatever Ḥaninah prohibited in order to embarrass him.[77] The Stammaitic comment immediately following this story in the Bavli intimates a point of criticism of the messengers' tactics:

> בשלמא הוא מטהר והם מטמאין לחומרא, אלא הוא מטמא והם מטהרין, היכי הוי? והא תניא: **חכם שטמא אין חברו רשאי לטהר, אסר אין חברו רשאי להתיר?**[78] קסברי: כי היכי דלא נגררו בתריה.
>
> It is well if he [Ḥaninah] declares pure and they [the visitors] declare impure [since they are] more stringent. But if he declares impure and they declare pure, how can this be? Have we not learned: **If a sage declares impure, his colleague may not declare pure; if he prohibited, his colleague may not permit?**[78] They reasoned that [it was justified] so that they [the Jews in Babylonia] would not be drawn after him.[79]

The Stam questions how the messengers could permit what their colleague had already prohibited. They explain that the messengers reasoned that such controversial behavior was justified in order to discourage the masses from following Ḥaninah. The Bavli thus seems to justify

75. *B. Nid.* 24b reports a dispute between Ḥanina and Rabban Gamaliel II on a different issue.

76. *Y. Sanh.* 1:2 (19a) and *b. Ber.* 63a-b. See the original texts in chart 5.2 below, p. 283.

77. For more on this and other differences between the Yerushalmi and the Bavli versions, see Rubenstein, *Culture*, 24–25, 82–83, and 160–61; and Aharon Oppenheimer, "The Attempt of Hananiah, Son of Rabbi Joshua's Brother, to Intercalate the Year in Babylonia: A Comparison of the Traditions in the Jerusalem and Babylonian Talmuds," in *The Talmud Yerushalmi and Graeco-Roman Culture II*, ed. Peter Schafer and Catherine Hezser (Tübingen: Mohr Siebeck, 1998), 255–64.

78. *T. ʿEd.* 1:5 and see parallels above, p. 134 n. 26.

79. *B. Ber.* 63b.

these extreme polemical tactics but not without first noting a potential condemnation of them.[80]

Compare this with the ending of the Yerushalmi *sugya* wherein Ḥananiah, after consulting with R. Yehudah b. Betera, rides on a horse to inform his constituents in Babylonia of his changed ruling. The Yerushalmi adds: "Those [places] he reached, he reached [and informed them to follow the Palestinian authorities]. Those places he did not reach observe a corrupt [calendar]."[81] While the Bavli makes no explicit indication of whether Ḥananiah acquiesced, the Yerushalmi has him riding on a horse to inform everyone of his error. The Yerushalmi adds a further rather extreme formulation that those who did not hear of Ḥananiah's ruling practiced in error. The Yerushalmi thus completely negates Ḥananiah's previous calendar without compromise even *post factum*.

Another contrast between the two Talmuds is found in Ḥananiah's citation/consultation of elder authorities in each story. In the Yerushalmi, Ḥananiah consults R. Yehudah b. Betera, who affirms the supremacy of the patriarchal authority. The Bavli, on the other hand, omits this scene and instead has Ḥananiah recall R. Akiba intercalating the calendar in Babylonia (*m. Yebam.* 16:7), thus offering a precedent for extra-patriarchal authority.

Thus, the Yerushalmi deems Ḥananiah's calendar completely invalid, portrays Ḥananiah's retraction as absolute, and gives no hint of criticism of the Palestinians. The Bavli, by contrast, does not mention Ḥaninah's retraction but does offer potential criticism of the Palestinian messengers and cites a precedent for intercalation in Babylonia. One could explain the different portrayals in the two Talmuds based simply on geographical bias and power struggle; the Yerushalmi completely denigrates the Babylonian position and dishonors its leader, while the Bavli, though largely agreeing that calendrical power must be centralized in Palestine, nevertheless shows discomfort with the Palestinian political maneuvering. In light of the thesis of this book, however, one could suggest another explanation for the differences between the two Talmudic tellings of this story. Perhaps the Yerushalmi portrays Ḥananiah's rulings and retraction so starkly because its redactors demanded uniformity of practice in all areas of halakha, and especially regarding the calendar. The Bavli, on the other hand, while agreeing that uniformity of practice is important, especially regarding the calendar, nevertheless also takes into consideration other values

80. Even the Stam's response is presented only as the reasoning of the messengers (קסברי), which may indicate that the Stam itself did not necessarily agree with that assessment. Still, that the *sugya* ends on this note does point toward an overall, but perhaps qualified, endorsement of the messenger's actions.

81. *Y. Sanh.* 1:2 (19a). Translation from Jeffrey Rubenstein, *Rabbinic Stories* (New York: Paulist, 2002), 91.

that have the potential to trump the value of uniformity. In this case, uniformity comes at the expense of collegiality (the visitors' subversive intent), respect for local authority (contradicting Ḥaninah's prior rulings), and truth (offering false rulings).

In sum, diversity of practice in matters pertaining to the calendar can be particularly dangerous to the unity and stability of a community. If one rabbi and his followers perform some action on Shabbat in the privacy of their homes and other rabbis declare it prohibited, the social ramifications are minimal. If, however, one group celebrates a holiday on a day different from the date accepted by others, then the potential for creating factionalism is great.[82] The Mishnah, Yerushalmi, and, perhaps to a lesser extent, the Bavli all seem to agree on the need to use forceful tactics in order to impose uniformity regarding the calendar.

Deposition of Rabban Gamaliel

Rabban Gamaliel is said to have used (or abused) his power to impose unity on his colleagues in other matters as well. Much has been written about the story of Rabban Gamaliel's deposition told in *y. Ber.* 4:1, 7c-d (= *y. Taʿan.* 4:1, 67d), and *b. Ber.* 27b-28a. (See the text in chart 5.3 below, p. 287.) We will here focus only on what the two versions of this story might reveal about the attitude of the Yerushalmi and Bavli toward multiplicity of practice.

The trigger of this story is a controversy between Rabban Gamaliel and R. Yehoshua concerning whether the *arvit* prayer is mandatory or optional. A student asks both sages for their halakhic opinions about this matter and informs Rabban Gamaliel that R. Yehoshua disagrees with him. Rabban Gamaliel thereupon challenges R. Yehoshua in a public session. R. Yehoshua lies about his own opinion but is unsuccessful at hiding his dissent, and Rabban Gamaliel forces R. Yehoshua to stand during his lecture, causing him great embarrassment. The crowd cannot tolerate Rabban Gamaliel's heavy-handed leadership and decides to depose him. They see this incident as the last straw in a pattern of behavior.

The two Talmuds describe this pattern in slightly different terms. The Yerushalmi [D] quotes the crowd's complaint: ועמדו כל העם על רגליהם ואמרו לו כי על מי לא עברה רעתך תמיד—"All the people[83] stood on their feet and said to him [Rabban Gamaliel], '*Who has not suffered from your constant malice?*'"[84] In the Yerushalmi, Rabban Gamaliel is accused of mistreating all of the

82. See above, p. 33.

83. On the phrase "all the people" as a reference to the sages, see Miller, *Sages and Commoners*, 242–44.

84. A quote from Nah 3:19, which refers to the evils committed by Assyria.

rabbis, and indeed he is only restored after he apologizes to all of them. The Bavli, on the other hand, specifies three specific instances of dispute over halakhic practice in which Rabban Gamaliel caused distress to R. Yehoshua. Devora Steinmetz sees this as just one instance of a larger difference between the two versions of this narrative:

> Although the [Palestinian] narrative begins with a legal dispute between R. Gamaliel and R. Yehoshua, that dispute is not the reason for the patriarch's deposition. In the BT, the people recognize a pattern of R. Gamaliel in conflict with R. Yehoshua over legal questions, but here [in the PT] they accuse the patriarch of mistreating everyone, and, indeed, R. Gamaliel later goes to apologize to all of the rabbis.[85]

Another striking difference between the versions is found in the controversy over the number of benches in the study house. The Yerushalmi quotes two opinions about whether there were eighty or three hundred benches there, noting that this does not include those "standing beyond the fence." It is not readily apparent why this dispute is mentioned here. H. Shapira suggests that it is a later addition, perhaps based on the Bavli.[86] It may, however, serve some literary function in this narrative. First, it introduces the *baraita* about R. Eleazar ben Azariah teaching at "the vineyard in Yavneh," which is explained as referring to the benches set up in rows like a vineyard. Second, it emphasizes how great R. Yehoshua's embarrassment was and how monumental was the scene of booing down Rabban Gamaliel, which happened in front of so many sages.

In the Bavli, this tradition is completely transformed. Rather than a dispute about how many benches were already in the study house, the Bavli discusses how many benches were added after Rabban Gamaliel was deposed. Rabban Gamaliel's exclusionary policy included placing a guard at the door to limit entrance. The Bavli continues to report that as a result of the influx of sages in the study house on that day, "there was not a single law pending in the academy that they did not resolve." Thus, the Bavli makes the claim that an inclusive policy that allows for all to participate in the debate is a positive value and leads to better understanding of Torah.

In the same vein, Rubenstein points out a difference between the two Talmuds regarding the criteria for choosing R. Eleazar as a replacement:

> In the Yerushalmi R. Eleazar is appointed on the basis of his ancestry, that he is tenth generation in descent from Ezra. R. Akiba observes that

85. Devora Steinmetz, "Must the Patriarch Know *`Uqtzin?*: The *Nasi* as Scholar in Babylonian *Aggada*," *AJS Review* 23 (1998): 178.

86. Hayyim Shapira, "The Deposition of Rabban Gamaliel—Between History and Legend," *Zion* 64 (1999): 7 n. 8 (Hebrew).

> R. Eleazar knows less Torah than he but is "more a descendant of great men." The Bavli attributes R. Eleazar's selection to a combination of wisdom, wealth, and ancestry. Significantly, the type of wisdom required for a position of leadership is dialectical skill, R. Eleazar's ability to solve objections. Note again that academic status is contingent on skill in debate.[87]

Perhaps the most important difference between the two versions of this narrative is the process by which Rabban Gamaliel regains his position. In the Yerushalmi, Rabban Gamaliel "immediately" goes to each and every sage's house to apologize, including that of R. Yehoshua, who castigates him for not being aware of the hardships faced by his adherents. The sages forgive him and fully restore his position, demoting R. Eleazar ben Azariah to a secondary position.

In the Bavli, by contrast, Rabban Gamaliel must go through a complete transformation of character to become more accepting of others and to better appreciate the value of debate. First, Rabban Gamaliel himself, on seeing the added participation in the study house, is said to regret his exclusionary policy. He is falsely reassured in a dream that he acted properly; but this is just a temporary comfort to assuage his guilt. Next comes the real test of Rabban Gamaliel's repentance. An Ammonite proselyte asks the sages whether he may marry into the Jewish nation; Rabban Gamaliel says no but R. Yehoshua says yes. So far this situation is similar to that which triggered the deposition in the first place. Rabban Gamaliel, however, is no longer able to wield his authority to silence R. Yehoshua but is now forced to engage in an honest debate. R. Yehoshua wins out, and the Ammonite is permitted to marry.[88] It is only at this point that Rabban Gamaliel recognizes his error and proceeds to apologize to R. Yehoshua. Paradoxically, and perhaps this is the point of this entire narrative, Rabban Gamaliel's heavy-handed demand for uniformity and stifling of debate in the opening scene ends up causing great conflict, while tolerance for free debate results in solving problems and coming to an agreement.

Unlike in the Yerushalmi, where R. Eleazar is demoted in order for Rabban Gamaliel to regain his position, in the Bavli, Rabban Gamaliel is forced to share his seat of power with R. Eleazar ben Azariah. Steinmetz explains: "The conclusion of the Babylonian narrative ensures that multiple voices will be heard in this *beth midrash;* the division of teach-

---

87. Rubenstein, "Thematization," 79.

88. Of course, the Bavli did not compose this story anew but rather copied it from *m. Yad.* 4:4. The most immediate connection to this context is that the Mishnah begins with בו ביום. Nevertheless, the decision by the Bavli editor to include any source here and to choose this tradition over others that begin with בו ביום should encourage us to find a more substantial connection between the Mishnah and the larger story.

ing duties institutionalizes the values of the new leadership, assuring that never again will R. Gamaliel's voice silence other scholars from voicing their halakhic positions or their Torah interpretations."[89] Steinmetz summarizes the values promoted by the Bavli:

> The [Babylonian] Berachot narrative argues forcefully for the power of free debate. The patriarch, here, is not taken to task for ignorance; he is taken to task for behavior which limits the growth and free expression of ideas. The first glimpse which we are given of the *bet midrash* shows R. Yehoshua lying about his point of view concerning a question of halakha. R. Gamaliel has not only closed the doors in the face of potential students, he has closed the doors in the face of honest debate. The BT, which so clearly values both the process and the products of unfettered debate, disposes of the patriarch who rejects this value. R. Gamaliel can return only when he recognizes the value of debate, and he returns on the *bet midrash*'s new terms: not only are potential students allowed access to torah, not only does debate continue freely until resolution is reached, but the very arrangement at the narrative's conclusion—the division of teaching responsibilities between R. Gamaliel and R. Eleazar b. Azariah—guarantees that never again will a single voice dominate the *bet midrash*.[90]

In this narrative, tolerance for open debate and multiple opinions go hand in hand with tolerance for differing halakhic decisions and diversity of halakhic practice. Rabban Gamaliel, who bars sages from the debate in the study house, also demands that R. Yehoshua conform to his halakhic decisions. In the end, Rabban Gamaliel learns his lesson regarding both issues. He learns to appreciate the value of including many opinions in the debate of the study house. He also accepts that someone else's halakhic decision may be based on better proofs than his own; he is, therefore, required to allow others to teach from his pulpit rather than silence them, as he had done previously.

In sum, the Yerushalmi story addresses political power and the relationship between the patriarch and the rabbis. While it is a halakhic debate that sparks the deposition, debate itself is not the central issue. The Bavli, on the other hand, focuses the narrative on the value of debate, inclusiveness of multiple opinions, and the right of an individual rabbi to dissent. Although much of the Bavli narrative concentrates on debate and diversity of opinion, the opening scene suggests that diversity of practice is also being addressed. The Bavli version thus reflects a positive view of halakhic pluralism on the part of the Bavli narrators.

---

89. Steinmetz, "Must the Patriarch," 181.
90. Ibid., 188–89.

Standardizing Liturgy

Rabban Gamaliel is also portrayed as a unifying force regarding the daily liturgy of the *Eighteen Blessings*. Barry Freundel sees Rabban Gamaliel's push to make *arbit* mandatory, as seen above, as just one part of his larger agenda to suppress spontaneous individual prayer in favor of standardized public liturgy.[91] In *m. Ber.* 4:3, Rabban Gamaliel states that "every day one must pray eighteen [blessings]." Other Tannaim, including R. Yehoshua, R. Akiba, and R. Eliezer, resist Rabban Gamaliel's decree.[92] The *Eighteen Blessings* became the standard daily prayer in Palestine during the Amoraic period while rabbis in Babylonia resisted the standardization of liturgy in favor of spontaneous prayer.[93] Freundel concludes as follows:

> As we approach the end of the Mishnaic period, Rabban Gamaliel's "eighteen" appears to win broad approval as mandated personal prayer in Palestine. In the Amoraic period we never again find a Palestinian source that opposes daily recitation of the "Eighteen".... Just the opposite is true in Babylonia. Through the first three Amoraic generations, all the evidence points to universal rejection of the *Shmoneh `Esrei* as daily mandated personal prayer in that community except on special occasions such as the New Moon and fast days. Babylonia seems unwilling to accept Rabban Gamaliel's authority in this matter and from even later in the Amoraic period we hear of continued resentment.... Down to at least the sixth Amoraic generation, opposition remains to this practice in Babylonia.[94]

Freundel's analysis of the development of the *Eighteen Blessings* confirms our own findings regarding the role of Rabban Gamaliel as a unifying force as well as the difference between Palestinian and Babylonian reactions to Rabban Gamaliel. Palestinian rabbis accept the unified liturgy proposed by Rabban Gamaliel while Babylonian rabbis prefer the diversity of liturgy that sprouts forth from spontaneous prayer.[95]

---

91. Barry Freundel, "Formalization of Individual Prayer Around the Shmoneh `Esrei in the Talmudic Period, Patterns of Acceptance, Rejection and Modification" (Ph.D. diss., Baltimore Hebrew University, 2004), 108–13

92. Ibid., 113–37

93. Ibid., 146f.

94. Ibid., 237–38

95. Freundel's methodology, however, is different than that used throughout this book. Freundel distinguishes between statements of Palestinian and Babylonian sages regardless of whether they appear in the Yerushalmi or the Bavli. He even looks to the biography of each sage taking into account where they studied and where they traveled. Accordingly, Rav, although a Babylonian, reflects some Palestinian tendencies on account of his having studied there. My own methodology is to focus on where a statement appears and to place less emphasis on who said it. See pp. 36–39.

Akavia ben Mahalalel and *Mishnah ʿEduyyot*

Another prominent rabbinic dissident is Akavia ben Mahalalel. The story of his disagreement with the sages and subsequent excommunication in *m. ʿEd.* 5:6–7 must be read in context of the entire tractate of *ʿEduyyot*. Anthony Saldarini and Devora Steinmetz have convincingly shown that the Akavia narrative is strategically placed within *m. ʿEd.* by its redactor as part of a larger effort to establish uniformity of practice based on majority rule.[96] This effort is evident already in the first chapter, beginning with *m. ʿEd.* 1:5–6 (cf. *t. ʿEd.* 1:4):

> ולמה מזכירין את דברי יחיד בין המרובין הואיל ואין הלכה אלא כדברי המרובין שאם יראה בית דין את דברי היחיד ויסמוך עליו...
> אמר רבי יהודה אם כן למה מזכירין דברי היחיד בין המרובין לבטלן שאם יאמר האדם כך אני מקובל יאמרו לו כדברי איש פלוני שמעת:
> Why do they [Tannaitic traditions] mention the words of the individual within the majority considering that halakha only follows the majority? So that if a [future] court agrees with the words of the individual it can rely on him. . . .
> R. Yehudah said: If so, why do they mention the words of the individual within the majority [who will] nullify them [the words of the individual]? So if someone should say, "Such have I received," they will tell him, "You heard according to the words of so-and-so [who is an individual and so your tradition is not significant]."[97]

This text makes it clear that only one opinion, that of the majority, is viable for halakhic practice. The dispute here concerns whether the prior majority can ever be overturned in favor of the minority opinion; but all agree that only one opinion can be legitimate at any given time. The narrative about Akavia ben Mahalalel in *m. ʿEd.* 5:6–7, which is found near the center of the tractate, then comes to exemplify the principle of majority rule and show the consequences of violating it:

> עקביא בן מהללאל העיד ארבעה דברים אמרו לו עקביא חזור בך בארבעה דברים שהיית אומר ונעשך אב בית דין לישראל אמר להן מוטב לי להקרא שוטה כל ימי ולא ליעשות שעה אחת רשע לפני המקום שלא יהיו אומרים בשביל שררה חזר בו.
> ...ונדוהו ומת בנדויו וסקלו בית דין את ארונו...

96. On the structure of the tractate and the placement of the Akavia story within it, see Anthony J. Saldarini, "The Adoption of a Dissident: Akabya ben Mehalalel in Rabbinic Tradition," *Journal of Jewish Studies* 33 (1982): 549; and Steinmetz, "Distancing and Bringing Near," 51–68.

97. Text follows ms. Kaufmann. See the discussion of this text in Halbertal, *People of the Book*, 51–52; and Fraade, "Rabbinic Polysemy," 19–21.

> בשעת מיתתו אמר לבנו בני חזור בך בארבעה דברים שהייתי אומר אמר לו ולמה לא חזרת בך אמר לו אני שמעתי מפי המרובים והם שמעו מפי המרובים אני עמדתי בשמועתי והם עמדו בשמועתן אבל אתה שמעת מפי היחיד ומפי המרובין מוטב להניח דברי היחיד ולאחוז בדברי המרובין.
>
> Akavia ben Mahalalel testified to four opinions. They said to him, "Akavia, retract those four opinions that you have said and we will make you *'av beth din leYisrael* (the chief of the court of Israel)." He responded, "Better that I be called a fool all my life and not become wicked for even a moment before God; let it not be said that I retracted for the sake of attaining an office."
>
> ...They excommunicated him and he died in the state of excommunication and the court stoned his coffin....
>
> In the hour of his death, [Akavia] said to his son: "My son, retract the four opinions that I used to say." He answered: "Why did you not retract yourself?" He responded: "I heard [my view] from the majority and they heard [their views] from the majority. I stood firm in the tradition I heard and they stood firm in the tradition they heard. But you have heard from an individual and from the majority. It is better to let go of the opinions of the individual and hold on to the opinions of the majority."[98]

It is evident from this narrative that these disputes were not just theoretical but that Akavia ruled in practice according to his opinions.[99] The first consequence of his nonconformity is that he is prevented from attaining a prestigious appointment. He is subsequently excommunicated for life because of his refusal to conform.[100]

The last paragraph further concretizes the principle of majority rule by quoting Akavia himself as he instructs his son to follow the majority. He reveals that the only reason he dissented from the current majority was because he followed the majority of the previous generation; thus, ironically, his current dissent actually supports the principle of majority rule. Saldarini summarizes the argument of this text: "The editors of the Mishnah used Akavia for their own purposes and tightly control the presentation of traditions concerning him. They are concerned with uniting

---

98. Translation adapted from Saldarini, "Adoption of a Dissident," 548–49.

99. When listing the four issues under dispute (not cited here), the Mishnah uses language that describes actual rulings: "He used to declare impure...."

100. Both Talmuds explain that Akavia was excommunicated for showing disrespect to Shemaiah and Abṭalyon by doubting that they used authentic *soṭah* waters; see *y. Moʿed Qaṭ.* 3:1 (81d) and *b. Ber.* 19a. However, the four cases of disagreement should probably be read parenthetically; see the structure used in the translation by Rubenstein, *Rabbinic Stories*, 69; and see Steinmetz, "Distancing and Bringing Near," 53 n. 15. Even according to the Talmudic interpretation, Akavia's dissent must have been a contributing factor in his excommunication.

dissident views into a working and harmonious whole and with establishing proper authority to maintain law."[101] The little discussion in the Yerushalmi about this story is repeated in the Bavli,[102] and so these sources are not useful for ascertaining the Talmuds' view on the matter.

The negative attitude toward pluralism of practice found in the Akavia narrative and in *m. ʿEd.* 1:5–6 can also be detected in *m. ʿEd.* 8:7, which states that according to R. Shimon, Elijah will come at the end of days in order to "resolve controversy."[103] This goal is also cited in *t. ʿEd.* 1:1, which introduces this tractate as an attempt at Yavneh to preserve the Torah.[104] The fear is not only that Torah will be lost but that the proliferation of controversy will become unmanageable until a day comes when one will search for Torah and find that "not one word of Torah resembles another."[105] These statements share a negative view of controversy, which would ideally not exist. Although this tractate records many controversies, they ideally should be resolved and certainly must not lead to diversity of practice. Taken together, the paragraphs cited above demonstrate a concerted push for uniformity of practice and intolerance for dissent by the redactors of tractate *ʿEduyyot*.[106]

R. Eliezer ben Hyrcanus—Oven of Akhnai

Another dissident rabbi is R. Eliezer ben Hyrcanus, who disagreed with his colleagues regarding the purity of a coiled oven and issued practical rulings in accordance with his own opinion. *T. ʿEduyyot* 2:1 mentions only that "controversy multiplied in Israel" on account of the dispute over this oven, but does not give any further details. Both Talmuds fill in the story. The story about the oven of Akhnai has been analyzed too many times to require a fresh analysis here.[107] I will thus focus only those points

---

101. Saldarini, "Adoption of a Dissident," 551.

102. See above, n. 100. Akavia is also mentioned in *b. Sanh.* 88a in context of the rebellious elder; see below, p. 324.

103. See further in Steinmetz, "Distancing and Bringing Near," 58–68.

104. Jeremy Wieder, "Mishnah Eduyot: A Literary History of a Unique Tractate" (Ph.D. diss., New York University Press, 2005), 4–5.

105. Cf. *Sifre Deut., pisqa* 48 (ed. Finkelstein, 113); *b. Šabb.* 138b-139a; and see further at Naeh, "Structures," 583–85; and Steinmetz, "Distancing and Bringing Near," 64–65 nn. 40, 43, and 44.

106. This may not be true of the entire Mishnaic corpus. See the discussion of *m. Yebam.* 1:4 above, pp. 189–90.

107. See references at Rubenstein, *Talmudic Stories*, 314–15 nn. 1–3. Other recent treatments include Fisch, *Rational Rabbis*, 78–88; Boyarin, *Border Lines*, 168–74; Steinmetz, "Agada Unbound," 311–37; and Michael Novick, "A Lot of Learning Is a Dangerous Thing: On the Structure of Rabbinic Expertise in the Bavli," *HUCA* 78 (2007): 91–107.

in each story that shed light on the attitude toward diversity of practice reflected in each Talmud.

According to both the Yerushalmi (*y. Moᶜed Qaṭ.* 3:1, 81c-d) and the Bavli (*b. B. Meṣᶜia* 59a-b) versions of the story, R. Eliezer is excommunicated by his colleagues. However, each version makes a very different comment about the justification of the ban. The Yerushalmi narrative is set within a series of stories about people being banned for various reasons. R. Eliezer is banned for refusing to submit to the majority, and the Yerushalmi gives no indication that his punishment was undeserved.

The Bavli narrative, on the other hand, is set within a larger discussion of wrongdoing with words. In this context, the oven of Akhnai story presents an example of a sage, R. Eliezer, being wrongfully treated by his colleagues. The Bavli introduces Rabban Gamaliel into the narrative as the party responsible for the harsh treatment of R. Eliezer. It seems that Rabban Gamaliel is typecasted for this role because of his reputation in the narratives discussed above as one who forces unity by quashing debate.[108] Rabban Gamaliel is able to temporarily stave off punishment by announcing, "Master of the world, it is revealed and known to you that I acted not for my honor, nor did I act for the honor of my father's house, but I acted for your honor in order that disagreements do not multiply in Israel." However, this claim of pure intentions ultimately proves insufficient, and Rabban Gamaliel dies after R. Eliezer cries out in anguish. The narrative ends with a statement already quoted in the earlier discussion regarding the severity of verbal wrongdoing, "All the gates have been locked except for the gate of [grievances caused by] wrongdoing." The Bavli does not defend R. Eliezer's dissent and fully upholds the principle of majority rule even in the face of a heavenly voice. Nevertheless, the Bavli does call for greater tolerance in the way dissent is handled.[109]

---

108. This explanation for the choice of Rabban Gamaliel is proposed by Steinmetz, "Agada Unbound," 321f.

109. This reading of the Bavli story follows Rubenstein, *Talmudic Stories*, 34–63, and the first explanation of Steinmetz, "Agada Unbound," 324–26. According to this interpretation, the Bavli story is doubly anti-authoritarian: the rabbis "defeat" the authority of God's own ruling, and the rabbis, in turn, are criticized for their jurispathic exclusion of a minority interpretation. See further in Stone, "Pursuit," 857–58.

Rubenstein, *Talmudic Stories*, 64–102, also compares the Yerushalmi and Bavli treatments of Elisha ben Abuya, the sinning sage. Elisha does not fit into the topic of this chapter since he did not follow an alternate interpretation of halakha but rather violated halakha explicitly. Nevertheless, it is interesting to note that the Yerushalmi portrays Elisha ben Abuya in a very negative light on account of his apostasy while the Bavli version is somewhat more sympathetic. Further research is needed to see if the Bavli is generally more tolerant than the Yerushalmi of halakhic violation and apostasy. The results of that research could shed light on the Bavli's greater tolerance for halakhic diversity, i.e., the Bavli may have had not only a different conception of the halakhic system but also a general attitude of political tolerance even for that which is completely wrong.

Ya'aqov of Kefar Nevoraia

All of the dissidents discussed above were Tannaim. However, one Amoraic figure stands out for his radical halakhic views. The teachings of Yaʿaqov of Kefar Nevoraia are discussed in *Genesis Rabbah, parashah* 7:[110]

[A] יעקב איש כפר נבוריה הורה בצור דגים טעונים שחיטה
שמע ר׳ חגי אמר ליה תא לקי
אמר ליה בר נש דאמר מילה דאוריתא לקי אתמהא
אמר ליה מניין היא אוריתא
אמר ליה דכתיב ישרצו המים שרץ נפש חיה ועוף יעופף וגו׳[111] מה העוף טעון שחיטה אף דגים טעונין שחיטה
אמר ליה לא הורית טבות
אמר ליה ומן הן את מודע לי
אמר ליה רביע לך ואנא מודע לך
אמר ליה כתיב הצאן ובקר ישחט להם וגו׳ [אם את כל דגי הים יאסף.[112] ישחט אין כתיב כאן אלא יאסף]
אמר ליה רציף ליה דהיא טבא בגלעה.
[B] יעקב איש כפר נבוריה הורה בצור מותר למול בנה שלנכרית בשבת
שמע רב חגאי אמר ליה איתא לקי
אמר ליה מן מר מילי אוריה לקי אתמהא, ומהו אוריא, אמר ליה דכתיב ויתילדו על משפחותם לבית אבותם[113]
אמר ליה לא הורית טבות
אמר ליה ומן הן את מודע לי
אמר ליה רביע לך ואנא מודע לך, אמר ליה כתיב ועתה נכרות ברית לאלהינו להוציא כל נשים והנולד מהם וגו׳[114]
אמר לו ומן הקבלה אתה מלקני אתמהא
[אמר ליה וכתורה יעשה][115]
אמר ליה רצוף ריצפך דהיא טבא באולפנא.

[A] Yaakob of Kefar Nevoraia issued a ruling in Tyre that fish require slaughtering [in order to be eaten]. R. Ḥaggai heard this; he told him [Yaʿaqov], "Come and receive lashes." He [Yaʿaqov] responded in astonishment, "Someone who utters a word of Torah receives lashes!" He [R. Ḥaggai] told him, "Where is it in

110. Hanokh Albeck and Judah Theodor, *Midrash Bereshit Rabbah: Critical Edition with Notes and Commentary* (Jerusalem: Shalem Books, 1996), 1:50–52. The *sugya* is paralleled in *Pesiqta de-Rav Kahana, Parah 'adumah, pisqa* 4:3, (ed. Mandelbaum, 1:64). Part B is paralleled in *y. Yebam.* 2:6 (4a) and *y. Qidd.* 3:12 (64a) (and cf. *y. Šabb.* 19:5 (17b) noted above, pp. 199–200 n. 133). In the Yerushalmi version, Yaʿaqov only intends to rule leniently but changes his mind before issuing the ruling. For further discussion of Yaʿaqov of Kefar Nevoraia, see Ir-Shai, "Yaakov 'Ish Kefar Nevoraia," 153–66; Miller, *Sages and Commoners*, 192–95, 436–40, and passim; and Steven Fine, "A Cosmopolitan 'Student of the Sages': Jacob of Kefar Nevoraia in Rabbinic Literature," in *Maven in Blue Jeans: A Festschrift in Honor of Zev Garber*, ed. S. Jacobs (West Lafayette, IN: Purdue University, 2009), 35-43.

> the Torah?" He responded, "As it is written, *Let the waters bring forth swarms of living creatures and birds that fly....*[111] Just as the birds require slaughtering so too the fish require slaughtering." He [R. Ḥaggai] told him, "You have not ruled well." He responded, "From where can you prove this to me?" He told him, "Lie down [to receive lashes] and I will tell you." He [R. Ḥaggai] said to him, "It is written, *Could enough flocks and herds be slaughtered ... or could all the fish of the sea be gathered....*[112] It does not say 'slaughtered' [regarding fish] but rather 'gathered.'" He [Yaᶜaqov] said, "Lay it on me because it [your proof] is a good argument."
> [B] Yaᶜaqov of Kefar Nevoraia issued a ruling in Tyre that one is allowed to circumcise the son of a Gentile woman [and a Jewish man] on Shabbat. R. Ḥaggai heard this; he told him [Yaᶜaqov], "Come and receive lashes." He [Yaᶜaqov] responded in astonishment, "Someone who utters a word of Torah receives lashes!" What is [the verse from] the Torah? He [Yaᶜaqov] told him, "As it is written, *They were registered by their families according to the houses of their fathers.*"[113] He [R. Ḥaggai] told him, "You have not ruled well." He responded, "From where can you prove this to me?" He told him, "Lie down [to receive lashes] and I will tell you." He [R. Ḥaggai] said to him, "It is written, *Now then, let us make a covenant with our God to expel all these women and those who have been born to them....*"[114] He responded in astonishment, "Do you give me lashes based on the tradition [recorded in the Writings, not in the Pentateuch]!" He said, "*and let the Torah be obeyed.*"[115] He [Yaᶜaqov] said, "Lay on me your hammering because it [your proof] is a good teaching."

Yaᶜaqov of Kefar Nevoraia rules that fish require ritual slaughter[116] and that one may circumcise the son of a Jewish man and a Gentile woman on Shabbat, thus declaring that the child is Jewish. R. Ḥaggai subpoenas Yaᶜaqov to be whipped. A debate then ensues between them, each citing different prooftexts. At the end, Yaᶜaqov is convinced regarding both issues and willingly receives lashes. The punishment here is therefore jus-

---

111. Genesis 1:20. Compare the use of this verse in *b. Ḥul.* 27b.

112. Numbers 11:22.

113. Numbers 1:18.

114. Ezekiel 10:3.

115. Ibid.

116. A similar view is found in the Damascus Document (CD XII.13–14), which forbids the consumption of fish blood. See Ir-Shai, "Yaakov 'Ish Kefar Nevoraia," 164–65. It is not clear, however, whether the Dead Sea sect required ritual slaughter; see Fine, "Cosmopolitan," 42 n. 26, citing Louis Ginzberg, *An Unknown Jewish Sect* (New York: Jewish Theological Seminary of America, 1976), 79–80, 148, 346–47.

tified on account of Yaʿaqov having issued a mistaken ruling by his own admission. This is, therefore, not a case of halakhic multiplicity since even Yaʿaqov agrees in the end that his opinion is not valid. This text has no parallel in the Bavli, so it is difficult to assess its editorial intention. But even a literary reading of this text on its own makes it evident that these stories reflect a negative attitude toward minority opinions, at least toward such radical viewpoints as those of Yaʿaqov.[117] This Palestinian text reads as a warning against radical dissent; such dissidents deserve lashes even if they change their minds. Of course, without a Bavli parallel, one cannot say that this text reflects only a Palestinian point of view; the Bavli may very well have been just as intolerant of such extreme views.

Conclusion

Tannaitic sources record many instances of multiplicity of practice in which an individual rabbi opposes the majority opinion. In some instances, these dissidents are placed in a negative light, such as in stories about Akavia ben Mahalalel and Yaʿaqov of Kefar Nevoraia. But in other cases, their dissent is not commented on within the Tannaitic texts and seems to be acceptable, such as in the Rabban Gamaliel stories.

We have compared the Yerushalmi and Bavli treatments of these stories in an effort to extrapolate the Talmudic view of dissenting halakhic practice in general. In many instances, such analysis is not possible for one of three reasons: (1) the Talmuds do not comment on the Tannaitic sources (*t. Ber.* 4:15; *m. Roš Haš.* 2:8–9); (2) the two Talmuds have similar interpretations of the Tannaitic source (Akavia ben Mahalalel; *m. Pesaḥ.* 7:2; *m. Beṣah* 3:2); or (3) the story appears in only one of the Talmuds (Yaʿaqov of Kefar Nevoraia).

Fortunately, some of these stories are discussed in both Talmuds and are sources of fruitful analysis. Most significant is the extended discussion concerning *m. Ber.* 1:1 found at *y. Ber.* 1:1 (3a). This *sugya* directly addresses the subject of diversity of halakhic practice and concludes definitively that the Tannaim never practiced their own opinions against their colleagues. The problematic nature of that *sugya*'s proofs, as well as the implausibility of its conclusion, makes the *sugya* all the more significant because it reveals its redactors' ideology. According to this *sugya,* diverse practices are not to be tolerated and the possibility that individual Tannaim did practice against their colleagues must be interpreted away. A similar line

117. Miller, *Sages and Commoners*, 192–95, argues that the harsh treatment of Yaʿaqov was due to his provenance from a village. The rabbis from the cities guarded their exclusive authority to resolve matters of halakha.

of questioning against Rabban Gamaliel and other Tannaim is found in other Yerushalmi *sugyot* as well (*y. Pesaḥ.* 7:2 (34b); *y. ʿAbod. Zar.* 3:10 (43b); *y. Demai* 3:3 (23c); and *y. Beṣah* 3:2 [62a]) suggesting that this viewpoint is not localized to *y. Ber.* 1:1 (3a) but reflects the view of the Yerushalmi's redactors.

Rabban Gamaliel's authority to set the calendar seems to have been generally accepted. Strong tactics used by him and Rabbi to stop dissent are reported in the Mishnah and both Talmuds with little criticism. However, his attempts at forcing uniformity regarding laws of prayer and liturgy are considered highly problematic in the Bavli. This is seen in the Bavli's retelling of Rabban Gamaliel's deposition, where the focus on halakhic debate is more pronounced than in the Yerushalmi version, as well as in the Bavli's rejection of Rabban Gamaliel's standardization of liturgy, which is accepted in the Yerushalmi. Similarly, the Yerushalmi approvingly reports on the ban of R. Eliezer b. Hyrcanus for his dissenting practices, while the Bavli is sympathetic to R. Eliezer and introduces Rabban Gamaliel as the wrongdoer who deserves no less than death for his heavy-handed quashing of a dissident.

In this set of cases, the Bavli admits that there was diversity of practice among the Tannaim and criticizes attempts to force unity while the Yerushalmi denies many instances of diversity and praises attempts at unification. Assuming that the Talmuds portray the past to accord with their picture of an ideal halakhic society, the outcome of this analysis confirms the findings of other chapters in this study that the Bavli is more tolerant of diversity of halakhic practice than is the Yerushalmi. To be sure, neither Talmud takes an extreme position on this matter; the difference between them may only be relative, but it is still significant. The next two chapters turn from narrative sources to legal treatments of how to deal with dissenting practices.

Chart 5.1 Calendar controversy of Rabban Gamaliel. Text of *m. Roš Haš.* 2:8–9[118]

[A] Another time, two [witnesses] came and said, "We saw it at the appropriate time. But the following night it could not be seen"—and Rabban Gamaliel accepted them. R. Dosa b. Harkinas said, "They are false witnesses. How can one testify about a woman who gave birth, and the next day her belly is between her teeth?" R. Yehoshua said to him [Dosa]: "I see your words."	[A] ועוד באו שנים ואמרו ראינוהו בזמנו ובליל עבורו לא נראה וקבלן רבן גמליאל אמר רבי דוסא בן הרכינס עדי שקר הן היאך מעידים על האשה שילדה ולמחר כריסה בין שיניה אמר לו ר׳ יהושע רואה אני את דבריך.
[B] Rabban Gamaliel sent to him [R. Yehoshua], "I decree that you come to me with your staff and your money on the day on which Yom Kippur falls according to your [calendrical] reckoning."	[B] שלח לו רבן גמליאל גוזרני עליך שתבא אצלי במקלך ובמעותיך ביום הכפורים שחל להיות בחשבונך.
[C] R. Akiba went to him [R. Yehoshua] and found him in distress. He [Akiba] said to him, "I can demonstrate that every decision made by Rabban Gamaliel is valid. For it says, *These are the festivals of the Lord, the sacred occasions, that you shall declare* (Lev 23:4): whether at their proper times, whether not at their proper times, I have no festivals other than these ones [that *you* declare]."	[C] הלך ומצאו רבי עקיבא מיצר אמר לו יש לי ללמוד שכל מה שעשה רבן גמליאל עשוי שנאמר (ויקרא כג:ד) אלה מועדי ה׳ מקראי קודש אשר תקראו אתם בין בזמנן בין שלא בזמנן אין לי מועדות אלא אלו.
[D] He [R. Yehoshua] approached R. Dosa b. Harkinas. He [Dosa[118]] said to him, "If we go and question the [decisions of the court of Rabban Gamaliel, we should also question [the decisions] of every single court that existed from the time of Moses until now. For it says, *Moses, Aaron, Nadav, Avihu and seventy of the elders of Israel ascended* (Exod 24:9). Why were the names of the elders not specified? To teach that every group of three who stood as a court for Israel—behold, they are like the court of Moses."	[D] בא לו אצל רבי דוסא בן הרכינס אמר לו אם באין אנו לדון אחר בית דינו של רבן גמליאל צריכין אנו לדון אחר כל בית דין ובית דין שעמד מימות משה ועד עכשיו שנאמר (שמות כד:ט) ויעל משה ואהרן נדב ואביהוא ושבעים מזקני ישראל ולמה לא נתפרשו שמותן של זקנים אלא ללמד שכל שלשה ושלשה שעמדו בית דין על ישראל הרי הוא כבית דינו של משה.
[E] He [R. Yehoshua] took his staff and money in his hand, and he went to Yavneh to Rabban Gamaliel on the day that Yom Kippur fell according to his reckoning. Rabban Gamaliel stood up and kissed him on his head. He said to him, "Come in peace, my master and my student. My master in wisdom, and my student in that you accepted my words."	[E] נטל מקלו ומעותיו בידו והלך ליבנה אצל רבן גמליאל ביום שחל יום הכפורים להיות בחשבונו עמד רבן גמליאל ונשקו על ראשו אמר לו בוא בשלום רבי ותלמידי רבי בחכמה ותלמידי שקבלת דברי.

118. Translation from Rubenstein, *Rabbinic Stories*, 86-87, with slight modification.
119. See above, n. 70.

Chart 5.2 Calendar controversy in Babylonia. Comparison chart for *y. Sanh.* 1:2 (19a) from ms. Leiden (= *y. Ned.* 6:8, 40a) and *b. Ber.* 63a–b[120]

***b. Ber.* 63a-b**	***y. Sanh.* 1:2 (19a)**
אמר רב ספרא, רבי אבהו הוה משתעי: כשירד חנינא בן אחי רבי יהושע לגולה היה מעבר שנים וקובע חדשים בחוצה לארץ.	חנניה בן אחי רבי יהושע עיבר בחוצה לארץ
שגרו אחריו שני תלמידי חכמים רבי יוסי בן כיפר ובן בנו של זכריה בן קבוטל. כיון שראה אותם, אמר להם: למה באתם? אמרו ליה: ללמוד תורה באנו. הכריז [עליהם]: אנשים הללו גדולי הדור הם, ואבותיהם שמשו בבית המקדש, כאותה ששנינו: **זכריה בן קבוטל אומר: הרבה פעמים קריתי לפניו בספר דניאל** (משנה יומא א:ו).	שלח ליה רבי ג׳ איגרן גבי ר׳ יצחק ורבי נתן בחדא כתב לקדושת חנניה
התחיל הוא מטמא והם מטהרים, הוא אוסר והם מתירים. הכריז עליהם: אנשים הללו של שוא הם, של תהו הם. אמרו לו: כבר בנית ואי אתה יכול לסתור, כבר גדרת ואי אתה יכול לפרוץ.	
אמר להם: מפני מה אני מטמא ואתם מטהרים, אני אוסר ואתם מתירים? אמרו לו: מפני שאתה מעבר שנים וקובע חדשים בחוץ לארץ. אמר להם: והלא עקיבא בן יוסף היה מעבר שנים וקובע חדשים בחוץ לארץ? אמרו לו: הנח רבי עקיבא, שלא הניח כמותו בארץ ישראל. אמר להם: אף אני לא הנחתי כמותי בארץ ישראל.	
אמרו לו: גדיים שהנחת נעשו תישים בעלי קרנים, והם שגרונו אצלך. וכן אמרו לנו: לכו ואמרו לו בשמנו: אם שומע מוטב, ואם לאו יהא בנדוי. ואמרו לאחינו שבגולה: אם שומעין מוטב, ואם לאו יעלו להר, אחיה יבנה מזבח, חנניה ינגן בכנור, ויכפרו כולם ויאמרו: אין להם חלק באלהי ישראל. מיד געו כל העם בבכיה ואמרו: חס ושלום! יש לנו חלק באלהי ישראל.	וחדא כתב גדיים שהינחת נעשו תיישים ובחדא כתב אם אין את מקבל עליך צא לך למדבר האטד ותהי שוחט ונחוניון זורק
	קרא קדמייתא ואוקרון תנייתא ואוקרון תליתא בעא מבסרתהון אמרין ליה לית את יכיל דכבר אוקרתנין
וכל כך למה? משום שנאמר כי מציון תצא תורה ודבר ה׳ מירושלים.	קם רבי יצחק וקרא באורייתא אלה מועדי חנניה בן אחי רבי יהושע. אר׳ מועדי יי׳ (ויקרא כג:ד) אמר לון גבן קם רבי נתן ואשלים כי מבבל תצא תורה ודבר יי׳ מנהר פקוד אמרין ליה כי מציון תצא תורה ודבר יי׳ מירושלם (ישעיהו ב:ג) אמר לון גבן

120. Translation from Rubenstein, *Rabbinic Stories*, 90–92. The first and last lines of the Bavli are my translation. Boldface indicates a Tannaitic source.

	אזל קבל עליהון קמי רבי יהודה בן בתירה לנציבין אמר ליה אחריהם אחריהם א"ל לי נא ידע מה תמן מה מודע לי דאינון חכמין מחשבה דכוותי. מכיון דלא ידעי מחשבה דכוותיה ישמ־עון ליה. ומכיון דאינון חכמין מחשבה דכוותיה ישמע לון. קם ורכב סוסיא הן דמטא מטא והן דלא מטא נהגין בקילקול
בשלמא הוא מטהר והם מטמאין—לחומרא, אלא הוא מטמא והם מטהרין. היכי הוי? והא תניא: **חכם שטמא אין חברו רשאי לטהר, אסר—אין חברו רשאי להתיר**? קסברי: כי היכי דלא נגררו בתריה.	

b. Ber. 63a-b	*y. Sanh.* 1:2 (19a)
R. Safra said, R. Abbahu used to relate that when Ḥananiah the nephew of R. Yehoshua went down to the diaspora [Babylonia], he used to intercalate years and fix new moons outside of the Land [of Israel].	Ḥananiah the nephew of R. Yehoshua intercalated outside of the Land [of Israel].
They sent to him two scholars, R. Yose b. Kefar and the grandson of Zecharia b. Qevuṭal. When he saw them he said to them, "Why have you come?" They said to him, "We have come to study Torah." He announced concerning them, "These men are the luminaries of the generation, and their ancestors served in the Temple, as we learned, **Zecharia b. Qevuṭal said, "Many times I read to him [the high priest] from the Book of Daniel"** (*m. Yoma* 1:6).	Rabbi [Yehudah the Patriarch] sent three letters to him with R. Isaac and R. Natan. In one he wrote, "To his holiness Ḥananiah."
He began to rule impure and they ruled pure. He forbade and they permitted. He announced concerning them, "These men are fraudulent. [These men] are vacuous." They said to him, "You have already built and you cannot destroy. You have already fenced in and you cannot break apart."	

He said to them, "Why do I rule impure and you rule pure, I forbid and you permit?" They said to him, "Because you intercalate years and fix new moons outside of the Land [of Israel]." He said to them, "Did not Akiba b. Yosef intercalate years and fix new moons outside of the Land [of Israel]?" They said to him, "leave [the case of] R. Akiba, for he left behind no equal [in Torah] in the Land of Israel." He said to them, "I too left behind no equal in the Land of Israel."	
They said to him, "The kids you left have become goats with horns, and they sent us to you. They said to us thus: 'Go and speak to him in our name. If he listens—good. If not let him be under a ban. Speak also to our brethren in the diaspora. If they listen—good. If not, let them go up the mountain. Let Aḥia build an altar, let Ḥananiah play the lute, and let them all be heretics and say, "We have no share in the God of Israel."'" Immediately all the people broke out in weeping and said, "God forbid! We have a share in the God of Israel."	And in one he wrote, "The kids you left behind have become goats." And in one he wrote, "If you do not accept [that the intercalation must be done in the Land of Israel], then go out to the wilderness of Atad. You be the slaughterer [of sacrifices], and let Neḥunyon sprinkle [the blood on the altar]."
	He [Ḥananiah] read the first and honored them [R. Isaac and R. Natan]. He read the second and honored them. He read the third and wanted to dishonor them. They said to him, "You cannot, for you already honored us."

Why all this? Because it says *For Torah shall come forth from Zion, the word of God from Jerusalem* (Isa 2:3).	R. Isaac rose and read [in the Torah], "These are the set times of Ḥananiah the son of R. Yehoshua's brother." They [the people said to him, "[No! It says,] *The set times of the Lord* (Lev 23:4)." He said to them, "[That is the reading] with us [but apparently not with you]." R. Natan rose and read the *haftarah* [from the Prophets], "For Torah shall come forth from Babylonia and the word of God from Nehar Pekod." They said to him, "[No! It says,] *For Torah shall come forth from Zion, the word of God from Jerusalem* (Isa 2:3)." He said to him, "[That is the reading] with us [but apparently not with you]."
	He [Ḥananiah] went and complained about them to R. Yehudah b. Betera in Nisibis [a city in Babylonia]. He [R. Yehudah b. Betera] said to him, "[The calendar is set] according to them, according to them." He [Ḥananiah] said to him, "Do I not know what I left behind there? What assures me that they know how to calculate [the calendar] as [accurately] as I do?" [He said to him,] "And [just] because they do not know [how to calculate as accurately] as he [=you], will they listen to him? [But as it is,] because they do know how to calculate [as accurately] as he, he should listen to them." He arose and rode on his horse. Those [places] he reached, he reached [and informed them to follow the Palestinian authorities]. Those places he did not reach observe a corrupt [calendar].
It is well if he [Ḥananiah] declares pure and they [the visitors] declare impure [since they are] more stringent; But if he declares impure and they declare pure, how can this be? Have we not learned: **If a sage declares impure, his colleague may not declare pure; if he prohibited, his colleague may not permit?** They reasoned that [it was justified] so that they [the Jews in Babylonia] will not be drawn after him.	

Chart 5.3 Deposition of Rabban Gamaliel. Comparison between *y. Ber.* 4:1 (7c–d) and *b. Ber.* 27b–28a.[121]

***b. Ber.* 27b–28a**	***y. Ber.* 4:1 (7c–d)**
תנו רבנן: [a] **מעשה בתלמיד אחד שבא לפני רבי יהושע, אמר לו: תפלת ערבית רשות או חובה? אמר ליה: רשות.** **בא לפני רבן גמליאל, אמר לו: תפלת ערבית רשות או חובה? אמר לו: חובה. אמר לו: והלא רבי יהושע אמר לי רשות! אמר לו: המתן עד שיכנסו בעלי תריסין לבית המדרש.**	[A] מעשה בתלמיד אחד שבא ושאל את רבי יהושע תפילת הערב מהו אמר ליה רשות בא ושאל את רבן גמליאל תפילת הערב מהו אמר ליה חובה אמר לו והא רבי יהושע אמר לי רשות אמר לו למחר כשאכנס לבית הוועד עמוד ושאול את ההלכה הזאת
[b] **כשנכנסו בעלי תריסין, עמד השואל ושאל: תפלת ערבית רשות או חובה? אמר לו רבן גמליאל: חובה.** **אמר להם רבן גמליאל לחכמים: כלום יש אדם שחולק בדבר זה? אמר ליה רבי יהושע: לאו. אמר לו: והלא משמך אמרו לי רשות! אמר ליה: יהושע, עמוד על רגליך ויעידו בך!**	[B] למחר עמד אותו תלמיד ושאל את רבן גמליאל תפילת הערב מהו אמר לו חובה אמר לו הא רבי יהושע אמר לי רשות אמר רבן גמליאל לר' יהושע את הוא אומר רשות אמר ליה לאו אמר לו עמוד על רגליך ויעידוך
[c] **עמד רבי יהושע על רגליו ואמר: אלמלא אני חי והוא מת יכול החי להכחיש את המת, ועכשיו שאני חי והוא חי היאך יכול החי להכחיש את החי?**	
[d] **היה רבן גמליאל יושב ודורש, ורבי יהושע עומד על רגליו, עד שרננו כל העם ואמרו לחוצפית התורגמן: עמוד! ועמד.** אמרי: עד כמה נצעריה וניזיל? 1. בראש השנה אשתקד צעריה, 2. בבכורות במעשה דרבי צדוק צעריה, 3. הכא נמי צעריה, תא ונעבריה!	[D] והיה רבן גמליאל יושב ודורש ורבי יהושע עומד על רגליו עד שרינננו כל העם ואמרו לר' חצפית התורגמן הפטר את העם אמרו לרבי זינון החזן אמור התחיל ואמר התחילו ועמדו כל העם על רגליהם ואמרו לו כי על מי לא עברה רעתך תמיד
מאן נוקים ליה? 1. נוקמיה לרבי יהושע? בעל מעשה הוא; 2. נוקמיה לרבי עקיבא? דילמא עניש ליה, דלית ליה זכות אבות; 3. אלא נוקמיה לרבי אלעזר בן עזריה, דהוא חכם והוא עשיר והוא עשירי לעזרא. 1. הוא חכם—דאי מקשי ליה מפרק ליה, 2. והוא עשיר—דאי אית ליה לפלוחי לבי קיסר אף הוא אזל ופלח, 3. והוא עשירי לעזרא—דאית ליה זכות אבות ולא מצי עניש ליה.	הלכו ומינו את רבי אלעזר בן עזריה בישיבה בן שש עשרה שנה ונתמלא כל ראשו שיבות והיה רבי עקיבה יושב ומצטער ואמר לא שהוא בן תורה יותר ממני אלא שהוא בן גדולים יותר ממני אשרי אדם שזכו לו אבתיו אשרי אדם שיש לו יתד במי להתלות בה וכי מה היתה יתידתו של רבי אלעזר בן עזריה שהיה דור עשירי לעזרא

121. Translations from Rubenstein, *Rabbinic Stories*, 98–103. See further literature cited there, p. 270 n. 6. Boldface indicates a Tannaitic source. Determination of what is a Tannaitic source is chosen solely on the basis of introductory terminology (תנו רבנן or תנא) even though some of these texts may be Amoraic pseudo-*baraitot* and the terminology may be post-Talmudic. See idem, *Talmudic Stories*, 261–62.

[e] אתו ואמרו ליה: ניחא ליה למר דליהוי ריש מתי־בתא? אמר להו: איזיל ואימליך באינשי ביתי. אזל ואמליך בדביתהו. אמרה ליה: דלמא מעברין לך? אמר לה: יומא חדא בכסא דמוקרא ולמחר ליתבר. אמרה ליה: לית לך חיורתא. ההוא יומא בר תמני סרי שני הוה, אתרחיש ליה ניסא ואהדרו ליה תמני סרי דרי חיורתא. היינו דקאמר רבי אלעזר בן עזריה: **הרי אני כבן שבעים שנה,** ולא בן שבעים שנה.	
[f] תנא: **אותו היום סלקוהו לשומר הפתח ונתנה להם רשות לתלמידים ליכנס. שהיה רבן גמליאל מכריז ואומר: כל תלמיד שאין תוכו כברו—לא יכנס לבית המדרש.**	
[g] ההוא יומא אתוספו כמה ספסלי. אמר רבי יוחנן: פליגי בה אבא יוסף בן דוסתאי ורבנן, חד אמר: אתוספו ארבע מאה ספסלי; וחד אמר: שבע מאה ספסלי.	[G] וכמה ספסלין היו שם רבי יעקב בן סיסי אמר שמונים ספסלים היו שם של תלמידי חכמים חוץ מן העומדין לאחורי הגדר רבי יוסי ביר׳ אבון אמר שלש מאות היו שם חוץ מן העומדין לאחורי הגדר
[h] הוה קא חלשא דעתיה דרבן גמליאל, אמר: דלמא חס ושלום מנעתי תורה מישראל. אחזו ליה בחלמיה חצבי חיורי דמליין קטמא. ולא היא, ההיא ליתובי דעתיה הוא דאחזו ליה.	
[i] תנא: **עדיות בו ביום נשנית,** וכל היכא דאמרינן בו ביום—ההוא יומא הוה. ולא היתה הלכה שהיתה תלויה בבית המדרש שלא פירשוה.	[I] כיי דתנינן תמן **ביום שהושיבו את רבי אלעזר בן עזריה בישיבה** (משנה ידים ג:ה וד:ב) תמן תנינן **זה מדרש דרש רבי אלעזר בן עזריה לפני חכמים בכרם ביבנה** (משנה כתובות ד:ו) וכי כרם היה שם אלא אילו תלמידי חכמים שהיו עשויין שורות שורות ככרם
[j] ואף רבן גמליאל לא מנע עצמו מבית המדרש אפילו שעה אחת, דתנן: **בו ביום בא יהודה גר עמוני לפניהם בבית המדרש, אמר להם: מה אני לבא בקהל?** **1. אמר לו רבן גמליאל: אסור אתה לבא בקהל; אמר לו רבי יהושע: מותר אתה לבא בקהל.** **2. אמר לו רבן גמליאל: והלא כבר נאמר:** (דברים כג:ד) **לא יבא עמוני ומואבי בקהל ה׳! אמר לו רבי יהושע: וכי עמון ומואב במקומן הן יושבין? כבר עלה סנחריב מלך אשור ובלבל את כל האו־מות, שנאמר: ואסיר גבלות עמים ועתודותיהם שושתי ואוריד כאביר יושבים** (ישעיהו י:יג), וכל דפריש—מרובא פריש. **3. אמר לו רבן גמליאל: והלא כבר נאמר: ואחרי כן אשיב את שבות בני עמון נאם ה׳** (ירמיהו מט:ו)—**וכבר שבו. אמר לו רבי יהושע: והלא כבר נאמר: ושבתי את שבות עמי ישראל** (עמוס ט:יד)—**ועדיין לא שבו.** **מיד התירוהו לבא בקהל** (משנה ידים ד:ד).	

[k] אמר רבן גמליאל: הואיל והכי הוה, איזיל ואפייסיה לרבי יהושע. כי מטא לביתיה, חזינהו לאשיתא דביתיה דמשחרן. 1. אמר לו: מכותלי ביתך אתה ניכר שפחמי אתה. אמר לו: אוי לו לדור שאתה פרנסו, שאי אתה יודע בצערן של תלמידי חכמים במה הם מתפרנסים ובמה הם נזונים. 2. אמר לו: נעניתי לך, מחול לי! לא אשגח ביה. 3. עשה בשביל כבוד אבא! פייס.	[K] מיד הלך לו רבן גמליאל אצל כל אחד ואחד לפייסו בביתו אזל גבי ר' יהושע אשכחיה יתיב עביד מחטין אמר ליה אילין את חיי אמר ליה ועד כדון את בעי מידעי אוי לו לדור שאתה פרנסו אמר לו נעניתי ליך
[l] אמרו: מאן ניזיל ולימא להו לרבנן? אמר להו ההוא כובס: אנא אזילנא. שלח להו רבי יהושע לבי מדרשא: מאן דלביש מדא ילבש מדא, ומאן דלא לביש מדא יימר ליה למאן דלביש מדא שלח מדך ואנא אלבשיה? אמר להו רבי עקיבא לרבנן: טרוקו גלי, דלא ליתו עבדי דרבן גמליאל ולצערו לרבנן.	[L] ושלחון גבי רבי אלעזר בן עזריה חד קצר ואית דמרין רבי עקיבא הוה
[m] אמר רבי יהושע: מוטב דאיקום ואיזיל אנא לגבייהו. אתא, טרף אבבא. אמר להו: מזה בן מזה יזה, ושאינו לא מזה ולא בן מזה יאמר למזה בן מזה: מימיך מי מערה ואפרך אפר מקלה? אמר לו רבי עקיבא: רבי יהושע, נתפייסת? כלום עשינו אלא בשביל כבודך! למחר אני ואתה נשכים לפתחו.	[M] אמר לו מי שהוא מזה בן מזה יזה מי שאינו לא מזה ולא בן מזה יימר למזה בן מזה מימיך מי מערה ואפרך אפר מקלה אמר לו נתרציתם אני ואתם נשכים לפתחו של ר"ג
[n] אמרי: היכי נעביד? 1. נעבריה—גמירי: מעלין בקדש ואין מורידין! 2. נדרוש מר חדא שבתא ומר חדא שבתא—אתי לקנאויי! 3. אלא: לדרוש רבן גמליאל תלתא שבתי, ורבי אלעזר בן עזריה חדא שבתא. והיינו דאמר מר: שבת של מי היתה—של רבי אלעזר בן עזריה היתה.	[N] אף על פי כן לא הורידו אותו מגדולתו אלא מינו אותו אב בית דין
[o] ואותו תלמיד רבי שמעון בן יוחאי הוה.	

b. Ber. 27b-28a	*y. Ber.* 4:1, 7c-d
[a] Our rabbis taught: **Our sages have taught: Once a certain student came before R. Yehoshua. He said to him, "The evening prayer—optional or obligatory?" He said to him, "Optional." He came before Rabban Gamaliel. He said to him, "The evening prayer—optional or obligatory?" He said to him, "Obligatory." He said to him, "But did not R. Yehoshua say to me, 'Optional.'" He said to him, "Wait until the shield-bearers [the sages] enter the academy."**	[A] Once a certain student came and asked R. Yehoshua, "The evening prayer—what is its status?" He said to him, "Optional." He went and asked Rabban Gamaliel, "the evening prayer—what is its status?" He said to him, "Obligatory." He said to him, "And yet R. Yehoshua said to me, 'Optional.'" He said to him, "When I enter the assembly house tomorrow, stand up and ask about that law."
[b] **When the shield-bearers entered, the questioner stood up and asked, "The evening prayer—optional or obligatory?" Rabban Gamaliel said to him, "Obligatory." Rabban Gamaliel said to the sages, "Is there anyone who disagrees on this matter?" R. Yehoshua said to him, "No." Rabban Gamaliel said to him, "But did not they say to me in your name, 'Optional'?" He said to him, "Yehoshua! Stand on your feet that they may bear witness against you."**	[B] The next day that student stood up and asked Rabban Gamaliel, "The evening prayer—what is its status?" He said to him, "Obligatory." He said to him, "And yet R. Yehoshua said to me, 'Optional.'" Rabban Gamaliel said to R. Yehoshua, "Are you the one who said 'Optional'?" He said to him, "No." He said to him, "Stand on your feet that they may bear witness against you."
[c] **R. Yehoshua stood on his feet and said, "If I were alive and he [the student] dead—the living could contradict the dead. Now that I am alive and he is alive—how can the living contradict the living?"**	

[d] **Rabban Gamaliel was sitting and expounding while R. Yehoshua stood on his feet, until all the people murmured and said to Ḥuṣpit the *turgeman*, "Stop!" and he stopped.** They said, "How long will he [Rabban Gamaliel] go on distressing [R. Yehoshua]? (1) He distressed him last year on Rosh HaShana. (*m. Roš Haš.* 3:8–9.) (2) He distressed him in [the matter of] the firstling, in the incident involving R. Zadoq. (Cf. *b. Bek.* 36a.) (3) Now he distressed him again. Come let us depose him. Whom will we raise up [in his place]? (1) Shall we raise up R. Yehoshua? He is involved in the matter. (2) Shall we raise up R. Akiba? Perhaps he [Rabban Gamaliel] will harm him, since he has no ancestral merit. (3) Rather, let us raise up R. Eleazar b. Azariah, for he is wise, and he is wealthy, and he is tenth [in descent] from Ezra. (1) He is wise—so that if anyone asks a difficult question, he will be able to solve it. (2) He is wealthy—in case he has to pay honor to the emperor. (3) And he is tenth in descent from Ezra—he has ancestral merit and he [Rabban Gamaliel] will not be able to harm him."	[D] Rabban Gamaliel was sitting and expounding while R. Yehoshua stood on his feet until all the people murmured and said to Ḥuṣpit the *meturgeman*, "Dismiss the people." They said to Zenon the *hazzan*, "Say 'Begin.'" He said "Begin," and all the people stood on their feet and said to him [Rabban Gamaliel], "*Who has not suffered from you constant malice?* (Nah 3:19)." They went and appointed R. Eleazar b. Azariah to [lead] the assembly. He was sixteen years old, and his entire head became full of white hair. Rabbi Akiba was sitting and feeling upset [that he was not selected]. He said, "Not that he knows more Torah than I, but he is the descendant of greater men than I. Happy is the man whose ancestors have gained merit for him. Happy is the man who has a peg on which to hang." And what was the peg of R. Eleazar b. Azariah? He was tenth generation [in descent] from Ezra.

[e] They said to him, "Would our Master consent to be the head of the academy?" He said to them, "Let me go and consult with the members of my household." He went and consulted his wife. She said to him, "Perhaps they will depose you?" He said to her, "[Let a man use] a valuable cup for one day even if it breaks on the morrow." She said to him, "You have no white hair." That day he was eighteen years old. A miracle happened for him and he was crowned with eighteen rows of white hair. (This explains what R. Eleazar b. Azariah said [elsewhere], **Behold I am as seventy years old…** (*m. Ber.* 1:5), and not "[I am] seventy years old").	
[f] It was taught: That day they removed the guard of the gate and gave students permission to enter. For Rabban Gamaliel had decreed, "Any student whose inside is not like his outside may not enter the academy."	
[g] That day many benches were added. R. Yoḥanan said, "Abba Yosef b. Dostenai and the sages disagree. One said, 'Four hundred benches were added.' And one said, 'Seven hundred benches were added.'"	[G] And how many benches were there? R. Yaᶜaqov b. Sisi said, "Eighty benches of students were there, excluding those standing beyond the fence." R. Yose b. R. Avun said, "Three hundred were there, excluding those standing beyond the fence."
[h] Rabban Gamaliel became distressed. He said, "Perhaps, God forbid, I held back Torah from Israel." They showed him in a dream white casks filled with ashes. But that was not the case, they showed him [the dream] only to put his mind at peace [but he really had held back Torah.]	

[i] It was taught, "They taught [Tractate] *ʿEduyyot* on that day." And anywhere that it says *On that day* [in the Mishnah]—[refers to] that day. And there was not a single law pending in the academy that they did not resolve.	[I] (This refers to what we have learned elsewhere, **On the day they seated R. Eleazar b. Azariah in the assembly** (*m. Yad.* 3:5). We learned elsewhere, **R. Eleazar expounded this interpretation to the sages at the vineyard there in Yavneh** (*m. Ketub.* 4:6). But was there a vineyard there? Rather, these are the students who used to assemble in rows like a vineyard.)
[j] And even Rabban Gamaliel did not hold himself back from Torah. For it was taught: **On that day Yehudah the Ammonite proselyte stood before them in the academy. He said to them, "Am I [permitted] to enter the congregation of Israel [=to convert]?" Rabban Gamaliel said to him, "You are forbidden." R. Yehoshua said to him, "You are permitted." Rabban Gamaliel said, "Is it not written, *No Ammonite or Moabite shall be admitted into the congregation of the Lord* (Deut 23:4)"? R. Yehoshua said to him, "And are Ammon and Moab in their [original] places? Sennacherib King of Assyria has since come and mixed up all the nations, as it says, *I have erased the borders of peoples; I have plundered their treasures and exiled their vast populations* (Isa 10:13).** And whatever separates, separates from the majority." **Rabban Gamaliel said to him, "Has it not already been said, *I will restore the fortunes of the Ammonites—declares the Lord* (Jer 49:6), and they have already been restored?" R. Yehoshua said to him, "Has it not already been said, *I will restore my people Israel* (Amos 9:14), and they have not yet been restored?" Immediately they permitted him to enter the congregation** (*m. Yad.* 4:4).	

[k] Rabban Gamaliel said, "I will go and appease R. Yehoshua." When he arrived at his house, he saw that the walls of his house were black. He said to him, " From the walls of your house it is evident that you are a smith." He said to him, "Woe to the generation whose chief you are, for you do not know the distress of the scholars, how they earn a living and how they subsist." He said to him, "I apologize to you. Forgive me." He [R. Yehoshua] paid no attention to him. [Rabban Gamaliel said,] "Do it for the honor of my father's house." He said to him, "You are forgiven."	[K] Immediately Rabban Gamaliel went and apologized to each and every one in his own house. He went to R. Yehoshua and found him sitting and making needles. He said to him, "From these you make your living?" He said to him, "You did not know this until now? Woe be the generation whose chief you are!" He [Rabban Gamaliel] said to him, "I apologize to you."
[l] They said, "Who will go and tell the rabbis [that we have reconciled]?" A certain laundryman said, "I will go." R. Yehoshua sent [word] to the academy, "Let him who wears the robe wear the robe. Should one who does not wear the robe say to one who wears the robe, 'Take off your robe and I will wear it'?" R. Akiba said, "Lock the doors so that the servants of Rabban Gamaliel cannot come in and distress the sages."	[L] They sent in a certain laundryman to R. Eleazar b. Azariah, and some say it was R. Akiba.
[m] R. Yehoshua went and knocked on the door. He said, "Let a sprinkler, the son of a sprinkler, sprinkle. Should he who is neither a sprinkler nor the son of a sprinkler say to a sprinkler, the son of a sprinkler, your water is cave water and your ashes are common ashes?" R. Akiba said to R. Yehoshua, "Have you been appeased? We acted only for the sake of your honor. Tomorrow you and I will rise early to his [Gamaliel's] door."	[M] He said to him, "Let a sprinkler, the son of a sprinkler, sprinkle. Should he who is neither a sprinkler nor the son of a sprinkler say to a sprinkler, the son of a sprinkler, your water is cave water and your ashes are common ashes?" He [R. Eleazar b. Azariah] said to them [the sages], "If you are satisfied, let you and me rise early to the door of Rabban Gamaliel."

[n] They said, "What shall we do? (1) Shall we depose him [R. Eleazar b. Azariah]? There is a tradition, **One raises the level of holiness but does not diminish it** (*m. Menaḥ.* 7:11). (2) Shall this master expound on one Shabbat and that master on the next? He [Rabban Gamaliel] will not accept that since he will be jealous of him." (3) Rather, they ordained that Rabban Gamaliel would expound three Shabbats and R. Eleazar b. Azariah one Shabbat. This explains the tradition, **Whose Shabbat was it? It was [the Shabbat] of R. Eleazar b. Azariah** (*t. Soṭah* 7:9).	[N] Nevertheless, they did not demote him [R. Eleazar b. Azariah] from his high office but appointed him head of the court.
[o] And that student [who asked the original question] was R. Shimon bar Yoḥai.	

6

Rebellious Elder: Tannaitic and Amoraic Transformation of a Biblical Institution

One way in which the rabbis grounded their authority to legislate halakha for all of Israel is by appropriating for themselves the positions previously held by the judges and priests during Temple times. Deuteronomy 17:8–13 grants full judicial authority to the high court in Jerusalem, which can mete out the death penalty for anyone who disobeys its decision. The Tannaim and Amoraim reinterpret various aspects of these verses so that the law refers to their own halakhic rulings. It is interesting to note that the rabbis use this law not so much to assert their authority over the masses but rather to suppress dissenting rabbis from breaking away from the mainstream rabbinic rulings. While no Tanna or Amora goes to the extreme of advocating the death penalty for a colleague who disobeys the majority decision, there is still a wide range of opinions about how fully the biblical law should be mapped onto rabbinic disputes.

The extent to which various rabbis confine the law to the biblical context, prop it up as a theoretical model, or attempt to use it in practice can reveal their general attitude toward dealing with rabbis who espouse divergent halakhic practices. In this chapter, we trace the ways in which the Tannaim, and Palestinian and Babylonian Amoraim transformed the biblical law with an eye toward how this transformation reflects on their attitude regarding halakhic pluralism. We will show that while Palestinian texts attempt to extend the law of rebellious elder into the rabbinic period, the Bavli greatly limits its application to the point of being almost completely obsolete. This reflects the Yerushalmi's relative intolerance for diversity compared to that of the Bavli.

The Biblical Law

As part of its regulation of the judicial branch of the government, Deuteronomy requires all regional courts to answer to a central high court.[1] Deuteronomy 17:8–13 details the process and punishments involved:

(ח) כִּי יִפָּלֵא מִמְּךָ דָבָר לַמִּשְׁפָּט בֵּין דָּם לְדָם בֵּין דִּין לְדִין וּבֵין נֶגַע לָנֶגַע דִּבְרֵי רִיבֹת בִּשְׁעָרֶיךָ וְקַמְתָּ וְעָלִיתָ אֶל הַמָּקוֹם אֲשֶׁר יִבְחַר יְהֹוָה אֱלֹהֶיךָ בּוֹ:
(ט) וּבָאתָ אֶל הַכֹּהֲנִים הַלְוִיִּם וְאֶל הַשֹּׁפֵט אֲשֶׁר יִהְיֶה בַּיָּמִים הָהֵם וְדָרַשְׁתָּ וְהִגִּידוּ לְךָ אֵת דְּבַר הַמִּשְׁפָּט:
(י) וְעָשִׂיתָ עַל פִּי הַדָּבָר אֲשֶׁר יַגִּידוּ לְךָ מִן הַמָּקוֹם הַהוּא אֲשֶׁר יִבְחַר יְהֹוָה וְשָׁמַרְתָּ לַעֲשׂוֹת כְּכֹל אֲשֶׁר יוֹרוּךָ:
(יא) עַל פִּי הַתּוֹרָה אֲשֶׁר יוֹרוּךָ וְעַל הַמִּשְׁפָּט אֲשֶׁר יֹאמְרוּ לְךָ תַּעֲשֶׂה לֹא תָסוּר מִן הַדָּבָר אֲשֶׁר יַגִּידוּ לְךָ יָמִין וּשְׂמֹאל:
(יב) וְהָאִישׁ אֲשֶׁר יַעֲשֶׂה בְזָדוֹן לְבִלְתִּי שְׁמֹעַ אֶל הַכֹּהֵן הָעֹמֵד לְשָׁרֶת שָׁם אֶת יְהֹוָה אֱלֹהֶיךָ אוֹ אֶל הַשֹּׁפֵט וּמֵת הָאִישׁ הַהוּא וּבִעַרְתָּ הָרָע מִיִּשְׂרָאֵל:
(יג) וְכָל הָעָם יִשְׁמְעוּ וְיִרָאוּ וְלֹא יְזִידוּן עוֹד:

[8]If a case is too baffling for you to decide, be it a controversy over homicide, civil law, or assault—matters of dispute in your courts—you shall promptly repair to the place that the LORD your God will have chosen, [9]and appear before the levitical priests, or the magistrate in charge at the time, and present your problem. When they have announced to you the verdict in the case, [10]you shall carry out the verdict that is announced to you from that place that the LORD chose, observing scrupulously all their instructions to you. [11]You shall act in accordance with the instructions given you and the ruling handed down to you; you must not deviate from the verdict that they announce to you either to the right or to the left. [12]Should a man act presumptuously and disregard the priest charged with serving there the LORD your God, or the magistrate, that man shall die. Thus you will sweep out evil from Israel: [13]all the people will hear and be afraid and will not act presumptuously again.[2]

A number of issues present themselves when interpreting this pericope. These issues are discussed in rabbinic sources, medieval commentaries, and modern scholarship. We will first try to recover the original intent of the biblical law in order to better appreciate how it was later transformed by the rabbis.

1. This court may have had larger legislative and executive duties as well, but this passage emphasizes the role of the court as final deciders in difficult cases or making the law in the absence of any other precedent. It was not a court of appeals in the sense that they overruled a decision of a lower court, but rather was consulted when the local authorities could not come to a decision.

2. NJPS translation.

First, it is not clear to whom the law is being addressed. The first two verses address a local judge who does not know the law regarding a particular case, "If a case is too baffling for you...."[3] However, vv 10–13 seem to address the citizen of Israel who is to carry out the teaching of that high court in practice. Verse 12 clearly refers to "the man who acts," that is, the litigant, not the judge.[4] It would be strange for a local court to refuse to decide according to the ruling of the high court to whom it deferred. If the local court felt strongly about a case it would not have needed to request a decision from the higher court in the first place. Even if the judges are the ones charged to go to the high court, however, the severe punishment must be aimed at the litigants as a deterrent for the rest of the nation. It seems clear that it is one of the litigants who is most likely to reject the pronouncement of the high court on a new law that does not go in his favor. The passage begins addressing the local court, for it is they who will refer the case to the high court. But the focus of the law applies to the litigants themselves.

Second, who is to sit on the court? Deuteronomy 17 envisions a court made up of a combination of priests and nonpriests, which would be natural in Jerusalem—the city of priests. The relationship between the priests and the nonpriestly judges, however, is not clear.[5] Third, the location of

---

3. Peter C. Craigie, *The Book of Deuteronomy* (Grand Rapids, MI: Eerdmans, 1976), 252, writes that "the local judges were to inquire about the case" not the litigants, but see n. 6 there. See also Jeffrey Tigay, *The JPS Torah Commentary: Deuteronomy* (Philadelphia: Jewish Publication Society, 1996), 164, who compares the judges who bring cases to the high court with the elders who bring cases to Moses in Deut 1:17. The chiefs similarly bring the difficult cases to Moses in Exod 18:22. The existence of local courts is mandated by Deut 16:18–20. The word "בשעריך—in your gates" in Deut 17:8 refers back to the same word in 16:18 and probably denotes not just "your cities" in general but rather the courts or councils of elders, which would meet at the city gate.

4. See Tigay, *Deuteronomy*, 165.

5. Regarding the placement of priests on the high court, a feature reiterated in Deut 19:17 and 21:5, it is obvious throughout the Bible that priests dealt with more than just the cult. Leviticus 10:11 commands them to teach the people all of the laws, and Deut 17:18, 31:9 and 24 place them in charge of safekeeping the scroll of the Torah. Ezekiel 44:24 attributes adjudication of both ritual and civil laws to the levitical priests. In later times, 1 Chron 23:4 counts 6,000 Levites as officers and judges. It may have been the common practice to have priests and lay judges together as seen in 2 Chron 19:8–11, where Jehoshaphat makes a court in Jerusalem with priests, Levites, and laymen. In that case there seems to be some separation of powers between the head priest who presides over matters of God and the head of the house of Judah who presides over royal matters.

Craigie, *The Book of Deuteronomy*, 252, suggests that "the particular function of the priests would be to legislate on matters of ceremonial law, and that of the judge to legislate on matters of civil and criminal law" (even though he rejects such a clear distinction in a theocracy so both priests and judges saw all cases). However, we see the priest being part of the judgment in a civil case in Deut 19:17. Deuteronomy 21:5 also says about the priests that "by their word every dispute and every assault shall be settled." S. R. Driver, *Deuteronomy*, International Critical Commentary (Edinburgh: T. & T. Clark, 1978), 209, commenting on v.

the court is confined to "the place that the Lord your God will have chosen," as part of the Deuteronomic program of centralization. This requirement, however, will be questioned in rabbinic texts.

Finally, what types of cases were reviewed by this court? The plain meaning of "between blood and blood" here connotes different types of injury or killing; the court may have difficulty distinguishing between murder and manslaughter in a particular case.[6] נגע can mean leprosy when joined with a modifier, as in נגע צרעת;[7] but, by itself, it means a blow[8] or affliction.[9] The latter definitions better fit the rest of v. 8, which introduces and concludes the list of items with words relating to civil laws, namely, משפט and ריבת.[10] Questions of purity and impurity were usually decided by an individual priest and did not require deliberation before a court.[11] Therefore, this high court dealt primarily with matters of civil and criminal dispute. The Midrashim and Talmuds will address all of these issues.

12, suggests that although the priests and lay judges were involved in all cases, "the verdict was delivered sometimes by the ecclesiastical president of the board, sometimes by its civil president; the procedure may have varied according to the nature of the case under consideration."

Other scholars resort to source criticism and find two strands of court traditions here. Some say that the priests are original while others argue that the judges are original. Steuernagel says two independent traditions are combined here. Originally there were two types of courts, but then both types were combined because of centralization. These views are summarized in Moshe Weinfeld, *Deuteronomy and the Deuteronomic School* (Oxford: Clarendon, 1972), 235–36. See also Yehezkel Kaufmann, *History of Israelite Religion from Antiquity to the End of the Second Temple*, 3 vols. (Jerusalem: Mosad Bialik, 1955–1960), 2:466–67 (Hebrew); and Alexander Rofe, *Introduction to Deuteronomy* (Jerusalem: Akademon, 1988), 75–85 (Hebrew).

6. The phrase בין דם לדם is interpreted by *Sifre* 152, cited below p. 312, to refer to purity laws regarding different categories of uterine bleeding. However, there is no indication that such cases require any judgment by a priest or outside authority. Unlike Leviticus 13–14, where a decision by a priest is required, Leviticus 15 assumes that a woman can determine the status of blood on her own based on its timing. See also Rashbam, Ibn Ezra, and Ramban to Deut 17:8.

7. Leviticus 13:2. When נגע stands alone in this chapter, it usually has a definite article, thus referring to the specific affliction in question to decide whether or not that affliction is a case of leprosy. Only in Lev 13:22 is נגע used alone to refer to the impurity of the affliction, but even here it only has this specific connotation because of the context. Generally, the word means any affliction, whether impure or not.

8. See Deut 21:5. Cf. Gen 26:11; and 32:26, 33. See also Tigay, *Deuteronomy*, 373 n. 37.

9. See Exod 12:1; 1 Kings 8:37–38; Ps 38:12; and Prov 6:33.

10. For ריב in a civil context see Exod 21:18. Ibn Ezra, Ramban, and Shadal already explain Deut 17:8 to refer only to civil and criminal law. See also Isaac Sassoon, *Destination Torah* (Hoboken, NJ: Ktav, 2001), 292–95.

11. See Leviticus 13–14.

Rabbinic Interpretation of Biblical Passages

Tannaitic sources on this passage are found in *Sifre Deuteronomy* 152–155, *m. Sanh.* 11:2–4, and *t. Sanh.* 3:4, 7:1, 11:7, and 14:12. This law comes to be known as *zaken mamre*, rebellious elder, in these sources. This name itself is a significant departure from the original law, as we will see below. In both Talmuds, the major discussion of this topic is presented as commentary on *m. Sanh.* 11:2–4.[12] Other references to and stories involving the rebellious elder will be discussed below.

Tannaitic sources begin to reinterpret this passage in various ways and transform it into a law that would be relevant to their contemporary circumstances. The original biblical law spoke to the needs of a sovereign nation in need of a civil and criminal judicial authority in order to maintain peace and justice. The rabbis, under foreign rule and without a centralized judicial system, transposed this passage to the realm of rabbinic dispute and halakhic decision making. *M. Sanhedrin* 11:2 sets forth the basic procedure of this case:

[A] זקן ממרא על פי בית דין שנאמר כי יפלא ממך דבר למשפט וגו'
[B] שלשה בתי דינין היו שם אחד יושב על פתח הר הבית ואחד יושב על פתח העזרה ואחד יושב בלשכת הגזית באים לזה שעל פתח הר הבית ואומר כך דרשתי וכך דרשו חבירי כך לימדתי וכך לימדו חבירי אם שמעו אומרים להם
ואם לאו באין להם לאותן שעל פתח העזרה ואומר כך דרשתי וכך דרשו חבירי כך לימדתי וכך לימדו חבירי אם שמעו אומרים להם
ואם לאו אלו ואלו באים לבית דין הגדול שבלשכת הגזית שממנו יוצאת תורה לכל ישראל שנאמר מן המקום ההוא אשר יבחר ה'
חזר לעיר ושנה ולימד כדרך שהיה למד פטור ואם הורה לעשות חייב שנאמר והאיש אשר יעשה בזדון אינו חייב עד שיורה לעשות
[C] תלמיד שהורה לעשות פטור נמצא חומרו קולו:

[A] An elder who rebels against the court as the verse says, "If a matter of law should be too exceptional for you…" (Deut 17:8).
[B] There were three courts there. One sat at the entrance to the Temple mount, one sat at the entrance to the courtyard, and one sat in the chamber of hewn stone.[13] They came to that which was

12. Chapter 11 of the Mishnah became the tenth chapter in most manuscripts and all printed editions of the Bavli. On the history of this change see Mordechai Sabato, *A Yemenite Manuscript of Tractate Sanhedrin and Its Place in the Text Tradition* (Jerusalem: Yad Izhak Ben-Zvi, 1998), 220–21 (Hebrew).

13. On the meaning of this location see Guttmann, *Rabbinic Judaism in the Making*, 27. We must agree with Guttmann that "These Mishnah passages show that the Tannaim did not intend to describe the 'Sanhedrin' of Javneh, nor to give a historical account of the Sanhedrin of Jerusalem, but rather attempted to describe the *ideal* Sanhedrin" (ibid., 23). This chapter

at the opening of the Temple mount and he says, "Such have I interpreted and such have my friends interpreted; such have I taught and such have my friends taught." If they learned [that law previously] they tell them.
If not, they come to those at the entrance to the courtyard and he says, "Such have I interpreted and such have my friends interpreted; such have I taught and such have my friends taught." If they have learned [that law previously] they tell them.
If not, these and those come together to the great court in the chamber of hewn stone from which Torah comes forth to all of Israel, as the verse says, "*From that place that God will choose*" (Deut 17:10).
If he returns to his city and repeats and teaches just as he had taught before, he is innocent. However, if he issues a practical ruling, he is liable, as the verse says, "*Should a man act presumptuously*" (Deut 17:12). He is not liable until he issues a practical ruling.
[C] If a student teaches in practice he is innocent. His stringency turns out to be his leniency.

Whom Does the Law Address?

The Mishnah labels the subject of this law a "rebellious elder," and quotes the passage beginning in Deut 17:8, even though the verse makes no mention of an elder. Part C of the Mishnah explains further that the law does not apply to a student but only to one who has authority to decide halakha, whom the Mishnah calls a זקן, "wise elder."[14] A similar limitation is also found in *Sifre* 152 on that same verse:

---

too will not deal with the history of the Sanhedrin or of the institution of the rebellious elder but rather will trace the intellectual history of what the Tannaim and Amoraim taught about how a theoretical Sanhedrin would deal with a hypothetical rebellious elder. For a discussion of the historical Sanhedrin, see above p. 7 n. 21; and Hugo Mantel, *Studies in the History of the Sanhedrin* (Cambridge: Harvard University Press, 1965), 54–101.

14. *Zaken* is used in the sense of a high judge in *m. Zebaḥ.* 1:3; *t. Sukkah* 4:6; *t. Šeqal.* 3:27; *t. Sanh.* 7:11; 8:1; *t. Ḥul.* 2:24: *t. ᵓOhal* 17:12; *t. Yad.* 2:18; *Semaḥot* 3:10; 8:7; and 11:19. It is used in the sense of a great scholar in *y. ᶜAbod. Zar.* 2:8 (42a) (see text below, p. 329 n. 104) and as an honorific, as in Shammai ha-Zaken, Hillel ha-Zaken, Rabban Gamaliel ha-Zaken, etc. The term derives from the seventy elders who assisted Moses in Exod 19:7; Num 11:16–17; and Deut 27:1. See further at Mantel, *Sanhedrin,* 99; Hezser, *Social Structure,* 277–86; and Miller, *Sages and Commoners,* 438.

The description of the elder as "ממרא—rebellious" may predate the Mishnah. See Aharon Shemesh, "Halakha u-nevu'ah: navi sheqer ve-zaqen mamre," in *Renewing Jewish Commitment: The Work and Thought of David Hartman,* ed. Avi Sagi and Zvi Zohar (Jerusalem: Shalom Hartman Institute and Hakibbutz Hameuchad, 2001), 925 n. 6. Shemesh traces the

כי יפלא, מלמד שבמופלא הכתוב מדבר.

"If … too baffling": This teaches that Scripture speaks of a *mufla* (senior legal authority).

While the original biblical law holds any person of Israel who disobeys the court's ruling in contempt and liable to capital punishment, the Mishnah and the *Sifre* restrict the scope of the law to only a זקן, "wise elder," or מופלא, "exceptional judge."[15] This shift directs the law toward discouraging dissent among the intellectual leadership rather than toward disobedience by laypeople.

This point can be supported by comparing part B of this Mishnah to a closely parallel Tosefta at *t. Sanh.* 7:1. (See a side-by-side comparison below in chart 6.1, p. 334.) The Tosefta recalls ancient times when there was allegedly no rabbinic controversy since all matters were settled by the great court:

אמר ר' יוסי בראשנה לא היו מחלוקות בישראל אלא בבית דין[16] של שבעים ואחד בלשכת

---

term ממרא back to the Dead Sea scrolls. 4Q159 reads, "ביד ".ואשר ימרה...יומת אשר עשה ביד רמה רמה is a common substitute for מזיד in the scrolls. More interesting is the use of the verb ימרה whose usage is similar to that of the term זקן ממרא. This would presage the midrashic transfer of the high court's authority to the rabbis based on Deuteronomy 17. However, Moshe Bernstein, in the forthcoming revision to John M. Allegro and Arnold Anderson, *Qumran Cave 4.1 (4Q158–4Q186)*, Discoveries in the Judean Desert V (Oxford: Clarendon, 1968), argues that 4Q159 borrows language from Josh 1:18, in which Israel promises not to rebel against Joshua, thus transferring Joshua's authority to the contemporary court.

15. The meaning of *mufla* is somewhat obscure. The word may derive from פלא, meaning "extraordinary" (see Francis Brown et al., *The Brown-Driver-Briggs Hebrew and English Lexicon* [Peabody: Hendrickson, 2001] 810) to refer to one whose knowledge is exceptional and deep, able to understand that which is hidden to others (see *b. Ḥag.* 13a). Alternatively, it may come from פלא meaning "to swear" (see Lev 22:21; Num 15:3, 8), מופלא meaning "one who can swear" (see *b. Naz.* 29b, 62a). Perhaps these officially recognized judges underwent a swearing-in ceremony. See further in Albeck, *Mishnah, Nezikin*, 503–5.

Mantel, *Sanhedrin*, 135–39, argues that *mufla* signifies a judge ordained by the great court of Jerusalem and ceased to be used after the destruction of the Second Temple. In the former period, a court could be populated with nonordained judges as long as there was at least one officially ordained judge present. See *m. Hor.* 1:4, *Sifra Ḥoba, parashah* 4:4 (Louis Finkelstein, *Sifra on Leviticus*, 5 vols. (Jerusalem: Jewish Theological Seminary of America, 1983–1992), 2:141–42 (Hebrew)), and *t. Hor.* 1:2. According to Mantel's theory, the Mishnah states the same basic idea as the Sifre except that it uses *zaken* instead of *mufla*, thus updating the language of the Sifre, which reflects a more ancient system, to the newer post-destruction terminology. For further scholarly literature on this term, see references in Fraade, *From Tradition to Commentary*, 236 n. 51.

16. This text follows ms. Erfurt. Mss. Erfurt and Vienna of *t. Sanh.* 7:1 and ms. Erfurt of *t. Ḥag.* 2:9 read, בבית דין, which connects this clause with the preceding, as translated here. According to this version, one would still have to distinguish between the factionalism of the Houses, wherein each side practiced differently, with the division within the high court, which agreed by vote to follow only one practice. Mss. Vienna and London of *t. Ḥag.* 2:9, the

הגזית ושאר בתי דינין של עשרים ושלשה היו בעיירות של ארץ ישראל ושאר[17] בתי דינין
של שלשה שלשה[18] היו בירושלם אחד בהר הבית ואחד בחיל
נצרך אחד מהן הלכה הולך לבית דין שבעירו אין בית דין בעירו הולך לבית דין הסמוך
לעירו אם שמעו אמרו לו[19] אם לאו הוא ומופלא[20] שבהם באין לבית דין שבהר הבית אם
שמעו אמרו להן ואם לאו הן[21] ומופלא שבהן באין לבית דין שבחיל אם שמעו אמרו להן
ואם לאו אילו ואילו הולכין לבית דין הגדול שבלשכת הגזית...
נשאלה שאילה אם שמעו אמרו להם ואם לאו עומדין למינין רבו המטמאין טימאו רבו
המטהרין טהרו משם היה יוצאת הלכה ורווחת בישראל
משרבו תלמידי שמאי והילל שלא שימשו כל צורכן הרבו מחלוקות בישראל.

R. Yose said: At first there were no divisions within Israel except within the court of seventy-one members in the chamber of hewn stone. And there were other courts of twenty-three members in the cities of the land of Israel. And there were other courts of three each in Jerusalem, one on the Temple mount and one at the *ḥel* (rampart).

If one[22] was required [to learn] a halakha, he would go to the court in his town. If there was no court in his town, he would go to the court in the next town. If they had heard [the law], they told him. If not, he and *mufla* among them would come to the court that was on the Temple Mount. If they had heard [the law], they told them. And if not, they and the *mufla* among them would come to the court that was at the *ḥel*. If they had heard they told them, and if not, these and those would go to the high court that was in the chamber of hewn stone....

---

first edition of *t. Sanh.* 7:1, as well as the version of the Tosefta in *y. Sanh.* 1:4 (19c) and *b. Sanh.* 88b read בית דין or סנהדרין without the preposition. In these versions the high court is not an exception to the condition of unity but rather it begins the list of various courts. See partial translation on p. 167. This list introduces the next part of the Tosefta, which delineates the procedure for moving from the lowest to the highest court. See Rosen-Zvi, "Ha-umnam," n. 140, who argues that the versions without the preposition are original.

17. Ms. Vienna and the first edition of *t. Sanh.* 7:1, mss. Erfurt and London and first edition of *t. Ḥag.* 2:9, *y. Sanh.* 1:4 (19c) and *b. Sanh.* 88b read ושני. Ms. Vienna of *t. Ḥag.* 2:9 reads שני.

18. *B. Sanh.* 88b reads עשרים ושלשה. Ms. Vienna and first edition of *t. Sanh.* 7:1 read שלשה only once.

19. Mss. Erfurt and London of *t. Ḥag.* 2:9 and *y. Sanh.* 1:4 (19c) also read לו. Ms. Vienna and first edition of *t. Sanh.* 7:1 and the first edition of *t. Ḥag.* 2:9 read להם. Ms. Vienna of *t. Ḥag.* 2:9 and *b. Sanh.* 88b read להן.

20. Ms. Erfurt of *t. Ḥag.* 2:9 reads מופלג.

21. The parallel in *t. Ḥag.* 2:9 has הוא in ms. Vienna but הן in ms. Erfurt.

22. The Tosefta literally translates, "if one of them requires a halakha." The pronoun here seems *prima facie* to refer to the immediately preceding list of courts. However, it would not make sense to say that if the court requires a halakha then it should go to the court. Therefore, the referent must be to any individual.

A question would be asked. If they heard they told them. If not, they would take it to a vote. If those who declared it impure had the majority, they declared it impure; if those who declared it pure had the majority, they declared it pure. From there did the law emanate and spread throughout Israel. Once the students of Shammai and Hillel, who did not serve sufficiently, became numerous, divisions multiplied in Israel.[23]

Part B of the Mishnah is a modified excerpt from this Tosefta. The Tosefta seems to be more original because it provides a more detailed account of the court system and the entire description integrates more smoothly with the context of the Tosefta.[24] The Tosefta describes the ideal system of old where every local controversy would be decided at some point in the judicial hierarchy. In the Mishnah, however, the description is somewhat superfluous, since all we need to know is the final stage of the *zaken* receiving instruction from the supreme court. [25]

That the Mishnah must be derived from the Tosefta is most evident when analyzing the subjects of the verb in each. The Tosefta does not deal with litigants but rather with one who "was required [to learn] a halakha." That person goes to the local court. If the local court does not know, then the inquirer goes along with the *mufla* of the local court to the court at the Temple Mount. The Tosefta starts with a single person, נצרך אחד מהן הלכה הולך, and turns to the plural at the next stage once the *mufla* of the local court joins him, הוא ומופלא שבהם באין. If that court also does not know, the inquirer and the *mufla* of the local court go along with the *mufla* of the court at the Temple Mount to the court at the *ḥel*. If they too do not know, then "these and those—אלו ואלו" go to the highest court. Albeck explains that אלו ואלו refers here to the previous group of the inquirer and two *mufla* judges along with the entire court at the *ḥel*.[26]

The Mishnah, however, skips the first stage of the Tosefta that takes place at the local court. The Mishnah begins with a single person, זקן ממרא,

23. *T. Sanh.* 7:1. See pp. 167–69 for further analysis of parts of this Tosefta. Parallels are found in *t. Ḥag.* 2:9, *y. Sanh.* 1:4 (19c), and *b. Sanh.* 88b.

24. Brandes, "Beginnings of the Rules," 94 n. 1, assumes that the longer Tosefta must include later additions to the earlier Mishnah. I disagree for the reasons spelled out in this and the next paragraphs.

25. Note that the biblical law does not necessarily refer to a permanent court but rather could be an ad hoc council put together when necessary. The first reference to a permanent court in the context of this law is Josephus, *Antiquities*, 4.8.14, who says that difficult cases go to the holy city where "the high priest, the prophet, and the council of elders (*gerousia*)" determine it. Josephus adds the reference to a court, thus predating this aspect of the interpretation found in the Mishnah. See also Steve Mason, ed., *Flavius Josephus: Translation and Commentary* (Leiden: Brill, 2000), 3:410–11; and Goodblatt, *Monarchic Principle*, 95–97.

26. Albeck, *Mishnah, Nezikin*, 458.

but then jumps to the plural, באים, without explanation, even though the continuation offers only the voice of a single person in front of the court, כך דרשתי וכך דרשו חברי כך לימדתי וכך לימדו חבירי. The next stage at the court situated at the entrance of the courtyard presents the same problem of the plural, באין, followed by the statement of only a single person. The Mishnah removes any mention of the *mufla* here, thus causing confusion about who joins the litigant in going to the next court.[27] At the final stage of the Mishnah, the plural is doubled to אלו ואלו באים. It is not at all clear to which two groups of people this refers since nobody besides the elder himself is mentioned beforehand as coming to the next court. Rather, the Mishnah seems to have kept the language of the Tosefta even though the singular and plural nouns and verbs no longer fit into the new context, which removes the *mufla.*[28]

More significant than these procedural details, however, is the change in context between the two texts. The Tosefta, making no explicit reference to Deuteronomy 17, deals with legal controversy and how it was resolved through the judicial system during ideal times.[29] The Mishnah, on the other hand, codifies the laws stemming from Deuteronomy 17, which deals with civil suits and individual cases. By importing the Tosefta's discussion of legal controversy into the context of the rebellious elder, the Mishnah effectively rewrites the law of Deuteronomy 17 to be one concerning not the masses and their lawsuits but the rabbis themselves and their controversies. As was mentioned above, this is evident just from giving Deuteronomy 17 the title of זקן ממרא, which itself limits the applicability of the law to senior rabbis. This textual appropriation from a context of rabbinic controversy realizes even further the rewriting of the biblical law to adapt it to rabbinic ideology.[30] If, according to the biblical law, it is the litigants who go to the high court, in the Tannaitic reinterpretation, it is the judges (Sifre) or the rabbis (Mishnah) who go to the court.

The substance of the cases is also different. The Mishnah inserts into the Tosefta a sample query of the court: ואומר כך דרשתי וכך דרשו חבירי כך לימדתי

---

27. The version of the Tosefta in *b. Sanh.* 88b has already been updated to conform to the Mishnah by removing *mufla* and adding "ואומר כך דרשתי וכך...חבירי." The Bavli also substitutes the court at *ḥel* mentioned in the Tosefta with the court at the entrance to the *`azarah,* which is mentioned in the Mishnah.

28. The removal of the word *mufla* from the Mishnah's quotation of *t. Sanh.* 7:1 may be part of the same updating as the replacement of *mufla* in Sifre 152 with *zaken* in *m. Sanh.* 11:2, as noted above n. 15.

29. The Tosefta is likely based on the outline of Deuteronomy 17, in which a local person who does not know the law goes to inquire at the Temple court. See Rosen-Zvi, "Ha-'umnam," who calls the Tosefta a "concealed midrash" to Deuteronomy 17. Still, the Tosefta does not deal with the law of the rebellious elder but rather focuses only on the normal procedure of the court.

30. For an unconvincing treatement of the differences between this Mishnah and Tosefta, see Fisch, *Rational Rabbis,* 66–68.

וכך לימדו חבירי. The content of the dispute does not involve any litigants but rather interpretations of Scripture (כך דרשתי) or traditional teachings (כך לימדתי). The language used in this Mishnah does not fit well with the context of a baffled court. "Such have I interpreted and such have they interpreted" sounds not so much like a speechless court that cannot come up with an answer but rather like a study session where there are too many opinions. This is not a group of baffled judges but a clash between a majority and a minority group of rabbis. The Mishnah ends, "if he goes back and teaches as he used to." This deals not with a citizen involved in litigation but rather an interpreter and teacher of the law. The important matter is not how he himself practices when he goes back to his town, as the verses imply, but rather how he teaches others to practice.[31]

Fraade's comments on *Sifre* 152 are equally true for the Mishnah: "The intellectual and teaching role of the central courts is emphasized, rather than their strictly juridical function and authority. The central courts decide not so much between conflicting parties in a civil or criminal dispute as between *sages* who differ in their legal interpretations."[32]

Where Does the Law Apply?

As part of their reapplication of Deut 17:8–13 from the context of a national high court to the *beth midrash*, the Tannaim also discuss whether the law of the rebellious elder applies to the rabbinic court/council at Yavneh or any other central place where the rabbis met after the destruction of the Temple. Even though the verse limits the law to Jerusalem, "the place that God shall choose," *Sifre Deut. pisqa* 153 finds an extra word to include Yavneh: ובאת לרבות בית דין שביבנה—"*And you shall come* (Deut 17:9): this includes the court at Yavneh."[33] This has the effect of extending the law, which might have become irrelevant with the loss of Jerusalem, into the rabbinic era.

The next *pisqa* of the *Sifre*, however, takes a step back by adding that

---

31. This point is also expressed by *t. Sanh.* 14:12 and *y. Sanh.* 11:3 (30a), which similarly stress teaching others, although they also require that the elder has practiced or will practice himself. However, *Sifre Deut., pisqa* 155 (ed. Finkelstein, 207) requires that the judge actually perform an action against the high court and does not require that he teach: "אשר יעשה—על מעשה הוא חייב ואינו חייב על הוריה" (ed. Finkelstein, 207). It is possible to explain the end of the Sifre as "he is not liable if he [only] teaches." I.e., the Sifre's case is similar to the case of "הורה ולא עשה פטור" in the Tosefta and Yerushalmi and requires both practicing *and* teaching. *B. Sanh.* 88b, on the other hand, holds one liable whether he performs *or* teaches "תנו רבנן: אינו חייב עד שיעשה כהוראתו, או שיורה לאחרים ויעשו כהוראתו." See Daniel Sperber, "Sugya aḥat be-masekhet Horayot," *Sinai* 70 (1972): 3 n. 13, for a slightly different categorization of these sources.

32. Fraade, *From Tradition to Commentary*, 85. Italics are in the original.

33. Ed. Finkelstein, 206. "*The place that God shall choose*" is always assumed by the rabbis to be Jerusalem, and therefore an extra word is required to include any other location.

only rebellion against the high court in Jerusalem warrants the death penalty: ועשית על פי הדבר על הורית בית דין הגדול שבירושלם חייבים מיתה ואין חייבים מיתה על הורית בית דין שביבנה—"*You shall act according to the words* (Deut 17:10): One is liable to death for [disobeying] the ruling of the great court in Jerusalem but one is not liable to death for [disobeying] the ruling of the court at Yavneh."[34] Even though no rabbi was allowed to disobey the majority at Yavneh, the Yavnean council could not sentence a colleague to death for doing so.[35] This interpretation provides a lower level of authority for the Yavnean court.

The Yerushalmi, however, adds a gloss after quoting this same midrash, which may offer a slightly different explanation: ובאת לרבות בית דין שביבנה. רבי זעירא אומר לשאילה—"*And you shall come*: including the court at Yavneh. R. Zeira says, for an inquiry."[36] That is, if an elder rebels against a decision made concerning "an inquiry" asked of the Yavneh court, then that elder is liable to death. However, the Yavneh court itself may not punish him. Only the Jerusalem court can mete out the punishment, perhaps so that the punishment will be made more public[37] or perhaps because this law concerns the judicial system of the nation as a whole and so requires the adjudication at the highest court.[38] Either way, the Yerushalmi maintains that the reason one is not liable to death for disobeying the Yavneh court is not because it has any less authority but only because that court lacks the means to practically execute the punishment.[39] At a theoretical level, however, the Yavneh court may hold the same authority and demand the same level of obedience as the high court of Jerusalem.[40]

---

34. *Sifre Deut., pisqa* 154 (ed. Finkelstein, 207).

35. This reading takes the two statements of the Sifre as complementing each other, not disagreeing. See ibid., 206, comment on line 10, for this reconciliation. It would be incorrect to interpret the second statement to mean that one is not liable in Yavneh and therefore permitted. It is clear from the next line in that *pisqa* that a distinction is being made between חייבים מיתה and a general prohibition. See more on this below.

36. *Y. Sanh.* 11:3 (29d).

37. *M. Sanh.* 11:4 rules that the rebellious elder is not killed in a local or Yavnean court but only in the high court in Jerusalem on a festival so that the punishment will be more public and serve as an example to deter others from doing the same. This is the opinion of R. Akiba, while R. Yehudah, who says one kills him immediately, would presumably also dispense with the need to bring him to the Jerusalem court. *Pene Moshe* interprets that R. Zeira seeks to reconcile the Midrash that includes Yavneh with the opinion of R. Akiba.

38. *M. Sanh.* 1:8 lists many laws that can be decided only by the high court of seventy-one. A common denominator between these cases is that they all concern national interests. The law of the rebellious elder, however, is not listed here.

39. Perhaps this is part of a larger reluctance or inability to use the death penalty after losing national sovereignty. See texts cited by Hammer-Kossoy, "Divine Justice in Rabbinic Hands: Talmudic Reconstitution of the Penal System," 14–19. The Romans did not authorize Jewish courts to mete out the death penalty. See Guttmann, *Rabbinic Judaism in the Making*, 19–21; and Aharon Oppenheimer, "Jewish Penal Authority in Roman Judaea," in *Jews in a Graeco-Roman World*, ed. Martin Goodman (Oxford: Clarendon, 1998), 181–91.

40. See Finkelstein, *Sifra*, 5:57. Finkelstein argues that the redaction of Sifre Deuteron-

We see in the *Sifre* and the Yerushalmi a move to extend the law of the rebellious elder, even if only a limited version, to the rabbinic court at Yavneh. There seems, however, to be an alternate view among the Tannaim. The Bavli version of the midrash, which is also included in *Midrash Tannaim*,[41] focuses not on the word ובאת—"and come" (v 9) to include Yavneh, but rather on the words "to the place" (v 8), to exclude any place but the Temple. *B. Sanhedrin* 87a reads: אל המקום מלמד שהמקום גורם—"*To the place*, this teaches that the place determines." Bavli *Sanhedrin* 14b elaborates further:

> תניא כוותיה דרב יוסף: **מצאן אבית פאגי והמרה עליהן, כגון שיצאו למדידת עגלה, ולהוסיף על העיר ועל העזרות, יכול שתהא המראתו המראה—תלמוד לומר וקמת ועלית אל המקום מלמד שהמקום גורם.**
>
> It was taught in accordance with Rav Yosef: **If one found them [the court] at Beth Page and rebelled against them, for example, if they went for the measurement for a heifer or to extend a city or the Temple courts, is it possible that his rebellion is considered a [formal act of] rebellion? The text therefore states, *You shall arise and go to the place*, this teaches that the place determines.**[42]

This *baraita* discusses a case when the high court of Jerusalem itself happens to meet at an alternate location for some reason. In such a case, an act of rebellion is not only unpunishable but is not considered an act of rebellion at all.[43] This *baraita* ties the power of the court to its location within the Temple. Therefore, even the same members at a different location, and cer-

---

omy began in Yavneh during the time of Yoḥanan ben Zakkai. This would explain the push in the *Sifre* to raise the status of the Yavneh court. The Mekhilta on Debarim may have had different origins and therefore reflected a different attitude towards Yavneh. This is impossible to prove, however, without a reliable edition of the Mekhilta. See next paragraph.

41. David Hoffmann, *Midrasch Tannaim zum Deuteronomium* (Berlin: H. Itzkowski, 1909), 102, on Deut 17:8.

42. See parallels in *b. Sanh.* 87a; *b. Soṭah* 45a; and *b. ʿAbod. Zar.* 8b.

43. This follows my translation above, which I think follows the Hebrew most literally. By contrast, Soncino (to *b. Soṭah* 45a) translates "… it is possible to think that his act of rebellion is punishable…. This teaches that the place determines [whether the act of rebellion is punishable]." According to this translation, one is prohibited from disobeying the court even when not at their location but one is not given the death penalty for such action. According to this explanation, one could reconcile this Midrash with the Sifre. However, this translation is not faithful to the Hebrew, adding more commentary than is warranted. In any case, even if one does interpret this *baraita* as addressing only the punishment aspect of the law, the rhetorical force of each statement is still significantly different. The Sifre goes out of its way to include Yavneh in a blanket statement and then adds a caveat about the limitation of the punishment, while the Bavli *baraita* simply limits the law to Jerusalem with no mention of Yavneh at all.

tainly a newly formed court at Yavneh, would not have the same authority to punish dissenters. By raising the central court to unique authority as if the location itself provides them with exclusive power, this *baraita* ironically ends up degrading every other court.

We thus find differences of opinion in the Tannaitic and Amoraic sources regarding the application of the law of the rebellious elder to the court at Yavneh, and perhaps later courts as well.[44] The original discussion, as reflected in the *Sifre* and Yerushalmi *baraita,* on the one hand, and *Midrash Tannaim* and the Bavli *baraita,* on the other, may reflect tensions by the Tannaim living after the destruction about the status of Yavneh itself. However, this issue would not have been relevant in Amoraic times. It therefore seems significant that the Yerushalmi quotes the *Sifre* version, which includes Yavneh, while the Bavli's *baraita* excludes any other court besides that in the chamber of hewn stone.

We do not know whether both interpretations were available to the redactors of the Talmuds or whether each Talmud already included different versions of the Tannaitic material in their proto-formats. One can conceive of at least three possibilities for the provenance of the Bavli *baraita*: (1) The Bavli redactors received a version of the *Sifre*, ignored it, and created an artificial "*baraita*" to counter it. (2) The Bavli redactors received two Tannaitic traditions and chose the more restrictive versions. (3) The Bavli redactors received only the *baraita* that was part of the proto*sugya*. According to the first two possibilities, one can posit that the redactors of the Bavli, where multiple practices were tolerated, ignored the version of the *Sifre* and Yerushalmi in favor of a restrictive interpretation that relegated the entire law of the rebellious elder to an unrecoverable past and understood it as significant only for theoretical discussion. According to the third option, the presence of the restrictive *baraita* in the Bavli and not in the Yerushalmi may be based either on an accident of transmission history or on the decision (perhaps subconscious) of Amoraim to prefer this tradition over the *Sifre* version. Similarly, we do not know whether the Yerushalmi redactors had a choice of two alternate traditions or whether they only received the *Sifre* version. Thus, we cannot posit with certainty that the difference between the two Talmuds is a result of purposeful redactional choices based on differing attitudes toward diversity. However, having analyzed many examples in previous chapters of this study of the Talmuds making redactional choices based on their respective views toward diversity—evidence that relies on explicit statements and on readily evident redactional choices—we propose that this is yet another such

44. For the way the Talmudic discussion plays out in the writings of Maimonides, who extends the authority of the Sanhedrin, and Nahmanides, who limits it, see Yonason Sacks, "The Mizvah of 'Lo Tasur': Limits and Applications," *Tradition* 27, no. 4 (1993): 49–60, and other essays in that same volume.

example. Whatever the prehistory of each *sugya*, it seems significant that the interpretations found in each Talmud fit into the general pattern of the Yerushalmi furthering the cause of uniformity by extending the law of the rebellious elder and the Bavli tolerating diversity by limiting the same law.

Who Sits on the Court?

The next line of *pisqa* 153 in the *Sifre* continues to update the law of the rebellious elder to fit in with the rabbinic era. Deut 17:9 specifies that הכהנים הלוים—"the levitical priests" are to be part of the tribunal. The Midrash, however, explains that it is preferable to have priests and Levites on the tribunal, but not necessary:

> אל הכהנים הלוים, מצוה בבית דין שיהיו בו כהנים ולוים יכול מצוה ואם אין בו יהא פסול תלמוד לומר ואל השופט, אף על פי שאין בו כהנים ולוים כשר.
> *To the Levitical priests:* It is a commandment that a court should include priests and Levites. Can it be a commandment and if there are no [priests and Levites] on it is it invalid? The verse teaches, *and to the judge*: even if there are no priests and Levites it is valid.[45]

While priests had some important roles in the courts of the rabbinic era, their status was greatly diminished from that assumed in the Bible and Second Temple era.[46] It therefore became impractical or anachronistic

45. *Sifre Deut., pisqa* 153 (ed. Finkelstein, 206). The phrase הכהנים הלוים, which occurs in several places in Deuteronomy (besides 17:9, it also occurs in 17:18; 18:1; 24:8; 27:9), does not mean the priests and the Levites but rather "the Levitical priests." According to Deut 18:6–8, all sons of Levi were eligible to be priests. See Moshe Weinfeld, ed., *Debarim*, Olam haTanakh (Tel-Aviv, 1999), 142. The midrash, however, regards priests and Levites as separate categories.

46. The Damscus Document (CD X, 4–7) mentions a requirement that the courts have "four of the tribe of Levi and Aaron" in each court of ten members. The Temple Scroll (LVII, 11–14) similarly states, "Twelve princes of his people shall be with him [the king of Israel], and twelve priests and twelve Levites, who shall sit together with him for judgement and for the law." A fragment of the *Aegyptiaca* of Hecataeus of Abdera describes the priests as "judges in all major disputes." See Ginzberg, *An Unknown Jewish Sect*, 48–49; Daniel Tropper, "The Internal Administration of the Second Temple of Jerusalem" (Ph.D. diss., Yeshivah University, 1970), 123–47; idem, "Bet Din Shel Kohanim," *JQR NS* 63, no. 3 (1973): 204–21; Lawrence Schiffman, *Sectarian Law in the Dead Sea Scrolls: Courts, Testimony and the Penal Code* (Chico, CA: Scholars Press, 1983), 26–27; and Reuven Kimelman, "Ha-'oligarkiah ha-kohanit ve-talmide ha-ḥakhamim bi-tqufat ha-Talmud," *Zion* 48, no. 2 (1983): 135–48. *M. Ketub.* 1:5 and *t. Sanh.* 4:7 mention a court of priests, and *t. Sanh.* 7:1 assigns special authority to priests and Levites in matters of marriage law. *M. Sanh.* 4:2 also requires that judges in a capital case be "priests, Levites, or Israelites marriageable to priests." Rava states in *b. Yoma* 26a, "You

to require priests and Levites on every court. The *Sifre* accordingly deems their presence optional.

Pisqa 153 then continues by addressing the quality of the judges themselves:

> אשר יהיה בימים ההם, אמר רבי יוסי הגלילי וכי עלת על דעתך שתלך אצל שופט שאינו בימיך אלא שופט שהוא כשר ומוחזק באותם הימים.
>
> *Who will be in those days* (Deut 17:9): R. Yose the Galilean said: Would it occur to you to go before a judge who is not in your own days! Rather, [this refers to] a judge who is qualified and reputable in those days.[47]

This Midrash predicts that people in later times will look back with nostalgia to the great judges of old and will consequently not hold their contemporary courts in high esteem. The Midrash therefore grants the courts of each generation the same high status and encourages the masses to submit to their authority. This is yet another way in which the Midrash seeks to have some semblance of the biblical court system continue into its own days.[48]

To What Types of Cases Does the Law Apply?

Another step in the transformation of the biblical law from the context of a national judicial system to rabbinic controversies involves expanding it from the realm of civil law to encompass all aspects of halakha. This is seen most clearly in *Sifre* 152:

> ממך, זו עצה. דבר, זו הלכה. למשפט, זה הדין. בין דם לדם, בין דם נדה לדם יולדת לדם זיבה. בין דין לדין, בין דיני ממונות לדיני נפשות לדיני מכות. בין נגע לנגע, בין נגעי אדם לנגעי בגדים לנגעי בתים. דברי, אלו ערכים וחרמים והקדשות. ריבות, זו השקית סוטה ועריפת עגלה וטהרת מצורע. בשעריך, זה לקט שכחה ופיאה.
>
> "*From you*": This refers to counsel.[49] "*A case*": This refers to a

---

will not find any rabbinical scholar giving decisions who is not a descendant from the tribe of Levi or Issachar." However, even though a remnant of the ancient requirement for priests to be part of the judicial system still lingers in these rabbinic texts, it remains only a vestige and never an obligation. See Urbach, *The Halakhah*, 55–57.

47. Ed. Finkelstein, 206. Cf. *b. Roš Haš.* 25b.

48. See similarly in Michael S. Berger, *Rabbinic Authority* (New York: Oxford University Press, 1998), 35–37 and 43–49.

49. Fraade, *From Tradition to Commentary*, 237 n. 52, takes this to mean another person, an advisor. He is influenced by the Bavli reading, which is discussed below. But the reading

> matter of halakha. "*To decide*": This refers to logical inference. "*Between blood and blood*": Between menstrual blood, the blood of birthing, and the blood of a flux. "*Between plea and plea*": Between cases requiring material punishment, cases requiring capital punishment, and cases requiring corporal punishment. "*Between stroke and stroke*": Between plagues [of "leprosy"] that affect humans, and plagues that affect houses, and plagues that affect clothing. "*Matters of*": These refer to valuations, and devotions, and consecrations. "*Disputes*": This refers to the bitter waters that the suspected wife is made to drink, the breaking of the heifer's neck, and the purification of the leper. "*In your courts (lit., gates)*": This refers to gleanings, the forgotten sheaf, and the corner of the field.[50]

Each word of this verse is atomized to include another subject of Jewish law. This Midrash is also quoted with minor variations as a *baraita* at the opening of both the Yerushalmi's and the Bavli's discussions on the law of the rebellious elder.[51] *Sifre* and Yerushalmi say that ממך—"from you" refers to "counsel" so that even nonlegal matters such as advice are also enforceable by the court. In the Bavli version, the same words refer to a type of person, יועץ—"advisor," who, as is explained later in the Bavli, is an expert on matters of the calendar.[52] If this is not a quotation from an alternative Tannaitic Midrash,[53] then it may be part of a larger Bavli strategy to limit the scope of the rebellious elder. Perhaps the Bavli redactors were too uncomfortable applying capital punishment to the rejection of

---

here means that one must listen to the court's advice on any matter, contrasting with matters of strict halakha, which are inferred in the next term. For עצה in a similar usage see *m. Yebam.* 12:6, where the court suggests to a *yabbam* whether it is proper for him to perform *yibbum* or *ḥaliṣa*. See also Albeck, *Mishnah, Nezikin*, 504.

50. Finkelstein, *Sifre*, 205–6. Translation based on Fraade, *From Tradition to Commentary*, 84. This section continues the line quoted above, p. 303. At the same time that the Tannaim limit those who can be given the death penalty for disobeying the high court, i.e., only senior rabbis, they also expand the jurisdiction of this high court beyond civil cases.

51. *Y. Sanh.* 11:3 (30a) and *b. Sanh.* 87a. See comparison in chart 6.2, p. 335. Cf. *Sifre Deut., pisqa* 351 (ed. Finkelstein, 408).

52. This is backed up in *b. Sanh.* 87a by a verse from Nah 1:11, which, besides containing the words ממך and יעץ, sheds no light on the connection between these words. The meaning of יועץ as "a calendar expert" derives from a similar explanation in *b. Ḥag.* 14a.

53. This same version does appear in *Midrash Hag-gadol* (ed. Fisch, 5:386) and *Midrash Tannaim* (ed. Hoffman, 102), however those Midrashim may themselves be citations from the Bavli and cannot reliably be assumed to represent the original Mekhilta to Deuteronomy. Another possibility is that originally, even the Bavli read the *baraita* with עצה. However, after this was reinterpreted by Rav Papa (*b. Sanh.* 87a) to mean יועץ, later copyists inserted that Amoraic interpretation back into the Bavli *baraita*.

mere advice from the great court and so interpreted it to refer to calendrical matters.

The *Sifre* and Bavli versions continue to include "halakha," presumably ritual laws, and "*din*," civil laws. The Yerushalmi version instead adds "*aggada*," which may include all of the stories, parables, and moral sayings of the rabbis.[54] *Aggada* as well as advice are clearly not the usual grist of the high court. All of these interpretations serve to transform the original law from the context of the national judiciary to the context of the *beth midrash*.[55] Courts typically adjudicate matters of civil, criminal, and family law. In the *Sifre*'s rereading, however, this institution becomes a legislative body whose jurisdiction encompasses all of Jewish law. Included are laws from each Seder of Mishnah: *Zeraim* (*Pe*ʾ*ah*), *Mo*ʿ*ed* (calendar in Bavli version), *Nashim* (*Soṭah*), *Nezikin* (monetary, capital, and corporeal punishments),[56] *Qodashim* (ʿ*Arakin, Temurah*), and *Ṭeharot* (*Niddah, Zabim, Nega*ʿ*im*). There is testimony that the Temple court in the decades before 70 C.E. already dealt with various ritual cases,[57] but it is unlikely that the court envisioned by the Bible fulfilled this role. Fraade once again summarizes the effect of the *Sifre*:

> The overall effect of this dissection and deictic specification is to transform the supreme tribunal from one that adjudicates difficult cases of intra-Israelite conflict, to one whose primary purpose is to decide between the conflicting views of the sages in matters of specialized legal exegesis and differentiation, especially with regard to proximate legal categories. We have here what might be thought of as the intellectualization (or rabbinization) of the functions of the central judiciary of Deuteronomy.[58]

Sifre 154, however, defines the jurisdiction of the court in different terms:

> [A] על פי התורה אשר יורוך, על דברי תורה חייבים מיתה ואין חייבים מיתה על דברי סופרים.
> [B] ועל המשפט אשר יאמרו לך תעשה, מצות עשה.
> לא תסור מן התורה אשר יגידו לך, מצות לא תעשה.
> [C] ימין ושמאל, אפילו מראים בעיניך על ימין שהוא שמאל ועל שמאל שהוא ימין שמע להם.

54. Finkelstein, *Sifra*, 5:61–83, attempts to explain other divergences between the Sifre and Yerushalmi versions. He argues that the Yerushalmi version derives from a Midrash from the school of R. Ishmael.

55. Sassoon, *Destination Torah*, 294, comments, "The baraitha's inclusion of ritual should not be attributed to the mention of priests in the passage that it is engaged in elucidating, but rather to the ecclesiastical character of the rabbinic *beth din*."

56. To this category should be added the last line of *Sifre Deut.*, *pisqa* 153, "ודרשת והגידו לך את דבר המשפט—אלו דקדוקי משפט" (ed. Finkelstein, 207).

57. See the statement of R. Ṣadoq, who lived during the Second Temple period concerning laws of *Miqva*ʾ*ot* in *m.* ʿ*Ed.* 7:4. See also *m. Pe*ʾ*ah* 2:6, *m. Mid.* 5:4, and *t. Soṭah* 9:1.

58. Fraade, *From Tradition to Commentary*, 84.

> [A] *In accordance with the instruction given to you* (Deut 17:11): One is liable to the death penalty for [disobeying the court regarding] biblical laws but one is not liable for [disobeying the court regarding] laws of the scribes.
> [B] *And the ruling handed down to you, you shall act:* A positive commandment. *You must not deviate from the verdict that they announce to you:* A negative commandment.
> [C] *To the right or to the left:* even if they show you that right is left and that left is right you must obey them.[59]

Line A excludes all of rabbinic law from the death penalty. A rebellious elder presumably still may not rebel against a ruling of the court regarding a rabbinic law, but such a violation would not warrant the death penalty.[60] This creates two levels of possible violation of the law of the rebellious elder and, by doing so, somewhat weakens its force. The biblical verse makes no distinction as to whether the court's ruling is based on a Pentateuchal code or simply a matter of the court's discretion. All cases, even those based only on the court's reasoning and without scriptural proof, carry the threat of the death penalty in the original law in order to deter others from disobeying the court, thus upholding its authority. Limiting the penalty to only biblical laws changes the nature of the entire law of the rebellious elder. It now takes on a retributive character as an especially harsh penalty for disobeying biblical laws, which are more serious than rabbinic laws. The importance of maintaining the authority of the court for its own sake, no matter what happens to be the substance of their ruling, is diminished.

It is not clear how this Midrash relates to the earlier one in *pisqa* 152, which expanded the law of the rebellious elder to include all of civil, criminal, and ritual law. Do these two sections of Midrash represent opposing Tannaim or are we to assume in reading *pisqa* 152 that only the portion of those laws based in the Pentateuch are punishable by death while the rabbinic amendments are not?[61] It is furthermore not clear how lines A and B relate to line C of *pisqa* 154. Line B simply reinforces the strength of

---

59. Ed. Finkelstein, 207.

60. This line comes immediately after the line quoted above, p. 308, that one is only liable for the death penalty for disobeying the high court in Jerusalem. Since these two lines share the same structure, "על...חייב מיתה ואין חייבין מיתה על...," both should be interpreted the same way as dealing specifically with the application of the death penalty and not the prohibition itself. Contrast this with two lines in *Sifre Deut., pisqa* 145, which share a different structure, "על...חייב ואינו חייב על...." That section limits not only the punishment but the entire prohibition.

61. Shemesh, "Halakha u-nevu'ah," 925, notes the tension between the two statements and takes them both as part of the struggle the Tannaim had to uphold their contemporary courts with authority and at that same time allow for individual intellectual freedom.

the verse by pointing out that it includes both a positive and a negative commandment and seems to simply clarify the view in line A. Line C says even if they say something that is obviously wrong—that right is left—you must obey. Lines A and B, which limit the law to biblical ordinances, seem to contradict line C, which expands the law to any teaching of the court, even an illogical one.[62]

If lines A and B seem incompatible with line C and *pisqa* 152, they outright contradict *m. Sanh.* 11:3:

> חומר בדברי סופרים מבדברי תורה האומר אין תפילין כדי לעבור על דברי תורה פטור חמשה טוטפות להוסיף על דברי סופרים חייב.
>
> There is a greater stringency regarding teachings of the scribes than regarding teachings of the Torah. If one says, there is no precept of *tefillin*, such that a biblical law would be transgressed, he is exempt. [But, if he rules that the *tefillin* must contain] five compartments, thus adding to the words of the scribes, he is liable.

Line A of *Sifre* 154 says that one is liable only regarding biblical laws and not rabbinic laws while Mishnah says the opposite. The Mishnah interprets the law as directed specifically toward upholding rabbinic laws, which lack the same intrinsic authority that Torah laws do and require this added cautionary measure.[63] The Tannaitic texts leave us confused about whether and how to reconcile these various statements. Fortunately, a *baraita* that is found only in the Bavli can help us reconstruct the Tannaitic scene. *B. Sanhedrin* 87a reads:

> תנו רבנן: זקן ממרא אינו חייב אלא על דבר שזדונו כרת ושגגתו חטאת, דברי רבי מאיר.
> רבי יהודה אומר: על דבר שעיקרו מדברי תורה ופירושו מדברי סופרים.
> רבי שמעון אומר: אפילו דקדוק אחד מדקדוקי סופרים.

---

62. For further discussion on the meaning of line C, see below p. 342f.

63. *Y. Sanh.* 11:4 (30a) (=*y. Ber.* 1:4, 3b) elaborates on this point by citing a number of Amoraic teachings echoing the promotion of rabbinic law; among them is the following:

> רבי בא בר כהן בשם ר׳ יודה בר פזי תדע לך שדברי סופרים חביבין מדברי תורה שהרי רבי טרפון אילו לא קרא לא היה עובר אלא בעשה ועל ידי שעבר על דברי בית הלל נתחייב מיתה על שם ופורץ גדר ישכנו נחש.
>
> R. Ba bar Kohen [said] in the name of R. Yehudah bar Pazzi: Know that the words of the scribes are more beloved than the words of the Torah for behold had R. Ṭarfon not recited [the *shema*] at all he would have only transgressed a positive commandment, but because he transgressed the words of Beth Hillel he was liable to death as per the verse, "*He who breaches a fence will be bitten by a snake*" (Eccl 10:8).

The rabbis consider R. Ṭarfon (*m. Ber.* 1:3) liable to death because of Eccl 10:8. This verse is used in a similar sense of threatening those who disobey the rabbis in *t. Ḥul.* 2:23, *Abot de-Rabbi Natan* B:3 (ed. Schechter, 14), *y. Ber.* 1:1 (3a) (above, p. 247); *b. Šabb.* 110a, et al. The goal of such death threats is to uphold rabbinic law as defined by the majority or mainstream group of rabbis. This curse acts as a substitute for the judicial process of the rebellious elder in the absence of legal authority to punish. See further discussion below, p. 326.

> Our rabbis taught: A rebellious elder is liable only for a matter for which one is liable to *karet* for purposeful transgression and a sin-offering for accidental transgression. This is R. Meir's view.
> R. Yehudah said: For a matter whose root is biblical, but whose interpretation is from the scribes.
> R. Shimon said: Even for a single detail from the detailed interpretations of the rabbis.

This *baraita* should warn us from trying to reconcile all of the various Tannaitic sources because it presents views of Tannaim ranging from one extreme to the other. Even though this *baraita* is found only in the Bavli and not in any Tannaitic source, the first opinion of R. Meir is also found in *Midrash Hag-gadol* in the name of Rabbi:[64]

> רבי אומר כי יפלא ממך דבר למשפט כלל בין דם לדם ובין דין לדין ובין נגע לנגע פרט דברי ריבות חזר וכלל כלל ופרט וכלל ואין אתה דן אלא כעין הפרט מה הפרט מפורש דבר שחייבין על זדונו כרת ועל שגגתו חטאת אף כל דבר שחייבין על זדונו כרת ועל שגגתו חטאת.
>
> Rabbi says, *"If a matter of judgment is too baffling"*—a generality, *"between blood and blood, between claim and claim, between wound and wound"*—specifics, *"matters of dispute"*—another generality. Whenever one finds a generality, specifics, and a generality one interprets the generalities to be similar to the specifics. Just as the specifics list matters for which one is liable to *karet* for purposeful transgression and a sin-offering for accidental transgression, so too [this law applies to] all cases for which one is liable to *karet* for purposeful transgression and a sin-offering for accidental transgression.[65]

This quotation from *Midrash Hag-gadol,* which Hoffman includes in *Midrash Tannaim,*[66] likely derives from a Tannaitic Midrash. That R. Meir's opinion is found in this Midrash argues for the authenticity of the Bavli *baraita.*[67] R. Meir is even more limiting than line A of *Sifre* 154. Not only

64. Finkelstein, *Sifra,* 5:70, suggests that R. Meir is the correct reading in *Midrash Tannaim* as well since copyists often confused R. Meir with Rabbi. Alternatively, the text may originally have read דבר אחר, was abbreviated to ד"א, and then the *dalet* was mistaken for a *resh* and then expanded to "Rabbi says."

65. Shlomo Fisch, *Midrash hag-gadol* (Jerusalem: Mosad Harav Kook, 1975), 5:389. It is not clear why the Midrash assumes that the פרט section in the middle contains only laws whose violation deserves *karet/haṭṭat*. See Finkelstein, *Sifra,* 5:70–71, who explains that this *derasha* is working off of an original Midrash from the school of R. Ishmael where only *karet* violations are listed.

66. Hoffmann, *Midrasch Tannaim,* 102.

67. None of the opinions in the *baraita,* except the second (see below, p. 322), are found

does R. Meir exclude rabbinic laws, he even excludes most biblical laws. He limits the cases in which the rebellious elder would warrant capital punishment to some of the most severe biblical laws. These laws number thirty-six and are listed in *m. Ker.* 1:1.[68] Many of these laws warrant death by stoning, the most severe form of capital punishment, when performed on purpose and in the presence of witnesses.[69] Thus, if an elder disobeyed the court and performed work on Shabbat, his punishment for that violation itself (stoning) would be greater than his violation by the law of the rebellious elder whose punishment is only strangulation. The punishment of the rebellious elder would apply only when the elder taught others a permissive law that he did not perform himself.[70] R. Meir's opinion is therefore the most retributive. An elder is liable to death only for performing (or teaching) a law whose penalty is often death in any case.

---

elsewhere as Amoraic sayings. Since the *baraita* quotes such far-ranging opinions, it has no obvious agenda that could indicate that some Amora or Stam composed it and then ascribed to it Tannaitic authority. The *baraita* therefore seems to be an authentic remnant from a Tannaitic Midrash such as Mekhilta to Deuteronomy.

68. This category is also used as a limitation in the context of *Horayot*: "A court is not liable until they rule in a matter that is punishable by *karet* if done on purpose and requires a sin-offering if by mistake" (*m. Hor.* 2:3). The connection to *Horayot* is made explicit in *b. Sanh.* 87a:

> מאי טעמא דרבי מאיר? גמר, דבר דבר, כתיב הכא: כי יפלא ממך דבר למשפט, וכתיב התם ונעלם דבר מעיני הקהל. מה להלן דבר שחייב על זדונו כרת ועל שגגתו חטאת, אף כאן דבר שחייב על זדונו כרת ועל שגגתו חטאת.
>
> What is the derivation of R. Meir? He learns *dabar dabar*. It is written here, *"If a case (dabar) is too baffling for you to decide"* (Deut 17:8), and it is written there, *"And the matter (dabar) escapes the notice of the congregation"* (Lev 4:13). Just as there [the law applies to] a matter for which one is liable to *karet* for purposeful transgression and a sin-offering for accidental transgression, so too here [the law applies to] a matter for which one is liable to *karet* for purposeful transgression and a sin-offering for accidental transgression.

In fact, a similar *gezerah shavah* is used in *t. Hor.* 1:7 and *b. Hor.* 4a where דבר in both paragraphs teaches that just as in the rebellious elder, one is only liable for transgressing part of a law but not the whole of it (which is never mentioned in context of rebellious elder), so too in cases of a mistaken court. It is interesting that these cases are viewed as being similar even though they are actually on opposite sides of the table; in *Horayot* the court is mistaken while the rebellious elder wrongly disobeys a court's valid decision. While *b. Sanh.* 87a derives the category for the rebellious elder from *Horayot*, *Midrash Hag-gadol* (ed. Fisch, 5:389) derives it within the context of the rebellious elder and without reference to *Horayot*. *Sifra, Ḥoba, parasha* 1, *parshata* 1:7 (ed. Finkelstein, 2:120), on the other hand, derives the category for *Horayot* from within its own context without reference to the rebellious elder. For more on the relationship between the two sets of laws see the next chapter, esp. p. 364 n. 66.

69. See *m. Sanh.* 7:4.

70. *B. Sanh.* 88b similarly asks, "if he acts according to his ruling he is already liable to death and now he is [again] liable to death?" This question assumes the opinion of R. Meir, even though that is not stated.

B. Sanhedrin 87a-88a already questions the relationship between R. Meir and the Midrash found in *Sifre* 152. While the solution is a feat of "stupendous effort and virtuosity,"[71] it is patently not the plain meaning of the Midrash. By forcing *Sifre* 152 into R. Meir's definition, the Bavli greatly limits the number of cases included in the law of the rebellious elder and muffles the rhetorical force of *Sifre* 152, which is to expand the law into all cases. As we will see below, this is only one of several ways in which the Bavli limits the applicability of the rebellious elder.[72]

At the other extreme of R. Meir is the view of R. Shimon that every jot and tittle of rabbinic law is included: אפילו דקדוק אחד מדקדוקי סופרים.[73] In this view, the law of the rebellious elder is not retributive, for why should one be liable to death for violating a minor rabbinic decree. Rather, the purpose of the law is to uphold the authority of the court/rabbis no matter what they say. Punishment of even, and especially, the most minor of misdemeanors sends a strong signal to deter any other disobedience of the rabbis' decision. R. Shimon is rhetorically closest to line C of *Sifre* 154, which even adds cases where the rabbis teach something that seems illogical.

R. Yehudah adopts a middle opinion, which explains that the purpose of the law of the rebellious elder is to uphold the rabbis' authority to interpret Scripture. The second example given in *m. Sanh.* 11:3, of five *ṭoṭafot* in the *tefillin,* fits into this category of a rabbinic interpretation of something based in Scripture.[74] The first example, "one who says there is no precept of *tefillin*" could refer to those who, like Rashbam, interpret the biblical verses figuratively, that we should keep these words in mind, and not that we physically bind them on our body.[75] The literal interpretation, which requires physical *tefillin,* is not unique to the rabbis since it was so

---

71. Sassoon, *Destination Torah,* 294.

72. One could argue that the Bavli's extended exercise to explain Sifre 152 according to R. Meir does not reveal any ideological agenda but is rather an attempt to reconcile differing opinions or simply a mechanical exercise to display virtuosity. However, as mentioned above in n. 70, a *sugya* found later in the Bavli still assumes the position of R. Meir, which suggests that the Bavli's redactors accept his opinion, at least to some degree. If so, the attempt to explain Sifre 152 according to R. Meir indicates support for his opinion rather than simply an exercise in reconciliation. See also below, p. 333 n. 117. The term תרגמה/תרגמא/מתרגם is found dozens of times in the Bavli to reconcile contradictory sources by "translating" or reinterpreting one of the sources to fit with the other. See Wilhelm Bacher, *'Erkhe midrash* (Jerusalem: Karmi'el, 1969), 2:320–22. The choice of which source to reinterpret and how extensively this explanation changes the prior understanding of the law must surely reflect some vision as to which is deemed preferable, rather than simply a mechanical reconciliation. However, the usage of this term requires further study.

73. A similar phrase is found in *t. Demai* 2:5 in the context of a convert who, according to one opinion, must accept every jot and tittle of halakha.

74. See *b. Sanh.* 88b.

75. R. Shmuel ben Meir (ca. 1085–ca. 1174) on Exod 13:9.

interpreted by such prerabbinic groups as the Samaritans and the Dead Sea sect as well as the *Letter of Aristeas* (line 159), Philo, and Josephus (*Ant.* 4.8.13).[76] In *b. Sanh.* 33b and *b. Hor.* 4a, the Talmud uses Sadducean interpretation as the barometer for what is explicit in the biblical text.[77] Assuming that the Sadducees did wear *tefillin,* one who denies this precept does not violate rabbinic law but the literal meaning of a biblical verse.[78]

The view that *tefillin* must contain five *ṭoṭafot* may simply be a theoretical example, or it may refer to an actual sectarian view. Although the *tefillin* found among the Dead Sea scrolls contain either one or four compartments, like the rabbinic *tefillin,* it is interesting that the sect included more biblical passages than are prescribed by the rabbis.[79] Maintaining five *ṭoṭafot* may refer to this or similar practices.[80] If so, the aim of the law of the rebellious elder in the view of some Tannaim may be to reign in sectarian deviations among the rabbis. Explicit biblical laws have intrinsic authority accepted by all on account of their presence in Scripture. It is the rabbinic interpretation of Scripture, however, which was hotly contested by various detractors. The category set out by R. Yehudah lends itself to issues subject to controversy between the rabbis and other sects. The Mishnah has a similar polemical tone. The Mishnah, therefore, may very well represent the opinion of R. Yehudah.

Furthermore, if we assume that the entire pericope of *Sifre* concerning the rebellious elder (*pisqa'ot* 152–155) is an integrated unit from the hand of one author or school, then we can reconcile both *pisqa'ot* 152 and 154 lines A and C with the opinion of R. Yehudah. Line A does not deal with explicit laws in the Torah, which the rabbis would not have the power to contradict, but rather with rabbinic definitions of the biblically based law.[81] If line C is not merely exaggerated rhetoric, it seems to contend that even if the rabbis teach an illogical or nonliteral explanation of a biblical commandment, one must still follow their ruling.[82] Similarly, *pisqa* 152 only means to spell out the range of topics included within the law of the rebel-

---

76. See Albeck, *Mishnah, Nezikin,* 459; Naomi Cohen, "Philo's Tefillin," *World Congress for Jewish Studies* 9A (1986): 199–206; and John Bowman, "An Arabic Hijab Manuscript and Jewish and Samaritan Phylacteries," *Abr-Nahrain* 32 (1994): 53–56.

77. See below, p. 341.

78. See Hirsh Mendel Pineles, *Darkah shel Torah* (Vienna, 1861), 20.

79. There are also one or two tefillin with three compartments but none with five. See Yigal Yadin, "Tefillin shel rosh me-Qumran," *Erez Israel* 9 (1969): 76, and Yehudah Cohn, *Tangled Up in Text: Tefillin and the Ancient World* (Providence, RI: Brown Judaic Studies, 2008), 56.

80. See further in Jacob Mann, "Changes in the Divine Service of the Synagogue Due to Religious Persecutions," *Hebrew Union College Annual* 4, nos. 241–310 (1927): 289–99; however, Cohn, *Tangled,* 130, disagrees.

81. Shemesh, "Halakha u-nevu'ah," 928, suggests that R. Yehudah's opinion, as quoted in the Talmuds, is meant to reconcile the Mishnah with the Sifre.

82. *Y. Hor.* 1:1 (45d) has a version of line C that states the reverse. We will analyze the laws of *Horayot* and their relationship to the rebellious elder in the next chapter.

lious elder, even though only the rabbinic interpretations of those biblical laws would be punishable.[83] However, even if we can reconcile some of the various texts in terms of their practical implications, it is clear that they each serve a different rhetorical purpose.

To sum up the Tannaitic opinions, R. Meir and *Midrash Tannaim* are at one extreme, putting the greatest limitations on the law of the rebellious elder, who is punished only for teaching against the court in very serious cases. At the other extreme is R. Shimon, who puts no limitations on the type of case for which the rebellious elder can be punished. Even a detail of rabbinic law must be defended in order to uphold the authority of the central court. In the middle is the opinion of R. Yehudah, who sets forth two conditions: a case must be based in the Torah so that it meets a minimum threshold of severity, but it also must depend on rabbinic interpretation. Other statements seem to agree, more or less, with R. Yehudah. The examples presented in *m. Sanh.* 11:3 fit into the conditions of R. Yehudah. *Sifre* 154 line A emphasizes the first condition while line C and the Mishnah stress the second. All opinions except R. Meir seem to agree with *Sifre* 152 that the court is not limited only to civil and criminal cases but has authority to decide all matters of Jewish praxis.

The opinions of R. Yehudah and R. Shimon reflect another example of how the original biblical law has undergone a rabbinic transformation. If the original law upheld the *court's* authority to interpret biblical laws, R. Yehudah reinterprets it to apply to the authority of the *rabbis* to interpret biblical law—ופירושו מדברי סופרים. R. Shimon expands the law to all rabbinic enactments and uses a similar phrase: דקדוקי סופרים. The Mishnah focuses the rabbinic aspect of the law with even greater emphasis than the other formulations by specifically excluding דברי תורה and including, once again, דברי סופרים. These formulations suggest a polemical antisectarian motive.

Extending the law into the realm of rabbinic law bolsters the authority of the rabbinic majority while at the same time suppressing minority opinion. The law no longer applies to a defiant litigant, but to a learned elder who disagrees with the mainstream rabbinic opinion. This might be a fellow rabbi with a minority position, a member of a nonrabbinic sect, or perhaps someone on the border of the two camps. In any case, the Tannaitic sources show a certain discomfort with allowing any rabbi or wise elder to decide halakha against the majority. It is improbable that there

83. The medieval commentators suggest various strategies to reconcile or choose between the Mishnah, Sifre 152, R. Meir, and R. Yehudah. See Tosafot *b. Sanh.* 88b, s.v. ואין; Nissim Gerondi, *Hidushe ha-Ran: masekhet Sanhedrin* (Jerusalem: Mosad ha-Rav Kook, 2003), 570–77; Rambam, *Mishneh Torah, hilkhot mamrim,* 4:2, and commentators ad loc.; and the heated correspondence between R. Meir Abulafia and the rabbis of Lunel reprinted in Shalom Yungerman, *Qobeṣ shiṭot qama'e: masekhet Sanhedrin* (Zikhron Yaʿaqov: ha-Makhon le-Hosa'at Sefarim ve-Kitve Yad she-leyad ha-Merkaz le-Hinukh Torani: 2007), 1,466–68.

existed a Sanhedrin with the power to inflict capital punishment at any time during the Tannaitic period,[84] and so this law was not meant to be practical. Nevertheless, this reinterpretation of the law, even if only theoretical, reflects a desire on the part of the Tannaim to allow for freedom of debate but limit diversity of practice.

Turning to the Amoraic treatment of this issue, the Yerushalmi (*Sanh.* 11:4, 30b) cites the words of R. Yehudah[85] but in the name of R. Hoshaiah and elaborates on them:

> רבי בא רבי יוחנן בשם רבי הושעיה אינו חייב עד שיורה בדבר שעיקרן מדברי תורה ופירושו מדברי סופרים כגון הנבילה כגון השרץ שעיקרן מדברי תורה ופירושן מדברי סופרין
> אמר רבי זעירא לעולם אינו חייב עד שיכפור ויורה בדבר שעיקרו מדברי תורה ופירושו מדברי סופרין כגון נבילה וכגון שרץ שעיקרן מדברי תורה ופירושן מדברי סופרים והוא שיגרע ויוסיף בדבר שהוא מגרע והוא מוסיף
> R. Ba [said in the name of] R. Yoḥanan in the name of R. Hoshaiah: "One is not liable until he rules in a matter whose root is biblical and whose interpretation is from the scribes such as carrion and such as reptiles whose root is biblical and whose interpretation is from the scribes."
> R. Zeira said: "He will never be held liable until he denies and rules on a matter whose root is biblical and whose interpretation is from the scribes such as carrion and such as reptiles whose root is biblical and whose interpretation is from the scribes provided that he diminishes or adds in a matter that he will diminish and he will add."

R. Zeira adds another requirement on top of that of R. Hoshaiah, that the rebellious elder should add to or diminish from the law in a way that will cause the law to be both augmented and reduced. R. Zeira seemingly wishes to exclude a case where the rebellious elder adds a requirement that does not impinge on any previous definition of the law. Such a rul-

84. See references above, p. 7 n. 21.

85. Significantly, besides this statement based on the view of R. Yehudah (who is not cited by name in the Yerushalmi), the Yerushalmi only cites the expansive views presented by Sifre 152. The Yerushalmi also adds a whole section here praising the value of rabbinic law as more beloved than biblical law in order to bolster *m. Sanh.* 11:3, and thereby R. Yehudah's opinion as well. The Yerushalmi, however, does not include the limiting opinions of R. Meir and those found in Sifre 154 and Midrash Tannaim. While one cannot prove that the Yerushalmi knew of these sources and purposely omitted them, it is nevertheless noteworthy that all of the most limiting opinions are not found in the Yerushalmi. Perhaps these traditions were unwittingly repressed over time in the Yerushalmi's environment that demanded halakhic uniformity and sought an expansive view of the law of the rebellious elder. See, however, R. Zeira in the next paragraph who limits the law of rebellious elder in a different way.

ing would not threaten the authority of the majority. Only if the elder's addition in some way conflicts with and diminishes the majority opinion is he liable. The Talmud continues to discuss which specific cases would fall into this category and ends up with instances within the laws of impurity of carrion and creeping things, the size of a leporous spot, *tefillin,* and *mezuzah.*[86] Presumably other cases can also be found to fit the criteria. While the Yerushalmi thus greatly limits the law of the rebellious elder, the Bavli contains a parallel *sugya* that almost eliminates the law altogether. *B. Sanhedrin* 88b states:

> אמר רבי אלעזר אמר רבי אושעיא: אינו חייב אלא על דבר שעיקרו מדברי תורה ופירושו מדברי סופרים, ויש בו להוסיף, ואם הוסיף גורע. ואין לנו אלא תפילין אליבא דרבי יהודה.
>
> R. Eleazar said in R. Oshaia's name: He is liable only for a matter whose root is biblical and whose interpretation is from the scribes and one can add to it in such a way that the addition will be a subtraction. The only precept we have [that fulfills these conditions] is *tefillin.* This follows R. Yehudah.

R. Eleazar's wording is obviously a variation of R. Zeira but is not identical.[87] R. Eleazar requires that the rebellious elder argues with a rabbinic interpretation of a biblical law that is quantifiable such that by adding to it one nullifies it. An anonymous gloss adds that this follows the opinion of R. Yehudah and that *tefillin* is the only possible case that fits these requirements.[88] The *sugya* continues to suggest other possible cases such as *lulav* and fringes, but they are all rejected. R. Eleazar's requirement seems almost arbitrary. He seems to require that the elder does not simply offer an alternate to the court's explanation, but that he actually undermines them by changing a quantity that they have specified and that is an intrinsic part of the commandment. Whatever the reasoning is, it is significant that the Bavli limits the entire law of the rebellious elder to the one case that it *must* include since it is the example given in the Mishnah. This *sugya* effectively writes the law out of existence and curbs the possibility for Babylonian Amoraim to use the law against their cantankerous colleagues.

---

86. Disagreement about the distribution of oil in a thanksgiving offering and the length of fringes do not qualify.

87. In the Bavli, R. Eleazar quotes in the name of R. Oshaia, who is the same as R. Hoshaiah in the Yerushalmi, the author of the statement before R. Zeira.

88. This gloss does not seem to be a continuation of R. Eleazar's statement since it is not found in R. Zeira's words in the parallel Yerushalmi. Also, R. Eleazar's statement is entirely in Hebrew and the gloss contains Aramaic (אליבא).

Rav Kahana, in another Bavli *sugya,* limits the law of the rebellious elder in yet another way. *B. Sanhedrin* 88a relates a dispute:

> אמר רב כהנא: הוא אומר מפי השמועה והן אומרין מפי השמועה אינו נהרג, הוא אומר כך הוא בעיני והן אומרין כך הוא בעינינו אינו נהרג. וכל שכן הוא אומר מפי השמועה והן אומרין כך הוא בעינינו אינו נהרג, עד שיאמר כך הוא בעיני והן אומרים מפי השמועה. תדע, שהרי לא הרגו את עקביא בן מהללאל.[89]
>
> ורבי אלעזר אומר: אפילו הוא אומר מפי השמועה, והן אומרין כך הוא בעינינו נהרג, כדי שלא ירבו מחלוקות בישראל. ואם תאמר: מפני מה לא הרגו את עקביא בן מהללאל? מפני שלא הורה הלכה למעשה.
>
> Rav Kahana said: If he says, "[I base my ruling] on tradition," and they [the judges of the court] say "[We base our ruling] on tradition," he is not executed. If he says, "Thus it appears to me," and they say, "Thus it appears to us," he is not executed. All the more so, if he says, "[I base it] on tradition," and they say, "Thus it appears to us," he is not executed. He is executed only when he says, "Thus it appears to me," and they say, "[We base our ruling] on tradition." The proof is that they did not execute Akavia ben Mahalalel.
>
> R. Eleazar said: Even if he says. "[I base my ruling] on tradition," and they say, "Thus it appears to us," he is executed, so that division should not spread in Israel. And if you should argue, "Why did they not execute Akavia ben Mahalalel?", [I would answer] because he did not issue a law to be put into practice.

Rav Kahana says that the rebellious elder is not killed as long as he argues his case from equal footing, be it from tradition or his own reasoning. Even if the elder bases his opinion on his own subjective rationale, but the court also has no received tradition, he is not killed since they are both on equal ground. This limitation completely undermines the nature of the original law. If the biblical law is meant to uphold the authoritative status of the court, then it should make no difference on what their or the elder's opinion is based. It is illogical to think that the court could allow anyone to disobey it as long as the dissenter claims to have a received tradition. This would lead to anarchy in a national judicial system. Rather, Rav Kahana clearly has in mind the world of the *beth midrash*. When the rabbis are disputing an issue, various kinds of arguments hold different weight. A received tradition about an issue holds more validity than an individual rabbi's subjective outlook. If both sides of an argument have a received tradition, then no matter how many rabbis heard one side or the other, as long as the minority knows that its position is based on a reliable tradition,

89. See the discussion of Akavia above, pp. 274–76.

they need not cede. No majority can disqualify an authentic tradition. Similarly, if both sides use their own logic, then the majority cannot claim to have better logic than the minority. Even if a national court attempts to recover the traditional halakha, its ultimate purpose is to issue a law that it can impose on the nation regardless of the law's "truth." The goal of the *beth midrash,* on the other hand, at least according Rav Kahana, is to arrive at truth. Truth cannot be decided by a vote but is rather determined by the best sources and arguments. Therefore, only if the majority has the force of tradition behind it can they force an individual's subjective rationale to bend to their will.[90]

R. Eleazar takes the opposite extreme, arguing that the basis for each position makes no difference. The minority must always bow to the majority "in order that dissention should not proliferate in Israel." R. Eleazar maintains uniformity of practice as the highest value above arriving at truth or preserving tradition. The final conclusion of the Stam (perhaps based on a majority vote) is that uniformity wins out, lest sectarianism begin to spread. This leads into the next *sugya,* which, quoting *t. Sanh.* 7:1, contrasts the glory days before Beth Shammai and Beth Hillel when there was uniformity with later times when the Torah has become two.[91] However, even though Rav Kahana's extreme position is rejected in practice, his view may still represent an important theoretical basis for the Bavli's more tolerant agenda. Rav Kahana does not simply limit the cases in which the law of the rebellious elder applies; he undermines its theoretical basis, namely that the high court has ultimate authority. He argues instead that the court, or the majority, holds authority only to the extent that it can achieve the truth based on received tradition.

Rebellious Elder in Talmudic Narratives

Based on the extensive discussion of the rebellious elder in the eleventh chapter of *Sanhedrin,* we might expect it to come up again in various discussions throughout the Talmud in relation to the many controversies between majority and minority practices found therein. Surprisingly, however, the term זקן ממרא occurs in only a handful of halakhic discussions,[92] and there is no recorded case of anyone killed as a rebellious elder even though there were surely many people who did not listen to the ruling

90. According to Rav Kahana, the weight of the majority also must be factored in since an individual with a tradition cannot subdue the logic of the majority. Perhaps a tradition remembered by only one person loses some of its reliability and therefore is on the same footing as the majority's rationale.

91. See above, pp. 303–4.

92. *Y. Soṭah* 4:2 (19c) (and parallels in *y. Sanh.* 8:6 [26b]; *b. Soṭah* 25a and *b. Sanh.* 88b); *b. Sanh.* 14b (quoted above, p. 309, and see parallels there in n. 42); *b. Sanh.* 16a; and *b. Hor.* 4a.

of the rabbinic majority. There are, to be sure, stories of dissident rabbis being excommunicated[93] or cursed;[94] excommunication in rabbinic times replaces the death penalty.[95] The term זקן ממרא itself, however, is used in a narrative only twice in the Yerushalmi and never in the Bavli.[96] In both Yerushalmi stories, one rabbi threatens to brand a colleague as a rebellious elder. One narrative concerns the laws of *yibbum* and is found in *y. Yebam.* 10:4 (11a):

> יבמה שנישאת בלא חליצה
> רבי ירמיה אמר זה חולץ וזה מקיים
> רבי יודה בר פזי בשם רבי יוחנן תצא
> רבי יוסי בשם רבי הילא תצא
> רבי יוסי שאיל לרבי פינחס היך סבר רבי אמר ליה כרבי ירמיה אמר ליה חזור בך דלא
> כן אני כותב עליך זקן ממרא
>
> If a widow without children [who is obligated to perform levirate marriage] marries without *ḥaliṣa*:
> R. Yirmiah says, this one [the surviving brother] performs *ḥaliṣa* and this one [her husband] remains.
> R. Yehudah bar Pazzi [says] in the name of R. Yoḥanan, she must divorce [her husband].
> R. Yose [says] in the name of R. Hila, she must divorce.
> R. Yose asked R. Pinḥas, "What does the master think?" He told him, "In accordance with R. Yirmiah." He said to him, "Retract, for if not, I will write that you are a rebellious elder."[97]

In a discussion on one detail of the laws of *yibbum*, R. Yirmiah takes a lenient position regarding a widow who believed she was free to marry another man but after remarrying found out that she was obligated to perform *yibbum*. R. Yirmiah allows her to perform *ḥaliṣa* whenever she finds out her *yibbum* obligation and remain married to her second hus-

---

93. *B. Sanh.* 88a does ask why Akavia ben Mahalalel was not killed (presumably as a rebellious elder). See above, p. 324.

94. See above, p. 316 n. 63.

95. See Hammer-Kossoy, "Divine Justice in Rabbinic Hands," 434; and Steinmetz, "Distancing and Bringing Near," 53 n. 14. *Y. Sanh.* 8:6 (26b) distinguishes between two stages of punishment for the rebellious elder, "זקן ממרא הדא דתימר שלא להורגו אבל להחזירו לא היו מחזירין אותו למקומו—[The statement that] the rebellious elder [can be forgiven] is only stated to mean that we do not execute him, but we still do not return him to his position." Before the elder is killed, he is first removed from his place. This likely refers to some type of excommunication.

96. Gray, *Talmud in Exile*, 114, makes the same observation: "Of seven occurrences of the term זקן ממרא in the Bavli, none involves one sage using the term against another, while of six occurrences of the phrase in the Yerushalmi there are four occurrences (two stories and their parallels) in which one sage uses the term against another."

97. The *sugya* is copied in *y. Giṭ.* 8:6 (49c) but is original here. See Lieberman, *Tosefta ki-fshuṭah*, 6:112, to *t. Yebam.* 11:7

band, while his colleagues state that the second husband must divorce her. The stringent colleagues are R. Yoḥanan and R. Hila, second- and third-generation Palestinian Amoraim, who are quoted by their students R. Yehudah bar Pazzi and R. Yose, third- and fourth-generation Amoraim. R. Yirmiah himself is contemporary with these students. R. Yose, who just reported the stringent view in the name of R. Hila, then turns to his contemporary, R. Pinḥas, to inquire concerning his opinion. When R. Pinḥas agrees with R. Yirmiah, R. Yose commands him to retract under the threat of being named a rebellious elder.[98] We are not informed what the consequences of this would be, perhaps excommunication, perhaps less formal social ostracism. We are also not told whether or not R. Pinḥas retracted his opinion. However, a similar story is reported in *y. ʿAbod. Zar.* 2:8 (41d) (=*y. Šabb.* 1:4, 3d) in which the threat is reported to have worked:

מי אסר את השמן
רב יהודה אמר דניאל אסרו וישם דניאל על לבו וגו׳
ומי התירו ר׳ התירו ובית דינו...
רבי אחא רבי תנחום בר חייה בשם רבי חנינה ואמרי לה בשם ר׳ יהושע בן לוי שהיו עולין
להר המלך ונהרגין עליו[99]
יצחק בר שמואל בר מרתא נחת לנציבין אשכח שמלאי הדרומי יתיב דרש **רבי ובית דינו**
התירו בשמן[100]
שמואל אכל[101] רב לא קביל עליה מיכול
אמר ליה שמואל אכול דלא כן אנא כתב עליך זקן ממרא
אמר ליה עד דאנא תמן אנא ידע מאן ערר עליה שמלאי הדרומי
אמר ליה מר בשם גרמיה לא בשם רבי יודן נשייא אטרח עלוי ואכל

Who forbade the oil [of Gentiles]?
Rav Yehudah said, Daniel forbade it: *Daniel resolved [not to defile himself with the king's food or the wine he drank]* (Dan 1:8).

98. The opinion of R. Yirmiah is rejected not because he opposed *m. Yebam.* 10:3. That Mishnah follows the opinion of R. Akiba while the sages disagree (see *t. Yebam.* 11:7, quoted in the continuation of the Yerushalmi *sugya*). Rather, R. Yirmiah interprets the opinion of the sages differently from his colleagues. The sages say that the children from the second marriage are not *mamzerim*. R. Yirmiah interprets this liberally to mean that the marriage is legitimate and she may remain married. His colleagues say that the children are not *mamzerim* because the prohibition of marrying another while under the obligation of *yibbum* is less severe (only a negative prohibition), but her second marriage is still illegal and she must be divorced. See *Pene Moshe*; *b. Yebam.* 92a; Maimonides, *Mishneh Torah, Nashim, Hilkhot Yibbum* 3:19; and Lieberman, ibid.

99. *Pene Moshe* explains that Rabbi permitted the oil of gentiles because Jews would risk their lives to gather olives from the king's mountain in order to make their own oil and were sometimes killed there.

100. *T. ʿAbod. Zar.* 4:11. See further below, n. 106.

101. Ms. Leiden reads אבל, which must be a simple scribal error. See Sussman, *Talmud Yerushalmi*, 1391, line 44. Cf. Gray, *Talmud in Exile*, 108 n. 27, who also suggests emending this phrase based on the parallel in *y. Šabb.* 1:4 (3d). Ms. Leiden also adds אמר at the beginning of this line, but Sussman, ibid., suggests that it be omitted.

> And who permitted it? Rabbi and his court permitted it....
> R. Aḥa, R. Tanḥum bar Ḥiyya [said] in the name of R. Ḥaninah, and some say in the name of R. Yehoshua b. Levi, they were ascending to the king's mountain and were being killed on it.[99]
> Isaac bar Shmuel bar Marta went down to Nisibis. He found Simlai the Southerner sitting and expounding: **Rabbi and his court permitted oil [of Gentiles].**[100]
> Shmuel ate [oil of Gentiles]; Rav did not accept upon himself [permission] to eat.
> Shmuel said to him [Rav], "Eat, for if you do not do so, I shall write that you are a rebellious elder."
> He [Rav] said to him, "When I was there [in Palestine], I learned that Simlai the Southerner rejected it [the prohibition against oil of Gentiles]."
> He [Shmuel] said to him, "Did the master [Simlai] say this in his own name? Did he not cite it in the name of R. Yehudah the Patriarch?" He [Shmuel] badgered him about it until he [Rav] ate.

R. Yehudah says that the origin of a prohibition against using the oil of Gentiles goes back to Daniel. However, Rabbi and his court subsequently allowed it.[102] Rav wanted to stick with the stringency. Rav, it seems, was generally stringent in this area as seen in the continuation of the *sugya*, אמר רבי יוסי בי רבי בון והדא מן חמירתא דרב רב נחת לתמן חמתון מקללין וחמר עליהון — "R. Yose b. R. Bon said: This is one of the stringencies of Rav. Rav went down [to Babylonia], saw they were lenient, and issued stringencies on them." Apparently, Palestinians were generally stricter in laws regarding separation from Gentiles than were the Babylonians. In fact, Isaac bar Shmuel bar Marta learns that Rabbi's court permitted it only when he traveled to Nisibis in Babylonia. This could explain why Shmuel, the Babylonian, permitted while Rav, though also a Babylonian, seems to have taken on certain stringencies during his studies in Palestine, which he then imported to Babylonia.

While there is no surprise that Rav and Shmuel should argue on a halakhic matter, what is striking in this *sugya* is the confrontation at the end of the *sugya*. Shmuel commands Rav to eat from the oil of Gentiles and threatens to "write" (an edict?) that Rav is a rebellious elder if he does not concede. Once again, this threat probably involves social ostracism rather than a formal indictment. Rav protests that the source of the

102. This *sugya* states twice that Rabbi's court allowed oil. The second is from Simlai in Nisibis. The first is at the beginning of the *sugya* but it is not clear if that is an anonymous statement or a continuation of Rav Yehudah's words after an interjection by an anonymous questioner. If the latter, then both this statement and that of Simlai have their provenance in Babylonia.

permissive law is Simlai himself, not Rabbi. Shmuel counters that Simlai only reported what Rabbi enacted. Perhaps Shmuel is so adamant in this case because Rabbi's authority itself is at stake. Although unstated, Rav may have held onto this stringency in order to send a message that Rabbi had no right to undo an ancient prohibition.[103] Unlike the story in *y. Yebam.* 10:4 (11a), this story provides us with a conclusion. Shmuel continued to insist and Rav finally gave in and ate.[104] Also unlike the story at *y. Yebam.* 10:4 (11a), this story has a revealing parallel at *b. ʿAbod. Zar.* 35b-36a:[105]

שמן: רב אמר: דניאל גזר עליו, ושמואל אמר: זליפתן של כלים טמאים אוסרתן. אטו כולי עלמא אוכלי טהרות נינהו? אלא, זליפתן של כלים אסורין אוסרתן.

א"ל שמואל לרב: בשלמא לדידי דאמינא זליפתן של כלים אסורין אוסרתן, היינו דכי אתא רב יצחק בר שמואל בר מרתא ואמר, דריש רבי שמלאי בנציבין: **שמן ר' יהודה ובית דינו נמנו עליו והתירוהו**,[106] קסבר: נותן טעם לפגם מותר; אלא לדידך דאמרת דניאל גזר עליו, דניאל גזר ואתא רבי יהודה הנשיא ומבטל ליה? והתנן: **אין בית דין יכול לבטל דברי בית דין חבירו אלא א"כ גדול הימנו בחכמה ובמנין?**[107]

א"ל: שמלאי לודאה קא אמרת? שאני לודאי דמזלזלו.

א"ל: אשלח ליה, איכסיף.

אמר רב: אם הם לא דרשו, אנן לא דרשינן? והכתיב: וישם דניאל על לבו אשר לא יתגאל בפת בג המלך וביין משתיו.[108] בשתי משתאות הכתוב מדבר, אחד משתה יין ואחד משתה שמן.

רב סבר: על לבו שם ולכל ישראל הורה, ושמואל סבר: על לבו שם ולכל ישראל לא הורה.

Regarding oil [of gentiles], Rav said: Daniel decreed against it. But Shmuel said: The residue of impure vessels prohibits it. Does everyone eat only pure food? Rather, the residue of prohibited vessels prohibits it.

---

103. In fact, the next line of the *sugya* wonders how Rabbi could have permitted what a greater court prohibited.

104. It is interesting to compare Shmuel's insistence with Rav's tolerance in a similar case found a few lines after this one (*y. ʿAbod. Zar.* 2:8, 42a): "תורמוסין שלהן מה הן רבי אוסר גניבה מתיר אמר רבי אני זקן והוא זקן אני עלת על ליבי לאסור והוא עלת על דעתו להתיר—Lupines of Gentiles, what is their status? Rabbi prohibits, Geniva permits. Rabbi said, 'I am an elder and he is an elder, I decided in my heart to prohibit and he decided in his mind to permit.'" Although ms. Leiden reads רבי, Rav is the more likely colleague of Geniva. In this case, Rav recognizes that his opponent is also of high rank (perhaps Rav is being humble here) and both parties have authority to rule as they deem proper. Perhaps, however, Rav's tolerance here is not so much a function of a more easy-going personality than Shmuel but rather due to the different circumstances. Shmuel needed to uphold the authority of Rabbi's court, while Rav was simply stringent on an unclear case.

105. For a thorough comparison between the Yerushalmi and Bavli versions of this story see Gray, *Talmud in Exile*, 112–16.

106. *T. ʿAbod. Zar.* 4:11. Boldface indicates a Tannaitic source. See further below, n. 106.

107. *M. ʿEd.* 1:5.

108. Daniel 1:8.

> Shmuel said to Rav: It is alright for me since I say that the residue of prohibited vessels prohibits it; that is why when R. Isaac bar Shmuel bar Marta came, he said: R. Simlai expounded in Nisibis, **"Oil [of Gentiles], R. Yehudah and his court voted on it and permitted it."**[106] He reasoned, [a prohibited substance that] gives a foul taste is permitted. But for you who says that Daniel decreed against it, how could R. Yehudah the Patriarch come and nullify what Daniel decreed? Behold we have learned: **No court may nullify the ruling of another court unless it is greater than it in wisdom and number?**[107]
> He replied: Did you quote Simlai from Lyyda? Lyddians are different for they make light [of halakhic matters].
> He said to him: Should I send a message [to R. Simlai about what you said]? Rav was embarrassed.
> Rav said: If they have not expounded should we not expound? Behold Scripture states: "*Daniel resolved not to defile himself with the king's food or the wine he drank.*"[108] The verse mentions two drinks: one is drink of wine the other is drink of oil.
> Rav reasoned, he [Daniel] resolved for himself and ruled for all of Israel. Shmuel reasoned, he resolved for himself and did not rule for all of Israel.

In the Bavli, Rav says that the prohibition against the oil of Gentiles dates back to Daniel while Shmuel refutes this and argues that the original prohibition was just a matter of the oil being mixed with nonkosher residue, which Shmuel permits. The Bavli adds more detail about why Rav rejected the testimony of Simlai.[109] Simlai was from Lydda, a city with a reputation for disregarding some parts of halakha.[110] Rav then continues

109. It is not clear whether Rav doubts the reliability of the report altogether or just does not think that Rabbi had the authority to permit. Rav evidently did not know of *t. ʿAbod. Zar.* 4:11. Most editions and manuscripts of *m. ʿAbod. Zar.* 2:6 also say that Rabbi permitted oil; however, these words are a late addition transferred from the Tosefta; see Epstein, *Mavo le-nusah ha-Mishnah*, 949. The continuation of the dialogue indicates that Rav had a problem on both accounts. Shmuel's response, "Should I send a message to him"—even assuming that the pronoun refers to Simlai and not Rabbi himself—quells the first doubt since Simlai will make it clear that he did not permit oil himself but is only passing on a tradition. This first exchange between Rav and Shmuel is paralleled in the Yerushalmi. Rav's counter that he will interpret the verse from Daniel even if Rabbi did not do so indicates that he also disagreed with Rabbi's decision.

110. See Schwartz, "Tension Between Scholars," 102–9; and Miller, *Sages and Commoners*, 126 n. 31, 249 n. 127, and 282. R. Simlai is also denigrated by R. Yonatan in *y. Pesaḥ.* 5:3 (32a) (= *b. Pesaḥ.* 62b), on which see Miller, ibid., 130–34. Lydda in the Bavli is usually called "the South" in the Yerushalmi. Uzi Weingarten, personal communication, suggests that R. Simlai's reputation here may be related to his antinomic midrash in *b. Mak.* 23b-24a. Evidently, however, this generalization by Rav and R. Yonatan was not true of all citizens of

to defend his position based on Scripture. Most significantly, only in the Yerushalmi does Shmuel threaten to call Rav a *zaken mamre*.[111] In both Talmuds, Shmuel rebukes Rav for making a snide remark about R. Simlai. Only in the Yerushalmi, however, does Shmuel continue to pressure Rav until he gives in and eats from the Gentile oil. To the contrary, in the Bavli, Rav goes on to give further arguments as to why he stands by his position.

It is difficult to assess which story, if any, better represents the historical reality. On the one hand, the story involves Babylonian rabbis, and so the Bavli does not suffer from transmission across locales. On the other hand, the Yerushalmi is still redacted much earlier than the Bavli and so suffers less from transmission across time.[112] But regardless of the history, it is still significant to compare the way the story was transmitted and recorded by the two Talmuds. In the Yerushalmi version, Shmuel forces Rav to accept his position, which is based on the authority of Rabbi, and Rav does so. In Bavli, they argue and continue to argue, but there is no threat and no indication that Rav gave in. If the Yerushalmi reflects the original version, then it is revealing that the Bavli removed the references to the *zaken mamre* and to Rav's "repentance." If the Bavli reflects a more original version of the story then it is also revealing that the Yerushalmi would insert the *zaken mamre* line.[113] Either way, this example fits in with the trend we have seen in other cases of the Yerushalmi tending to push rabbis toward conformity to the position of the majority or, in this case, of the patriarch, while the Bavli is more tolerant of diverse practices. Alyssa Gray summarizes this difference between the Talmuds as follows:

> Whereas *y. Avodah Zarah*'s Rav yields to Shmuel and eats the Gentile oil, *b. Avodah Zarah*'s Rav offers an interpretation of Dan 1:8 that justifies his continued avoidance of the oil. Rav's refusal to yield to Shmuel in b. Avo-

---

Lydda, which was a major Jewish center and was the home of many great rabbis, nor was it true of all times. See *b. Šabb.* 29b; Ze'ev Safrai, "Yiḥudo shel ha-yishuv be-'ezor Lod-Yafo bi-tqufat ha-Mishnah veha-Talmud," in *Ben Yarkon ve-Ilan* (Ramat Gan: Bar-Ilan University, 1983), 53–72; Aharon Oppenheimer, "Jewish Lydda in the Roman Era," *Hebrew Union College Annual* 59 (1988): 115–36; and Dov Herman, "The Different Approaches of the Rabbis in Yavneh, Lod, and Galilee regarding the Ninth of Av as Reflected in the Laws of the Day," *Hebrew Union College Annual* 73 (2002): 1–29 (Hebrew).

111. Gray, *Talmud in Exile*, 114, explains why the Bavli may have added a reference to Rav's embarrassment (איכסיף) based on the significance given to shame in the Bavli in general, as discussed by Rubenstein, *Culture*, 67–79. However, this still does not explain why the Bavli does not include the threat of Rav being labeled a rebellious elder.

112. In addition, the general tendency of the Bavli storytellers is to take great liberties in using their source material to create new narratives. More than the Yerushalmi, the Bavli redactors regularly rework their sources in order to fit into the literary and didactic context of the *sugya*. The Bavli is therefore generally less useful for reconstructing history than the Yerushalmi. See further above, p. 38.

113. This position is taken by Ben-Menahem, *Judicial Deviation*, 91.

> dah Zarah certainly makes sense in light of the greater decentralization of the Babylonian amoraic movement and the differences between Babylonia and Palestine on the issue of the diversity of practice and/or opinion.[114]

Gray's explanation for the difference between the two stories in terms of the Bavli's greater decentralization and greater acceptance of "diversity of practice" matches my own conclusions here as well as at the end of chapter 3.[115]

Conclusion

In sum, the history of interpretation surrounding Deut 17:8–13 reveals some general patterns of thought by the rabbis concerning authority and dispute. The basic assumption throughout the laws of the rebellious elder, unlike the laws of *Horayot* discussed in the next chapter, is that every Jew must follow the decision of a court or else suffer the penalty associated with each individual law—which may be a fine, lashes, or something more severe. But beyond the punishment required for that individual transgression, some people in some circumstances are further punished with the death penalty for rebelling against the high court's decision as mandated by Deuteronomy 17. The extent to which the court can prosecute a fellow rabbi for disobeying their decision acts as a litmus test for their degree of intolerance or pluralism toward their detractors.

While various opinions existed among the rabbis of every generation concerning the details of the law of the rebellious elder, some generalizations about each era can be made based on the sources. The Tannaim modified every aspect of the biblical law in order to transfer it from a statute upholding the authority of the national judicial system to a mostly theoretical model of how to deal with halakhic disputes among the rabbis. Every detail of the law is reworked: who (the litigants of the Bible become the wise elder or high judge, the priests on the court are replaced with sages), where (the Temple court is expanded to include Yavneh), and what (from only civil laws in the Bible to all of halakha with emphasis on rabbinic interpretation of the law). In reality, the Tannaim tolerated hundreds of differences of opinion, as is evident throughout rabbinic literature, and they even lived with a good deal of multiplicity of practice, as evident in numerous narratives.[116] Nevertheless, the extension of the law

114. Gray, *Talmud in Exile*, 115, based on Kalmin, *The Sage in Jewish Society*, 11, on which see above, p. 158.

115. See above, pp. 153–61.

116. See examples analyzed in chapters 4 and 5.

of the rebellious elder reveals the desire of the Tannaim for a high degree of uniformity. If only they had the political means and the intellectual courage, they would force that unity on their dissenters, especially those with sectarian attitudes.

The Yerushalmi, for the most part, continues the line of thinking found in Tannaitic literature but limits the type of case to quantitative changes in rabbinic interpretation of biblical laws. The Bavli, by contrast, almost completely writes the law out of existence by limiting it to the one example in the Mishnah, *tefillin,* and confining the applicability of the law to the Jerusalem court. This is not to say that the Bavli eschews any concept of authority. The overall picture of the Bavli must include a rhetorical reading of its entire commentary on *m. Sanh.* 11:2–4.

The Bavli on *m. Sanh.* 11:2 is not structured as a step-by-step logical argument. It is structured as a commentary on each phrase of the Mishnah rather than as an expository essay. Nevertheless, we can trace some rhetorical flow in the movement from one *sugya* to the next. The first *sugya* quotes *Sifre* 152. The next *sugya* introduces three Tannaitic opinions including that of R. Meir, the Tanna who limits the law of the rebellious elder to the greatest extent. The next *sugya* forces the expansive *Sifre* into the narrow definition of R. Meir. The rhetorical message is that *Sifre* 152 is rejected in favor of R. Meir.[117] R. Meir relegates the authority of the court to a small corner of biblical laws already deserving severe punishment. Rav Kahana, in the next *sugya*, goes a step further and questions the very concept of authority itself. Rav Kahana's extreme position is rejected for fear of disunity, and ancient days of unity are remembered as an ideal. The Bavli on the next Mishnah then limits the law to the one case of *tefillin*.

The Bavli recognizes that a court must have authority in order for the community to hold together. However, the Bavli is not willing to uphold the model of the rebellious elder in which that authority is forced on the individual sage. This is clearly exemplified by comparing the two Yerushalmi narratives, which employ the threat of *zaken mamre,* with the total absence of a *zaken mamre* threat in the Bavli versions. Argumentation and reasoning are the only tools the Bavli will allow, which necessarily leads to a more tolerant outlook. Overall, the Bavli prefers persuasion over power.

---

117. One could argue that the Bavli's motivation is simply to reconcile two opposing Tannaitic views but does not mean to reject Sifre 152. However, considering that the continuation of the Bavli *sugya* finds two more ways to limit the types of cases to which the law of rebellious elder applies, I consider all of these interpretations as one unit with a single motivating force—to constrict the application of the law of the rebellious elder. See also above, p. 319 n. 72.

Chart 6.1 Comparison chart for *m. Sanh.* 11:2 and *t. Sanh.* 7:1

***m. Sanh.* 11:2**	***t. Sanh.* 7:1 (ms. Erfurt)**
זקן ממרא על פי בית דין שנאמר כי יפלא ממך דבר למשפט וגו'	
שלשה בתי דינין היו שם אחד יושב על פתח הר הבית ואחד יושב על פתח העזרה ואחד יושב בלשכת הגזית	א"ר יוסי בראשנה לא היו מחלוקות בישראל אלא בבית דין של שבעים בלשכת הגזית ושאר בתי דינין של עשרים ושלשה היו בעיירות של ארץ ישר' ושאר בתי דינין של שלשה שלשה היו בירושלם אחד בהר הבית ואחד בחיל
	נצרך אחד מהן הלכה הולך לבית דין שבעירו אין בית דין בעירו הולך לבית דין הסמוך לעירו אם שמעו אמרו לו
באים לזה שעל פתח הר הבית ואומר כך דרשתי וכך דרשו חבירי כך לימדתי וכך לימדו חבירי אם שמעו אומרים להם	אם לאו הוא ומופלא שבהם באין לבית דין שבהר הבית אם שמעו אמרו להן
ואם לאו באין להם לאותן שעל פתח העזרה ואומר כך דרשתי וכך דרשו חבירי כך לימדתי וכך לימדו חבירי אם שמעו אומרים להם	ואם לאו הן ומופלא שבהן באין לבית דין שבחיל אם שמעו אמרו להן
ואם לאו אלו ואלו באים לבית דין הגדול שבלשכת הגזית שממנו יוצאת תורה לכל ישראל שנאמר מן המקום ההוא אשר יבחר ה'	ואם לאו אילו ואילו הולכין לבית דין הגדול שבלשכת הגזית בית דין שבלשכת הגזית אף על פי שהו של שבעים ואחד אין פחות מעשרים ושלשה נצרך אחד מהן לצאת רואה אם יש שם עשרים ושלשה יוצא ואם לאו אין יוצא עד שיהו שם עשרים ושלשה היו יושבין מתמיד של שחר עד תמיד של בין הערבים ובשבתות ובימים טובים באין לבית המדרש שבהר הבית נשאלה שאילה אם שמעו אמרו להם ואם לאו עומדין למינין רבו המטמאין טימאו רבו המטהרין טהרו
חזר לעיר ושנה ולימד כדרך שהיה למד פטור ואם הורה לעשות חייב שנאמר והאיש אשר יעשה בזדון אינו חייב עד שיורה לעשות תלמיד שהורה לעשות פטור נמצא חומרו קולו:	
	משם היה יוצאת הלכה ורווחת בישראל משרבו תלמידי שמאי והילל שלא שימשו כל צורכן הרבו מחלוקות בישראל.

Chart 6.2 Comparison chart for *Sifre Deut.* 152 and parallels at *y. Sanh.* 11:3 (30a) and *b. Sanh.* 86b.

		1	2	3	4	5	6	7	8	9	10
1	ספרי			כי	יפלא,	מלמד				שבמופלא	
	ירושלמי	כתיב		כי	יפלא	ממך	דבר	למשפט	מגיד	שבמופלא	שבבית
	בבלי	תנו	רבנן:	כי	יפלא	ממך	דבר			במופלא	שבבית
2	ספרי		הכתוב	מדבר.		ממך,	זו	עצה.			
	ירושלמי	דין	הכתוב	מדבר		ממך	זה	עצה			
	בבלי	דין	הכתוב	מדבר.		ממך,	זה	יועץ,	וכן	הוא	אומר:
3	ספרי									דבר,	זו
	ירושלמי									דבר	זו
	בבלי	ממך	יצא	חשב	על	ה׳	רעה	יעץ	בליעל.	דבר	זו
4	ספרי	הלכה.	למשפט,	זה	הדין.	בין	דם	לדם,	בין	דם	נדה
	ירושלמי	אגדה				בין	דם	לדם	בין	דם	נידה
	בבלי	הלכה,	למשפט	זה	הדין.	בין	דם	לדם	בין	דם	נדה,
5	ספרי				לדם	יולדת	לדם	זיבה.			
	ירושלמי	לדם	בתולים	בין	דם	נידה	לדם	זיבה	לדם	צרעת	
	בבלי				דם	לידה,	דם	זיבה.			
6	ספרי	בין	דין	לדין,	בין	דיני	ממונות	לדיני	נפשות	לדיני	מכות.
	ירושלמי	בין	דין	לדין	בין	דיני	ממונות	לדיני	נפשות		
	בבלי	בין	דין	לדין	בין	דיני	נפשות,	דיני	ממונות,	דיני	מכות,
7	ספרי										
	ירושלמי	בין	דין	לדין	בין	הנסקלין	לנשרפין	לנהרגין	ולנחנקין		בין
	בבלי										

8	ספרי								בין	נגע	לנגע,
	ירושלמי	נגע	לנגע	בין	מצורע	מוסגר	למצורע	מוחלט	בין	נגע	לנגע
	בבלי								בין	נגע	לנגע
9	ספרי	בין	נגעי	אדם	לנגעי	בגדים	לנגעי	בתים.	דברי	אלו	ערכים
	ירושלמי	בין	ניגעי	אדם	לניגעי	בגדים	ולנגעי	בתים	דברי		
	בבלי	בין	נגעי	אדם,	נגעי	בתים,	נגעי	בגדים,	דברי	אלו	החרמים
10	ספרי	וחרמים		והקדשות.		ריבות,	זו	השקית	סוטה	ועריפת	עגלה
	ירושלמי						זו	השקיית	סוטה	ועריפת	העגלה
	בבלי	והערכין		וההקדשות.		ריבת	זו	השקאת	סוטה,	ועריפת	עגלה,
11	ספרי	וטהרת	מצורע.								
	ירושלמי	וטהרת	המצורע		ריבות	אילו	הערבים	והחרמים	והתמורות	וההקדישות	
	בבלי	וטהרת	מצורע.								
12	ספרי	בשעריך,	זה	לקט	שכחה	ופיאה.		וקמת	מיד,	וקמת	בבית
	ירושלמי							וקמת		וקמת	מבית
	בבלי	בשעריך	זו	לקט	שכחה	ופאה.		וקמת			מבית
13	ספרי	דין,	מיכן	אמרו	שלשה	בתי	דינים	היו	שם	אחד	על
	ירושלמי	דין									
	בבלי	דין,									
14	ספרי	פתח	הר	הבית	ואחד	על	פתח	העזרה	ואחד	בלשכת	הגזית
	ירושלמי										
	בבלי										

15	ספרי	באים	לזה	של	שער	הר	הבית	ואומר	כך	דרשתי	וכך
	ירושלמי										
	בבלי										
16	ספרי	דרשו	חבריי	כך	לימדתי	וכך	לימדו	חבריי	אם	שמעו	אמרו
	ירושלמי										
	בבלי										
17	ספרי	להם	ואם	לאו	באים	לזה	שעל	פתח	העזרה	ואומר	כך
	ירושלמי										
	בבלי										
18	ספרי	דרשתי	וכך	דרשו	חבריי	כך	לימדתי	וכך	לימדו	חבריי	אם
	ירושלמי										
	בבלי										
19	ספרי	שמעו	אמרו	להם	ואם	לאו	אלו	ואלו	באים	לבית	דין
	ירושלמי										
	בבלי										
20	ספרי	הגדול	שבלשכת	הגזית	שמשם	תורה	יוצאה	לכל	ישראל	שנאמר	מן
	ירושלמי										
	בבלי										
21	ספרי	המקום	ההוא	אשר	יבחר	ה׳.					
	ירושלמי						ועלית	זו	העלייה	דבר	אחר
	בבלי										

22	ספרי	וקמת	ועלית,	מגיד	שארץ	ישראל	גבוהה	מכל	הארצות	ובית	המקדש
	ירושלמי		ועלית	מיכן						לבית	הבחירה
	בבלי		ועלית	מלמד						שבית	המקדש
23	ספרי				גבוה	מכל	ארץ	ישראל			
	ירושלמי	שלא	יבנה	אלא	בגובהו		של	עולם	מה	טעמא	כי
	בבלי				גבוה		מארץ	ישראל,			
24	ספרי										
	ירושלמי	בהר	קדשי	בהר	מרום	ישראל	אשתלנו	ונשא	ענף	ועשה	פרי
	בבלי										
25	ספרי							ובאת,			לרבות
	ירושלמי	וגומ›						ובאת			לרבות
	בבלי		וארץ	ישראל	גבוה	מכל	הארצות.		אל	המקום	מלמד
26	ספרי			בית	דין	שביבנה.					
	ירושלמי			בית	דין	שביבנה					
	בבלי	שהמקום	גורם.								

7

The Relationship between the Laws of the Rebellious Elder and *Horayot*: A System of Checks and Balances

Introduction

Tractate *Horayot* deals with a court that issues a mistaken ruling. In such a case, unknowing laypeople who act in accordance with the court's erroneous decision are not liable, but those who know the court is mistaken but still act upon its decision are liable. What is the relationship between this *Horayot* law and the law of the rebellious elder examined in the previous chapter? If a sage believes that a court issued a mistaken ruling, then the law of rebellious elder requires him to obey the court regardless while the law of *Horayot* requires him to disobey it. The *Horayot* law seems to contradict the law of the rebellious elder and potentially opens the door to recognizing legal pluralism. This law allows for the possibility that the court and the laypeople will follow one law while dissenting judges and students can and must legitimately follow another.[1] Close analysis of the sources, however, will show that the law of *Horayot* does not contradict the law of the rebellious elder but rather complements it to form a unified system of checks and balances that, at least in its Tannaitic formulations, does not allow for any legitimate diversity of halakhic practice. We trace the development of the law of *Horayot* within the Talmuds and note how this development, especially in the Bavli, opens the possi-

1. In a standard case of the court making a blatant error, the court's ruling is invalid, and those who follow it are not liable only because they are not at fault for making the error. In such a case, only the practice of the dissenter is legitimate. However, if the dissenter continues to maintain that the court is in error even after the court confirms that its decision is correct, then it is no longer clear which side is wrong, and so both practices can claim legitimacy. See further below, p. 353.

bility for both the court and the dissenter to act on opposing but equally valid halakhic standpoints.

The law of the rebellious elder restricts the right of an individual rabbi to disobey the majority ruling of the high court. This law implies that the high court has absolute authority to make and interpret law and thus impose uniformity of practice on the Jewish community. The previous chapter analyzed various opinions about when the elder is punished or not, but no source there encouraged or even permitted him to disobey the court. Avi Sagi considers this law as an example of a "deontic model" of Jewish law, wherein the court's authority is based not on any characteristic of the members of the court (for example, intelligence or lineage) but rather on the court's official position of power. That position may be granted by community consent or by the legal system itself. Once granted, though, its authority is absolute and demands "unconditional obedience, even when apparently wrong."[2] Since the court's authority is independent of its knowledge or abilities, it can never be mistaken. This system leaves no room for individual disagreement. The law of the rebellious elder, at least as put forth in Tannaitic sources, assumes an authoritarian system where there is no real room for dissent or diversity, at least regarding those cases adjudicated by the court.

The laws in the first chapter of Mishnah *Horayot*, on the other hand, present the flipside of the law of the rebellious elder where a rabbi who believes the court is in error not only *may* but *must* disobey the ruling. *M. Horayot* 1:1 teaches that if a court makes a ruling in error and the masses follow it, the followers are not liable since they relied on the court's decision. Instead, once the court realizes its mistake, it must bring a sacrifice on behalf of the community:

> הורו בית דין לעבור על אחת מכל מצות האמורות בתורה והלך היחיד ועשה שוגג על פיהם ... פטור מפני שתלה בבית דין.
>
> If a court issues a ruling to transgress any one of the commandments expressed in the Torah and an individual goes ahead and practices mistakenly in accordance with their ruling ... he is exempt because he relied on the court.

This is based on the rabbinic understanding of Lev 4:13–20. The continuation of *m. Hor.* 1:1 adds an important exception:

> הורו בית דין וידע אחד מהן שטעו או תלמיד והוא ראוי להוראה והלך ועשה על פיהן ...
> הרי זה חייב מפני שלא תלה בבית דין
> זה הכלל התולה בעצמו חייב והתולה בבית דין פטור.

2. Avi Sagi, "Models of Authority and the Duty of Obedience in Halakhic Literature," *AJS Review* 20, no. 1 (1995): 11.

> If a court issues a ruling and one of them [the judges] or a disciple who is competent enough to issue legal decisions knows that they erred but still goes out and practices in accordance with their ruling ... he is liable because he did not rely on the court.
> This is the general principle: One who relies on himself is liable but one who relies on the court is exempt.

A judge or a student who knows that the court has made a mistake may not rely on that court's decision. Indeed, in some cases, this responsibility to check the court applies to laymen as well. If the decision contradicts a blatant verse, a law "with which even the Sadducees would agree,"[3] then the court is not liable because even a layperson is expected to know better and disobey the court. It is significant that the Bavli in the name of Shmuel holds all individuals, whether learned or not, liable for following a wrong decision in all cases unless the majority of the people follow it.[4] This is one way in which the Bavli expands the right and obligation of individuals to disobey the court, which can lead to legitimate diversity of practice when the individual and the court each follows its own opinion. This Bavli expansion may relate to the Bavli's greater tolerance for diversity in general.

While Sagi considers the law of the rebellious elder as an example of the deontic model, he points to *Horayot* as an example of the "epistemological model." According to this model, the authority of the court is based only on its ability to arrive at the truth. Once a colleague or a student recognizes that the court has erred, the court loses its authority, and so he must disobey the mistaken ruling. Sagi writes: "The binding duty of a Jewish individual is, first and foremost, to the Torah rather than to the sages, whose authority rests on their knowledge rather than on an arbitrary power to command whatever they wish."[5] Sagi therefore draws the

---

3. *B. Hor.* 4a; cf. *b. Sanh.* 33b. The Sadducees allegedly accepted only biblical law. See Josephus, *Antiquities*, 13.10.6. *B. Nid.* 57a similarly recognizes that the Samaritans interpret Lev 19:14, "Do not put a stumbling block before the blind," literally and reject the rabbinic interpretation that it prohibits offering misleading advice. See Halivni, *Peshat and Derash*, 10–13.

4. *B. Hor.* 2b–3a. See Zvi Aryeh Steinfeld, "Yahid she-ʿasah be-hora'at bet din," *Sidra* 10 (1994): 131–64, for the origins of this *sugya*. Even if the historical Shmuel never made such a statement, the Bavli redactors did.

5. Sagi, "Models," 5. This idea is also expressed nicely by Jose Faur, "One-Dimensional Jew, Zero-Dimensional Judaism," *Review of Rabbinic Judaism* 2 (1999): 35–36:

> Those in charge to administer and interpret the Law may err, implying, thereby, that there is an objective law independent of governmental bureaucracies and institutions. Thus, the king, the high priest, and the Supreme Court of Israel are subject to judicial error and must bring an expiatory sacrifice. An entire Talmudic Tractate Horayot deals with the niceties of this principle. In this defining principle Jewish law differs from other legal systems. The Constitution of the USA, for example, is what the Supreme Court declares. Therefore, it can never commit

conclusion that, "every individual is equally entitled to make judgments concerning their truth."[6] The epistemic model implies tolerance for diversity of practice, since evaluation of truth is subjective and each individual is entitled to his own evaluation and need not pay heed to an authoritative decision.[7] Richard DeGeorge, upon whom Sagi bases his theoretical model, classifies epistemic authority as nonexecutive in the sense that it "does not involve any right to command or to act on or for another."[8] Since the court's legitimacy stems only from its success at arriving at the truth, it in effect has no independent power.

These two laws, then, seem to reflect two different models of authority, and each model has a different view about tolerance for diversity of halakhic practice.[9] The rebellious elder who *disobeys* the high court is punished; in *Horayot*, the rabbi who *obeys* the court is punished. Indeed, a dissenting rabbi must make a choice between these two extreme requirements; either he must follow and uphold unity or he must not follow and create multiplicity. Since both of the laws are present and prominent in the Mishnah, Midrashim, and Talmuds, they are not likely to be the works of two different schools of thought. How, then, can these two sets of laws be reconciled? What is a dissenting rabbi to do?

The difference between these two laws is most succinctly represented by comparing *Sifre Deut.* 154, "*To the right or to the left* (Deut 17:11)—even if they point out to you that right is left and left is right, obey them,"[10] which is said in the context of the rebellious elder, with *y. Hor.* 1:1 (45d):

> דתני יכול אם יאמרו לך על ימין שהיא שמאל ועל שמאל שהיא ימין תשמע להם תלמוד לומר ללכת ימין ושמאל[11] שיאמרו לך על ימין שהוא ימין ועל שמאל שהיא שמאל
> For it was taught: Can it be that if they [the judges] tell you that right is left and that left is right then you should obey them? [Therefore the verse] comes to teach, "*to walk right or left*"[11]—only if they tell you that right is right and that left is left.

---

a judicial mistake. "We are under a Constitution," declared Charles Evans Hughes (1862–1948), one of the most perceptive Chief Justices of the United States, "but the Constitution is what the judges say it is."

6. Sagi, "Models," 3.

7. See ibid., *'Elu va-Elu'*, 199–202.

8. Richard DeGeorge, *The Nature and Limits of Authority* (Lawrence: University of Kansas, 1985), 26.

9. A parallel to the deontic model may be found in general legal theory in the view of Owen Fiss, "Objectivity and Interpretation," 755–58. Fiss writes: "Judicial interpretations are binding whether or not they are correct" (p. 755). The epistemological model, on the other hand, finds resonance in the outlook of Robert Cover; see below, p. 369.

10. Ed. Finkelstein, 207. See above, p. 315.

11. Deuteronomy 28:14, although, the word ללכת comes *after* the words ימין ושמאל in the verse. Cf. Deut 5:28 and 17:11.

Beforehand, the Yerushalmi *sugya* wonders how "a disciple who is competent enough to issue a legal decision" (*m. Hor.* 1:1) could have been so ignorant of a law as to follow the court's mistake. The Talmud's first answer is that he knew the correct law but his mistake was in assuming that he was required to follow the court even though he knew the court was in error. This assumption is encapsulated in the *sugya* by the phrase התורה אמרה אחריהם אחריהם—"the Torah said 'follow them, follow them.'"[12] The *sugya* then rejects the possibility that the competent disciple could make such an assumption based on the above-quoted *baraita*, which is strikingly similar in wording, though opposite in meaning, with *Sifre* 154.[13]

It is clear from the context that the *baraita* in the Yerushalmi is not simply a corrupt version of the *Sifre*, but rather seems to represent a fundamentally different view. The *Sifre* and Yerushalmi *baraita* should also not be understood as deriving from opposing schools of thought. They are only representative statements that summarize the viewpoint of their respective contexts. The *Sifre* passage is found in the context of the law of the rebellious elder, a law whose goal is to maximize the authority of the court. The *baraita* is found in Yerushalmi *Horayot*, where the individual is called on to disobey the faulty court. Both categories of law are discussed by the same rabbis within the same corpus of rabbinic writings, and so there should be some way to reconcile them. At issue for our purposes is

12. This phrase is also found in *y. Beṣah* 4:3 (62c) and *y. Sanh.* 1:2 (19a) = *y. Ned.* 6:8 (40a). In the latter, R. Yehudah b. Betera urges R. Ḥanina to follow the rabbis of Palestine and cease from declaring the new moon in Babylonia; see above, pp. 266–69. In that case the issue is not that R. Ḥanina disagreed with the Palestinian court's decision as much as that he felt himself more competent. The context of the story there is a law that requires the new moon to be declared in Israel. This phrase is equivalent to the rule מצוה לשמוע דברי חכמים in the Bavli (*b. Hor.* 2b; *b. Yebam.* 20a; *b. Qidd.* 50a; *b. B. Bat.* 48a; *b. Sanh.* 53b; and *b. Ḥul.* 106a). See also Menahem Lorberbaum, "Toᶜeh be-miṣvah li-shmoaᶜ be-divre hakhamim," in *Ben samkhut le-otonomiah be-masoret Yisrael*, ed. Z. Safrai and A. Sagi (Tel-Aviv: Hakibbutz Hameuchad, 1997), 352–63.

13. Based on this *baraita*, the Yerushalmi rejects the possibility that a knowledgeable student could possibly err by adhering so mindlessly to the "follow them, follow them" principle. It therefore ends with another response of R. Yose in the name of R. Hila that just as an individual layman who mistakenly relies on the court is completely free of punishment, even though he should be liable to a guilt offering like any inadvertent transgressor, so too this student who violates intentionally will also get a reduced sentence of a sacrifice rather than the full punishment due to the intentional transgressor.

The Bavli curiously ends with the first response without mention of the Yerushalmi's second response. According to the Yerushalmi, a dissenter who obeys the court knowing that it is mistaken still brings a sacrifice as one who sins by mistake. According to the Bavli, the dissenter may only bring a sacrifice if he thought he must follow the court even when it is mistaken. If, however, he was aware of *m. Hor.* 1:1 that he must not follow the mistaken court and he follows it nevertheless, then he has sinned intentionally and may not bring a sacrifice. The Bavli deals with the too-submissive dissenter more harshly than does the Yerushalmi. Perhaps this is part of a trend in the Bavli to push for greater individual responsibility to check the court.

whether the Talmud prohibits diversity, as would seem from the law of the rebellious elder, or whether it requires it, as would seem from the laws of *Horayot*.

Past Solutions

Commentators have long noted the conflict between these two sets of laws and have attempted various reconciliations. In an attempt to survey the range of possible explanations, Gerald Blidstein and Avi Sagi[14] have gathered the various interpretations found in medieval and premodern Jewish commentaries. Because they take a more topical and philosophical approach, Blidstein and Sagi do not focus on the original intent of the Talmudic sources. Many of the solutions proposed there rely on one or two selected statements of the Talmud but do not satisfy a comprehensive reading of both sets of laws. Modern commentators have also proposed various explanations, each of which has its own problems. We will present a short review of the solutions proposed by the premodern and modern scholars as a framework on which to base a hopefully more convincing resolution of the Talmudic sources.[15]

---

14. Gerald Blidstein, "'Even if He Tells You Right is Left': The Validity of Moral Authority in the Halakha and Its Limitations," in *Studies in Halakha and Jewish Thought Presented to Rabbi Prof. Menachem Emanuel Rackman on his 80th Anniversary*, ed. Moshe Beer (Ramat-Gan: Bar-Ilan University Press, 1994), 221–41 (Hebrew); and Sagi, "Models," 1–24.

15. Finkelstein, *Sifra*, 1:201–2 and 5:79, proposes a historical explanation for the difference between the two sets of laws. He argues that the law of *Horayot* began in pre-Hasmonian times when the Sanhedrin was populated by Hellenizers and corrupt priests. In those times, the Hasidim wanted to limit the authority of the Sanhedrin, which they did not trust and often disagreed with. Accordingly, the midrash on Deut 17:11 in the Yerushalmi, which says that one only needs to listen to the court when they say that right is right, comes from this time period. After the Hasmonean takeover, the Sanhedrin was populated by Hasidim and Pharisees. During this time period, the law of the rebellious elder was propped up so that the newly reliable Sanhedrin would have complete authority. In this later time period the midrash was reversed, as is recorded in *Sifre* 154.

This reconstruction is highly conjectural, as it assumes many facts about the existence and nature of the Sanhedrin during the second and third centuries B.C.E. for which we have little evidence. Furthermore, there is barely any indication in either set of texts connecting them to these historical events. Indeed, one could equally argue that *Horayot* reflects the view of the Pharisees during late Second Temple times when they did not have control of the Sanhedrin, and the rebellious elder is a creation of the Yavnean Sanhedrin when the rabbis did have full control. Even if one could find some historical basis for the development of each law under different political circumstances, it still would not answer the literary question of why the Mishnah and the Talmuds include both sets of laws in neighboring tractates without any note that they are in tension. We find examples of individual Mishnaic laws that contradict one another, but not entire categories of law and not without a Talmudic discussion of the problem.

Nahmanides' solution is to sustain the law of the rebellious elder while redefining the laws of *Horayot* to be almost nonexistent. In so doing, he chooses a path that requires the most uniformity of practice. Nahmanides quotes the *Sifre* in both his commentary on Deut 17:11 as well as in his more lengthy discussion on the subject in his gloss on Maimonides' first principle in *Sefer Hamiṣvoth*. He explains that all Jews must follow the court, even if they do not agree with it, in order to preserve unity. Nahmanides contends with tractate *Horayot* by relegating it to a minor stipulation:

> ויש בזה תנאי יתבונן בו המסתכל בראשון שלהוריות בעין יפה, והוא שאם היה בזמן הסנהדרין חכם וראוי להוראה והורו בית דין הגדול בדבר אחד להתר והוא סבור שטעו בהוראתן אין עליו מצוה לשמוע דברי החכמים ואינו רשאי להתיר לעצמו הדבר האסור לו אבל ינהג חומר לעצמו וכל שכן אם היה מכלל הסנהדרין יושב עמהן בבית דין הגדול ויש עליו לבא לפניהם ולומר טענותיו להם והם שישאו ויתנו עמו ואם הסכימו רובם בבטול הדעת ההוא שאמר ושבשו עליו סברותיו יחזור וינהוג כדעתם אחרי כן לאחר שיסלקו אותו ויעשו הסכמה בטענתו. וזהו העולה מן ההלכות ההם. ומכל מקום חייב לקבל דעתם אחר ההסכמה על כל פנים.
>
> There is a stipulation here that the reader will discover if he carefully examines the beginning of *Horayot*, which is: If a sage fit to issue decisions lived at the time of the Sanhedrin, and the Sanhedrin rules that a certain matter is permitted and he believes that they made a mistake in their ruling, he is not obligated to heed the sages and he is not permitted to allow himself something forbidden. Rather, he must be strict with himself. This is all the more so true if he himself is a member of the Sanhedrin and sits on the great court. He must come before them and present his argument to them, which they will discuss and debate with him. If the majority of them reject his view and show the error of his reasoning, he must retract and act in accordance with their ruling after they have dismissed him [and after] having come to an agreement regarding his claim. This is what emerges from these rulings. In all cases, he must accept their ruling after they have considered it.[16]

If a sage believes the court to be in error, he has an obligation to come and inform them of it. The entire law of *Horayot*, according to which the sage must follow his own understanding, only applies to the brief window of time before he gets a chance to go argue with the court.[17] Once

---

16. Charles Ber Chavel, *Sefer ha-mitsvot la-Rambam* (Jerusalem: Mosad Ha-Rav Kook, 1981), 17. Translation from Sagi, "Models," 14.

17. Even within this window, Nahmanides only gives the example of where the court ruled leniently and the dissenter wishes to be stringent. In that case, he may be stringent on himself before he goes to the court. It is not clear why the sage may not be stringent on himself even after the court disagrees with his objection, since he violates no law by being

the court hears his complaints and maintains its decision, the sage must submit himself to the court. Nahmanides does allow for the possibility that the court can make a mistake. For this reason, the sage is required to inform them of it so that, if indeed the court made an error in their logic or overlooked an important source, it can be rectified. However, he assumes that if the court considered the possible error and nevertheless stuck with its opinion, then that opinion is authoritative and any objection no longer matters.[18]

It is clear that Nahmanides believes the high court should have absolute authority in order to suppress multiple practices and prevent the Torah from becoming two Torahs. It is that belief that dictates his reading of the Talmud. The Talmud itself, however, never makes any distinction between before and after the sage goes to the court. In fact, the Talmud never mentions a requirement for the sage to consult the court at all.[19] If our goal is to understand how the Tannaim and Amoraim themselves reconciled the two sets of laws, then Nahmanides' reconciliation is not adequate.

Zvi Aryeh Steinfeld thinks that *m. Hor.* 1:1 is generally misinterpreted and that it does not ever give permission to anyone to disobey a court. He argues that the words והלך ועשה על פיהן, in the second half of *m. Hor.* 1:1, do not refer to the judge or student but rather to the individual—יחיד—

---

stringent. (Although, Shmuel does force Rav to be lenient and eat the oil of Gentiles, perhaps because Shmuel felt that Rav's personal stringency weakened the force of Rabbi's court; see above, pp. 327–32.) If the court ruled stringently, however, would Nahmanides allow the disagreeing sage to be lenient until he comes to the court? Presumably not. If so, the disagreeing sage must always be stringent on himself, even before he comes to the court. The only case in which *m. Hor.* 1:1 would actually require the sage to act against the court would be a case where neither option is more stringent than the other, such as a civil case where a leniency for one party is a stringency for the other.

For commentators who use the distinction between passive and active actions to resolve the tension, see Blidstein, "Even If," 234–36. Ḥayyim ben ʿAṭṭar, *Ḥefeṣ Hashem*, (Amsterdam, 1732), for example, says one must listen to the court's stringencies even if he disagrees with them. This is the law of the rebellious elder. However, if the court commands one to do an action that he thinks is wrong then he must refrain. This is the law of *Horayot*. Of course, not all cases will fit so easily into either category, and so this resolution is not sufficient on its own.

18. *M. Hor.* 1:4 shows that the court can still be mistaken even if someone objects. In that case, one of the judges informs the court that they are mistaken. They overrule him and give a decision anyway. If, at a later point, the court realizes their mistake, they are not liable for those who followed their ruling in the interim. Nahmanides may argue that even if the court may be objectively in error, their ruling is still binding until they overturn it because unity is of higher value than truth.

19. See Eliezer Berkovits, *Ha-halakha, koḥah ve-tafqidah* (Jerusalem: Mosad Ha-Rav Kook, 1991), 158. For further analysis of Nahmanides' view see Avi Sagi, "The Dialectic between Decision-Making and Objective Truth in the Halakhah—Some Considerations regarding the Philosophy of the Halakhah," *Dine Israel* 15 (1999–2000): 30–38 (Hebrew); and Blidstein, "Even If," 230–31.

already mentioned in the first half of the Mishnah. In this reading, this Mishnah simply echoes the law of *m. Hor.* 1:4 that if one member of the court knows it is mistaken and he notified the rest of the court, then the court's decision is not an official ruling and the court is exempt from any sacrifice. *M. Horayot* 1:1 similarly teaches that if one of the members of the court or a qualified student knew that the court was mistaken and then a layperson follows the court's decision, the layperson is liable.[20] This is not convincing, however, since it does not fit well into the wording. We would assume that the subject of the verb והלך would be the immediately preceding noun, אחד מהם ... או תלמיד. More importantly the reason, מפני שלא תלה בבית דין, is not accurate according to Steinfeld's interpretation. The court's decision may not have been valid but the individual did rely on the court. If it is the judge or student himself who acts on the court's ruling, as is the usual interpretation, then he is liable because he knew the court was mistaken and therefore cannot claim to have relied on the court.[21] Rather, it is clear that *m. Hor.* 1:1 does in fact mandate that a judge or qualified student who knows that the court is wrong may not rely on the court's decision. Once again, we return to the contradiction between this law and that of the rebellious elder.

If the Talmudic sources do not explicitly make a distinction between the two laws, then perhaps we need to look for a more fundamental distinction that is assumed in the very definition of each category and that therefore did not need to be stated. The rebellious elder, as we can see just from his title, is one who defies the authority of the court. His punishment is so severe not because of the specific matter of dispute but because his actions threaten to undermine the court. The dissenter in *Horayot*, on the other hand, generally respects the court but still feels that it is mistaken about a certain matter. To some extent, the distinction between the two may be based on the individual's intention or prior relationship with the court establishment.[22] However, since intention is difficult to gauge and

---

20. Zvi Aryeh Steinfeld, "On the Clarification of a Mishna in Tractate Eduyot," *Bar Ilan* 13 (1976): 84–106 (Hebrew).

21. Steinfeld is correct to question the Bavli's explanation of why the dissenting judge should be correct to bring a sacrifice if he intentionally transgressed. The Bavli's explanation that the judge mistakenly thought he must follow the rabbis even when they are wrong is also rejected by the Yerushalmi. However, just because the Bavli gives a forced explanation, that is not a good reason to reject the plain meaning of the Mishnah. Steinfeld could instead assume the better explanation of R. Yose in the name of R. Hila (*y. Hor.* 1:1 [45d]; see p. 342 above) that since the inadvertent transgressor incurs no punishment in this case, by analogy the intentional transgressor should be treated like an inadvertent sinner. For more problems with Steinfeld's explanation, see Avraham Walfish, "Haṭat ha-ʿedah ve-'aḥrayut ha-yaḥid: ʿiyyun be-darkhe ha-ʿarikhah shel Mishnat Horayot pereq 1," *Netuʿim* 6 (2000): 19 n. 41.

22. R. Eliyahu Mizraḥi expresses this idea by comparing the rebellious elder with a Sadducee: לא תסור אינו אלא במי שממרה בדבריהם ובהוראתן ואינו כפוף להם כמו הצדוקין והבייתוסין ודומיהם, ולא

no Talmudic source takes prior relationship into account, various commentators have attempted to identify a more objective means of distinguishing between the two types of dissenters.

Hanina Ben-Menahem suggests that the official status of the dissenter is what distinguishes the two laws:

> The desire to eliminate schism is one manifestation of the ongoing attempt to unify the halakhah. The main threat to the unity of the halakhah is a situation where contradictory rulings are issued by different organs within the system. Awareness of this danger led to the creation of an absolute obligation on the part of subordinate organs to obey all rulings of the supreme court. By contrast, individuals who do not partake in the decision-making process, and who are not responsible for the enforcement of the law, do not constitute a threat to halakhic unity. Consequently, they are not under the same absolute obligation as are judges. Accordingly, the *sugya* in *b. Hor.* 2b implies that there is no duty, indeed no right, on the part of individuals to obey erroneous pronouncements of the central court.[23]

Blidstein expands on the reasoning behind this distinction.[24] Only an elder

---

במי שהוא כפוף למצוותן ועובר עליהם—"'Do not deviate' (Deut 17:11) only applies to one who rebels against their words and rulings and is not submissive to them such as the Sadducees and the Boethusians and the like, but [it does] not [apply] to someone who is [generally] submissive to their command and transgresses their ruling [in a particular case]." See Blidstein, "Even If," 237. It is unlikely that Maimonides would agree with this formulation since he clearly distances the rebellious elder from the Sadducees in Mishneh Torah, *Hilkhot mamrim* 3:3–4. Nevertheless, Blidstein uses this as an explanation of how Maimonides distinguishes between the two laws. In *Horayot,* the dissenter argues about the content of the law while the rebellious elder does not take issue with their ruling—perhaps he has no opinion about it or perhaps he even agrees with it. The rebellious elder simply refuses to obey their decision. Such a scenario could fit with the biblical description of the law where the judge does not know the law, goes to ask the high court, but then refuses to obey. If this judge had his own opinion or tradition on the matter then he would not have needed to go to the court. He does not take issue with the content of the court's decision but rather refuses to submit to the court's authority. This scenario, however, does not fit with the Mishnah's description (*m. Sanh.* 11:2) of the case where the judge comes before the high court and says, "Such have I taught and such have my colleagues taught." Blidstein's formulation therefore does not work for the Mishnah where both the rebellious elder and the dissenter in *Horayot* disagree with the content of the high court's decision.

23. Ben-Menahem, *Judicial Deviation*, 170; and see larger discussion at 165–73.

24. Blidstein, "Even If," 233. Blidstein also names Rabbis Ḥayyim Palachi, Moshe Margaliot, and David Hoffman as subscribing to this view. However, I have not been able to find any statements in their writings that clearly express this view. Hoffman does say that the rebellious elder is a judge, but does not mention the case of *Horayot.* Moshe Margaliot's comment is not lucid. Ḥayyim Palachi, *Semikha le-ḥayyim* (Saloniki, 1826), *Even ha-ʾezer, siman* 9, 62d–63a, distinguishes not between the status of the dissenter but rather between whether or not he discussed his case with the court. The rebellious elder goes through the various levels of the judicial system until he finally presents his case to the high court. If all of these

of the court has the status to threaten the authority of the court. We do not look to the intention of the dissenter but rather to the effect his actions will have on the masses who will view the elder's dissent as a rebellion and a sign that the court has lost its authority. If a lower judge or qualified student, on the other hand, disobeys the court, there are no serious political ramifications. *M. Horayot* 1:1 therefore allows, and even requires, that a judge or a qualified student disobey a court if he thinks it is wrong. As mentioned above, the Bavli goes so far as to impute guilt to individual laypeople, as long as they remain a minority of the nation, if they obey a mistaken ruling. This solution, however, does not square with the Mishnah. As Blidstein points out, *m. Hor.* 1:1 includes members of the high court itself among those who must disobey the mistaken court.[25]

Others distinguish between different categories of law. R. Yehudah b. R. Eliezer, a Tosafist, limits the law of the rebellious elder to decrees and enactments that the court has the authority to make in order to safeguard the halakha or for the general good of the community. These decrees need not be based on biblical or traditional sources but are rather based on the will of the court. One who disobeys such a decree therefore rebels against the court's legislative authority. The law of *Horayot*, on the other hand, deals with the court's interpretations of biblical and rabbinic law. In these cases, the court's authority derives from the traditional sources themselves. Therefore, if one thinks they have misinterpreted the sources, he has every right to disobey them.[26]

Along the same lines, Shlomo Havlin and Eliezer Berkovits distinguish between types of laws but draw the line in a slightly different place.[27] They point out that the *Sifre* comments on Deut 17:11, which deals with rabbinic law where one must follow what they say even if it not logical. The Yerushalmi, on the other hand, includes the word ללכת in its quota-

courts heard his arguments and still disagreed, it is not likely that they are all mistaken, and so the individual must accede. In the case of *Horayot* the dissenter has not gone through that process, and so he may, and must, assume that the court is mistaken and practice his own view. This view ends up being similar to that of Nahmanides, as Palachi himself notes.

25. Blidsein, "Even If," 234, quotes ʿAṭṭar, *Ḥefeṣ Hashem*, comment on *b. Hor.* 2b, s.v. דטעו, who suggests an opposite distinction. Only a judge or a competent student may disobey the mistaken court since they know better. Laypeople, on the other hand, do not have the requisite knowledge to responsibly disagree with the court. This distinction could work for the biblical description of the rebellious elder where it is the litigant, and not the judge, who disobeys the court. However, it does not work for the Talmudic sources, which limit the rebellious elder to the judge and which also expand *Horayot* to laypeople.

26. See *Rabotenu baʾale ha-Tosafot ʿal ha-Torah*, (Warsaw: N. Shriftgisser, 1876), on Deut 17:11, and Blidstein, "Even If," 227.

27. See Shlomo Zalman Havlin, "Al 'ha-ḥatimah ha-sifrutit' ke-yesod ha-ḥaluqah litqufot ba-halakha," in *Mekhqarim be-sifrut ha-talmudit*, ed. Shemu'el Re'em (Jerusalem: Ha-ʾakademiah Ha-leʾumit Ha-yisreʾelit Le-madaʿim, 1983), 164 n. 71, and Berkovits, *Ha-halakha, koḥah ve-tafqidah*, 159–61.

tion of the verse and therefore must refer to Deut 28:14, which deals with biblical laws that are commanded by God directly, אשר אנכי מצוה אתכם. In such cases, as explained in tractate *Horayot*, one must disobey the court when they are mistaken. In this view, the court has full authority to make decrees and decide rabbinic law as they wish, but their authority to interpret biblical law is only valid to the extent that they interpret it correctly.[28]

These reconciliations, however, do not take into account what the Talmudic sources themselves say about which categories of law apply to each case. *M. Horayot* 3:1 says that the law of *Horayot* applies only to the partial abrogation of a law. The examples cited there are all biblical laws but are also all based on rabbinic interpretation. These easily fit into the category of laws "whose essence is from the Torah but whose explanation is from the rabbis," which is the criterion for the rebellious elder according to R. Hoshaiah (*y. Sanh.* 11:4, 30b) and R. Yehudah (*b. Sanh.* 87a).[29] Even if one could argue that Mishnah *Horayot* deals only with biblical laws, אחת מכל מצות האמורות בתורה—"one of the commandments mentioned in the Torah," certainly the Babylonian Talmud expands the category to include rabbinic law of various types (*b. Hor.* 4a-b).

Furthermore, no Talmudic source limits the rebellious elder to rabbinic decrees. Only *m. Sanh.* 11:3 seems to limit the law of the rebellious elder to rabbinic laws, though even it uses an example of a rabbinic defi-

28. See also Jose Faur, *Studies in the Mishne Torah: Book of Knowledge* (Jerusalem: Mossad Harav Kook, 1978), 21–25 (Hebrew). Commenting on Maimonides, Faur similarly explains that Horayot only applies to laws received by Moses about which there is no controversy, i.e., those he would count in the 613 biblical precepts. Maimonides uses the term גוף תורה, which means received biblical laws in other contexts as well. The rebellious elder applies to laws derived by the rabbis or laws newly created by them, i.e., all rabbinic derivations and decrees not counted in the 613. See the five categories of oral law that Maimonides lists in his introduction to the *Commentary on the Mishnah* (ed. Yosef Kafiḥ, *Mishnah with the Commentary of Rabbenu Moshe ben Maimon* [Jerusalem: Mossad Harav Kook, 1963–67], *Zeraᶜim*, 11–12 [Hebrew]). This model has a benefit that *Horayot* applies only to clear-cut cases about which there is no controversy, and so it can be clearly determined that the court made an error. All cases that include controversy fall into the realm of the rebellious elder such that once the court decides between the various positions, the elder must accept their authoritative ruling. Unfortunately, this model does not actually fit into the words of Maimonides. Faur writes, דין העלם דבר חל רק על דבר שהוא גוף תורה—"the law of forgetting something (Horayot) applies only to something that is part of the Torah (biblical)" (p. 22). However, see *Mishneh Torah, Hilkhot shegagot,* 14:1–2; the court is only responsible when they make a ruling about that which is not explicit in the Torah. In fact, Maimonides writes that *Horayot* applies only to commandments that are punishable by *karet*; see his introduction to *Horayot* in his *Commentary on the Mishnah* (ed. Kafiḥ, *Neziqin*, 305). This is the same category of laws that applies to the rebellious elder; see *Commentary on the Mishnah to Sanhedrin* 11:2 (ibid., 148) and *Mishneh Torah, Hilkhot mamrim* 3:5 and 4:1.

29. See above, pp. 322 and 317. Rav Ashi (*b. Hor.* 4a) in fact links the two laws by deriving the category of laws for *Horayot* from the law of the rebellious elder. See more on this below, p. 363.

nition of how to fulfill the biblical law of *tefillin*. Most sources apply it only to biblical laws proper.[30] *Sifre Deut.* 154 is the most explicit, stating, "One may be sentenced to death for transgressing the ordinances of the Torah, but not for transgressing ordinances of the Scribes." This statement appears immediately before the line that Havlin explicates, "even if they point out to you that right is left and left is right, obey them." It is thus clear that in the Talmudic view, and certainly in the view of the author of *Sifre Deut.* 154, the law of rebellious elder applies to biblical laws and is not limited to rabbinic decrees or interpretations.

Legitimate Dispute or Outright Error

Instead, one can suggest a more nuanced distinction between the categories of law that apply to each case. Those who distinguish between biblical and rabbinic laws are aiming toward a deeper feature of these two types of laws. *Horayot* deals with cases in which it is clear that the court made an error by deciding against a source that they have no authority to challenge. The rebellious elder, on the other hand, disagrees with a court that decided in favor of one side of a controversial issue where the court does have the authority to determine which view should become normative.

While it may be true that there exists less controversy and the courts have less authority regarding biblical laws as opposed to rabbinic laws, this is not always the case. The very category of biblical law is itself defined by the rabbis, and it is often not clear from the Talmud which details of a law were considered biblical or not. The Tannaim and Amoraim themselves, predating the Geonic penchant to count the biblical commandments, do not always distinguish carefully between the two.[31] Furthermore, there may be many rabbinic opinions that are so well established that a later court would not have the authority to contest them. The essential distinction is not between biblical and rabbinic laws, nor is it between court decrees and interpretations of previous laws. Rather, the distinction is based on whether the court's opinion has some validity though the dissenter has an alternative view, interpretation, or tradi-

30. See above, pp. 312–25. *Sifre Deut.* 152 (ed. Finkelstein, 205–6) lists biblical laws, and R. Meir in *b. Sanh.* 87a limits it to biblical laws that carry *karet* as their punishment. R. Yehudah at *b. Sanh.* 87a limits it to rabbinic interpretation of biblical laws, which are nevertheless biblical in origin, and *m. Sanh.* 11:2 itself includes an example of biblical interpretations כך דרשתי—"such have I interpreted." R. Shimon's definition in *b. Sanh.* 87a, "Even for a single detail arising out of the subtle interpretations of the rabbis," includes rabbinic laws but does not limit the rebellious elder only to that category.

31. See Halivni, *Peshat and Derash*, 14–15.

tion—in which case he must submit to the court's authority—or whether the court is utterly and objectively mistaken—in which case the dissenter must disobey the court.

That this distinction is assumed by the Talmudic sources is evident in the language it uses. Compare the first Mishnah in each context. *M. Sanhedrin* 11:2 describes a case where the dissenter comes before the high court and says, כך דרשתי וכך דרשו חבירי כך לימדתי וכך לימדו חבירי. There are multiple views here, each theoretically legitimate, vying for normative status.[32] Even though the dissenter disagrees with his colleagues, he still calls them חבירי—"my colleagues" and acknowledges their opinion. *M. Horayot* 1:1, on the other hand, describes the case where הורו בית דין וידע אחד מהן שטעו.[33] The word טעו—"erred" by itself is never used regarding someone who rules according to one side of a rabbinic controversy.[34] No matter how vehemently one side of a *maḥloqet* disagrees with the other, it is rare that either side will be called erroneous. Rather, this word usually applies to a ruling for which there is simply no source and, in most cases, the proponent of the mistaken view will presumably admit to his error once it is pointed out.

The Yerushalmi, commenting on *m. Hor.* 1:1, describes a case of *Horayot* in revealing terms. *Y. Horayot* 1:2 (45d) states:

> רבי אימי בשם רשב״ל מתניתא כגון שמעון בן עזאי יושב לפניהן מה נן קיימין אם בשסילקן תבטלו הורייתן ואם בשסילקו אותו תבטל הורייתו אלא כי נן קיימין בשזה עומד בתשובתו וזה עומד בתשובתו הורייתן אצלו אינה הוראה שלא סילקו אותו אצל אחרים הורייה שלא סילקן
>
> R. Immi in the name of R. Shimon ben Laqish [said], "The Mishnah speaks of [a disciple of] the caliber of Shimon ben ʿAzzai who was sitting before them [the court]." Now how shall we explain this? If he has rejected their [the court's] position, then their decision is void. And if they have rejected his [position] then his instruction is void. Rather, we assume that it is a case where both [the disciple and the court] remain firm in their decisions. Their decision is not applicable to him since they did not reject him but it is applicable to others since he did not reject them.

32. See Berkovits, *Ha-halakha, koḥah ve-tafqidah,* 160, who also makes this point and adds further proof from *b. Sanh.* 88a where Rav Kahana and R. Eleazar discuss the relative merits of various types of arguments (see discussion above, pp. 324–25). Both sages are in agreement, however, that neither arguments from tradition nor arguments from subjective reasoning are mistakes. They only disagree about which type of argument wins out when wielded by either the minority or majority.

33. The verb טעו is used again in *m. Hor.* 1:2, and 4.

34. Late Babylonian Amoraim do use the phrase טעות בדבר משנה in this sense, but the unqualified word טעות, which is found in Tannaitic sources, is never used regarding one who follows a rejected minority opinion. See discussion below, pp. 356–63.

Once the dissenter begins to argue with the court, the initial assumption is that one of them will succeed in disproving the other's position. This describes not a dispute between two legitimate halakhic positions about which should be normative but rather a clash about which position is correct and which is mistaken. The verb סלק—"to reject" is used in this sense in other contexts as well.[35] If after great deliberation, the two parties cannot convince each other of their error, then the court's decision is legitimate for all others but not for the dissenter. We end up with a situation that tolerates the existence of two opposing views that are practiced simultaneously. If this were a common *maḥloqet* between two legitimate viewpoints, then the dissenter would have to recognize the validity of the majority viewpoint and follow it or else become a rebellious elder. But in this case, it is precisely because the dissenter thinks the majority view is a complete error that he may not follow it, as per *m. Hor.* 1:1, ironically creating a scenario wherein opposing practices are both legitimately followed.

The distinction between legitimate dispute and outright error explains the contradiction between the two versions of the Midrash on Deut 17:11. Both Midrashim use the symbols of right versus left as a metaphor. But the exact meaning of the metaphor differs in each text. *Sifre Deut.* 154 takes right versus left to include any difference of opinion between legitimate views while the Yerushalmi version uses it to refer to objective errors. The meaning of the metaphor in each case can be established only by looking at the context of each. *Sifre Deut.* 154, in the context of the rebellious elder, emphasizes the authority of the court while Yerushalmi *Horayot* emphasizes the responsibility of the individual to check on the court.

Requirement for Unanimity

This distinction explains the rationale behind an otherwise curious requirement that the court's decision must be unanimous in order for it to be liable when it makes a mistake. This requirement is spelled out in many Tannaitic sources:

> הורו בית דין וידע אחד מהן שטעו ואמר להן טועין אתם ...הרי אלו פטורין.
>
> If a court issues a ruling but one of its members knows that they erred and he told them, "You are in error," ... then they are not liable.[36]

35. See above, p. 225 n. 196.
36. *M. Hor.* 1:4.

לא היה מופלא של בית דין שם או אמר אחד מהם איני יודע או שאמר להם טועין אתם,
יכול יהו חייבין תלמוד לומר עדת ישראל ישגו עד שיורו כלם.

If the *mufla*[37] of the court was absent or if one of the members [of the court] said, "I do not know," or if he said, "You are in error," can it be that they [the judges] are liable? Therefore Scripture teaches, "*the whole community of Israel*" (Lev 4:13); [they are not liable] until all of them issue a [unanimous] ruling.[38]

חומר בהוראה מה שאין כן בדיני נפשות ... שבהוראה עד שהורו כולן ובדיני נפשות
הולכין אחר הרוב.

There is an aspect of the law of Horayot that is more stringent than laws of capital punishment … for the law of Horayot [applies] only if all [the judges] rule [unanimously], but in the laws of capital punishment we follow the majority.[39]

Y. Horayot 1:1 (45d) quotes this same law in the name of R. Manna bar Tanḥum, דר' מנא בר תנחום אמר נכנסו מאה עד שיורו כולן—"For R. Manna bar Tanḥum said: If one hundred [judges] enter [the court, the law of *Horayot* does not apply] until they all rule [unanimously]." *B. Horayot* 3b quotes similar words in the name of R. Yonatan. Generally, a simple majority is sufficient for an authoritative ruling. In this case, however, should there be any disagreement among the judges then we assume that the dissenting judge would be successful in pointing out the error. If, for some reason, the majority ignores the warning and votes in error, this cannot be considered a mistaken ruling. The other judges can no longer claim ignorance for they should have heeded the warning and deliberated further. Rabbi David Pardo (1718–1790) explains: היכא דחד חולק ואמר להן טועין אתם לא הוה להו לסמוך ולהורות הלכה למעשה עד שיצרפו וילבנו הדבר מתוך הויכוח לברר האמת—"When one disagrees and tells them, 'you are mistaken,' nobody should have relied [on the court] and legislated in practice until they processed and clarified the matter by discussion to arrive at the truth."[40] Therefore, the judges, who have sinned deliberately, cannot bring a sacrifice, and the masses are responsible for following their mistaken ruling.[41]

It is clear from these sources that the dissenter in a case of *Horayot* does not have merely an alternate point of view, a different tradition, or another angle on a difficult issue. If that were the case, then how could

37. See analysis of this term above, p. 303 n. 15.
38. *Sifra, Ḥoba, parasha* 4:4 (ed. Finkelstin, 2:141–42).
39. *T. Hor.* 1:3.
40. David Pardo, *Ḥasde David* (Jerusalem: Vagshal, 1994), 5:913.
41. This case would fall into the category of a court that deliberately issues a wrong ruling and the masses mistakenly follow it, מזידין ועשו שוגגין, about which *m. Hor.* 1:4 rules that the court is exempt from sacrifice.

we expect the majority of judges to know that the dissenter is objectively right? If, however, we are dealing with a case where the court has simply overlooked a source or missed a logical step in their argument, then we are dealing with objective right and wrong. If every member of the court makes even a blatant mistake, we can still consider it an inadvertent error because even responsible people sometimes just slip up. However, once even a single member of the court points out the mistake, we expect the rest of the members to review the matter and recognize their error.[42]

Both Talmuds question the relationship between the requirement for unanimity and the second half of *m. Hor.* 1:1. In *m. Hor.* 1:1, there is a dissenter so that according to the unanimity requirement the court cannot bring a sacrifice. Yet the court still brings a bullock to atone for the masses who inadvertently followed the ruling.[43] The Yerusahlmi explains that the dissenting member of *m. Hor.* 1:1 was not present at the time of the ruling.[44] The Bavli says that he was present but did not express his disagreement, כגון שהרכין ההוא אחד בראשו—"for example, he nodded his head."[45] This is a variation on the Yerushalmi, but instead of not being physically present, only his argument is not present.

At the end of the Bavli *sugya*, however, R. Mesharsheya completely rejects the unanimity requirement, citing the ruling that if the majority of the community cannot bear a rabbinic decree then the decree is void. Just as in the case of rabbinic decrees we consider the majority even though the verse says, "the entire nation,"[46] so too here the majority should be suf-

---

42. *B. Sanh.* 17a applies the same reasoning to a unanimous guilty decision in a capital case, "Rav Kahana said: If the Sanhedrin unanimously find [the accused] guilty, he is acquitted." If not one member of the court could find reason to acquit, then we suspect that they have not given a fair trial and have not tried hard enough to look at the merits of the defendant's case. However, if there is a dissenting opinion, then we know that the dissenter has argued for acquittal and the rest of the court must have taken all of those arguments into account. Even if the majority still found him guilty, at least we know they performed proper deliberation and gave a fair trial. This does not guarantee that the court's decision is correct, but it does insure that the court considered both sides thoroughly and offered a careful response. Here, too, just as in *Horayot,* the assumption is that a unanimous court might easily overlook an important argument or source while the decision of a non-unanimous court is deliberate and fair.

43. One could explain that the court only brings a bullock in the case in the first half of *m. Hor.* 1:1 but not in the second half. However, both Talmuds read the Mishnah as two parts of one case. *B. Hor.* 3b expresses this in a midrashic formula, ה"ז חייב, מפני שלא תלה בב"ד; האי הוא דחייב, הא אחר פטור. If others are not liable it can only be because the court has brought a bullock on their behalf. On the tendency of the Bavli Stam to use midrashic exegesis on the Mishnah, see Avinoam Cohen, "'Minyana le-meʿute maiʾ u-ʾminyana lama liʾ: min ha-sheʾeloth ha-Talmudiyot ha-noseʾot ʿofi Sevoraʾi," in *Meḥkarim ba-lashon ha-Ivrit ub-sifrut ha-Talmudit,* ed. M. Kadari (Ramat-Gan: Bar-Ilan University Press, 1990), 92 n. 50.

44. See *y. Hor.* 1:2 (45d).

45. *B. Hor.* 3b.

46. Malachi 3:9.

ficient even though the verse states, "If all of the nation of Israel should transgress by mistake." It is not clear how R. Mesharsheya can so easily reject a Tannaitic tradition,[47] nor is his motivation apparent.[48]

Other Cases of a Court Making a Mistake

The distinction between a mistake and a disagreement is very subtle and difficult to determine. It may therefore be instructive to look at some other cases in the Talmud where the word טעות is applied in order to get a better sense of its semantic field. *T. Horayot* 1:6 distinguishes between a legitimate decision and a mistaken one in the case of an observable fact: הורו בין דין שהוא מוצאי שבת ואחר כך זרחה חמה אין זו הוראה אלא טעות—"If a court legislates that Shabbat is over and the sun appears thereafter, this is not a legitimate decision but rather an error." This is a case of misjudging an empirical reality.[49]

טעות can also refer to a mistaken tradition. *T. Zebaḥim* 2:17 reports that Issi ha-Babli remembered a certain tradition he heard from Rabbi but was unsure of the tradition because nobody else could confirm it: חיזרתי על כל חבריי ולא מצאתי לי חבר הייתי סבור שמא טעות הוא ביד רבי—"I went around to all of my colleagues and I did not find a corroborating tradition. I was convinced that it may have been an error made by Rabbi." He was afraid it was a "mistaken" tradition until R. Eleazar finally was able to corroborate it. *B. Šabbat* 63b reports that Rav Dimi quotes a certain statement in the name of R. Yoḥanan. After Abaye rejects it based on a *baraita*, Rav Dimi replies that he misquoted R. Yoḥanan: שלח להו: דברים שאמרתי לכם טעות הם בידי,

47. Curiously, however, the Talmuds do not quote any of the Tannaitic sources but Amoraic statements instead.

48. Perhaps R. Mehsarsheya felt that many cases of *Horayot* are not in fact so clear cut and so it is not fair to assume that the court is deliberately misguiding the masses if they do not at first agree with the dissenter's view. In fact, the Yerushalmi expands the cases that fall into the *Horayot* category from those given in the Mishnah. The Bavli accepts those expansions and even adds a few more examples; see below, p. 362 n. 61. In these more subtle cases, it may not be obvious that the court is mistaken even though one member tells them they are wrong.

49. It may not always be clear what matters are purely factual and which are decisions of halakhic status. For example, *b. Yebam.* 92a deliberates on whether the court's decision is valid in a case where a husband goes away, the court rules that his wife may remarry, and then the husband comes back. Clearly the court was mistaken factually, but Rav Naḥman holds that the decision still has *halakhic* validity and so the wife is exempt from a sacrifice. In general, however, when a ruling is an obvious mistake, such as in *t. Hor.* 1:6, or when the court rules against an explicit verse, then their ruling is not valid and whoever follows it is responsible. When a ruling is not an obvious mistake then it is a valid הוראה and whoever follows it is not held responsible.

ברם כך אמרו משום רבי יוחנן—"He sent to him: What I told you was an error; but rather, this is what they said in the name of R. Yoḥanan…."[50]

The word טעות also is used to refer to a misinterpretation or misapplication of a source. *B. Sanhedrin* 5b tells of the people of a certain town who would use water while kneading and still consider the dough pure. Rabbi questioned them and they explained that a student once told them this law. In fact, the student only said that מי ביצים—"eggs" do not make food ready to receive impurity but they heard מי בצעים—"pond water."[51] The continuation of the story is introduced by the words וטעו נמי בהא—"they also erred in this." The citizens also misapplied *m. Parah* 8:10: "The waters of Keramyon and Pigah, because they are ponds, are unfit for purification purposes." The people of this city assumed that since pond waters cannot be used for purification they also do not make food ready to receive impurity.

טעות is also used in more complex halakhic matters where the error is less obvious, such as in *m. Naz.* 5:4:

> מי שנדר בנזיר והלך להביא את בהמתו ומצאה שנגנבה אם עד שלא נגנבה בהמתו נזר הרי זה נזיר ואם משנגנבה בהמתו נזר אינו נזיר וזו טעות טעה נחום המדי כשעלו נזירין מן הגולה ומצאו בית המקדש חרב אמר להם נחום המדי אלו הייתם יודעים שבית המקדש חרב הייתם נוזרים אמרו לו לא והתירן נחום המדי וכשבא הדבר אצל חכמים אמרו לו כל שנזר עד שלא חרב בית המקדש נזיר ומשחרב בית המקדש אינו נזיר.
>
> One who vowed to be a Nazirite and went to bring his animal [to sacrifice] and found that it was stolen, if he vowed to be a nazirite before the animal was stolen then he is a nazirite. If he vowed to be a nazirite after his animal was stolen then he is not a nazirite. Naḥum the Mede made an error on this matter when nazirites came up from the Diaspora and found the Temple in ruins. Naḥum the Mede said to them, "Had you known that the Temple was destroyed would you have vowed to be nazirites?" They said to him, "No," whereupon Naḥum the Mede released them [from their vow]. When the matter came before the sages, they said to him [Naḥum the Mede], "Whoever vowed to be a nazirite before the destruction of the Temple is a nazirite. [Whoever vowed to be a nazirite] after the destruction of the Temple is not a nazirite.

---

50. The same phrase is also found in similar contexts at *b. ʿErub.* 16b, 104a; *b. B. Bat.* 127a; *b. Zebaḥ.* 94b; *b. Ḥul.* 56a; and *b. Nid.* 68a. See also *y. Ketub.* 4:11 (29a).

51. This story about the citizens of the city confusing "eggs" with "water" is also found in *y. Šeb.* 6:1 (36c) = *y. Giṭ.* 1:2 (43c) where the citizens do not use pond water but water in which eggs were boiled. The Bavli makes the story more interesting by introducing the word play. Rosental, "Mesorot Ereṣ-Yisraeliyot ve-darkan le-Bavel," 15, explains that this word play was only possible in Babylonia where the letter *ʿayin* was not pronounced.

Naḥum the Mede holds a mistaken view and rules based on it. When the rabbis find out about his mistaken ruling they correct it. Presumably, Naḥum the Mede agreed once he realized his error. In fact, *b. Naz.* 32b wonders how R. Eliezer in *m. Ned.* 9:2 could have held the same mistaken view as that of Naḥum the Mede. The Bavli therefore assumes that the rabbis must have forced R. Eliezer to agree with them, אמר רבה: שטפוהו רבנן לר' אליעזר ואוקמיה בשיטתייהו—"Rabbah said, the rabbis swamped R. Eliezer and made him agree with their opinion."

A number of sources use the word טעות with a modifying phrase, טעות בדבר משנה—"a mistake regarding a teaching from tradition" and טעות בשיקול הדעת—"a mistake in reasoning." In general, if a court awards money to one party of a dispute but makes a mistake in reasoning, then its judgment holds inasmuch as the awardee does not have to return the award, although the judges themselves may have to pay the wrongly accused party from their pockets. If the court made a mistake regarding a tradition, however, then the decision is not valid and the awardee must return the money.[52]

The phrase טעה בדבר משנה is used in cases where the judge completely ignores an authoritative source. In *b. Bek.* 28a = *b. Sanh.* 33a, the Talmud uses the term to refer to R. Ṭarfon's mistake in deeming nonkosher an animal whose womb was cut out, thus ignoring an explicit Mishnah.[53] Similarly, the Gemara at *b. Ketub.* 100b says of a court that disregarded the proper procedure as set forth in a Mishnah, נעשו כמי שטעו בדבר משנה.[54] Rav Ashi at b. Sanh. 33a states that טעה בדבר משנה can apply to violation of any Tannaitic or even Amoraic ruling:

> אמר ליה רבינא לרב אשי: אפילו טעה ברבי חייא ורבי אושעיא? אמר ליה: אין. אפילו בדרב ושמואל? אמר ליה: אין. אפילו בדידי ודידך? אמר ליה: אטו אנן קטלי קני באגמא אנן?
>
> Ravina said to Rav Ashi, "[Is a judge's ruling invalid] even if he erred regarding [a tradition from] R. Ḥiyya or R. Oshaia?" He said to him, "Yes." [He asked further,] "Even regarding [a tradition from] Rav and Shmuel?" He said to him, "Yes." [He asked further,] "Even regarding [a tradition] from me and you?" He said to him, "Are we just reed choppers in the swamp?"

---

52. This is the opinion of Rav Assi (some mss. read Ammi) in *b. Sanh.* 6a, 33a and R. Yoḥanan in *y. Ketub.* 9:2 (33a). However Resh Laqish in the latter source says that the ruling is valid in both categories. See text below.

53. *M. Ḥul.* 3:2. Of course, it would be anachronistic for R. Ṭarfon to know a Mishnah, unless the term refers to a collection of teachings that predates Rabbi's Mishnah. More likely, "Mishnah" can refer to any teaching from tradition. See next note.

54. See also *b. Šeb.* 38b where the phrase is used by Rava and Rav Papa about a court procedure that is not specified in the Mishnah. Here too, "Mishnah" simply means "a teaching from tradition"—even traditions not included in the Mishnah.

This expansive definition is also found in the Yerushalmi (*Ketub.* 9:2, 33a):

> הכל מודין שאם טעו בשיקול הדעת שאין מחזירין, מדברי תורה מחזירין
> מה פליגין בטעות משנה שרבי יוחנן אמר בטעות משנה שיקול הדעת, רבי שמעון בן לקיש אמר טעות משנה דבר תורה
> היא טעות משנה היא טעות זקינים
>
> Everyone agrees that if they erred in reasoning, they do not return [the money], and [if they erred] in a matter of Torah law then they do return [it].
> About what do they argue? If they erred regarding a [rabbinic] tradition: R. Yoḥanan says a mistake regarding a tradition [is the same as a mistake in] reasoning. R. Shimon ben Laqish says a mistake regarding a tradition [is the same as a mistake regarding] a law of Torah.
> A mistake [regarding] a Mishnah is the same as a mistake regarding something learned from elders.

This *sugya* sets out three categories of error: טעות בשיקל הדעת, טעות משנה, and טעות בדברי תורה—a mistake in reasoning, a mistake regarding a rabbinic tradition and a mistake regarding a matter of Pentateuchal law. The last line says that טעות משנה is the same as an error about any matter learned from the elders, that is, any rabbinic teaching. It is seems clear from this grouping that טעות משנה is meant to include any violation of an explicit and generally accepted rabbinic law, whether Tannaitic or Amoraic.

In other cases, טעות בדבר משנה applies even to a ruling that follows an opinion that is recorded in the Mishnah but that is not the generally accepted normative view. In *b. Ketub.* 84b, the term is applied by the Stam to a court that ruled according to R. Ṭarfon in a monetary case where the normative view is accepted to be that of R. Akiba. In *b. Ketub.* 100a even a decision by Rabbi that agrees with the majority opinion (חכמים) at *m. Ketub.* 11:5 is labeled by the Stam as טעות בדבר משנה since the halakha is established according to R. Shimon ben Gamaliel. טעות here is not used in the sense of an objectively identifiable mistake, as in the sources above, but rather as any case in which one contradicts a generally accepted ruling.

טעות בשיקול הדעת has a variety of definitions in different sources. In *b. Bek.* 28b = *b. Sanh.* 33a it refers to R. Ṭarfon's misjudging the scientific fact that animals can live without their wombs.[55] Rav Papa redefines the term to mean not cases of reason but cases of controversy where one follows the view that is not customarily followed, even though there is no strictly legal decision about which view is normative.[56]

---

55. The Gemara says that R. Ṭarfon erred in both דבר משנה (see above, n. 53) as well as שיקול הדעת.

56. *B. Sanh.* 6a and 33a.

In sum, the word טעות unqualified always refers to an outright mistake in which a decision or teaching is based on a false understanding of reality, or it contradicts or misinterprets an authoritative tradition. It is also used dozens of times in the phrases מקח טעות, קדושי טעות, נשואי טעות and נדר טעות—"mistaken sale, mistaken engagement, mistaken wedding, and mistaken vow," also in the sense of an invalid transaction because of some mistake in the process. The phrases טעות בדבר משנה and טעות בשיקול הדעת are also generally used in the same sense. These phrases refer sometimes, especially for the later Babylonian Amoraim (Rav Papa) and the Stam, to decisions according to one side of a legitimate controversy in which the other side has been widely accepted to be the halakha. Evidently, the late Babylonians and the Stam view these long-ago-rejected opinions as invalid, and so one who rules according to them is simply in error. This, however, is a different usage from the unqualified טעות and the way the word is used in Tannaitic[57] and early Amoraic passages. *M. Horayot* 1:1 and 4 use the unqualified word טעו. Based on the above discussion, we should understand the nature of the court's mistake in the sense of an objectively identifiable error rather than simply a ruling with which a given rabbi disagrees.

To What Types of Cases Does the Law Apply?

That *Horayot* deals with cases where the court makes a patent mistake is further evident from the types of cases mentioned as examples in the Mishnah. *M. Horayot* 1:1 opens the subject with הורו בית דין לעבור על אחת מכל מצות האמורות בתורה—"If a court issues a ruling to transgress any one of the commandments enjoined in the Torah." This certainly sounds like a case of violating a clear-cut biblical commandment. *M. Horayot* 1:3 elaborates further:

> הורו בית דין לעקור את כל הגוף אמרו אין נדה בתורה אין שבת בתורה אין עבודה זרה בתורה הרי אלו פטורין
> הורו לבטל מקצת ולקיים מקצת הרי אלו חייבין כיצד אמרו יש נדה בתורה אבל הבא על שומרת יום כנגד יום פטור יש שבת בתורה אבל המוציא מרשות היחיד לרשות הרבים פטור יש עבודה זרה בתורה אבל המשתחוה פטור הרי אלו חייבין שנאמר ונעלם דבר דבר ולא כל הגוף:
>
> If a court issued a ruling to uproot an entire body [of halakha]: if they said there is no law regarding the menstruant in the Torah; there is no Shabbat in the Torah; there is no law of idolatry in the Torah, then they [the judges] are exempt.

57. See, for example, *m. Sanh.* 5:5 and *t. Pesaḥ.* 7:17.

> If they issued a ruling to nullify part and retain part then they are liable. How so? If they say there is a law regarding the menstruant in the Torah but one who has intercourse with a woman who needs to watch [for blood] one day corresponding to [having seen blood] one day is exempt; there is Shabbat in the Torah but one who carries from private domain to public domain is exempt; there is a law of idolatry in the Torah but one who [only] prostrates is exempt, they [the judges] are liable, for the verse states, "*the matter is forgotten*," the matter and not the entire body.[58]

The reason why a court is not responsible when it uproots an entire body of halakha is that we expect the masses to know these broad categories of explicit biblical law and so they cannot claim to have relied on the court. However, if the court abrogates only part of a biblical law then they are responsible to bring a sacrifice. The Mishnah brings three examples of blatant errors.[59]

---

58. See parallel at *Sifra Ḥoba, parasha* 4:7–8 (ed. Finkelstein, 2:142).

59. Finkelstein wonders how any court could make such blatant errors. He concludes that the examples derive from pre-Hasmonian times when the Sanhedrin was in the hands of Hellenizers. We have already noted above, n. 15, that this reconstruction is problematic. To the extent that one can historicize at all, it is more likely that these examples are issues about which there was sectarian controversy during late Second Temple times. Goldberg, *Commentary to the Mishna Shabbat*, 3, argues, based on this Mishnah, that carrying on Shabbat was a matter of sectarian controversy. He proposes that tractate *Shabbat* begins with the subject of transporting on Shabbat as a polemic against the Sadducean view. (For other explanations, see Yehudah Shaviv, "Maduaʿ patḥa masekhet Shabbat bi-mlekhet hoṣaʾah," *Sinai* 105 (1990): 220–30. Haym Soloveitchik, "*Mishneh Torah:* Polemic and Art," in *Maimonides after 800 Years: Essays on Maimonides and His Influence*, ed. Jay Harris (Cambridge, MA: Harvard University Press, 2007), 327–43, makes a similar argument for the order of the laws of *Shabbat* in Maimonides' *Mishneh Torah*. The Karaites differed from the rabbis concerning the laws of cooking, lighting candles, and having Gentiles do work. Maimonides therefore addresses these three issues in chapters 3 to 6 even before he introduces the thirty-nine categories of work in chapter 7.)

Albeck, *Mishnah, Moʿed*, 435, similarly argues based on *m. ʿErub.* 6:2 that the Sadducees did not prohibit transporting objects from the house to the courtyard. The Damascus Covenant (CD XI, 7–8) clearly prohibits carrying on Shabbat: "No one may remove [anything] from the house to outside or [bring it] from outside into the house." However, the Sadducees of the late Second Temple were very different from the earlier Sadducean Zadokite priesthood that formed the Dead Sea sect. See Lawrence Schiffman, *The Halakhah at Qumran* (Leiden: Brill, 1975), 114; and idem, *Reclaiming*, 89. Ginzberg, *An Unknown Jewish Sect*, 65–66, writes, "According to a statement in the Talmud, Horayot 4a, the Sadducees forbade only carrying something out of the house (on Shabbat) but not carrying something into it. Accordingly our author [of the Damascus Covenant], who forbade both acts, would seem to be in agreement with the Pharisees as against the Sadducees. Nevertheless, it is clear from the Talmud itself that this statement has no basis in fact but is purely scholastic speculation and is offered only as a hypothesis by the Talmud itself." Regardless of whether the historical Sadducees in fact allowed carrying into the courtyard, it is significant that *m. ʿErub.* 6:2 attributes this view to them and that *m. Hor.* 1:3 also uses carrying as an example.

The Talmuds wonder about the obviousness of the examples of the Mishnah. *Y. Horayot* 1:2 (46a) questions the examples cited at *m. Hor.* 1:3 of partially uprooted laws since they seem to actually uproot entire categories of law.[60] *B. Horayot* 4a-b similarly wonders about the examples of the Mishnah since they contradict explicit verses. Both Talmuds proceed to reread the Mishnah's examples and modify them to be much more subtle details of each law.[61] These later rabbinic sources provide examples that

---

CD V, 6–7, records that there was a difference of opinion between the sectarians and the Pharisees regarding laws of female impurity: וגם מטמאים הם את המקדש אשר אין הם מבדיל כתורה ושוכבים עם הרואה את דם זובה—"They also defile the Temple for they do not separate according to the Torah and they lie with a woman who sees her blood flow." The scroll does not specify the details of the argument and the sectarians are in any case more stringent regarding this law. However, this does indicate that menstrual laws were a subject of dispute between the sects and this Mishnah may likely be making reference to such a dispute. More research is needed to see if the laws of idolatry also might have been matters of sectarian controversy. A similar inquiry could explain the three examples mentioned in *t. Hor.* 1:7, which all relate to the Temple sacrifices, such as what the exact punishment is for eating blood.

Another indication that the law of *Horayot* had antisectarian undertones is the statement of Shmuel in *b. Hor.* 4a (the statement is also quoted in the name of R. Yoḥanan in *b. Sanh.* 33b):

> אמר רב יהודה אמר שמואל: אין בית דין חייבין עד שיורו בדבר שאין הצדוקין מודין בו. אבל בדבר שהצדוקין מודין בו—פטורין. מאי טעמא? זיל קרי בי רב הוא.
>
> Rav Yehudah said in the name of Shmuel: A court is only liable if they rule in a matter about which the Sadducees disagree but in a matter that the Sadducees agree with they are exempt. What is the reason? It is a matter [about which you can say,] Go read it in the master's house.

The court is liable only if its ruling disagrees with the Sadducees, i.e., if it is not explicit in the Torah (see above, p. 341 n. 3). It is extraordinary that the Sadducean law should be the criterion for defining a category in rabbinic halakha. The Sadducees were long gone in Shmuel's days and it would have been anachronistic for him to refer to their interpretation of law. If Shmuel is repeating an older tradition, then his statement may reflect a polemical aspect of the law of *Horayot*.

If it is true that the law of *Horayot* was directed against sectarian authority in its early history, a speculative but nevertheless appealing possibility, then the distinction between the law of *Horayot* and that of the rebellious elder becomes clear. From the point of view of the rabbis and their Pharisaic predecessors, the views of sectarian groups were outside the bounds of legitimacy and were therefore deemed outright errors. The rebellious elder, on the other hand, addressed controversy internal to the rabbis where multiple valid opinions coexisted. In later times, when sectarianism diminished, the two categories remained but needed to be redefined. As I point out in the next paragraph, the Talmuds update the Mishnah's examples and the entire law of *Horayot* to be still relevant to post-sectarian times. It accomplishes this by distinguishing legitimate controversy among the rabbis from blatant errors that can sometimes occur even in a rabbinic court.

60. Distinguishing between categories and details involves the issue of individuation of laws, on which see Joseph Raz, *The Concept of a Legal System: An Introduction to the Theory of Legal System* (Oxford: Clarendon, 1980), 70–92; and Hanina Ben-Menahem, "Maimonides' Fourteen Roots: Logical Structure and Conceptual Analysis," *Jewish Law Annual* 13 (2000): 3–30.

61. It is interesting to note that the laws presented in the Bavli are extremely subtle

are more realistic to their age.[62] It is significant, however, that all of the new interpretations are also matters about which there exists no rabbinic controversy.[63] Thus, there remains a clear distinction between the categories of law applicable to either *Horayot* or the rebellious elder.

Parallel Laws

As discussed above, *m. Hor.* 1:3 defines the category of law for which a court is liable as partially abrogated laws. *T. Horayot* 1:7 repeats this definition but adds a curious biblical derivation. The Tosefta connects the word דבר in Lev 4:13 with the same word in Deut 17:8:

> נאמר כאן דבר ונאמר להלן דבר מה דבר האמור להלן דבר מקצתו ולא כולו אף דבר האמור כאן מקצתו ולא כולו אתה אומר דבר מקצתו ולא כולו או אינו אלא כולו תלמוד לומר בין דם לדם ולא כל דם בין דין לדין ולא כל דין בין נגע לנגע ולא כל נגע.
> Scripture states here *"matter"* (Lev 4:13) and it states there *"matter"* (Deut 17:8). Just as *"matter"* that is stated there means part of it but not all of it, so too *"matter"* that is stated here means part of it but not all of it. Do you say *"matter"* means part of it but not all of it or does it only mean all of it? Scripture therefore comes to teach, *"between blood and blood"* (ibid.) but not the entire blood, *"between judgment and judgment,"* but not the entire judgement, *"between affliction and affliction,"* but not the entire affliction.[64]

We have been approaching the laws of *Horayot* and rebellious elder as two opposites in tension over the conflicting values of authority and truth. By making a *gezerah shavah* between the two laws, the Tosefta reveals that it views the two laws as being closely related, perhaps even parallel to each

---

nuances of halakha, even more so than the Yerushalmi examples. The Bavli thus expands the category of cases about which one must disobey the court from only blatant examples in the Mishnah to even very subtle errors. This may be connected to the Bavli's greater tolerance for diverse practices in general, since dissent from the court results in multiplicity of practice by the dissenter and everyone else. Of course, the Bavli's search for more subtle cases may be simply a consequence of its greater penchant for dialectics and thus not connected with the issue of tolerance.

62. See above, n. 59.

63. Although *m. Šabb.* 12:1 records a controversy regarding throwing an object over public domain from one private domain to another, all agree that throwing from public to private domain or vice-versa is prohibited. Therefore, a ruling to the effect that any throwing or passing is allowed has no support and is simply a blatant error, even though it contradicts no biblical verse and does not represent a category of law.

64. *T. Hor.* 1:7. Curiously, this qualification is not mentioned anywhere in context of the rebellious elder. Perhaps this qualification is related to the rule in *b. Sanh.* 87a that the rebellious elder only applies in a case where the essence is biblical but the explanation is rabbinic.

other. The same derivation is repeated by Rav Ashi in *b. Hor.* 4a. *B. Sanhedrin* 87a uses the same *gezerah shavah* in the opposite direction to prove that just as in *Horayot* the court is liable only for laws that oblige *karet* or a sin offering,[65] so too the rebellious elder is only killed for disagreeing about those types of laws. These derivations are especially interesting because they are not necessary; one could derive the same conclusions in other ways.[66]

The connection between the two laws is also apparent regarding the issue of where the law of *Horayot* applies. The *Sifra*[67] establishes from the language of Lev 4:13 that the law of *Horayot* applies only to the Great Sanhedrin in the chamber of hewn stone. This is also the opinion of the sages in *m. Hor.* 1:5, which includes a similar derivation. This limitation is also assumed by *t. Hor.* 1:4. *Y. Horayot* 1:1 (45d), however, provides another derivation:

> אין חייבין עד שתהא הורייה מלישכת הגזית אמר רבי יוחנן טעמא דהך תנייא מן המקום ההוא אשר יבחר יי׳.
>
> One is not liable unless the ruling is from the chamber of hewn-stone. R. Yoḥanan said, the source of this teaching is: "*from that place that the Lord will have chosen*" (Deut 17:10).[68]

R. Yoḥanan quotes Deut 17:10 from the context of the rebellious elder to prove that the law of *Horayot* applies only to the Great Sanhedrin, as if the two laws are interchangeable.[69]

As noted, Sagi proposes that the law of the rebellious elder assumes a deontic view of Jewish law while the law of *Horayot* assumes an epistemic view. According to this understanding, the two laws stand in tension with each other, and it is surprising that the rabbis would apply laws from one context to the other. Rather, it seems that the rabbis themselves thought of Jewish law as neither completely deontic nor entirely epistemic. Certainly, the courts and the rabbis have great authority to define biblical laws, create rabbinic laws, and interpret tradition. However, their power is nev-

65. See *m. Hor.* 2:3.

66. *M. Hor.* 1:3, *Sifra Ḥoba, parasha* 4:8 (ed. Finkelstein, 2:142), and *b. Hor.* 4a use Lev 4:13 by itself to derive that the law of *Horayot* applies only to a partial abrogation of a law. *Midrash hag-gadol* derives that the rebellious elder is killed only for laws obliging *karet* or a sin offering from Deut 17:8 alone; see above p. 317 n. 65.

67. *Ḥoba, parasha* 4:2 (ed. Finkelstein, 2:141).

68. This law with the same biblical derivation is repeated at *y. Hor.* 1:6 (46a) (= *y. Pesaḥ.* 7:6, 34c) in the name of R. Yose. If that attribution is correct, then "R. Yoḥanan" in *y. Hor.* 1:1 (45d) may be a mistaken expansion of an abbreviation.

69. See also Sperber, "Sugya aḥat be-masekhet Horayot," 157–62, who suggests that Rav Dimi's ruling in *b. Hor.* 2a—that the court is liable only for a normative *halakhic* decision—is derived from a similar requirement regarding the rebellious elder.

ertheless limited. They may not pass certain boundaries, such as negating biblical law, canceling well-established decrees of previous courts, or abandoning longstanding Pharisaic-rabbinic interpretations of laws.[70]

Taken together, the laws of the rebellious elder and of *Horayot* are not in opposition but rather actually complement each other to create a system of checks and balances. The law of the rebellious elder grants the high court greater authority than all individual opinions and prevents the Torah "from becoming two Torahs."[71] The law of *Horayot* ensures that the high court itself remains true to tradition and does not veer from the halakhic system, so that Torah does not become divorced from its roots. The court has ultimate authority, but only if it remains within the bounds of basic Torah norms.

Just as the rebellious elder protects against individual rabbis disobeying the law as decided by the high court, the law of *Horayot* protects against a wayward court that disobeys the law of the Bible as interpreted by longstanding Pharisaic-rabbinic tradition. In fact, the two laws have the same force. Both laws agree on a judicial hierarchy wherein ultimate authority lies in the Torah and the sources of oral law, which are interpreted by the high court. They both assume that the court has authority to *interpret* the law but never to *ignore* the law. Neither source allows for any true diversity of practice. Either the court is correct and the rabbis must all obey, or it is mistaken and they must all disobey. These two laws are actually two parts of a unified system.

Conclusion

Rather than viewing the laws of rebellious elder and *Horayot* as contradictory, we argue that they complement each other to create a unified system. The law of *Horayot* supports dissent against an objectively erroneous decision of a court while the law of the rebellious elder prohibits dissent from a court that issues a legitimate, even if controversial, decision. This unified system leaves very little room for diversity of halakhic practice. If the court is within its right to legislate, then nobody may disobey, and if they are outside their right, then everyone must disobey. Of course, this system assumes the existence of a universally recognized Sanhedrin. In a decentralized judiciary, the laws of *Horayot* and rebellious elder lose much of their legal force. A rebellious elder can still be excommunicated if

---

70. Of course, one could find Talmudic examples violating each of these sources of authority. But in those cases, the deviation is usually justified with some loophole, *okimta* (limiting the law to only certain cases), rereading of the source, or alternate tradition. On this topic, see further in Hayes, "Abrogation of Torah Law," 643–74.

71. See references below, p. 386 n. 68.

he disobeys the majority of rabbis, and a dissenter may still refuse to abide by the majority ruling if he is convinced they are wrong. But the laws will not be applied consistently to every case nor will they have the same effectiveness in limiting diversity of practice.

In practice, it may be difficult for an individual who disagrees with the court to decide whether the court is objectively mistaken and has gone beyond the limits of its authority or whether they hold a legitimate alternate opinion that he just vigorously opposes. Still, it will be up to individual dissenters to use their best judgment about whether to disobey the ruling and risk becoming a rebellious elder, or submit to the ruling and be liable for knowingly following a mistaken ruling. Following a similar line of thinking, Rabbi Issachar Baer Eylenburg (1550–1623) looks to the subjective judgment of the dissenter to decide whether to follow *Sifre Deut.* 154 or the Yerushalmi version of the Midrash:

> דהא דאמרו בספרי אפילו מראים בעיניך על שמאל שהוא ימין הכי פירושו, אפילו תחשב בלבך על פי שקול הדעת שטעו בדין ואמרו על שמאל שהוא ימין, אבל לא שהוא יודע בודאי שטעו בדין.
>
> That their saying in the Sifre, "even if they point out to you that right is left," means that even if in your heart and according to your own reasoning you think they were mistaken in judgment and said about left that it is right, but not if he knew for certain that they were wrong.[72]

At a theoretical level, there must be some border between a legitimate halakhic stance that is within the court's authority to uphold and what is beyond their jurisdiction and power to legislate. However, there is no clear indication where to draw this line in practice. All of these distinctions depend on meta-halakhic categories, and there exists no meta-authority above the Sanhedrin who could decide such matters. These holes in the system will cause *de facto* diversity of practice. As noted earlier in the Yerushalmi, when the court and the dissenter both insist that the other is utterly mistaken, they will each have to follow their own opinions. Those stories in which we sense the greatest tension between the rabbis, such as *m. Roš Haš.* 2:8–9[73] and the oven of Akhnai,[74] are often centered around the nebulous territory between the two categories of legitimate controversy and objective error.

This system is only upheld to its full extent in the Tannaitic sources.

---

72. Issachar Baer Eylenburg, *Be'er Sheva'* (Warsaw, 1890), 7. Translation from Sagi, "Models," 23. See also Ya'akov Algazi, *Sefer she'erit Ya'aqov* (Brooklyn: Beth Hasefer, 1989), 3:425.

73. See above, pp. 264–66.

74. See above, pp. 276–77.

As seen in the previous chapter, the law of the rebellious elder is greatly watered down in the Bavli. Regarding the law of *Horayot*, we see that the Yerushalmi, and to a greater extent the Bavli, enlarges the number of cases in which one must disagree with the court. The three blatant examples of error in *m. Hor.* 1:3 are interpreted to be more subtle aspects of these laws in Yerushalmi and more examples are added in the Bavli.[75] While in the Mishnah, only a judge or a competent student may disobey the court, Shmuel, according to the Bavli, holds every individual liable for following a mistaken court as long as the dissenters remain a minority.[76] By limiting the rebellious elder and increasing the right of people to disobey the court, the tight system of checks and balances in the Mishnah becomes loosened. The Bavli especially opens the possibility for more diversity of practice by reducing instances in which a dissenter could be branded as a rebellious elder and at the same time permitting individuals to assert their right to disobey the court in more cases.

75. See above, p. 362 n. 61.

76. See above, 341. The Bavli also increases the punishment for one who follows the court knowing they are mistaken and knowing that he should not submit to their authority. See above, p. 343 n. 13.

Conclusion

Every social group and legal system must deal with the tension between exclusivity and inclusively, between unity and diversity, and ultimately between truth and peace. A group that is too inclusive will cease to be a group, for every community needs boundaries. If everyone is included then nothing defines its members. On the other hand, a legal system that tolerates no deviation from a single interpretation of the law will similarly cease to exist since indeterminacy built into all legal codes necessarily triggers multiple understandings. Legal theory has long been grappling with these issues and searching for models that best represent how law—with the theoretical and practical pluralism it engenders—functions as a coherent system. As we have seen in the introduction,[1] opinions range from legal centralism, staunchly maintained by Owen Fiss, among others, to legal pluralism, articulated most expansively by Robert Cover.

How does halakha, as encoded in the literature of the Tannaim and Amoraim, deal with halakhic diversity? When two rabbis inherit different traditions from legitimate sources or derive opposing rulings using commonly accepted exegetical methodology, does the halakhic worldview allow for both interpretations to be practiced or does it impose uniformity on its members?

Predictably, rabbinic literature offers a spectrum of responses to the question of how to approach diversity of halakhic practice. We find institutions such as the law of the rebellious elder that assume a model of legal centralism. According to this law, the central court retains sole legislative authority, "Even if they point out to you that right is left and left is right."[2] Fiss similarly argues that "An interpretation is binding even if mistaken"[3] and may therefore be rightfully enforced by the state. The law of *Horayot*, on the other hand, grants all worthy sages the right to interpret the law as they see fit such that when a court is deemed mistaken the dissenters may and even must follow their own legitimate view. This law would surely be a central tenet in Cover's utopia. While these two models stand apart in legal theory, rabbinic literature manages to integrate both of them

1. See above, pp. 3–15.
2. *Sifre Deut.* 154; see above, p. 314.
3. Fiss, "Objectivity and Interpretation," 758.

into a complex system of checks and balances.[4] Different circumstances will require the application of one rule or the other in order to maintain a healthy balance between the central authority and the legitimate interpretations of its dissenters.

Just as tolerance for diversity shifts depending on individual circumstances, it also varies from one issue to the next. Certain topics, such as the setting of the calendar, are particularly sensitive because of their potential to cause social rifts or because of the polemics involved. On the other hand, diversity in matters of custom is much more tolerable than in halakhic issues. The amount of tolerance shown by one rabbi to an opposing rabbi may have more to do with their relative status[5] or personal tensions[6] than about the halakha in question. Thus, rabbis are usually more tolerant of their colleagues than of their students.[7] The very same sage may be tolerant toward the opposing practice of one person regarding one issue but then use all his power to stifle diversity practiced by a more threatening personality regarding a more sensitive issue.

Yerushalmi and Bavli Compared

While the factors listed above are grounds for even a single sage or a single work of rabbinic literature to present a wide array of attitudes toward legal pluralism, we have also found that the sages represented in the Yerushalmi generally maintain a more negative attitude toward diversity when compared with their counterparts in the Bavli. We have seen explicit examples of this in nearly every chapter. R. Yoḥanan creates a universal system of rules for deciding between disputing Tannaim; the Bavli rejects these rules flat out.[8] Resh Laqish applies "Do not make factions" quite broadly to prohibit any diversity of halakhic practice; Abaye and Rava, on the other hand, limit the prohibition to diversity within one city or even within members of one court.[9] The Bavli says, "Each river follows its own course,"[10] and describes how certain rabbis had jurisdiction over certain areas yet respected differences in other jurisdictions;[11] no such phenomenon is found in the Yerushalmi. The

4. See above, pp. 363–67.

5. See above, p. 153 n. 75. See also Richard Kalmin, "Collegial Interaction in the Babylonian Talmud," *Jewish Quarterly Review* 82, no. 3–4 (1992): 383–415, on the expectation of junior sages to show deference to senior sages.

6. See above, p. 153 n. 77.

7. See above, p. 153 n. 76.

8. See above, pp. 43–62.

9. See above, pp. 97–120.

10. See above, pp. 129–32.

11. See above, pp. 132–44.

Yerushalmi suggests that Beth Shammai never practiced its own opinions while the Bavli proves definitively that it did.[12] The Yerushalmi at *Ber.* 1:1 (3a) constructs a lengthy *sugya* proving that no Tanna practiced differently from his colleagues.[13] In fact, the Yerushalmi cites a number of Tannaitic sources that portray individual Tannaim practicing against the mainstream halakha but consistently reinterprets them under the assumption that such diversity is historically impossible. The Bavli, on the other hand, reports diverse practices among the Tannaim without apology.

We have also seen how this difference of attitude affects the formation and editing of Bavli and perhaps even Yerushalmi *sugyot*. Such more subtle, though no less important, differences can be found when comparing the Talmudic treatments of factionalism in custom versus law, narratives about diversity between the Houses and among other Tannaim, and the rebellious elder. Analysis of the form of these *sugyot* and of the way the Bavli borrows and changes Yerushalmi formulations demonstrates just how deeply entrenched are the different attitudes of the two Talmuds.

This also provides a window into how the Stam worked. Having established different attitudes in each Talmud based on only explicit statements, we can gain insight into the more subtle methods used by the Talmuds, especially the Bavli, to suppress or highlight a certain viewpoint. Specific examples may be ambiguous, but generally one can point to the following methods: omitting parts of a *sugya*, adding explanations to received traditions, changing the context of a *sugya* by moving it to a different tractate, changing the order of statements, changing details of stories, and providing different answers to questions already addressed in prior sources. If we find such methods used in other contexts we should similarly look for the agendas motivating such changes.

Of course, the differences in attitude between the Talmuds are only general trends, and exceptions can be found in both directions.[14] Some of these are discussed herein and further investigation will no doubt discover more. We should not think of the entire Yerushalmi or Bavli as monolithic. They were not redacted by one person or even one group or school. The Yerushalmi and Bavli include tractates with different styles, and the existence of parallel *sugyot* within the same corpus—often at odds with one another—points to what may be competing editors.[15] Nevertheless, we do find at least a general trend of more tolerance in the Bavli than in the Yerushalmi.

12. See above, pp. 99 and 205.

13. See above, pp. 246–47.

14. See, for example, *y. Ber.* 7:3 (11c) and *b. Šabb.* 50a, discussed above, pp. 138–40.

15. See Abraham Goldberg, "The Palestinian Talmud," in *The Literature of the Sages, Part One*, ed. Shmuel Safrai (Philadelphia: Fortress, 1987), 313–14; and Strack and Stemberger, *Introduction*, 171–75, 94–97.

Modern theories regarding the composition of the Bavli show that it was redacted by fifth- to seventh-century anonymous rabbis. Since much of our evidence comes from the way the Bavli reworks Yerushalmi *sugyot*, we can assume that the Stammaim are responsible in large part for the difference between the Talmudic portrayals of the attitudes of the Tannaim and Amoraim. However, a number of Amoraic statements, assuming they are reliably attributed, already show evidence of differing attitudes between the Palestinian and Babylonian Amoraim. Rav Mesharsheya, a fifth-generation Babylonian, rejects the decision-making rules of R. Yoḥanan's school, which reflects a fundamentally different attitude toward unity of halakha versus individualism. The interpretations of *lo titgodedu* by Abaye and Rava are examples of fourth-century Babylonian Amoraim making a bold reversal of the Yerushalmi interpretation. The phrase "Each river follows its own course" is quoted by Rav Huna and Rav Yosef, Babylonians from the second and third generations. Assuming that these formulations are not themselves inventions of the Stammaim, and there is no reason to suspect that they are, the differences between the Talmuds can already be traced back to the Amoraim themselves. Of course, it is possible that the Stammaim used their editorial license to give tolerant statements of Amoraim more prominence while repressing or reinterpreting intolerant statements. Nevertheless, it seems that there were already significant differences between the Palestinian and Babylonian Amoraim, which were amplified by a possibly stronger pluralistic bent of the Stammaim. Therefore, when looking for historical causes for the difference in attitude between the Talmuds, we can look to both the period of the Amoraim as well as that of the Stammaim.

Various explanations can be given for this split, some more convincing than others. One set of explanations looks to the ambient culture in each country to explain rabbinic attitudes. One such explanation is given by Hanina Ben-Menahem, who argues that in Palestine, the existence of sectarianism and the spread of Christianity created a threat to the authority of rabbinic halakha. Thus, "The Destruction and the religious confusion that followed, and the additional problem of a continuously growing dissident sect, forced the Rabbis to take defensive measures in order to preserve the authority of the halakhah."[16] These measures included enforcing strict adherence to a unified definition of halakha, which would not tolerate potentially dangerous sectarian-like alternatives. Ben-Menahem recognizes that sectarianism did not continue into the Amoraic period and does not claim that "one can find a Christian background wherever the Yerushalmi insists on strict adherence to the law."[17] Rather, he says that even though the historical circumstances that led to the push to unify hal-

16. Ben-Menahem, *Judicial Deviation*, 96.
17. Ibid., 98.

akha disappeared, this effort continued into the Amoraic period because of the momentum gained in the earlier period. In Babylonia, on the other hand, "the pagan climate of the outside world did not pose an immediate threat to the integrity of the halakhah,"[18] and so the Bavli was able to be more tolerant of deviation and diversity within halakha.

This explanation is somewhat speculative because it assumes, first, that the reaction of the rabbis at Yavneh to the post-destruction events was to unify their own camp by excluding all diversity, a debatable claim.[19] Besides, it further assumes that the attitude in these early decades continued on its own trajectory for the next few centuries, a rather tenuous proposition. I agree that the threat of Second Temple sectarianism likely lies behind rationales for monism, such as, "so that division should not spread in Israel," mouthed by late Second Temple sages.[20] However, Second Temple sectarianism does not sufficiently account for the Yerushalmi's general intolerance for pluralism.

Another explanation that looks to the rabbis' ambient cultures derives from events contemporary with the rabbinic period. Rather than focus on how the Jews were treated in each land, whether by the governments or by the dominant religions,[21] one can look to the legal cultures of each country for the most relevant historical contexts. As discussed above,[22] during the centuries in which the Tannaim and Amoraim were active, Roman law was undergoing a sustained program of codification. Many of the methods found in Roman codes have interesting parallels in Palestinian Talmudic sources. Even if the rabbis were not aware of the specifics of Roman jurisprudence, a legal atmosphere that fears the disorder and confusion created by disunity and places a high value on codification could certainly have permeated the thinking of the Palestinian rabbis and caused them to work toward the codification and uniformity of halakha. Ironically, the codificatory projects of both the Romans and the Palestinian Amoraim led to a broadening of the category of custom and an increase in its role in the legislative process.[23]

In the realm of religion as well, Christianity, already in the second century, was developing a formal set of theologies and a hierarchical leadership structure. A negative attitude toward diversity is evident from con-

18. Ibid., 96–97.

19. See above, pp. 34–36. How would this explain, for example, the existence of and tolerance for Beth Shammai and Beth Hillel in the Mishnah and Tosefta?

20. See below, p. 386. For other sectarian-related statements and laws, see above, p. 169 n. 20.

21. Persian and Roman governments were both fairly tolerant of diversity within their empires toward whoever paid their taxes and did not cause trouble. See Garnsey, "Religious Toleration in Classical Antiquity," 1–27; and Friedenberg and Gold, *Sasanian Jewry*, 7–8.

22. Pp. 77–80.

23. See above, p. 119.

troversies about the date of Easter, forgiveness of sin, and Christology, as well as from intense anti-Gnostic polemics and from the proto-orthodox writings of Irenaeus and Tertullian.[24] The many ecclesiastical councils of the fourth century attempted to enforce a universal creed on all Christians, and Nicene orthodoxy emerged as a dominant force.[25] This negative view of diversity and the perpetual push toward uniformity may have also contributed to similar attitudes by Palestinian rabbis.[26]

The situation in Sasanid Persia was very different. We have already seen that Sasanian law, as far as we can tell from extant sources, did not produce any code, nor did it legislate any rules for dealing with controversy.[27] Thus, we must presume that Persian legists did not find it particularly troubling that various authorities and opposing opinions were sometimes quoted in their legal texts.[28] Zoroastrianism, the dominant religion of Sasanian Persia, also seems to have been tolerant of internal disputes. Philip Kreyenbroek cites the following from the *Epistles of Manushchihar*, a Zoroastrian text dating to 881 C.E.:

> On account of the depth and much intricacy of the religion they mention many opinions and well-considered decrees which were likewise formed devoid of uniformity, and the utterance of the different opinions of the priests is with the reciters of the Nasks; but even among themselves the most supremely just high-priests were of a different opinion, different judgment, different teaching, different interpretation, and different practice only in the peace, mutual friendship, and affection which they had together.[29]

---

24. See Harold Attridge, "Christianity from the Destruction of Jerusalem to Constantine's Adoption of the New Religion: 70–312 C.E.," in *Christianity and Rabbinic Judaism*, ed. Hershel Shanks (Washington, D.C.: Biblical Archaeology Society, 1992), 151–94.

25. See Dennis Groh, "The Religion of the Empire: Christianity from Constantine to the Arab Conquest," in *Christianity and Rabbinic Judaism*, ed. Hershel Shanks, 267–303; and John Behr, "The Question of Nicene Orthodoxy," in *Byzantine Orthodoxies: Papers from the Thirty-sixth Spring Symposium of Byzantine Studies*, ed. Andrew Louth and Augustine Casiday (Burlington, VT: Ashgate, 2002), 15–26.

26. To be sure, Christianity also exerted influence on Babylonian Jewry; see Herman, "Exilarchate," 281–319; and Michal Bar-Asher Siegal, "Literary Analogies in Rabbinic and Christian Monastic Sources" (Ph.D. diss., Yale University, 2010). However, such influence could not have been as strong as that in Palestine.

27. See above, pp. 79–80.

28. As noted above, p. 1 n. 2, Persian texts do contain some controversy but much less so than in rabbinic literature.

29. *Sacred Books of the East*, vol. 18, *Pahlavi Texts*, part II; trans. E. W. West (Oxford, 1882), available online at http://www.avesta.org/mp/epm.htm. See alternate translations at Bemanji N. Dhanbar, *The Epistles of Manushchihar* (Bombay: Trustees of the Parsee Panchayat Funds and Properties, 1912); and Philip Kreyenbroek, "On the Concept of Spiritual Authority in Zoroastrianism," *Jerusalem Studies in Arabic and Islam* 17 (1994): 10.

Kreyenbroek adds,

> In a number of Pahlavi books—notably those dating from the post-Sasanian era—three accepted "teachings" are mentioned.... A characteristic feature of most of the texts where judgments from such teachings are discussed is that these judgments are mentioned side by side, without comment on the intrinsic merits of each. Traditionally, it seems, all rulings by recognized dastwars were held to be valid, and could not be abrogated even though a different judgment might later be officially preferred.[30]

What emerges is that the attitudes of the rabbis in each empire toward diversity parallels the attitudes of their surrounding legal and religious cultures. Palestinian rabbis displayed intolerance toward religious diversity as did their Christian neighbors and began projects of codification like their contemporary Roman jurists, while Babylonian Amoraim mirror the tolerance of their Sasanian Zoroastrian neighbors.

Other possible contributing factors are more internal to Jewish society. One may look toward the difference in Jewish self-governance in each country by comparing the role of the patriarch to that of the exilarch. Summarizing *b. Sanh.* 5a, Gedaliah Alon writes: "By contrast to the Exilarch, who is seen as a merely secular leader, the Patriarch in Eretz Israel is perceived as Head of the Academy too."[31] Alon further writes that the patriarch presided over the Sanhedrin, which settled disputes between the sages.[32] Lee Levine adds that the patriarch maintained close ties with the sages.[33] The exilarch, on the other hand, was criticized by many, if not most, Babylonian sages.[34] Kalmin similarly writes: "The patriarch in Palestine presided over institutions which linked diverse rabbis from diverse localities; the Exilarch in Babylonia did not unify the rabbinic movement

30. *Sacred Books of the East*, vol. 18, *Pahlavi Texts*, part II. Although these texts postdate the Talmudic period, there is no reason to doubt that a similar situation also prevailed in earlier Zoroastrian law.

31. Alon, *The Jews in Their Land*, 317. Alon further calls the exilarch, "a purely temporal official in the Persian Empire" (ibid., 724). He summarizes: "Judah I was able to unite Palestinian Jewry into one organic whole under the political, social and religious leadership of the Patriarch and the Sanhedrin. That structure was to endure for something like two hundred years" (ibid., 716–17). Lee Levine, "The Jewish Patriarch (Nasi) in Third Century Palestine," in *Aufstieg und Niedergang der römischen Welt II, 19/2*, ed. H. Temporini and W. Haase (Berlin and New York: de Gruyter, 1979), 28, also describes the patriarchate as "a public office which commanded authority in a great many areas—political, social, communal, and religious."

32. Alon, *The Jews in Their Land*, 467.

33. Levine, *Rabbinic Class*, 139–91. He summarizes: "Instances of positive ties and contacts are far more numerous than incidents of friction and tension" (ibid., 190). See also Goodman, *State and Society*, 111–18, especially regarding the close connection between the rabbis and R. Yehudah the Patriarch.

34. See Herman, "Exilarchate," 217–66; Gafni, *Jews of Babylonia*, 94–104; and Jacob Neusner, *A History of the Jews in Babylonia* (Leiden: Brill, 1965–70), 3:41–94, 4:73–124.

to the same degree."[35] The differences between the Talmuds could accordingly be explained based on the existence of the Sanhedrin and the patriarch as the religious leader, which acted as unifying forces of halakha in Palestine, but without counterparts in Babylonia.

Critical analysis, however, shows that this possibility lacks foundation. In fact, there likely did not exist one centralized Sanhedrin in Palestine after 70 C.E.,[36] and the patriarch was not universally recognized by the sages as a halakhic authority.[37] In any case, even if there was a strong patriarch recognized by most sages during the Talmudic period, there is still no indication that the patriarch used, or even could have used, his power to promote unified halakhic practice in any areas other than setting the calendar. This explanation is therefore unconvincing as a contributing factor to the difference between the Talmudic attitudes toward diversity.

Still, even if the patriarch and exilarch may not be relevant here, there were other factors at work that pushed for unity or made room for diversity among the rabbis. In chapter 3, we showed that one important reason for the difference in attitudes between the Talmuds is simply the geographic distribution of the rabbis in each country. We had occasion there to cite David Kraemer;[38] we quote him again more extensively:

> The rabbis in Babylonia were distributed over a greater geographical area than their Palestinian counterparts, constituting small groups in a larger, often nonrabbinized Jewish population.... By contrast, the rabbis in Palestine were concentrated in the north, particularly in Tiberias and its environs. By virtue of this concentration, the movement could demand greater uniformity of its adherents. Unlike their Babylonian counterparts, the rabbis of Palestine were less compelled to tolerate diversity of opinion or practice. Moreover, because of the smaller geographical extent of Palestine, the smaller Jewish population (at least in the latter centuries of

---

35. Kalmin, *The Sage in Jewish Society*, 12.

36. See above p. 7 n. 21.

37. Against Levine (*Rabbinic Class*, 33), Schwartz, *Imperialism*, 104, writes that the patriarchs "acquired much of their influence precisely by replacing their ties to the rabbis and allying themselves instead with Palestinian city councilors, wealthy Diaspora Jews, and prominent gentiles." See also Albert Baumgarten, "The Politics of Reconciliation: The Education of R. Judah the Prince," in *Jewish and Christian Self-Definition: Volume Two, Aspects of Judaism in the Graeco-Roman Period*, ed. E. P. Sanders (Philadelphia: Fortress, 1981), 213–25, regarding tensions between patriarchs and the Akibans. For a comprehensive treatment of the status of the patriarch, see Hezser, *Social Structure*, 405–49, who writes, "Most rabbis were not particularly concerned with the patriarchate. The patriarch's lack of influence on rabbis' legal opinion and practice and some rabbis [*sic*] opposition against his rulings and lifestyle is further indicated by a number of legal statements, discussions, and stories" (p. 429). Alon bases much of his opinion on Talmudic reports about Rabban Gamaliel II and R. Yehudah the Patriarch, which cannot be used as historical sources; see above, p. 15, and ch. 5. For more on the patriarchate, see above, p. 242 n. 5.

38. Above, p. 154 .

> this era), and the fact that the rabbis had once controlled the office of the patriarch, it is likely that they exerted greater power here than did their counterparts in Babylonia.[39]

Kraemer begins to describe the difference between Palestine and Babylonia in terms of power. Rabbis in both places may have wished for unity, but the rabbis in Babylonia did not have the means to enforce unity over a diffuse population. This tolerance is not a reflection of an epistemological stance concerning multiple truths, the indeterminacy inherent in interpretation, or an appreciation of the richness in having many sets of laws; the Babylonian rabbis would have preferred uniformity. Rather, Kraemer's tolerance has more to do with political practicalities of not being able to impose uniformity on one other. Where the rabbis felt they had the right and the power to impose uniformity, they did so.[40] In Palestine, however, where Jews were concentrated in the north,[41] the rabbis could exert authority not only on the laypeople but even on dissenting colleagues.

My own study of the interpretation of the law of *lo titgodedu* (Deut 14:1) and stories about traveling rabbis confirms that geography played an important role in explaining the difference between the Talmuds. However, I find that geographical distance in Babylonia does not so much inhibit power as much as it decreases the tension caused by proximity to differing practices. As Kimelman notes in a slightly different context, "Plural options stir minimal dissonance when there is little contact between them. Generally, local uniformity is sufficient for the appearance of Jewish unity."[42] The more distance there is between groups following different practices, the less contact and communication there will be between them, and thus the diversity will not be very noticeable or bothersome. The concentration of the Jewish population in Palestine due to migrations after the Roman wars and urbanization during the third century C.E. brought diverse groups into close proximity.[43] In this environment, it is likely that

39. David Kraemer, *Responses to Suffering in Classical Rabbinic Literature* (New York: Oxford, 1995), 221.

40. This view may be supported by the intolerance shown by teachers of divergent opinions or practices of their students. See above, p. 153 n. 76 .

41. Palestinian society was more concentrated in the conglomerate of northern cities and villages centered around Tiberias and Sepphoris. Of course, there were important population centers and rabbis in southern cities as well. Elman, "Argument for the Sake of Heaven," 278, points to the redaction of *Sifre Zuṭa* and *Yerushalmi Neziqin* as proofs for this. However, these were still small centers orbiting the larger one in the north. See above, pp. 278–80, on Yaʿaqov of Kefar Nevoraia who lived outside the main camp and whose views were not tolerated by R. Ḥaggai who was in the center.

42. Kimelman, "Judaism and Pluralism," 132.

43. On the urbanization of the rabbis, see Miller, *Sages and Commoners*, 446–66, and passim; Satlow, *Jewish Marriage in Antiquity*, 40; Yoram Tsafrir, "Some Notes on the Settlement and Demography of Palestine in the Byzantine Period: The Archaeological Evidence,"

dissonance was felt when groups with differing practices pressured one another to assimilate to their own practices, and an atmosphere of intolerance arose.

Because the Jewish population was spread across the country in various cities, each city contained a small number of sages at a time, one of whom was recognized, by his colleagues and/or by the populace, as the local authority for that city.[44] This gave each local authority a great degree of autonomy to teach and practice as he saw fit without intervention from colleagues in neighboring towns. When one rabbi did go to visit the town of a colleague, the visitor maintained respect for the rulings of the local rabbi. This social reality is most explicitly stated in *b. Ketub.* 54a, which actually maps out the jurisdictions belonging to Rav and Shmuel.[45] This map traces the same administrative regions imposed by the Sasanian government and also mirrors the feudal structure of Sasanian society.[46]

Furthermore, the role of the rabbi as local authority in Babylonia correlates with the findings of Isaiah Gafni that the rabbis served as administrators over charity and education in Babylonia.[47] The Babylonian rabbis, who were diffuse enough that each major personality could carve out his own turf, were able to wield that power as administrators as well. In Palestine, on the other hand, these roles were filled by layleaders. Rabbis in Palestine were not recognized as exclusive authorities, neither in matters of community administration nor in matters of halakha. The mimetic traditions of the community trumped the halakhic arguments of the rabbis, and whatever power a rabbi did have in the area of halakha was shared by many nearby colleagues.[48]

The above-noted factors contributing to the differences between the Talmuds are based on historical circumstances dating from the Amoraic period. These factors can help explain differences between the Talmuds found at the Amoraic level. However, much of the evidence presented in the above chapters stems specifically from the redactional activities of the Bavli, either in anonymous statements of the redactors or in the forms of the *sugyot*. We therefore turn to factors that led to the Stammaitic views

---

in *Retrieving the Past: Essays on Archaeological Research and Methodology in Honor of Gus W. Van Beek*, ed. Joe D. Seger (Winona Lake, Ind.: Eisenbrauns, 1996); Shaye Cohen, "The Place of the Rabbi in Jewish Society of the Second Century," in *The Galilee in Late Antiquity*, ed. Lee Levine (New York: Jewish Theological Seminary, 1992), 160–64; idem, "The Rabbis in Second-Century Jewish Society," 966–71; Daniel Sperber, *Roman Palestine 200–400: The Land* (Ramat-Gan: Bar-Ilan University Press, 1978), 119–35; and A. Jones, "The Urbanization of Palestine," *The Journal of Roman Studies* 21 (1931): 78–85.

44. See above, pp. 154–58.
45. See above, p. 155.
46. See above, p. 156.
47. See above, p. 159.
48. See above, pp. 159–61.

regarding pluralism. In this regard, the view of the Stammaim toward diversity of halakhic practice seems to grow out of their acceptance of diversity of opinions. As discussed in the introduction, the scholarly consensus is that the Bavli—especially in its Stammaitic layer—reflects greater tolerance for multiple opinions and uses argumentation in a qualitatively greater degree than does the Yerushalmi.[49] We should therefore incorporate here reasons scholars have proposed for differences between the Talmuds regarding diversity of opinion and predilection for argumentation. Here are two summaries of the differences between the Talmuds in this regard by David Halivni and Jeffrey Rubenstein, respectively:[50]

> It has often been pointed out that the Babylonian Talmud differs from the Palestinian Talmud in that the argumentational material of the former is more complex, more dialectical, richer and more variegated in content, more removed from the *peshat* (the simple meaning) of the texts it discusses. This is true even when the same opinion of the same sage is discussed in both Talmuds. Indeed, the discussions are qualitatively different. Z. Frankel has already noted that the argumentational [*sic*], the "give-and-take" of the Palestinian Talmud is qualitatively not unlike that of the early generations of Amoraim (I would add also that of the middle-generation Amoraim) in the Babylonian Talmud, in those instances where we can ascertain with a high degree of certainty that the "give-and-take" is actually from the Amoraim. Both are simple, narrow in focus, responding to the question at hand, and without a unique style, whereas the argumentational [*sic*] in the Gemara of the Babylonian Talmud is colorful, pulsating, outreaching, often presenting an interwoven and continuous discourse with a distinct, identifiable style of its own.[51]

> Bavli argumentation, far more than that of the Yerushalmi, focuses on minority opinions, which have no bearing on practical law. Extended dialectical discussions probe different Amoraic opinions, testing, hypothesizing, and investigating various possibilities, and then conclude much where they start, often failing to arrive at any resolution whatsoever. The Bavli features contrived arguments that satisfy the structural needs of the *sugya* but add little substance to the discussion. We find spurious questions and forced answers as literary devices to emphasize aspects of the debate. Sections of the give-and-take may be repeated verbatim for rhetorical or pedagogical purposes. In many cases, rhetoric and style, more than substantive law or final conclusions, motivated the construction of argumentation. Rarely are these phenomena found in the Yerushalmi.[52]

---

49. See above, pp. 17–26.

50. See similar summaries quoted at Hayes, *Between the Babylonian and Palestinian Talmuds*, 184–85.

51. Halivni, *Midrash*, 82.

52. Rubenstein, *Culture*, 3.

These two Talmudists explain that the argumentation of the Bavli is the creation of the post-Amoraic editorial layer of the text.[53] The Amoraim transmitted only apodictic statements, while it is the Stammaim who constructed the rhetorical style of the Bavli. It is they who investigated minority views and who retold various stories and statements that reflect a pluralistic attitude. The difference between the Talmuds regarding diversity of practice found in this study thus parallels the difference between the Talmuds regarding diversity of opinion, as set out in the introduction.[54] Therefore, the explanation for the latter may also apply to the former.

Rubenstein explains that the change from the Amoraic period to the Stammaitic period was caused by the rise of the rabbinic academy.[55] During the Amoraic period, rabbis would gather in small circles of disciples that disbanded when the teacher died or moved. It was not until the fifth century that larger institutions of learning began to arise that transcended the individual sages who presided over them.[56] The shift in academic setting brought with it a change in self-perception from individuality to corporate identity and personal anonymity. Rubenstein elaborates:

> [The Stammaim] evidently saw themselves as living in a postclassical period after the conclusion of the era of their predecessors, the Amoraim. That they ceased attaching their names (or their teachers' names) to statements points to a substantive break with the past, a sense that prior modes of activity had to come to an end.... The Stammaim thus viewed the body of Amoraic legal rulings as a closed corpus. They accordingly dedicated themselves to the rigorous analysis and explanation of earlier sources. They attempted to reconstruct the reasoning that justified Amoraic rulings, since the bulk of the reasoning had not been considered worthy of preservation or transmission during the Amoraic period. The Stammaim constructed hypothetical arguments to justify contradictory Amoraic opinions and formulated possible responses to those arguments. These types of activity involved dialectics, the formulation of "objections and responses," hence discursive argumentation became the dominant practice and most highly valued ability in Stammaitic times.[57]

At this time, more than ever before, the study of halakha became intellectualized. Precisely because they were not creating any new apodictic

---

53. See Halivni, Midrash, 76–92; and Rubenstein, *Culture*, 2–7. See also further references above, p. 36 n. 139.

54. To be sure, even the Bavli does not go so far as to celebrate diversity of practice as do many rabbinic statements regarding multiplicity of opinion (forty-nine arguments revealed to Moses, seventy interpretations, etc.). Nevertheless, the Bavli does generally show significantly greater tolerance for diversity of practice than does the Yerushalmi.

55. Rubenstein, *Culture*, 22–23.

56. See Goodblatt, *Rabbinic Instruction in Sasanian Babylonia*.

57. Rubenstein, *Culture*, 47–48.

formulae but saw themselves as only interpreting prior statements, they could stand back from their material and see it as an object of study.[58] More than the rabbis before them, the Stammaim sought to categorize, conceptualize, and rationalize the mass of material that they received from tradition.[59]

Along with this level of objectification and conceptualization of prior Amoraic material comes the emphasis on reason over tradition. Whereas Amoraim could argue about who received a more reliable tradition from their teachers, the Stammaim shared the same pool of traditions. Therefore, their contribution was to sort through these traditions, compare versions, note incongruities, cite proofs, and use their rational powers to justify and explain difficulties. The "Uprooter of Mountains" took

---

58. In explaining why the Bavli includes more argumentation than previous rabbinic literature, Kraemer, *Mind*, 117, writes: "Unlike the earlier documents, the Bavli also had the amoraic tradition on which to build. In the presence of the rulings and interpretations of the amoraim, the gemara was free to speculate on the meanings and relationships of these various elements of the tradition. Thus, amoraic interpretation gave way to the even more liberal interpretive enterprise of the Bavli itself."

59. Moscovitz, *Talmudic Reasoning*, 347–52, finds an increase in conceptualization already during Amoraic times, especially among later Babylonians. "However," he writes, "the markedly increased use of explicit, sophisticated conceptual formulations in the anonymous stratum, and especially the extensive multiple application of existing principles to new cases, is so striking that this stylistic (and quantitative) difference ultimately takes on qualitative dimensions" (p. 350). Moscovitz does not provide an explanation for this qualitative shift. However, he does write the following with regard to the increased conceptualization from the Tannaitic to the Amoraic periods:

> Why such a striking transition should have occurred at this time is not fully clear, although it might be attributable, at least in part, to the canonical or quasi-canonical status which the Mishnah (and, perhaps to a lesser extent, other tannaitic works) acquired during this period. For once these works were deemed authoritative—as study books, if not as legal codes—the need to interpret and analyze them led naturally, perhaps even ineluctably, to the conceptual analysis of these works. The development of amoraic conceptualization thus seems to be intimately bound up with the development of Mishnah exegesis; as noted frequently in the course of this study, there is a strong affinity, even an inseparable bond, between conceptualization and exegesis (ibid., 347).

A similar explanation is proposed by Jeffrey Rubenstein, "On Some Abstract Concepts in Rabbinic Literature," *Jewish Studies Quarterly* 4 (1997): 71. The same explanation applies even more so to the shift from Amoraic to Stammaitic activity. Once the Amoraic period came to an end (see Rubenstein, *Culture*, 5, on *b. B. Meṣiʿa* 86a), their traditions took on a canonical quality and became the objects of exegesis for the Stammaim. But, whereas the Amoraim continued using individual attributions—in fact, the split between late Tannaim and early Amoraim is rather blurry—the Stammaim saw themselves as so distinct from their predecessors that they began to speak with a collective voice. This led to the quantum increase in conceptualization, argumentation, and intellectualization found in the Stammaitic layers of the Bavli.

precedence over "Sinai." Dialectical ability became more important than memory.[60]

In such an environment, all participants shared a common base of material and methodology; they agreed on a language of discourse—that of argumentation. Thus, even though they disagreed, for no two people think alike, there was a recognition that there exists more than one way to conceptualize a specific example, and there are many possible interpretations of a given phrase. This realization brought with it a certain amount of tolerance.[61] The belief that more than one theoretical interpretation can contain truth opened up the possibility that more than one halakhic practice could be equally valid as well.

This Stammaitic development is not an entirely new innovation but rather picks up on and extends the difference between the Talmuds regarding the role of *minhag,* as discussed in chapter 2. Palestinian Amoraim, and, perhaps to some extent, early Babylonian Amoraim as well, saw halakha as more of a mimetic tradition. They sought to preserve accurately the law as they received it from their predecessors. Therefore, *minhag*—the actual practice of the people—was held in high esteem. It could not be easily changed and was an important factor in determining law, sometimes even more important than traditions passed on in the study hall. In this environment, the goal of study was to retrieve the original or most faithful

---

60. See Rubenstein, *Culture,* 48–51; and idem, "Thematization," 83. In some ways these two methods parallel what Avi Sagi calls the "discovery model" and the "creative model." See Avi Sagi, "Halakhic Praxis and the Word of God: A Study of Two Models," *Jewish Thought and Philosophy* 1 (1992): 305–29. It is also similar to what Halbertal calls the "retrieval view" and the "constitutive view." See Moshe Halbertal, *People of the Book,* 54–72. In the first side of each pair, the interpreter seeks to discover or retrieve the original sense of the text; he simply wants to recover the pristine meaning of the source as given at Sinai. In the second half of each pair, the interpreter makes use of the wealth of meaning inherent in the words of the text to dynamically create halakha. Memory is more important for the first activity while dialectical ability is essential for the second. Of course, this is only a very rough mapping that ignores many nuances of these theories and skips over the variety of activity found in all layers of the Talmud. I bring it only as a heuristic schema.

61. As Perelman and Olbrechts-Tyteca, *The New Rhetoric,* 1, write: "The very nature of deliberation and argumentation is opposed to necessity and self-evidence, since no one deliberates where the solution is necessary or argues against what is self-evident. The domain of argumentation is that of the credible, the plausible, the probable, to the degree that the latter eludes the certainty of calculations."

This is cited by Kraemer, *Mind,* 99, who applies the theories of Perelman and Olbrechts-Tyteca to the Bavli's forms of argumentation, use of authority and need for justification. Kraemer writes: "Deliberation/argumentation is, as a form, opposed to self-evidence and confident assertion of a single truth. If truth were readily evident, then no reasonable person would argue against that truth. Assuming that the deliberations we are discussing involve reasonable and not irrational parties, we must conclude that their willingness to engage in argumentation is evidence of their recognition that the answer to a given question or problem is not necessary or self-evident. To the contrary, if they are willing to debate the issue, they must agree that there are at least two possible answers or solutions" (ibid., 102).

interpretation of a prior source and to arrive at the correct legal decision. For later Babylonian Amoraim, and certainly for the Stammaim, the living day-to-day practice of halakha was less important than the results of rational argumentation of the rabbis.[62] Therefore, the importance of *minhag* was checked in favor of reasoned conclusions based on interpretation, conceptualization, and discussion of traditional sources.[63]

According to this line of thought, the difference between the Talmuds is based partly on their respective views about the nature and politics of halakha. This may be an overgeneralization, but I think it does encapsulate an essential distinction between the Talmuds. The Yerushalmi focuses on the practical and communal aspect of halakha as a set of rules that governs the masses of Jews. As such, it is important to create restrictions on dissent and uphold a unified system of decision making in order to generate unified communal practice. The Bavli, on the other hand, focuses

62. This movement continues the trend already in motion from the Second Temple to rabbinic times, as noted by Siverstev, *Households, Sects, and the Origins of Rabbinic Judaism*, 272–74:

> In the early decades of the Second Temple period families and family-based halakhic observances were central elements in Jewish religiosity and piety.... Toward the end of the Second Temple period a new type of religious discourse begins to crystallize in which family-owned traditions are increasingly abandoned and transformed in favor of more universal, eternal, and abstract modes of presentation.... This transition from household to disciple study circle as the basic unit within Judaism is what, I would argue, marks the transition from Second Temple to Rabbinic Judaism.... Tannaitic and early Amoraic periods in Roman Palestine witnessed the gradual transition from family-dominated to school-dominated modes of religious consciousness. Throughout this time both modes more or less equally contributed to the development of Rabbinic Judaism. Only by the fourth century (if not later) did classical Rabbinic Judaism come of age when study sessions became the predominant social form embodying rabbinic tradition.

63. These two conceptions of halakha are similar to the mimetic and text-based forms of halakhic instruction described by Haym Soloveitchik, "Rupture and Reconstruction: The Transformation of Contemporary Orthodoxy," *Tradition* 28, no. 4 (1994): 64–130. There is, however, an important difference between the modern text-based model and the Bavli intellectualization. Concerning the former, Soloveitchik writes, "One confronts in Jewish law, as in any other legal system, a wide variety of differing positions on any given issue. If one seeks to do things properly (and these "things" are, after all, God's will), the only course is to attempt to comply simultaneously with as many opinions as possible. Otherwise one risks invalidation. Hence the policy of 'maximum position compliance,' so characteristic of contemporary jurisprudence, which in turn leads to yet further stringency" (p. 72). We have seen in chapter 1, however, that one of the Bavli's strategies for dealing with differing positions where no clear decision has been handed down is to allow the individual to choose between the equally valid possibilities. Therefore, a move to text-based learning can lead to unification of halakha around the most stringent position, but it can also lead to more diversity by recognizing the legitimacy of multiple options.

Cf. also idem, "Religious Law and Change: The Medieval Ashkenazic Example," *AJS Review* 12, no. 2 (1987): 205–21, on the strict adherence of the medieval Franco-German community to custom versus other communities where Talmudic law trumped local custom.

on the theoretical and intellectual/conceptual aspect of halakha as a distillation of the most convincing opinions and best verified traditions from among the expansive set of prior traditions. This outlook necessarily produced an environment where diversity of practice was common and even tolerated.[64]

To summarize, we can delineate three primary factors contributing to the differences found between the Yerushalmi and the Bavli. The first two factors assume that the differences in the Talmuds reflect historical differences during the Amoraic period. The first factor points to efforts at codification in Roman law and the dogmatic nature of fourth-century Christianity, on the one hand, and the tolerance and lack of codificitory projects in Sasanian/Zoroastrian law.

The second factor is that Palestinian Jews are concentrated in small geographical areas with many rabbis vying with one another for dominance, while Babylonian Jews are spread over a large area with only one dominant rabbi in any given location. The Babylonian rabbis are able to create "fiefdoms" on the model of the feudal system in Sasanian Babylonia using the same borders designated as Sasanian administrative provinces. Divergent practices are allowed to continue between each of these regions where the local rabbinic authority is recognized as such and has no need or ability to impinge on the region of his colleague. In Palestine, on the other hand, the concentration of rabbis within one administrative province under central Roman rule deprived the rabbis of the ability to each lead his own followers and ignore his colleagues. This resulted in their diminished power, a stronger layleadership, an emphasis on mimetic halakha, and less social, political, or rational bases for tolerating halakhic diversity.

The last reason does not make any historical claim about the views of the Amoraim but, rather, locates the different attitudes in the Talmuds to their redactional strata. The Babylonian Talmud continued to be redacted for about two centuries after the close of the Palestinian Talmud. These Stammaim who were now working within the context of an institutional yeshiva viewed themselves as anonymous commentators on a set of received traditions. These traditions already had a semicanonical status such that these Stammaim could edit, organize, and interpret them but not add to them. The Stammaim were aware that they no longer retained the legislative status of the Amoraim.[65] The Stammaim valued argumentation above all, were

---

64. Of course, the Yerushalmi does utilize learned argumentation, but not to the same extent as the Bavli. It is also true that the Bavli does sometimes take the general practice of the common people into consideration; however, such instances are fewer and less consequential. See Miller, *Sages and Commoners*, 381.

65. See *b. B. Meṣiʿa* 86a: "Ravina and Rav Ashi are the end of authoritative teaching." See further in Richard Hidary, "Ashi," *Encyclopedia Judaica* 2 (2007): 565–66.

loath to dismiss any received tradition, and therefore displayed tolerance for diversity of opinion, which promoted halakhic pluralism in practice as well.

To bring these factors together, in the Roman Empire we find a general atmosphere of legal and religious discomfort with diversity and long-lasting projects of codification. Within this atmosphere, the Palestinian rabbis are living in close proximity, which both highlights differences of practice and increases competition. These factors lead them to oppose halakhic pluralism. In addition, a general view of halakha as mimetic tradition rather than rabbinic legislation and a preference for *minhag* over legal reasoning provided little theoretical basis to justify diverse practices. In Babylonia, on the other hand, we find a legal and religious atmosphere that is not particularly anxious about diversity and where there is little trace of codificatory projects. Babylonian Amoraim are spread out geographically, which both serves to mask diverse practices from the everyday experience of non-travelers and also decreases competition among the rabbis. In addition, halakha in Babylonia increasingly developed within a structure of legal reasoning that provided a good theoretical basis for explaining and justifying the existence of pluralism of both opinion and practice.

Theoretical Basis of (In)tolerance

In the introduction, I set forth a range of views from universal monism to universal pluralism along with the theoretical assumptions behind each attitude. I will now use this model to categorize the texts and topics analyzed in these seven chapters. While a topical arrangement of chapters was necessary in order to analyze each text within its legal and literary context, we can now step back and gather together all those texts that share each theoretical attitude. This will allow us to characterize the nature of rabbinic tolerance and intolerance and find the underlying rationales behind their views. I will focus on those texts that reveal, sometimes explicitly and other times more subtly, the motivation behind their attitudes in order to gain a more nuanced understanding of the nature and goals of rabbinic monism and pluralism.

Perhaps the clearest example of universal monism is the law of the rebellious elder, especially as set forth in Palestinian sources; one who disobeys the court's decision incurs nothing less than the death penalty. Although there are no reports of this law ever having been carried out, the Yerushalmi does retell two instances in which one rabbi threatens to label the other a rebellious elder.[66] The goal of this law is twofold: (1) to uphold

66. *Y. Yebam.* 10:4 (11a) and *y. Šabb.* 1:4 (3c). See above, pp. 326–27.

the authority of the court in particular, and the rabbis generally;[67] and (2) to limit diversity of practice since it leads to factionalism. The latter goal is mentioned explicitly by R. Yehudah b. Betera who prohibits a court from forgiving the rebellious elder, "*so that division should not spread in Israel*."[68] The same phrase is also uttered in the name of R. Eleazar: "Even if he [the rebellious elder] says, '[I base my ruling] on tradition,' and they say, 'Thus it appears to us,' he is executed, *so that division should not spread in Israel*."[69]

The most extreme instance of intolerance is the tradition that students of Beth Shammai murdered students of Beth Hillel.[70] The narrator does not defend their actions and even adds: "That day was as difficult for Israel as the day the [golden] calf was made." But, at least some members of Beth Shammai are portrayed as universal monists. Along these lines, though less severe, is Yonatan b. Harkinas who pelts the Hillelite rabbis with pebbles to wake them up and, presumably, also to insult them.[71] Both of these events are not found in the Bavli versions of these narratives.

Other narratives involving interactions between the Houses include verbal attacks and complete delegitimization of the other side. R. Ṭarfon is castigated by his colleagues for following Beth Shammai.[72] Beth Shammai tells R. Yoḥanan ben Haḥorani that he never fulfilled the commandment of *sukkah* in his life because he practiced according to Beth Hillel.[73] Some opinions in the Talmuds similarly state that if one follows Beth Shammai, "his actions are worthless," and "is deserving of death."[74]

In narratives involving other Tannaim, one finds universal monism on the part of the rabbis who excommunicate Akavia ben Mahalalel for his dissenting views[75] (which he presumably also put into practice), as well as those who excommunicate R. Eliezer b. Hyracanus.[76] In the Bavli version of the latter story, Rabban Gamaliel defends this excommunication using the same phrase quoted above regarding the rebellious elder, "*so that division should not spread in Israel*."[77] Yaᶜaqov of Kefar Nevoraia is whipped for

67. The former is already suggested in the biblical verses. The latter is evident in those sources that apply the law of rebellious elder to rabbinic laws and interpretations; see especially *m. Sanh.* 11:3, cited above, p. 316, and discussion there.

68. *Y. Sanh.* 8:6 (26b) and parallels in *b. Sanh.* 88b, *b. Soṭah* 25a, and *Midrash Tannaim* to Deut 17:13.

69. *B. Sanh.* 88a; see above, p. 324. This goal is also evident in *m. Sanh.* 11:2, which describes the hierarchy of courts. That Mishnah derives from *t. Sanh.* 7:1 (above, pp. 303–6), which explicitly bemoans the factionalism created by the absence of the courts.

70. See above, p. 178.

71. *Y. Yebam.* 1:6 (3a). See above, p. 198.

72. *M. Ber.* 1:3. See above, p. 171.

73. *M. Sukkah* 2:7. See above, p. 170.

74. *Y. Yebam.* 1:6 (3b) and *b. Ber.* 11a. See above pp. 201 and 222–23.

75. *M. ᶜEd.* 5:6–7. See above, pp. 274–75.

76. See above, pp. 276–77.

77. *B. B. Meṣiᶜa* 59b.

his dissenting rulings.[78] Rabban Gamaliel forces R. Yehoshua to conform to his ruling and on another occasion punishes R. Yehoshua for teaching an opposing law.[79] These stories do not necessarily reflect a general monistic attitude in all halakhic debates; they may be based on some antagonism directed toward a specific practice, person, or group. Nevertheless, one finds a pattern in the tone the Talmuds take when retelling these and other stories about the Houses and the Tannaim. As shown in chapters 4 and 5, the assumption of the Yerushalmi is that multiple practices lead to tension. If this is taken as a projection of the Yerushalmi redactors' own views, then it implies that, for the Yerushalmi, there can only be one valid law and other practices will be protested or lead to tension. By contrast, the Bavli versions of most of these narratives are more critical of forceful tactics directed against dissenting rabbis.

If one defines universal monism as a case in which one side of a dispute physically or verbally protests the other side, then most narratives involving conversations between practitioners of two opposing laws will fall into the category of universal monism. Stories about those who passively ignore the opposing practice, even though they consider it illegitimate, will largely go unrecorded. However, we do find examples of particular monism at *t. Moᶜed Qaṭ.* 2:15–16 where various rabbis confront stringent practices that they consider invalid but still choose not to protest. According to the Bavli, the visiting rabbis did not protest because providing them with a leniency might cause them to disregard other, more serious, laws as well. Thus, even though their practice itself has no halakhic validity, it does still serve some good and is therefore tolerated.[80]

M. ᶜEduyyot 1:5–6 and its parallel at *t. ᶜEd.* 1:4 present a complex picture.[81] One view there claims that minority opinions are recorded in the Mishnah in order to reject one who cites a tradition similar to the minority opinion. This thorough rejection of minority views is closest to universal monism. The other view in these sources claims that minority opinions are recorded so that they can be reinstated by a future court. This view attributes some theoretical validity to minority views but still provides no leeway for both opinions to be practiced simultaneously. These two views thus disagree about the theoretical value of minority opinions but agree that only one may be practiced. The second view, however, does seem more tolerant of the minority view.

Another group of texts takes a negative view of diversity, though it is not clear whether it considers the opposing practice invalid or just an unfortunate but legitimate reality. The line between particular monism

78. *Genesis Rabbah* 7. See above, p. 278.

79. See above pp. 269–72.

80. See above, pp. 85–93.

81. See text above, p. 274.

and particular pluralism is often blurry since both are passive stances. The law of "Do not make factions," especially as interpreted in Palestinian texts, explicitly prohibits multiplicity of practice, but does not suggest that either side of a controversy is deemed invalid. This law intends to prevent minority groups from opposing the majority practice and encourages unity through uniformity. However, in none of the texts analyzed in chapter 2 was one side deemed illegitimate; in fact, the Yerushalmi specifically excludes one who practices rejected views from the prohibition against making factions.[82] Therefore, this law best represents an attitude of particular pluralism but with a negative view toward the existence of diversity.

T. Ḥagigah. 2:9 pines after the good old days when there "were no divisions within Israel" because the supreme court decided all matters of practice, and laments the subsequent divisions into factions even as it accepts their reality.[83] This text does not go to the extreme of invalidating the practice of either House and so also represents particular pluralism but, again, with a negative view of diversity.

The Yerushalmi also makes a number of statements reflecting negative particular pluralism. The negative attitude toward diversity presented in *t. Ḥag.* 2:9 is echoed and even amplified in *y. Ḥag.* 2:2 (77d).[84] *Y. Berakot* 1:1 (3a), reading various sources against the grain, denies multiplicity of practice on the part of various Tannaim.[85] *Y. Sanhedrin* 4:2 (22a) says that the Torah tolerates multiple interpretations and was given without "clear-cut decisions"; nevertheless, it is up to the sages to decide on one law by following the majority.[86] The Yerushalmi in four places quotes the *baraita*, "These and these are the words of the living God, but halakha follows Beth Hillel."[87] Both views are theoretically true, but only one is valid in practice.

The rules of decision-making created by R. Yoḥanan's school impose uniformity on all halakhic rulings. None of these texts states explicitly that a minority practice that does create a faction or that ignores a rule of R. Yoḥanan is considered invalid. In the case of R. Yoḥanan's rules, the Bavli discusses whether they are even meant to decide halakha definitely or are only guidelines indicating which opinions are generally preferred. Even in the Yerushalmi, many exceptions to these rules can be found. Thus, texts that advocate these rules also represent negative particular pluralism.

---

82. See above p. 99.

83. See above, p. 167. This assumes that מחלוקת is a faction, not an argument; see above, p. 167 n. 12.

84. See above, p. 169.

85. See above, pp. 246–47.

86. See above, p. 28.

87. See citations above, p. 201 n. 136.

What are the theoretical assumptions and rationales behind those who take a negative view toward diversity, whether in the form of monism or negative particular pluralism? One who invalidates multiple practices might do so because he thinks there is only one truth, that is, only one valid opinion even at a theoretical level. However, one is hard pressed to find any rabbinic text that explicitly rejects the validity of multiple opinions.[88] Even regarding a strong monistic law such as that of the rebellious elder, *m. Sanh.* 11:2 teaches that the dissenter "is not liable until he rules in practice," but he may teach his opinion theoretically—thus recognizing multiple truths.[89] The only text that may indicate that the other view is invalid even theoretically is *b. Ber.* 36a: "Beth Shammai, when in conflict with Beth Hillel, is not a [valid] Mishnah," though such an interpretation is doubtful.[90]

Rather, a negative attitude toward diversity of practice may be based on a negative attitude toward multiple opinions. *Sifre Devarim, piska* 48 reads:

> הרי הוא אומר (עמוס ח:יב) ישוטטו לבקש את דבר ה׳ ולא ימצאו רבותינו התירו שהולכים מעיר לעיר וממדינה למדינה על שרץ שנגע בככר לידע אם תחילה הוא אם שניה
> רבי שמעון בן יוחי אומר אם לומר שהתורה עתידה להשתכח מישראל והלא כבר נאמר (דברים לא:כא) כי לא תשכח מפי זרעו אלא איש פלוני אוסר איש פלוני מתיר איש פלוני מטמא איש פלוני מטהר ולא ימצאו דבר ברור.
>
> Behold the verse states: They will run to and fro seeking the word of the Lord but they shall not find it (Amos 8:12). [These are the words of the Torah.][91] That they will walk from city to city and from country to country concerning a reptile that touched a loaf to find out if it is [impure] in the first degree or the second degree.
> R. Shimon ben Yoḥai says, if this means that the Torah will be forgotten from Israel, but behold the verse states, For it will never be forgotton from the mouth of their offspring (Deut 31:21). Rather, this person prohibits and that person permits, this person declares impure and that person declares pure and they will not find the matter clear-cut. [92]

88. The statement that comes closest to this view is *t. Ḥag.* 2:9 = *t. Sanh.* 7:1; see above, pp. 167 and 303–4, which states that there was no controversy before the proliferation of the students of Shammai and Hillel. Even in this source, however, there is clearly multiplicity of opinion among the sages of the lower courts. The high court decides the monolithic practical ruling but does not necessarily invalidate the theoretical value of all other opinions. See above, p. 168 n. 15. In any case, even this source would agree that valid multiple opinions coexist after the demise of Shammai and Hillel.

89. See above, pp. 28 and 301.

90. See above, p. 224 n. 190.

91. This follows the emendation of Finkelstein, *Sifri*, 112.

92. This tradition is also cited at *b. Šabb.* 138b.

M. Baba Batra 9:10 similarly bemoans the existence of multiple opinions, but still does not invalidate them:

> נפל הבית עליו ועל אמו אלו ואלו מודים שיחלוקו אמר רבי עקיבא מודה אני בזה שהנכ־
> סים בחזקתן
> אמר לו בן עזאי על החלוקין אנו מצטערין אלא שבאת לחלק עלינו את השוין!
> If the house collapsed upon someone and upon his mother, [Beth Shammai] and [Beth Hillel] both agree that [the estate] should be divided equally. R. Akiba said, "I agree that [according to Beth Hillel] the property remains with its present possessor."
> Ben Azai told him, "We lament over matters already in dispute and now you come divide what we held to be in agreement!"

Ben Azai laments the existence of even theoretical dispute. Nevertheless, the Mishnah does include multiple opinions on every subject, thus recognizing the existence of more than one valid opinion.[93]

Most often, negative attitudes toward diversity are based on the assumption that multiple truths do exist, and perhaps even must exist, but that the halakhic system should decide on a uniform practice.[94] This is evident in *t. Ḥag.* 2:9, where various opinions of rabbis and lower courts are decided by the higher court. This idea is most clearly formulated in *y. Sanh.* 4:2 (22a), where, after being told that the Torah must contain multiple opinions in order to exist, the Talmud reports that "Moses said before Him, 'Master of the universe, inform me what is the halakha?' He responded, '*Incline after the majority.*'"[95] This assumption is also evident in *m. ʿEd.* 1:5–6 and the law of "Do not make factions." The need for decision making between competing views is evident in the rules of R. Yoḥanan as well as in those Yerushalmi and Bavli *sugyot* that end with a halakhic conclusion, whether based on R. Yoḥanan's rules or not. There may be many valid theoretical options, but the community must decide on only one.

Two general motivations drive the attitudes of monism and negative particular pluralism. First, a desire for social unity of the Jewish people so that division does not spread in Israel and they not become factions. This requires uniformity of practice, especially regarding communal matters such as the calendar and upholding the authority of the central judiciary. The shadow of Second Temple sectarianism is especially felt in statements

---

93. To be sure, the Mishnah does often limit the number of opinions it cites compared with the Tosefta. Thus, the Mishnah seems to begrudgingly accept diversity of opinion while seeking to limit it whenever possible. Still, one cannot deny that the Mishnah accepts multiple opinions.

94. For further analysis of this rationale, see Ben-Menahem, "Is There," 167–68; and Ben-Menahem et al., *Controversy and Dialogue in the Jewish Tradition: A Reader*, 20–21.

95. See above, p. 28.

defending this position.[96] Second, uniformity is important in order to preserve the authority and unity of the Torah, so that the Torah not become "two Torahs."[97] The rebellious elder is prosecuted even for a minor issue, and even if he has no following; the problem with him is not the threat of social factionalism but rather the challenge to central authority. There may be many theoretically valid positions, but law should ideally settle on one practice at any given time based on majority rule or some other authority structure. Conflicting practices lend an air of randomness to the system and diminish its authority.

The Bavli echoes many of the above-quoted statements reflecting a negative view of diversity. However, it also coins other statements that reflect particular or universal pluralism that do not judge diversity in a negative light. The Bavli statement "Each river follows its own course" expresses particular pluralism; multiple practices are valid for the groups who follow them (even if one group may not follow the practice of the other), because there is more than one way to get to a destination. The reality of diversity of practice is deemed acceptable with no hint that it ought to be otherwise. The *baraita* quoted in the Bavli concerning R. Yose the Galilean's town eating poultry and milk and R. Eliezer's town violating Shabbat for circumcision preparations reflects particular pluralism, again with no hint that such diversity is problematic.[98] Many of the stories about visiting rabbis similarly reflect nonnegative particular pluralism. Statements such as "Leave him alone, he reasons according to his master" reflect particular pluralism without negativity.[99] An explicitly positive attitude toward diversity is found in one Bavli story where a city is praised for following a minority opinion.[100] The existence of multiple practices in different locales is not portrayed as being negative in any of these narratives.

The Bavli also shows a more positive attitude toward diversity in its interpretation of "Do not make factions," the law of rebellious elder, the rules of R. Yoḥanan, and the way it retells narratives about Tannaim. The Bavli's rejection of rules of decision making, as discussed in chapter 1, seems to reflect an especially positive view of pluralism. One who views diversity negatively, even if he tolerates it, would welcome R. Yoḥanan's system of unifying halakhic decisions. The rejection of these rules in the Bavli in favor of case-by-case adjudication shows that uniformity was not the Bavli's priority.

---

96. See above, p. 169 n. 20.
97. See references above, p. 167 n. 14.
98. *B. Šabb.* 130a. See above, p. 148.
99. *B. Šabb.* 12b, 53b; and *b. Pesaḥ.* 106b (above, pp. 140 and 141 n. 41).
100. *B. Šabb.* 130a. See above, p. 149.

Examples of universal pluralism, in which the other practice is fully acceptable as an alternative or at least the decisions of the other group are accepted, are rarer than examples of particular pluralism, but they do exist. The Bavli's recognition of cases of indeterminacy and its openness to choosing any option in some cases reflect universal pluralism.[101] *M. Yebamot* 1:4, depending on its interpretation, attests to perhaps the most radical example of universal pluralism.[102] The Houses married each other and mixed their vessels together despite their substantial halakhic differences. They did not simply accept that the opposing view is valid for the other group; they went a step further and acted on the results of the other group's rulings, although they themselves would have ruled differently in the very same case.

T. Yebamot 1:10–11 elaborates on the motivations of such strong tolerance by quoting two verses.[103] Despite numerous arguments over various aspects of marriage laws, the Houses still married each other because "they practiced truth and peace between them, as the verse states, '*Truth and peace they love*'" (Zech 8:19).[104] The Houses valued peaceful relations between their two populations more than the truth value of their respective halakhic positions. This verse is quoted again in the Yerushalmi and Bavli versions of the Tosefta.[105] The Bavli adds, "This is to teach you that they showed love and friendship toward one another."

Furthermore, states the Tosefta, the Houses "did not abstain from handling pure objects one upon the other to fulfill what is stated, '*All the ways of a man seem right to him, but the Lord probes motives*' (Prov 16:2)." Each House was able to accept the other party's decisions despite their fundamental disagreements because they recognized that the other party also had sincere motives. Each group arrived at a certain understanding of law based on what seemed correct in their eyes; but ultimately, since God values one's motives, each group also valued the motives of the other. One must be careful not to read too much into these prooftexts since the Tosefta does not elaborate on their interpretation and the Talmuds greatly limit the extent of tolerance implied by these statements; nevertheless, these justifications are significant as theoretical models.

The theoretical assumption behind positive particular pluralism and universal pluralism is that there is not always a need for the halakhic system or central judiciary to decide on one law for all Jews. In some cases, it is sufficient for a local authority to decide the law for his jurisdiction.

---

101. See above, pp. 62–72.

102. See above, p. 189.

103. See above, p. 191.

104. This verse is also cited in *b. Sukkah* 32b to decide a halakhic point, thus showing that it was used as a legal principle.

105. See above, pp. 201 and 208.

In other cases, no need is felt for any decision making altogether. Texts supporting positive and universal pluralism are also mostly found in the Bavli, which encourages theoretical debate more than earlier Palestinian texts. Although, as noted above, no rabbinic text invalidates multiplicity of opinion, the Bavli goes beyond previous texts in its positive view of multiplicity of opinions. This also informs its nonnegative, and sometimes even positive, attitude toward pluralism of practice.[106] Just as God's Torah is polysemous, so, too, the rabbis' halakha can be pluralistic. The motivation directing attitudes of pluralism is peace, that is, communal unity through acceptance of diversity. This tolerance is achieved through recognition of sincere motives and validation of competing truth values even at the level of practice.[107]

Monists and pluralists share the same goal of achieving unity within Judaism. Both also generally agree that there exists more that one theoretically legitimate law. The essence of their disagreement, rather, is twofold. First, whether communal unity is best achieved by forcing uniformity or by tolerating and including diversity. Second, whether law should speak with a single, authoritative, and clear voice, or whether law can and should be multifaceted, robust, and able to speak to varied groups in a polyphonous but hopefully harmonious voice. Different circumstances and issues may call for greater emphasis on one over the other, but an overemphasis on either can rupture the system. Talmudic law, like all systems of law, exists and thrives by balancing between the poles of the ever-present dialectic of uniformity versus diversity.

---

106. See view of Rav Kahana in *b. Sanh.* 88a above, p. 324, who states that the equivalent truth value of a minority opinion necessarily leads to tolerance for one who puts that opinion into practice.

107. These values are similar to those mentioned by Cover as the tools used by the imperial model to maintain the community; see above, p. 11. What Cover names "the mirror of critical objectivity" corresponds to the validation of competing truths arrived at through recognized halakhic principles. What Cover calls "the constraint of peace on the void at which strong bonds cease" is equivalent to the value of peace mentioned in rabbinic sources to justify one group recognizing the halakhic decisions of its rivals.

Bibliography

Albeck, Hanokh. *Introduction to the Mishna*. Jerusalem: Mossad Bialik, 1959 (Hebrew).

———. *Introduction to the Talmud Bavli and Yerushalmi*. Tel-Aviv: Dvir, 1987 (Hebrew).

———. *Six Orders of Mishnah*. 6 vols. Jerusalem: Mossad Bialik, 1959 (Hebrew).

Albeck, Hanokh, and Judah Theodor. *Midrash Bereshit Rabbah: Critical Edition with Notes and Commentary*. Jerusalem: Shalem Books, 1996.

Alexander, Elizabeth Shanks. *Transmitting Mishnah: The Shaping Influence of Oral Tradition*. New York: Cambridge University Press, 2006.

Algazi, Yaᶜakov. *Sefer she'erit Yaᶜaqov*. Brooklyn: Beth Hasefer, 1989.

Allegro, John M., and Arnold Anderson. *Qumran Cave 4.1(4Q158–4Q186)*. Discoveries in the Judean Desert 5. Oxford: Clarendon, 1968.

Alon, Gedaliah. *The Jews in Their Land in the Talmudic Age (70–640 C.E.)*. Translated by Gershon Levi. Jerusalem: Magnes, 1984.

Amit, Aharon. *Talmud ha-Igud: BT Pesaḥim Chapter IV*. Jerusalem: Society for the Interpretation of the Talmud, 2009.

Ashkenazi, Duberush. *Shaᶜare Yerushalmi*. Warsaw: N. Schriftgisser, 1866.

Atlas, Samuel. *Pathways in Hebrew Law*. New York: American Academy for Jewish Research, 1978 (Hebrew).

Aṭṭar, Hayyim ben. *Hefeṣ Hashem*. Amsterdam, 1732.

Attridge, Harold. "Christianity from the Destruction of Jerusalem to Constantine's Adoption of the New Religion: 70–312 C.E." In *Christianity and Rabbinic Judaism*, edited by Hershel Shanks, 151–94. Washington D.C.: Biblical Archaeology Society, 1992.

Austin, John. *Lectures on Jurisprudence; or, The Philosophy of Positive Law*. London: John Murray, 1885.

Avery-Peck, Alan, and Jacob Neusner, editors. *The Mishnah in Contemporary Perspective*. Leiden: Brill, 2006.

Avi-Yonah, Michael. *The Holy Land from the Persian to the Arab Conquests (536 B.C. to A.D. 640)*. Grand Rapids: Baker Book House, 1966.

Azulai, Hayyim Yosef David. *Sefer birke Yosef*. Jerusalem: Siaḥ Yisra'el, 2000.

Bacher, Wilhelm. *ᶜErkhe midrash*. Jerusalem: Karmi'el, 1969.

Bar-Asher Siegal, Michal. "Literary Analogies in Rabbinic and Christian Monastic Sources." Ph.D. diss., Yale University, 2010.

Baumgarten, Albert. *The Flourishing of Jewish Sects in the Maccabean Era: An Interpretation*. Leiden: Brill, 1997.

———. "The Politics of Reconciliation: The Education of R. Judah the Prince." In *Jewish and Christian Self-Definition: Volume Two, Aspects of Judaism in the Graeco-Roman Period,* edited by E. P. Sanders, 213–25. Philadelphia: Fortress, 1981.

Behr, John. "The Question of Nicene Orthodoxy." In *Byzantine Orthodoxies: Papers from the Thirty-sixth Spring Symposium of Byzantine Studies,* edited by Andrew Louth and Augustine Casiday, 15–26. Burlington, VT: Ashgate, 2002.

Ben-Menahem, Hanina. "Is There Always One Uniquely Correct Answer to a Legal Question in the Talmud?" *Jewish Law Annual* 6 (1987): 164–75.

———. *Judicial Deviation in Talmudic Law*. New York: Harwood Academic Publishers, 1991.

———. "The Second Canonization of the Talmud." *California Law Review* 28, no. 1 (2006): 37–51.

———. "Talmudic Law: A Jurisprudential Perspective." In *The Cambridge History of Judaism IV: The Late Roman-Rabbinic Period,* edited by Steven Katz, 877–98. Cambridge: Cambridge University Press, 2006.

Ben-Menahem, Hanina, et al. *Controversy and Dialogue in Halakhic Sources*. 3 vols. Boston: Boston University School of Law, 1991–2002 (Hebrew).

———. *Controversy and Dialogue in the Jewish Tradition: A Reader*. New York: Routledge, 2005.

Ben-Shalom, Israel. *The School of Shammai and the Zealots' Struggle against Rome*. Jerusalem: Yad Izhak Ben-Zvi and Ben-Gurion University of the Negev Press, 1993 (Hebrew).

Benovitz, Moshe. *Talmud ha-Igud: BT Berakhot Chapter I*. Jerusalem: Society for the Interpretation of the Talmud, 2006 (Hebrew).

Berger, Michael S. *Rabbinic Authority*. New York: Oxford University Press, 1998.

Berkovits, Eliezer. *Ha-halakha, koḥah ve-tafqidah*. Jerusalem: Mosad Ha-Rav Kook, 1991.

Biale, Rachel. *Women and Jewish Law*. New York: Schocken Books, 1984.

Bitman, Avigdor. "Le-ṭivo shel ha-kelal halakha ke-Beth Hillel." *Sinai* 82 (1988): 185–96 (Hebrew).

Blidstein, Gerald. "ʿAl hakhraʿat ha-halakha bi-zman ha-zeh: ʿiyyun ba-Rambam hilkhot mamrim 1, 5." *Dine Israel* 20–21 (2001): 3–12.

———. "'Even If He Tells You Right Is Left': The Validity of Moral Authority in the Halakha and Its Limitations." In *Studies in Halakha and Jewish Thought Presented to Rabbi Prof. Menachem Emanuel Rackman on his 80th Anniversary,* edited by Moshe Beer, 221–41. Ramat-Gan: Bar-Ilan University Press, 1994 (Hebrew).

Boccaccini, Gabriele. *Roots of Rabbinic Judaism: An Intellectual History, from Ezekiel to Daniel*. Grand Rapids, MI: Eerdmans, 2002.

Botwinick, Aryeh. "Underdetermination of Meaning by the Talmudic Text." In *Commandment and Community: New Essays in Jewish Legal and Political Philosophy*, edited by D. Frank, 113–40. New York: State University of New York Press, 1995.

Bowman, John. "An Arabic Hijab Manuscript and Jewish and Samaritan Phylacteries." *Abr-Nahrain* 32 (1994): 47–58.

Boyarin, Daniel. "Anecdotal Evidence: The Yavneh Conundrum, *Birkat Hamminim*, and the Problem of Talmudic Historiography." In *The Mishnah in Contemporary Perspective*, edited by Alan Avery-Peck and Jacob Neusner, 1–35. Leiden: Brill, 2006.

———. *Border Lines: The Partition of Judaeo-Christianity*. Philadelphia: University of Pennsylvania Press, 2004.

———. *Intertextuality and the Reading of Midrash*. Bloomington: Indiana University Press, 1990.

Brandes, Yehuda. "The Beginnings of the Rules of Halachic Adjudication: Significance, Formation and Development of the Rules Concerning the Tanaic Halacha and Literature." Ph.D. diss., Hebrew University, 2002 (Hebrew).

Brauner, Ronald. "Some Aspects of Local Custom in Tannaitic Literature." *Jewish Civilization* 2 (1981): 43–54.

Brody, Robert. *The Geonim of Babylonia and the Shaping of Medieval Jewish Culture*. New Haven and London: Yale University Press, 1998.

Brown, Francis, et al. *The Brown-Driver-Briggs Hebrew and English Lexicon*. Peabody, MA: Hendrickson, 2001.

Bruns, Gerald. "The Hermeneutics of Midrash." In *Hermeneutics Ancient and Modern*, 104–23. New Haven: Yale University Press, 1992.

Büchler, Abraham. "Halakhot le-ma'aseh ke-Beth Shammai bi-zman ha-bayit ve-'aḥar ha-ḥurban." In *Sefer ha-yovel li-khevod R. Mosheh Aryeh Bloch*, edited by Sámuel Krausz and Miksa Weisz, 21–30. Budapest, 1905.

Burgansky, Israel. "Masekhet Sukkah shel Talmud Bavli: mekoroteha ve-darkhe ʿarikhatah." Ph.D. diss., Bar-Ilan University, 1979.

Carter, James Coolidge. *Law: Its Origin Growth and Function*. New York: G. P. Putnam's Sons, 1907.

Chavel, Charles Ber. *Sefer ha-miṣvot la-Rambam*. Jerusalem: Mosad Ha-Rav Kook, 1981.

Chernick, Michael. "An Analysis of BT Berakhot 7a: The Intersection of Talmud Criticism and Literary Appreciation." In *Through Those Near to Me: Essays in Honor of Jerome R. Malino*, edited by Glen Lebetkin, 257–65. Danbury, CT: United Jewish Center, 1998.

———. *Midat "gezerah shavah": ṣuroteha ba-Midrashim uva-Talmudim*. Lod: Habermann Institute, 1994.

Claman, Richard. "A Philosophic Basis for Halakhic Pluralism." *Conservative Judaism* 54, no. 1 (2002): 60–80.

Cohen, Aryeh. *Rereading Talmud: Gender, Law and the Poetics of Sugyot*. Atlanta: Scholars Press, 1998.

Cohen, Avinoam. "'Minyana le-meᶜute mai' u-'minyana lama li': min ha-she'eloth ha-Talmudiyot ha-nose'ot 'ofi Sevora'i." In *Meḥkarim ba-lashon ha-'Ivrit ub-sifrut ha-Talmudit*, edited by M. Kadari, 83–101. Ramat-Gan: Bar-Ilan University, 1990.

Cohen, Naomi. "Philo's Tefillin." *World Congress for Jewish Studies* 9A (1986): 199–206.

Cohen, Shaye. *From the Maccabees to the Mishnah*. Philadelphia: Westminster, 1987.

———. "Patriarchs and Scholarchs." *Proceedings of the American Academy for Jewish Research* 48 (1981): 57–85.

———. "The Place of the Rabbi in Jewish Society of the Second Century." In *The Galilee in Late Antiquity*, edited by Lee Levine, 157–73. New York: Jewish Theological Seminary, 1992.

———. "The Rabbis in Second-Century Jewish Society." In *The Cambridge History of Judaism. Vol. 3: The Early Roman Period*, edited by W. Horbury, W. D. Davies, and J. Sturdy, 922–90. Cambridge: Cambridge University Press, 1999.

———. "The Significance of Yavneh: Pharisees, Rabbis, and the End of Jewish Sectarianism." *Hebrew Union College Annual* 55 (1984): 27–53.

———. "A Virgin Defiled: Some Rabbinic and Christian Views on the Origins of Heresy." *Union Seminary Quarterly Review* 36 (1980): 1–11.

Cohn, Yehudah. *Tangled Up in Text: Tefillin and the Ancient World*. Providence: Brown Judaic Studies, 2008.

Cover, Robert. "Nomos and Narrative." In *Narrative, Violence, and the Law: The Essays of Robert Cover*, edited by Martha Minow, Michael Ryan, and Austin Sarat, 95–172. Ann Arbor: University of Michigan Press, 1995.

———. "Obligation: A Jewish Jurisprudence of the Social Order." In *Narrative, Violence, and the Law: The Essays of Robert Cover*, edited by Martha Minow, Michael Ryan, and Austin Sarat, 239–48. Ann Arbor: University of Michigan Press, 1995.

Craigie, Peter C. *The Book of Deuteronomy*. Grand Rapids, MI: Eerdmans, 1976.

Daube, David. "Dissent in Bible and Talmud." *California Law Review* 59 (1971): 784–94.

———. "Rabbinic Methods of Interpretation and Hellenistic Rhetoric." *Hebrew Union College Annual* 22 (1949): 239–64.

Davies, William D. *The Setting of the Sermon on the Mount*. Cambridge: Cambridge University Press, 1966.

DeGeorge, Richard. *The Nature and Limits of Authority*. Lawrence: University of Kansas, 1985.

Dhanbar, Bemanji N. *The Epistles of Manushchihar*. Bombay: Trustees of the Parsee Panchayat Funds and Properties, 1912.

Dishon, David. *Tarbut ha-maḥloqet be-Yisra'el: ʿiyyun be-mibḥar meqorot*. Jerusalem: Schocken, 1984.

Dorhman, Natalie. "Reading as Rhetoric in Halakhic Texts." In *Of Scribes and Sages: Early Jewish Interpretation and Transmission of Scripture*, edited by Craig Evans, 90–114. London: T&T Clark International, 2004.

Driver, S. R. *Deuteronomy*. International Critical Commentary. Edinburgh: T&T Clark International, 1978.

Efron, Joshua. *Studies on the Hasmonean Period*. Leiden: Brill, 1987.

Elman, Yaakov. "Acculturation to Elite Persian Norms and Modes of Thought in the Babylonian Jewish Community of Late Antiquity." In *Netiʿot le-David: Jubilee Volume for David Weiss Halivni*, edited by Yaakov Elman, Ephraim Halivni, and Zvi Aryeh Steinfeld, 31–56. Jerusalem: Orhot, 2004.

———. "Argument for the Sake of Heaven: The Mind of the Talmud: A Review Essay." *Jewish Quarterly Review* 84, no. 2–3 (1994): 261–82.

———. "Order, Sequence, and Selection: The Mishnah's Anthological Choices." In *The Anthology in Jewish Literature*, edited by D. Stern, 53–80. New York: Oxford University Press, 2004.

———. "Scripture Versus Contemporary Needs: A Sasanian/Zoroastrian Example." *Cardozo Law Review* 28, no. 1 (2006): 153–69.

Elon, Menachem. *Jewish Law: History, Sources, Principles*. Philadelphia: Jewish Publication Society, 1994.

Epstein, Y. N. *Mavo le-nusaḥ ha-Mishnah*. Jerusalem: Magnes, 1948. Reprint, 2000.

———. *Mevo'ot le-sifrut ha-Tannaim, Mishnah, Tosefta, u-midreshe halakha*. Edited by E. Z. Melamed. Jerusalem: Magnes, 1947.

———. "Sifri zuṭa, parashat parah." *Tarbiz* 1 (1930): 46–78.

Eylenburg, Issachar Baer. *Be'er Shevaʿ*. Warsaw, 1890.

Faur, Jose. *Golden Doves with Silver Dots: Semiotics and Textuality in Rabbinic Tradition*. Bloomington: Indiana University Press, 1986.

———. "Law and Hermeneutics in Rabbinic Jurisprudence: A Maimonidean Perspective." *Cardozo Law Review* 14 (1992–93): 1657–79.

———. "One-Dimensional Jew, Zero-Dimensional Judaism." *Review of Rabbinic Judaism* 2 (1999): 31–50.

———. *Studies in the Mishne Torah: Book of Knowledge*. Jerusalem: Mossad Harav Kook, 1978 (Hebrew).

Fine, Steven. "A Cosmopolitan 'Student of the Sages': Jacob of Kefar Nevoraia in Rabbinic Literature." In *Maven in Blue Jeans: A Festschrift in*

Honor of Zev Garber, edited by S. Jacobs, 35–43, West Lafayette, IN: Purdue University Press, 2009.

Finkelstein, Louis. *The Pharisees: The Sociological Background of Their Faith.* Third edition. Philadelphia: Jewish Publication Society, 1962.

———. *Sifra on Leviticus.* 5 vols. Jerusalem: Jewish Theological Seminary of America, 1983–1992 (Hebrew).

———. *Sifre on Deuteronomy.* New York: Jewish Theological Seminary of America, 1969 (Hebrew).

Fisch, Menachem. *Rational Rabbis: Science and Talmudic Culture.* Bloomington: Indiana University Press, 1997.

Fisch, Shlomo. *Midrash hag-gadol.* Jerusalem: Mosad Harav Kook, 1975.

Fiss, Owen. "Objectivity and Interpretation." *Stanford Law Review* 34 (1982): 739–63.

Fonrobert, Charlotte. "From Separatism to Urbanism: The Dead Sea Scrolls and the Origins of the Rabbinic Eruv." *Dead Sea Discoveries* 11, no. 1 (2004): 43–71.

———. *Menstrual Purity: Rabbinic and Christian Reconstructions of Biblical Gender.* Stanford, CA: Stanford University Press, 2000.

———. "The Political Symbolism of the Eruv." *Jewish Social Studies* 11, no. 3 (2005): 9–35.

———. "Review of *The Pluralistic Halakhah.*" *Review of Biblical Literature* 6 (2004): 350–53.

Fraade, Steven. *From Tradition to Commentary: Torah and Its Interpretation in the Midrash Sifre to Deuteronomy.* Albany: State University of New York, 1991.

———. "Rabbinic Polysemy and Pluralism Revisited: Between Praxis and Thematization." *AJS Review* 31, no. 1 (2007): 1–40.

Frankel, Zechariah. *Mevo ha-Yerushalmi.* Breslau: Schletter, 1870.

Frenkel, Yonah. "Hermeneutic Problems in the Study of the Aggadic Narrative." *Tarbiz* 47, no. 3/4 (2001): 139–72 (Hebrew).

———. *Sippur ha-agadah, aḥdut shel tokhen ve-ṣurah: koveṣ meḥqarim.* Tel Aviv: Hakibbutz Hameuchad, 2001.

Freundel, Barry. "Formalization of Individual Prayer Around the Shmoneh ʿEsrei in the Talmudic Period, Patterns of Acceptance, Rejection and Modification." Ph.D. diss., Baltimore Hebrew University, 2004.

Friedenberg, Daniel, and Norman Gold. *Sasanian Jewry and Its Culture.* Chicago: University of Illinois Press, 2009.

Friedman, Mordechai Akiva. "Teshuva be-ʿinyane tefilah mi-zemano shel Rav Saʿadia Gaon." *Sinai* 109 (1992): 125–44.

Friedman, Shamma. *Pereq ha-'isha rabbah ba-Bavli.* Jerusalem: Jewish Theological Seminary of America, 1978.

———. "Some Structural Patterns of Talmudic Sugyot." *Proceedings of the Sixth World Congress of Jewish Studies* 3 (1977): 389–402 (Hebrew).

———. *Tosefta ʿatikta: masekhet pesaḥ rishon*. Ramat-Gan: Bar-Ilan University Press, 2002.

Furnish, Dale. "Custom as a Source of Law." *American Journal of Comparative Law* 30 (1982): 31–50.

Gafni, Isaiah. *The Jews of Babylonia in the Talmudic Era: A Social and Cultural History*. Jerusalem: Zalman Shazar Center for Jewish History, 1990 (Hebrew).

Garnsey, Peter. "Religious Toleration in Classical Antiquity." In *Persecution and Toleration*, edited by W. J. Sheils, 1–27. Oxford: Ecclesiastical History Society, 1984.

Gerondi, Nissim. *Ḥidushe ha-Ran: Masekhet Sanhedrin*. Jerusalem: Mosad ha-Rav Kook, 2003.

Gilat, Yitzhak D. "Eleazar (Eliezer) ben Zadok." *Encyclopedia Judaica* (2007): 6:309.

———. "Le-maḥloqet Beth Shamai u-Beth Hillel." In *Yad le-Gilat*, 156–66. Jerusalem: Bialik Institute, 2002.

———. "Lo titgodedu." *Bar Ilan* 18–19 (1981): 79–98.

———. *The Teachings of R. Eliezer Ben Hyrcanos and Their Position in the History of the Halakha*. Tel Aviv: Dvir, 1968 (Hebrew).

Ginzberg, Louis. *A Commentary on the Palestinian Talmud*. 4 vols. New York: Jewish Theological Seminary of America, 1941 (Hebrew).

———. *On Jewish Law and Lore*. Philadelphia: Jewish Publication Society of America, 1955.

———. *An Unknown Jewish Sect*. New York: Jewish Theological Seminary of America, 1976.

———. *Yerushalmi Fragments from the Genizah: Vol. I, Text with Various Readings from the Editio Princeps*. Jerusalem: Jewish Theological Seminary of America, 1909.

Goldberg, Abraham. *Commentary to the Mishna: Shabbat*. Jerusalem: Jewish Theological Seminary of America, 1976 (Hebrew).

———. "The Mishna—A Study Book of Halakha." In *The Literature of the Sages: Part One*, edited by Shmuel Safrai, 211–51. Philadelphia: Fortress, 1987.

———. *The Mishna Treatise Eruvin*. Jerusalem: Magnes, 1986.

———. "The Palestinian Talmud." In *The Literature of the Sages, Part One*, edited by Shmuel Safrai, 303–19. Philadelphia: Fortress, 1987.

———. "Ṣimṣum maḥloqet eṣel Amora'e Bavel." In *Meḥqere Talmud* 1, edited by Yaakov and David Rosental, 135–53. Jerusalem: Magnes, 1990.

Goodblatt, David. "The End of Sectarianism and the Patriarchs." In *For Uriel: Studies in the History of Israel in Antiquity Presented to Professor Uriel Rappaport*, edited by M. Mor, J. Pastor, Y. Ashkenazi, and I. Ronnen. Jerusalem: Zalman Shazar Center for Jewish History, 2005.

———. "Local Traditions in the Babylonian Talmud." *Hebrew Union College Annual* 48 (1977): 187–217.

———. *The Monarchic Principle: Studies in Jewish Self-Government in Antiquity*. Tübingen: Mohr Siebeck, 1994.

———. *Rabbinic Instruction in Sasanian Babylonia*. Leiden: Brill, 1975.

Goodenough, Erwin R. *Jewish Symbols in the Greco-Roman Period*. New York: Pantheon, 1953.

Goodman, Martin. "The Function of 'Minim' in Early Rabbinic Judaism." In *Geschichte—Tradition—Reflexion I*, edited by Peter Schäfer, 501–10. Tübingen: Mohr Siebeck, 1996.

———. "The Roman State and the Jewish Patriarch in the Third Century." In *The Galilee in Late Antiquity*, edited by Lee Levine, 107–19. New York: Jewish Theological Seminary of America, 1994.

———. *State and Society in Roman Galilee, A.D. 132–212*. Totowa, NJ: Rowman & Allanheld, 1983.

Gordis, David. "Two Literary Talmudic Readings." In *History and Literature: New Readings of Jewish Texts in Honor of Arnold J. Band*, edited by William Cutter, 3–15. Providence: Brown Judaic Studies, 2002.

Graetz, Heinrich. *History of the Jews*. 6 vols. Philadelphia: Jewish Publication Society of America, 1891–98.

Gray, Alyssa. *A Talmud in Exile: The Influence of Yerushalmi Avodah Zarah on the Formation of Bavli Avodah Zarah*. Providence: Brown Judaic Studies, 2005.

Green, William Scott. "Romancing the Tome: Rabbinic Hermeneutics and the Theory of Literature." *Semia* 40 (1987): 147–68.

Griffiths, John. "What Is Legal Pluralism?" *Journal of Legal Pluralism* 24 (1986): 1–55.

Groh, Dennis. "The Religion of the Empire: Christianity from Constantine to the Arab Conquest." In *Christianity and Rabbinic Judaism*, edited by Hershel Shanks, 267–303. Washington DC: Biblical Archaeology Society, 1992.

Gunzberg, Aryeh Leib. *Sha'agat 'aryeh*. New York: Israel Wolf, 1958.

Guttmann, Alexander. "The End of the 'Houses.'" In *The Abraham Weiss Jubilee Volume*, 89–105. New York: Abraham Weiss Jubilee Committee, 1964.

———. "Hillelites and Shammaites: A Clarification." *Hebrew Union College Annual* 28 (1957): 115–26.

———. "Participation of the Common People in Pharisaic and Rabbinic Legislative Processes." *Jewish Law Association Studies* 1 (1985): 41–51.

———. *Rabbinic Judaism in the Making*. Detroit: Wayne State University Press, 1970.

Halbertal, Moshe. *By Way of Truth: Nahmanides and the Creation of Tradition*. Jerusalem: Hartman Institute, 2006 (Hebrew).

———. *Interpretive Revolutions in the Making: Values as Interpretive Considerations in Midrashei Halakhah*. Jerusalem: Magnes, 1999 (Hebrew).

———. "Jews and Pagans in the Mishnah." In *Tolerance and Intolerance in Early Judaism and Christianity*, edited by G. Stanton and G. Stroumsa, 159–72. Cambridge: Cambridge University Press, 1998.

———. *People of the Book: Canon, Meaning, and Authority*. Cambridge: Harvard University Press, 1997.

Halevy, Isaak. *Dorot ha-rishonim*. Berlin: Binyamin Ha-aretz, 1920. Repr., Jerusalem, 1966.

Halivni, David. "Aspects of the Formation of the Talmud." In *Creation and Composition: The Contribution of the Bavli Redactors (Stammaim) to the Aggada*, edited by Jeffrey Rubenstein, 339–60. Tübingen: Mohr Siebeck, 2005.

———. *Meqorot u-mesorot*. 6 vols. Tel Aviv: Dvir; Jerusalem: Jewish Theological Seminary of America and Magnes, 1968–2003.

———. *Midrash, Mishnah, and Gemara: The Jewish Predilection for Justified Law*. Cambridge: Harvard University Press, 1986.

———. *Peshat and Derash*. Oxford: Oxford University Press, 1990.

———. "The Reception Accorded to Rabbi Judah's Mishnah." In *Jewish and Christian Self-Definition: Volume Two, Aspects of Judaism in the Graeco-Roman Period*, edited by E. P. Sanders, 204–12. Philadelphia: Fortress, 1981.

———. "The Role of the Mara D'atra in Jewish Law." *Proceedings of the Rabbinical Assembly of America* 38 (1976): 124–29.

Halivni, Ephraim. *The Rules for Deciding Halakha in the Talmud*. Lod: Mekhon Haberman le-Meḥqere Sifrut, 1999.

———. "Yom ṭov sheni." *Sinai* 106 (1990): 41–45.

Hallewy, E. E. "The First Mishnaic Controversy." *Tarbiz* 28 (1958): 154–57 (Hebrew).

Hamitovsky, Itzhak. "Rabbi Meir and the Samaritans: The Differences Between the Accounts in the Yerushalmi and the Bavli." *Jewish Studies, an Internet Journal* (2009): 1–26 (Hebrew).

Hammer-Kossoy, Michelle. "Divine Justice in Rabbinic Hands: Talmudic Reconstitution of the Penal System." Ph.D. diss., New York University, 2005.

Handelman, Susan. "'Everything Is in It': Rabbinic Interpretation and Modern Literary Theory." *Judaism* 35, no. 4 (1986): 429–40.

———. "Fragments of the Rock: Contemporary Literary Theory and the Study of Rabbinic Texts - A Response to David Stern." *Prooftexts* 5 (1985): 75–95.

———. *The Slayers of Moses: The Emergence of Rabbinic Interpretation in Modern Literary Theory*. Albany: State University of New York Press, 1982.

Hart, H. L. A. *The Concept of Law*. Oxford: Oxford University Press, 1994.

Hartman, David. *A Heart of Many Rooms: Celebrating the Many Voices within Judaism*. Woodstock, VT: Jewish Lights, 1999.

Havlin, Shlomo Zalman. "Al 'ha-ḥatimah ha-sifrutit' ke-yesod ha-ḥalukah li-tqufot ba-halakha." In *Mekhqarim be-sifrut ha-talmudit*, edited by Shemu'el Re'em, 148–92. Jerusalem: Ha-'akademiah Ha-le'umit Ha-yisre'elit Le-madaʿim, 1983.

Hayes, Christine. "The Abrogation of Torah Law: Rabbinic *Taqqanah* and Praetorian Edict." In *The Talmud Yerushalmi and Graeco-Roman Culture I*, edited by Peter Schäfer, 643–74. Tübingen: Mohr Siebeck, 1998.

———. *Between the Babylonian and Palestinian Talmuds: Accounting for Halakhic Difference in Selected Sugyot from Tractate Avodah Zarah*. New York: Oxford University Press, 1997.

———. "Legal Truth, Right Answers and Best Answers: Dworkin and the Rabbis." *Dine Israel* 25 (2008): 73–121.

———. "Theoretical Pluralism in the Talmud: A Response to Richard Hidary." *Dine Israel* 26–27 (2009–2010): 257–307.

Heger, Paul. *The Pluralistic Halakhah: Legal Innovations in the Late Second Commonwealth and Rabbinic Periods*. Berlin: de Gruyter, 2003.

Heinemann, Isaak. *Darkhe ha-'aggada*. Jerusalem: Magnes, 1970.

Heinemann, Joseph. "The Nature of the Aggadah." In *Midrash and Literature*, edited by Geoffrey Hartman and Sanford Budick, 41–55. New Haven: Yale University Press, 1986.

———. "Profile of a Midrash: The Art of Composition in Leviticus Rabba." *Journal of the American Academy of Religion* 31 (1971): 141–50.

Henshke, David. "Minhag mevaṭel halakha? (Le-ishushah shel hashʿarah)." *Dine Israel* 17 (1994): 135–54.

———. "R. Joshua's Acceptance of the Authority of Rabban Gamaliel II: A Study of Two Versions of the Same Event." *Tarbiz* 76, no. 1–2 (2007): 81–104.

Herman, Dov. "The Different Approaches of the Rabbis in Yavneh, Lod, and Galilee regarding the Ninth of Av as Reflected in the Laws of the Day." *Hebrew Union College Annual* 73 (2002): 1–29 (Hebrew).

Herman, Geoffrey. "The Exilarchate in the Sasanian Era." Ph.D. diss., Hebrew University, 2005 (Hebrew).

Herr, Moshe, and Menachem Elon. "Minhag." *Encyclopedia Judaica* (2007): 14:265–78.

Hezser, Catherine. "The Codification of Legal Knowledge in Late Antiquity: The Talmud Yerushalmi and Roman Law Codes." In *The Talmud Yerushalmi and Graeco-Roman Culture I*, edited by Peter Schäfer, 581–641. Tübingen: Mohr Siebeck, 1998.

———. "Social Fragmentation, Plurality of Opinion, and Nonobservance of Halakha: Rabbis and Community in Late Roman Palestine." *Jewish Studies Quarterly* 1 (1993–94): 234–51.

———. *The Social Structure of the Rabbinic Movement in Roman Palestine.* Tübingen: Mohr Siebeck, 1997.

Hidary, Richard. "Ashi." *Encyclopedia Judaica* 2 (2007): 565–66.

———. "Classical Rhetorical Arrangement and Reasoning in the Talmud: The Case of Yerushalmi Berakhot 1:1." *AJS Review* 34, no. 1 (April 2010): 33–64.

———. "Right Answers Revisited: Monism and Pluralism in the Talmud." *Dine Israel* 26–27 (2009–2010): 229–55.

———. "Tolerance for Diversity of Halakhic Practice in the Talmuds." Ph.D. diss., New York University, 2008.

Hobbes, Thomas. *Leviathan*. Cambridge: Cambridge University Press, 1904.

Hoffmann, David. *The First Mishna and the Controversies of the Tannaim; The Highest Court in the City of the Sanctuary*. New York: Maurosho Publications of Cong. Kehillath Yaakov, 1977 (Hebrew).

———. *Midrasch Tannaim zum Deuteronomium*. Berlin: H. Itzkowski, 1909.

Honoré, Tony. *Law in the Crisis of Empire, 379–455 AD: The Theodosian Dynasty and Its Quaestors*. Oxford: Clarendon, 1998.

Horovitz, Hayyim Saul. *Sifre d'Be Rab: Sifre on Numbers and Sifre Zutta*. Jerusalem: Shalem Books, 1992.

Ir-Shai, Oded. "Yaʿaqov 'Ish Kefar Nevoraia—Ḥakham she-nikhshal be-minut." *Meḥqere Yerushalayim be-Maḥshevet Yisrael* 2, no. 2 (1983): 153–68.

Ish-Horowicz, Moshe. "Religious Tolerance and Diversity in Judaism." In *Jerusalem—City of Law and Justice,* edited by Nahum Rakover, 249–62. Jerusalem: Library of Jewish Law, 1998.

Ish Shalom, Meir. *Sifre de-ve Rav*. Vienna, 1864.

Jackson, Bernard. "Is Diversity Possible within the Halakhah?" *L'Eylah* 29 (1990): 35–38.

———. "Jewish Law or Jewish Laws." *Jewish Law Annual* 8 (1989): 15–34.

Jacobs, Louis. *Structure and Form in the Babylonian Talmud*. Cambridge: Cambridge University Press, 1991.

Jacobs, Martin. *Die Institution des jüdischen Patriarchen: Eine quellen- und traditionskritische Studie zur Geschichte der Juden in der Spätantike.* Tübingen: Mohr Siebeck, 1995.

Jaffee, Martin. "The Babylonian Appropriation of the Talmud Yerushalmi." In *The Literature of Early Rabbinic Judaism,* edited by Alan Avery-Peck, 3–27. Lanham MD: University Press of America, 1989.

———. *Torah in the Mouth: Writing and Oral Tradition in Palestinian Judaism 200 BCE - 400 CE*. Oxford: Oxford University Press, 2001.

Jolowicz, H. F., and B. Nicholas. *Historical Introduction to the Study of Roman Law*. Cambridge: Cambridge University Press, 1972.

Jones, A. "The Urbanization of Palestine." *Journal of Roman Studies* 21 (1931): 78–85.

Kahn, Paul W. "Community in Contemporary Constitutional Theory." *Yale Law Journal* 99 (1989–1990): 1–85.

———. "Interpretation and Authority in State Constitutionalism." *Harvard Law Review* 106, no. 5 (1993): 1147–68.

Kalmin, Richard. "Collegial Interaction in the Babylonian Talmud." *Jewish Quarterly Review* 82, no. 3–4 (1992): 383–415.

———. *The Sage in Jewish Society of Late Antiquity*. New York: Routledge, 1999.

———. *Sages, Stories, Authors, and Editors in Rabbinic Babylonia*. Atlanta: Scholars Press, 1994.

Kanter, Shamai. *Rabban Gamaliel II: The Legal Traditions*. Chico, CA: Scholars Press, 1980.

Karlin, Aryeh. *Divre sefer: masot*. Tel Aviv: Maḥbarot le-Sifrut, 1952.

Katzoff, Binyamin. "Ha-yaḥas ben ha-Tosefta veha-Yerushalmi le-masekhet Berakhot." Ph.D. diss., Bar-Ilan University, 2004.

———. "The Relationship Between the Baraitot in the Tosefta and Their Talmudic Parallels: The Evidence of Tractate Berachot." *Hebrew Union College Annual* 75 (2004): 1–24 (Hebrew).

Kaufmann, Yehezkel. *History of Israelite Religion from Antiquity to the End of the Second Temple*. 3 vols. Jerusalem: Mosad Bialik, 1955–1960 (Hebrew).

Kautzsch, E., and A. E. Cowley. *Gesenius' Hebrew Grammar*. Oxford: Clarendon, 1910.

Kellner, Menachem. *Must a Jew Believe Anything?* London: Littman Library of Jewish Civilization, 1999.

Kelsen, Hans. *Pure Theory of Law*. Translated by Max Knight. Berkeley: University of California Press, 1967.

Kimelman, Reuven. "*Birkat Ha-Minim* and the Lack of Evidence for an Anti-Christian Jewish Prayer in Late Antiquity." In *Jewish and Christian Self-Definition: Volume Two, Aspects of Judaism in the Graeco-Roman Period*, edited by E. P. Sanders, 226–44, 391–403. Philadelphia: Fortress, 1981.

———. "Ha-'oligarkiah ha-kohanit ve-talmide ha-ḥakhamim bi-tqufat ha-Talmud." *Zion* 48, no. 2 (1983): 135–48.

———. "Judaism and Pluralism." *Modern Judaism* 7, no. 2 (1987): 131–50.

———. "Rabbi Yohanan of Tiberias: Aspects of the Social and Religious History of Third Century Palestine." Ph.D. diss., Yale University, 1977.

Kiron, Arthur. "Golden Ages, Promised Lands: The Victorian Rabbinic Humanism of Sabato Morais." Ph.D. diss., Columbia University, 1999.

Kirschenbaum, Aaron. "Jewish Penology: Unanswered Questions." *Jewish Law Annual* 18 (2008): 123–30.

———. "The Role of Punishment in Jewish Criminal Law: A Chapter in Rabbinic Penological Thought." *Jewish Law Annual* 9 (1991): 123–43.

Kohat, Hanah. "Ben 'aristoqratyah le-demoqratyah—Rabban Gamaliel ve-Rabbi Yehoshua." In *Sefer yeshurun*, edited by Michael Shashar, 213–28. Jerusalem: Shashar, 1999.

Kraemer, David. "Composition and Meaning in the Bavli." *Prooftexts* 8, no. 3 (1988): 271–91.

———. *The Mind of the Talmud*. Oxford: Oxford University Press, 1990.

———. "The Mishnah." In *The Cambridge History of Judaism IV: The Late Roman-Rabbinic Period*, edited by S. Katz, 239–315. Cambridge: Cambridge University Press, 2006.

———. "New Meaning in Ancient Talmudic Texts: A Rhetorical Reading and the Case for Pluralism." *Proceedings of the Rabbinical Assembly* 49 (1988): 201–14.

———. *Reading the Rabbis: The Talmud as Literature*. Oxford: Oxford University Press, 1996.

———. *Responses to Suffering in Classical Rabbinic Literature*. New York: Oxford, 1995.

Kreyenbroek, Philip. "On the Concept of Spiritual Authority in Zoroastrianism." *Jerusalem Studies in Arabic and Islam* 17 (1994): 1–15.

———. "Ritual and Rituals in the Nerangestan." In *Zoroastrian Rituals in Context*, edited by Michael Stausberg, 317–32. Leiden: Brill, 2004.

Kugel, James. "Two Introductions to Midrash." *Prooftexts* 3 (1983): 131–55.

Lamm, Norman, and Aaron Kirschenbaum. "Freedom and Constraint in the Jewish Judicial Process." *Cardozo Law Review* 1 (1979).

Lapin, Hayim. "Early Rabbinic Civil Law and the Literature of the Second Temple Period." *Jewish Studies Quarterly* 2 (1995): 149–83.

———. "Rabbis and Cities in Later Roman Palestine: The Literary Evidence." *Journal of Jewish Studies* 50, no. 2 (1999): 187–207.

———. "Rabbis and Cities: Some Aspects of the Rabbinic Movement in Its Graeco-Roman Environment." In *The Talmud Yerushalmi and Graeco-Roman Culture II*, edited by Peter Schäfer and Catherine Hezser, 203–17. Tübingen: Mohr Siebeck, 1998.

Leiser, Burton. "Custom and Law in Talmudic Jurisprudence." *Judaism* 20 (1971): 396–403.

Levine, Lee. "The Jewish Patriarch (Nasi) in Third Century Palestine." In *Aufstieg und Niedergang der römischen Welt II, 19/2*, edited by H. Temporini and W. Haase, 649–88. Berlin and New York: de Gruyter, 1979.

———. *Judaism and Hellenism in Antiquity: Conflict or Confluence?* Peabody, MA: Hendrickson, 1999.

———. *The Rabbinic Class of Roman Palestine in Late Antiquity*. Jerusalem: Yad Izhak Ben-Zvi, 1989.

———. "The Status of the Patriarch in the Third and Fourth Centuries: Sources and Methodology." *Journal of Jewish Studies* 47, no. 1 (1996): 1–32.

Lewin, Benjamin. *Iggeret Rav Sherira Gaon*. Jerusalem: Makor, 1972.

Lieberman, Saul. *Ha-Yerushalmi ki-fshuṭo*. Jerusalem: Hoṣa'at Darom, 1934.

———. *Hellenism in Jewish Palestine*. New York: Jewish Theological Seminary, 1962.

———. "Kakh hayah ve-kakh yihyeh." *Cathedra* 17 (1981): 3–10 (Hebrew).

———. *Texts and Studies*. New York: Ktav, 1974.

———. *Tosefeth rishonim*. New York: Jewish Theological Seminary of America, 1999.

———. *The Tosefta According to Codex Vienna ...* Jerusalem: Jewish Theological Seminary of America, 1955.

———. *Tosefta ki-fshuṭah*. New York: Jewish Theological Seminary of America, 1955–1988.

Lightstone, Jack N. *The Rhetoric of the Babylonian Talmud: Its Social Meaning and Context*. Waterloo: Wilfrid Laurier University Press, 1994.

Liss, Abraham. *The Babylonian Talmud with Variant Readings*. Jerusalem: Yad Harav Herzog, 1983 (Hebrew).

Locke, John. *A Letter Concerning Toleration*. Indianapolis: Hackett, 1983.

Lorberbaum, Menahem. "Toʿeh be-miṣvah li-shmoaʿ be-divre hakhamim." In *Ben samkhut le-otonomiah be-masoret Yisrael,* edited by Z. Safrai and A. Sagi, 352–63. Tel-Aviv: Hakibbutz Hameuchad, 1997.

Lowy, S. "The Extent of Jewish Polygamy in Talmudic Times." *Journal of Jewish Studies* 9 (1958): 115–38.

Mack, Hananel. "Torah Has Seventy Aspects—The Development of a Saying." In *Rabbi Mordechai Breuer Festschrift: Collected Papers in Jewish Studies,* edited by Moshe Bar-Asher, 2:449–62. Jerusalem: Aqademon, 1992.

Macuch, Maria. *Das sasanidische Rechtsbuch "Matakdan i hazar datistan" (Teil II)*. Wiesbaden: Deutsche Morgenländische Gesellschaft, Kommissionsverlag, F. Steiner, 1981.

———. *Rechtskasuistik und Gerichtspraxis zu Beginn des siebenten Jahrhunderts in Iran: Die Rechtssammlung des Farrohmard i Wahraman*. Wiesbaden: Otto Harrassowitz, 1993.

Malinowitz, Chaim, et al., eds. *The Schottenstein Edition: Talmud Yerushalmi*. Brooklyn: Mesorah Publications, 2005.

Mann, Jacob. "Changes in the Divine Service of the Synagogue Due to Religious Persecutions." *Hebrew Union College Annual* 4 (1927), 241–310.

Mantel, Hugo. *Studies in the History of the Sanhedrin*. Cambridge: Harvard University Press, 1965.

Mason, Steve, ed. *Flavius Josephus: Translation and Commentary*. Leiden: Brill, 2000.

Matthews, John. *Laying Down the Law: A Study of the Theodosian Code*. New Haven: Yale University Press, 2000.

de Menasce, J. P. "Zoroastrin Pahlavi Writings." In *The Cambridge History of Iran, Volume 3(2): The Seleucid, Parthian and Sasanian Periods*, edited by Ehsan Yarshater, 1166–95. Cambridge: Cambridge University Press, 1968.

Mill, J. S. *On Liberty*. Indianapolis: Hackett, 1978.

Miller, Stuart. "R. Hanina bar Hama at Sepphoris." In *The Galilee in Late Antiquity*, edited by Lee Levine, 175–200. New York and Jerusalem: Jewish Theological Seminary of America, 1992.

———. "Roman Imperialism, Jewish Self-Definition, and Rabbinic Society: Belayche's *Iudaea-Palaestina*, Schwartz's *Imperialism and Jewish Society*, and Boyarin's *Border Lines* Reconsidered." *AJS Review* 31, no. 2 (2007): 329–62.

———. *Sages and Commoners in Late Antique Eretz Israel*. Tübingen: Mohr Siebeck, 2006.

Montgomery, James Alan. *The Samaritans: The Earliest Jewish Sect, Their History, Theology and Literature*. New York: Ktav, 1968.

Moore, George Foot. *Judaism in the First Centuries of the Christian Era, the Age of the Tannaim*, 1927. Reprint, New York: Schocken Books, 1971.

Moscovitz, Leib. *Talmudic Reasoning: From Casuistics to Conceptualization*. Tübingen: Mohr Siebeck, 2002.

Mousourakis, George. *The Historical and Institutional Context of Roman Law*. Burlington, VT: Ashgate, 2003.

———. *A Legal History of Rome*. London: Routledge, 2007.

Naeh, Shlomo. "'Make Yourself Many Rooms': Another Look at the Utterances of the Sages about Controversy." In *Renewing Jewish Commitment: The Work and Thought of David Hartman*, edited by Avi Sagi and Zvi Zohar, 851–75. Jerusalem: Shalom Hartman Institute and Hakibbutz Hameuchad, 2001 (Hebrew).

———. "On Structures of Memory and the Forms of Text in Rabbinic Literature." In *Meḥqere Talmud* 3, no. 2 (2005): 543–89 (Hebrew).

Neusner, Jacob. *Eliezer Ben Hyrcanus: The Tradition and the Man*. 2 vols. Leiden: Brill, 1973.

———. "From Biography to Theology: Gamaliel and the Patriarchate." *Review of Rabbinic Judaism* 7 (2004): 52–94.

———. *A History of the Jews in Babylonia*. Leiden: Brill, 1965–70.

———. *Judaism in Society: The Evidence of the Yerushalmi: Toward the Natural History of Religion*. Atlanta: Scholars Press, 1991.

———. *Rabbinic Traditions about the Pharisees before 70*. Vol. 2. Leiden: Brill, 1970.

———. *Reading and Believing: Ancient Judaism and Contemporary Gullibility*. Atlanta: Scholars Press, 1986.

———. *The Tosefta*. Peabody, MA: Hendrickson, 2002.

———. "Why We Cannot Assume the Historical Reliability of Attributions: The Case of the Houses in Mishnah-Tosefta Makhshirin." In *The Mishnah in Contemporary Perspective*, edited by Alan Avery-Peck and Jacob Neusner, 1:190–212. Leiden: Brill, 2006.

Noam, Vered. "Beth Shammai veha-halakha ha-kitatit." *Madaᶜe ha-Yahadut* 41 (2002): 45–67.

———. *Megillat Taᶜanit: Versions, Interpretation, History with a Critical Edition*. Jerusalem: Tad Ben-Zvi, 2003 (Hebrew).

Novick, Michael. "A Lot of Learning Is a Dangerous Thing: On the Structure of Rabbinic Expertise in the Bavli." *Hebrew Union College Annual* 78 (2007): 91–107.

Oppenheimer, Aharon. "The Attempt of Hananiah, Son of Rabbi Joshua's Brother, to Intercalate the Year in Babylonia: A Comparison of the Traditions in the Jerusalem and Babylonian Talmuds." In *The Talmud Yerushalmi and Graeco-Roman Culture II*, edited by Peter Schäfer and Catherine Hezser, 255–64. Tübingen: Mohr Siebeck, 1998.

———. *Babylonia Judaica in the Talmudic Period*. Wiesbaden: Ludwig Reichert, 1983.

———. *Between Rome and Babylon: Studies in Jewish Leadership and Society*. Tübingen: Mohr Siebeck, 2005.

———. "Jewish Lydda in the Roman Era." *Hebrew Union College Annual* 59 (1988): 115–36.

———. "Jewish Penal Authority in Roman Judaea." In *Jews in a Graeco-Roman World*, edited by Martin Goodman, 181–91. Oxford: Clarendon, 1998.

Palachi, Hayyim. *Semikha le-ḥayyim*. Saloniki, 1826.

Pardo, David. *Ḥasde David*. Jerusalem: Vagshal, 1994.

Parker, Kunal. "Context in History and Law: A Study of the Late Nineteenth-Century American Jurisprudence of Custom." *Law and History Review* 24, no. 3 (2006): 473–518.

Perelman, Chaim, and L. Olbrechts-Tyteca. *The New Rhetoric: A Treatise on Argumentation*. Notre Dame, IN, and London: University of Notre Dame Press, 1969.

Perikhanian, A. G. *The Book of a Thousand Judgements (A Sasanian Law-Book)*. Translated by Nina Garsoian. Costa Mesa, CA: Mazda, 1997.

———. "Iranian Society and Law." In *The Cambridge History of Iran, Volume 3(2): The Seleucid, Parthian and Sasanian Periods*, edited by Ehsan Yarshater, 627–80. Cambridge: Cambridge University Press, 1968.

Petuchowski, Jakob. "Plural Models within the Halakhah." *Judaism* 19 (1970): 77–89.

Pineles, Hirsh Mendel. *Darkah shel Torah*. Vienna, 1861.

Poste, Edward. *Institutes of Roman Law by Gaius*. Oxford: Clarendon, 1904.
Quint, Emanuel, and Niel Hecht. *Jewish Jurisprudence: Its Sources and Modern Applications*. New York: Harwood Academic Publishers, 1986.
Rabotenu baʿale ha-Tosafot ʿal ha-Torah. Warsaw: N. Shriftgisser, 1876.
Rackman, Emanuel. "Secular Jurisprudence and Halakhah." *Jewish Law Annual* 6 (1987): 45–63.
Ravitzky, Aviezer. "She'elat ha-sovlanut be-masoret ha-datit-ha-Yehudit." In *Ben samkhut le-oṭonomiah be-masoret Yisra'el*, edited by Z. Safrai and A. Sagi, 195–224. Tel-Aviv: Hakibbutz Hameuchad, 1997.
Rawls, John. *A Theory of Justice*. Cambridge: Harvard University Press, 2005.
Remer, Gary. "Hobbes, the Rhetorical Tradition, and Toleration." *Review of Politics* 54, no. 1 (1992): 5–33.
Robinson, O. F. *The Sources of Roman Law: Problems and Methods for Ancient Historians*. London: Routledge, 1997.
Rofe, Alexander. *Introduction to Deuteronomy*. Jerusalem: Akademon, 1988 (Hebrew).
Rosen-Zvi, Ishay. "Ha-'umnam 'protocol' bet ha-din be-Yavne? ʿIyyun meḥudash be-Tosefta sanhedrin perek 7." (forthcoming).
Rosenak, Avinoam. *The Prophetic Halakhah: Rabbi A.I.H. Kook's Philosophy of Halakhah*. Jerusalem: Magnes, 2007 (Hebrew).
Rosensweig, Michael. "Elu Va-Elu Divre Elokim Hayyim: Halakhic Pluralism and Theories of Controversy." *Tradition* 26, no. 3 (1992): 4–23.
Rosental, David. "Mesorot Ereṣ-Yisre'eliyot ve-darkan le-Bavel." *Cathedra* 92 (1999): 7–48.
Rosental, E. S. "Masoret halakha ve-ḥidushe halakhot be-mishnat ḥakhamim." *Tarbiz* 63 (1994): 321–74.
Rosenthal, Gilbert S. "'Both These and Those': Pluralism within Judaism." *Conservative Judaism* 56, no. 3 (2004): 3–20.
Rubenstein, Jeffrey. *The Culture of the Babylonian Talmud*. Baltimore, MD: Johns Hopkins University Press, 2003.
———. "On Some Abstract Concepts in Rabbinic Literature." *Jewish Studies Quarterly* 4 (1997): 33–73.
———. "Perushe meqorot Tanaiim ʿal yede ʿeqronot kelaliim u-mufshaṭim." In *Netiʿot le-David: Jubilee Volume for David Weiss Halivni*, edited by Yaakov Elman, Ephraim Halivni, and Zvi Aryeh Steinfeld, 275–304. Jerusalem: Orhot, 2004.
———. *Rabbinic Stories*. New York: Paulist, 2002.
———. "Social and Institutional Settings of Rabbinic Literature." In *The Cambridge Companion to the Talmud and Rabbinic Literature*, edited by Charlotte Fonrobert and Martin Jaffee, 58–74. Cambridge: Cambridge University Press, 2007.
———. *Talmudic Stories: Narrative Art, Composition, and Culture*. Baltimore: Johns Hopkins University Press, 1999.

———. "The Thematization of Dialectics in Bavli Aggada." *Journal of Jewish Studies* 54, no. 1 (2003): 71–84.

Sabato, Mordechai. "Qeri'at shemaʿ shel R. Ishmaʿel ve-shel R. 'Eleazar ben ʿAzariah veha-hakhraʿah ke-Beth Hillel." *Sidra* 22 (2007): 41–55.

———. *A Yemenite Manuscript of Tractate Sanhedrin and Its Place in the Text Tradition*. Jerusalem: Yad Izhak Ben-Zvi, 1998 (Hebrew).

Sacks, Yonason. "The Mizvah of 'Lo Tasur': Limits and Applications." *Tradition* 27, no. 4 (1993): 49–60.

Safrai, Shmuel. "Bet Hillel and Bet Shammai." *Encyclopedia Judaica* (2007): 3:530–33.

———. "Ha-hakhraʿah ke-Beth Hillel be-Yavneh." *Proceedings of the Seventh World Congress of Jewish Studies: Studies in the Talmud, Halacha, and Midrash*. Jerusalem, 1981, 21–44.

———. "Ha-ṣibbur ke-gorem bi-qviʿut ha-halakha." In *Ben samkhut le-oṭonomiah be-masoret Yisra'el*, edited by Z. Safrai and A. Sagi, 493–500. Tel-Aviv: Hakibbutz Hameuchad, 1997.

Safrai, Ze'ev. *The Jewish Community in the Talmudic Period*. Jerusalem: Zalman Shazar Center for Jewish History, 1995 (Hebrew).

———. "Yiḥudo shel ha-yishuv be-'ezor Lod-Yafo bi-tqufat ha-Mishnah veha-Talmud." In *Ben Yarqon ve-'Ayalon*, 53–72. Ramat Gan: Bar-Ilan University Press, 1983.

Sagi, Avi. ""Both Are the Words of the Living God": A Typological Analysis of Halakhic Pluralism." *Hebrew Union College Annual* 65 (1995): 105–36.

———. "The Dialectic between Decision-Making and Objective Truth in the Halakhah—Some Considerations regarding the Philosophy of the Halakhah." *Dine Israel* 15 (1999–2000): 7–38 (Hebrew).

———. *'Elu va-Elu': A Study on the Meaning of Halakhic Discourse*. Tel-Aviv: Hakibbutz Hameuchad, 1996 (Hebrew).

———. "Halakhic Praxis and the Word of God: A Study of Two Models." *Jewish Thought and Philosophy* 1 (1992): 305–29.

———. "Models of Authority and the Duty of Obedience in Halakhic Literature." *AJS Review* 20, no. 1 (1995): 1–24.

Saldarini, Anthony J. "The Adoption of a Dissident: Akabya ben Mehalalel in Rabbinic Tradition." *Journal of Jewish Studies* 33 (1982): 547–56.

———. *Pharisees, Scribes and Sadducees in Palestinian Society: A Sociological Approach*. Wilmington, DE: Michael Glazier, 1988.

Sanders, E. P. *The Historical Figure of Jesus*. New York: Penguin Books, 1993.

———. *Jewish Law from Jesus to the Mishnah: Five Studies*. London: SCM, 1990.

———. *Judaism: Practice and Belief, 63 BCE-66 CE*. London: SCM, 1992.

———. *Paul and Palestinian Judaism*. Philadelphia: Fortress, 1977.

Sarason, Richard. "Interpreting Rabbinic Biblical Interpretation: The Problem of Midrash, Again." In *Hesed ve-Emet: Studies in Honor of Ernest*

S. Frerichs, edited by Jodi Magness and Seymour Gitin, 133–54. Atlanta: Scholars Press, 1998.

Sassoon, Isaac. *Destination Torah*. Hoboken, NJ: Ktav, 2001.

Sassoon, Solomon D. *Sefer halakhot pesuqot*. Jerusalem: Ḥebrat Meqiṣe Nirdamim, 1951.

Satlow, Michael. *Jewish Marriage in Antiquity*. Princeton, NJ: Princeton University Press, 2001.

Schalit, Abraham. *Roman Administration in Palestine*. Jerusalem: Mosad Bialik, 1937 (Hebrew).

Schiffman, Lawrence. *The Halakhah at Qumran*. Leiden: Brill, 1975.

———. "Inter- or Intra-Jewish Conflict? The Judaism of the Dead Sea Scrolls Community and Its Opponents." In *Qumran and Jerusalem: Studies in the Dead Sea Scrolls and the History of Judaism*, 353–64. Grand Rapids, MI: Eerdmans, 2010.

———. "Jewish Sectarianism in Second Temple Times." In *Great Schisms in Jewish History*, edited by Raphael Jospe and Stanley Wagner. New York: Ktav and University of Denver Press, 1981.

———. *Reclaiming the Dead Sea Scrolls*. New York: Doubleday, 1994.

———. *Sectarian Law in the Dead Sea Scrolls: Courts, Testimony and the Penal Code*. Chico, CA: Scholars Press, 1983.

———. *Who Was a Jew?: Rabbinic and Halakhic Perspectives on the Jewish-Christian Schism*. Hoboken, NJ: Ktav, 1985.

Schremer, Adiel. "How Much Jewish Polygamy in Roman Palestine?" *Proceedings of the American Academy for Jewish Research* 63 (2001): 181–223.

———. "Qumran Polemic on Marital Law: CD 4:20–5:11 and Its Social Background." In *The Damascus Document*, edited by Joseph Baumgarten, Esther Chazon, and Avital Pinnick, 147–60. Leiden: Brill, 2000.

Schürer, Emil. *A History of the Jewish People in the Time of Jesus Christ*. New York: Charles Scribner's Sons, 1896.

Schwartz, Daniel. "From Priests at Their Right to Christians at Their Left?: On the Interpretation and Development of a Mishnaic Story (M. Rosh Hashanah 2:8–9)." *Tarbiz* 74, no. 1 (2005): 21–41 (Hebrew).

Schwartz, Joshua. "Tension Between Palestinian Scholars and Babylonian Olim in Amoraic Palestine." *Journal for the Study of Judaism* 11 (1980): 78–94.

———. "Tension Between Scholars from Judea in the South and Scholars of the Galilee during the Era of the Mishna and Talmud (After the Bar-Kochba War)." *Sinai* 93 (1983): 102–9 (Hebrew).

Schwartz, Seth. *Imperialism and Jewish Society, 200 B.C.E. to 640 C.E.* Princeton, NJ: Princeton University Press, 2001.

———. "The Patriarchs and the Diaspora." *Journal of Jewish Studies* 51, no. 2 (2000): 208–318.

Shapira, Hayyim. "Beit ha-Midrash (the House of Study) during the Late

Second Temple Period and the Age of the Mishnah: Institutional and Ideological Aspects." Ph.D. diss., Hebrew University, 2001 (Hebrew).

———. "Bet ha-din be-Yavneh: maʿamad, samkhuyot ve-tafqidim." In *ʿIyyunim be-mishpaṭ ʿIvri uva-halakha: dayyan ve-diyyun*, edited by Yaʿaqov Ḥabah and ʿAmiḥai Radziner, 305–34, 2007.

———. "The Deposition of Rabban Gamaliel—Between History and Legend." *Zion* 64 (1999): 5–38 (Hebrew).

Shaviv, Yehudah. "Maduaʿ pathạ masekhet Shabbat bi-mlekhet hoṣa'ah." *Sinai* 105 (1990): 220–30.

Shemesh, Aharon. "Halakha u-nevu'ah: navi sheqer ve-zaqen mamre." In *Renewing Jewish Commitment: The Work and Thought of David Hartman*, edited by Avi Sagi and Zvi Zohar, 923–41. Jerusalem: Shalom Hartman Institute and Hakibbutz Hameuchad, 2001.

Shepansky, Israel. "Torat ha-minhagot." *Or ha-Mizraḥ* 40, no. 1 (1991): 38–58.

Siverstev, Alexei. *Households, Sects, and the Origins of Rabbinic Judaism*. Leiden: Brill, 2005.

Smallwood, E. Mary. *The Jews under Roman Rule from Pompey to Diocletian*. Leiden: Brill, 1981.

Smith, Morton. "What Is Implied by the Variety of Messianic Figures?" *Journal of Biblical Literature* 78 (1959): 66–72.

Sofer, Amos. "Ha lan ve-ha le-hu." *Sinai* 113 (1994): 84–89.

Sokoloff, Michael. *A Dictionary of Jewish Babylonian Aramaic of the Talmudic and Geonic Period*. Ramat-Gan: Bar Ilan University Press, 2002.

———. *A Dictionary of Jewish Palestinian Aramaic of the Byzantine Period*. Ramat-Gan: Bar Ilan University, 1992.

Soloveitchik, Haym. "*Mishneh Torah:* Polemic and Art." In *Maimonides after 800 Years: Essays on Maimonides and His Influence,* edited by Jay Harris, 327–43. Cambridge, MA: Harvard University Press, 2007.

———. "Rupture and Reconstruction: The Transformation of Contemporary Orthodoxy." *Tradition* 28, no. 4 (1994): 64–130.

Sperber, Daniel. *Minhage Yisrael: Meqorot ve-toladot*. Jerusalem: Mosad Harav Kook, 1990.

———. *Roman Palestine 200–400: The Land*. Ramat-Gan: Bar-Ilan University Press, 1978.

———. "Sugya aḥat be-masekhet Horayot." *Sinai* 70 (1972): 157–62.

Spiegel, Jackob. "'Amar Rava hilkheta'—piske halakha me'uḥarim." In *Iyyunim be-sifrut Ḥazal ba-miqra ub-toledot Yisrael,* edited by Y. D. Gilat, 206–14. Ramat Gan: Bar-Ilan University Press, 1982.

———. "Later (Saboraic) Additions in the Babylonian Talmud." Ph.D. diss., Tel Aviv University, 1975 (Hebrew).

Steinfeld, Zvi Aryeh. "On the Clarification of a Mishna in Tractate Eduyot." *Bar Ilan* 13 (1976): 84–106 (Hebrew).

———. "Yaḥid she-ʿasah be-hora'at bet din." *Sidra* 10 (1994): 131–64.

Steinmetz, Devora. "Agada Unbound: Inter-Agadic Characterization of Sages in the Bavli and Implications for Reading Agada." In *Creation and Composition*, edited by Jeffrey Rubenstein, 293–337. Tübingen: Mohr Siebeck, 2005.

———. "Distancing and Bringing Near: A New Look at Mishnah Tractates ʿEduyyot and ʾAbot." *Hebrew Union College Annual* 73 (2002): 49–96.

———. "Must the Patriarch Know *ʿUqẓin?*: The *Nasi* as Scholar in Babylonian *Aggada*." *AJS Review* 23, no. 2 (1998): 163–90.

Stern, David. "Anthology and Polysemy in Classical Midrash." In *The Anthology in Jewish Literature*, edited by idem, 108–39. New York: Oxford University Press, 2004.

———. "Midrash and Hermeneutics: Polysemy vs. Indeterminacy." In *Midrash and Theory: Ancient Jewish Exegesis and Contemporary Literary Studies*, 15–38. Evanston, IL: Northwestern University Press, 1996.

———. "Moses-cide: Midrash and Contemporary Literary Criticism." *Prooftexts* 4 (1985): 193–213.

Stern, Sacha. "Rabbi and the Origins of the Patriarchate." *Journal of Jewish Studies* 54, no. 2 (2003): 193–215.

Stollman, Aviad. "Halakhic Development as a Fusion of Hermeneutical Horizons: The Case of the Waiting Period Between Meat and Dairy." *AJS Review* 28, no. 2 (2004): 1–30 (Hebrew).

Stone, Suzanne Last. "In Pursuit of the Counter-text: The Turn to the Jewish Legal Model in Contemporary American Legal Theory." *Harvard Law Review* 106, no. 4 (1993): 813–94.

———. "Sinaitic and Noahide Law: Legal Pluralism in Jewish Law." *Cardozo Law Review* 12 (1991): 1157–213.

———. "Tolerance Versus Pluralism in Judaism." *Journal of Human Rights* 2, no. 1 (2003): 105–17.

Strack, H. L., and G. Stemberger. *Introduction to the Talmud and Midrash*. Translated by Marcus Bockmuehl. Minneapolis: Fortress, 1992.

Sussman, Yaakov. "The History of Halakha and the Dead Sea Scrolls: Preliminary Observations on *Miqsat Maʿase ha-Torah* (4QMMT)." *Tarbiz* 59 (1990): 11–76 (Hebrew).

———. *Talmud Yerushalmi According to Ms. Or. 4720 (Scal. 3) of the Leiden University Library with Restorations and Corrections*. Jerusalem: Academy of the Hebrew Language, 2001.

Ta-Shma, Israel. *Early Franco-German Ritual and Custom*. Jerusalem: Magnes, 1999 (Hebrew).

Talmon, Shemaryahu. "The Calendar Reckoning of the Sect from the Judean Desert." In *Aspects of the Dead Sea Scrolls*, edited by C. Rabin and Y. Yadin, 162–99. Jerusalem: Magnes, 1958.

The Theodosian Code and Novels and the Sirmondian Constitution. Translated by Clyde Pharr. Princeton, NJ: Princeton University Press, 1952.

Tigay, Jeffrey. *The JPS Torah Commentary: Deuteronomy*. Philadelphia: Jewish Publication Society, 1996.
Tropper, Amram. "Avot." *Encyclopedia Judaica* (2007): 2:746–50.
———. "'Ub-lekhtekha ba-derekh': Beth Hillel ke-darkan." (forthcoming).
Tropper, Daniel. "The Internal Administration of the Second Temple of Jerusalem." Ph.D. diss., Yeshivah University, 1970.
Tsafrir, Yoram. "Some Notes on the Settlement and Demography of Palestine in the Byzantine Period: The Archaeological Evidence." In *Retrieving the Past: Essays on Archaeological Research and Methodology in Honor of Gus W. Van Beek*, edited by Joe D. Seger. Winona Lake, Ind.: Eisenbrauns, 1996.
Tushnet, Mark. "Anti-formalism in Recent Constitutional Theory." *Michigan Law Review* 83 (1984–85): 1502–44.
Urbach, E. E. *The Halakhah: Its Sources and Development*. Givᶜatayim: Yad La-Talmud, 1984 (Hebrew).
———. *The Sages: Their Concepts and Beliefs*. Jerusalem: Magnes, 1971 (Hebrew).
———. "Self-Isolation or Self-Affirmation in Judaism in the First Three Centuries: Theory and Practice." In *Jewish and Christian Self-Definition: Volume Two, Aspects of Judaism in the Graeco-Roman Period*, edited by E. P. Sanders, 269–98. Philadelphia: Fortress, 1981.
Uter, Alan. "Is Halakhah Really Law?" *Jewish Law Annual* 8 (1989): 35–52.
Wacholder, Ben-Zion. "Sippure Rabban Gamaliel ba-Mishna uba-Tosefta." *World Congress for Jewish Studies* 4, no. 1 (1967): 143–44.
Wald, Stephen. *BT Pesahim III: Critical Edition with Comprehensive Commentary*. New York: Jewish Theological Seminary, 2000.
———. *BT Shabbat Chapter VII*. Tamud Ha-Igud. Jerusalem: Society for the Interpretation of the Talmud, 2007 (Hebrew).
———. "Mishnah." *Encyclopedia Judaica* (2007): 14:319–31.
Walfish, Avraham. "Ḥaṭat ha-ᶜedah ve-'aḥrayut ha-yaḥid: ᶜiyyun be-darkhe ha-ᶜarikhah shel Mishnat Horayot pereq 1." *Netuᶜim* 6 (2000): 9–36.
Watson, Alan. "An Approach to Customary Law." *University of Illinois Law Review* 561–76 (1984).
Weinfeld, Moshe, ed. *Debarim*, Olam haTanakh. Tel-Aviv: Divre ha-Yamim, 1999.
———. *Deuteronomy and the Deuteronomic School*. Oxford: Clarendon, 1972.
Weiss, Moshe. "The Authenticity of the Explicit Discussions in Bet Shammai-Bet Hillel Disputes." *Sidra* 4 (1988): 53–66 (Hebrew).
———. "Traces of Pre-Bet Shammai—Bet Hillel Explicit Halakhic Decisions." *Sidra* 8 (1992): 39–51 (Hebrew).
Wieder, Jeremy. "Mishnah Eduyot: A Literary History of a Unique Tractate." Ph.D. diss., New York University, 2005.
Wurzburger, Walter S. "Plural Modes and the Authority of the Halakhah." *Judaism* 20, no. 4 (1971).

Yadin, Azzan. "Rabban Gamliel, Aphrodite's Bath, and the Question of Pagan Monotheism." *Jewish Quarterly Review* 96, no. 2 (2006): 149–79.
———. *Scripture as Logos: Rabbi Ishmael and the Origins of Midrash*. Philadelphia: University of Pennsylvania Press, 2004.
Yadin, Yigal. "Tefillin shel rosh me-Qumran." *Erez Israel* 9 (1969): 60–85.
Yungerman, Shalom. *Qobeṣ shiṭot qama'e: masekhet Sanhedrin*. Zikhron Yaʿaqov: ha-Makhon le-Hoṣa'at Sefarim ve-Kitve Yad she-leyad ha-Merkaz le-Ḥinukh Torani, 2007.
Zeni, Eliyahu. *Rabanan Sabora'e u-kelale ha-hora'ah*. Haifa: Ofaqim Reḥabim, 1992.
Zimmels, H. J. "The Controversy about the Second Day of the Festival." In *The Abraham Weiss Jubilee Volume*, 139–68. New York: Abraham Weiss Jubilee Committee, 1964.
Zlotnick, Dov. *The Iron Pillar—Mishnah: Redaction, Form, Intent*. Jerusalem: Bialik Institute, 1988.
Zussman, Yaakov. "Ve-shuv le-Yerushalmi neziqin." In *Meḥqere Talmud* 1, edited by Yaakov and David Rosental, 55–133. Jerusalem: Magnes, 1990.

Index of Passages

Index of Subjects

Gafni, Isaiah, 157n93, 159, 375n34, 378
Gaius, 78, 79
  Institutes, 79
Galilee, 43
  concentrated population of, 154, 158, 160
  as district, 156-57
  practices of, 99
Gamaliel of Yavneh, Rabban, 87n21, 376n37, 386-87
  against accepted opinion, 241-42, 259-63
  on the calendar, 264-66, 282t
  deposition of, 219, 269-72, 287t,
  following Beth Shammai, 187-88, 211
  and local customs, 87-88, 91
  portrayal of: in Tannaitic literature, 280; in Yerushalmi and Bavli, 280-81
  on reciting *Shema*, 243-49, 258
  standardizing liturgy, 273
  on trapping animals, 261-63
  as unifier, 15, 34, 41, 264
Gentiles, 35n135, 36, 86-88, 91, 93n41, 261-62, 263n67, 361n59, 376n37. *See also* laws concerning, food, oil of Gentiles; laws concerning, Shabbat, circumcision on, for son of a Gentile woman
Geonim, 45n9, 61, 108nn90-91, 109n97, 111n103, 117n121, 169n23, 172n33
Gilat, Yitzhak D., 46n10, 97n53, 98, 105n77, 108n90, 166n9, 187n90, 188n102
Ginzberg, Louis, 44n5, 46n10, 71n90, 87n22, 193n117, 176 195n126, 247n29, 249n31, 250n33, 254n43, 255n47, 256n49, 257n54, 260n61, 279n116, 311n46, 361n59
Goodblatt, David, 7n21, 7n22, 155n80, 157n93, 158n93, 380n56
Goodman, Martin, 34, 35, 35n134, 156n86, 158n98, 159n103, 188n100, 243n6, 375n33
Graetz, Heinrich, 180
Griffiths, John, 3n7, 8, 9n28
Guttmann, Alexander, 12n46, 44n5, 163-64n3, 301n13

Hadrian, 43, 77, 78, 119
Haggai, R., 200n133, 278-79, 377n41
halakha. *See also* codification 8n27, 9, 18n66, 29, 390
  in absence of state, 12-13
  deciding, 390-93: on ad hoc basis, 15, 43, 58, 151; avoidance in Bavli, 22-23; either-or option, 63-70, 74-78, 383n63, and *see* Beth Shammai and Beth Hillel, permission to choose between; maintaining status quo, 71-72; by majority, 151, 388, 391; maximum position compliance, 72, 383n63; role of laypeople and women in, 82n6, 12n46; by rules. *See* rules for deciding halakha; "whoever is stronger prevails," 71, 72n95, 73
  definition of, 81
  indeterminacy in, 3, 13-14, 62-77
  individuation of, 362n60
  as a legal system, 5n10
  and mimetic tradition, 145, 154, 157, 159-60, 378, 382, 383n63, 384-85
  and reason, 120, 154, 380-84
  role of custom in creating. *See* custom, role in legislation
  vs. custom. *See* custom, *vs.* halakha
Halbertal, Moshe, 1n1, 18n65, 33n127, 93n38, 169n23, 195n123, 274n97, 382n60
Halivni, David, 18-19n66, 22, 24, 30, 37n139, 44n5, 52n21, 56n29, 108, 110, 112nn107-8, 133n22, 134n24, 136n27, 149n66, 194n119, 341n3, 379, 379n51, 380n53
Halivni, Ephraim, 53, 54, 56n31, 59, 61, 96n47, 222n186, 224n190, 228n204
Handelman, Susan, 18n65, 27
Hart, H. L. A., 5n10, 62n62, 83n7
Hartman, David, 21
Havlin, Shlomo, 349, 351

polysemy. *See also* multivocality, 18n65, 19, 20nn70-71, 26, 28n99, 393
priests, 33, 75, 82n5, 128n6, 189-90, 192-93, 199-200, 211, 244, 284, 297-300, 305n25, 311-12, 332, 341n5, 361n59
Principate, 77
prophecy. *See also* revelation; Beth Shammai and Beth Hillel, and the heavenly voice, 1, 199-200, 218, 220-22
Pumbedita, 111n106, 129-30, 131n15, 139, 144, 155n80, 156, 158n93, 223

Qumran. *See* Dead Sea Sect

Rabbi. *See* Yehudah the Patriarch, R.
rabbis
  centralization of. *See* Palestine, concentration of Jews in; Babylonia, geographic separation of Jews in
  as local authorities: in Babylonia, 132-44, 153-61, 375, 378; in Palestine, 145-53, 155n79, 158-61, 332, 375-76, 378, 383n62, 384
  urbanization of, 377n43
  relationship with: laypeople, 90-91, 140-41, 256-57; priests, 82n5; students, 133-34, 144n50, 146n58, 153, 173, 370
Rav, 128n4, 205-6, 223n189, 225, 261-62,
  on Beth Shammai's practice, 106, 202-3
  on bird's leg, 129
  law follows, 61
  on Lyddians, 330
  Palestinian tendencies, 273n95
  as rebellious elder, 328
  and Shmuel. *See* Shmuel, and Rav
  and R. Yohanan's rules, 48-53, 55-57, 58n44,
Rava, 68-69, 72n96, 92, 102, 139-41, 143, 206,
  defending rabbinic positions, 24n88
  on *lo titgodedu*, 106, 110-13, 115, 117-18, 120, 127, 153n74, 161, 370, 372
rebellious elder, 41, 369, 371, 391
  in the Bible, 297-301
  court membership, 311-12
  differences between Talmud Yerushalmi and Talmud Bavli interpretations, 310, 323, 331, 333
  and the law of *Horayot*. See *Horayot*, and rebellious elder
  narratives of, 274-76, 325-22, 385
  reason for, 386
  and sectarianism. *See* sectarianism, and rebellious elder
  and theoretical pluralism, 28, 389
  types of cases, 312-25
  where it applies, 307-11
  whom it applies to, 204n141, 302-7
Resh Laqish,
  on circumcision, 150
  on *lo titgodedu*, 99, 105, 107-12, 114, 116, 117n121, 370
  and R. Yohanan, 46n10, 75-76, 107-12, 137-38, 145, 147-48, 359
  on the patriarch, 46n10
revelation. *See also* prophecy, 17, 20n71, 29-30, 130n12, 169n23, 227, 382n60
rhetoric. *See* Perelman, Chaim and L. Olbrechts-Tyteca; Talmud, rhetorical reading of
Roman Empire
  and Jewish sovereignty, 13
  Palestine in, 156-57
  strong central government, 158
Roman law
  codification of, 43-44, 77-80, 119, 373, 375, 384-85
  conflicting opinions in, 1n2
  constitutio Antoniniana, 119
  custom and *ius non scriptum,* 119
  jurists of, 46n10, 78, 375
  Justinian's *Digest,* 77
  Law of Citations, 78
  Twelve Tables, 77
Rubenstein, Jeffrey, 7n22, 24, 25n93, 27, 38n145, 164n3, 182n72, 200n134, 213n163, 216n171, 218n175, 219n180, 256n51, 267n77, 268n81, 270-71, 275n100, 276n107,

CPSIA information can be obtained at www.ICGtesting.com
Printed in the USA
BVOW02s0310240916

463189BV00001B/21/P

9 781930 675919